THE
EVERYTHING.
GUIDE TO
COPING WITH PERFECTIONISM

Dear Reader,

It is a cosmic stroke of luck that I have been invited to share with you some thoughts, experiences, and discoveries about the slippery topic of perfectionism. For me, being perfect at many things brought momentary pleasure, even honors, prizes, and awards, but at what cost? As I've gone through situations where it is important to cooperate with others, as in a marriage, child-parent relationship, working within a group or with a client, I see that doing things perfectly is not such a great asset.

Being 100 percent on top of things makes others uncomfortable. Always being on time or a few minutes early makes latecomers nervous. Always having a good answer can make others feel incompetent or unimportant. It can be an act of grace to be an accepting, attentive presence and smooth out the kinks later on.

If you have a monster within you that shouts you're not doing things fast enough, perfectly enough, or whatever else enough, this book can help quiet that voice. We can work together to lighten up unrealistic expectations, and in the process, open the door to the incredible wonder of life and people around you, however quirky and flawed.

Appreciatively,

Ellen Bowers, PhD

Welcome to the EVERYTHING® Series!

These handy, accessible books give you all you need to tackle a difficult project, gain a new hobby, comprehend a fascinating topic, prepare for an exam, or even brush up on something you learned back in school but have since forgotten.

You can choose to read an Everything® book from cover to cover or just pick out the information you want from our four useful boxes: e-questions, e-facts, e-alerts, and e-ssentials.

We give you everything you need to know on the subject, but throw in a lot of fun stuff along the way, too.

We now have more than 400 Everything® books in print, spanning such wide-ranging categories as weddings, pregnancy, cooking, music instruction, foreign language, crafts, pets, New Age, and so much more. When you're done reading them all, you can finally say you know Everything®!

QUESTION

Answers to
common questions

FACT

Important snippets
of information

ALERT

Urgent
warnings

ESSENTIAL

Quick
handy tips

PUBLISHER Karen Cooper

MANAGING EDITOR, EVERYTHING® SERIES Lisa Laing

COPY CHIEF Casey Ebert

ASSOCIATE PRODUCTION EDITOR Mary Beth Dolan

ACQUISITIONS EDITOR Kate Powers

ASSOCIATE DEVELOPMENT EDITOR Eileen Mullan

EVERYTHING® SERIES COVER DESIGNER Erin Alexander

THE

EVERYTHING®

GUIDE TO
COPING WITH
PERFECTIONISM

Overcome toxic perfectionism, learn to embrace your
mistakes, and discover the potential for positive change

Ellen Bowers, PhD

Adams media

Avon, Massachusetts

The Everything® Guide to Coping with Perfectionism
is dedicated to my friends, family, clients, and coworkers
who have tolerated my own perfectionism. Thank you.

An Everything® Series Book.
Everything® and everything.com® are registered trademarks of F+W Media, Inc.

Published by Adams Media, a division of F+W Media, Inc.
57 Littlefield Street, Avon, MA 02322 U.S.A.
www.adamsmedia.com

ISBN 10: 1-4405-5160-X
ISBN 13: 978-1-4405-5160-4
eISBN 10: 1-4405-5182-0
eISBN 13: 978-1-4405-5182-6

Printed in the United States of America.

10 9 8 7 6 5 4 3 2 1

Library of Congress Cataloging-in-Publication Data
Bowers, Ellen.
  The everything guide to coping with perfectionism / Ellen Bowers.
      p. cm.
  Includes bibliographical references and index.
  ISBN-13: 978-1-4405-5160-4 (pbk. : alk. paper)
  ISBN-10: 1-4405-5160-X (pbk. : alk. paper)
  ISBN-13: 978-1-4405-5182-6 (ebook : alk. paper)
  ISBN-10: 1-4405-5182-0 (ebook : alk. paper)
  1. Perfectionism (Personality trait) 2. Interpersonal conflict. 3. Adjustment (Psy-
chology) I. Title.
  BF698.35.P47B69 2012
  155.2'32–dc23

                                2012030651

This book is intended as general information only, and should not be used to diagnose or treat any health condition. In light of the complex, individual, and specific nature of health problems, this book is not intended to replace professional medical advice. The ideas, procedures, and suggestions in this book are intended to supplement, not replace, the advice of a trained medical professional. Consult your physician before adopting any of the suggestions in this book, as well as about any condition that may require diagnosis or medical attention. The author and publisher disclaim any liability arising directly or indirectly from the use of this book.

Many of the designations used by manufacturers and sellers to distinguish their products are claimed as trademarks. Where those designations appear in this book and Adams Media was aware of a trademark claim, the designations have been printed with initial capital letters.

This book is available at quantity discounts for bulk purchases.
For information, please call 1-800-289-0963.

Contents

Acknowledgments

The first thank you is to Kate Powers of Adams Media, who saw the tremendous need and potential for a book of this sort. Her enthusiasm and skill helped enormously to shepherd this work into fruition. The next thank you is to numerous friends and family members who contributed ideas, examples, and even begged to be case studies for the book. I am immensely appreciative of so much kindness and generosity, and I am grateful to know so many perfect people. Another thank you goes to the fabulous resources of the Glendale and Pasadena public libraries. I cannot live without you. And finally I wish to thank Fay, Orchid, Jeanine, and my stalwart Sunday group for consistent interest and support.

Top 10 Signs of Suffering from Perfectionism

1. Never feeling relaxed or at peace.

2. Always wanting to be the best, the first, the greatest.

3. Feeling driven to have the last word in arguments or conversations.

4. Feeling deeply tired much of the time.

5. Believing that your accomplishments are of little or no value.

6. Wanting to chuck everything and start over with a new job or new spouse.

7. Physical symptoms such as insomnia, heart palpitations, skin disorders.

8. High anxiety because of having so many things to do.

9. Your closest relationships lack warmth and comfort.

10. The sensation of having an enormous hole in your soul.

Introduction

MOST PEOPLE THINK of perfectionism as a good thing. What's wrong with working hard to reach lofty goals? But perfectionism can go too far—much farther than pulling all-nighters to hand in the perfect paper or cleaning the house until it shines. Toxic perfectionism can result in obsessive behavior, damaged self-esteem, depression, and even physical ailments.

Perfectionism is rampant in modern culture. The pressures of the media, working hard to sustain a career, the rising cost of living combined with dwindling job opportunities, somewhat fragmented families, and the faster pace of life all contribute to unrealistic expectations of oneself and others. The result can be a sort of dark, pervasive irritability and short-temperedness in every conversation and human exchange.

Have you eavesdropped lately on anyone ordering his or her favorite latte? More than likely, the instructions are delivered in a clipped, terse voice, and the barista is doomed if he uses 2 percent milk instead of soy. Have you overheard a young parent giving last-minute instructions to a beleaguered child as she is dropped off at school or daycare? "Don't mess up your new dress," and "Remember what I said about being friendly to little Mike who has just joined the class," or "Eat all your vegetables, and remember to phone me at four o'clock, and don't lose the cell phone." All this for a five-year-old!

The faster pace of communication, availability of infinite amounts of information in print or on the Internet, and the constant blasts of media cause people to feel that they are always behind, not quite up on the latest news, or impossibly inept at following the latest fashion trend or movie releases. It makes a person tired before he or she even begins the day. Even enormously bright, capable people are overwhelmed by the perfectionistic standards of today's society. And then there are those who simply give up trying.

Perfectionism can be a huge motivating factor for tremendous achievement. A young pianist memorizes and performs the entire repertoire of

Bach's Preludes and Fugues. An aspiring skater practices every day and competes in the Olympics. Ordinary people diet and work out in order to be a little healthier. A young, eager husband engages in therapy in order to learn more effective ways to communicate with a delicate-natured wife. A traveler memorizes dozens of sentences in a foreign language before taking an adventurous trip.

These instances are not necessarily harmful, unless other aspects of life are so neglected that something is sacrificed. If the young pianist has ulcers, the aspiring skater has no friends, the health enthusiasts are scheduled for numerous plastic surgeries, and the willing husband is lying awake at night to the point of not being able to function at work, then perfectionism is at play. Of course, people have a wide range of talents and capabilities. While an average person cannot memorize so much music, perhaps there is some-one who can do so without adverse effects. The important thing is whether or not the person is truly happy with the accomplishment, and trickier still— where does the motivation come from?

A key component in identifying perfectionism in oneself is the question: "Is it important to be perfect in this situation, or am I making myself unhappy?" Getting at the root causes of the dark world of impossible, pervasive perfectionism can lead to a detective search into childhood experiences, buried traumas, and unconscious agendas. The quest is worth it, as the result is a happier, sane, pressure-free life. Perfectionism is not a curse. With enough information and a bit of curiosity and willingness, even years of perfectionistic thinking and behavior can be untangled and laid to rest. However, it will take some courage to do such an investigation, and tenacity in forming some different habits and responses. The rewards are great.

CHAPTER 1

The Basics of Perfectionism

Perfectionism is when high standards have become impossible to reach. For sometimes unknown reasons, a person is driven to be the most beautiful, top one's sales records month after month, attain perfect As in school, and become a Nobel Prize winner. Perfectionism has an element of compulsivity, and anything short of perfection is seen as a failure. Think of high standards on steroids. A desire for mastery is certainly admirable and can lead to a fulfilled life. However, perfectionism, whether in what one imagines others expect or in what is expected of a child, mate, or coworker, ultimately leads to the erosion of relationships.

Definition: What Is Perfectionism?

Merriam-Webster's online dictionary offers the following definitions of *perfectionism*:

First, there is the theological view that a perfect moral character allows a person to attain the highest good. Next, theology says that perfection is a state of freedom from sin. The third definition is more the focus of this book: a personal disposition that inclines one to see anything short of perfection as unacceptable.

Perfectionism can be broken into two types. First, there are behaviors such as checking, correcting, categorizing, and organizing. Second, one has difficulty making decisions, gives up efforts too quickly, or procrastinates. Both types are burdensome to the individual and others who live or work near the person.

Perfectionists tend to screen out positive options, almost always focusing on the negative. Perfectionists sense a host of "shoulds" careening through their mind most of the time. Perfectionists adversely compare themselves to others and make many wrong assumptions, imagining that they can read minds and that others can read their minds. There are core beliefs of not being okay, not being valuable or lovable. The result is a lot of spinning wheels and wasted time and energy.

Well, What's Wrong with That?

* Perfectionism causes unhappiness—ill feelings within the self and in relation to others. It creates a life seemingly fraught with danger at every turn because the high standards believed to be important can never be met. This creates a tired, discouraged person, always on the brink of satisfaction and achievement but never quite making it. Perfectionistic parents raise nervous children, those kids who hover around the edges of something fun, afraid that they will do something wrong and get yelled at.

Perfectionistic spouses create a "walking on eggshells" atmosphere in the home, as the significant other never knows when the next verbal barb will fly. Should the car have been washed on the way home? An impromptu luncheon planned for the corporate wives? Should the carpet have been cleaned before the holiday dinner? A perfectionistic spouse can create an impossibly elusive checklist of tasks that was never discussed or agreed upon with his or her significant other. In the significant other's mind, this list becomes paramount with keeping the other person momentarily happy.

FACT

Perfectionism leads to a preoccupation with others. One's own needs get shifted to the back burner, resulting in personal neglect, even physical illness. Others may thrive on all that attention, but the self atrophies.

The Appeal of the Imperfect

Have you noticed that in recent years handmade items are very popular and indeed sought after? A hand-hewn chair may be a cherished souvenir from travels and is favored over something less expensive from an assembly line. There is something very personal and attractive in an art or craft that comes from the efforts of an individual. The flaws add to the character of the piece.

ESSENTIAL

Often the direction one is going is the only thing that is really important. Perfection is unattainable, so it makes perfect sense to simply keep taking actions in the direction of the desired goal. The results will take care of themselves.

This could be true for people, as well. The flaws in appearance or character add to the artistry of the human being. Can you imagine Frida Kahlo without her heavy eyebrows? But no biographies relate trips to the salon for waxing and tweezing.

Staying Out of the Affairs of Others

Straightening out other people is so appealing to perfectionistic people. There are so many potential projects! However, nagging and criticizing does not create happy, wholesome relationships, and one soon finds others turning the other way when one enters a room. Redirecting the focus to one-self is appropriate.

There is much to do in terms of developing a life of satisfying activities. The result is a well-rounded person who brings a relaxed glow to relationships. Such a person has a great deal of appeal, whether in romantic relationships or in a work group. Old habits may resist change, but catching that inclination to correct or fix can create a much more peaceful life.

Understanding Perfectionism and Its Effect on Your Life

Perfectionism can be a deadly detriment to enthusiasm, satisfaction, and happiness. It destroys relationships as people pick, pick, pick at each other, whether it is in a marriage or between parent and child. Children of perfectionistic parents tend to carry the mantle forward and become unreasonable taskmasters toward themselves and others, and the unhappy legacy is passed on. With perfectionistic people, often the unreasonable need to be right is lorded over others, much to the detriment of friendships and working relationships. Have you ever heard a very bright, small child lecturing someone in the sandbox about the correct way to make sand cookies? This is a future perfectionist, and someone not so easy to be around comfortably.

ESSENTIAL

It has been said that a person who isn't making mistakes isn't making much of anything. Life is constant trial and error, a series of discoveries about what works and what doesn't work. Mistakes are a natural part of the process.

What are some of the effects of perfectionism?

- Difficulty setting realistic goals and taking steps toward them
- Inability to relax and enjoy an ordinary day
- Extreme sensitivity to criticism
- Tendency to look at problems rather than solutions

- Strained relationships or inability to have relationships
- Tendency to escape into fantasy or various addictions
- A sense that life is passing by without participating
- Insomnia and other psychosomatic conditions
- Social isolation, shame, fear about even simple things
- Creating rituals to overcome the blocks to action

A tendency toward perfectionism makes it nearly impossible to even think about trying something new, let alone actually doing it. What if one has a yearning to work in a foreign country? The thought is daunting because of the impossibility of knowing the language and culture ahead of time. Not acting on desires creates a feeling of great loss. Who knows—people in that country may find it quite endearing to interact with a foreigner speaking their tongue at a toddler level of expertise. Many happy diplomatic memories could result from various blunders.

Toxic Perfectionism

Toxic perfectionism is the extreme edge of perfectionism where the person is frozen in paralyzed inaction. There is such a high degree of fear of failure that it becomes impossible to do anything because it is certain to be wrong! This state of paralysis leads to depression in fairly short order. It is difficult to reason with a person in this paralyzed state of mind, even if you are trying to convince yourself to do something differently. All you will hear is "Yes, but . . ." Even the most highly intelligent person cannot see that the way out of intense immobilization is to take any action, however lame and imperfect. This would be a good time to try something mediocre, as it releases the log-jam of shame and self-recrimination.

FACT

Fear of abandonment often underlies toxic perfectionism. One is deathly afraid that if something is not done perfectly, the situation or relationship will simply fall apart. The emotions around this are akin to life-threatening terror, often based in childhood where, in fact, one might have been told that something had to be perfect in order for the child to remain in the family.

Toxic perfectionism works like an insidious poison that can wither even the most gorgeous day or luscious experience. It's like Eeyore's sighing even when the sun is shining and friends have gathered for his birthday celebration. Toxic perfectionism is like a foggy lens of perception. Everything will be musty and moldy because of the lens, not because of the nature of the actual experience or situation. This is quite difficult to understand when one is in it. It helps to have trusted people—spouse, friend, or therapist—who can point it out.

Toxic perfectionism can be especially deadly for substance abusers or those with behavioral addictions, as one is apt to totally "go for broke" when in that impaired state of thinking. The gambler will slip the last twenty dollars into the slots, even though it is part of the rent money, and the compulsive overeater will finish off the half gallon of ice cream because the diet has been ruined anyway with some small slip. The drinker will finish three bottles of wine, simply because they are there, staring at him, speaking to him for some action. The all-or-nothing, black-and-white thinking and action is the hallmark of toxic perfectionism. It is difficult to even imagine small increments of anything positive in such a state of mind.

The Lurking Culprit—Fear

Hiding behind toxic perfectionism is a huge amount of fear. It may even be hidden from the perfectionist. Though all their excuses may seem completely rational, hidden fear is their motivator. It protects the perfectionist from failure—ultimate and colossal failure of the most public sort or even minuscule mistakes that aren't worth the bat of an eyelash. Sometimes a person can sense that fear and even face it by taking one small step in the direction of the desired goal.

ALERT

A different version of the familiar adage could be, "Anything worth doing is worth doing badly." No one is an expert at the beginning of a new undertaking. Often there is much to learn in the early processes of something different, and it can be quite fun to mess around with materials or strange circumstances.

For example, if you'd like to earn your living as an artist, place a sketch pad and drawing materials near your work space and reach for it when you get a little free time. You might find that the small action of reaching for the lovely colors and textures brings on a barrage of admonitions and emotions. "No! That's a waste of time! Doing art is frivolous! You'll never amount to anything! Nobody wants to see your art!" If you can continue the positive action in spite of the negative chatter, it does subside. The positive action becomes easier and the buried fear is no longer so powerful. Sometimes the emotions are incredibly strong and scary, like that of a child in danger. Those out-of-proportion fears are a clue that the irrational beliefs about perfection were learned in childhood.

The Extremes of Toxic Perfectionism

At the farthest extreme of toxic perfectionism, people commit suicide over a large or small crisis. For example, a straight-A student gets a B and loses a scholarship. A family breadwinner suffers a large financial loss and does not see how the family can survive. If the whole identity and self conception rides on being the perfect student or the perfect provider, the situation is precarious indeed. Death may seem the only way out, as the individual is momentarily incapable of accepting that another direction could possibly become fruitful. The student could get a part-time job or the family breadwinner could ask for help and support from the spouse, or possibly consider a different career direction. These avenues would not be clearly evident to a person suffering from toxic perfectionism.

The Urge to Complete at All Costs

Perfectionism can take some strange turns, causing the afflicted person to do completely irrational things. For example, an entrepreneur has botched an investment deal, and there is considerable financial loss. He goes to the extreme of taking the rest of his money and splurging it on a wild weekend in Las Vegas.

The urge to complete at all costs shows up with eating disorders. The undereater refuses to eat at all or binges and purges so there is no nourishment for the body. The overeater goes to the extreme of eating whole cakes in the middle of the night or ordering a family-sized pizza and finishing it off while watching a video alone. It is not hunger driving the action. It is the need to completely finish it off.

FACT

> The compulsion toward perfection sometimes arises from distressed families where doing or saying something perfectly momentarily takes the heat off the situation. The problematic person sets aside anger for a few moments and appreciates the effort to dissolve tension. However, the dynamic quickly shifts and the perfectionist has to do something else perfectly. The expectation of perfection in the overeager family member is a ruse to keep the attention off the flaws of the troubled individual.

Sometimes the urge to complete at all costs is found in domestic violence situations. For example, the abused spouse senses that the partner is gathering steam for a destructive outburst. She is quite aware of the nuances of behavior in herself and in the spouse, knowing that saying just the perfect crude remark will send him over the edge. At least, she thinks, the episode is finished then, even if it ends up with a visit to the emergency room. In this case, the two participants share the perfectionistic thinking and behavior, sharing responsibility for bringing the cycle to its culmination. It's perfectly horrible, but the energy between them sought completion.

A Matter of Perspective

Sometimes perfectionism is a case of misplaced emphasis. Imagine that when you are entertaining a friend for coffee, you discover that there is no creamer in the refrigerator. The perfect host or hostess would be embarrassed. However, the point of the visit is to enjoy each other's company, not to create a Martha Stewart moment. No one will remember in a month whether or not the hostess offered creamer or not.

Perhaps an individual is interested in taking on a community volunteer effort for a cause that seems really important. However, without a background in fundraising, event planning, or working on committees, it is natural to feel inept and reluctant. Truthfully, there are no Nonprofit Police gauging the degree of competence when someone takes on a new task. One is likely to find that others in the organization are quite happy to have new energy directed toward the work. Part of the enjoyment is learning the ropes of the situation. One's humanness makes an endearing contribution.

Can I Change My Mind?

The urge to complete something at all costs precludes the possibility of changing course along the way. For example, a young college student studies art history for three years, aiming for a career as a university professor. During the course of studying her required courses she finds out that art history seems a little dry, compared to the fun that the studio students seem to be having. If she changes her major, more time in college will be required. Is it worth it to shift gears? Most likely yes, as it is illogical to continue on a course that would not be enjoyable. Most probably, the additional art history background would be quite enriching to the studio artist, adding an historical depth to her work.

The Seduction of Praise

In close relationships, one has to be very careful and selective with the use of praise, as others with perfectionistic tendencies can become dependent upon it and feel quite frightened if everything is not praiseworthy. Of course, this is an unrealistic way to live, hanging on the possibility of a word from the significant other or boss. Parents who praise their children constantly may feel that it is a right thing to do, but moderation would be in order.

A steady diet of praise is like a steady diet of candy and cookies—ultimately harmful for the person. One hopes that each person within the relationship, whether adult or child, is able to generate positive reinforcement from within. The child puts away the toys because it is the accustomed thing to do in that family. The family chef prepares a nice meal out of loving kindness, not for the dangling carrot of syrupy thank-yous.

Classical conditioning says that intermittent reinforcement is the most powerful way to shape attitudes and responses. An occasional comment of gratitude is much more powerful than a constant stream of praise. Praise makes the other person dependent on that feedback, leading to false behaviors of all kinds and too many perfection-motivated actions.

Certain very strong individuals are impervious to praise or criticism, understanding that often the other person has an underlying motive to control. You might think that praise would always be welcome, but not if the intent is to manipulate. It might be an interesting idea to try, even for only one day, to be oblivious to others' comments of praise and criticism, to simply be secure within oneself no matter what is said.

The Symptoms of Perfectionism

To err is completely human, but perfectionistic people have surreal, completely different standards, behaviors, and beliefs. Some of the following are typical symptoms of perfectionism:

- Anxiety
- Fear of making mistakes
- Depression
- Procrastination
- Fear of criticism
- Critical of self and others
- Overemphasis on minute things
- Great difficulty prioritizing relative importance of tasks
- Interpersonal difficulties
- Persistent negative thinking
- Social phobias

- Substance or behavioral addictions

Other difficulties may include being unusually slow in one's tasks or not doing them at all, having seemingly well-thought-out excuses for not doing what is expected, and behaving in irrational, emotional ways when the situation does not require such.

But It's Important to Do It Right!

Perfectionism can be an elusive difficulty to understand, as the American culture rewards hard work, commitment to results, putting in long hours, and high achievement. However, striving for excellence is different from striving for perfection. Perfection is hopeless; it is virtually unattainable.

It is easy to forget that perfection is a matter of fantasy. French writer Nicolas Chamfort quipped that bachelors' wives and old maids' children are always perfect.

Excellence is a different matter—simply bringing all that is possible to the task at hand and then letting it go, assuming that it is completely acceptable. A person who is not perfectionistic is able to view herself as a completely worthwhile individual, regardless of what is attained or not. The perfectionist, however, has a deeply felt belief that one has to be perfect in order to be acceptable as a person. Of course, this almost never happens, resulting in fragile self-esteem.

FACT

There is a belief among Navajo weavers that perfection provokes the wrath of the gods. For that reason, an intentional mistake is cleverly woven into each beautiful rug. Thus, the gods are appeased for the moment. The hidden knot is generally only known by the weaver.

Struggles with Negativity

The perfectionist is rarely happy. There is a persistent undercurrent of dissatisfaction with oneself and life. Whatever achievements there are bring only fleeting joy. Then they are dismissed as trivial or marginal. There is the element of control with perfectionism, where one is provoked to seek particular outcomes, even when they are impossible. Food addicts often have ritualistic, controlling behaviors around their meals and food, veering into perfectionism, even if it means perfectly consuming all that is available at the moment. Perfectionists can exhibit extreme apathy and hopelessness, as nothing seems right or good enough. Such despair may take the form of unresolved grief.

Overcompensating

It can be tempting to try to become perfect in order to compensate for something that seems wrong or missing in life. Perhaps a young woman came from a terrible family. Her sense of security was shattered by her parents' difficult divorce and resulting experiences of being shunted from relative to relative during her formative years. She might create a goal to have a happy family—actually a perfect family to make up for what was lost before. The unsuspecting groom does not realize that he will be playing a part in an unknown play, rather than spontaneously creating a life together based on the needs of both persons. He becomes a puppet, willed by the wife to behave in a certain way, do only certain types of work, and relate to her in specified, rigid ways.

Someone else may try to create something fantastic to overcome perceived imperfections, such as the colorful DJ played by Wolfman Jack in the film *American Graffiti*. In a *Wizard of Oz* manner, he creates a strong persona, one who is almost entirely invisible, in order to be important in the lives of the high school students in the story.

Risk

To counteract some of the effects of perfectionism it is helpful to become more comfortable with risk. Imagine life as a grand adventure, and it's up to you to explore and participate. Yes, there may be setbacks and temporary embarrassments when trying something different, but the pleasures of new experiences are mostly likely worth it. Maybe you have always wanted to shop in the markets of Kathmandu. Maybe you would like to work with a hot-air balloon crew and silently drift over the mountains, looking at miniature coyotes and rabbits below. Maybe you would like to fly in a helicopter over the Grand Canyon. These types of things entail risk but could bring new life and energy into the deadened sensibilities of perfectionism.

CHAPTER 2

The Root Causes of Perfectionism

Perfectionism doesn't spring from nowhere. People with perfectionism, if they take the time to investigate their personal history and do a careful appraisal of their environment, will see that it's no accident that they have perfectionistic tendencies. Some of the origins might be genetic, which, of course, are completely out of a person's control, and others are found in the surroundings and significant relationships that impact a person's life. If you want to discover the roots of your perfectionism, think of tracing the causes of being too perfect not as a mystery, but as a bit of an adventure.

Domestication and the Big Dream of Society

The popular writer Don Miguel Ruiz clarifies some of the struggles that modern people endure, especially in his bestseller, *The Four Agreements*. One of his helpful concepts is that strong forces act on small children to "domesticate" them, to make them fit into society in a smooth way. Well-meaning parents condition the child to act, speak, move, and believe in the ways of the prevailing culture. A Navajo child or a Korean child might be given a lot of freedom up to the age of four or five, as it is assumed that children are naturally good and don't need any serious correction. Caucasian children in Western society might be more severely directed—"Do this," "Do that"—and have to learn a lot of rules of the household, Grandma's household, school, and church in order to behave in a customary manner. The child is innocent and takes on, wholesale, the beliefs of the parents and culture as the absolute truth. It takes years of effort in adult life to examine those beliefs and accept or delete, one by one.

FACT

In the Inuit culture there is no word equivalent to the English word "discipline," as within that society it is incomprehensible that small children would misbehave. They are simply being small children, doing what babies and toddlers do in a quite natural, uninhibited way.

Ruiz's idea of the Big Dream of society helps one to understand the roots of perfectionism. The society, group, clan, or family is more or less sold a bill of goods in terms of the prevailing values of the bigger surrounding culture. This is true around the globe; otherwise, chaos would prevail. However, sometimes beliefs get reduced to the lowest common denominator and work to a person's detriment. For example, in Mexican culture a woman is often praised if she is compliant, meek, and subservient toward men. What if she wants to be an engineer or construction manager? She will have a lot of opposition and work to do to overcome the Big Dream of her society. There may be a lengthy time of ostracism while she finds a new tribe of like-minded individuals to encourage her in her life's true calling.

In terms of perfectionism, it is natural for children to want to please their parents. A child learns at a very young age what is okay with the big people and what is not. There is a strong drive to be in harmony with the caretakers, even if the situation is logically impossible. For example, if one comes from a family where higher education is revered, the children will likely make good grades in school and become literate and conversant on intellectual matters. If such a child wants to chuck everything and backpack around the world at the age of twenty, there will be a conflict of drives. She will want to complete something educational in order to please the parents but still follow her own curiosity about, say, the Great Wall of China and the exotic plants of Costa Rica rain forests. A conflict arises within the person because she is going against the Big Dream of her formative years. This can be rough to endure, sometimes leading to hopeless efforts at pleasing people when the original aim is buried but not forgotten.

ESSENTIAL

Don Miguel Ruiz's dictum of don't take things personally, no matter what, helps greatly when dealing with others who are perfectionistic. The boss may come down really hard because a report is not formatted *her* way. It's not personal. The mother-in-law may have a fit about a new career plan that's outside of the family reality, but it's not personal.

Family of Origin Causes

Dysfunctional families are fraught with possibilities for the development of perfectionism. If alcoholism or other substance abuse is present, relationship dynamics are distorted in incomprehensible ways to a child or even adults. The drinker may be sweet and accommodating during the sober times, and the child works very hard to please. When the drinking starts, the child still wants to please, possibly in order to stop or curb the drinking as it creates such chaos in the household.

The spouse in such a situation may believe that keeping the house completely clean and the children quiet will prevent drinking or at least prevent violent outbursts during the binge weekends. Such magical thinking perpetuates perfectionism in the spouse and in the children as they work very hard to control the uncontrollable. It is not a true cause-and-effect situation, but no one sees that.

High-Achievement Perfectionism

In families where high achievement is revered, but there is actually little warmth and true emotional caring, children may learn that getting a good report card will bring a fleeting bright spot of praise. This can be mistaken for love. The wrong association becomes deeply imbedded in the child's mind, and he tries harder and harder to keep the straight-A average going, even at the cost of immense stress and limited social life. Because the perfection is elusive, the distorted mind of the youngster propels the individual to keep at it, constantly grasping for the invisible goal. Such children often take a career path advised by the parents, perhaps falling into an arduous life of medicine and law, somewhat innocently, because the true interests and talents are clouded over by the dynamic of the parents' control over what is lauded and what is not.

Parents who are mentally ill, whether with narcissistic personality or other disorders, will likely unwittingly foster perfectionism in their children. For example, a man who has become a compulsive gambler recalls that his mother attempted suicide several times during his young years. He never knew whether she would survive or not. Such an insecure atmosphere makes the individual grasp at straws, believing that the next big win will solve all his problems and he'll have a perfect life. He can even put together a perfect betting plan, based on the number of tries and strategies in order to perfectly outwit the casinos.

The relationship between a daughter and a narcissistic mother can be a particularly damaging one. Such a mother sees a daughter not as a separate entity but as an extension of herself. This kind of maternal narcissism makes any genuine bond almost impossible. It also gets in the way of the daughter's ability to grow into a strong, independent, and capable woman. A narcissistic mother often sets impossibly high standards for her daughter, and the daughter's struggles to meet perfectionistic standards go unrewarded or punished. Narcissistic mothers can be envious of their daughters' youth and beauty, and this jealousy can take the form of aggression and cruelty.

Narcissistic Personality Disordered Parents

Narcissistic parents sometimes live through their children, especially if they are highly talented, and the child becomes accustomed to planning her days around the quixotic needs of the demanding parent. "Make me a cup of tea. Paint me a picture. Show me the poem you wrote. Come over here and keep me company." The litany emitting from the bottomless pit keeps the child quite busy, much to the detriment of normal development. There is always the hope that *this time* the parent will be satisfied and happy. This is almost never the case, and the child dances faster and faster, likely on a perfectionistic bent for life.

Addictions in the Childhood Home

Any addictions in the family of origin—workaholism, sex and porn, shopping, playing the stock market, overeating, overachieving, incest, alcohol, or drugs—will likely lead to a degree of perfectionism in the children, as the emotional needs are not met during the formative years. The addiction always is the most important relationship for the addict, and the family's emotional needs are a far second down the ladder. The child, however, does not understand that and wants so very much to make Daddy stay home for a while, take a few minutes away from the computer screen, or put down the beer and barbequed dinner for a while.

There becomes a drive of desperation that is the norm for the person who evolves from such a family environment. Being perfect seems, subconsciously, to right the wrong of not having enough of the right kind of attention as a child. A young professional adult can be driven to do her job so well that she will never provoke any criticisms from her supervisor or coworkers. Of course, this is an unrealistic hope, but it feels life-threatening, as the emotions are that of a child, the child who wanted to make the parents stop fighting and drugging by being the best little girl. It is, sad to say, a futile effort.

ALERT

Persons who are unmothered or unfathered may, according to Dr. Clarissa Pinkola Estes, become unrealistic in their desires for perfect high achievement, attempting to go to great impossible lengths of earning numerous PhDs or ascending to the top of Mount Everest. Being "unmothered" or "unfathered" means that the parent was not available to emotionally nurture the child. Such parents may be preoccupied with their own lives or in some manner stunted in their development. Persons who are unparented may have had parents who were physically or emotionally absent, neglectful, or abusive. The result is a gaping psychological scar.

Societal Causes

Living in present times is fraught with pressures, deadlines, and a plethora of digital and electronic gadgetry demanding maintenance. Schedules are complicated, involving multiple careers in the household and the children's round of extra activities. Financial pressures loom, and at the same time, there is the push to provide everything for oneself and one's family that seems "normal"—designer clothes, wholesome food, and enough culture and entertainment to keep up. In urban areas, traffic snarls are a predictable part of daily life and workers are often on call, tethered to unrelenting responsibilities by cell phones or the Internet. It is impossible to perfectly keep up with all this, but people try. The frantic pace is the new norm.

ESSENTIAL

Persistence, even in the face of opposition, is a good way to make progress on cherished personal goals. Imagine a woodcutter chopping down a redwood tree or Michelangelo chipping away at his sculpture of David. The first dozen attempts will have little effect, but cumulatively, each effort adds to the glorious result. The trick is to remain focused on the mundane, or, on each little action of chipping away.

Even the closest relationships are different in the twenty-first century compared to two or three generations ago. These days, everyone watches TV talk shows or reads self-help books to glean the secrets of being happy with someone. Expectations are high in terms of hoped-for happiness with a significant other. It's easy to constantly miss the mark and come up feeling not good enough, attractive enough, or clever enough for that special someone. It's hard work to be so perfect in one's romantic life.

QUESTION

Why are arranged marriages sometimes more enduring than those unions based on romantic love?
During past times in the United States and in even somewhat recent years in Asian countries, partners were chosen by the parents in terms of compatible family values and harmonious goals. The role of each person was clear, and expectations were in line with reality.

Effects of School and Church

Although the original meaning of the word *educate* meant "to draw out from what is within the student," one does not often experience that luxury in schools these days. From preschool through postgraduate degrees, time is regimented and the learning process is heavily controlled. Pressures are enormous at every stage of schooling, even to the point that some parents of preschoolers are cultivating the child's spot in an Ivy League college! The emphasis is most often on results—grades, reports, starring in a play, scoring the most in sports—and potential for perfectionism is abundant.

Education and Perfectionism

Children and youth are vulnerable. They are learning their place in the world, and school is a big part of their life during those years. Their self-esteem is fragile, and having the wrong backpack or pair of shoes can seem like the end of the world. A frown from a disgruntled teacher can ruin a child's day. Peer approval is so important and fleeting in its demands. Having the perfect app for the iPhone may be the ticket for a coveted friendship. Having access to money and a car for a teenager makes it possible to have the perfect date. It's an unwieldy house of cards, but everyone involved tries to negotiate their way through it without injury. A persona can be somewhat shaped by the right clothing, friends, and manner of speaking in order to fit in with the best crowd. The criteria are fluid, creating a lot of stress for a sensitive teenager just trying to keep up and learn what is going on.

FACT

Patience for oneself, and eventually with others, is a marvelous antidote for the effects of society, school, and church pressures. Imagine that you are your own encouraging teacher or spiritual guru, and you gently and quietly support yourself in small triumphs. Such compassion for the self is a great role model for those in your world, as societies' institutions teach quite the opposite.

For those on the highest academic track, families pressure students to perform well so they can get into good schools and perhaps bring the family acclaim. This is especially treacherous if the family is troubled and a student's success is the only way the family can feel good about itself. This leads to a hopeless type of perfectionism, as the youth takes on the burden of making the sinking ship float a little longer, producing great anxiety about one's worth.

Church and Perfectionism

Depending on a person's spiritual and religious orientation, one can feel the weight of sin and a watchful patriarchal God who is constantly assessing one's position in the scheme of things between heaven and hell. Even in adult years, one can hear the cautionary voices of the nuns and priests, or remember a smack on the hand for momentarily having a daydream or flirting with someone of the opposite sex. The church, as an institution, is a big part of the Big Dream, working diligently to keep people in line so that society will function in an orderly way.

In his book, *Perfection: Coming to Terms with Being Human*, writer Michael J. Hyde says that philosophers such as Hume were critical of the church because it used "their own esteemed notions of perfection in a fanatical way to manipulate and persecute the masses." Many philosophers of the Enlightenment period saw the church as a threat to freedom of thought. Why would churches try to control people with a perfectionistic view of God and sin? Perhaps to keep the treasury coffers full, or to simply keep the conservative aspects of society in place, preserving order.

Trying to be perfect so that one is worthy of love from God is another hopeless road to travel. It can seem life-threatening if those early influences were fraught with threat and fear. Many people go through a lengthy period of examining the true nature of their spirituality, sloughing off the punitive aspects of the early teaching. Some find it easier to stay closer to the first teachings, finding comfort in the finite predictability of it. This is a personal matter. However, if one wonders if God is angry and disapproving a good amount of the time, one can likely find perfectionistic habits and thinking going along for the ride.

FACT

One way to strengthen spirituality if one is recovering from harmful early religious influences is to read dramatically different spiritual books. Volumes by Hafiz and Rumi are chock full of celebratory love from God, completely untainted with punitive judgment. If you are interested in this topic, you might want to sample *The Gift*, by Hafiz, and *The Illuminated*, by Rumi.

It takes effort to untangle a mature spiritual value system, but it is very much worth it. Keeping family harmony with previous generations who hold conservative, set views can be accomplished if one is not too argumentative or defensive about one's new direction. Ultimately, if you are comfortable with what you believe, those around you will likely be at ease as well. After all, God created flowers and animals in enormous variety. Why not paths to enlightenment? Perfectionism will be less troubling if one cultivates a belief in some sort of higher self that is nonjudgmental, loving, embracing, and noncritical.

Effects of the Media

The hype of advertising, emphasis on celebrity, and rampant consumerism all combine to make a person feel inadequate and insecure without the particular product being touted. Think about it. An ad for a great product flashes on the TV, perhaps a breath freshener or dental whitener. It is presented as if it will be the answer to all a person's relationship challenges. The weight control industry is quite prosperous, as 50 percent of the entire Western Hemisphere slowly becomes obese. In parts of the United States, plastic surgeons advertise in elegant, slick magazines, persuading the reader to consider just one more nip or tuck in order to be more perfect.

QUESTION

Is less than perfection actually more attractive and appealing?
The famous writer, Adrienne Rich, says that "our friends were not unearthly beautiful, nor spoke with tongues of gold; our lovers blundered now and again when we most sought perfection. . ." Do you love your friends because they are perfect? You probably love them because they are kind, generous, and fun to be around—sounds like Adrienne Rich was on to something!

The entire industry of advertising operates on the premise that consumers will perceive that they have a need or inadequacy that can be filled with the offered product or service. Eat this and you'll be satisfied! Drive this car and you will automatically attract a new mate! Go to this particular theme park and create happy family memories! Of course, in a fast-paced society, it is helpful to have numerous goods and services available to make life easier, but not to the point of never feeling like you have enough or are enough.

The effects of the media are especially strong if one is vulnerable for some reason, as many are, such as adolescents, women who hope to keep a fragile marriage together, persons in the entertainment industry, or people who are otherwise constantly in the public eye. Celebrity news is full of instances of anorectic spouses or girlfriends, hoping that the perfect weight will bring the attention wanted from the significant other. Actresses have been told by their agent or director that they need to lose ten pounds in order to have a chance at the coveted part. Dancers go without eating in order to look svelte in their roles and not be too heavily weighted while executing the demands of their roles.

This creeping perfectionism, the mask of appearance and image, requires huge expenditures of energy and money. It is, in fact, exhausting. Such effort is good for the gross national product, but is it good for self-esteem? Sometimes, perhaps, yes. If you think that you would be more confident in interviews with a new implant or teeth whitening session, then that is a possible direction toward self-esteem. If one imagines that a full mouth of replaced teeth and veneers are required even before the initial headshots are sent out, this could be perfectionism. The key is whether the aim is real or imaginary, attainable or always out of reach.

Adolescents are especially impressionable, imagining that the perfect case for their iPhone or great pair of boots will enhance their social status or even wrangle an invitation to a cool party. For decades, the tobacco industry preyed on youth, enticing them with interesting characters and jingles, offering the way to the "in" crowd and assured peer acceptance. Of course, the result was otherwise—possibly a shorter life, even the devastation of emphysema.

ALERT

The personal characteristic of never asking for help can be a route to isolation and unhappiness. Those who openly share their struggles and ask friends, family, and professionals for information and support are more connected socially and emotionally, creating a life of better overall health and well-being.

When one is tempted to go to the knockoff clothing store in search of the perfect item to ratchet up one's self-esteem, it might be more beneficial to call a friend, visit an elderly relative, or participate in useful volunteer work. Instead of a diminished bank account, appreciation is the result.

The media sometimes preys on young parents in insidious ways, pushing products and services to ensure that they will have perfect children. The answers to the parents' insecurities are offered in the form of DVDs to increase the child's intelligence, home-schooling programs to teach foreign languages, and every kind of educational learning, martial arts, music lessons, play environments, behavior modification for less-than-perfect children, and even medication, when all else seems to have failed. One probably knows consciously that it is not possible to buy confidence or perfection in whatever form one would desire in a child, but the corporations are uncanny in their ability to tap into that nagging belief that just this one time the right product or service will rectify the situation.

FACT

The Journal of Pediatrics reported a study of infants who watched the popular video series, Baby Einstein, actually regressed in their language development. Disney offered full refunds to those who bought the videos between 2004 and 2009. Apparently, even high quality recorded poetry and music is not a substitute for quality time with parents.

If one seems to be particularly susceptible to the media forces, it can be helpful to take a break from the various avenues that are customarily seen as entertainment. For example, a family could think of marvelous ways to interact without TV for an entire weekend. The overachiever could make a commitment to stay off of the Internet after 7:00 P.M. for a week. The zealous shopper could take a different route home from work, going to the gym instead of looking for perfect clothing.

You may notice as you work to counteract the effects of early programming and the conditioning of society, schools, and churches that your problems tend to recycle. The second spouse may be better than the first, but still there are the echoes of the nagging parents. One might expect personal growth to follow a steady positive trajectory, but it almost never happens that way.

It is tempting to berate oneself as errors and poor choices are repeated over and over again, but these patterns present an opportunity to learn, and eventually to teach others. Think of it as getting a graduate degree in a particularly annoying habit. You will be the expert in learning how not to do that, and you can assist others who have similar struggles.

Moving out of perfectionism is an example of slowly spiraling growth. Improvement may become apparent in one part of life but become slippery in another. Choices of husbands and boyfriends may improve, but a drastic sugar addiction takes over! You stop drowning your woes in sodas and ice cream, but start bouncing checks! It seems the nature of life is that there is always something to work on. The trick is to remain steady in the effort. Focus on the next thing, and the ultimate result will be visible progress.

CHAPTER 3

The Limiting Effects of Perfectionism

Extreme perfectionism is deadly. An extreme perfectionist is unable to determine priorities for a single day. Bills are ignored and mail is unopened because one cannot perfectly measure up to the task of handling life's administration. Suicide is considered rather than a career change. This extreme black-or-white mindset pushes out a wide range of gray options. One never goes out on a date because the wardrobe is lacking. Someone else might not earn a college degree because of the fear of being the wrong age or level of intelligence.

Getting Out of Negative Cycles

One technique for getting out of a negative trend is to stop everything and start over. You can start your day at any time, even if everything that went before was chaotic and distressing. If the day is a shambles because of traffic, unreasonable demands from work, or conflicting household schedules, stop everything and begin the day at that point, even if it is three o'clock in the afternoon. Perhaps, after quietly enjoying a nourishing snack (with the phone turned off), read something inspirational, do a few minutes of yoga, or walk for a while in someone's rose garden. Then, and only then, take the challenges one by one.

Take It to the Journal

Writing has long been known as a highly effective way of teasing out the wrinkles of the mind. If you can sit down with pen and page, the deeper issues will sometimes jump out and surprise you. The human mind has a way of layering information and beliefs so that some are deeply hidden. The act of writing, especially the old-fashioned way with pen and paper, will often allow the buried thought, feeling, or memory to emerge. If you're in a quandary about what to write, ask yourself some questions, such as "What is bothering me today?" "What do I want?" "What am I so angry about?" "What am I afraid of?" Often just getting started with any sentence will bring forth the stream of what needs to flow out. There may be a situation that needs attention. There may be an impossible circumstance that you have to walk away from. There may be deeply held goals, longings, and talents that are crying out for expression.

Spend Time with a Hobby

It may seem cliché to imagine that a hobby could eradicate your negative trend, but actually, it can. The brain can only do one thing at a time, and if you shift gears to something that you completely enjoy, the brain can no longer go along the negative track. It's a physical impossibility. Those thoughts and emotional trends are streams of electrical synapses, and once you get into a groove, the current tends to stay in that groove. It may seem like turning around the *Titanic* to go a different direction, but it certainly is worth it in order to change the tone of the day.

Do you have long-forgotten interests and hobbies that you enjoyed at a different stage of your life? Maybe you enjoy puzzles, the larger and more complicated, the better. Sitting down with the puzzle quiets the mind and allows different, healthier thoughts and emotions to come forth. Do you have a passion for dance? Turn on some music and dance, volunteer at a dance academy, or sign up for a hot salsa class. When your physical body is happy and expressive, it is impossible to feel negative.

ALERT

Watch out for the tendency to be perfectionistic and competitive even in hobbies and recreation. You do not have to be the best archer, golfer, chef, or karaoke diva. The point is to relax and enjoy life in a way that enhances your happiness, even for a few minutes. The pleasure will spill over into other aspects of life that might be challenging.

Increase Your Exercise

Studies show that regular exercise decreases the tendency toward depression. The chemistry of the body is arranged so that using the body, as it is intended, creates a release of dopamine, the happiness drug that is naturally manufactured in your brain. Doing something physical outside in the sun doubles the benefit, as the added melatonin makes you feel good.

The additional exercise may also improve the quality of your sleep, thereby improving the overall quality of your existence. It is difficult to feel negative if you are fit and well-rested, looking forward to the day. You may find that you need to increase the amount of sleep you get each night, perhaps cutting back on overworking or oversocializing.

Improve Your Nutrition

Entire books have been written about healthy nutrition, and you may want to investigate some of them in order to shift from negativity to a life that is more positive. It is quite difficult to change eating habits, as they are deeply set in one's culture and personal history. However, some foods tend to leave one with a heavy, lethargic feeling, more conducive to that creeping dark mood. Think of a family sitting around after Thanksgiving dinner. There's a reason that is not the customary diet every other day of the year.

Other foods make you feel sparkly and alive. It can be fun to browse through an outdoor farmers' market or upscale health food store, trying samples of unusual things. It can be fun to try a different restaurant to see what they offer and how you feel after eating it. You may discover that you love sushi, Mediterranean, vegan, or vegetarian!

Caffeine and sugar tend to create a temporary spike in the mood, making a person feel uplifted, but there may follow a mood crash, requiring more of the uplifting substance. A caffeine or sugar junkie can sometimes gradually diminish the amount of intake without having to endure terrible detox symptoms. It can be difficult to give up the pleasurable rituals around these favorites, but the reward is a lesser tendency to get lost in negative emotions.

And alcohol in moderation is better, of course, than drowning one's woes in drinking. The answer is not in the bottom of the glass.

Perfectionism, Procrastination, Paralysis

These three Ps can absolutely immobilize a person. They are intertwined in a tricky way that can baffle even the most intelligent mind. Imagine your highly capable, creative, and intelligent friend who wants to start a business. First he has to get his finances straightened out. Then he has to check all his social media sites. Then he has to help a friend move. Then he has to change the oil in the car. Then he has to clean out the garage. Each of these actions is completely forward-moving on their own, but the trend is that of a person who is putting off taking even the smallest action toward launching a new business. The result is remorse, self-criticism, and hopelessness.

If you work in one of the arts and tend to immobilize yourself with panic at the beginning of a project, called the blank canvas syndrome, just throw anything on the canvas to get some momentum going. Whatever you do at the beginning can be changed later, and using some energy to get going will bring other ideas to bear on the project. Make friends with those pesky Ps, so they don't stop you in your tracks. You have waited long enough to begin your novel. Open the document and give it a title. You have intended forever to catalog a large bin of family photographs. Take down the bin and start putting the photos in piles according to branch of the family and time period. It will take shape after you make the start.

Another Visit to Fear

Often it is not easy to see the underlying fear that motivates inaction or perfectionism. If one never takes the steps toward a desired goal, then one never has to experience the consequences, whether they are positive or turn out completely wrong. It is easier mentally to keep it in the abstract, the world of fantasy. You may have known people who have a goal that is actually a fantasy, the actual aim of their life that will be fulfilled when certain other circumstances have changed. One can bet that that fantasy will still be in place at the very end of life because it is a protection against the hard knocks that result from actually trying something different.

The underlying fear is often learned. Perhaps one grew up in a home where the children were criticized if they made a mess, brought home poor grades, made too much noise, or had emotional needs when the parents were too tired, preoccupied with their own lives, or simply incapable of being genuinely attentive to needy children. Parents often yell and lash out when they feel unable to meet the requirements of parenting. Those loud voices become deeply imbedded in the brain and may come out when a person wants to try something quite different. Go traveling in Europe with a backpack? "You'll be overcome by bandits!" Take a job in sales with a high income potential? "Sales is not a respectable profession! Stick with something we can be proud of!" Leave a relationship that has long since lost its bloom? "In our family we don't have any divorces! What will we tell the neighbors?!" These old voices haunt a person far into adulthood, especially when there's an inclination to try something new.

Breaking the Logjam

Paralysis results from an extreme amount of perfectionism and procrastination. At this extreme, it can be helpful to get assistance from others, whether a friend, a support group, or someone in the helping professions. For example, a woman experiences the sudden loss of a boyfriend. He died while visiting a relative in a distant state, surprisingly at a young age with no apparent underlying disease. The woman accepts the daily phone call of a friend who asks what she's going to do that day. The unbearable grief becomes a stream instead of a river, and eventually a trickle, because of the daily need to come up with a plan for the day.

Meeting with others who have similar difficulties can alleviate the isolation and self-recrimination involved with paralyzing perfectionism and procrastination. Others have found a way out, providing a hopeful example. Certain techniques are shared. Perhaps one calls a friend to make a verbal commitment to take a particular action.

Another decides to join a professional group that networks at regular intervals in order to learn how to create a website for a new business. Another decides to let go of a volunteer position that has become a hotbed of political backbiting, creating more time and energy for the direction of his or her true calling. These examples of others' actions and reconnection with humanity take away the luring sting of perpetual procrastination.

Willingness and Readiness

It is one thing to realize one's tendency to get lost in habits of perfectionism, procrastination, and paralysis, but it is quite another to be willing to release those inclinations and embrace something different. This can seem as traumatic as welcoming a brain transplant, but it is the crux of the matter in terms of letting go of the harmful constraints of the three Ps. Imagine small steps that you are willing to take that are different. Imagine yourself free from the grip of unhealthy thinking. Accept that you are a free, fluid, flexible person, and move into that self with grace.

ESSENTIAL

Whenever you can, celebrate small victories in moving through the abyss of perfectionism. Mark each success with a pleasurable outing or a little treat for yourself. It can be private or shared, small or generous. Gold stars may be enough for one person, and another may desire a five-course dinner with a violin trio. The trick is to make it meaningful to you so you deeply feel the reward.

Substituting Other, More Satisfying Behaviors

Many times you can sidestep the crush of perfectionism by taking your inclination in a different direction. If you're inclined to overeat, prepare a delicious, attractively served meal for a friend. If you're apt to overshop, offer your services to a convalescing or elderly friend. Do their shopping instead of buying more of what you don't need. If you are a writer or editor who tends to agonize over your own projects, consider offering your editing skill to a friend who is finishing a novel. The momentum of extending your skills to others moves back into your own work in a positive way.

Pencil It In

If you tend to cram too many things into your planning calendar, try for a month or so writing your commitments in pencil. Erase things as you change your mind or see that you have included too many things in the day. Maybe you change your mind and don't find something as appealing as when you first had the idea. Erase it. That lunch date doesn't seem as purposeful, now that you think about it. Erase it. You will find yourself becoming less perfectionistic and more relaxed about time and how you use it. Always keep in mind that you are at the helm of your life. You're the decision-maker, and you don't need to spend a lot of energy defending your choices. This is definitely a time when action speaks louder than words.

Redirect Your Talents

Do you tend to compulsively clean your house? There are undoubtedly many people in your life who would tremendously value your skill and energy in sprucing up their place. It is much easier to be detached when it's not your own environment. You will probably find it easier to stop. Do you tend to obsessively wander around the Internet, looking up random topics? There are many who would be happy to have your research skill devoted to their travel plans, medical concerns, or possible schools for their son or daughter.

Marshal Your Marvelous Creativity

Everybody is creative in some way, even if we do live in a culture that tends to only notice the stars in various fields, making them the best and minimizing the creativity of the average person. You, dear reader, have marvelous things to contribute in your life. What do you do naturally? Maybe you make a wonderful homemade soup or play a mean riff on an electric guitar.

ESSENTIAL

Control can often be an illusion. It may seem like one has control or would like to have control. Giving up control and all pretense of control over others and outside circumstances brings enormous freedom. Suddenly there is more free time. People are more interesting. Even the sky is a brighter blue and music sounds more enchanting.

Maybe you are the happiest when you're doing the East Coast Swing to the oldies. Do you have a flair for reading stories to children or inventing stories off the cuff? Do you spontaneously interact with strangers using humor? Harness your talent and express it, even if it seems small in scale and not very important. It *is* important because it tempers that monster voice of perfectionism. No one cares what ingredients you add to the soup, as long as it tastes good, and no one cares what exact tone of modulation you use to read a story, because everyone around is enjoying it. That's the aim—joy for yourself and those you serve with your creativity.

The Perils of Black-and-White Thinking

Extremist ideas about others, life's challenges, and oneself can lead down a dangerous road of self-destruction and poor self-esteem. During the Asian economic crisis several years ago, it was heart-breaking to hear of family breadwinners who chose to jump from skyscrapers rather than try to determine a different way to support their families. Similar events occurred during the stock market crash of 1929.

FACT

One of the tenets of Buddhist thought is that suffering is caused by attachment to particular people, places, identities, situations, or even personal constructs. For example, believing that one will only be okay if a particular candidate wins a presidential election is not a good route to happiness. Having a good day only if it doesn't rain could set you up to have a terrible day. Believing that one can be happy only with one particular lover creates a fragile life. Imagine complete freedom from all the tethers that seem like security.

Imagine a situation where a woman overhears her employer talking on the phone about the status of her position. Her mind takes the essence of the conversation and strings it out to the max—she will be fired and have to file for bankruptcy the very next day! An aspiring guitar player masters his craft and does many presentable gigs around a major city, but at the realization that he will never be famous he wants to stop playing. What's the use?

Thinking in black and white disallows perfectionists to see possible options within the gray. There are always other choices, but the perfectionistic mind gyrates back and forth between extremes like a pendulum gone wild. Often the perspective of trusted people can point out the gray possibilities, assuring the friend or family member that all is well if neither the black or white extreme occurs.

What Can You Do Instead?

It helps to settle in with a sobering awareness of the effects of perfectionism. Journaling regularly or frequent conversations with a caring person can keep the results of perfectionism at the forefront of the mind and emotions. This can be painful, but it's not a permanent state of affairs. The awareness is the first step to getting a handle on that difficulty.

FACT

Often the simple act of cutting back on commitments will diminish the effects of perfectionism. Having fewer things to do will relax a person, and there is more time to enjoy them. Perfectionists tend to have an unrealistic view of time and what they can accomplish in a given amount of time. Less could turn out to be more.

Accepting the tendency toward perfectionism does a lot to diminish the yammering self-criticism. Some people tell the internal committee to be quiet for a while. If it's the voice of a critical parent, one can ask her to sit in the car while an important interview is going on. Everyone is flawed in some manner, and the varieties of characteristics add to the flavor of life. You might have a tendency toward perfectionism. You can laugh about it when you are thirty minutes early for an event. Laugh again when you ask your spouse one more time to look for the lint roller and go over your outfit that is already perfect.

Trying new actions after the awareness and acceptance stages will be a good final step to gaining some mastery over the destructive aspects of perfectionism. Perhaps you are strongly motivated to stop correcting your children, as you notice that they have become super sensitive and tend to tune you out. When you're about to criticize them, take a deep breath and wait. In the grand scheme of things, how important is the small thing you were going to bring up? In ten years will it matter? Instead, give your children a hug and tell them you love them.

ESSENTIAL

Putting off things that one enjoys indicates negative self-worth. Now is the best time to do that fun thing! You're absolutely worth it. Take the kids fishing, plan that trip to Paris, take some steps toward a different career, or make a serious commitment to a yoga and Pilates schedule. It can even be something small like seeing a movie you've had your eye on, or getting a pedicure at a fancy salon. You will feel great about yourself.

People who are inclined to work late at the office can designate one day that they absolutely will leave at five o'clock. They can then see how that feels and then add another day of leaving at five o'clock the following week. Those who tend to work on their laptops in bed can decide on a time to shut it down and read a book or chat with the spouse.

It is pleasurable to approach each day with the question, "What can I do today to make myself happy?" This will move a person toward activities that are closer to the heart, truer to the essence of the self. And isn't that the purpose of life—to express joy? Being a joyful presence among others is a powerful catalyst for cultural and societal change. It could begin with you, this very moment.

FACT

Talented inventors and creators, such as Socrates, Leonardo da Vinci, Benjamin Franklin, and Thomas Edison, were fearless in trying new things and solving practical societal problems. One doubts that they worried whether their creations were perfect. They were relentless in their motivation to constantly experiment in new directions.

Those who are considering a career change, but are fearful of not being competent in the new endeavor, can take on a small part-time volunteer effort to see how it feels. Is it satisfying? Is it fun? Perhaps a small freelance opportunity could give the dissatisfied person a taste of the new direction. The perfectionistic person tends to think that she has to have an MBA from Harvard and a long resume of accomplishments in the chosen field before going the new way. It simply is not true. Competence, willingness, and reliability are so much more important than any particular background.

The key is whether one is happy or unhappy with the direction chosen, moment by moment within each day. With a certain amount of objectivity, it is possible to catch oneself in the act of thinking and behaving perfectionistically. That split second pause can be the beginning of a new direction, even within a single day. One can pause and ask, "Is this next thing making me happy?" If not, think of something else. Pause and do nothing for awhile as the mind clears. Something truer to the self will emerge.

Do everything you can to acknowledge and celebrate small successes. It might be enjoyable to mark on a particular calendar the actions taken to overcome perfectionism and procrastination. Small actions count. Speak gently and kindly to yourself and note when you pause instead of launching into perfectionistic thinking or actions. A person doesn't become perfectionistic overnight, and reversing the trend will also take some time.

CHAPTER 4

The Difficulties of Perfectionism

The consequences of perfectionism are devastating to mental conditions, intimate and social relationships, and even one's physical health. The deep belief that one is never good enough counteracts happiness. Those who try to get along with perfectionistic mates or supervisors will attest to the lack of joy in such an endeavor (walking on eggshells or waiting for the next complaint is certainly no fun). And ulcers, high blood pressure, obesity, and diabetes are the dire results of compulsive worry or behavior.

Pressure to Be Perfect

Pressures to be a particular way or do certain things can come from within the person or from others. It takes some ongoing reflection and sensitivity to ignore the internal drive to perfection. It seems so normal, especially if the person has been that way for a lifetime! Bit by bit, however, honest self-inquiry will tease out the particular statements that seem to be running the show.

ALERT

Perfection is not necessarily a positive goal. Leonard Cohen says it this way, "Forget your perfect offering. There is a crack in everything; that's how the light gets in."

Learning to deflect outside criticisms or otherwise harmful forces will also take some practice. If your mother-in-law always has a sharp dig to make during the weekly phone conversation, a short bookend call to a friend before and after will diminish the pressures from your mother-in-law's comments.

It is possible to dramatically decrease one's susceptibility to the pressures of the media or culture at large by simply cutting down on the exposure to these pressures. For example, spending fewer hours on the Internet or watching TV will take some of the heat off. Replacing those hours with activities that are truly enjoyed rebuilds what is lost from too much conditioning by outside forces. If working with needlepoint or bargello while listening to Vivaldi is the ultimate form of relaxation, then that is what should be frequently woven into your schedule. A person's uniqueness often comes out when he or she remembers and actually does what is deeply pleasurable.

It helps to deliberately reframe your mindset regarding the attractiveness of perfection. What exactly will perfectionism accomplish? The love of a cherished someone? Fame and fortune? Actually, it is more than likely that you will be loved if you can laugh at and own your flawed actions and attributes. Comedians realize this and craft many of their jokes around their own foibles. And fame and fortune come as a result of sincere interest and service to others. Although one may work very hard to master the essentials of a profession, being perfect is not usually a part of the equation.

FACT

How many times did Thomas Edison fail in his quest to invent a light bulb? The story goes that he said, "I did not fail 1,000 times. I successfully discovered 1,000 ways not to create a light bulb." How many times did the Wright brothers attempt to fly a plane? Historical accounts range from four to dozens. Creating something important is a developmental process.

Dan Kuiper describes the cycle of perfectionism in his blog, *www.findingfatherslove.com*. Unrealistic expectations of the self inevitably lead to bad results. Blaming oneself for disappointing consequences, such as not making the big sale, getting a date with a coveted person, or winning love of one's parents, leads to procrastination, guilt, diminished confidence, and defensiveness. Productivity is lowered. One forces oneself to repeat the steps of the process, this time with higher standards of performance than they had before, and one is back to where they started, harboring unrealistic expectations of the self, leading to guaranteed negative results.

Investment in Identities

In the United States, there is a deep investment in the connection between identity and career. Very young children are asked what they want to be when they grow up. Almost every casual conversation between new acquaintances contains the question, "What do you do?" A quirky answer in the realm of, "I eat, I sleep, and I talk with my children," will cause puzzlement and discomfort. We are a society of human doings instead of human beings.

If one is deeply invested in a particular type of business or work and the economy shifts, it can become a personal crisis to adapt to something different and new. This process can be akin to a death or divorce, bringing up feelings of grief, hopelessness, and sorrow. A broader, balanced life, with many avenues for self-esteem, can provide a buffer. This buffer can greatly help a person during times of dramatic loss or change.

QUESTION

Why do men sometimes have more of a life crisis with retirement compared to women?
Men are generally more deeply invested in their career identity. Women generally live more diverse lives, juggling work, household duties, and community service. While men are lost with nothing to do, women shift gears and priorities more easily.

It can be interesting and informative to sit down with a journal or piece of blank paper and brainstorm answers to the question, "Who am I?" After the first predictable roles flow onto the page—parent, spouse, worker, career person—be open to what might come next. Perhaps you're a warrior, visionary, gatekeeper, whistleblower, joker, peacemaker, diplomat, scavenger, or inventor. Maybe you're a healer, designer, appreciator, gardener, listener, wizard, aerial artist, or keeper of the stories. None of these ideas are bound by gender or age, and they can be interpreted metaphorically rather than literally. You may strongly identify with something that is not usually what you think of as a part of your identity. This could be a direction to explore.

The Power of Choice

Although it doesn't seem like it when one is in the throes of perfectionism gridlock, one always has choices—always. For example, a woman who was threatened by a rapist calmly said to him, "Why would a handsome fellow such as you have to resort to these extreme measures?" They discussed the extremes of his motivation, and he went on his way. In another case, an elderly minister was accosted by a robber in an urban parking lot. The minister asked what the robber needed the money for, and when the man said that he was unable to pay his rent, the white-haired gentleman wrote out a check for two months' rent and gave it to the robber.

Given these examples, one can see that a large part of choice is keeping mental composure. Yes, emergencies happen. Attaining the mental discipline of poise under any circumstance brings freedom from perfectionism. Yes, the circumstances of external life may be chaotic, unpleasant, and fast-changing, but a calm, deliberate person can usually find something sensible to do, even under duress.

A compulsive overeater feels compelled to eat the juicy Danish, simply because it is sitting there on the plate, calling for attention. The usual reflex action is to reach for the Danish and eat it. Another choice would be to pause and ask the question, "Do I want the momentary pleasure of the Danish or a more slender body?" Sometimes the answer will go one way and sometimes another, but it is good to make the choice deliberate rather than automatic.

A college music student preparing for a solo recital is expected to practice four or five hours a day for several months. She receives an invitation to visit someone in another state during spring break and feels that it is an impossible situation. She wants to have the music perfectly prepared for the concert, only a few short months in the future. The perfectionistic choice would be to decline the invitation and practice daily during the spring break. Another choice would be to accept the invitation and study the music visually and mentally while vacationing, sitting down at various pianos that are available during her travels. It takes a relaxed, creative mind to see that there truly are other choices.

Sometimes a person is compulsively perfect in one aspect of life but not in another. A professional designer finds that she concentrates on each aspect of work to an extraordinary degree, but in her hobby of playing wind instruments in various community ensembles, she is relaxed and carefree, even if she is playing a solo. This freedom is the result of giving herself mental and psychological permission to be less than perfect. It is a hobby, so she doesn't feel so pressured to do it exactly right. She is more open to the pleasure of making music with others and enjoying the spirit of community while doing so.

React or Respond?

It seems that other people and outside circumstances are generally beyond your personal control, but it is important to remember that, almost always, you have the ability to respond to situations however you choose. For example, if a less-than-favorite relative calls with a litany of demands, one might react with an argument, only to repeat numerous other arguments that have happened over decades. Or one might respond with a neutral, "That's interesting. I'd never thought of it in quite that way." The other person will be dumbfounded and the argument is over.

Let It Go and Walk Away

Another interesting choice is simply not to engage and go the other direction. For example, if you get irate e-mails from friends or coworkers, hinting that a response is urgent, try just letting the e-mail sit there. No response can be a response. You can choose not to engage with something or someone that is not going to be beneficial to you. Even in political or social movements that you passionately endorse, there are some issues or problems that you can walk away from. You can't fight every battle yourself. Others can pick up the torch and do some of the campaigning.

Perhaps a friend or relative is mired in an impossible life situation. She is bullied at work and at home. It seems that there is no way out of either situation. You would like to be a savior and rectify the situations, but you find yourself tired after each long conversation. Unless you are a professional social worker, it is not up to you to rescue others. You can gather as much pertinent information as you feel inclined to do, give it to the person, and ask her to call you after she has made up her mind. You are available for her to check in with from time to time but unavailable as a daily therapist. Walking away will result in the person seeking out other internal and external resources, possibly resulting in solutions that you would have never considered.

Internal Locus of Control

Those who have a strong sense of motivation originating from within are said to have an internal locus of control. Such strength enables the individual to make choices and decisions based on what is truly inside instead of reacting to demands and stimuli coming from the outside. This sense of control is a big help when coping with perfectionism. If you are comfortable in your own skin, so to speak, advertising, culture, and the demands of other people will be less likely to cause behavior that is not in harmony with your personal values.

ALERT

Seeking approval is the antithesis of an internal locus of control. A person who is constantly thinking of ways to please others is likely a perfectionist imagining what is going to keep that other person in line. This can actually be a subtle form of manipulation and control. It would be best to turn that controlling, pleasing inclination back to the self.

An externally driven life would be the opposite. A life that is governed by style, fashion, the stock market, or the requests of family members (regardless of how outrageous) can possibly bring material comfort, but it is not a path to serenity or freedom from perfectionism.

Extremism in Hobbies or Volunteer Work

The perfectionist can create a nightmare for himself even when the activities are intended to be fun. Joining the gym evolves into becoming the most talented weightlifter in a fifty-mile radius and entering contests to show off the muscles. The weekend gardener enters the rose competition of the local charity and creates high levels of anxiety around whether she will win or not.

The talented elementary school gymnast starts working out after school with a coach, giving up her social life and family gatherings because she wants to enter the Olympics. This is not to say that goals are not important and that high achievements can be quite fulfilling, but is there happiness? Is there joy in the endeavor or agony? Is the person losing sleep and leading an unbalanced life? Sometimes young gymnasts, dancers, and skaters resort to bulimia in order to maintain the weight that is desired for the work. This, of course, is damaging to the body and is an example of perfectionism that is unhealthy in terms of the person's whole life.

In modern Western culture, higher education is highly revered. Those who find success in academia can take it to an extreme, becoming a professional student, earning degree after degree, much to the detriment of their bank account, often resulting in insurmountable student loans. Such an individual makes learning a hobby, which is innocent enough, but as a lifestyle, especially if the scholar is constantly seeking awards, mentions in all the right publications, and more and more honors along with the degrees, perfectionism is seen in all the diplomas.

What Can You Do Instead?

The limits of perfectionism are not a life sentence. They can be deeply imbedded in the personal psyche, but with effort, there is always a way out. One woman found that she could handle her perfectionism by having several creative projects going at once around the house. For her, it felt harmless to have all of these projects relatively unfinished, and she could pick up each one in turn, giving it some attention when she felt in the mood. These small projects gave her a way of balancing the demands of her business, and she didn't feel the need to make each hobby into another business.

It's a Wrap

In her book, *Refuse to Choose*, Barbara Sher suggests that people who feel the unreasonable need to complete each creative endeavor should wrap the project up in an incomplete form and label the project, including information about what has been completed and what could be done next. In this way, the individual can have many interests and approach life in a relaxed, exploratory way without feeling the perfectionistic drive to complete each and every project to the maximum potential. This frees the individual to choose other interests or to focus on those that are most satisfying.

Lower Your Expectations

It can be fun to try some things with no intention of reaching a mastery level. Maybe you have always been curious about Sufi dancing or modern dance. Seek out a group to explore those pursuits. Many people undertake learning a foreign language as adults with no aspiration of becoming fluent. They only have the goal of being able to communicate pleasantries with people they meet in their travels or neighbors who might be from other countries. Maybe there is a neighborhood French pastry shop with a cashier who would exchange a few words of French with you as you purchase your croissant. Such small, imperfect explorations can bring enormous pleasure into life. Others enjoy seeing people try things and screwing up. Everyone laughs at a bit of clownish self-deprecation.

Indulge the Senses

When you can, indulge in sensory luxury and pleasure. If you think you can't afford top-of-the-line indulgences, seek out free or nearly free experiences. Spend some time at the perfume counter in your favorite department store to see what is available. Enjoy a makeup consultation. Sometimes massage training programs are looking for subjects for the students to practice on. They need to accumulate hours toward accreditation and are happy to give you an almost professional massage, probably at no cost.

Mother Nature

Almost always, time in nature will relax a person and bring a new perspective. A day trip to an outdoor nature preserve brings new insight and focus. Walking on pine needles brings different sensations and thoughts compared to walking on a concrete sidewalk. Riding a horse creates a feeling of unity with other life forms, quite different from the experience of driving a car on the freeway. Observing wild deer in the redwoods brings awe and peace of mind.

New Friends

Even befriending people outside your age range can be fun and enlightening. Maybe there is a nearby seven-year-old who would like to tell you about her day at school and her American Girl collection. Maybe there is a ninety-year-old who has incredible stories to tell about World War II or the Great Depression. Such friendships are enormously enriching and take the focus off the inclination to be perfect. All that is required is to listen and be present for the other person, your new friend.

The Internet holds many possibilities for forums on various topics. It is easy to connect with people all over the world on any topic that is of mutual interest. One can develop real friendships in cyberspace, greatly enriching life for all involved. Many people have e-mail friendships that have been ongoing for years, sometimes resulting in travels and in-person visits.

Flex Your Decision-Making Muscle

Stop yourself when you see that you're second-guessing decisions you have already made—a college degree, choice of spouse, career path. Energy is wasted by going over these life choices.

Perfectionists agonize over decisions, whether small or large. What to prepare for dinner, which gift to get for a secretary. What is behind this anguish? The fear of failure. The wrong choice could jeopardize those important relationships, creating an insurmountable loss. A perfectionist's tendency toward insecurity creates self-doubt.

All you can do is bring everything you know to the situation and give it your very best guess. At some other time in the future, a new decision might be in order if new factors come to light. Alice Domar, author of the book, *Be Happy Without Being Perfect*, also suggests the following:

- Tell yourself that most of your decisions are good.
- Consider the pros and cons of any possible direction.
- Realize that what is right for others may not be right for you.
- You are in the best position to look out for your best interests.
- Changing old traditions can be fun.
- Set aside bias and discrimination toward others.
- Stop approval-seeking in its tracks.
- Adapt to unexpected circumstances.
- Forget about the Joneses and suit yourself.

ESSENTIAL

Accept the fact that every decision means the loss of possibility. This is the nature of life. Focusing on regret slows down the decision-making process. One can embrace the unknown and be accepting of good enough progress. Try to relax while making a decision, as anxiety gets in the way. In the grand scheme of things, many decisions are not especially important, such as which clothes to wear or what to order at the restaurant. Have you ever eaten with people who ask everyone in the group what they are going to have and then grill the long-suffering waiter about every offered dish? Try to spare your companions that waste of time.

Sometimes people who grow up with rigid, controlling parents marry someone who likes to make all the decisions in the family. If this is the case in your life, start asserting yourself in small ways, perhaps voicing a preference for a particular movie. Then progress beyond baby steps to choosing a vacation destination. Flexing the decision-making muscle makes it stronger, and those in your world will learn to respect it.

Sometimes it is impossible to know which one is actually preferred. In this case, there is nothing wrong with the old method of eeny, meeny, miny, mo. It could be that the result of this time-honored technique will show you that you really want the other one!

CHAPTER 5

The Concept of the Adult Child

The concept of the adult child arose in the 1980s with the work of John Bradshaw, Claudia Black, Robin Norwood, and Susan Forward. These self-help writers made Virginia Satir's work on family systems accessible to mass audiences, essentially becoming a part of the personal growth culture of the 1980s and early 1990s. Satir's work was based on that of Murray Bowen, the first researcher who observed that the difficulties of one family member dramatically impacted everyone in the family.

Effects of Alcoholism and Other Family Dysfunction

Entire books and university specialty programs, not to mention twelve-step programs and other self-help support groups, have arisen because of the effects of alcoholism on the family. Resources are listed in the Appendix if you would like to delve more deeply into this topic.

Adult children of alcoholics tend to choose mates who are emotionally unavailable, as that was the tone in the childhood home. One becomes distressed that the addicted partner is not really tending to the relationship and tries harder and harder to win the person with increasingly perfect behavior.

It has only been as recent as the latter half of the twentieth century that professionals became aware that having an alcoholic, or some other dysfunction in the family, tremendously impacted the family as a whole. Prior to that time, difficult family members were more or less shrugged off as "the town drunk," "the gambler," or "the womanizer." However with the work of pioneers such as Virginia Satir and Murray Bowen, it has become common knowledge that dysfunction or substance abuse stresses the entire family, creating all sorts of compensating behaviors.

In one of his studies, Murray Bowen found that when a hospitalized schizophrenic daughter showed improvement and seemed able to start living a normal life, the mother became very uncomfortable and wanted the young woman to remain sick and hospitalized. This was the beginning of Bowen's insight that sickness is sometimes purposeful, and others adjust to it in ways that meets their own needs.

Growing up with alcoholism is far from relaxing, and sometimes the only result is a determination to survive. For example, a woman who grew up with alcoholic parents said that she would have been fine if she had been instantly self-supporting, right out of the womb. Children in such circumstances often take on adult responsibilities—cooking and doing housework for the family, caring for younger children, or even physically caring for their parents when they are drunk. Some adult children, especially in rural parts of the United States, have memories of driving the family car without a driver's license, as young as ten years old, going from bar to bar in a small town, looking for the errant parent.

The Paradox of Adult Children

The concept of adult children arose as professionals began to discover that adults who survived a very difficult family life in which there was alcohol, other substance abuse, incest, gambling, workaholism, excessive debt, pornography, religious addiction, or sex addiction tended to retain certain characteristics as grown adults. The Adult Children of Alcoholics, a twelve-step program that addresses these difficulties, lists the following characteristics:

- Fear of people and authority figures
- Approval seekers
- Frightened by angry people
- Become alcoholic or marry someone alcoholic or otherwise compulsive
- Overdeveloped sense of responsibility
- Feel guilty when standing up for oneself
- Addicted to excitement
- Confuse love with pity
- Repress feelings
- Low self-esteem
- Terrified of abandonment
- Have alcoholic characteristics, even without drinking
- Reactors rather than actors (having a knee-jerk reaction rather than a thoughtful response; being passive in life rather than action-oriented)

Adult children tend to be stuck in their emotional development, often recreating the original family dynamic in their personal lives or in the workplace. The unreasonable, demanding supervisor may be a repeat of an authority figure in childhood who was virtually unpleasant. The spouse may turn out to be an eerie twin of a narcissistic mother.

FACT

Adult children of alcoholics often have an overdeveloped sense of responsibility. They tend to take care of tasks that others do not want to do, look after family details, and carry out plans as promised. They are excellent workers. It is important to be aware of this trait, especially if it is excessive to the point of exhaustion. One has to be alert for those who might take advantage.

The emotions felt during conflict are often as strong as those of a child, creating a fearful, uneasy, restricted lifestyle. It is often a challenge to move out of such an uncomfortable state because it feels normal. This is the norm for a person who grew up in a tenuous, quickly shifting environment.

Adult children are often stuck in isolation, torn between silent despair and outward rebellion. Often lifelong indecision is a part of the picture, as no one ever taught the person how to intelligently make decisions. It is quite difficult to face the reality of childhood neglect and abuse. It is easier to hide in denial and exist in isolation and fantasy.

Adult children often do not have a strong sense of what is normal. The norm in the addicted household was skewed, but an intelligent, adaptive child will become adjusted to that and carry the off-center norm into his or her adult life. Sometimes one guesses what is normal from TV or movies. "That family seems to do things this way, so maybe I'll try that." Observant children learn from friends' families about how other people do things and try a little here and there. Many adult children have a sense that they are acting out a part in life, somewhat on the sidelines. It all seems like being an actor or actress because there was no solid grounding in the family foundation. To a certain extent, the technique of "acting as if" is a way to move into different areas of confidence and competence, but it can be grueling for the person who had no solid mentoring at all during the younger years. It becomes a full-time job to learn how to be a grownup.

Fine-Tuned Sensitivity

Children growing up in an alcoholic or otherwise dysfunctional home develop a fine-tuned sensitivity to the moods and actions of everyone in the household. They are little barometers, able to determine by a gesture when violence might erupt. They can tell by the tone of voice over the phone whether the parent has been drinking or not. If so, that might be a night that the children will prepare their own dinner, even if it is only a bowl of cereal. Individuals with this kind of background can become quite empathetic and skilled at negotiation as adults, if the emotional damage has been repaired through therapy or other focused work. It is not a negative trait to be keenly attuned to the nuances of other people.

Adult Children and Perfectionism

Children who survive a troubled family carry a deep fantasy that somehow they can correct the problem. If they only can achieve enough, be pretty enough, get a perfect batting record in baseball, or clean the house well enough, the family will become whole, loving, and well. One can see that this deeply imbedded drive would lead to perfectionism. The theme of trying over and over again to make it right for significant others becomes a hidden mantra of life, usually with disappointing results, as the original (and possibly current difficulties) are out of the control of the individual.

Birth Order

If you combine birth order, or how a person turns out according to family position, with the adult child/alcoholic family dynamic, one gets a very interesting pot of stew! Generally, oldest children turn out to be high achievers, good at leadership, and comfortable around adults of all kinds, as their first world as a child was that of adults.

First-Born Children

Oldest children in troubled families can sometimes turn out to be the most injured, as likely the parents were quite young and oblivious to their obsessive difficulties. In this case, the oldest adult child can be withdrawn from life and eventually work out a way to just get by without having to participate very much. He may retire at a young age or find a way for someone else to support him. He may feel troubled and ill at ease in social situations, feeling that he does not fit in anywhere. Much of his existence may be endured in isolation, even within a family.

Middle Children

Middle children are sometimes lost in the shuffle, as they never were top banana. The attention is usually on the older one, and later, the younger ones. Middle children learn to negotiate, play both sides of a situation, adapt, and accommodate. In a troubled, dysfunctional family, middle children can become martyrs, more or less selling their soul to the most difficult family member, trying for decades to make everything okay for that person.

FACT

Being a middle child does not always mean that a person is lost in the shuffle. Some famous middle children include people such as Charles Darwin, the Dalai Lama, John F. Kennedy, Abraham Lincoln, Ernest Hemingway, Warren Buffett, and Bill Gates. Middle children can also sometimes develop the skills of leadership and peacemaking.

This role can persist for a lifetime, and sometimes the individual sacrifices life goals and personal happiness in the futile effort to bring healing to the sick family member. The middle adult child hopes that one more birthday party or family celebration will at last make the difficult parent happy. One can squander time and money in the impossible quest, hoping that the effort will have a perfect result.

ESSENTIAL

Many adult children find that their core emotions are shame, guilt, self-hate, and a pervasive feeling of failure. These feelings must be faced, felt, and grieved before the adult child can find maturity and freedom.

Youngest Children

The youngest child is often a bit more carefree, as the parents' dysfunction may have matured and dissipated somewhat through the years. The youngest child has older siblings to help take care of her, and in some ways, take the heat off. She might be indulged and catered to, and in adult years can be charming and clownish. However, in youngest adult children from dysfunctional families there can be a gnawing personal emptiness, as if one never quite knew what was going on. She may marry inappropriately and not understand why she is unhappy.

She may be such an inveterate people pleaser that she has never truly explored her own interests, falling into jobs and pursuits that are lukewarm at best. She tries to be the perfect hostess, sibling, or daughter, but has a nagging feeling that she has missed the mark. The result can be a retreat into depression.

FACT

The experience of isolation is commonly felt in adult children. Such individuals learn that other people are not trustworthy and have a hard time developing emotionally intimate relationships, even personal friendships. This situation is exacerbated by the fact that the isolation is unrecognized. It is assumed that everyone else feels the same way.

The Only Child

The only child will have many of the same characteristics as the first-born child, turning out to be a rather adultlike, responsible high-achiever at a young age. However, if there is alcohol abuse or other severe family problems, the only child may find herself in an intense pressure cooker, unwittingly taking on the emotional work of maintaining the family equilibrium. Sometimes, troubled parents look to the child for love and solace, and the child has no choice but to deliver. Such an individual really has no opportunity to enjoy childhood, as there are jobs to do from the very early years onward.

Beware of the Internalized Critical Parent

Much of the drive toward perfectionism is an attempt to please the deeply imbedded voices of the authority figures from childhood. For example, a mother may have nagged about wearing muddy boots in the house or keeping one's clothes clean, even while playing in the sand box. A father may have shouted, "I'm not made of money!" when the child asked for lunch money, making him feel guilty for even the most basic of human needs. When a child is dependent upon dysfunctional people for survival, what they say is taken as truth. Those irrational criticisms can become an almost permanent part of a person's psyche, unless one takes the time to unravel and face them.

QUESTION

What is the origin of the term "critical parent"?
Eric Berne, the originator of transactional analysis theory, was one of the first to use this term. He described the characteristics of this internal voice as judgmental, punitive, patronizing, and posturing. The points mentioned are often either/or with no safe middle ground.

It takes effort to tease out those voices, as they seem real, true, and factual. Yes, money does not grow on trees, but does this mean that it is normal to be wracked with economic insecurity in even the best of times? Years of admonishments to "clean your plate because there are starving children in Ethiopia" makes it seem like a federal offense to leave unwanted food, perhaps leading to unnecessary overeating.

Superhero Parents

Adult children have an especially difficult time making their own way if their parents are famous. Would you want to trade places with Lisa Marie Presley, Chaz Bono, Sean Lennon, Ziggy Marley, Chelsea Clinton, or any of the Kennedys? When the parent has been perfect in some aspect of life, such as an extremely gifted achiever that has become a household name, the legacy wreaks with possibilities for the development of a perfectionistic child.

It is likely that to rise to those heights of recognition, the adult was, at times, preoccupied with his endeavors, perhaps neglecting the child's needs. The child may have had some dim awareness that the father was famous and known outside the home, but he may just want some quiet time with his daddy to play a game of Scrabble or share a sandwich. The lingering unmet needs combined with the impossibly long list of accomplishments and credits to the famous parent means that the young adult will always fall short, always. This is a difficult family history to overcome. The adult child is sometimes doomed to live in the shadow of the parent, even if there might be financial comfort. However, it is human to wish for a separate identity, one that is not defined in terms of someone else, even if that person is deeply loved. Some of these types of adult children move to a different country and go into a different type of work. Stella McCartney's fashion success is an example of this way of creating an individual life of her own, in spite of the renown of her father.

Arrested Development

Persons who come from troubled families often have difficulty maturing emotionally. It's no one's fault really. It is just the consequence of a family environment that focused on the needs of the addicted person to the detriment of other family members. The result is that adult children have the task of growing up when their chronological age would seem to indicate that they should already be grown up.

ESSENTIAL

Persons who become addicts, whether with a substance or a behavior, often stop growing emotionally at the point that the addiction began. For example, if a drinker started in high school, he will retain the emotional maturity of a teenager throughout his drinking years. If he chooses sobriety, he can start the maturing process from the adolescent level forward. This aspect of being stunted by any obsessive behavior can cause numerous relationship and life challenges.

If one is stuck in the past, dwelling on injustices and nursing resentments, it can be similar to imagining that the wake behind the boat is driving the boat. An impossibility! The wake follows the boat, but it doesn't propel the boat. The same is the case with various emotional rough spots having to do with personal history. It is useful to learn about each aspect, then take action to improve the situation.

Concept of the Inner Child

The idea of a buried inner child arose in the therapeutic community and in the popular culture in the 1980s. Although professionals before that time had a sense that parts of a self could be split off, especially when injured, the term "inner child" provided a way for people to talk about the idea of a younger self, one who was vulnerable, shattered, and scared.

FACT

Charles L. Whitfield, MD, was one of the first to coin the term "inner child." His book *Healing the Child Within* has become a classic in the field of psychology, especially within the specialties of recovery from substance abuse and other addictions.

Reparenting Oneself

Many people embrace the idea of reparenting oneself if the home background is one of emotional deprivation or even abuse. John Bradshaw's book, *Homecoming*, includes a very useful chart at the end of each stage of life with suggested activities for repairing the damage done at that particular age. For example, a person who experienced horrible deficits at the preschool age may enjoy simple walks outdoors, looking at plants and animals and naming them. No goal implied, just the fun of looking at interesting things.

A person who experienced deprivation and painful experiences during the elementary school age may enjoy mastering new skills, as developmentally that is what occurs in a healthy family. One might enjoy getting a new bicycle and riding along a boardwalk. It might be satisfying to learn inline skating or to try a part in community theater. Keeping the cautionary note in mind, it is not a goal to be perfect with these new pleasures but to fill in the missing aspects of child development that occurred because of family dysfunction.

Openness to love will be a part of the reparenting process. Love may, at first, feel dangerous, as in the dysfunctional home people lied about love, or their actions did not match the words. An irate parent may have beaten the child, saying, "I'm only doing this because I love you." However, courageously embracing love will open the doors to freedom, warmth, and wonders of the world outside the self-imposed walls of self-hate. Trust starts to build and a social web of support gradually forms. The warm affection that adult children feel for each other heals the old inner pain. These new friendships provide a framework where individuals mirror for one another the value and self-worth that was absent in the childhood home.

Adult children often enter adult life with little or no social skills. They need to learn the basics—how to introduce people to each other, how to make small talk at a gathering, how to make and receive phone calls, how to ask questions and listen to the answers. Situations with strong, safe parameters sometimes become a practice ground for social skills that eventually will become useful in the larger life outside the therapy session or support groups. Adult children need help in determining who is safe for a friend and who might not be.

Gratitude

When one embarks on looking at so much past history and repairing the psychological damage, it is tempting to simply be angry or depressed. The situation is unfair, and it is a lot of work to undergo a major overhaul of the human personality. Many people stay rageful or depressed throughout much of their lifetimes. However, this represents a loss in human potential and opportunities for a good life and deep happiness, regardless of the past.

ESSENTIAL

A useful tool for healing from the adult child syndrome is to write a daily gratitude list. It helps to shape perception so that, gradually, one starts to see all the incredible good in life, instead of all the problems. The list can include simple things, such as good weather, a full refrigerator, or a bright blue sky. This daily habit is useful for developing ongoing peace of mind.

A focus on gratitude pulls the person back into the present time and forces awareness. Some people make a daily grateful list as a part of their morning journaling. Such things as food, clothing, and shelter; cherished friends and family members, regardless of how quirky; good health; good weather; and opportunities for creative expression could fall on the list. It will be unique to each person and certainly change from day to day and year to year.

Impatience with Children

It is highly likely that the adult child will find it difficult to let her own child be a child. In the troubled family home, there was no room for the normal learning curve for life's necessary tasks. One had to instantly know how to do things, without asking for or receiving help and encouragement. It is a miracle that children can survive such a harsh environment, but often they do accommodate, sometimes with the help of teachers or other adults in the extended family.

Small children need a lot of time and repetition in order to learn the tasks of getting along in life. They need to learn how to tie their shoes, button and unbutton their clothing, put on rain boots, speak courteously to others, manage simple cooking tasks in the kitchen, and take care of their belongings. An adult child who becomes a parent may need help from older, mentor-type friends, as he or she does not have any internalized role model. The built-in knee-jerk reaction is one of impatience and intolerance for a child who is struggling to master something new. It takes a great deal of concentration to break the chain of the negative legacy, but it is worth it to raise children who do not become perfectionistic.

What Can You Do Instead?

The quagmire of adult childhood is not a place to live forever, merely an important place to visit on the journey of self-discovery. It might be tempting to retreat into the world of psych hospitals and social services, but, ultimately, this does not lead to a satisfying life.

ALERT

Watch for procrastination in work and recreational pursuits, even in managing money. Sometimes putting things off forever is a way to forestall the hidden voices of disapproval for not doing the task perfectly enough. If it's not done, ever, it can remain in the fantasy world of being perfect sometime in the future.

All kinds of resources are available to help the sincere person who wants to create a good life, regardless of past injuries. There are twelve-step programs to help with any addiction, many of which offer telephone meetings by conference calls. Such programs are virtually free, only asking for voluntary donations when the participant is able. The loving mentoring of a successfully recovering sponsor can offer consistency and gentle support.

Therapy can work wonders in moving through the feelings of a frustrated child. It is most helpful if the therapist has some understanding of the dynamics of alcoholism or other severe family dysfunction. During an initial consultation, it is permissible to ask questions about a counselor's experience with alcohol, domestic violence, incest, substance abuse, or whatever might be needed. Sometimes referrals from friends can reap good benefits with a therapist that might be compatible. For an adult child, this relationship could turn out to become his or her first trusting, intimate relationship.

For a time, it could be advisable to decrease work responsibilities, as the reparation work of adult children is an unpaid job in and of itself. Strong emotions will spill forward, and it might be difficult to concentrate on a full-time career while working on intense emotional issues. Some clients shift to part time or downsize their lives and take an easier job for a time. The actual work is looking into the subterranean regions of the psyche for a few months or years, and the day job supports that work. Now that is being a grownup!

ESSENTIAL

As one moves through the process of healing from childhood deprivation, it is helpful to know the now classic stages of grief. Watch for the stages of shock and denial, pain and guilt, anger and bargaining, depression and loneliness, reconstruction and integration, and, finally, hope and acceptance.

One has to be courageous about doing grief work. Much of what was lost in the process of becoming an adult child was the rightful experience of being a cherished child. As the layers are peeled away, one can be astonished at the volume of tears. This is a phase of thawing out. Strong emotions were repressed for years, even decades, as survival was the main goal. As life's circumstances become more secure, it is safe to feel those old emotions. It helps to have the companionship of people who understand and do not judge.

From time to time, take a break and notice beauty in your surroundings. Pull yourself into today, letting your mind rest from the intense work of examining the effects of growing up in a challenged family. A walk in a botanical garden or spending a holiday weekend in a woodland retreat will do wonders to heal your sensibilities. Take in cultural events in your community, including museums and festivals, and enjoy the interesting diversity of life. A stroll through a farmers' market is a feast for all the senses, especially if local musicians add their talents to the celebratory event of shopping for fresh foods. Appealing to your senses helps the injured, deprived aspects of one's background to heal.

An important element of adult child healing is to emotionally separate from the parents and even other family members. This does not mean to stop relating and loving them. It means that eventually one will be able to detach, break some of the umbilical cords, and develop a separate life with interests unique to the individual. There may be guilt and longing during the earlier phases of this work, but truer interests come to the forefront, replacing the perfectionistic tendencies to try to do everything correctly to remedy the problems of the family. This thankless task can be set aside, once and for all, and one finds the perfectionism receding.

Giving Up Addictions

In general, adult children find that they have used various addictive substances and behavior to mask intense feelings of sorrow, panic, and fear. Often these feelings are repressed, as they are too scary to face. Using legal substances, such as alcohol, sugar, nicotine, and caffeine, dulls the emotional pain, and survival is possible. Some adult children space out with various defenses of the mind. Perfectionism can be such a defense. Other ways might be projecting or rationalization, such as "It really wasn't that bad. I wasn't beaten every day."

ALERT

Suicide is a danger for adult children of alcoholics and other families with dysfunction. The combination of isolation, exhaustion from keeping defenses in place, and propensity to addictions of substance and behavior are cause for alert. The range of choices can seem quite narrow to an adult child. The world can seem like a dangerous and hostile place.

Some adult children become addicted to excitement. They use high levels of feeling to keep deeper fears at bay. Excitement could come from high-risk activities, such as adventure sports or racecar driving. It could come from gambling. It could come from choosing mates who are indulging in dangerous activities—substance abuse, crime, and other chaotic behavior. The adult child then becomes addicted to the other person.

At times the adult child may force the body to shut down and physically block out normal sensation. The mind can train the body to not feel normal pain. Intuition is lost, and a sort of physical armor makes it possible to exist in the world. The person may be overweight or just exhibit a stiff posture and gait.

Emotional sobriety—the creation of an inner and outer life characterized by serenity, poise, maturity, and acceptance—is a worthy goal for the adult child. Of course, some days can always seem better than others, but after the past is examined and released, even the worst of days are not as bad as the terror and violence of the childhood home. The individual learns to distinguish what is past and what is present and to become aware of personal triggers that send him or her zooming into past emotions. It might be the sound of a slammed door or a particular postural stance of a feared authority figure. Over time, the intensity of the triggers will lessen, becoming only the whisper of a memory. The current, present life moves more to the forefront as the old emotions recede.

Some adult children find that holidays have to be carefully managed. One adult child learned to hate Easter because her father gave up alcohol for Lent and then went on a huge bender on Easter day. Another associated Christmas with the violence of her alcoholic brother. One learns to make alternative plans—quiet, enjoyable times with safe, sane people. Associations with blood relatives may still be a part of holidays but in measured amounts. Many adult children insist on having their own transportation to and from family events and a stay in a hotel room rather than with a relative.

CHAPTER 6

The Relationship of Perfectionism to Obsessive-Compulsive Personality Disorder

Obsessive-Compulsive Personality Disorder (OCPD) is closely linked with perfectionism. The person suffering with this mindset seems to have a built-in "checker" that does not quit. One gets stuck on repetitive thoughts and behaviors that are difficult to halt, and then becomes fearful that if certain behaviors are not accomplished, something terrible will happen. Examples of OCPD thoughts and behaviors can include things like avoiding sharp corners on a table or repeatedly straightening pictures that are a millimeter off.

What Is Obsessive-Compulsive Personality Disorder?

Obsessive-compulsive personality disorder is characterized by a preoccupation with orderliness, perfectionism, and mental and interpersonal control. This disorder, which begins in early adult years, leaves little room for openness, flexibility, or satisfying efficiency in behaviors. Roots for the disorder are often found in some type of addiction in the childhood home. The child learned to try to be perfect to make the problem go away.

Characteristics of OCPD

People with this disorder create and follow extensive rules, attend to details and procedures, and compile lists and schedules that are beyond what the average person would consider, sometimes forgetting the original purpose of the act. Projects are often left unfinished because they cannot be perfect. Workers with this obsessive disorder may turn down invitations for a vacation because they believe they cannot take time away from their projects.

Hobbies and leisure pursuits are viewed as tasks instead of activities to enjoy. What should be seen as fun is overlaid with rules and perfectionistic procedures. It is difficult for the individual with obsessive-compulsive personality disorder to have fun.

Behaviors

Individuals with OCPD are overly critical of themselves and merciless in dealing with others. They have extremely high standards for themselves and other people. Humanitarian thinking does not enter into dealings with others—only rules and the correct procedures. Even if a friend or stranger needs help, the individual with obsessive-compulsive personality disorder will not offer it if it is against any rule.

Such rigidity translates to moral rules and values, with the individual seeing it as their duty to follow rules and help others to do so.

ALERT

If you tend toward obsessive-compulsive behavior, become aware of triggers that provoke obsessive-compulsive episodes. Try to mentally step back, pause, breathe, note the high emotions and rapid thinking, but sit still with it. Perhaps take a walk or a hot bubble bath. Let the aftermath of the trigger move through you with no action on your part. It will pass.

For example, if someone wants to borrow money for a hamburger, a person with OCPD would not loan any money because debt is harmful, and he or she would not think of the nutritional needs of the person.

No Arguing

Individuals with this disorder see themselves as right and feel that their way is the only way to do something. They steadfastly insist on their own views and do not delegate well to others, thinking that they are the only one who can do a good job. They are rarely open to the ideas of others. It is difficult for them to listen to others with genuine interest.

Decisions can be painstaking and very slow, sometimes resulting in nothing getting done. Perfectionism and procrastination are prevalent. Certain authority figures are given undue respect, and others not respected are ignored or resisted. This type of individual is not affectionate and does not easily give compliments. He has difficulty expressing feelings and may not even know what they are.

Resulting Difficulties

Persons with OCPD have trouble letting go of things because they believe they might need them in the future. This can run to the extreme of things seeming to take over a house with no room for a person to actually live. This type of individual may not want to be in intimate relationships with others because he does not understand and cannot negotiate the emotional terrain of closeness.

Obsessive-Compulsive Personality Disorder in the Family

The person with OCPD can be quite challenging to live with, as he obsessively pursues perfection. They want a perfect image of themselves and need everyone and everything around them to be well-ordered. Of course, this almost never happens, and the nearby family members suffer with the forcefulness of the OCPD person's aims.

People with OCPD can appear detached, emotionally cold, and machine-like, and they can be described as control freaks. However, they do have empathy for others. They can be deeply compassionate, especially toward others who do not see the need for control of the chaos around them.

ALERT

Watch for unconscious sabotage in yourself and others. Obsessive-compulsive persons may periodically derail something that is going perfectly well because of the need for chaos. It may be difficult to enjoy an ordinary day.

People with OCPD do form lasting personal relationships, although sometimes with challenges. Women with obsessive-compulsive personality disorder are more likely to seek help than are men.

You Can Choose Your Friends, But Not Family

Family relationships are usually not chosen, as one is born into a home with perhaps disordered parents and siblings who were already on the scene. In these relationships, one usually cannot just leave because it is unsatisfactory. A certain amount of accommodation has to occur with whoever is there, and only later during the adult years can one make independent choices regarding who is to be in one's household.

Growing up with OCPD family members can skew a child's perception of what is normal and acceptable. One can be inclined to make poor choices in life mates or career for lack of appropriate role modeling. Trust and self-esteem may suffer. If the family member with OCPD is a child, other siblings may resent the focus on that child and feel neglected. Parents of such a challenged child may become depleted, forgetting to take time out for themselves and to give quality time to the other children.

Case Study

David, a single man in his midforties, was interviewed for this book. He admits to being perfectionistic. He commented that he was fearful that he would not say completely accurate things about his condition and that a reader of the book might be somehow harmed if he didn't say things perfectly. It's going to be in print, and he would feel guilty if anything were misleading. Also, he related that he spent quite a bit of time deciding where to park his car so the degree of sunlight or shade would not harm his iPhone.

David's father was an engineer of German heritage, a recovered alcoholic who was particular in his life and work but not compulsively perfectionistic. He usually had a right way to do things.

His mother, who is still living, has had times of drinking and times of sobriety, as well as times of emotional stress and other times of what could be termed "emotional sobriety." His mother was very perfectionistic about clothing and about protecting a good image. Appearances were paramount for her and other members of the family.

David recalled that if he was not picked up at school at 3:00 P.M., his mother was probably going into a drinking bout and his father would come at around 5:00 P.M. The family shifted into a different routine for the duration of the mother's binge.

He was embarrassed by his mother's emotional outbursts and tried to create a composed, moderate emotional temperament for himself. The family home atmosphere was a mixture of loving, fun times and angry times surrounding his mother's drinking. His parents divorced when David was fifteen. He sought attention through negative actions up until about eighteen years of age and shifted into getting positive attention as a young adult.

David commented that he believes there are genetic components to perfectionism and also learned components. His mother's father was an engineer who built radio stations. He was precise and careful in his work, but always ended the day at 6:00 P.M. He drank an occasional beer, but there was no drinking to excess. David's grandmother, who is still living at ninety-four, was one of ten children. Her father drank, but stopped of his own accord, and one sibling became a drinker but eventually found sobriety.

David's obsessive-compulsive behaviors started during his teen years when he became excessively interested in hygiene. He did not want to contaminate various objects, such as his guitar. He began repeated hand washings during those years. There was always an undue concern for the care of clothing and material things, and he worked out excessively, wanting his body to be perfect. Any asymmetry of the pectoral muscles was disturbing to him. During his younger years, he had a sense that he wanted to master his own life, to be great at something.

When David was a young adult, he became obsessed with his eyesight. For twelve years he wanted desperately to have perfect eyesight and developed a repetitive habit of taking off his glasses and putting them back on. He read numerous books on healing vision and tried various methods of eye exercises. Finally a friend did an intervention and helped him to accept imperfect vision.

Perfectionism and obsessive behaviors continue to be a part of David's current life, although in a more moderate fashion. He uses his attention to detail in a positive way in his work, checking contracts until they are exactly right. His company has a good record because of his attention to detail. David is also a musician, sometimes doing hundreds of takes on a song. He has learned to practice a song twenty or thirty times and than let it go, revisiting it on another day, and miraculously it sounds fine! Good enough is acceptable.

David is still concerned with complete accuracy in his speech. He wants everything to be communicated in a perfect way so that nothing is misunderstood. He becomes anxious about any error in articulation or word choice. He ruminates over the ramifications of being misunderstood and causing harm in someone's life.

He has had ongoing bodily concerns, worrying about things that could go wrong and sometimes do go wrong. He is passionate about sharing his experience with others who might unnecessarily suffer with similar anguish, going in mental circles with obsessive thoughts.

He wonders if perfectionism is a way to keep the lid on feelings that are too difficult to face, and has a sense that changes in behavior can lead to moderation of uncomfortable emotions and thoughts.

Obsessive-Compulsive Personality Disorder in Yourself

A person with OCPD is not a relaxed, peaceful person. She believes that she is correct and has great difficulty allowing others to do things, as they might do something wrong. She is preoccupied with rules, lists, and accurate ways of performing tasks. She is not a generous soul, tending toward miserliness, and she tends to keep material things, even when they are no longer useful. She is worried and fearful much of the time.

Is This You?

One lives with secrecy, hoping that one's constructed self looks acceptable to the outer world. One has to work to maintain cursory relations with the store clerks, mail carrier, and tellers at the bank. Can they imagine the underlying fears, the constant anxiety? It seems to be written on the forehead.

FACT

Panic attacks can be a part of the obsessive-compulsive constellation. Brief, intense episodes of fear and terror are accompanied by physical symptoms of sweating, tremors, and accelerated heart rate.

Do you find yourself being obsessed with hygiene? Are you checking your receding hairline every day? Do you push others to adhere to your standards of perfection? Do you become mistrusting of others when you see that they do not adhere to your rules or standards?

There is usually an undercurrent of evaluation going at all times, a mental monologue about how one is doing in comparison to others and how others are doing in reference to one's internal standards and rules. The monologue isn't verbalized out loud, but it can be a time-consuming mental preoccupation, a deep habit that leaves one exhausted.

Conversational Style

You may find your conversations peppered with many "always" and "nevers." "Should" appears frequently in your dialogue with others. You quite painfully discover that you alienate others when you coldly cut them off as you decide they do not measure up to what you had in mind at an earlier stage in the relationship. You find yourself manipulating others, distorting information in order to get your way in an effort to feel secure and in control.

You may be angry a lot of the time with a pervasive feeling that you have been wronged, invalidated, and abused. Others do not seem to share this view of your situation, causing further anger. This anger can give your voice an edge that puts people off.

ALERT

Watch out for mood swings that have nothing to do with external circumstances. Efforts to moderate the world within do wonders for a more orderly, serene existence in the outer realm.

Relationships

You find that you withdraw from relationships when you expect to be hurt or rejected. The other person senses your withdrawal and criticizes. It seems you can't win in your efforts to be close to another.

You find that you describe much of your experience as a catastrophe and that others do not share your view. It is annoying when they do not share your sense of the importance of the situation. You participate in endless circular arguments about these things and endure enormous frustration when the other person will not come around to your point of view.

Others have told you that your early experiences, or current situation, were enough to cause serious difficulty, even posttraumatic stress disorder, but you continue to deny that anything really awful happened.

But It Seems So Important!

Individuals with OCPD have a sense of entitlement that is often inappropriate for the given circumstances. They want favorable treatment and living conditions at all times, even if unwarranted or unearned. Reason does not help, as the OCPD person feels she absolutely must have the corner office, the paid parking, and the expense account, regardless of the department budget. It seems like a personal right.

Material items that are valued can turn into hoarding, and no amount of arguing or persuasion can help the obsessive person see that the situation has deteriorated to one of cancelled house insurance, police visits to determine the health of animals and people living with you, and arguments about what is and is not a fire hazard. It's as if a lens has clouded the perception of the individual, making each item a treasure instead of fodder for the local landfill.

Urgency/Emergency

A person with OCPD describes every event as a histrionic catastrophe. It is difficult to have an ordinary, calm conversation with such an individual, as she keeps pulling the conversation back to the disastrous nature of the event, trying to pull in the emotional engagement of the other person. They overreact to bad news or disappointments, often failing to see underlying difficulties that contributed to the deterioration of the situation. Much of this effort is an attempt to draw attention to the self, as if they are starved and this is the only way to be fulfilled. It can be tiring for those who attempt to befriend such a person.

People with OCPD may bait others into viewing a situation according to their opinion or best interests. Such conversations will have little reciprocal give and take, and the other person may walk away feeling as if she has been hit by a hurricane. The agenda for the exchange was not laid out at the beginning but covertly sneaked in after the conversation had begun. Because of these many interpersonal difficulties, it is a challenge for the obsessive-compulsive individual to form and maintain friendships.

What Can You Do Instead?

Be alert for a no-win scenario when you are involved with someone with OCPD. Only two unattractive options are considered, with considerable force to choose one or the other. With help, you can possibly see other choices, even if they are quite different from what could have been imagined by the obsessive-compulsive disordered person.

Resist Objectifying Others

With effort, other people can be seen as true individuals rather than objects. And it is not necessary to hold others to criteria that they have not agreed upon. This pressure causes others to become angry, and they may leave the situation, resulting in continued loneliness.

Try direct requests rather than resorting to passive-aggressive manipulations. Most intelligent people are insulted by such tactics. If there is a situation where you are feeling pressured by guilt or some other less than upfront method, catch it in the bud and decide whether it is something that is of interest to you. A lengthy discussion is not necessary, just a direct statement or request about what you would like to see occur.

Be alert to projection, the act of attributing traits, motivations, or assumptions to another person when they are actually believed or felt within the originating individual. For example, a jealous boyfriend shouts at his girlfriend, "You knew you should not have worn that sexy dress to the party! It caught every guy's attention in the room and made me look like a fool!" The woman had no such intention. She simply selected an attractive dress to wear to a party. Let the other person be a real person with his or her own characteristics and beliefs, not what might have been projected upon him or her.

Resist Miserliness

Do your best to keep unnecessary material objects to a minimum in your home and office. Although it may seem dangerous to get rid of things that you might need in the future, it's quite possible that, when that future moment arrives, you will have what you need.

Make an effort to be a little more financially generous with yourself and others. Miserliness can be a type of hoarding, a behavior and attitude that makes close relationships with others difficult. Try to imagine that life is always going to be generous to you, and no matter what, you will be able to provide for yourself and those close to you.

Aim for acceptance in terms of values, morals, ethnicity, and lifestyle cherished by others. Perhaps others really know what is best for themselves, and you become a more attractive person when you are not molding and judging others, however silently within yourself.

Selective memory is a habit of retrieving only part of a relevant situation that substantiates a bias or a particular point of view. Such behavior causes arguments and is detrimental to loving relationships. No one likes to have a particular reality dictated to them.

Be Gentle and Kind—Toward Yourself!

Carve out time for leisure and important relationships, even when you have a lot of work to do. It could be that some relaxation will enhance your enjoyment of your career and lessen the overemphasis on impossibly perfect details.

Make an agreement with yourself to work on a task for a finite length of time. However it turns out at that point is good enough, even if it's not perfect. Perhaps hand it off to a coworker at that point for a few finishing touches. This will enable you to complete work without getting stuck in the paralysis of perfection. You can breathe easier and enjoy a more relaxed life.

Continue Therapy

David, the subject of the case study, continues to check in with a therapist who knows him well. There are few crises in his life these days, but he appreciates the support of someone who has been with him on his journey to overcome compulsive perfectionism.

Perfection is not all that it is cracked up to be. Winston Churchill said it this way, "The human story does not always unfold like a mathematical calculation on the principle that two and two make four. Sometimes in life they make five or minus three; and sometimes the blackboard topples down in the middle of the sum and leaves the class in disorder and the pedagogue with a black eye." These types of incidents bring welcome comic relief.

CHAPTER 7

The Relationship of Perfectionism to Overeating and Other Eating Disorders

Researcher and writer Alice Domar noted in her book, *Be Happy Without Being Perfect*, that there are approximately 11 million people in the United States with the disorders of anorexia nervosa or bulimia nervosa. As a people, Americans are approaching the 50 percent mark in terms of obesity. Perfectionism plays a part in these tendencies. A study at the University of North Carolina at Chapel Hill identified obsessionality (the psychology term for perfectionism) as a behavior trait of overweight people. Many persons suffering from eating disorders have perfectionistic tendencies in terms of diet, exercise, body image, and weight.

Overeating in the Family

Certain variables in the family home can set up a propensity toward overeating at some point in adult life. Was there a tone of insecurity at home when you were young? One woman in a weight-control journaling group remembered that her alcoholic mother would sometimes fix dinner for her and sometimes not. On the afternoons she was passed out on the couch, the little girl would eat whatever she could find in the cupboards. This set up a dynamic of insecurity around food that was still present in her adult years. Nervously, she planned each meal and snack as if it might disappear.

Influences of the Mother

According to Domar, mothers who are perfectionistic and insecure have a detrimental effect on their daughters' body image. Such a mother may not feel attractive. She is never satisfied with herself or others, puts others down, never admits when she is wrong, is afraid of making mistakes, and is preoccupied with her weight and appearance.

ESSENTIAL

An interesting journal topic to explore is kitchen memories. Descriptions of those childhood scenes can sometimes unearth a surprising variety of memories and emotions. Who was there? Who did the cooking? What was the emotional tone? What are the fragrances? How do these almost forgotten associations influence you now?

This type of mother teaches insecurity to her daughters, increasing their risk for eating disorders. Mothers influence daughters' eating habits, body image, interest in physical activity, and level of self-esteem.

Scarcity Mentality

Were any of your relatives dramatically affected by the Great Depression or otherwise inclined to be excessively frugal? Scarcity around food or money can lend itself to overeating. If one is taught to waste not, want not, it ends up going to the waist. Overeating can be generational. If your parents were taught by their parents that food was hard to come by, those attitudes were part of the family legacy, which affects your shopping and food consumption today.

Incest

Were there conditions of incest in the home? In those types of families, layers of body fat can provide a protection against unwanted advances. Relationships are not a possibility because one does not feel attractive enough.

FACT

Research shows a relationship between incest and overeating. One may tend to bury unwanted memories and truths with the sedating aspects of food, or one may be tremendously dissatisfied with the physical body because it was misused by others. Or, if the child or youth felt physical pleasure during the unwanted act, there may be feelings of betrayal by the body, and often tremendous anger, which is numbed by consuming food.

Sex is not necessarily enjoyed if it was experienced under conditions of force at too young of an age for there to be mutual consent. Often persons with incest issues don't remember the incidents until they lose weight, as the memories are pushed underground. As the person gathers strength in the direction of having a positive body image, the psychological strength comes forward to handle the emotions of incest recovery work.

Anorexia and Control

Perfectionism in relation to eating disorders can become apparent in teenagers with anorexia when their behavior is about control. If the family environment is such that the family is constantly harping on the youngster, the one thing the child can control is what to eat and not eat. It can be the only out for a teenager who is controlled in every other aspect of life, sometimes bringing attention that is deeply desired, even if more negative than positive.

Criticism from other relatives dramatically impact a child and teenager. Were there instances in your childhood years when someone made comments about your weight? Were you measured, touched, or criticized in a bodily sense? This can set up hypersensitivity to weight-related topics in your adult years. One expects criticism, so it becomes internalized as a self-fulfilling prophecy.

Parental Example

Was food used as an abused substance by any of your parents, stepparents, or grandparents? A child who sees others binge learns that this is an acceptable way to pass time and endure difficult emotions. If weekend mornings included frosted doughnuts without fail and entertainment was eating in front of the TV, the die is cast in terms of the role of overeating for the children in the family.

What's Your Eating Style?

The following questions were developed by the National Eating Disorders Association to help people determine whether or not they have a problem with eating. An answer of "yes" to more than two could indicate the need for professional help in this area.

1. Do you prefer eating alone?
2. Do you constantly calculate calories?
3. Do you weigh yourself often?
4. Do you exercise because you have to, not because you want to?
5. Are you afraid of gaining weight?
6. Do you ever feel out of control when you are eating?

7. Do your eating patterns include extremes of dieting, food preferences, rituals, or secretive binging?
8. Has control over food become one of your primary concerns?
9. Do you feel guilty, disgusted, or ashamed after eating?
10. Do you worry about the size or shape of your body?
11. Do you feel as if your value is based on how you look and what you weigh?
12. Is it an emergency if you gain or lose a few pounds?

ALERT

Most people think that the biggest cause of death among persons with mental illness is suicide, but, in fact, more people die from eating disorders than other psychiatric illnesses. Exact figures are elusive because some die from associated disease, such as diabetes. One source estimates that 350,000 Americans die from eating disorders each year.

Numerous studies show a relationship between perfectionism and eating disorders. The person needs to feel perfect, and it comes out in exercise and eating patterns. Eating disorders are far more common than one would realize, and many are hidden, even from family and friends.

Usually the difficulty arises during the adolescent years, taking the form of starving, exercising excessively, forced vomiting, or purging with laxatives, enemas, or diuretics. Many people with eating difficulties look quite normal.

FACT

Victorian social thinking and art critic John Ruskin said, "All things are literally better, lovelier, and more beloved for the imperfections which have been divinely appointed."

How do you talk to yourself about your body and weight? Perfectionistic people may indulge in negative self-talk that could include the following statements.

- My thighs are too fat.
- My belly is too large.
- My weight is too high.
- I'm out of shape.
- My hair looks awful.
- I look ten years older than my actual age.
- My friends look better than I do.
- I'm disappointed in my body.
- I should be on a diet.
- I should have a higher sex drive.
- I am a pig.
- I am a failure, a disgusting mess.

Substitute a More Pleasurable Activity

Food is such a primitive pleasure that it may seem like a challenge to think of other things that could be as rewarding. It may take some time to trade food rewards for other rewards. It sometimes helps to think of other sensory rewards. Often participating in something highly creative will bring as much pleasure as favorite foods.

Black-and-White Extremes with Food

Do you find yourself going on an occasional or frequent fling of binging because you ruined the day with one extra snack? You may have added a pastry to your midmorning coffee break and find yourself bulldozing through the rest of the day with pizza, candy, cookies, chips, and a nighttime snack of ice cream out of the carton. The day was shot anyway and you can always start again tomorrow. Literally, this is true, but it is also possible to stop the trend after the first unneeded snack without going to the extremes of indulgence. Distorted thinking is behind such actions.

FACT

Magical thinking and fantasy can sometimes be a part of perfectionism and weight difficulties. "When I'm down to my perfect weight, I'll find the perfect mate." "After I've lost my extra twenty pounds, I will look for a more satisfying job." "Getting down to the weight I had as a newlywed will solve all my marriage problems." One knows subconsciously that these things are not true, but the emotions are too difficult to face. The result is inaction and stagnating in the status quo.

One can also find distorted thinking in regard to exercise. There is a hesitation to exercise for only ten minutes, as everyone knows that one has to exercise thirty minutes three times a week to have any effect. Any exercise is always better than none, and some studies reveal that short exercise sessions spaced throughout the day are quite effective in lowering blood pressure.

Set Some Realistic Goals

It probably is not possible to attain the appearance and weight you had in high school. A size four is not the answer to happiness. Sometimes it works well to set weight-loss goals in increments. A pound a week is usually manageable. One can reach a plateau, become comfortable with it, and then set a new goal.

Some people are less perfectionistic about weight loss if they stay off the scale and focus on forming different habits, especially with exercise. One can decide to use the stairs rather than the elevator and park at the edge of the parking lot instead of close to the office door.

Some individuals find that focusing on one health change at a time brings good long-term results. A person might decide not to eat while watching television, or to perhaps drink coffee black instead of with sugar and cream. It might be fun to take over the dog-walking responsibilities from the children and enjoy the added exercise. Physical exercise is a wonderful substitute for formerly unhealthy habits because it decreases stress, one of the triggers for excessive snacking.

Learning Some New Sensory Pleasures

If food is the only pleasure or the most significant sensory pleasure in life, it helps to learn others. Then excess food won't be missed so greatly. It can be a slow process, building a larger repertoire of things that are satisfying to the senses. Some of the senses may be dulled, due to years of overeating.

What about Sex?

Perfectionistic people assume that everyone is having mind-blowing sex, as the characters in popular media seem to have that sort of lifestyle. In actuality, the sex drive waxes and wanes throughout different stages of life. It is normal during times of great stress or crisis for the sex drive to be at almost zero. Having a baby, going through a job layoff, or divorce can plummet the libido.

Here are some thoughts for enjoying sex, even if you don't have a perfect body:

- The opposite sex does not need for you to look perfect in order to enjoy sex with you.
- More than likely, you are more critical of your appearance than your partner is.
- Actions are more important than appearance, and if you feel sexy, you will be sexy.
- Sometimes sex isn't perfect, but it still can be enormously enjoyable.
- Self-pleasuring is a good way to learn one's specific preferences for arousal, which then can be communicated to the partner.
- Read books to learn about sexuality, especially if you are in a category that is usually ignored (handicapped, ill, or aging). There are many useful, adaptive suggestions out there.
- Consider therapy if you feel intense shame, guilt, remorse, or fear around sexual activity.

Focus on the Aesthetics

Have you ever had an opportunity to eat while immersed in the rituals of another culture? Often the meals are pleasurable because of the beauty of the process, the dishes and utensils, or the marvelous companionship involved. For example, the Japanese tea ceremony is lengthy and quite beautiful, focusing on the honor of the person served. It is deeply satisfying to be the recipient in the ceremony. Korean people sometimes use communal service dishes, as each individual at the table takes bite-sized pieces with chopsticks. This custom adds to the fellowship of the occasion.

When you eat alone, set yourself a fine table, using attractive dishes, tablecloth, and cloth napkin. Caution yourself against rushing through to the end of the meal. The slower you savor the experience, the less you will be inclined to eat. If you eat alone in a restaurant, you can enjoy the ambiance of the place, the service, and the presence of others dining, even if you are not directly talking with them. Perhaps there is live music to add another layer of sensory delight.

When you cook at home, aim for a variety of colors, temperatures, and textures on your plate. Balance something mild with something a bit spicy. Bright colors are satisfying to the eye. Surprises in texture delight the senses involved in taste, chewing, and swallowing.

ALERT

Different cultures have different temperature and taste rhythms that are customary during a meal. If you're missing that "certain something" to satisfy yourself, it could be a part of that cultural meal rhythm. You can eat your way through a lot of food, trying to find the missing taste or satisfaction. In western European and American dinner culture, a meal usually concludes with a hot drink and something sweet. A cup of hot tea and a dish of sliced fresh fruit might be satisfying.

If a dish is meant to be hot, serve it hot, not lukewarm. Although it is natural to gravitate toward preferred favorites, it can be enjoyable to try something different. Kale chips are flavorful and healthy. Mediterranean figs wrapped in grape leaves are surprisingly delicious. It might be fun to partner with a friend to explore a different ethnic restaurant once a month and then try to prepare similar foods at home.

Pack Your Lunch

If too many business lunches are wrecking your waistline as well as your bank account, it makes sense to plan your food at home and take it to work. The old days of baloney sandwiches and potato chips are long gone. Carry over your new-found enjoyment of the aesthetics and ritual of food to your lunches at your desk. Focus on the same variety of color, texture, and temperature that you enjoy in your own home. Such self-care can provide you with a psychological lift that protects you from hitting the vending machines at 3:00 P.M. Broccoli florets, hummus with pita, and herbal tea nurture the spirit as well as the body.

Focus on Sharing Rather Than Eating

If you love to cook but want to minimize the risk of overeating your creations, it can be very enjoyable to prepare meals or snacks for others. The emphasis is on what they enjoy rather than what you're consuming. Most people love to be catered to in this way, as it recalls associations of being provided for in their mother's or grandmother's kitchen. You can solidify important relationships be preparing good food and serving it.

ESSENTIAL

Cooking as a creative act is marvelous. The cook will enjoy experimenting, and the praise will make the cook feel appreciated. One might develop a specialty of homemade breads, soups, or party cakes. Mistakes are almost always easily fixed. Too much seasoning is rectified by adding more flour or liquid, and the fallen cake layer can be propped up with toothpicks, marshmallows, or stiff frosting.

Others may be interested in learning cooking skills from you. When your kitchen, heart, and talents are open to others, everyone benefits, and the heat is off your perfectionistic tendencies with food and eating. The focus is on learning something new and enjoying the communal pleasures of preparing food together and having a friendly meal.

Explore Your Other Senses

It can be a wonderful adventure to fully indulge senses apart from taste. It might be interesting to get a season ticket to a symphony series or seek out strange music in hole-in-the wall venues. Imagine a stroll in the French Quarter of New Orleans. Although the wonderful food is certainly present, the focus is on the luscious sounds of Louisiana jazz. Be aware of summer music events in park bandstands or farmers' markets, often free.

Consider getting a museum membership so that you can satisfy your eye and intellect with marvelous creations arranged beautifully. A long visit to a museum store can be as fun as a stroll through a gallery, and you might find a journal that will make your self-exploration appealing rather than another chore.

If you have never considered massage as a typical part of your life, at least think about enjoying this type of attention occasionally. It can be interesting to sample the various modalities of bodywork. You might like Trager, Reiki, or heavy duty Swedish. Try a hot stone massage at least once. It can be great to work with a massage therapist who includes rituals from various healing cultures, incorporating fragrances and healing totems.

What Can You Do Instead?

It might be interesting to go on a media diet. Refuse television for a week or so and cut down on magazines. One has to realize that hundreds of people apply for positions in the public eye, and the producers choose the most attractive ones. Even models themselves say that when they see a perfectly airbrushed photo of themselves, they exclaim that they do not really look like that image. It helps to stay away from it for a while, as it is natural to compare oneself to those unrealistic portrayals of the human form.

Writer and researcher Alice Domar offers a checklist to determine whether an individual is preoccupied with an unrealistic body image. See what you think about these statements in connection to what you believe about yourself and your body:

- I am completely aware of what I eat.
- When I interact with a very attractive person, I feel inferior.

- I point out my flaws when I speak with others.
- I don't enjoy shopping because nothing looks good on me.
- People say I exercise too much.
- I don't believe people when they say I am attractive.
- I believe I should have self-control over what I eat.
- The thinner I am, the more I like myself.
- My anxieties about how I look interfere with my enjoyment of sex.
- I don't like seeing pictures of myself.
- I am disappointed with myself when I become sick.

These beliefs are clues to an unrealistic perception of one's physical self. Such attitudes can be corrected with effort. Try to catch yourself making silent, perfectionistic statements to yourself, and offer a loving comment instead.

Balance Solitary Eating with Social Meals

If you discover that most of your temptation to overeat comes when you are alone, remember to include others in your mealtimes. Such social experiences take away the taboo nature of food, as everyone is eating and enjoying themselves. The emphasis is on the conversation rather than the specific foods and how much is eaten. On the other hand, if you have found yourself with a crowd of friends or family members who tend to overeat as entertainment, you might want to pull away from that and eat alone some of the time, find more health-conscious eating buddies, or join the overeaters only for coffee.

What about Meals While Traveling?

What can you do when you travel, visiting family, friends, or a business conference? These occasions require some advance planning. For friends and family, you might offer to prepare some of the meals, so you have some of the decision-making control of what goes into the meal. Offer to shop with family members, and if necessary, fix your own meal apart from those indulging in the ten-cheese burritos. It doesn't hurt to pack along some of your healthy snacks in an airline carry-on tote. Often business conference chefs are quite able to prepare adaptive meals for special preferences—low sodium or fat, gluten free, vegan or vegetarian. Watch out for the temptation to eat whatever is available simply because it is covered by the expense account.

Remember Self-Forgiveness

Perfectionists with eating issues tend to be so very hard on themselves. One little mistake and the day is shot, offering an excuse to eat oneself through the remainder of the day, starting anew tomorrow. Instead, practice self-forgiveness with each infraction, regardless of how small or large. Think in terms of which foods are healthy for your body and which are unhealthy, making your eating decisions accordingly. Consider changing your self-talk, eliminating statements such as, "I was bad today" or "I was good today" in reference to whether you had a candy bar or a handful of baby carrot sticks. The things you eat do not define a person, and certainly no eating action makes an individual bad or good. Such extremism lends itself to many errors and too much self-criticism.

Substitute Exercise for Eating

In recent years exercise has taken so many specific new directions that it seems overwhelming to think of beginning a new physical habit. Pilates seems so challenging, and all of the participants already look perfect and do not even need the class. Yoga might require that you twist yourself into a pretzel while chanting "Om," and the hikers expect you to be able to walk five miles, which, of course, requires a whole different wardrobe of hiking gear.

FACT

A type of exercise that is enjoyed is more likely to be repeated, and ultimately embraced, as a longer-term part of a balanced life. It takes about twenty-one repetitions for a new activity to become a habit.

Such perfectionistic perceptions are apt to stop a person even before the new habit is begun because it seems to be a sheer impossibility. What about choosing something that you actually like to do? Remember some of your childhood pursuits when you did physical things for fun? Maybe you loved the roller rink. See if your local rink has an adult night and try it once. Did you enjoy a swim club? Look for a pool where you can pay as you go without committing yourself to a membership. Perhaps social dance is your forte. This type of event combines exercise with socializing, which is marvelous for your overall well-being.

A simple walk each day requires no special clothing or shoes and raises your mood while lowering your blood pressure. Even an outing of twenty minutes connects you with nature and your neighbors. It can be quite pleasurable to breathe deeply, lengthening the stride, and swinging your arms rhythmically.

Part of the challenge of managing perfectionism as an aspect of an overeating difficulty is that one has to eat in order to survive. It is not an obsessive substance such as alcohol or cigarettes, where one can completely eliminate the culprit and lead a normal life.

Consider Gardening

Working with your hands in the soil can be a soothing antidote for difficulties with eating issues. The elements of nature are calming, and you may attain a sense of peace as your actions increase the health and beauty of your flowers or homegrown herbs.

Famous transcendentalist Ralph Waldo Emerson said, "When I go into my garden with a spade, and dig a bed, I feel such an exhilaration and health that I discover that I have been defrauding myself all this time in letting others do for me what I should have done with my own hands."

It might be satisfying to cultivate your own vegetable garden, even if you only have a bit of balcony space in a busy urban environment. Raised beds are popular and do not require a lot of ground space, as you can walk around all four edges of the perimeter. Once you have tasted fresh tomatoes directly from the garden, you will wonder how you ever could eat supermarket tomatoes that have been trucked thousands of miles and artificially ripened.

Getting Support

As perfectionism in connection with eating is one of the more difficult obsessions to manage, it is helpful to seek out individuals and groups who can assist you along the way. If you work in an office where everyone heads for the break room and double chocolate brownies during the afternoon coffee break, you may want to find at least one coworker who will agree to keep you company as you forgo the temptations. It is difficult to endure the questions and teasing when one changes a habit. A walking buddy can give you attention as you share your successes and struggles, and someone you could check in with by phone when you are battling with a stressor.

The thriving weight-loss industry provides many choices in individual help and group offerings. It may take some time to investigate the many alternatives to see what feels comfortable in terms of the personal value system and pocketbook. Overeaters Anonymous is free, except for voluntary donations. There is no pressure to contribute. Weight Watchers has been thriving for decades, as its simple program teaches the participants new tastes and portion sizes compatible with a healthy weight.

CHAPTER 8

The Relationship of Perfectionism to Alcoholism

More is known about alcoholism than other addictions. Since the 1930s and the inception of the worldwide program of Alcoholics Anonymous, alcoholics, their friends and family, and professionals in the field of substance abuse continue to learn about the complex nature of what is now termed a disease, not a moral weakness. Alcoholism seems to be a multifaceted affliction, a disease with spiritual, emotional, mental, and physical components. Genetics play a role, as alcoholism moves through generations, more often affecting males. Perfectionism is an aspect of the puzzle of alcoholism.

Perspective of John Bradshaw's Work

John Bradshaw's books and seminars brought a greater understanding of alcoholism into public awareness. *On the Family*, *Healing the Shame That Binds You*, and *Homecoming* fully explore the far-reaching tentacles of the disease and how these tentacles damage each person in the family in ways that continue through adult life and generationally, unless each person makes the effort to heal. Numerous recovery programs and therapeutic specialties have arisen from this work in the 1980s.

Family Roles

Bradshaw makes it very clear that the presence of an addiction or major dysfunction in a family splinters the group, and each person is likely to take on a role so that the organism can function as a whole, though in a halting, faulty way. Some of the family roles he recognized are as follows:

1. Star or Hero

The Star in the alcoholic family is the high achiever who wins acclaim and some positive attention for the group. She is a straight-A student, known and respected in the community, and is likely multitalented, earning prizes, newspaper accounts, and praise from teachers. She is expected to be perfect because her job is so important.

FACT

Alcoholism is often connected with a child trauma. In the case of Bill Wilson, the founder of Alcoholics Anonymous, his parents separated and divorced. He lived with his grandparents while his mother went to medical school. He had little contact with either parent and became obsessed with learning to play the violin.

The family has so many difficulties that it is up to this one person to rectify the situation by creating something positive. If she fails, the family is likely to disintegrate, so there is a lot of pressure inherent in the situation. This role can be akin to that of a sacrificial lamb, as the role does not allow for self-inquiry, fooling around, or simply doing things because they bring joy. It is almost as if the whole purpose of the Star's existence is to make the family okay or to make the alcoholic okay. The personality has been seriously hijacked for other uses.

2. Clown

This role brings comic relief, as everyone in an alcoholic family is stressed, tired, worried, and frightened. The Clown, sometimes the youngest child, is finely attuned to the alcoholic dynamic and knows with perfect timing when to crack a joke or accidentally on purpose fall off a chair in order to dissipate tension and divert attention. Everyone in the family depends on this person to do this job without fail. It seems a pleasant enough role, but limiting in the long run. It is difficult for the family clown to be taken seriously in life. She may want to pursue a demanding profession, but the family minimizes her goals, seeing her only as the fluffy goof-off. This role can be taken into the work environment. The person might be very well liked, but her contributions to the board meeting are often restated by another person, who then takes credit for the idea. The Clown's input is likely to be trivialized both personally and professionally.

3. Rebel

This person in the alcoholic family is similar to the Star, but in a more negative way. Often a son, he draws attention away from the alcoholic problem by getting into trouble himself. He may be truant from school, in trouble with the law, dabble in illegal or legal substances, or involved in crime at a young age. He is perfect in his ability to create a diversion when the family is wound up to the breaking point over the difficulties caused by an alcoholic.

ALERT

Alcoholics sometimes create diversions with accusations and other provoking actions. This is to take the attention away from their drinking. It is wise not to react to such tactics, as the arguments are futile. If one topic isn't successful, the alcoholic will toss out another. It is best not to engage.

The Rebel's job is as important as any other role, and as with the other roles, it is limiting. He has difficulty growing out of the bad boy image, even when the role has been outgrown. He, like other members with a role, is denied the freedom to experiment, to try various ways of living and solving problems in order to meet his needs. Sometimes he drops out of school and is handicapped in choosing a career, turning to crime in adult years.

4. Lost Child

Like the family Hero, the Lost Child is very good. She wouldn't dream of doing anything wrong because she is frightened of losing approval. She is somewhat invisible, as everyone is too busy putting out other brush fires in order to see that she even has any needs. She is average in many ways— appearance, personality, and school achievement. Sometimes she brings attention to herself by becoming sick. This type of diversion is not criticized, as it seems genuinely out of her control. A major illness can momentarily shift the family focus to this Lost Child and give her some needed attention. Sometimes the Lost Child continues being sick in adult life, as illness is perceived at the subconscious level to bring rewards. Persons with chronic illnesses in adult years may find that the role brought attractive goodies in the alcoholic home. If one develops a perfectly horrible illness, there is even more attention.

Codependency

All the family members are codependent with one another. Each one is finely tuned to the other, as needs are anticipated without them being spoken and pressures are exerted to keep everyone in their proper place. Often the partner of the alcoholic is highly codependent, imagining that making circumstances perfect in some way will have an effect on whether or not the person drinks. This type of magical thinking is exhausting and time-consuming, as the codependent spouse works harder, keeps the career going, ensures the children are clean and well-behaved, and presents a good face to the community. The situation is rampant with perfectionism, as none of the actions have the desired effect. One tries harder but can never succeed. Perfectionism is a quite common trait for the spouse of an alcoholic.

Alcoholism in the Family

Alcoholism devastates family relationships. Each individual has deep, unmet needs but does not realize it. Family pressures keep the dirty laundry within the home, and secrets are locked into each person. Older children sometimes take over the cooking, childcare, and management of the household.

Alcoholics are sometimes the type of person who tried very hard to do something but failed. The deep remorse pushes the person toward the bottle. Jim Rubens, author of *OverSuccess: Healing the American Obsession with Wealth, Fame, Power, and Perfection*, found interesting connections between perfect success and addictions of various kinds. Those who lose out, such as chronic gamblers and failures in the work force, turn to smoking and alcohol. Rubens cites figures of one in four Americans who are clinically addicted to a substance or behavior, indeed a high cost to being a part of the rat race of high success.

On the other hand, highly recognized success is no guarantee against the grip of addictions. Those who make it in a visible way can become oversensitized to perfection and seek an addictive outlet, such as pornography or cocaine. One sees examples of this in highly successful businesspeople or celebrities in the entertainment industry. To the outside viewer, it seems that such a high degree of success would bring enormous security and satisfaction, but sometimes the opposite is true. The material opulence brings forth deeper inner demons, and the tortured person seeks greater addictive experiences, such as hard drugs or dangerous behaviors. Rubens views the American culture's extreme emphasis on perfection and success as a costly social disease.

Denial, Not a River in Egypt

Sometimes called the elephant in the living room, denial is rampant in alcoholic homes. "The alcoholic is not drunk; she is taking a nap." "No, there wasn't a fight last night; you made that up." "I didn't go to your school play because you didn't tell me about it; how could you be so stupid?"

Each individual in the family used denial to protect themselves and each other from the surreal horror of the disease. Otherwise, nobody could function.

Denial is prevalent even among highly intelligent people when alcoholism is very much part of the picture. It can be a protection so that the person can function in life, as the bald truth would be devastating. The spouse may realize on some level that there will ultimately be a divorce but feels unable to accept the idea at the moment. Sometimes, with the help of therapy or recovery groups, the layers of resistance are peeled away, one at a time, generally at the pace that the person can accommodate new understandings.

Isolation

Each person is emotionally isolated, and the family as a whole is isolated from the community at large. The family members are ashamed about the alcoholism and its effects, often blaming themselves for the problem. It is common to see people in an alcoholic family spending large periods of time alone in separate rooms in the house, or in the same room but each plugged in to his own electronic device.

Because they don't have the emotional support to help with their burdens, children in alcoholic families suffer socially. They realize that they are different, although may not be able to pinpoint exactly how. They are discouraged from bringing friends home from school, as they never know if the parent will be drunk or not. They are embarrassed by unpredictable violence or inappropriate verbal outbursts. Some clever children in these types of families form close alliances with teachers or parents of their friends, easing some of the discomfort of the alcoholic dynamic.

Distorted Communication

Communication in alcoholic families is badly distorted or nonexistent. Children are punished for speaking up about their wants and needs, so they learn not to have wants and needs. The exception to the pressures against honest talk is that the alcoholic generally has free rein, shouting orders to everyone or plaintively manipulating from the sick bed.

Alcoholism, sometimes termed an obsession of the mind, twists all channels of communication within the family. The alcoholic can be very quick to divert the attention from his wrongdoing, thus persuading others in the family to doubt their perceptions and blame themselves for being mistaken about something. What seems true is untrue, and something else is deemed to be true. This distortion afflicts even the brightest members of the alcoholic family and can take years of effort to untangle. Some people with alcoholic relatives who have died still feel unspoken directives from the grave.

FACT

Stepping Stones, the home of Bill Wilson and Lois Wilson in New York State, is now a museum where visitors can see materials from the early days of AA and Al-Anon, enjoy the simple household furnishings of the influential couple, and visit Bill's writing cabin, where he wrote some of the AA books. Lois Wilson was the founder of Al-Anon, the sister program to AA, which helps friends and families of alcoholics.

Persons in an alcoholic family are quick to accuse each other of wrongdoing, and no one is encouraged to own up to mistakes. Some people become very meek, while others mask their insecurities with bravado. Perfectionism and other addictions become rampant, but nobody speaks of them. All these outlets and compensations are necessary to keep the family functioning. These tendencies increase in intensity as the disease runs its course, becoming progressive with ensuing problems of greater severity.

Compulsivity and Perfectionism

Compulsivity and perfectionism go hand in hand with alcoholism and the effects on other family members. The alcoholic tends to be an all-or-nothing kind of person. If she has a bottle of wine, she is driven to finish it off. Alcoholics are famous for "closing the joint" when they are out enjoying themselves with other drinkers. Those close to the alcoholic become compulsive in other ways. Most of the addictions of substance and behavior find their roots in the presence of alcoholism or some other addiction in the childhood home. Those in the family try to cope with the distress of alcoholism in a variety of ways. They may become people pleasers, workaholics, overachievers, substance abusers, obsessed with fame and attractiveness, or struggle with money issues, such as debt or gambling.

ESSENTIAL

Anxiety drives perfectionism in the members of an alcoholic family. Each individual hopes that she can control the drinker's behavior by doing something perfectly. As this, of course, is never going to happen, the anxiety becomes a deeply ingrained motivator for behavior. Even though the cycle is futile, the individual keeps trying unless outside information and help is sought.

Self-esteem is lacking within each person in the family, although it will be difficult for the alcoholic to admit it. Sometimes basic survival needs are barely met, not to mention the niceties of emotional support and spiritual sustenance. Therapists' and psychiatrists' offices are filled with clients whose difficulties originated in alcoholic homes, as the effects touch every aspect of life far into adult years. As those effects are invisible, it takes tremendous tenacity to trace them.

One person may become a compulsive cleaner, never satisfied until there is not a spot of dust anywhere in the home. Another becomes obsessive-compulsive, washing his hands until they are raw. Another may become a dropout from society, as he could never measure up to the idea of what his parents expected in a son. He languishes in his camper home, randomly reading books, as life passes him by.

Compulsivity and perfectionism are present in persons with the disorders of narcissistic personality disorder and borderline personality disorder, both of which have possible roots in alcoholic or other dysfunctional homes. Narcissists demand that everyone cater to their needs and expectations, requiring that circumstances be perfect in order to feel okay. Borderline personality people have no tolerance for error, in themselves or others, creating a dynamic that is challenging in relationships at work and at home.

ESSENTIAL

Persons who come from alcoholic homes tend to select mates who are unavailable in some way, thus creating the drive to make things right in the family of origin. The workaholic spouse is too busy to spend time together, and the Internet-addicted partner has more important things to do than enjoy a romantic evening. One may develop a pattern of relationships with people who are already married. The neglected one tries very hard to win over the other, repeating the earlier pattern from the childhood home.

Alcoholics perhaps tend toward perfectionism because of low self-esteem themselves. They are quick to judge—especially others. In order to try to feel good about themselves, they want to be the smartest and the best at whatever they do. It is difficult for the alcoholic personality to accept the idea of being an equal among equals or to simply put in a day's ordinary work for an ordinary wage. Often very creative, charismatic people, they expect themselves and others to be at the top of their game at all times. The trait of perfectionism in alcoholics and those who are closely associated with them can be taxing and wearing. The challenge is that the alcoholic perfectionist sees this position as a good thing. She believes that at least one person has to do quality control in the situation.

Are You a Drinker?

Alcoholics Anonymous created a list of Twenty Questions, which is a quick checklist for possible alcoholism. The list, one of the early pieces of AA literature, is as follows:

1. Do you lose time from work due to drinking?
2. Is drinking making your home life unhappy?
3. Do you drink because you are shy with other people?
4. Is your drinking affecting your reputation?
5. Have you ever felt remorse after drinking?

FACT

As of January 2012, there were 114, 070 Alcoholics Anonymous groups worldwide with over 2,133,842 members. The organization is supported by the voluntary donations of members at the meetings.

6. Have you ever gotten into financial difficulties as a result of drinking?
7. Do you turn to lower companions and an inferior environment when drinking?
8. Does your drinking make you careless of your family's welfare?
9. Has your ambition decreased since drinking?
10. Do you crave a drink at a definite time?
11. Do you want a drink the next morning?
12. Does drinking cause you to have difficulty in sleeping?
13. Has your efficiency decreased since drinking?
14. Is drinking jeopardizing your job or business?
15. Do you drink to escape from worries or trouble?
16. Do you drink alone?
17. Have you ever had a complete loss of memory as a result of drinking?
18. Has your physician ever treated you for drinking?
19. Do you drink to build up your self-confidence?
20. Have you ever been to a hospital or institution because of drinking?

This list is often used in hospitals and recovery centers to determine whether the patient is possibly an alcoholic. Generally, within the recovery movement it is presumed the decision of the alcoholic to determine whether or not he is an alcoholic. He is apt to be quite resistant to others labeling him as such, an aspect of the trait of denial. The trait of defiance may become painfully evident with year after year of protest.

Learning Other Ways to Have Fun and Be with Others

After becoming sober, the alcoholic has to learn new ways to enjoy herself. While drinking, the alcohol was necessary to smooth over human interactions, as often the alcoholic is somewhat shy, feeling ill at ease in many social settings. With drink in hand, the person feels instantly charming, clever, and wise. It is quite difficult for alcoholics to give up the social crutch of liquor, as the uncomfortable emotions and lack of social skills have to be faced and overcome.

Those who become sober in the context of a recovery center or AA club will find many alcohol-free events to enjoy, especially around holiday weekends when alcoholics tend to feel vulnerable and at risk for drinking again. Often with the help of a sponsor, a person who mentors the newly sober alcoholic through the Twelve Steps and through life's various challenges, the alcoholic learns to enjoy new activities.

FACT

In the context of safe recovery settings, alcoholics can learn social skills—extending a hand to newcomers, introducing fellow members to each other, and getting together before and after meetings for extra fellowship. The comfort of commonality gives the newly sober individual a bit of courage in speaking to others without alcohol coursing through his or her veins.

Sometimes in the company of fellow sober people, the alcoholic travels, undertakes hobbies, or throws himself into service for the benefit of other new people in sobriety. Some become quite active on the speaker circuit, sharing their recovery stories with others who are just starting their journey.

Sex and Sobriety

Many alcoholics have never had sex without the relaxing effects of alcohol. Inhibitions are set aside with the help of the bottle. Within the context of sobriety, one has to learn new ways of being intimate, learning not to be afraid of strong, complex emotions that emerge in the close presence of another person. Some programs in recovery centers and some meetings with twelve-step programs focus on the challenges of intimacy after the effects of alcoholism, both for the alcoholic and those other members of the family who have been scarred by alcoholic behavior. Some speaker events spotlight the success of a particular couple who is doing well to maintain their relationship within the context of sobriety from alcohol. Others shun sex, finding it too frightening, focusing instead on the daily challenge of staying sober.

Redefinition of Fun

For the person who has only realized pleasure as being drunk and high, it is an enormous culture shock to imagine life without the chaos and commotion surrounding substance abuse. One has to find different friends, as their former buddies are still drunk and high. More time is available for leisure, as one is not preoccupied with getting the next drink and figuring out who is going to pay for it. The alcoholic may have to become accustomed to more subdued levels of pleasure—expressing oneself on the dance floor or going on a sober cruise. The wonders of nature may bring more appeal, as weekend binges are replaced with trips to the beach. Another may become fascinated with books and literacy, seeking out similar friends or online groups for the discussion of ideas found in books.

What Can You Do Instead?

For alcoholics, substituting one thing for another can be tricky, as it could veer into the dangerous thinking of substituting beer for hard drinks, drinking only on weekends, or only drinking at home. These are the attempts of the clever mind to sidestep the progressive nature of the disease. Unlike food as an addictive substance, alcohol has to be completely given up in order to arrest its devastating course. Abstinence means no alcohol. However, those in sobriety discover that there are other ways to enjoy life.

Sports and Fitness

After years of abuse to the body, it can be enjoyable to shift gears and cherish the miracle of the human form. Past enjoyable pursuits can be cultivated again—racquetball, swimming, horseback riding, or hiking. Many types of sports include the social aspects as well, counteracting the alcoholic's tendency to brood alone.

Service to Fellow AA Members

Service is generally a requirement of AA sponsors, but it can be up to the individual to take on more responsibility, possibly serving the fellowship above the group level. When one is a group representative at the state, national, or international level, the obsession with alcohol is redirected toward the good of the organization as a whole and its continued ability to assist others who are at a different stage of recovery.

FACT

Returning to school can be appealing to alcoholics after sobriety. Some find a satisfying niche in programs leading to certification as drug and alcohol counselors. Having "been there," the sober alcoholic can effectively combine service to others and a new, useful career.

There are panels to present in hospitals and institutions, and committees to plan numerous conventions. Whatever perfectionistic inclinations an alcoholic has can be focused on being friendly to every newcomer and offering coffee and snacks to each person who visits a convention hospitality room.

Healthy Relationships

Generally, alcoholics are advised to stay out of romantic relationships until after a year of sobriety. At some point, though, it can be appealing to form and maintain a close, sustained relationship with another person. If one is already in a relationship while achieving sobriety, one can recommit to that person in a healthy way, correcting problems that were a result of the drinking and emotional neglect.

ALERT

Sober alcoholics have to be constantly vigilant for the pattern of putting down one addiction only to pick up another—overeating, gambling, overworking, spending too much time on the Internet, or participating in compulsive relationships. In the early years of AA, the rooms were guaranteed to be filled with smoke, and sweet treats were, and still are, almost always available.

Many alcoholics find that they are most comfortable with a partner who has a similar path, someone from the same recovery program. Others prefer someone who has a commitment to another program, such as Al-Anon, which provides that family member with healthy tools for relating to an alcoholic. Both people in the relationship have to keep their perfectionistic traits in check, as the temptation is always there to criticize the other person. Those difficult characteristics are always easier to see in someone else!

Improvements in Career

Alcoholics are generally quite talented, capable people, and after the detrimental effects of daily drinking are removed, the attention can be shifted to meaningful work. Often there is a great deal of damage to repair—debts to be repaid and apologies to supervisors and clients. Or one might want to retool and move into a different type of work. Sometimes people in sales, for example, find that the temptations of expense accounts and life on the road are too great for a newly sober person. There is a bar in every hotel.

A life closer to home and familiar meetings contributes greater security. Traveling musicians often discover the same thing. The adulation of the concert audience creates a high that can lead to drinking and other excesses of all kinds, but the adulation of the toddler son at home has no such risk. The musician may shift to session work or special events, such as conventions or weddings, trading stability and sobriety for fame.

Often as an alcoholic becomes more emotionally mature, former ego-driven striving gives way to enjoyment of being a part of a group, whether family or the sober fellowship, and eventually the satisfactions of giving service to humanity as a whole, as directed by the Higher Self or the Divine Source, emerges as the main point of one's time on earth. It's never too late for a fresh start or even complete reinvention!

CHAPTER 9

The Relationship of Perfectionism to Other Addictions

Generally speaking, the United States is an addictive society. Numerous addictions are rampant, especially behavioral addictions. You may know highly addictive people without realizing it. Imagine a paralegal preparing yet one more brief before going home at 10:00 P.M., the philandering spouse making a rendezvous on the way home, the gambler losing his apartment because of his inability to use his rent money for its proper purpose, the scholar insisting upon being published in the best journals every year, and the shopper filling the emptiness she feels in her soul with a massive redecorating project while running up all the household department store accounts and credit cards. You probably know someone similar to those scenarios.

Workaholism

Workaholism is a difficult addiction to pin down. It's somewhat like overeating, as a person has to work in order to survive. Most people spend many hours a week and many years devoted to gainful employment. The American culture reveres the ethic of working hard, so it can be somewhat tricky determining if a person has gone over the line of working addictively to the detriment of other aspects of life.

Signs and Symptoms of Workaholism

David Krueger, MD, offers the following list of questions to determine whether or not workaholism is present:

- Is there a set time to end the work day and start the evening or weekend?
- Do phone calls, meetings, and projects erode leisure time?
- Do you have withdrawal symptoms when not working—anxiety or depression?
- Has someone close to you accused you of being a workaholic?
- Do you constantly second-guess decisions and replay conversations?
- Is your identity as a person deeply intertwined with your work? Do you not enjoy yourself when you're doing something not connected with work?
- Do you take work setbacks very personally?
- Do you try to prove your worth to yourself or someone else by working hard?
- Are you working to please someone else or to satisfy your own ideals?
- Is work an escape? From what?

There is nothing inherently wrong with being passionate about one's career, thoroughly enjoying almost every aspect of it. It becomes addictive when one cannot stop, feeling that there is some danger when not working. Workaholism is the inability to relax. Often, workaholics will feel a need to constantly engage with work. Workaholism interferes with satisfying functioning in other areas of life.

ALERT

Perfectionism in the office holds inherent dangers of job dissatisfaction, poor relations with coworkers, procrastination, poor performance reviews, and carrying stress home.

Workaholics may struggle with underlying feelings of inadequacy and poor self-esteem, trying desperately to fill in the gaps of a shaky identity. Workaholics even work while on vacation, doing deals over the cell phone or laptop while sitting next to a beautiful beach in an exotic location.

A workaholic's significant other eventually starts to complain, as the loved one is never truly available. It's as if work is the mistress and the worker is constantly on call, never giving quality attention to friendships, family, or other aspects of life such as community, health, and enjoyable hobbies. Resentment builds up, and at first it seems difficult to criticize the person who is working all the time as there is a tangible result—support of the family. But this comes at what price?

Alice Domar discusses several cognitive distortions of people who are perfectionists in their work. She calls these twisted, unrealistic ideas "auto-thoughts." Some examples are as follows:

1. I can't start the next project until my desk is clean.
2. Everyone else is more competent than I am.
3. If someone criticizes my work, I'm a failure.
4. I can't leave this job because there's nothing else for me out there.
5. My coworkers are stupid.
6. If I had a better boss, my life would be better. I would be happier.
7. If I take personal time off, I won't get a promotion.
8. I shouldn't ask for help.
9. I cannot ever fail.

It's quite likely that what you expect of yourself as a perfectionist is far more than what your manager or supervisor expects of you. Think about whether your time could be spent doing other things if you did "good enough" work and stopped there.

Sex Addiction

Dr. Patrick Carnes brought the field of sex addiction into public awareness in the 1990s with his landmark books *Out of the Shadows*, *The Betrayal Bond*, and later *In the Shadow of the Net*, and *Don't Call It Love*. His work with thousands of patients in clinics in Mississippi and Arizona brought greater understanding about this painful addiction.

What are the signs and symptoms of sex addiction? Following is a brief checklist:

1. Do you spend time thinking about sex when you don't want to?
2. Does paying for sex negatively impact your finances?
3. Do you regret the time and energy spent on sex and romance?
4. Do you buy or rent pornographic videos or magazines? Pay for phone sex?
5. Have you had sex with a prostitute or visited massage parlors for sex?
6. Do you stare at people in public, imagining having sex with them?
7. If married, have you had sex outside your relationship without your partner's knowledge?
8. Does your sexual activity put you at risk for disease, or loss of marriage or your job?
9. Do you feel guilty or depressed following your sexual activities?
10. Do you keep your sexual activities secret from family, friends, and coworkers?

These behaviors and feelings about the behaviors indicate a problem with sexual addiction. The sex addict feels unable to stop or control the behavior, in spite of the emotional, social, physical, or financial costs. They often do not have emotional ties to the partners sought for addictive sexual activity.

FACT

In the United States alone, it is estimated that there are more than 60 million men, women, and children involved in Internet pornography addiction. Pornography use has a dramatic impact on individual lives, families, and society as a whole.

Perfectionism seems to be at the core of most addictions, including sex addiction. The afflicted individual has a drive to seek the perfect experience at all costs, to be perfect in the eyes of the other or oneself, and if he or she does not measure up, there is always the next time. Sex addiction can be a way of compensating for a feeling of failure in other aspects of life. One didn't reach the heights of success imagined at an earlier age, so it is easy to retreat to the sex chat rooms on the Internet.

Gambling

In many ways gambling is a part of the historical fabric of the United States, embedded in the psyche as romantic images in Western saloons of the nineteenth century and backroom poker games in speakeasies during Prohibition. Like the cowboy, the gambler is an icon of masculine skill, with a bit of lure of danger.

The famous Shoshoni Native American woman Sacagawea, who accompanied Lewis and Clark on their great expedition across the country, was won by her first husband, Toussaint Charbonneau, in a gambling game.

As with the other behavioral addictions, when the activity takes over a person's life and one is unable to stop, the line has been crossed from pleasurable fun to problematic addiction. A well-situated attorney may keep his racetrack diversions secret from his wife, and she cannot figure out why they seem to never have any money, even though they both earn good salaries. A wealthy landowner plays the stock market every day, even though the bottom line shows a loss for several years in a row.

Signs of Gambling Addiction

Some signs of gambling addiction include:

1. Inability to stop gambling or cut back, even when losing.
2. Compulsive thinking about gambling.

3. Continued gambling despite loss of marriage, job, and good opportunities.
4. Needing more frequent and larger wagers in order to get the mental rush.
5. Withdrawal symptoms of irritability and depression when not gambling.
6. Using gambling for mood alteration and to attempt to win back losses.
7. Stealing and other fraudulent actions to get money for gambling.
8. Borrowing money in order to continue gambling.
9. Lying to friends and family about the extent of gambling.
10. Mood swings.

Like alcoholics, compulsive gamblers tend to show progression in their struggle with the grip of the addiction. Some suffer life-threatening situations before admitting that they have a problem. Others steadily deteriorate over a long period of time. Sometimes gambling runs in families with the children copying the patterns of gambling parents, or choosing a spouse with a gambling habit. One habitual sports bettor describes the childhood incident where he won $3.75 on a horse in the company of his father and uncle, setting a pattern that extended throughout his adult years.

What Does Research Say?

A study done at the University of Toronto and University of Winnipeg found a strong link between perfectionism and procrastination, with the added correlation of fear of failure. This could provide an explanation why the gambler continues, even with the losses piling up. There seems to be a belief that the next play will overcome all the losses and spare the person from failure. Other issues linked to problem gambling are poor impulse control, hoarding, and high-risk taking.

ESSENTIAL

Research studies show relationships between uses of substances and gambling activity. One shows that the brain activity of a cocaine user is similar to that of a gambler in the midst of gambling. Another shows that persons who smoke or use other substances addictively are more likely to continue gambling.

A Case Study

A middle-aged woman had a successful professional life as a researcher, but she was unable to maintain relationships with men because of her tendency to criticize and correct them. They would leave after a few months. During an outing to a casino with several girlfriends, the woman had her first experience of winning $200 at a slot machine. It seemed like heaven. She loved the trancelike feeling of sitting at the machine, hour after hour. The musical sounds of the machine calmed her perfectionistic thinking.

ALERT

Gambling is not age or gender specific. Some casinos in gambling towns have found that offering senior specialties will bring in large numbers of loyal customers. Loneliness seems to be a factor for isolated seniors, and having a meal and sitting at the machines or poker table becomes a habitual way to spend the afternoon and evening.

It was like a meditation that paid money. As months and years went by, she lost hundreds of dollars, but she also won many perks at the casino, such as a free hotel room and meals. One weekend she lost $2,000, and her stomach ulcer flared up. She was hospitalized and started treatment for chronic gambling. It was found that her perfectionism was the underlying difficulty that led to gambling. She attended Gamblers Anonymous, learned to be less critical of herself and others, eventually married, and was able to stay happily married.

Types of Gambling

There are many types of gambling, and compulsive gamblers generally settle on one that is most satisfying. The choices include casinos, sports betting, horse racing, video gambling, Internet gambling, playing the lottery, and playing the stock market. Often a person will go to extreme lengths in order to participate in his or her favorite form of gambling. Persons living in a rural area may drive hundreds of miles to a casino, even though the lottery is available at the corner convenience store.

Overachieving

In a success-driven society, it is difficult to imagine that achievement could be a negative thing, but for the person driven perfectionistically, overachievement can become a waking nightmare. This type of individual goes to the top at all costs, sometimes to the detriment of health, relationships, and self-respect. It would seem that one could glean a great deal of happiness from achievement, but sometimes the opposite occurs, and the final years of life are spent in isolation and tremendous loneliness.

Fame and Reclusiveness

One can see that high achievement does not necessarily bring happiness in the example of Howard Hughes, who only saw his physician and other paid companions during his final years, even buying the hotel he was living in so that he would not have to move out! Writer-anthropologist Carlos Castaneda was reclusive after his bestseller years, refusing interviews and public appearances, only leaving his house at night, and finally staying in his sickbed, only seeing his physician and long-term women friends. For years the public did not know if he was alive or dead as he studiously manipulated his image in the media, wanting to be seen in a positive light no matter what. He did not allow himself to be human.

Unrealistic Expectations

According to author Jim Rubens, younger Americans have become more and more self-entitled. They feel that they are very special and able to achieve whatever they imagine. The percentage of students who rank high on scales for narcissistic personality disorder has risen in recent decades, and if these students embrace the American value of meritocracy, they fully expect to be at the top of whatever field is chosen. This can be a brutal illusion, as there is only room for so many high achievers at the top of each profession. The illusion that everything is accessible is a unique part of the American culture that can bring a lot of pain and disillusionment.

Family History

The drive to achieve at all costs can sometimes be rooted in the family history. Something in the dynamic of the childhood home drives the person to keep repeating the effort to win, to please someone important, or to definitely make a mark. It often takes some psychological archeology to find the underpinnings of perfectionism in the high achiever. It is tricky because on the outside it seems a positive thing, resulting in a stellar resume that impresses everyone.

The Pressure to Succeed

American childhood is no longer a time of leisure and exploration. Time is strictly scheduled, especially for families in which both parents have full time jobs. Wealthy couples spend large amounts of money on special training and coaching for their children, as they have them already placed on a prestigious career track. There is enormous pressure to perform, and time dawdling in a creek or abandoned quarry is not a part of today's childhood.

ALERT

Parents are likely to have so little free time to spend with children that aspects of parenting are delegated. An enterprising person in New York, Aresh Mohit, has a thriving business teaching children how to ride a bicycle!

Millions of children compete in the National Spelling Bee. One father of a child who placed ninth in the competition paid 1,000 people to pray for his son. This was in addition to spending years with the boy, helping him to memorize root words in three languages. The 2002 documentary film, *Spellbound*, directed by Jeffrey Blitz, tells the story of the competition.

On the other end of the achievement scale, the top companies only recruit MBAs from Harvard, MIT, Stanford, Dartmouth, and other Ivy League schools. The most brilliant, charismatic candidates are chosen, and they are expected to work eighty-hour weeks. It seems that from preschool through the adult years, the pressure is on. Only perfection can prevail in this cultural mindset.

Overspending

Somewhat similar to gambling, the compulsion to shop combines perfectionistic tendencies with money. The answer to life's problems is found in the next department store or car dealership. It seems very rational and real to the shopper that the purchase will finally make the person happy. Interacting with clerks, cashiers, and salespeople eases loneliness and isolation, and there is a bit of power felt during the transaction of handing over a credit card or cash. Some compulsive shoppers prefer shopping over the Internet out of secrecy and shame.

Compulsive Debt

Often high levels of debt accrue when a person struggles with compulsivity about money. Some money addicts go in the complete opposite direction and are miserly in their dealings with money—not earning enough to take care of themselves and having great difficulty spending money on themselves, ignoring needs for medical or dental care, and not saving for retirement or other legitimate purposes.

Signs of Compulsive Debting

Debtors Anonymous, a twelve-step fellowship based on the model of Alcoholics Anonymous, offers the following checklist to determine whether or not a person is in trouble with money:

- Not knowing monthly balances, monthly expenses, interest fees, or contractual obligations.
- Borrowing items from others and not returning them.
- Poor savings habits, not being prepared for taxes and insurance payments.
- Compulsive shopping, leaving price tags on items and returning them later.
- Difficulty meeting one's basic financial needs.
- Feeling especially grownup when using a credit card.
- Bouncing checks, living in chaos and drama around money.
- Living on the edge, paycheck to paycheck, taking insurance risks.
- Embarrassed when discussing money.

- Using time inefficiently, taking jobs under one's education level.
- Unwilling to value oneself, living in self-imposed deprivation.
- Hope that someone will save the day, pick of the pieces of serious financial trouble.

Persons that have compulsive issues with money sometimes discover them after other addictions have been managed, finding that the core insecurities under other difficulties had to do with money.

Case Studies

According to Jim Rubens, author of *OverSuccess: Healing the American Obsession with Wealth, Fame, Power, and Perfection*, overspending is no laughing matter. He recounts the situation of Elizabeth Roch, a worker in an accounting firm, who was fired for embezzling $241,061 to support her shopping habit. A male addicted to shopping bought 2,000 wrenches. Uno Kim, a gambling addict now in jail, entered the home of two elderly people in New Hampshire, killed them, robbed them of $36,000 in cash, and drove to the Mohegan Sun casino.

What Can You Do Instead?

It is possible to moderate each of the behavioral addictions. In order to lead a more balanced life, consider the following suggestions.

But I'm Working!

Create a transition time at the end of each day. Think of it as a period at the end of a sentence. Close the computer, close the files, and turn off the cell phone. The work will still be there tomorrow.

Set a clear time that you will stop working, and honor your commitment to yourself. Remember that the mind works best if it has time for play or just goof off. Most creative ideas emerge when a person is relaxed. Shift that intense focus to your loved ones and reap the benefits of their presence. Learn to not take things personally, especially criticisms of something at work. What is said is only that person's opinion. It's not about you as an individual.

A recent study done by researchers at Harvard University and the University of Arizona found that men worry about three things every day—money, their job, and their family. Women worry about much more—money, their job, immediate family, extended family, friends, appearance of their home, etc. Women are spread much thinner.

Strive for a more reflective life. One does not have to go, go, go in order to be important in life. And watch for the tendency to talk about work excessively. Set down that burden and ask others how they are doing. What was eventful in their day? Personal relationships will rekindle with this type of attention.

On the job, take the advice of one supervisor who gently encouraged a perfectionistic employee, "Let it go. It's already quite good enough."

Don't lose sight of the big picture. It is not a catastrophe if your spouse neglects to write down one item in the check register.

Place a sign on your computer or work area that says, "Done is better than good." This will move you to completion on those days you're nitpicking over small details.

Instead of Addictive Sex

Therapy and support groups help enormously once the addiction is recognized. Any efforts toward building self-esteem will lessen the desire for the quick fix. Spending quality time with loved ones helps to build an inner reservoir of true caring, ultimately more satisfying than the fleeting pleasures of addictive sexual activity.

Taking time to learn about healthy sexuality lessens the inclination toward addiction. Twelve-step programs are available to help individuals with sex addiction, some offering meetings over the phone with conference calls.

It generally takes a significant event for a sex addict to admit that there is a problem—arrest, loss of a job or marriage—but when that occurs, the denial starts to lift, enabling the individual to face and remedy the problem.

Couples therapy can be beneficial if great care is taken to properly disclose information that impacts each of the individuals. The partner may elect to undergo individual therapy or a support group for partners of sex addicts.

Instead of Compulsive Gambling

Recovery programs specifically for gambling are relatively new. For example, one recovery center in Reno, Nevada, had, in recent years, several dozen beds for people overcoming drug and alcohol addictions, but only two beds for persons struggling with gambling. If formal intervention or therapy is undertaken, it generally is on an outpatient basis, often in conjunction with other addictions, especially to substances. Therapists with specialties in gambling are relatively scarce, and it would be good to ask many questions before undertaking extensive therapy with a counselor, learning first of the person's experience with chronic gambling.

FACT

Thought distortion is a part of the gambling dynamic. Otherwise highly intelligent and rational people develop systems that they believe will help them to win, such as counting wins per plays, switching machines and tables, or going with a seemingly intuitive hunch that it is going to be a winning night. Guidance and practice is needed to face and change such distorted thinking if it is deeply imbedded in the psyche.

As with the other addictions, replacing the activity with other pleasurable pursuits sometimes causes the gambling to recede. Physical exercise is especially good because it creates endorphins, the positive high that the brain interprets as satisfying as gambling.

Weekly support groups, whether twelve step or otherwise, help counteract the isolation and shame that surround the gambler's self-image. Friendships form, and the gambler has someone to check in with when lonely, agitated, and feeling on the brink of hitting the slots just one more time.

Gamblers often need help in structuring time, as during the gambling days and nights, long hours were spent in the casino or other gambling venue. An altered state of consciousness ensues and the concept of a normal day is eventually completely lost. Time management guidance—what to do with those days and nights—can ease withdrawal. Some gamblers become avid volunteers, doing service in community endeavors. Others go back to school and become addiction counselors, sometimes with a specialty in gambling addiction. It helps greatly to have one or more people who understand the details of the gamblers routine and triggers that may set off relapses. Such a trusting relationship can make the difference between a gambler who recovers and one who does not.

Moderation for Overachievers

Martha Beck, in her book, *The Joy Diet*, has interesting ideas for taming the person who strives too much. Some of her suggestions are as follows:

1. Spend a few minutes each day doing nothing. Be lazy; embrace your dark side, or what Beck calls "the lying scumbag." Love all parts of yourself.
2. Insist on fifteen minutes of privacy each day. Hang a sign on your door that says you are not to be disturbed. Get acquainted with your emotions and bodily sensations.
3. Find a place in nature and observe the natural elements. Let yourself relax.

ESSENTIAL

Lao Tzu, the father of Taoism, wrote about inner quietness in this poetic way: "We shape clay into a pot, but it is the emptiness inside that holds whatever we want."

4. Feast your senses on beautiful and luscious things. Take your time and be certain that each sensory feast is something you genuinely like.
5. Be very honest in your relationships. Ask yourself what you want in the relationship and if there are important things you are withholding from the other person.
6. Seek out opportunities to laugh. This could mean attending comedy clubs, browsing the humor section in the bookstore, or hanging out with your weirdest friend for a while.
7. Give yourself time to play and ask yourself honest questions about how your play relates with your work. Are they compatible? Are you doing what you want to do?

Writer Toni Raiten-D'Antonio offers wonderful suggestions for moderation in her book *The Velveteen Principles for Women*. Those who tend to overachieve can find solace in the following ideas:

1. Real people are ethical.
2. Real people are sexual.
3. Real people are generous and empathetic.
4. Real people are flexible, staying away from absolutes.
5. Real people face their emotions, even the dark unpleasant ones.
6. Real people are honest with themselves and others.
7. Real people know their mission in life and live it to the best of their abilities.

The overachiever with a perfectionistic drive can tone it down, with practice. It sometimes takes many attempts to change old habits, many of which have been refined for decades.

But There's a Sale This Weekend!

Perfectionists with money difficulties can turn their lives around with the help of others on the same path or a therapist who understands the core issue of anxiety around money. Some find that cutting up all the credit cards is a good start. Doing everything possible to live within one's means, however simple, will bring peace of mind. Keeping track of expenses and expenditures will bring clarity, and necessary adjustments become apparent. Lifelong dependencies on others can evolve into true self-sufficiency. Some find that they are interested in developing a new career or starting a business for themselves, something more enjoyable than the stressful work that led to unfortunate perfectionism.

Spiritual activities such as prayer, meditation, and meeting with like-minded friends help the stressed-out consumer feel more connected to a larger source, as if perhaps the weight of the world does not necessarily rest on one's shoulders after all.

CHAPTER 10

The Relationship of Perfectionism to Mental Illness

The early twenty-first century is a favorable time for those who struggle with mental illness or who find mental illness in their families. During even the not-too-distant past, there was considerable prejudice and misinformation about mental illness. Problems were hidden or spoken of in hushed tones, as if there were something shameful about emotional difficulties. Families accommodated difficult behavior as best they could, as help was not readily available. In these unfortunate situations, everyone in the family suffered.

Mental Illness in the Family

It is unknown whether there is a cause-and-effect relationship between mental illness and perfectionism or vice versa. What has been shown is that there is an overlap between the trait of perfectionism and such disorders as depression, anxiety, obsessive-compulsive disorder, and insomnia. Perfectionism is also linked with sexual dysfunction and relationship problems. Regardless of the exact cause, one mentally ill family member affects the entire family. Those tendrils of effects reach into every aspect of adult life, like the tenacious tentacles of an octopus.

Origins in the Childhood Home

Extremes of perfectionism seem to find their roots with parents who were critical and punitive. The child tries very hard to measure up, but the high standard demanded seems to be a moving target. The child wants so very much to please the authority figures, but it almost never happens. The seed of perfectionism is planted and grows out of control in the adult years.

Case Study

In 2009, the *Boston Globe* printed an article about a child, aged twelve, who had to stop doing homework with a pencil because he was tempted to erase whole lines of writing on his paper that were not perfect. Staff writer, Carey Goldberg, noted that he worked on individual letters, erasing over and over again until the paper was worn through. In a like manner, on tests, he would get stuck and spend an inordinate amount of time erasing marks that did not seem perfect. The child is now grown, working as a research coordinator, after receiving help to find the dividing line between high standards and mental distress. He is able to negotiate that terrain somewhat better for himself now. He was diagnosed with obsessive-compulsive disorder. His perfectionism caused him and his family great distress as he was growing up.

Identity and Mate Selection

Persons who grow up with a mentally ill parent have difficulty creating a well-balanced life for themselves, as that first important example becomes deeply imbedded in the psyche. If the mother struggles with narcissistic personality disorder, sons are likely to choose a mate with some kind of grave difficulty, and daughters will have a struggle creating a strong, solid life for themselves, as the illness seems intertwined with being female. They may understand rationally that the mother is a separate individual and there are possibly other ways of being, but emotionally it is as if the imprint sets a default mode, the place the daughter returns to during times of duress.

ESSENTIAL

Fragrance and tone of voice are powerful attractors. Be aware if you find the fragrances—alcohol, tobacco, a particular perfume or aftershave—of someone from the past who was problematic appealing. Do you gravitate to someone with a New York accent or a Southern drawl? Take note, remember those first associations, and decide if they really apply in the present time. It will be difficult, but you can reteach your olfactory and sound radar.

When there is any kind of mental illness in a parent, the children tend to choose partners with some kind of challenge, as it feels normal because of the childhood dynamic. There may be a perfectionistic drive to "help" the spouse or even to fix or cure them. This can lead to a lifetime of exhaustion and frustration. Usually helping the other person makes the helper weak and dependent, although at first she may seem appreciative.

Are You Mentally Ill?

Mental illness is a broad topic. It is often difficult to see problem traits within oneself. However the website *www.outofthefog.net* offers a list of traits that are helpful when observing others and even oneself. Some of the behavioral characteristics of mental illness noted are as follows:

1. Putting others down, constantly picking fights
2. Manufacturing chaos and catastrophes
3. Cruelty to animals
4. Dependency and depression

5. Stealing at home, taking things without permission
6. Emotional abuse and emotional blackmail; gaslighting

ALERT

Gaslighting is a term used to describe the behavior of systematically persuading another person to mistrust her perceptions. The word comes from the 1944 MGM movie, *Gaslight,* in which the female lead is made to feel crazy because the lights flicker and lower each day. Her husband says they do not.

7. Enmeshment and engulfment with others in the family (The person who is the target of someone else's enmeshment or engulfment may, at first, feel flattered. He calls several times a day and is interested in every nuance of your feelings and details of your day. Eventually the situation becomes cloying and you feel strangled, willing to do anything for some space and a breath of fresh air.)
8. Emptiness, feeling worthless
9. Frivolous litigation (suing people for sheer drama)
10. Hoovering (A term coming from a popular brand of vacuum cleaner, indicating a trait in which the person with the disorder temporarily improves her behavior and her significant other gets sucked back into a hopeful state regarding the relationship.)

Of course, a simple checklist is not enough to determine whether a person is mentally ill, but it can serve as a guide to prompt further investigation by professionals in the field, gathering a body of information over time. Mental illness is not an all or nothing situation. Conditions can occur along a continuum, with the individual exhibiting greater symptoms one day or one year and less at other times.

Just Act Normal

There is much to be said for the old adage of "acting as if." For example, if a person is extremely frightened of job interviews, one can act as if she is completely confident, able to have a pleasant conversation with the interviewer, fully expecting that she might get an offer because she believes that she has a lot to give to the employer. Often mentally ill persons are quite intelligent and have gathered a vast storehouse of information about what is normal from watching television and movies, noting what average people seem to say and do in a wide array of life situations. One can draw upon that knowledge and essentially become normal by acting in those learned ways.

It can be helpful to bookend calls to supportive friends when trying something new that seems especially daunting. Call or text the friend and tell him what you are about to do. Perform the new action, and then make a second call to the friend, telling him how it went. Bookending is a marvelous way to bolster confidence when embarking on new habits and behaviors.

ALERT

Presentation and confidence carry the day. In the film *Catch Me If You Can*, the main character, based on a true individual, was able to wend his way through many high-profile occupations without credentials, simply by procuring appropriate uniforms and learning the jargon of the profession.

Some challenged individuals find that pretending to be an actor or actress serves them well in challenging situations. For example, if a young man has tremendous fear of authority figures, especially the police because his abusive father was a law enforcement officer, when he is pulled over on the freeway, he can take a deep breath, imagine he's an actor playing a part in a film, and calmly answer the officer's questions.

Rethinking Relationship Choices

Selecting appropriate partners can be a landmine of difficulty for mentally ill persons. On the one hand, there is the deeply imbedded role model from the family of origin, which may have been less than ideal, and at the other extreme, one swears to find the perfect mate in order to overcome the past history. One can read all the self-help books and engage in years of therapy and still have trouble finding a suitable life partner. Couples therapy can offer wonderful support; it's like having a coach for your relationship.

Trial and Error

If one can view the dating game as an endeavor of trial and error, it can be somewhat fun. Each person and each relationship will have pros and cons, and it all is ultimately a learning process. It is not necessary to find the perfect spouse the first time out of the gate, especially if there is the handicap of a problematic background. One gentleman goes so far as to describe his first marriage as his "warm-up marriage," where he was somewhat learning the ropes, taking that knowledge into the next relationship.

Often one goes through various relationships working out the challenges of interacting with a partner who surprisingly seems just like the mother or father. It can be even humorous when the husband has traits identical to the mother, or the wife turns out to be the evil twin of an abusive father. Ultimately, tremendous healing can come from such discoveries. Don't view these experiences as failures. They are stepping stones to further knowledge about the self.

ESSENTIAL

Don't be too hard on yourself if a marriage or significant relationship ends. Keep in mind that the institution of marriage was designed centuries past when people hardly ever lived beyond forty years old. It is illogical to imagine that a partner selected at age eighteen will still be compatible at age fifty or sixty, although many couples do manage to negotiate many stages of individual and relationship change and growth.

There are bound to be wounds and a grieving period if a relationship does not work out as planned, but it does not have to immobilize a person for extended lengths of time. Sometimes there are buried feelings of abandonment left because of unresolved needs from the childhood home, and these can erupt when a relationship ends. The terror is that of a young child who is frightened about sheer survival, a most unpleasant sensation to feel as an adult. The feelings will pass, if the individual has the tenacity to feel them and not numb them out with a substance or addictive behavior. During these times of regression, try to be as gentle with yourself as you would be if you found a lost child at the airport.

Join Groups According to Your Interests

One way to find a compatible mate is to participate in various adult groups that run parallel to your deepest interests. Maybe you are passionate about travel. Attend travel lectures at the local travel specialty store. Travel as much as you can, even solo, and you will likely find interesting single people along the way.

If you are a book lover, join the local friends of the library association and mingle with other book people, organizing sales, or work in the used bookstore. Scan the local newspaper for events with a literary focus and go to them, even if you're confident the perfect person won't be there and you aren't perfect enough anyway. Just have fun, and view it as practice.

Maybe genealogy is your passion. Find others with a similar bent and compare notes. You can connect with people from lost branches of your family, forming significant friendships over the Internet. Some of these new friends may have a connection with someone who could be the perfect mate for you.

Groups that meet for an extended period of time work well for those who are quiet and rather slow to warm up to the opposite sex. A class at the local community college will enable you to observe others over a period of time, as will volunteer efforts along the line of whatever interests you. It is possible to get to know a person rather well just by observing and listening for a period of several weeks. You can decide whether the person might be a potential mate after you have seen plenty of positive qualities.

FACT

Although catering somewhat to the older crowd, Parents Without Partners is helpful to many singles who are looking for wholesome family activities. Long-term friendships form, perhaps with the possibility of romance and marriage. Through participation in events, it is possible to learn a person's character over time.

Keep in mind that some of your dating may feel odd and unnatural if you want to find a person who is quite different from your parents. That initial chemistry may not be there because you are wired in a different way, but over time, if there is emotional compatibility, the relationship can blossom.

Remember to ask questions about a person's relationship history. Are there patterns of brief, turbulent involvements? A lot of blame on the previous partner? Continuing anger? Red flags such as these can prevent you being a part of the person's story a couple of years in the future. Don't imagine for a minute that your caring for the individual will solve all those past problems. Instead, more than likely, over time those past difficulties will be 100 percent projected onto you. Keep looking.

Managing Anxiety

It can be very difficult to function in life while carrying a load of high anxiety. One loses sleep, avoids social situations, feels averse to risk of all kinds, and may spend a lot of money and mental energy in trying to manage the symptoms.

Detective Work

Look for the underlying emotions and beliefs in each situation that are terrifying you. Be patient with yourself, as such difficult parts of the psyche are often buried. Sit with your journal and jot down what you are feeling or what those voices are saying to you that makes a situation fraught with danger. Are you getting ready to board an airplane and you suddenly can't breathe normally and feel that you have to flee the airport? Patiently sit with that and see what comes to mind. Maybe you don't like confined spaces. Why would that be? Did your older brother trap you in a closet, tormenting you and ignoring your protests? Ease yourself through the memory of the past situation, and the present will become okay. Breathe. Don't forget to breathe, as the body relaxes with deep breathing.

A young woman, May, had nightmares that came with anxious emotions. She would wake up in a sweat and wonder where she was and what happened. The repetitious nightmares soon started to center around the theme of eyeballs. It was as if eyeballs were everywhere, looking at her and making her frightened. She talked about it with friends and was reassured that she was not crazy. Something would emerge. She remembered after a few months of the eyeball dreams and childlike terror that her brother and his buddies looked through a hole in the bathroom wall and watched her go to the bathroom. They sexually molested her, events that May had repressed until she was mature enough to handle the emotions accompanying such trauma. This example shows that such difficult emotions are there for a reason. Sitting with them until the root emerges takes tremendous personal courage, and the result is freedom.

Increase Your Exercise

As mentioned in other sections of the book, exercise contributes greatly to an overall sense of well-being. The body is meant to be used. If you can ramp up that use, doing things that you like to do, the anxiety lessens. That raw energy gets used up in a physical way so it doesn't hover around causing problems. Try swimming laps, walking around a track at a nearby school, bicycling, or dancing. Think about whether you want your exercise to be solitary or social and choose accordingly. You might like to have a running partner or, on the other hand, use the time in the outdoors to strengthen your spirituality. There is no one right way to do it. The main thing is to do physical things that you enjoy and repeat them enough that a positive habit is formed.

One Thing at a Time

It might seem superefficient to juggle the phone, the child, the stroller, the car keys, and the car, but this style does not create serenity. Deliberately do one thing at a time and see how your mind calms down. The brain can actually only handle one thing at a time, and the constant switching gears and direction contributes to anxiety. Breathe deeply, turn off the phone, take the child's hand, strap her into the car seat, load the stroller, and then check your keys before starting the car.

Multitasking is a popular skill these days, but it's to be avoided in your work or personal life if you wish to be free of anxiety. Doing several things at once is not something to aspire to, even if an attractive job description makes that a part of the package. Remember, you have a choice about what to do and how to live, and you don't have to be a multitasker to earn your living. Seek a situation where you can complete tasks from beginning to end, and there will be less anxiety.

What Can You Do Instead?

The National Alliance for the Mentally Ill (NAMI) has local and state branches, and often can refer you to other mental health organizations in a local or regional area. It is helpful to connect with others who have similar issues, especially the unique experience of growing up in a family with a mentally ill person.

Support groups such as Emotions Anonymous provide wonderful camaraderie and a structure for working through emotional difficulties. Strong friendships result from the common experience of having mental illness or surviving a family with a mentally ill member.

No Electronic Gadgets

Set aside a time period without a cell phone, e-mail, texting, or cruising the Internet. Turn off iTunes and just be. At first, see if you can manage an hour without anything digital. Then increase to two hours. Gradually increase your time away from gadgetry to see if you can enjoy an entire weekend of silence. You will discover new regions of your mind that are quite interesting. You may discover some freedom from perfectionism.

Spiritual Relief

Depending on how you conduct your spiritual life and the nature of any belief in a deity, you may find considerable solace by simply handing over stresses connected with perfectionism and mental illness to that higher source, however you envision it. You can sit quietly and imagine the negativity and fear flowing out with each breath. You can develop personal rituals that make sense to you, such as writing down difficult memories, entrenched habits, and stressful interpersonal situations on paper; burn them; and bury them as you say a few calming words. Truly imagine those past memories and emotions going into the earth completely apart from you from this moment forward.

CHAPTER 11

Perfectionism and Disease

It may be alarming to think of perfectionism actually having a part in health or illness, but it might possibly be the case. Think of the examphobic college student who breaks out in hives and cannot hold down food during finals week. She drinks coffee and suffers through insomnia, only barely able to take tests because her hands quiver so relentlessly. Consider the long-suffering person who had been the Rock of Gibraltar for her family, making herself the last priority, succumbing to cancer. Consider the patriarchs of the ice cream company Baskin Robbins who suffered early deaths from diabetes, inspiring the son, John Robbins, to teach consumers about health and a sane lifestyle.

But Isn't It about Germs?

It has been said that medicine is both an art and a science, but in Western cultures in recent decades, the trend has been skewed toward the scientific aspects of the human body. Alternative approaches abound, but they are usually not covered by insurance and are thus affordable only by those at the top of the earning curve.

ESSENTIAL

On a historical note, nurses who worked during war efforts found that patients healed better if caretakers washed their hands before working with their charges. Soon hand washing became a necessary part of preparation, and sterile, antiseptic conditions are required by the law and policing health organizations.

During past centuries it was not known that diseases were connected with microbes in the water, and, horrifying by today's standards, sewers were not kept separate from drinking or cooking water. Gradually, however, these pieces of relevancy came to light, and conventional standards of cleanliness have more or less eradicated some of the old diseases. Standard inoculations for children have also eradicated many common diseases.

Don't Germs Cause Illness?

According to the Mayo Clinic, germs are another name for bacteria, of which only 1 percent are harmful. Bacteria are in the human body all the time, and most of them are beneficial to the bodily processes. How then did germs get such bad press? Health education in elementary schools stresses the scary, negative aspects of germs, and children think of them as something like cooties, that you want to avoid at all costs. The importance of these little microbes gets blown out of proportion, and perhaps an obsessive hand-washing habit ensues.

Germophobia

Germophobes are people with obsessive-compulsive disorder who are compelled to act out rituals of washing and cleaning, sometimes to the detriment of being able to live a normal life, although many are able to contain the condition and function fairly well.

FACT

Mysophobia is another term for germophobia with Greek word components of "uncleanliness," and "fear." It is a pathological fear of contamination. Some observers think the United States has become obsessed with germs because hand sanitizers and alcohol handwipes are available at the entrance of every store and supermarket. Are we paranoid?

Some famous germophobes are the late Howard Hughes and Saddam Hussein, who reportedly sometimes required visitors to disrobe and wash with antiseptic solution. Comedian Howie Mandel makes fun of his germophobia in his routines, but he studiously does not shake hands with people, regardless of the situation.

Perfectionism and Stress

According to Alice Domar, perfectionists have a higher risk of various stress-related illnesses. For example, perfectionists are more vulnerable than the average person to postpartum depression, popularly called "the baby blues." A new mother expects that she will be the perfect mother and is discouraged when she feels tired and afraid. She assumes that she should instantly know how to breastfeed, change the baby, and understand the meaning of the baby's fussing.

As mentioned earlier in the book, perfectionism is a factor in the stress of eating disorders, as people have unrealistically high expectations of themselves in terms of appearance, exercise, and weight. They count calories, purge, and overexercise in order to attain a mythical perfect weight.

Stress and Illness

Stress is a factor in insomnia and gastrointestinal disorders. A mother with a special needs child is so stressed about the extra attention her child needs that she develops irritable bowel syndrome and temporomandibular joint disorder (TMJ).

Stress and Cancer

Cancer is a complex disease, and it is the focus of immense research and effort in the medical community. It is feared because of its unpredictability and how it seems to take on a life of its own once it starts. Even people with outwardly healthy lifestyles can find themselves with cancer. For example, a young graduate student, a vegan marathon runner and nonsmoker, came down with cancer. Though she was outwardly healthy, she was also perfectionistic about her body, doing everything possible to maintain a perfect weight and shape.

Some researchers found that those who were diagnosed with cancer often had a traumatic life experience within the previous eighteen months before the diagnosis—loss of a friend, severe financial loss, victim of a crime, or other life trauma. It is unknown exactly why some people's bodies succumb to cancer but not others. Some say it has to do with personal resiliency and the ability to remain relaxed under most conditions.

One survivor of breast cancer admitted that before cancer she was a perfectionist, but she changed her ways after overcoming her illness. She left dishes in the sink, left junk in the garage, and let the laundry go undone. Her children learned to make their own lunches, and she focused on rest and healing. She found that having cancer reduced her perfectionism. She now relaxes more, makes time for her children, knits, exercises, and cherishes times of doing nothing.

Perfectionistic people tend to blame themselves for the illness, going over past occurrences trying to determine where they went wrong. Perfectionists are accustomed to blaming themselves for everything, so why not cancer? Getting this dreaded disease seems like a breach of trust, and the entire house of cards falls down. How could everything go wrong when they did everything right? Perfectionists hate to be out of control, and cancer is definitely a situation where one has little control.

Dr. Harold Benjamin notes that prolonged stress is a component in the development of cancer. The body adapts to what is perceived as a worrisome situation with the fight-or-flight response, and it makes no difference whether the situation is real or imaginary, physical or emotional. The prolonged adaptation breaks down the normal bodily processes, and unhealthy cells have more room to maneuver. The healthy cells, which are the protectors, are unable to do their work, and the unhealthy cells start to reproduce.

More Research on Disease and Stress

Researcher and author Jim Rubens reports that a feeling of social defeat (not achieving as much as hoped for) leads to stress and disease. It has been found that when a person feels threatened, adrenaline surges, followed by cortisol, the master stress hormone. Cortisol is a steroid that helps people get through stressful situations, but it also suppresses the immune system, possibly to help reduce inflammation. One can see that a continuous stream of cortisol would not be good for one's health.

Glucose is released to prepare the person for an emergency. Blood pressure rises, heart rate increases, and breathing becomes rapid. Digestion and sex drive are diminished. Blood vessels constrict and the white blood cell count increases. Rubens quips that this may be helpful in escaping a buffalo stampede, but it is not useful in today's world.

The paradox is that today's experience of traffic jams, impossible work deadlines, conflicting roles, pressures for ever-increasing status, and the demands of constant contact with various communication devices cause enormous stress on the body, equal to that of the primitive man running from the tiger or bison.

ALERT

> Cartoonist Scott Adams advises entire days of "multi-shirking," just sitting around feeling mildly guilty for not keeping up with all the electronic communications. Enjoy a bit of sloth.

The brain rearranges itself to accommodate the stress load, resulting in the menu of modern diseases—obesity, insomnia, diabetes, atherosclerosis, depression, and decreased bone density. Other diseases related to stress are arthritis, allergies, and asthma. Another unfortunate result of prolonged stress is the brain's distortion of the emotion of fear, making the person chronically anxious.

Additional illnesses that are estimated to be 40–50 percent caused by stress are chronic fatigue, colds, flu, viruses, headaches, and migraines. Some persons in the medical community are skeptical about the relationship between stress and disease, only going so far to say that stress *contributes* to disease. Chronic stress makes a person *susceptible* to illness. These statements are somewhat different from the direct cause-and-effect supposition.

Are Stress-Related Conditions Inherited?

The United States has the seemingly positive myth and belief that anyone can make it to the top, creating a culture of high achievement, or at least the potential for such. What are some of the attributes that seem strongly related to genetics? According to Jim Rubens, the following conditions are connected to inheritance:

1. Depression
2. Extreme narcissism
3. Self-hatred
4. Autism
5. Schizophrenia
6. Bipolar disorder
7. Inclination toward addictions
8. Illegal drug use
9. Alcoholism
10. Obesity
11. Vision problems
12. High blood pressure

Rubens feels that these estimates are low, and that other physical and psychological difficulties may be highly connected to ancestry as well. So what's a perfectionistic person to do? Blame it on Mom and Dad and Uncle Charlie? It could be a case of forewarned is forearmed. Such knowledge may help you realize your propensity toward certain conditions. This does not mean that you should accept that developing these conditions is inevitable, but that you should create a lifestyle that will help ward off the genetic inclination.

The Immune System

The immune system is a delicate system of protection, finely tuned to destroy your body's invaders, such as microbes that enter through a cut in the skin, with something eaten, or negative influences in the air you breathed. The advent of AIDS made the general public more aware of the importance of a healthy immune system.

The immune system becomes depressed and weaker during times of prolonged stress and is thus unable to do its job of destroying unhealthy cells in the body. Thousands of medical studies have shown a correlation between stress and illness, although not everyone is convinced of a cause-and-effect relationship. In other words, stress and illness are present at the same time, but it is unknown whether stress is actually the cause of disease.

ESSENTIAL

Writer Martha Beck describes her mind as being like a "supercomputer possessed by the soul of a demented squirrel. It's constantly calculating, anticipating, remembering, fantasizing, worrying, hoarding, bouncing frenetically from thought to thought." Author Dwayne Dyer estimates that the human mind thinks about 60,000 thoughts a day.

The fight-or-flight response is a survival mechanism left over from primitive times when man lived very close to the earth and life was simple. If the caveman saw a tiger near his cave, he immediately got ready to fight it or run away. When danger is perceived, the mind and body work together to increase the heart and pulse rate, accompanied by a flood of adrenaline, so that the person can escape. The difficulty arises when there are numerous such incidents in modern life and everything is simply locked into the body. It's not necessary to run from the cave, but if your marriage is ending and your business is on the brink of bankruptcy, the dangers feel every bit as real as those of the caveman.

If one is still living out the aims of a perfectionistic parent (even if the parent has died) or responsible for the care of a family member with long-term illness, there is pressure on the immune system. Hormones flood into the bloodstream, the immune system is suppressed, and unhealthy conditions start to arise. Hans Selye, a researcher in the relationship between stress and illness, believes that if a lot of energy is used to handle emotional trauma, the body does not have enough resources left to take care of physical challenges. This information is good incentive to reduce mental trauma, so that energy is available to protect and heal the physical body.

The Social Component

During past generations, friends and extended family usually lived nearby, supporting all the members of a community during times of illness and stress. This is not the case in the twenty-first century, as many people live far from their blood relatives and move rather frequently during the course of their adult lives.

The experience of prolonged social defeat, as described by Jim Rubens, affects those in lower social classes with greater disease—lower birth weight, heart disease, lung disease, compromised mental health, cancer, and more days taken off from work. An unfortunate result of this lowered state of affairs is that such individuals are likely to compensate by taking up an addiction to make themselves feel better.

Don't the Doctors Know Everything?

American physicians are largely allopathic, meaning that they tend to view illness and the body in a scientific sense. Great emphasis is placed on symptoms and removing the symptoms. There is less interest in prevention and causes, and sometimes alternative methods of healing are disregarded because the physicians are not trained in these areas, and there is no way to get insurance reimbursement from approaches that are not mainstream.

Do Your Research

As the Internet has become available to almost everyone, patients have become more proactive, taking the time to research symptoms and diseases, and working with the physician as an equal team member. This can

Chapter 11: Perfectionism and Disease

require a degree of assertiveness that is not typical when interacting with a doctor, as culturally doctors are perceived as persons of authority. However, it is your body, and you have a complete right to ask questions and pursue whatever avenue seems in harmony with your belief system.

Explore Alternatives

Perhaps you have investigated meditation, yoga, and Ayurveda medicine, wanting to add these components to the conventional prescriptions doled out by clinic physicians. It would be wise to keep your team informed of what you are doing, but they may not fully understand.

Medical schools generally do not teach nutrition, so if you want to approach an illness with changes in the diet, such as eliminating meat and trying juicing for a few weeks, the physician may minimize this effort, but that doesn't mean that it's not worthwhile. Research has found that a plant-based diet works wonders with healing, but it is unlikely that your physician will write out a prescription for broccoli.

What Can You Do Instead?

It can be helpful to aim for an accepting view of the physical body, whatever its age and appearance. Your body has not turned against you if an illness develops. Perhaps it's a signal to slow down and shift gears, devoting loving, gentle care to the marvelous human form.

Don't Buy into Flawless Appearance

The entertainment industry spends more time and attention than ever on human perfection. Makeup artists extend cosmetics to the entire body—neck, arms, and legs. Cameras are sophisticated, and every detail has to be perfect—not a single wrinkle.

ALERT

Filmmakers expect to spend as much as $250,000 on postproduction work that removes blemishes and wrinkles from stars' faces, because with digital film, every imperfection is apparent.

With these images in the media, the average person is tempted to participate in the million-dollar plastic surgery industry. Consumers, mostly women, have breast lifts and augmentations, facelifts, as well as adjustments to other aspects of the anatomy. Attitudes have changed toward plastic surgery, and currently over half of the American population are in favor of such procedures. Hollywood's standards are tempting and ever-present, but what about being unique and somewhat ordinary? Individuality is always attractive and much healthier for overall wholeness and well-being.

Learn to Monitor Your Reactions to Stress

Dr. Harold Benjamin points out that everyone has stress, but one person's response might be different from another's. Keeping in mind the relationship between stress and illness, it would be quite beneficial to learn some ways to diminish the harmful bodily developments that occur because of stress.

It is possible to learn to control these emotions and behaviors, even under stressful conditions. Such control allows the immune system to do its natural work, and the body is not so apt to becoming ill. Think about which aspects of your lifestyle you have control over and make modifications wherever you can—shifting to a healthier diet, increasing exercise, avoiding ruminating over situations you cannot change, accepting the various aberrations of people and life with a sense of humor, expressing emotions as appropriate, and trying not to dwell overly long on negative feelings. Avoid self-blame and long-term resentment whenever possible.

Cultivate a degree of poise and composure that is unshakable. It will serve you well in severe emergencies and tragedies, allowing you to function in a helpful way toward others in crisis without endangering your physical health. Even if you are a fire fighter or emergency room technician, clear your mind at the end of the day and set aside your work until the next day. The technique of metaphorically putting a period at the end of the sentence would be useful. In your mind's eye, end the sentence, close the door, or put a lid on a box. Select an image that gives you the feeling of finality of the situation.

Visualization

Visualization has been found to be helpful for persons who are healing from various illnesses. This is a process, much like meditation, where the individual consciously relaxes each muscle group in the body and then imagines a vision of the location that needs to heal in its healthy form. Such a focus is powerful stimulus for the brain and subconscious mind. With repetition over time, the body responds and the healing is manifested.

Seek Out Joy

Is it possible to embrace the idea that you can be happy, even if you are healing from a serious illness? Joy does marvelous effervescent things to the immune system, quite the opposite of stress. Learn your own favorite repertoire for fun and freely indulge. Perhaps it's playing with your dog, strolling through a flea market, doodling with crayons, or tinkering with an antique automobile. Maybe you love reggae music but hardly ever go to a live concert. Make the time to find performances and attend. You will find kindred souls there, adding to the social well-being, which is a part of a healthy dynamic. Dismiss the mindset that all activity has to be purposeful.

Gather some children together—those from your family or neighbors—and make a big tub of soapy bubble solution. A little glycerin and dishwashing liquid will do the trick, and experiment with all kinds of utensils and toys to see what kinds of bubbles are possible. Have you ever made a bubble as large as a Hula-Hoop? That's an achievement!

Exercise Discernment in Relations with Others

You may find that when you are ill, some people bring you down and others build you up. There can be some surprises in the closest relationships. Some family members will bring doom and gloom to the discussion, and some of your best friends will avoid you if you are sick. It is impossible to control the emotional reactions of others, but you can make a conscious choice to interact only with people that make you feel better about yourself, those who encourage you and believe that you are fine no matter what you might be going through. You may find that it is more fun to chat with the quirky person you see at the coffee shop every week than with your relative who tells you all the scary statistics that have a bearing on your situation.

Don't Forget Sex!

Hold on to your sexuality if you become ill. Your perfectionistic voices may say that you're not attractive enough when you are sick, but your partner will feel differently. Having a disease does not mean that a person is no longer sexual. People can do sexy things together, even if intercourse is not possible because of an illness. Imagination and creativity bring new possibilities to the bedroom, if both partners are willing.

Both people may crave cuddling and embracing, especially the partner of the sick person if there has been a lengthy absence of affection. The diseased person may feel unattractive, but the genuine mutual caring will provide needed assurance.

ESSENTIAL

Not every sexual experience has to reach epic carnal heights or reverberate through history, like Antony and Cleopatra. Your perfectionism can be left outside the door so you can just focus on being together. Attention and kindness are always welcome.

Communication will help both people determine what has changed and what adaptations can occur so that needs are met. Every person, regardless of age or degree of health, has a need to be cared for and to share affection for another. You may have to be courageous and be the first to speak up. It is common to feel some loss of desire when coping with a serious illness. This can be accompanied by anxiety, as one fears the reaction of the loved one. Sometimes as healing begins, an amazing degree of tenderness and openness can ensue.

If pain is an issue, sometimes sex can be enjoyed right after the sick person has taken medication or done relaxation exercises. The couple can experiment with different positions to see what accommodates the situation.

The real challenge for the perfectionist will be the adjustment in body image. The body changes with serious illness and with age. However, the essence of the person remains intact, and that is what the partner loves: the shared experiences, memories, and emotional enjoyment of the union. This is not a time to be staring in the mirror. The partner of the sick person may be worried about hurting something or even feel guilty for having sexual needs. It seems selfish, but it is only human.

CHAPTER 12

Methods of Treatment

Even though perfectionism is not viewed as a specific disorder, there are many modes of therapy and education that can lessen the discomfort of the perfectionist. Cognitive therapy can help the individual recognize one's irrational thoughts and provide support while forming new ones. Psychoanalysis explores the roots of perfectionism, the underlying motives and issues. Group therapy is a method that provides a support system under the guidance of a trained professional, alleviating isolation. Humanistic therapy looks at the positive aspects of the situation and finds underlying meaning.

Perspective of Psychiatrists and Psychologists

Psychiatrists are MDs with a specialty in psychiatry, while psychologists hold a PhD or PsyD in psychology. Both do therapy and conduct research. Most states require that the psychologist do a supervised internship and gain licensure. Psychiatrists have attended medical school and studied further in the areas of assessment, diagnosis, treatment, and prevention of mental illness. Psychiatrists are able to prescribe medications, while in most states psychologists do not prescribe medications.

ALERT

Some tests available for measuring perfectionism are the Multidimensional Perfectionism Scale, the Perfectionistic Self Presentation Scale, the Almost Perfect Scale-Revised, and the Physical Appearance Perfectionism Scale. There is more investigative literature regarding the first three tests, compared to the final scale.

Sessions may be shorter with a psychiatrist, as they earn more money prescribing medications than doing therapy. Psychologists tend to do testing more than psychiatrists. You can expect that a psychiatrist will have a more scientific approach and perspective, and a psychologist will be somewhat broad in perspective. Of course, it is human to think that one's own perspective is superior, but the most important thing is that the patient gets the type of help desired. No one person has cornered the market on truth, and you have a right to enlist help that is in harmony with your values.

Some experts in the field believe that it does no good to encourage clients to lower their standards and try not to be so perfect. Clients have heard that from many sources already and will tend to tune out the professional. A better approach is to uncover the roots of the difficulty and focus on what is needed to feel loved, cared for, and completely okay without being perfect. Some clients have kept their imperfections secret for such a long period of time that they will stop therapy when the counselor gets close to the core of the matter.

How to Select a Therapist

Sometimes you have exhausted your inner resources and need assistance in coping with perfectionism. Ministers and mental health clinics often offer services at a nominal fee. Social service agencies may be of assistance, as well as marriage and family therapists. Clinical social workers often work as a part of a team. Psychologists and psychiatrists offer help, and the expense will be greater. When you meet with a counselor for the first time, ask lots of questions and try to determine whether you really feel comfortable with that individual. It's your prerogative to ask about the level of education, specialties, and whether the individual has experience with the specific issues you face. Investigate your insurance coverage and what documentation you will need for reimbursement.

ALERT

Don E. Hamachek of *psycnet.apa.org* discusses some differences between adaptive (normal) perfectionism and neurotic (maladaptive) perfectionism. Adaptive is believed by some to be more functional in terms of being appropriately careful, as in engineering or quality control work. Neurotic perfectionism is seen to be more debilitating. However, some professionals believe that adaptive perfectionism is harmful, as well.

Do not hesitate to shop around a bit and ask for referrals from friends and other mental health professionals in your life. The fit has to be correct in order for you to make progress with your perfectionism. Insurance may or may not cover therapy, but can you place a financial value on mental health for yourself and your future? Is it equal to a new TV or an upgrade on your car? A luxurious vacation?

In the short term, the therapist will try to tackle the immediate issues that likely brought the perfectionist in, such as difficulty maintaining relationships, obsession with success, fearful and self-critical thoughts. Then, the therapist usually begins to work on a long-term treatment strategy. The long-term strategy can involve an attempt to reshape the distorted image the client has of himself and the world around him, or to give him the skills he needs to function better.

ESSENTIAL

Individual Therapy

The ultimate goal of individual therapy is to help clients to unlearn negative patterns of behavior and to learn better ways to relate to others so that all the relationships in their lives can be more intimate, enjoyable, and rewarding.

QUESTION

What is the best kind of therapy for a perfectionistic person?
The success or failure of therapy depends less on the type of therapy used than on the relationship between the therapist and client. In any therapy, patients can learn, maybe for the first time, that they can safely express anger, or any emotion, with their therapists without the risk of rejection or fear that the therapist will stop treating them. Secure and comfortable in the relationship, these clients are then able to continue to discuss intimate secrets and painful issues that were locked away and previously not shared with anyone else.

Individual therapy sessions are designed to turn the mirror inward and allow the patient to better understand what it is that drives her to be competitive, distrustful, and driven to high standards. And then, with the light shining upon her inner demons, help her to find ways to better cope with them.

Individual therapy usually has three stages:

- It begins with the client and therapist going over specific thoughts or feelings in detail.
- The therapist and client work on identifying distorted views.
- The therapist works with the client to entertain new nondistorted ways of thinking.

Each week the therapist will likely give the client some specific homework assignments.

Psychotherapy

Another approach to individual therapy is the more classic method originated by Freud: psychoanalytical therapy. Classical Freudian, or psychoanalytic, therapy is not used as frequently today as other styles.

Psychoanalysis based on the psychodynamic model has changed somewhat since the time of Freud, but basically the Freudian model states that emotional disorders are based on inner unresolved conflicts between different aspects of one's psyche—the id, the ego, and the superego—or, more simply, between the conscious and unconscious mind. The goal of individual psychodynamic therapy is to reduce these conflicts, and in doing so, modify the personality of the individual for the better.

The therapist takes a less active role in this form of therapy. He remains fairly quiet and relies on the patient to reveal increasing amounts of distress buried in her subconscious.

Dreams are an important part of psychodynamic therapy. Freud believed that many subconscious conflicts are revealed in dreams. In this type of therapy, therapist and client will discuss dreams to gain insights into their meaning and what they show about the patient's inner struggles. Psychodynamic therapy can run from one year to as long as fifteen years or more.

Cognitive Behavioral Therapy (CBT)

The basic idea of cognitive behavioral therapy is to get the patient to recognize and identify untrue beliefs and negative behaviors, and replace these beliefs and behaviors with healthy, positive ones. The basis of this therapy is that our feelings and thinking play a major role in the way we behave and interact with people and the world around us.

The goal of cognitive behavioral therapy is to get patients to realize that while they cannot control every aspect of their lives and the world around them, they do have power over how they interpret and choose to deal with people, events, and objects in their environment.

With perfectionism, the thought patterns and feelings that cognitive behavioral therapy is trying to change are those of impossible expectations for the self and others. In order to deal with these destructive thoughts and behaviors, cognitive behavioral therapy begins by helping the client to see her problematic beliefs.

This first stage of the process is called functional analysis. The goal in this stage is to get the person to understand how thoughts, feelings, and situations contribute to negative behaviors. This can be a tough process, but when the therapist can break through the client's defenses and gain her trust, the self-discovery and insight that are essential to the treatment process can be achieved.

The second stage focuses on the actual behaviors that are making life miserable for the person and those around her. For example, the focus on perfection is creating a huge body image and appearance issue for her children. This stage can be especially difficult, as the client tends to believe there is nothing wrong with his behavior, and if those around him are taking offense, it's simply because they are too sensitive or even jealous. However, through intense cognitive behavioral therapy, a perfectionist can realize that not everyone shares her worldview and that her actions are harmful.

In the third and last part of the process, the client begins to learn and practice new skills that can be used to get different outcomes in real-world situations. For example, working on being average can be a goal. The CBT therapist can use several techniques to address this issue.

Role-playing, including role reversal, has been shown to be an effective technique. In these role-plays the therapist can get the person to see that there are other ways of relating to people and situations. Specific language will be used in the role-playing to bring about new belief statements and new thought patterns, such as "My best is good enough."

Cognitive behavioral therapy can be a challenging and rewarding method of treatment.

Find Groups of Like-Minded People

If you are looking for information about groups of people who are struggling with perfectionism, inquire at a hospital and social service agency. You may have to be creative in describing what you are looking for. The group might have a name something like "Personal Growth and Self-Esteem" or "Survivors of Trauma." Don't eliminate a group because it doesn't include the word "perfectionism." Numerous self-help twelve-step programs approach perfectionism and mental health from a variety of perspectives. There is no harm in dropping in on groups or calling the phone numbers listed on the web pages. Spending committed time in a group of people with similar suffering can lead to miracles in healing. One discovers that isolation is unnecessary, and a dozen heads are always better than one. Use your search tool and look around on the Internet to see what is available in your community.

What about Medication?

It would be unusual to use medication solely for the difficulty of perfectionism. However, if other disorders are a part of the picture, it is possible that medications could alleviate accompanying conditions, such as depression, anxiety, or other emotional distress. There isn't a known biochemistry for perfectionism, although one could expect the brain chemistry to be similar to that of the various addictions. It is unlikely that drugs will be developed specifically for perfectionism. One possible approach would be the combination of mood-stabilizing drugs for codisorders and therapy.

ALERT

Recent research suggests that some antidepressants, specifically selective serotonin reuptake inhibitors (SSRI) such as Prozac, may have the effect of creating serotonin overload. Serotonin regulates mood and levels of positive emotions. The risk is that increased levels of serotonin may also bring on false feelings of superiority.

Prescriptions could be a danger in the hands of a perfectionistic individual who also struggles with addictions. The temptation could be there to get the instant fix, even more than what is prescribed. In the long run, taking medications to feel better can result in feeling worse.

If you or someone you know tends toward depression, watch for the tendency to hoard medications for a possible suicide attempt. The prescribing physician will often suggest medications that are not addictive when such dangers are present. Throw out medications that are outdated, prescriptions for a different condition, or prescriptions for someone else.

There is no magic pill for dealing with core issues. Drugs alleviate symptoms, such as anxiety and mood swings. Persons with comorbid disorders may require medication to stimulate the brain so it reaches a normal balance and can function properly.

There is a tendency in today's medical field to overprescribe. A person who takes four or five medications has to be constantly on the alert for interactions and side effects. There is also the temptation to become overreliant on the drugs, avoiding psychotherapy that would help to unearth the underlying issues. Drugs tend to dull a person over time, leading to a situation where more and more is required for the same effect. It is important to recognize that some drugs cause challenges in thinking and performing certain tasks, such as driving a vehicle or operating machinery. The physician and patient have to work closely together to get the right balance.

ESSENTIAL

Let the prescribing doctor know if there are drug issues, and what other medications are being taken, as there may be interactions with unexpected side effects.

What Can You Do Instead?

Martha Beck suggests a way of quieting the mind called the Ticker Tape. Sit in a relaxed position as if getting ready to meditate. It is likely that you might not like meditating because of racing thoughts and complete inability to reach a Zenlike state of blank openness. The Ticker Tape exercise is perfect for this type of overthinking. With eyes closed, let the thoughts stream by, but place them on a thin strip of ticker tape as they go by behind your eyes. No judgment, just the ribbon of one thought after another. Spend a few minutes this way, and the mind and body will relax.

What Are Your Real Desires?

Mental illness can improve or simply disappear if a person gets honest about the truth of his life. Some self-inquiry can help. Ask yourself "When was I happy? What was I doing? What do I want now? What do I want to do with my time?"

One technique for accessing buried desires is to write a conversation between yourself and your inner child in a journal. Structure the writing as if it is a play, a conversation between the grown person and the inner child. It might look something like this:

Me: Hello, there.

Child: Hi.

Me: You sound mad.

Child: I am. You ignore me all the time.

Me: I'm sorry. What do you want?

Child: I do not want to work any more!

Me: I can understand that, but a certain amount of work takes care of things for us.

Child: Well then, not so much.

Me: What else would you like?

Child: Please don't make me listen to that woman with the scratchy voice. It makes my ears itch.

Me: Okay. Anything else?

Child: I just want to be outside somewhere and mess around. Look at leaves and twigs.

Me: There's an arboretum near here. Would you like to go there? They have incredible flowers.

Child: Yes. Thank you. I love you, Mommy.

Me: I love you, too, Sweetie.

This kind of dialogue calms a person down, and the simple desires come forth, sometimes leading to a new, more fruitful direction in life.

Reclaim Your Dreams

Was there a dream that you cherished as a child before you were rebuked, humiliated, and chastised out of having any authentic aspirations of your own? Some people from difficult family backgrounds learn to bury dreams because of the mistaken belief that keeping them hidden away will prevent pain. Actually, the opposite is true. Repressing one's longings ends up deadening the entire affect. Maybe there's less discomfort, but there is also less joy. This is not a happy way to live.

ALERT

Author Martha Beck suggests that those on a quest for a better, more satisfying, less perfect life should watch for the moment of *quickening*, the term used when a pregnant woman first feels the movement of the fetus in the uterus. Intense moments of awareness can be just like that—"I must work with paint;" "I have to get a divorce;" "I must live in a different house." Life's direction will smooth out after such an awakening.

Can you remember yourself at five or six years old? What did you think about and what did you like to do? What might you have done if your family had cued into your sincere interests a little more indulgently? What if there were no addictions in your family; how might you have cultivated some of your favorite pastimes? The essence of your personhood is the same now as it was then, and it's quite likely that what you enjoyed doing as a little tyke would still be enjoyed now.

Imagine the Ideal Lifestyle

Beyond winning the lottery, what seems attractive? You may be aiming for a new career, but how does it seem to be genuinely in that new career? For example, if you aspire to be a musician who receives an armful of flowers after a successful concert, would you equally enjoy the hours of preparation for public performance? The proportion of time spent alone with the instrument honing the craft is much greater than the time in the public eye. Be sure you would enjoy the entire lifestyle.

Maybe you want to travel all the time. Being an airline attendant might be fun. The travel privileges and always being on the go could be the lifestyle that satisfies you. Imagine going up and down the aisles, taking drink orders, soothing the whimpering child, answering tedious questions. Imagine handling a drunk or a potential terrorist. All this would be a part of the entire lifestyle. If you have children, would you be content with frequent phone conversations while you are flitting from place to place? Would you feel guilty that someone else was tending to the lunches and parent-teacher conferences?

Become a Risk Taker

In order to embrace your truest desires and dreams, it will become necessary to creep out of your comfort zone. This does not mean that you will be like Evel Knievel, eager to jump a motorcycle across the Grand Canyon. Small risks will suffice. Perhaps join Toastmasters in order to overcome a fear of public speaking. Sing karaoke while the club is still quiet enough to hear you. Then sign up at a neighborhood open mike. Agree to serve on the board of your favorite nonprofit, even if you have no patience for interpersonal politics.

The crux of risk taking is that you are afraid, and you face the fear and move forward. The fear subsides. Small successes and failures will make risk taking somewhat more palatable, and your life starts to blossom. You'd like to make a quilt from lovely vintage fabric handed down from the family ancestors, but machines frighten you. What if you sew your fingers to the fabric and ruin it with blood stains? It's likely that you can find a class with a patient teacher who would guide you through the process of crafting a new family heirloom.

Be Willing to Create

When you start claiming your true wants and desires and start taking risks, it becomes apparent that you are a creative person. In order to be happy you *must* create. Society has become so specialized that we imagine only a few people are unique enough to make something original. In actuality, everyone is creative. Unfortunately, this treasure of a human trait becomes stunted when too many people tell you to color within the lines.

Protect yourself from the naysayers and go forth with whatever it is that makes your soul sing. If it is ceramics, take a class and make little Zuni-style fetishes for all your friends. If it is real estate, buy a house and flip it. It's just arithmetic, right? If that's your love, go in that direction. Create a profit. The challenge will get your synapses buzzing again, and you will forget what it was like being depressed and immobilized with procrastination.

Be prepared for repetitious hard work.

ESSENTIAL

Hard work was a part of artist Michelangelo's life. Imagine laying on scaffolding under the ceiling of the Sistine Chapel for hours at a time, smelling paint fumes. He is quoted as saying, "If people knew how hard I work, they wouldn't find my achievements so remarkable." Artist Thomas Hart Benton made three-dimensional clay figures of each image in his massive murals. This was to ensure that the proportions would come out correctly.

Break Some Rules

A fair amount of self-inquiry eventually unearths one's personal rules. They may have come from parents, teachers, or the prevailing culture. It doesn't hurt to be aware of one's overriding values, as these are the beliefs that keep society from being completely chaotic. However, being a cookie-cutter person, someone with no individuality or character, could mean the death of your soul.

Maybe there's a family rule that it is not nice to outdo one particular person. The unspoken contract is agreed upon by everyone. Uncle Charlie always has the last word, and everything that is said about him is something positive. It might be fun at the next family reunion to say something after him, every time. A quiet comment to no one in particular, "Isn't Uncle Charlie a lovable bag of wind?" Say it again. Sit solidly while people look your way with a sharp intake of breath. It can be fun.

During holiday festivities, eschew the traditional tree and decorate your entire house in hues of purple. Go all out with candles, swags, blinking lights, and burgundy wine. Joke with friends who come over that you were stricken by the Sugar Plum Fairy and were obligated to fulfill her wishes until January 1. The strange looks won't hurt you.

FACT

Milarepa, a great hero of Tibetan Buddhism, encountered a host of demons, most of which he overcame with compassion. The meanest one simply would not leave. Milarepa climbed into the dragon's mouth and allowed himself to be swallowed. The dragon disappeared.

Be Naive

As you explore further and further afield outside your comfort zone, you might meet interesting people and wonder about certain aspects of their lives. Even if you don't usually strike up conversations with strangers, there is no harm in giving it a try. Ask your favorite barista how his day is going and ask what is selling well that day.

Ask a favorite (or feared) authority figure how she decided to go into her particular career. Did a certain mentor inspire her and help her? What was the path? Most people enjoy talking about themselves, and there could be something important to learn. When you're talking with someone and she uses a name or a word that is unfamiliar to you, stop and ask who that is or the meaning of that word. She will be happy to enlighten you.

Brag about Yourself

Find at least one person with whom you can exchange immodest bragging. Maybe it's a therapist, or maybe it's a best friend. Tell him in great detail how you slayed that dragon and got your proposal approved. You spoke up to your meddling neighbor. You made the dreaded phone call to the ex and apologized for your heinous behavior. You made a cake in the shape of a fire engine for your favorite nephew, without any pattern or instruction. When it's the other person's turn to brag, wholeheartedly cheer them on. Listen attentively and ask for details. You might even have a standing ovation at your little table for two in your favorite coffeehouse.

Be Childlike

There are situations in life where it is not necessary to be perfectly responsible and task oriented. It can be quite fun to occasionally set down the load of grown-up accountability and just be foolish. A woman takes her grandchild to the circus and wears a clown nose all day. A high-level architect has a secret collection of windup toys, and after especially stressful days of working with blueprints and specifications, she clears the dining room table and winds up all the little toys at the same time, enjoying the melee of color, sound, and collision.

Cultivate Partners in Crime

In order to enjoy yourself, you may need support during times when you experience opposition from significant others. Perhaps you just don't want to go across country to the wedding of the third cousin once removed, but it seems like a family obligation. Call up your friend and listen to her say, "If you don't want to go, don't go." Some of the objection may be within yourself, as you learn to align your actions with newly forming beliefs about what you want. At times it may feel like throwing the gears into reverse while you intend to move forward. Another person provides support in the new direction. Be careful in associations with those who might criticize or judge.

Perfectionism versus Authenticity

Perfection is an illusion; no one, or no thing, is or can ever be perfect. This is one of the realities that a person with perfectionism often has difficulty accepting. You have to learn to accept and embrace the imperfections in yourself, in others, and in your relationships.

This concept emphasizes authenticity as opposed to perfectionism. It stresses living authentically: having the strength and the courage to accept your own imperfections and vulnerabilities as being part of the "real you." In many ways it is a manner of living that also opposes everything perfect. When you are authentic in your own self-assessment, which includes flaws, fears, and things you may be ashamed of, you are able to be truly compassionate and empathetic toward others.

CHAPTER 13

A Thorough Self-Examination

It's fairly difficult to change something about yourself, such as modifying perfectionism, unless there is a grounded knowledge of your history and what has gone into making your personality. Instead of stumbling through a dark room without a flashlight, imagine being fearless as you look at all the parts of what has made you who you are today.

Family Rules and Values

It's not always easy to realize the truth about one's values and internalized rules because they seem so very true and normal! In fact, they are your norm and have been for many years. Often these deeply imbedded aspects of the self come to light when you start becoming close to other people and you discover how very different they are from you and each other. Their beliefs about what is important vary from yours. The variety can be interesting but unnerving.

Politics

Think about the political orientation of your parents and whether you have gone the same direction or veered the complete opposite. Maybe you're apolitical. Does your family have a tradition of becoming deeply involved with fundraising and campaigning for a particular party or person? Are politics discussed around the table during meals? Did your parents have divergent beliefs regarding politics, and did one defer to the other during election years? Did they discuss voting and informing themselves about the issues? Think about whether they read newspapers and magazines or listened to radio and television to formulate their voting strategies.

Recreational Patterns

How would you characterize your heritage in terms of having fun? Was it an Archie Bunker type of household with entertainment consisting of talking about the neighbors and bickering among the family members? What was a weekend like during your childhood or a typical holiday? Did your family travel, and were the children included?

ESSENTIAL

If you are in touch with older relatives in your family, it can be rewarding to talk with them about what sort of things they did for fun when they were young. Before media became the prominent source of entertainment, people were marvelously inventive in occupying themselves. You may hear about a vacant lot baseball team or a favorite country fishing hole.

Think about your mother's favorite things to do and your father's favorite pastimes. It's likely that you view these pursuits in a favorable light. What if you had wanted to start something completely different as a child, such as embark upon the study of sharks or collect bone fragments? How would this have been received? These types of questions help you to determine the attitudes in your household.

What were the tastes in music? Think about whether the norm in the household was Scarlatti or Johnny Cash, and where you place yourself in musical taste. Try to remember the pictures on the walls of your family home—portraits of family members, Currier and Ives prints, cherished children's art, Degas and Picasso prints, or original art created by friends or family members.

Some families are all work and no play. Children growing up in this type of environment can become perfectionistic in completing all the required tasks before allowing themselves to have fun. The dichotomy between work and pleasure can bring a negative attitude toward work, as it often is never done. Self-criticism about pleasure and being joyful in one's work are prevalent in these types of families.

Your Cultural Mandates

How would you describe the culture in which you grew up? What is your ethnicity? Are there particular "musts" that go along with being a part of that particular tribe? One of the best ways to become aware of one's culture is to visit another one! If you have been lucky enough to have an extended visit in a foreign country, think about what you learned in contrast to those local people. You can learn as much by becoming close friends with someone from a different culture.

Gender Rules

How are men and women taught to behave in your culture? Are there specific things that are expected and other things that are discouraged? Describe those things. For example, in Mexican culture, women are often taught to cater to men. Men are expected to work hard and provide for the entire family. Extended families are large and everyone is in on everyone else's news. Men are given more freedom, and women are expected to be good cooks.

FACT

Although the present generation is somewhat flexible, for years in South Korea it was tradition that once a woman married, she would no longer work outside the home. The man was the "outside person," and the woman was the "inside person," caring for all the domestic aspects of the family, including managing the finances.

You might be wondering how this could be important in this day and age, when so much is available to everyone. Gender stereotypes were eased during the social revolutions of the 1970s, and now each person can do what he or she wants. In general, that is true, but attitudes are handed down generationally, and your parents or grandparents may exert quite a lot of pressure or perhaps disapproval about certain aspects of your life. For example, if you are a woman coming from a Latina background, you might find yourself criticized if you opt for a career instead of marriage.

Education

What are the beliefs about education coming from your culture? Is it assumed that you will have an opportunity to attend college or university? Do the parents provide such an education for their children or are the children expected to work and search out scholarships? What careers are encouraged and what lines of work are scoffed at? If you decided to become a professional mime, how would that go over? Is there a cultural tradition of particular trades that are acceptable to your clan? What are they, and are you pressured to go in that direction? What happens if you want to learn something completely different?

ALERT

The Jewish culture has historically placed a great deal of emphasis on education, including girls' education, by the late nineteenth century and early twentieth century. However, people from other cultures, especially those of blue-collar socioeconomic groups, experience a particular type of discomfort if they are the first college-educated person in the family. This phenomenon is termed the imposter syndrome. Such individuals sometimes feel alienated from their families and have a sense professionally of being "found out," a bit defensive about the status they have achieved.

Is there a particular college that is favored by your family? Have many from your family or city gone to a certain university? What topics are considered useful to study and what is considered frivolous? Are you expected to get straight As, or are you encouraged to socialize and join a lot of campus clubs? Are you expected to excel in sports or in the arts?

What are your expectations regarding your children's schooling? Will they attend public schools or private? Do you home-school? What is your opinion about grades? Do you reward your children's good grades, or do you assume that they will excel because that is their job at school? These questions can help you tease out attitudes of perfectionism and high expectation concerning this aspect of your life.

Religion

In some cultures religion is synonymous with the culture. Think about your religious leanings and whether they came from your parents or your own self-inquiry and exploration. Automatically adhering to the religious beliefs of the culture in which you were raised can be a comfortable way to go, as you will have plenty of company. At the same time, it can be rewarding to acknowledge that foundation and deliberately try a different path, just out of curiosity, perhaps for a specific length of time.

Money

In your culture, what would be the prevailing beliefs about the importance of money? Do people generally save a certain portion that is earned, and what are the uses of the savings? At what age do children start to have their own money in your culture, and how do they spend it? Think about attitudes toward business—large corporations, small entrepreneurial efforts, and working from home. Some cultures favor one avenue, and others are inclined toward another. Think about a typical household within your culture and envision how the financial decisions are made.

ESSENTIAL

Money and power conventionally go hand in hand. It is good to be aware of the dynamics of power connected with money within one's family and within the culture. Such prevailing preferences can be changed within a relationship, but it will take considerable effort.

Who participates in the discussions and who has the final word? If teenagers need money to participate in school activities or other peer activities, how would the culture feel about that? Think about the prevailing cultural attitudes about banking and retirement and where you fit in terms of those cultural guidelines.

Blind Spots within Yourself

There is no foolproof way to discover blind spots, because, of course, they are hidden from your awareness! One way to think about this is to consider what friends and significant others have pointed out to you, either in exasperation or as a compliment. Think of comments that have included the words "You always . . ." or "You never . . . ." Are you always late because unconsciously you believe your time is more valuable than the other person's time? Do you think one sex is more important than the other, catering to one or the other in business settings? Should children be seen and not ever heard? Would you spend thousands of dollars on another college degree but have difficulty buying a new suit when yours becomes frayed? These are only a few examples. Try to be alert to what others say or their unspoken reactions when you relate to them. Over a period of time you may discover some blind spots.

Guidelines for Exploring Your Beliefs and Values

Writing is a good way to explore your history, background, beliefs, and values. Some people keep a separate journal for each aspect of their quest, and others devise a three-ring binder arrangement with separate categories for each part of their work. Yours will evolve over time as you get comfortable with the process. It is helpful to have a therapist, mentor, or close trusted friend to share your discoveries with as you progress through this important task. Spend a number of months to do the work, as realizations will occur to you along the way. One discovery leads to another, and momentum will build as the knowledge grows.

ESSENTIAL

Writing at the computer is somewhat different from handwriting in a journal. Handwriting seems to come from a deeper place in the brain and is useful for easing out unknown, buried attitudes, feelings, and memories. Keyboard writing is faster and a bit more analytical, perhaps using more of the left hemisphere of the brain. Make a conscious choice about which you prefer.

The twelve-step programs have an inventorying process that may work for you. The inventory can be a straightforward life story or a detailed listing of the chronology in each aspect of your life—relationships, career, spiritual growth, financial experiences. One woman remembered in a vague way that she had tremendously liked some of her homes and not so much others. She wrote a house inventory and discovered the interesting pattern that while living in the homes she did not like she was involved with dysfunctional mates! The mind is clever in how it stores information, and the writing process can tease it out in a highly beneficial way.

Your Autobiography

It may seem redundant to think of your life story again, especially if you have had years of therapy and other kinds of help. What else could possibly come to light? It never hurts to take a fresh look, as at different stages of life and maturity odd pieces of one's history are remembered with a new perspective and can be just the missing piece of the puzzle that helps you understand the perfectionistic patterns.

In her book, *Vein of Gold*, Julia Cameron recommends that the reader first write a timeline in five-year increments. "What?" you say in horror! Go ahead. Think about it. Consider making such a timeline with significant events noted under each section of your life. Then with a notebook or journal designated especially for this effort, write a thorough life story, focusing in five-year time blocks. Of course, you will not do it all in one sitting. This autobiography could take months to complete. Write about the significant happenings of each five-year increment. Were there tragedies? Traumas? Who were the significant people? What were you doing and how did you feel about it? What were your successes and failures? It will be interesting to complement your writing with photos of the places and people that were important for that time, as well as pictures of yourself. How did the six-year-old look as he went off to school? What are your memories of first driving a car? All these things are important aspects of your life story. When did you become perfectionistic? Whom did you hope to please? Were your efforts successful?

Feeling and Setting Aside Sorrow

Dr. Elisabeth Kübler-Ross brought the process of grief into mainstream awareness, mostly in connection with death, but the process is similar in facing injured and buried aspects of the self. If you lost a favorite nanny when you were five but were never allowed to grieve her exit from the family, the emotions that spew forth when you think about that will perhaps be that of a five-year-old. It will feel devastating. The same goes for the loss of a cherished pet, your trusty friend that would protect you and listen to all your stories.

American culture does not readily face or acknowledge the process of grief. Other cultures allow people to wail and take lengthy times away from usual responsibilities. It is unusual for Western workers to take more than a day or two when a family member is lost or there is some other major trauma. The stiff upper lip is expected as the worker quickly resumes normal responsibilities. Friends and coworkers may feel awkward, not knowing what to say to their peer. The truth is, difficult losses, even the loss of a fantasized idea of a perfect background, can take quite a long time to grieve—months or years even—as important anniversaries recur.

Following are the stages of grief that one can expect during a time of major transition:

- Shock and denial. You may feel numb and act as if you are on autopilot.
- Pain and guilt. This is a stage of unbelievable pain.
- Anger and bargaining. You may rant and rave, making deals with God.
- Depression and loneliness. The situation has happened and the loss is irrevocable.
- The turning point. The pain and depression begin to lessen.
- Reconstruction, adjustment, and working through. You start to look at practical considerations. With your new situation and new understanding, what has to change now? Is there a need for a financial overhaul? Do you want to sell your house and travel? Decisions are easier to make as you are more able to logically look at preferences and ramifications of each new direction.
- Acceptance and hope. At this stage the loss becomes integrated. It does not mean that you are thrilled with the loss, but you are calm and able to function in your life, even with a brand new set of circumstances. You no longer are preoccupied every waking moment with the devastation of the loss. You start to feel more comfortable about making plans for your future and actually believe that you will have a future, even without the old, previous misconceptions about where and how you are supposed to be perfect.

ALERT

Complicated grief is a deeply entrenched sorrow that has been stuck in the personality. The person was unable to complete the stages of grief. A person who is seemingly permanently sad should seek professional help to move the process along.

The grief process may not be as orderly as this list. There can be some looping back and being in more than one stage at a time. How long will it last? For major losses, it can take years, and the length of time increases if a person is unwilling to face the more difficult emotions. Those feelings of unresolved grief will pop up unexpectedly when there is another loss in the future. Then you will be grieving several things at once. It is better to be courageous and face each one as it occurs.

What Can You Do Instead?

Life does not have to be an uphill battle between the self or outside environment. It's unnecessary to be sad and tired all the time. Even if there is a background of difficult experiences, it is entirely possible to work them through and claim a joyful life. This shift in lifestyle does require effort and a willingness to set down habits of negative thinking.

ESSENTIAL

Researcher and life coach Brené Brown, PhD, LMSW, has coined a way of living authentically as being "wholehearted." Wholehearted people, as Dr. Brown describes, realize that what makes them vulnerable is also what makes them beautiful and allows them to connect to all of humanity, which shares similar pains, struggles, and vulnerabilities.

A Clear Look at Your Life

Here are ten ways you can learn to live more authentically:

- **Understand your purpose.** Does it feel like your life lacks direction? Do you think that health and prosperity will just come to you? You need to identify your life purpose. Think of it like a corporation's mission statement. Knowing your purpose means you will always have a way to find your authenticity.
- **Recognize your true values.** Make a list of the five things you value most. Then think about your goals. If your goals do not match up with your values, you are not living as authentically as you can or should be.

- **Embrace your own needs.** It is not a selfish act to take care of yourself. Having unmet needs can keep you from living authentically.
- **Know what you love or feel passionate about.** Recognize and embrace the things that make you genuinely happy. Whatever it is, from writing poetry to karaoke singing, if it makes your heart soar, do more of it!
- **Try living from the inside out.** Use yoga, meditation, or any other relaxation technique that can increase your awareness of your innermost thoughts and wisdom.
- **Accept your vulnerabilities, but respect your own strengths**. Recognize yourself for your positive traits and special talents. Make a list of at least three things that you know you are really, really good at. Honor your true self by doing things that express the strengths on your list.
- **Take time to relax.** You cannot be true to yourself or anyone else if you are burned out. Give yourself time to recharge by doing things just for fun, or by doing nothing at all.
- **Get rid of negative self-talk.** Listen to your internal dialogs. Are they supportive and encouraging, or negative and self-deprecating? Choose your mind's voice. Change negative messages into positive daily affirmations.
- **Inspire and encourage yourself.** Keep a journal of all your accomplishments, big and small, every day.
- **Do unto others as you would have them do unto you.** It is not just the Golden Rule, it is the way to live authentically. And once you are living authentically, giving to others becomes your natural state of being. Because if you are true to who you are, living purposefully and sharing the best of yourself with the world around you, you are giving back in every possible way.

Living more authentically will improve your own emotional health and will likely help you live better with others. Beyond that, once you have embraced living authentically, you will also be a good role model for others in your life.

The problem with trying to achieve any kind of perfectionism is that it negatively affects and impacts every effort. Take even an Academy Award–winning film or performance that has achieved Best Picture or Best Actor. There is something in that film or that performance that could still be judged as less than perfect. Ultimately, perfectionism, as opposed to authenticity, can be just a way to feel bad inside, no matter how great a job you may have done.

Perfectionism can be the enemy of everything good, because to the perfectionist, even the very good is not good enough. To someone who is able to live authentically, on the other hand, doing something very well will likely feel great!

Laughter Is Healing!

Writer and coach, Martha Beck, endorses laughter as a route to relaxed self-acceptance. She and her family are of Nordic ancestry, so when they get together for holidays, they don ridiculous Viking hats! An activity she suggests is to make collages with odd-looking photographic images and combine them with contradictory headlines from magazines or newspapers. For example, an innocuous photo of a tired, elderly grandmother could be combined with the caption, "The Colorless, Odorless Killer: In Cold Pursuit."

Self-deprecating humor is always attractive and endearing. Could it be fun to start to laugh at your perfectionism? Instead of shame and fear, bring it out into the open and embrace others in your humanness. You will be surprised at how others will identify with you and want to draw you closer as you own up to the frailties that accompany perfectionism.

Slay the Dragons

You do not need to be frightened by the labels—for example, "Here be dragons"—that were once put on maps to describe uncharted territories. According to whom? You may have heard the adage that the way out is through. Sometimes facing the dragons and not cowering to their hot breath brings on a huge spurt of energy and new level of growth. If you have a good idea for a new business and have fleshed out a good business plan, face the angel investors. Face the venture capitalists. What is the worst that could happen? They may decline the opportunity. This does not mean the same as verbally berating you for wasting their time with such a ridiculous idea. You will survive whether they say yes or no.

Physical Awareness

Along with the five senses, there is a kind of sensitivity that has to do with awareness of bodily position. Perhaps as you work, you can stop and do a few yoga stretches. During your daily walk, pull yourself up a little more erect and take longer strides. Swing your arms and enjoy the feeling of air on your skin.

If you like to dance or swim, take a particular delight in the awareness of your muscles as they harmoniously go through the paces of a smooth crawl or a finely executed East Coast Swing. The knowledge of where your body is, what it is doing in space, and the aesthetic and physical wonder of the rhythm and symmetry of it can be an unexpected source of joy.

Cultivate Intimacy

If you come from a background that created perfectionism, it is unlikely that true intimacy is a comfortable topic. This isn't necessarily sexual intimacy, although that might be included. Emotional intimacy is the elusive holy grail that is completely absent in a dysfunctional family. If you are perfectionistic, it is likely that intimacy is challenging for you.

Try being completely honest at first with just one or two completely warm, trustworthy people—perhaps a therapist or someone you have met in a support group. Test the waters. Tell them some of your darkest secrets, for example, that you have a ritual of lining up all the spice containers so the labels all face one direction.

Perhaps you check the coffeepot and the stove several times before leaving the house, and sometimes you call your spouse or neighbor to check if they are off because you cannot remember if you truly checked them or merely thought about it.

What else would you not want to share with another? These are the things that can be carefully shared as you discern the response of the trusted other. Is there any judgment? If not, you can proceed with what could be a truly intimate relationship. As you learn how to do this, you can slowly expand your social circle by adding more trusted friends.

ESSENTIAL

> "... Love for and understanding of one's own self cannot be separated from respect for and love and understanding of another individual. The love for my own self is inseparably connected with the love for any other self." —Erich Fromm

It is possible to be intimate with children, if you keep the perfectionism in check. No need to correct anything about them. Ask some interesting open-ended questions. What was the best part of your day so far? What would it be like to be invisible? Where would you go and what would you do? If you could travel in time, who would you like to visit?

It can be very rewarding to have long talks with elderly people. Open-ended questions yield much wisdom and perspective on life. What was your most memorable moment in your life? Who impacted you—public or private figure? If you could have done anything differently during your life, what would it have been? What was your most interesting mistake, and how did you recover? Ask them about perfectionism.

CHAPTER 14

Rebuilding Self-Esteem

Some persons from troubled backgrounds discover that they never actually *had* self-esteem, so it is a case of building esteem from ground zero. This stark realization gives the individual clarity, and new decisions are ready to be made. Some have said that esteem comes from doing esteemable acts. You may find that the old motivations for perfection subside somewhat as new, fresh actions move to the forefront of your life. The former frantic overachievement with its fleeting accolade is no longer as appealing as an honest, authentic moment with a treasured pet, friend, or relative.

Taking Back the Initiative in Your Life

The grips of perfectionism take away true control of your existence, as you are at the mercy of the old, outdated voices, whether yours or those of former authority figures. If you can muzzle those voices, it becomes possible to make decisions about your life that result in greater satisfaction.

Start Small

Perhaps you have been dominated by your spouse's lifestyle and social expectations that go along with a particular career. It has been seductive because there are many perks. First, select your own clothing when you are forced to attend one of those command performances. Maybe the invitation called for semiformal, but your favorite cardigan is calling to you. Snaz up the rest of the outfit to balance out the soft sweater, and see how comfortable you are truly being yourself. On another occasion, opt out completely and take a class or go to a cultural event that is more to your liking. Help your spouse fabricate a plausible excuse for your absence and promise some quality time together as a reward.

Take Bigger Initiatives

The confidence gained with small steps in your true direction lead to bigger steps toward your own happiness. You may find resistance among those closest to you. This is to be expected, as they are comfortable in their relationships with you and fear losing you to the new self that is emerging. It sometimes helps to keep plans quiet and let the actions speak for themselves. That way there is less room for arguing.

During your meditations and writing, new directions will emerge. Your essence will call to you once the heavy burden of perfectionism has been laid down. Do you long for the company of others who love flowers and other exotic plants? Spend some time haunting local nurseries and public gardens. Ask a lot of questions of the workers in such places. Offer to be of assistance in some way. Perhaps the local arboretum has a yearly sale and help is needed to publicize the event. The nursery manager may need a bookkeeper.

ESSENTIAL

George Washington Carver made the inspiring statement, "If you love something enough, it will reveal its secrets." Think of this when you feel a new direction calling. Spend time with it and see what secrets might be revealed.

There is something mystical about the process of going in a new direction. Doors open and a world is revealed that was formerly mostly unknown.

Being Part of the Human Race

Perfectionists try so hard to be good enough, better than, or the very best, when lurking in the psyche are the beliefs that one is not good enough at all. It is tortuous to keep doing things perfectly to quiet the demanding directives. As one lets go of perfectionism in the self, other people become more interesting and attractive. Fewer traits are annoying, and one can go forth and be a human among humans.

But I've Always Been an Alien!

Remember how lovable E.T. was? Being an alien might not be so bad, but joining the human race can be a comfort, as well. If you are on a treadmill from dawn until midnight crossing things off your "to do" list, set that aside and hang out in a public place with some fellow earthlings. Maybe go to a concert in the park and share your picnic with the family on the next blanket. Browse at your favorite bookstore and ask a fellow browser his opinion on a particular writer or subject. Try a lecture or seminar on a topic that seems intriguing but not your usual forte. Strike up conversations with other attendees about why they happened to be there. Follow up on interesting points with the presenters. When you're out for a walk in your neighborhood, take the time to exchange pleasantries with the neighbors about their remodeling projects or new puppies.

Without Competition I'm Nobody!

Others will find you infinitely more appealing as you become less perfect. This is hard to accept when one has lived an entire life on the treadmill of achievement and people pleasing. Try to reveal your foibles to others in small increments. If you burned the bagels one morning, tell everyone you encounter for the next hour or two. They will laugh and tell you of their own kitchen disasters.

Think of people in your world who make you feel absolutely fabulous. Is it the waitress at your favorite restaurant? How interested is she in your highest achievements? She wants to know what you would like to eat and likely already has something in mind for you because she knows your tastes. Neither of you are competing. Perhaps another favorite person is the custodian at a club you frequent. He cautions you to wait a moment while he cleans up a spill on the floor so you won't slip. He is never rushed and always has time to exchange a few pleasant words. This is not a competitive person and he is not interested in your achievements. Do you have a favorite cab driver who tells marvelous stories about his family's integration into American society? This person is not interested in your achievements, but you feel infinitely cared for as he amiably philosophizes on the way to your destination. Mutual respect is present when people are equals.

Giving Up Self-Punishment

Eventually your self-inquiries will lead you to recognize the critical voices within your mind, and the connection is made to perfectionism. It helps to write down the specific sentences that others said to you that have become a part of how you talk to yourself.

Critical Voices

Others have discovered sentences similar to the following:

1. You'll never amount to anything.
2. Nothing you do is important.
3. Your purpose is to support me. Don't bother me with your stories.
4. Why can't you be more like your sister?

5. You always were too much trouble.
6. You're just crazy.
7. Why don't you give up these strange things and just be normal?
8. Everything you do reflects upon the family.
9. Can't you see I'm busy? There's no time for you. Go away.
10. How dare you do that without discussing it with me!

These statements amount to verbal abuse, and the scary thing is, as an adult, those things continue to be said! Noticing the specific statements is a good first step. Then stop saying that specific thing when you catch it. It won't be instantaneous, as you undoubtedly have practiced the litanies for years.

Craft Some Affirmations

A good way to make use of critical statements is to write them down and then write down the exact opposite. The new sentence is your affirmation. For example, the criticism of "How dare you do that without discussing it with me!" becomes "You are an intelligent person who is free to create a life you love." "I'm too busy for you," becomes "You're important. Let's take the time to think about this together."

It is interesting to experiment with the voice of affirmations. Some people crave the affirmative directive, as if it is coming from the other person. Those "you" statements give the feeling of giving permission to think and feel in a new way. Others like to put the affirmation in the first person. The strong "I" statement gives the person a sense of centeredness and control.

Release Anxiety

As a person shifts from self-criticism to self-affirmation, the old nameless fears subside. The result is a much greater degree of calm as one moves through the day. Strangely enough, without the perfectionism, there are fewer real or imagined emergencies. It may feel odd not to be hyped up a lot, as if you are not important and your various tasks are not important. Anxiety can be a habit, and there is a bit of an adjustment in giving it up. When you feel that familiar tense posture and shallow breathing coming on, along with the racing thoughts, work with your breathing, tame your thoughts, and emphatically shift gears. It really is okay to be a calm, peaceful person.

Balancing Various Aspects of Your Life

If you tend toward perfectionism, it is quite likely that different parts of your life are out of balance. It is likely that a perfectionist works too hard or too long, spends too much time at the gym, or haunts the department store sales much too much. Compulsivity can take many forms. One way to approach a better balance is to think about what is being neglected. Have people in your life complained about something to you? Maybe you need to spend more time with friends. Strong social connections are a large component of mental health.

Possibly more leisure time is needed with the caution of not making the recreational pursuits something new to work on. It's not necessary to compete at Wimbledon to enjoy tennis.

ALERT

Beware of videogames and other role-playing online games as recreation! Jim Rubens notes that the average player clocks twenty-two hours a week in such games, and extremists play for up to eighty hours per week!

Some people find that keeping a time log for a few weeks shows where time is wasted or otherwise misspent. A simple notepad where the categories of life are listed with the length of time on each one, each day, is quite illuminating. Numbers show the graphic truth, and it becomes easier to grasp the necessity of reapportioning the currency of time. Some categories may be completely absent! It might help to look at your categories with a trusted friend or professional to get some support in shaving down the parts that are too large and reallocating time to other, neglected parts of your life. Undoubtedly, you will experience various emotions and attitude adjustments as you make those changes.

The Power of Positive Reinforcement

B. F. Skinner discovered that certain types of reinforcement are powerful conditioners for animals and humans. Now it is common knowledge that a pet can be trained to do certain tricks. So can you! You know your favorite rewards better than anyone. Be careful that your rewards are not something that could take you down another compulsive direction—overeating or shopping.

ESSENTIAL

Claiming true desires and accepting rewards for them can bring about a great deal of emotional pain if there has been a lifetime of self-deprivation. It is like a frostbitten limb thawing out. However, the benefits outweigh the discomfort if a person can withstand the process.

The areas that you discovered had been neglected might hold some ideas for helpful rewards. For example, if you tend to work too much, each day that you stop work at the specified time, reward yourself with ten minutes of dancing to energetic music. You have not danced in months or years! This is the reason to include the possibility of this as a reward.

It can be fun to discuss with your inner child what would be some good rewards. Surprisingly, something as simple as gold stars on the planning calendar might be enough to elicit that good feeling of acknowledgement. Perhaps the inner child wants to go to a comedic movie instead of another dreary docudrama. The indulgence can be very relaxing and fun. One author discovered at a book signing that almost all of her fans carried gel pens in glittery hues, a pleasant way to reward oneself.

According to classical conditioning, intermittent reinforcement is the strongest schedule because of its longer-lasting effects in shaping the behavior. You might find that when you are forming a new habit, a treat every time is needed to change the habitual direction. As it becomes a little more comfortable, a shift to a reward every few times becomes quite powerful.

Average Is Okay

Perfectionists abhor the idea of average. Actually, average is not so bad if it is accompanied by better health, better relationships, and greater peace of mind. Being average gives a person more room to experiment and to try various directions without being so afraid of not doing things well. Being an average Sunday painter might bring enormous pleasure. Singing in a chorus might provide the camaraderie of other music lovers and the safety of numbers. Not everyone has to be a soloist.

FACT

Being average is better for the health. One worker, who figuratively chained himself to the desk like a dog, never took breaks, and ate lunch at his desk, ended up with a ruptured ulcer.

Those aspects of life that have been neglected might be just the aspects that could bring happiness with average accomplishment. A fishing outing with younger relatives is fun, even if nobody catches any fish! The memories will be of the outdoors and shared moments.

Realistically, one is probably not going to become another Michael Jordan, Yo-Yo Ma, or the next winner of *American Idol*, although millions of Americans think it is possible. This is part of the American myth, that any person can reach the top. Olympist Michelle Kwan said it rather well, "I didn't lose the gold. I won the silver." Accepting the position of average is particularly difficult for baby boomers because that generation came of age when the average American did have greater options. It is especially essential for boomers not to become disillusioned but to refashion the idea of success in a way that is personal and real.

Rekindle Former Interests

What interests have you set aside because it seemed that your perfectionistic demands on yourself were so much more important? It might be fun to do some of those things again. Take a look at your Hot Wheels collection and remember how much fun you had selecting each little car. You might enjoy attending antique auto shows and refurbishing old cars. People who frequent those events may speak your same language.

Maybe life has become so impossibly busy that you have stopped cooking. Get out the cookbooks and browse through them. Think of which treasured people you'd like to cook for and plan a gathering. Shop for the best (but not perfect) ingredients and enjoy the leisurely process of preparing a meal for loved ones. Savor the textures and flavors. Create a table setting that pleases the eye, and choose background music according to the tastes of your guests. It might be fun to select a theme—a holiday or a particular type of ethnic food. This will give you an excuse to shop for exotic spices.

Has your social life suffered because of your devotion to a demanding job? Take some time and make phone calls just to catch up with friends you haven't spoken with recently. Remember who is sick or convalescing and send out some inquiries to see how those people are doing. Perhaps you like to make handmade greeting cards. Adding birthday notes to your planning calendar can spark interest in making something creative to send out for someone's birthday or other important event.

How to Manage Your Anger

It is likely that a lot of your anger is directed at yourself, because you are not perfect and do not perform perfectly. Underneath that anger is hurt and fear. If you can bear it, spend some time with yourself and find the true emotion under the anger. Are you hurt because a friend slighted you? Are you afraid that your parents or spouse will never love you the way you want to be loved? It can be sobering to face the truth of the emotion, but strangely, a person calms down a bit when clarity is reached.

Damage Control

When you feel tremendously out of sorts with anger and rage, direct that energy in another direction. Tell whomever you are with that you are taking a time-out. Go to another location and walk energetically for awhile. If you like to jog or cycle, this would be a good time to get the extra exercise.

Sometimes it helps to plug into your favorite music and be in a different zone for awhile. Perhaps you can clean out the garage or move the boxes of stored office records that you have ignored. Eliminate any thoughts of hurting yourself or others from your mind.

If you fear hurting a child while you are angry, keep close at hand, even in your cell phone, hotline numbers to prevent child abuse. Share honestly with the crisis worker how you feel and what you fear you might do. It helps, as well, to attend support groups for parents who fear that they will abuse their children. This is actually a common inclination for adults who were themselves abused as children. As you get to know those other group members, they can support you on those very difficult days.

Make Apologies as Necessary

As your anger becomes more under control, it helps to backtrack and say that you're sorry to each person that has been harmed by the outbursts. This will be quite difficult at first, as the anger seems so justified. However, with practice, getting back to the person right away humanizes the situation, and others can see that you own up to not being perfect. This can be a breath of fresh air for everyone concerned. It is especially important to make amends to children and others in very close relationships. Such sincere apologies keep the relationship channels clean and harmonious.

What Can You Do Instead?

It has been said that happiness is having something to do and someone to love. This could also be true of self-esteem. Enjoyable activities add so much to life, whether paid or unpaid, and being with persons who are genuinely cared for brings dimension and warmth to days that otherwise might be empty and barren. Perfectionists tend to suffer from loneliness.

ESSENTIAL

Maturity is the ability to work and the ability to love. Some aspects of maturity are accepting ambivalent situations and being able to cooperate with others, sometimes letting them have the final say in a decision.

Catch yourself on those good days and do a few more of the things that seem to enhance your self-esteem. As you let go of perfectionism, you will discover more about what truly makes you feel good about yourself. One good thing can lead to another, and these fine days compensate for the days when it seems that nothing goes according to plan.

Being of service to others is a sure route to self-esteem. In your work, think of the end result and how it truly meets the needs of the customers or clients. This is the heart of self-esteem—using your energy to provide something for another person who needs just what you deliver. If you are not currently employed, find a situation that cries out for your talents and give some time to others. It might be exercising and talking with animals at a humane society or sorting donations for a women's domestic violence shelter. If you like physical labor and construction sites, Habitat for Humanity is a possible place to do tremendous good.

On those days when it seems that perfectionism has the upper hand, one route to gaining self-esteem is to deliberately do things one at a time. Stop everything and do one simple thing—perhaps make a phone call or open the mail. People who do too much or try to do several things at once can experience nervous anxiety because none of the tasks they do feel complete or well done. Doing simple tasks around the home or workplace are good for calming down.

ALERT

Accept that each task requires a finite amount of time, and resist the temptation to try to do many things in a given span of time. It is frustrating, and leads to tension and anxiety.

Clearing out the inbox of old e-mails is mindless and calming. Sending a simple greeting card to a relative or friend bears fruit in self-esteem. Catching up on filing may not be the favorite task, but the feeling of accomplishment is a powerful reward.

CHAPTER 15

Perfectionism and the Only Child or Gifted Child

An only child or gifted child exists in an environment that can lead to the child trying to be perfect, and that situation often extends into adult years, resulting in a perfectionistic man or woman. The only child is the family's only shot at raising a child, and there can be intense pressure to get it right. The gifted child is so good at so many things that the temptation to be perfect is always there, both from within the child and from the parents. These inclinations continue into the adult experience.

Hazards Ahead!

Watch out for perfectionism! It can be deadly for the gifted child. Gifted children will likely be emotionally sensitive and easy to stunt with too much prodding or pushing. It's a good idea to remember that the quest of learning is what engages the mind, not the result. The result may be momentarily interesting, but the joy is in careening down the path to get there. Both parents and children need to keep in mind that it is the process that is valuable, not necessarily the result.

The child needs to understand that he is loved for who he is, not for what he does. The best prevention for the harms of perfectionism is to give the child plenty of unconditional love and affection. It also is sensible to let the child fail from time to time. Failure is definitely a part of life, and even a very young child can learn that he's okay, even if things don't turn out quite as expected.

Gifted Challenges

The exquisite sensitivity that enables gifted children to note subtle differences in texture, movement, color, and shape means that what others perceive as a blank wall can appear to them as a vibrant palette. Because they are constantly bombarded with sensory stimuli, they are more stressed. The extreme interpersonal sensitivity causes some children to tune into other people's feelings. They are aware of hints of criticism and displeasure that other children don't notice. Ironically, the combination of extreme sensitivity, high energy level, and reduced need for sleep are characteristics of children often diagnosed as hyperactive. There may be a lot of very misunderstood children out there! Gifted children can be perfectionistic in wanting to complete a task, but find to their utter frustration they do not have the physical strength or dexterity to carry it out.

Special Concerns for Adults and Children

From the beginning, an only child (who has only his parents for social company at home) is subject to peer pressure from parents that, in most cases, they aren't even aware they are exerting. The law of peer pressure is the same everywhere—conform to belong. Espousing the ruling norms of a group allows an individual member of that group to fit in, get along, and become a member in good standing.

FACT

Gifted adults often suffer from isolation and loneliness, and there is the temptation to dumb down, act normal and average, just to fit in with a social group. This quest can become a compulsion, trying over and over again to find the perfect tribe where the quick wit and curious mind will be accepted rather than scorned.

So the only child adjusts to parental ways, accepts parental terms, imitates parental actions, and acquires parental beliefs in order to be in good favor. In response, parental acceptance and approval is given. Gifted persons are sometimes similarly shackled, regardless of the age, feeling that everyone expects them to be a great problem-solver, charming and funny, and the one who always sees a project through. It can be a burdensome exercise in futile perfectionism.

Emotional Enmeshment

It's obvious to say, but important to remember, that parents and an only child grow extremely close emotionally. Their bonding is rooted in spending so much time together, keeping each other social company at home, caring so much for each other, and coming to know each other so intimately. Typically, their relationship is emotionally sensitized—parent and child being able to tell, without words, how the other is feeling. It is difficult to mask true feelings from each other.

If you remember the characters in the movie *White Oleander*, the mother fostered the enmeshment of the daughter in a very unhealthy way, refusing to let her develop as a separate individual. She insisted that the lost teenager remember that: "We are Viking women!" The mother said fairly often to the teenager, "You're perfect." This sets up unrealistic ideas in the child.

Feeling Tied to Each Other

Difficulty with such closeness arises when parents and child tie their own feelings to the well-being of each other. Harboring thoughts like the ones below is often a sign of emotional enmeshment.

- "I feel okay if you feel okay."
- "If you don't feel okay, then I don't feel okay."
- "If you don't feel okay, then I need to help you feel okay."
- "If I am unable to help you feel okay, then I won't feel okay."

ESSENTIAL

Emotional enmeshment comes at the expense of emotional independence, which allows one person to feel bad without the other automatically feeling bad in response. Someone who does not have emotional independence feels obliged to "fix" the unhappy other so they can both feel okay. This is a landmine for perfectionism because it is never possible to fix another person, although the youngster would like to.

Caution with Types of Reinforcement for Only Children

Since some degree of emotional enmeshment is very common between parents and an only child, the wrong comments can increase the pressure on this intense attachment. So when parents look at As on a report card and declare, "We must be doing something right!" the child links her personal performance to her parents' well-being. "How I do determines how my parents feel." This is a scary proposition, fraught with possibilities for perfectionistic thinking and behavior. Better for parents to have simply said, "Congratulations for how well you've done!" and express satisfaction for the child, rather than with themselves.

An only child or a gifted child can be quite sensitive to corrections, making you both unhappy. A parent may say, "It hurts me to give correction because I know it hurts my child." The child may say, "It hurts being corrected because that means I have failed to please my parents and now they are unhappy because of me." The child always wants to do the right thing and may try to second-guess what the parent wants, even if the parent does not clearly state what is expected.

Be careful of the temptation to attach your good feelings about yourself to the child's good behavior. Statements such as, "We're proud of you" or "You make us feel so proud" may increase perfectionistic pressure on the child to believe, "How well or badly I do determines how well or badly my parents feel about themselves." This gives unrealistic responsibility to the child concerning the parents' emotional health.

The Tyranny of Pleasing

Parents and their only child usually have mutual admiration for one another. Each side gives the other such high approval ratings that neither one can stand the thought of displeasing the other, or of not pleasing the other enough. This makes the give and take of getting along, with the inequities of age and power, especially hard to take.

Excessive pressure to please each other can create a "tyranny of pleasing." To reduce this tyranny of pleasing, parents should clarify for themselves and their only child the difference between love and approval. Love is a given. It is rooted in the parents' unconditional acceptance of the person their child is. Approval is earned. It is rooted in the parents' responsibility to conditionally evaluate their child's performance and to communicate how well or badly he or she is making decisions in life, completely separate from what the parents need from their own self-esteem.

ESSENTIAL

Explain to your child that love and approval are not the same. Love is a constant; approval varies with evaluation of the child's behavior. Love does not guarantee approval any more than disapproval means a loss of love. Keep dissipating the misconception that perfection is necessary for either love or approval.

You have a responsibility to evaluate your child's development and actions, but how you deliver your opinions makes the difference between fostering perfectionism or avoiding it. In fact, what you need to do is neutralize your evaluation when giving a correction by expressing it not as disapproval but as disagreement, as follows: "We disagree with the choice you have made, here is why, and this is what we need to have happen in consequence."

To keep the tyranny of pleasing from making it harder to assist your sensitive gifted or only child, you can communicate that your relationship will be displeasing sometimes, and that's okay.

- "We don't always have to agree with what the other believes."
- "We don't always have to like each other to get along."
- "We can disapprove of each other's actions and still love each other as much as ever."
- "We will both sometimes make decisions to please ourselves that we know will be displeasing to each other."
- "We are separate people and can please ourselves sometimes. This isn't selfish."

The tyranny of pleasing is not limited to children. Gifted adults, and adults who were only children, are similarly fine-tuned to the preferences of others, whether a spouse, close friend, coworker, or supervisor. The people-pleasing person is able to sense what the other wants, even before it is stated, and act on those things for the other person. This can be quite an attractive skill, to a point, but it sometimes gets out of hand, and the overly sensitive pleaser ends up having no life. All her efforts are extended toward others. This is especially the case if that was the dynamic in the person's childhood home.

The Expectation of Return

Parenting an only child is high-investment parenting. Everything that you have to give as parents is devoted to the welfare of a single child; all your hopes and dreams for parenthood ride on the shoulders of how that child grows through life. On the one hand, what you give, you give freely out of love. But because you are human, you do have some expectation of return for all the caring, time, energy, resources, and effort you have put in. The high investment parents make in an only child often comes with a high expectation of return. This setup includes dangers of perfectionism in both the parent and the child.

Sometimes, often in adolescence, the only child will object to the pressure he feels to make good on that return. "When you say you only want the best for me, what you really mean is that you want the best from me. The more you do for me, the more I'm expected to do for you, and most of all that means doing well! It's like I'm supposed to live my life to make you look good!" Be aware that a bright teenager in an emotionally healthy home will say such things, no holds barred!

Communicate to your only child that he or she does not owe you an unblemished and stellar performance in return for the dedicated care and support you provide. "All we expect from you is what we expect from ourselves—an honest effort to do what's right that results in a mixed performance of good decisions and bad, because none of us is perfect, only human."

Also, do not use the words "should" or "ought" when speaking to your child. Both words just encourage feelings of duty in a child who already carries a strong sense of obligation to you.

FACT

The only child's tendency to imitate and please parents who are very sensitive and understanding makes for a harmonious childhood most of the time. Come the more stormy adolescent years, however, the teenager may want to severely break out of the mold, especially if there have been tinges of perfectionistic expectations. Your good child may suddenly not be so good any more.

Unrealistic Standards of Performance

Being peers with parents not only leads the only child to develop more grown-up speaking and social skills at an early age, but all the adult association makes the boy or girl feel more adult. In consequence, the child will frequently lay claim to adultlike standing in the family.

Unhappily, this is where self-imposed performance pressure can begin for many only children. By presuming comparable standing to parents ("If I can act their equal, then I should have equal say"), the only child carries this equation one dangerous step further: "If I can act equally grown up, then I should be able to perform equally well." Does this sound like perfectionism?

But the child is not an adult, and so these standards are inappropriate and unreachable. "I can't do it as well as you," moans the only child when the more experienced parent does something better. Then, to ease this frustration, the parent may respond, "Don't be so hard on yourself, you're just a child." But this is not what the only child wants to hear, and now she feels put down and assigned inferior standing in the family.

To help keep your only child's unrealistically high standards from making it harder to relate to them, soften the stands you take by making honest explanations. "When we want you to take on additional responsibility, that doesn't mean you are not trying or working hard enough. It just means that as you grow there is more self-discipline to learn." "When we call you down for not doing what we feel you should, or for doing what we feel you shouldn't, that doesn't mean you don't do anything right. In fact, it's the exception that proves the rule: most of the time you conduct your life extremely well."

ALERT

Signs that your only child is putting unreasonable demands on himself include an intolerance of anything less than outstanding personal performance, extreme frustration with mistakes, severe self-criticism, and despondency after losing in competition or failing to achieve a goal.

Perfectionism can easily creep into the equation with an only child, as only children often are naturally high achievers. They have a lot of attention from the adults in their lives and can thrive in many ways. This is optimal, to a point, but not if the child becomes tense, absolutely *having* to be the best at everything. This is the route to an unhappy life.

Alice Miller's *Drama of the Gifted Child*

Alice Miller eloquently describes the painful hazards of a gifted child growing up in a situation where the parents have unhealthy needs that they attempt to fulfill through the sensitive, gifted child. This dynamic can be so insidious and twisted that it takes decades of therapy for the innocent individual to undo the psychological damage. Self-esteem must, by the very definition of the term, come from the self. Parents must have separate, fulfilled identities on their own, never leeching off the precious talents of the gifted child. If you have concerns about this dynamic, the book *The Drama of the Gifted Child* is a sober eye opener.

The situation is difficult for the child who wants to be perfect so the parents will feel okay about themselves. In a way, the child's personality and giftedness are hijacked by the parents, making it very challenging for the gifted child to develop self-knowledge and awareness. All she knows is that the parents depend upon her and it is best for everyone if she measures up accordingly.

FACT

According to a quotation from writer Pearl S. Buck, "The truly creative mind in any field is no more than this: A human creature born abnormally, inhumanly sensitive. To him a touch is a blow, a sound is a noise, a misfortune is a tragedy, a joy is an ecstasy, a friend is a lover, a lover is a god, and failure is death."

Adults who grow up with this kind of dynamic in their background often do not know their true interests and talents because the parents lived through them to such a great extent. The gifted adult is able to do many things very well and sometimes cannot distinguish between mastery and joy. Once the underlying dynamic has been discovered, the courageous adult can experiment with lost interests and talents, coaxing out tendrils of joy that were squelched by the needy parents.

What Can You Do Instead?

Only children and gifted children grow up in a pressure cooker environment. Conditions are likely that they can become arrogant, fearful, overly obligated, people pleasing, entitled, and perfectionistic. One has to be creative to overcome these tendencies, as everyone's aim in raising children (beyond the hope of surviving raising the child) is to raise a child who will be happy and functional in adult life.

Take a Time-Out from Only and Gifted

As paradoxical as it seems, these special children can get very tired of being special. The performance standards are intense, and everyone seems to be watching all the time. Enrichment can get tiresome. Some families have frank discussions with gifted children, asking them their preferences for placement in school or in summer programs. Some such children are remarkably self-aware and know when they need some time off. Sometimes they just want to be a kid. If grandparents are involved in the child's life, they often provide a mellow, tempering influence on the pressures of being so great.

Time Out from Parenting

Similarly, parents need time to simply be ordinary people. A weekend away alone or with the spouse provides marvelous respite from so much wonderfulness in the child. Parents can sleep when they want, eat whatever is desired, and watch shallow junky movies that might not be preferred fare for the child.

Parents who continue their own development tend to be happier at each stage of the child's growth. Eventually, when the only or gifted child strikes out on his own, the parent can still be happy, even if the favorite "project" has left the house. Passionate involvement in hobbies or work will continue, even after the most important years of parenting have come to an end.

Balance for Gifted and Only Adults

Like those special children, special adults have challenges in juggling the pleasures of a distinct status with that of being part of the human race. Sometimes such a person will set aside the braininess for a while and do something completely different, like work in a Buddhist bakery or join a volunteer crew of highway cleanup workers. Selection of a mate can be a challenge for exceptionally talented persons. Some join associations such as Mensa to find kindred souls, and others find them along the way in their professional associations.

If you happen to work with or otherwise are close with an only adult or gifted adult, compassion is always in order. Their perfectionism developed as a coping mechanism in a hothouse environment, and without it they would feel naked. After all, they didn't *choose* to be only or gifted. It was an accident of heritage.

CHAPTER 16

Deep Self-Acceptance

Self-acceptance is the antithesis of a perfectionist's usual self-critical frame of mind. However, it opens the door to the spiraling labyrinth of negativity. Self-acceptance slows down the mind, lowers the blood pressure, deepens the breathing, and eases a person into beautifully imperfect normalcy. With practice, the perfectionist catches the impossible demands on the self and mentally reframes them into something friendlier, more humane, more loving.

Julia Cameron's Ideas—The Artist's Date

Julia Cameron's books, *The Artist's Way* and *Vein of Gold*, are helpful resources for people working themselves out of a negative, unsatisfying life and into a life of creative expression and wholesome comfort. One of her marvelous suggestions is to take yourself on an artist's date once a week. The artist's date is a chance to go out alone and do something fun and nurturing for the creative inner artist. It doesn't have to cost money, but it does have to be alone, because having another person along diverts the focus of the outing.

Ideas for Artist's Dates

With practice, the artist's dates become quite fun, a little opportunity to goof off, play hooky, and generally be a little silly. Some possibilities might include the following, depending on what you really enjoy:

1. Go to the zoo and talk to the animals.
2. Buy some nice felt-tipped pens.
3. Buy stickers and put them in your journal every day.
4. Listen to and watch taiko drummers.
5. Go to an Aztec dance performance.
6. Go to a foreign market and buy foods you've never heard of before. Cook something with them.
7. Visit a stable and ride a gentle horse.
8. Check out children's books on your favorite topics and read them to yourself.
9. Ride a train to the end of the line, turn around, and come back home.
10. Attend a country auction and bid on something, and then eat homemade apple pie for lunch.

It is healing for the outings to be nonpurposeful, on purpose, as the brain and spirit relax with input from divergent directions. If you are a creative soul, as most people are, you may find that you get wonderful ideas during or following your artist's dates, but those ideas are not the purpose of the outing.

Watch for Self-Sabotage!

It is tempting to forget the artist's date, as you have too many other important things to do. This is the perfectionist-workaholic lurking around, trying to keep you from enjoying yourself. Think of it as medicine for the spirit, an IV for the soul that needs regular drips in order to keep all aspects of the balanced individual functioning well. You may have decades of self-deprivation to make up for, and the old punitive voices will try to derail your good intentions. If necessary, write the specific artist's date on your planning calendar and bookend it with someone in order for it to be a commitment that is as important as your work or doctor's appointments. Don't do the artist's date after everything else is finished, because that day never arrives.

Purpose for the Artist's Dates

How can these weekly outings be beneficial to a perfectionistic person? By definition, the artist's dates are little excursions with no purpose except to nurture the creative self. They are childlike, only intended for fun, but not a type of extravagant fun such as one would find in a theme park. A perfectionist has difficulty doing pleasurable actions for the self, and the artist's dates are a way to softly shave the edges off the perfectionism.

The artist's dates allow variety and innovation into the unbalanced obsessive life of the perfectionist, bringing respite to the digitally driven, time-driven, fast-paced life of accomplishment. There is no goal during the artist's date, except to enjoy oneself.

Comfortable in Your Own Skin

With more and more self-acceptance, you begin to find that you like yourself better, even without being perfect. There may be a time period of feeling vulnerable, slightly naked, as you go about your life with a less perfectionistic attitude, schedule, and lifestyle. You find yourself admitting errors and personal foibles to people and learn that they do not reject you. In fact, they are more accepting as your humanness evolves. Physically you become more relaxed, your mind slows down, and emotionally you are less wired.

You may find that you are apologizing less frequently. What a relief to be freer of unnecessary guilt, always beholden to others in a perfectionistic manner! When you feel the inclination to apologize, pause and check out the urge with someone else. It could be completely unnecessary.

Grieve the Perfectionistic Self

There may be a lengthy grief process for the loss of the perfect self. Actually, it is the idea or fantasy of the perfect self, as it can never be achieved. It was the effort that led to exhaustion and tremendous unhappiness. The predictable stages of the grief process may recycle a few times as the layers of false self and inhuman expectations fall away. Expect crying, sadness, and a need for extra rest. Some people find that they need extra nutrition, as grief is work. Think of it as hard labor for the spirit.

Where and How to Grieve

The American culture does not openly embrace grief, so finding safe places and people to support your grief can take some focused effort. Depending on their background and personalities, some therapists are able to be emotionally present when a person is grieving. Be alert for well-meaning individuals who are too quick to offer solutions, as they themselves are often quite uncomfortable with grief. Seek out friends who have walked a similar path and will not try to shape your experience for you.

FACT

Complicated grief is the term for a disorder in which the person who suffered a loss does not feel better after time has passed. The emotions of loss are as great as they were at the time of the loss, and the person has not resumed normal functioning.

It can be a tremendous comfort to have an understanding friend on the other end of a phone line when you need to cry or to tell a story about how your perfectionism tripped you up.

Support groups can be especially helpful during times of grief. Relationships are built over a period of weeks, months, or even years, and a network of genuine social support is the welcome result. Jim Rubens noted in his book, *OverSuccess*, that large numbers of people in the United States have no friends, at least no in-person friends. Social media may be relaxing and diversionary, but an actual person who can give you a warm hug is quite marvelous when one is grieving. Community bulletin boards sometimes display notices of special focus groups. Churches and hospitals offer various helpful groups, and neighborhood newspapers can be perused for possible groups during a time of specialized need.

I'm Afraid I'm Going Crazy!

The intense emotions of grief often frighten individuals who have kept them repressed for years. They might be the intense fear of a child who was reprimanded for demonstrating quite appropriate wants or needs. There may be intense longing for loving, aware, present relatives and experiences that should have been there but weren't. The good news is that those powerful feelings pass, if they are given time and space. If repressed, they do not pass. They pop out at embarrassing, inconvenient, inopportune times.

Some have been reassured that feeling crazy is actually a process of becoming uncrazy. It is a thawing out of frozen emotions that no longer want to be locked in. When a person reaches a place in life where the environment is safe, the people are safe, and one is resilient enough to withstand the torrents of tears, that's when the emotions come out.

Grief is rather organic, having an ebb and flow of its own. It's not something that you can schedule or sandwich in between getting married and finishing graduate school. It creeps up when the time is right. Sometimes an old grief will piggyback onto a current grief, especially if the former experience was not fully grieved at the time. At times an anniversary of a loss will precipitate an echo of the original loss.

There is certainly no harm in seeking professional help during times of intense grief. A familiar therapist can be of enormous comfort and support, or one can find a therapist with a specialty in grief work. Such therapeutic work can be short term or long term, depending on the needs of the individual.

If the following symptoms are present, the grieving individual may be stuck in complicated grief:

1. Intense longing for the person who died; a focus on their possessions and reminders
2. Difficulty accepting the death or loss
3. Feeling numb, preoccupation with sorrow
4. Bitterness, inability to enjoy life
5. Depression, not functioning in normal life
6. Withdrawal from social activities
7. Believing that life has lost meaning
8. Loss of trust in others
9. Feelings of guilt and self-blame
10. Wishing that one had died along with the person who was lost

These symptoms mostly refer to what might occur with the death of a loved one, but the loss of the idea of who one is as a perfect person, fulfilling some unknown, nameless requirements, can be just as devastating. It is always good to be aware of danger signals and when to reach out for help.

Pamper the Young, Inner Child

John Bradshaw's book, *Homecoming*, includes helpful charts for remedial activities for each developmental age of maturation. For example, the elementary school years are when we learn how to competently get along in the environment. If a parent was absent or preoccupied during that time, the adult may have a deficit in terms of feeling confident in knowing basic competencies and learning new ones. Loving parents encourage little ones as they try new things, and you can do that for yourself.

Pampering Ideas

The exact activities that are right for you will depend on what was missing during the young years and somewhat on your inclinations and interests. It may take some trial and error to discover what is truly pampering to your inner child. The following are some ideas that others have found helpful:

1. Sleep in sheets and blankets in colors and textures that you like.
2. Wear clothing that you like, especially at home.
3. Pay attention to food cravings and honor them if they are not self-destructive.
4. Reward yourself with a light-hearted movie.
5. Protect yourself from loud, dogmatic people.
6. Let your inner child know that you will get back to him in a specific amount of time if you have to do adult things for a while.
7. Talk to yourself in a calm, low, soothing voice.
8. Do fewer things and do them slowly.
9. Include nonpurposeful things in the day.
10. Stare at things and do nothing.

Giving Up Suffering

It can be quite difficult to give up the habit of suffering. It may have been a family role or the habit of an important role model, and it will seem disloyal or quite odd to think about the mantle of suffering sliding away. Will anything be left? What will become important without the effortful drudgery? Some families have a generational pattern of suffering, and one can feel quite strange embracing a joyful life. Will there be anything to discuss during family reunions?

Martyrdom

The types of families that foster perfectionism sometimes cultivate people who believe that martyrdom is an attractive aspiration. One parent may have been long-suffering, and everyone acknowledged what a good person he was to put up with everything that occurred in the dysfunctional house. Sighing may have brought positive solicitations and offers of attention and help. It's very difficult to get angry with the family martyr who is always of service to others and never complains.

ALERT

Perfectionists who tend toward martyrdom may subconsciously believe that if they do enough commendable things for many people, they will escape criticism. It is nearly impossible to criticize a person who seems so altruistic.

However, it is quite fine to live an enjoyable life without being a grind in the service of others. Notice if there is guilt when you do what you want instead of doing something that someone else would like you to do. That could be a clue to some lingering vestiges of martyrdom. Martyrs sometimes suffer depression and physical illness, as these are seemingly the only way to be deserving of a time-out from excessive responsibility.

Buddhist Thoughts on Suffering

Relief from suffering is at the heart of Buddhist teaching. Yes, life is full of change, sometimes welcome and sometimes not, and the human condition seems fraught with gain and eventual loss. How can one manage and still remain relatively sane and serene?

The practice of meditation greatly quiets the mind and makes the regular meditator less susceptible to the stresses of life. The daily quieting experience provides a healthy haven to which the person can return, instantaneously if necessary, without being caught up in the emergency of the moment.

The idea of attachment is central to the tenets of Buddhism, and attachment causes suffering. What are some types of attitudes, mindsets, things, people, or situations that create attachment and suffering?

1. Always getting one's own way.
2. The idea that a relationship will last forever.
3. A mental construct, such as politicians should selflessly serve their constituency.
4. But we've always done it this way! Difficulty with flexibility and change.
5. Feeling abandoned when a favorite friend or relative dies or moves away.
6. Addictive pleasures result in suffering when the source is removed.
7. Overemphasis on results, especially perfect results.
8. Relentless pursuit of sensory experiences requires an escalating schedule, as it is never enough. Not getting whatever is sought brings depression and anxiety.
9. Needing a certain identity or status to be acceptable to oneself.
10. Excessive material comfort, which can lead to a constant search for a new experience, such as the characters in the film *Eyes Wide Shut*.
11. Undue importance on a certain personal image.
12. Grasping at wrong ideas, such as "A mother has to stay home full time."
13. Dependence on rigid routines and rituals.

One can see that these ways of thinking, feeling, and behaving are interrelated, and it could be possible to wrestle with several at the same time. This results in a clinging to impossible results, and a great deal of personal unhappiness. Imagine, for example, that a very young, attractive woman marries a wealthy, somewhat older man. They have little in common. She could be thought of as a trophy wife. Her security in the situation depends upon being attractive and available to her husband. She becomes worried when she notices a few wrinkles and wonders if she should start a strict regimen of facial treatments. She undertakes a strict program of Pilates. She is completely image conscious, as she believes that without a certain physical image, her marriage will be over. One can imagine the suffering, anxiety, and mental anguish involved in trying to prevent aging. In this case, the profession of being a trophy wife did not lead to freedom, personal growth, and joy.

What Can You Do Instead?

Deep self-acceptance can gradually become a habit, and you may find that what was once tolerable in terms of overworking or overindulging in anything is no longer acceptable. Your days become a little more peaceful and you find fewer crises encroaching upon your life. People become more likable and interesting as you like yourself a little more.

Compromise with Imperfect Situations

One enterprising social worker was burned out in her profession but felt that she could not leave it. The earnings were good, and retirement benefits would have been lost if she made a midlife career change. She decided instead to embrace her creative nature and set up a miniature studio right outside her office cubicle. She set up interactive tasks for her coworkers who dropped by—a doodle notebook for squiggles in different colors, collage pieces on a day she asked people to make a collage with only white materials, and a photograph longing for whimsical cartoon captions. Her working relationships dramatically improved, and she decided she liked her job after all.

Thirty-Day Discipline

It can be very interesting to try any spiritual discipline for a set time period, such as thirty days. Some have added a daily meditation or made a commitment to themselves to read a passage from a specific text each morning. Others have decided to read everything they can find by Hafiz or Rumi. Hafiz was a fourteenth century Persian mystic and poet, and Rumi was a thirteenth century Persian poet, theologian, and Sufi mystic. The translations of their work have deeply inspired countless modern day spiritual seekers.

ALERT

The ancient science and art of yoga is a timeless way to attune the physical body with the spirit. It is pleasant to undertake a yoga practice in the company of others. Such classes are available in many levels of difficulty, often in community recreation programs, senior centers, as well as in private studios. Often the first class is free, and lessons are discounted if payment is made in advance for a series.

It can be illuminating to be aware of suffering and attachments, tracing each one to the source, letting go of whatever is the root dependency. A daily walk in nature can be a way of connecting to the larger world of the earthy elements. It can be an interesting discipline to do an unseen act of kindness every day for thirty days. One spiritual seeker embarked on a written gratitude list each day, listing ten new items each day. By the end of thirty days, he was grateful for air, electricity, and blood coursing through his veins and arteries.

Ease Up on Time Expectations

Many perfectionistic people plan too much to do within a given amount of time, forgetting that each task requires a finite amount of time to complete. It can be a beautiful habit of self-acceptance to pencil in fewer activities for each day, each week, and each weekend. If there is work to be done, shave off the other activities that are not closely work related.

If you are going across town to have lunch with a friend, allow plenty of extra time for unknown traffic conditions so you will arrive refreshed and ready to enjoy yourself instead of harried and frazzled. If you have a specific task that you anticipate will be tiring or irksome—perhaps jury duty—allow time to rest afterwards.

If you are grieving the loss of what you have mistakenly invested in a life of perfection, allow time to do the work. When the waves of grief wash over you, pause and let the mind do its healing work.

Constant Reinvention

If you're not a martyr or a perfectionistic workaholic, who are you? Some interesting people cultivate a life of continuous reinvention. Madonna created an image in the eighties that took her to the top of pop culture, and each decade of her life brings a different swath of creative expression, incorporating her mature womanliness in a deliberate, self-accepting way. Who would have thought that the young singer and dancer from Detroit could end up portraying Evita with such élan and bringing the idea of kabala to a wider range of followers?

Family Activities

As your inner child heals, you may go through a stage where you enjoy cultural activities intended for children. If you have a child to help you gain access, so much the better! If not, you can often quietly participate in family activities, and no one will notice that you are the adult child. Public libraries and museums have marvelous programs in literature, music, magic, puppetry, dance, and art. A storyteller weaves a marvelous web, and in the process, your wounded young self is enthralled.

CHAPTER 17

Choices

Volition is part of the human condition. Even in dire situations such as a hurricane, earthquake, or something as drastic as the events of September 11, 2001, a range of choices are available for human response. One can become irate, hysterical, and out of control, adding to the chaos of the situation, or one can remain poised, peaceful, and composed, focusing on service to others. Usually life is not so excessively demanding, and it is somewhat easier to examine a range of possibilities.

Readjusting Expectations

The perfectionist has unrealistic expectations for the self and others. This is more or less the definition of perfectionism—having unnecessarily high standards, even standards that are impossible to reach. Such a miserable outlook can be improved by looking at the underlying beliefs of such a mental state and considering some modifications.

Relationships

Toni Raiten-D'Antonio, author of *The Velveteen Principles for Women*, suggests that readers examine unrealistic beliefs, especially in the area of close relationships. Some unrealistic beliefs would include thoughts such as the following:

1. I am perfect for my partner, and she is perfect for me.
2. I can make him or her perfect for me.
3. This union will make us both happy for the rest of our lives.
4. People who love me can read my mind.

Raiten-D'Antonio cautions people to be conservative during the process of mate selection, taking the time to look beneath the veneer and allowing the other person to know you, including your flaws. Marriages based on appearances sometimes falter when the appearances start to crumble, as they inevitably do. No one is perfect, and the whirlwind courtship, quick engagement, and mad dash to the altar can result in a strange situation of looking at the other person and wondering who that stranger might be. Taking the time to learn whether the person is kind, generous, and flexible might lead to a happier union.

Adult children often have a pattern of choosing partners who are emotionally or otherwise unavailable. This is a choice because it feels similar to the dynamic in the home of childhood. One can ask if this pattern is satisfying and perhaps try a different way. The quality of life with someone who is really there can seem terrifying to one who is accustomed to barren, distant relationships. If it is a goal to have an emotionally present partner, one can start with friendships of the same sex, moving on to platonic relations with others of the opposite sex, and ultimately a relationship that has romantic and deeply loving potential. The vulnerability and sharing will be quite different from that of the childhood dynamic.

To Err Is Divine

There has to be room for human error, whether in marriage, child rearing, personal appearance, or in work. Some high achievers believe that the way to visible success is to make as many mistakes as possible, as that direction will eventually lead to a few things that work out very well. Tolerance for error can be difficult for a perfectionist. Sometimes one can warm up with one activity, where it doesn't matter how it is done, and the relaxed, carefree approach transfers to the next thing, where one is inclined to grit one's teeth during the entire experience.

ESSENTIAL

A few weeds do not ruin the garden. The stray grasses coexist fairly comfortably with the fruits, flowers, and vegetables, giving the gardener something to do when he feels like puttering among living things.

For example, if you're dreading writing a tedious report, toss together a salad of your own wild invention using the leftovers in the refrigerator, odd delicacies from the pantry, and a few choice items from your favorite market. You can call it deep greens, mixed nuts, and pickled plums with a side dressing of sweet chutney. Such fun will help you to approach the dry report with a touch of abandon.

It can be helpful to examine your beliefs about making mistakes. Do any of the following statements ring true for you?

1. It is dangerous to make mistakes.
2. I must do things perfectly the first time.
3. I cannot ask for help.
4. People will not like me if I screw up too badly.
5. Making mistakes will harm my reputation.
6. If I allow even a few mistakes, I will fall apart completely.
7. I'll never attract a mate if they know of my most serious mistakes.

It can be helpful to keep in mind that your choices reflect your opinion of yourself. If you are unnecessarily harsh with yourself, does it mean that you do not love yourself? Would you be so harsh with a cherished child or a very close friend who might be struggling? However you would treat a person that you love and respect is a good way to treat yourself, even while experimenting with mistakes and new behaviors. A little latitude and slack allows you to be human. During the course of your lifetime, one of the most important relationships is your relationship with yourself. You are always there, and it greatly enhances the quality of life if that relationship is cordial, loving, and accepting.

One cannot choose the family one is born into, but one can certainly choose a response to those circumstances. It may take years of therapy and numerous courses of various types of study to break free from perfectionism, but the choice is there. Try to deliberately think about what may be desirable response instead of a knee-jerk reaction. Not everyone has the stamina to embark upon such diligent inquiry, but the result is a life of freedom and satisfaction, no matter what the outside circumstances might be.

ESSENTIAL

Abraham Lincoln suffered numerous failures and setbacks before becoming president. He was defeated for the state legislature. He failed in business. His sweetheart died, and he had a nervous breakdown. He was defeated for Speaker of the House in the Illinois legislature. He was defeated for nomination to Congress. Once elected, he was defeated for renomination. He was defeated in his bid for the U.S. Senate. He was defeated in nomination for the presidency. He was again defeated in his bid to become a senator. But don't forget that, in 1860, he was elected as president and became one of the most famous figures in history.

Failures can point to a new direction just as clearly as successes. If something did not work out, then it becomes clear you must try a different tactic. Actually, life might be boring with a steady diet of stellar successes. Eventually one would want to try something novel, just in order to have a new experience. Failures make a person human, providing compassion for the self and others who undergo such humbling moments.

Catch Yourself in the Moment

Perfectionists tend to unnecessarily ruminate over details, thinking about what went wrong yesterday and planning everything that has to be done tomorrow, next week, and next month. There is no harm, of course, in being on top of things and accountable for one's time and efforts. However, the only thing that is truly available is the present moment. Too much worrying eradicates any possibility of joy in the present time.

FACT

> Choice is closely aligned with intention. Intention is aligned with strong desire. When these components are harmonized, life moves in the positive direction in harmony with the individual's deepest beliefs. The result is a satisfying experience, a satisfying life.

Next time you're rushing from here to there, pause and notice exact details in your environment. What types of clouds are in the sky? Do you remember those cloud names from elementary school science? Are there any shapes that remind you of an object?

What sounds are evident in the moment—traffic, neighbors, music, air conditioning? Is the coffeepot percolating? What snippets of other languages do you hear in your environment?

Shapes are interesting. Notice power lines, buildings, graffiti, even litter. What sorts of landscaping and trees are local to your work and house? Are there variations in color and texture? Notice the shapes of shadows. Observe people and their interactions. Is the young woman pregnant, and would you be able to guess her relationship to the two accompanying children? Perhaps they are a niece and nephew, or maybe first and second children awaiting a little brother or sister? Notice the types of clothing and hairstyles. This attention to detail is quite restful for the mind and gives you a needed vacation from obsessive dwelling on the impossible.

With the gift of twenty-four hours each day, how will you choose to use those hours and minutes? Segments of time are delicious morsels for you to expend however you decide. It doesn't have to be by rote or random, unconscious choice, often the unthinking way of the perfectionist. Each activity is yours alone, and it is up to you to make it satisfying, something that you can savor in memories you are creating.

Restart Your Day at Any Time

One aspect of personal choice is to start a new day at any point in the day. Who says it has to begin at 7:00 or 8:00 A.M.? This mental technique is especially useful on a challenging day. When too many requirements are colliding from too many directions, call a quick halt and make a decision to begin the day at that point. You may have some special rituals that give you the true feeling that a new day is beginning, perhaps an inspirational reading, a walk with your pets, or a tall glass of juice. Shift gears in a major way and let the day evolve from that point.

ESSENTIAL

Beware of the tendency to say that you will "try" to do something. Either you will do it or not do it. "Try" is a slippery word and one that can possibly be eliminated from the vocabulary, as it often genuinely means that you do not want to commit to whatever it is but do not want to tell the other person. It makes for more ease to simply say, "I'm sorry, but I won't be able to do that." It's a choice.

Gradually it becomes clear to a perfectionistic person that one always has the choice of attitude and response to life's circumstances. It may have become automatic for years or decades to respond in a certain passive, negative way when things don't go well, but it is enormously empowering to emphatically choose the thoughts that motivate daily actions. With this strong, centered stance, one is not blown around like a dandelion seed in the wind. It becomes much easer to negotiate quite complicated situations, and one becomes an asset to organizations of all kinds. You may find yourself being sought out for your calm demeanor under fire. A tranquil mind and a peaceful heart are always available to you.

Brainstorm When You're Stuck

Daily, monthly, and yearly choices make up the sum total of a person's character. There are large choices, such as whom to marry, where to live, what your career will be, and whether to have children and how many. Some of these choices seem irrevocable, and many cases that can be the case. At times, one has made a choice, and a new choice needs to be considered.

For example, a middle-aged woman living on the West Coast was concerned about her elderly mother in St. Louis. For several years she visited frequently, then for longer periods of time. At the end of her mother's life, she lived in the mother's home and handled the estate after the mother's passing, retaining her West Coast home to which she returned after the years of her mother's decline and death. Numerous choices were necessary during an approximate six-year time period.

ALERT

Being a victim is the opposite of having choices. Perhaps you were a victim in your family, and you had no choice but to accommodate the situation. However, in adult life, there are almost always choices, even if they seem scary or almost impossible. Victimhood is not a satisfying profession. Sometimes it helps to elicit the viewpoints of others when victimhood is lurking.

Can Change, Cannot Change

Sometimes it helps to make a list of situations in life that are irksome or uncomfortable. Then a chart can be fashioned with two columns—Can Change and Cannot Change. Looking at each item and asking the question about whether it can be changed or not sometimes opens some doors. Often the choices are opposite of what one has assumed! One cannot change the personality of the demanding boss, but a vacation or a transfer could lessen the difficulty.

ESSENTIAL

It can be very helpful to bluntly ask yourself, "What is the truth of this situation?" This stark question sometimes opens doors and circumstances shift. It might have seemed that the choice was in regard to one thing, but it turns out to be something completely different.

Choices that support serenity and the well-being of the whole person are always desirable, if not easy. For example, if you have a certain relative who always dominates the conversation, irrevocably bringing the attention back to himself even when others attempt to join in, you have several alternatives. You can choose not to go to the event. You can go but interact with other people in a different room. You can sit by him and enthusiastically nod every time he makes another important proclamation and congratulate yourself on how brave you were for those few minutes. You can think of blessings for this person, as something dreadful must be going on that he continues to demand attention like a toddler in a grown man's body.

It is always possible to choose one's perspective. Each individual has a lens of perception, and it is up to the person to decide what works in life. A perspective of doom and gloom, self-righteous judgment, and perfectionistic self-criticism leads to one type of a result. A perspective of acceptance, composure, and goodwill leads to another result. The individual perspective is the choice of each separate person.

Consult the Inner Child

Another way to brainstorm some ideas for new choices is to ask your inner child. Setting aside some time and journal pages to access that pure, innocent voice is an interesting way to tease out some gems. She might want to be surrounded by blue velvet, listen to sitar music, and learn how to kayak. Although seemingly impractical, brief side trips to accommodate those raw desires can ultimately lead to the evolution of new, interesting forks in the road.

It is freeing to choose to no longer be defined by the past and any unpleasant things that happened. The essence of your person, the lively inner child, is wise, joyous, and free, and he or she is able to be spontaneous with new choices. This child is witty, smart, and resilient and wants to guide you along some paths not yet explored. You might feel that if you take the hand of this child and try something different, you will permanently abandon your adult responsibilities. This is unlikely. The time with the inner child is temporary, only for checking out some deeper preferences and interests. With practice, you can form a trusting partnership and have more fun.

It is unlikely that the inner child is a perfectionist. Let her help you with choices that provide a range of responses. You might enjoy building a tall structure with Legos or dominoes. The child is completely comfortable making a random, somewhat purposeless structure, whereas the adult will want to build a bridge or a skyscraper that is a copy of something already known.

The inner child is often a quite good judge of character. Like household pets, he or she intuitively knows who is trustworthy and kind, and who is not. When you are in a quandary about which person to date or which job to pursue, ask the inner child. The inner child has ways of gleaning information that are more primitive, based on such nonverbal cues as eye contact, tone of voice, and physical mannerisms. Your inner child might not like the furtive edginess of the new potential client. She would prefer that you avoid such a cagey person.

Facing Fear of Outcomes

If one approaches choices with the confidence that things will evolve in a way that is ultimately positive, it becomes less unnerving to make a decision and move forward. Becoming locked up with fear of making a wrong choice leads to procrastination, immobilization, and depression. It is usually better to make any choice and see how it turns out.

Whenever possible, choose to have an open mind. A closed mind limits the range of choices quite drastically, and an open mind allows room for miracles and astounding new experiences.

Usually it is not too difficult to shift course, even if the result is something unexpected and unwanted. The movement through the consequences of the choice brings new information, and a different course becomes apparent along the way. It is somewhat like a courageous vacationer who takes off on country roads with no set destination in mind. She stops at roadside fruit stands, antique shops, and lavender farms, completely delighted at each juncture. This type of excursion has a completely different flavor from a highly planned outing where the traveler is white-knuckling it through the hour-by-hour schedule, looking more at the clock than the details of the sights.

Learning to be less fearful of outcomes frees up other people to be more relaxed with you and in their lives. Your social life and family life are an organic whole, and when one part improves or relaxes (you), others are somewhat let off the hook. They become less hard on themselves with you as an example. These shifts will not happen overnight, but even the possibility makes the effort very much worthwhile.

Trust is often an issue for persons who originate from troubled childhood homes. Often their perceptions were discounted, trivialized, and minimized, making it quite difficult to make discerning choices in later years. The environment may be chaotic, violent, and centered around the needs of the addicted adult. The child learns that inconsistency is the norm, making quick adaptation a more useful skill than trust in decision-making. Often for such children, what works one day to calm down the difficult parents or other family members will bring quite a different response another day. No wonder adults from such backgrounds have difficulty making choices when the outcome is unknown.

One way to gradually build confidence is to make choices in situations where the outcome is not especially important. For example, would the pasta taste better with tomato sauce or alfredo sauce? It really doesn't matter. Any choice will be fine. Sometimes choices of clothing or a movie to watch can be approached in a like manner. It doesn't matter what outfit is worn, and the choice of movie will be fine if everyone in the party reads the synopsis and a review or two. Even in the worst-case scenario, if the movie turns out to be terrible, everyone in the group can agree to leave the theater and do something else during the evening.

What Can You Do Instead?

Often choices are easier if one turns momentarily within, checking with the intuitive knowing aspect of the self. This could be called prayer. It might be a momentary meditation. It could be noticing the gut feeling about what should be next. These mental pauses require a bit of time, often something in short supply for the perfectionist, but the result is a course that is in greater harmony with the whole person.

Freely Choose Your Values

After considerable self-inquiry, one becomes at home with one's own values, even if there is somewhat of a departure from the beliefs of closest relatives or one's spouse. Most religious disciplines have a set of values, such as the Ten Commandments, that might have been the cornerstone for child-hood morals, but are the beliefs up to date? Is killing ever permissible—perhaps when defending a child?

Writer Toni Raiten-D'Antonio suggests that thoughtful persons examine a whole range of values and determine what is appropriate at that particular stage of life. Some possibilities could include:

Love	Honesty	Self-Reliance
Moderation	Flexibility	Restraint
Tolerance	Commitment	Wisdom
Acceptance of Others	Devotion	Strength
Faith	Self-Awareness	Compassion
Dependability	Interdependence	Interest in Others

A few moments of pondering the topics of adultery, theft, and lying might be useful in determining true beliefs, not the ideal that is unattainable.

Write a Mission Statement

You might cringe at the idea of a mission statement, thinking that would be the domain of MBAs from Ivy League universities, but actually, the endeavor of choosing a life that is satisfying to you is completely worthy of a serious statement, perhaps crafted over a period of time. If you are close with a mentor, coach, therapist, or deeply trusted friend, it will be useful to share the mission statement, after you have completed several drafts. You will want to address major life areas such as family relationships, financial stability, creative expression, health, service, and leisure. What do you see as your legacy? Some people go so far as to imagine an epitaph on the headstone of a grave, wondering what might have been said about a life well-lived.

A genuine calling can emerge from such a focus. Where do you feel generous, or where would you like to be generous? Writing and revising a mission statement over a time period of a few months or years enables a person to release old goals that are no longer appropriate. Maybe they were someone else's idea of what is important but no longer fit. Maybe the goals have been attained and something new would be more interesting and challenging.

Writer and world traveler, Rita Gelman Goldman, author of *Tales of a Female Nomad*, left an unsatisfactory Beverly Hills marriage when she was in her forties and embarked on a life of cross-cultural inquiry and tremendous service to needy children of other countries. Elizabeth Gilbert, author of *Eat, Pray, Love*, embarked on a parallel journey at a younger age, finding physical and spiritual health and a new life partner. Both of these women chose to depart from unsatisfactory lives and make something completely new.

Try Something Opposite

Perfectionists tend to do things in a habitual, somewhat rigid manner, as those ways seem to be the right ways. It can be fun to choose something completely opposite from time to time, just to see how it feels and decide if the outcome is enjoyable. Such experimentation frees up the synapses and tensions are released.

For example, if a person always journals and does spiritual reading in a particular chair, it can be interesting to take the journal and books to a neighborhood coffeehouse and start the day in a different place. If you always celebrate your birthday with a particular friend, it can be stimulating to choose a different friend and a different way of marking the importance of the day. The previous friend would probably be happy to celebrate with you over the phone. If you always read self-help books, pick up some diversionary fiction. If you usually watch serious dramatic films or television, try something completely shallow. You might enjoy it.

ALERT

Holidays can be problematic for persons from difficult families. Instead of doing the same dreary and unsatisfying round of dutiful fiascos, plan something completely different for yourself and a few cherished, close people. You might enjoy having a Cinco de Mayo party or a Day of the Dead celebration instead of a sugary Halloween. Instead of overeating on Thanksgiving, it might be interesting to join a group who serves a fine dinner for the homeless. It is your choice to mark these days however you choose.

Perfectionists often turn down personal invitations because they are too busy doing everything that seems especially important. One can be courageous and accept every invitation for a set length of time, perhaps a month, and see what adventures ensue. It is a practice of saying yes instead of no. One friend may invite you to hear a duo of folk musicians at a neighborhood bistro. Another wants to take you to the beach for a middle-of-the-week holiday. Another is involved in a group show and wants you to help with the guest book. The owners of your favorite ethnic restaurant may invite you to visit their relatives in a foreign country the next time they visit! Say yes, and mark the dates on your calendar.

Choose Transformation and Love

When you find yourself at a fork in the road and are genuinely in a quandary about which direction would be best, think of the long-term consequences of each choice. Think broadly in terms of what would be most transformational for you and most loving for others. That might be the course toward a more pleasing life.

CHAPTER 18

Decision-Making

Conscious decision-making and follow-up actions are the crux of a satisfying adult life. Perfectionists tend to be at the mercy of hidden, subconscious motives and drives, but with considerable self-inquiry, those fall away and the deliberate nature comes forth. Each day is a series of decisions—some small and some momentous. The key is awareness, the awareness that as an independent, volitional person, you have the power and right to make decisions that are good for you.

Clear the Slate and Start Anew

To a certain degree, life is cumulative, with each phase built upon the consequences of a previous phase. One decides on a basic set of values, chooses a profession and prepares for it, chooses a mate and general lifestyle, and life follows in the wake of those early adult decisions. Occasionally, though, you are thrown a curve ball that irrevocably changes everything. Perhaps a friend is lost in an accident, or someone close becomes seriously ill. A completely different opportunity is offered, somewhat from left field. The ability to quickly clear the slate and start fresh leaves you unencumbered to accept the surprises of life.

You might find it invigorating to move to a different state or country if you or your spouse is offered an interesting job. Children who have an opportunity to travel and experience other cultures become marvelously versatile. You might receive a grant, scholarship, or fellowship to study something completely different. A stimulating opportunity sometimes gives a person new energy and vigor.

Decide to Accept Sanity

No matter what occurred in the past or what traumas pile up in the present, one can always choose a rational, sane series of responses. As mentioned in previous paragraphs, it can be tempting to make a lifestyle of various diagnoses, learning the detailed language of all the disorders, but there aren't many job descriptions available for those particular qualifications. It can be a huge diversion, eating up precious decades of life. Instead, decide to dramatically shift gears and go the way of mature, intelligent living. It might feel like shedding a skin in order to move into new roles, but more than likely it will feel like releasing a weight of burden. It requires energy to hold dysfunction and limitation in place. Decide to be free of the seduction of the old ways.

Anticipate Positive Consequences

Instead of worrying about what could go wrong, with practice the procrastinator learns to look at the options and move toward the result that seems best at the moment. Gradually, anticipations become positive instead of negative. A liberating lifestyle ensues without the shackles of constrained perfectionism. It is as if blinders have been removed and the sky is bluer, the horizon wider, and life is a little sweeter. People seem more attractive and interesting, and every decision is not so momentous. Confidence grows and there is a sense of being carried along by the positive, unseen forces of life instead of being dragged down by darkness.

Think of Each Day as Moment by Moment

Perfectionists tend to overplan, jumping ahead mentally to the next hour, the next day, week, month, and year. A string of "what-ifs" rob the individual of the precious seconds of life. Details escape notice because of the cerebral preoccupation with planning and control.

ESSENTIAL

Different cultures have different perspectives on time. For example, Navajo Native Americans do not relate to the Caucasian fast-paced lifestyle. The language has no names for the time preoccupations of English-speaking people. Latino cultures are much more flexible with time commitments, taking each thing as it occurs and adjusting when necessary for unforeseen developments.

Within the framework of your own culture, think about time in some new ways—instead of strictly linear in finite blocks, perhaps little pearls or bubbles floating along. You can juggle the pieces in a playful way instead of being caught in the rigid chain of digital figures. Experiment with ignoring the clocks and time indications of computers and cell phones, perhaps for an entire Sunday afternoon. The body relaxes and breathing is easier. Such a moment-by-moment awareness opens the possibility for more spontaneous interaction with the environment, both within and without. Without a time obsession, the creative forces may bring you a new idea with great potential for development, and you have an adept nature to shift your course of direction.

The necessity for planned time zones instead of sun time or solar time arose in the late nineteenth century, especially in the United States and Canada, because of trains traveling rapidly across the continent. It was impossible to plan schedules without an agreed-upon system. Sir Sandford Fleming, a Canadian railroad planner, initiated the time zone system, resulting in the Meridian Conference of 1884 with delegates from twenty-seven nations. Because of the conference, now twenty-four time zones encompass the globe.

Automatic Pilot—Correct, Correct, Correct

The automatic pilot or robot pilot device on a plane serves to correct the course according to a preset set of instructions. In other words, the plane is flying exactly on course a small percentage of the time, but the automatic pilot constantly corrects, and the result is a landing at the desired destination. Humans, however, often have the delusion that it is necessary, or even desirable, to be 100 percent on target. Such unrealistic thinking creates tension and harsh perfectionism.

What would happen if you let up a little on yourself and think of decision-making as smaller bites of correction, like a plane moving thousands of miles in smaller bits of a corrected course? The quality of your thinking and actions shift a bit. You might have a general long-term or short-term aim in mind, but the increments to get there are smaller with considerable correction along the way. The corrections do not mean that something is wrong, only that the aircraft is jetting along with frequent adjustments.

Make a Vision Board with New Goals

Vision boards are an interesting way to create focus and direction. This goal-setting method, termed the Wheel of Fortune by metaphysical writer Catherine Ponder, has enabled many people to achieve manifestation of their hopes and dreams. No particular skill is required—merely the willingness to make decisions about images that represent aspects of various goals.

Materials for Your Vision Board

You will need some type of background. Poster board works well. Some people like large pieces of craft paper because it rolls up and is easy to transport. Others like foam core, and some ambitious planners enjoy working with a trifold display arrangement with hinges. You might enjoy browsing at an art supply store or office supply superstore to see what seems inspiring.

ALERT

Risk is a component of making decisions. The unknown looms, and results are unpredictable. However, without risk, there is no growth and development. The result might be worth the temporary discomfort.

Next, gather magazines representing topics that interest you—travel, homes, health and fitness. For example, an enterprising young man who hoped to get married, collected bride magazines. You will need scissors, glue, space to work, and a reasonable length of time, so you are not hurried.

How to Create a Vision Board

There are a couple of ways to approach the vision board task. Some prefer to make it conscious and focused, for example, choosing items that have to do with a beautiful work environment. Using this approach, you might look for pictures of furniture, perhaps a gorgeous loft studio, maybe a mockup of a profit and loss statement. Cut out those images and words that pertain to that goal and glue them down in whatever arrangement seems right to you.

Another way is to gather images that are appealing but seemingly unrelated. Choose pictures that speak to your soul—a gorgeous flower, a couple embracing on the beach in the sunset, a dolphin kissing a child. This approach is intuitive, letting the images come to you as if they need to be chosen. Collect them in a free, spontaneous way and group them however you wish on the solid background. This method is more like a collage. Sometimes the juxtaposition of items can surprise you. Relax and let your subconscious work with you in terms of relatedness that might not be available to your conscious mind just yet.

How to Use Your Vision Board

Keep your vision board in a visible place in your home, yet away from prying eyes of those who might criticize. You might like to have it on an altar, displayed as a piece of art in your office or wherever you relax at the beginning or end of the day. If there is a spot where you gaze and daydream, that might be a good place for the vision board. Let your eyes fall on it often.

Some meditators use the vision board as a focus prior to meditating, so those images will impress themselves on the subconscious mind during the quiet moments of meditation. Over time, the manifestation occurs. Those things or experiences move into a person's life, sometimes quickly, sometimes over a period of several months. It is enjoyable to work on vision boards in a group of like-minded people, sharing successes as they come into being.

ALERT

Beware of the inclination to sabotage your vision board work. Numerous people have the experience of creating a beautiful collage only to find that they spill coffee on it or accidentally crush it in the process of moving. Be aware that it is quite difficult to let numerous positive experiences into your life. It is the internal resistance that causes these "accidents." Do whatever you can to protect your vision board from your own destructiveness.

Prioritizing

Perfectionists have difficulty understanding the relative importance of various tasks, sometimes wasting large amounts of time doing things that could be relegated to another time or even completely set aside. It is sometimes necessary to get another person's input in order to do things in a sensible order.

First Things First

When looking at your To Do list on any given day, what is absolutely paramount? Usually items that have to do with a deadline come first. These could be work obligations, due dates on payments, or a loved one's birthday. There might be smaller priorities that are a part of the dated obligation. For example, a check has to be deposited in order to have funds in the account when you shop for the birthday gift. These are the things that shift to the top of the To Do list. Others are ready for your attention when the most important things are handled. Sometimes there is a series of small things that are convenient to do first. This has the effect of clearing the mind and releasing energy for the larger tasks.

How Important Is It?

A perfectionist has a talent for putting undue importance on things that are not especially important. Again, it helps to discuss these things with others to learn what is rational to others as you learn to prioritize. One meticulous housewife arranged the folds and pleats of the draperies every day in order that they appear perfectly symmetrical. Another vacuumed the carpets every day, making sure the lines of the vacuum were perfectly parallel and perpendicular on the nap of the carpet. Perhaps these things are not really so important.

ESSENTIAL

The perfectionist has to learn to leave some things undone. As impossible expectations are shrunk to a manageable reality, there simply isn't enough time to do everything one wants to do. In fact, there never was enough time to do all those tasks, but the frantic feeling of rushing around all the time became normal. It's okay to leave things undone or delegate some to others, and accept however they wish to do the tasks.

Actually, it is a matter of personal values to decide what is truly important and what is not. Usually relationships are important. Taking care of your health, financial stability, creative expression, and spiritual sustenance are important. You may have to juggle several high-priority items over a period of time in order to see that everything is adequately covered.

Perfectionists often neglect their health, as it seems that work is much more important. It might be better in the long run to prioritize the doctor's appointment, time for the health club or spa, or at a minimum, time for a daily walk to wind down. Perfectionists sometimes drastically neglect important relationships, feeling somehow that they will get to that later, after everything else is handled. Harry Chapin's folk rock song of 1974, *Cat's in the Cradle*, poignantly describes the situation where the father is constantly too busy for the little son, and then in reverse, the elderly father asks for time with the adult son, and he puts him off, saying he is too busy.

Bouncing Back from Failures

Failure is abhorrent to perfectionists. In fact, the entire thrust of perfectionism is to prevent failure. Of course, this effort is futile, as it often propels the individual into spirals of procrastination and time wasting, never getting any momentum toward actual achievement. The entire life is based on protection from failure and criticism, whether from within oneself or perceived from others.

If you think about failure as simply an experience on the way to the ultimate goal, it is not so bad. It can be an education in the way not to do things. For example, if a person has a pattern of choosing mates exactly like his or her abusive parent, those relationships could be seen as failures. These relationships are also thorough experiences in what happens with a mate of that type. One can think of it as a homeopathic inoculation in mate selection. Some things cannot be learned theoretically.

ESSENTIAL

The old adage of getting back on the horse after falling off has some truth to it, although not many people routinely ride horses in the twenty-first century. The key is to get going again rather quickly after a failure. Too much rumination can make the situation fester in your mind.

Once one gets over the fear of failure, it is freeing to simply do things as quickly as possible to see what works and what doesn't work. If you have had the opportunity to work in the vicinity of an artist or musician, you can see this process in action. The painter slathers on some color and then changes his mind, scraping it off and trying something else. The composer taps out a tune, makes some notes on the manuscript page, hums a bit, and tries something else. He does not jump immediately from the idea of the song to renting an orchestra and time in a recording studio. A lot of trial and error, with the emphasis on the error, is necessary to create a desired result, whether the result is something creative or a life well lived.

What Can You Do Instead?

Decision-making becomes easier with practice, like any other skill. It is wise to include other trusted friends and support persons in major life decisions—whether to leave a mate or stay, whether to make a career change, or whether to move to a new location. Often those with objectivity will have an enormously helpful perspective.

It's Not Life or Death

Perfectionists tend to think of decisions as black or white, this or that, and fear the consequences of making the wrong decision. Actually, many decisions are not that important—what to eat, what book to read, and what movie to attend. It doesn't matter if you get only six hours of sleep one night if you are able to make up for it the next subsequent nights.

A willingness to simply take action, to try a little of this and a little of that, will produce results that you can look at and see if they are what you expected or even want. One sometimes listens to young college freshmen agonizing over the appropriate major course of study, when it often happens that whole professions fall by the wayside and others are created in a short period of time. Several decades ago, no one ever heard of information technology, yet at the present time, IT work is very common.

Willingness is a large component of effective decision-making and moving away from the grip of perfectionism. Each action moves a person a little more out of bondage.

Skills and Knowledge Are Transferable

Trends come and go, but if one develops an attitude that whatever is learned will ultimately be useful in most situations, the perfectionistic tension somewhat subsides. For example, an eager person gets a degree in library science only to find that libraries are becoming digital. Entire collections are in e-book format, and older cataloging systems simply do not apply. However, the degree of intelligence and literacy required to get such a degree is immediately transferrable to learning about databases, e-reading devices, and methods of educating patrons about digital books.

Decision-Making in Groups

As you gain more confidence and practice with your own decisions, you may find yourself cooperating with others in group problem-solving challenges. Leadership perhaps is thrust upon you, and others look to you for help in resolving conflict. Decision-making is slower in groups, as it takes time for each person to express thoughts and opinions. It takes time to weigh all the ramifications and to consider the consequences of each course of action. If you are able to take a calm composure into the group process, sometimes surprising creative solutions will come forth, but only if everyone in the group feels safe. If a certain few usually dominate, the quieter ones will not voice an opinion. It helps greatly if the facilitator listens to each point of view and voices it back to the group, giving equal weight to each voice.

Decide to Trust a Spiritual Source

Much perfectionistic tension is released when the individual adopts a spiritual life and seeks help in decision-making. Some people call this the Higher Self, the Divine, or God. Others turn to animal totems, angels, or ancestors. All this is a matter of personal choice and completely up to the individual. The important thing is to develop *something*, some kind of spiritual partnership so that one is not alone in making decisions.

Trust in a higher being brings amazing serenity, as that partnership becomes the most significant one. Human relationships come and go, and all aspects of life are subject to flux, but the lynchpin of self-knowledge and firm cooperation with the spiritual guide makes decisions considerably less scary.

The Now Factor

Someday isn't a day of the week. When you make a commitment to do something, write it on your calendar and share it with someone trustworthy who is interested in your personal growth. If it is a decision requiring several steps, start working on the first increments. Of course, there is no harm in making short- and long-term plans, but sometimes putting things off, even for a little while, leads to a huge case of procrastination. Willingness and decision-making go hand in hand, leading to immediate action. This is a way to eliminate too much thinking about dire, negative results.

Imaginary Protective Clothing

A West Coast radio announcer occasionally asks her radio listeners to put on their Joy Jackets and get out into the day. If you tend to be fearful, think of wearing a magic flak vest that protects you from the slings and arrows of existence. It might be fun to look through your wardrobe and designate some of your favorite clothes as good luck outfits. When you're making difficult phone calls, attending a stressful meeting, or researching a scary possibility, wear the good luck clothing, and you might feel more relaxed.

CHAPTER 19

Spiritual Solutions

Ultimately, it becomes much easier to let go of perfection-ism if one embraces the idea of a spiritual life in a larger sense. Why are you here? Who are all these other beings, and what is the nature of your connection to them? How does a tree nourish itself from sunlight? How does an embryo "know" from the very beginning whether it will be a girl or a boy? These large questions about the nature of life lead one to embrace some kind of spirituality and a sense of a larger power. This can be a relief to a perfectionist. It gets tiresome being one's own God.

Meditation

Meditation is one way to develop a spiritual nature and confidence in a connection with a Higher Source. A Google search for your locale will possibly lead you to groups and teachers who are eager to help others. Churches, yoga centers, and hospitals often offer meditation classes. Be wary of taking perfectionism into the meditation experience, worrying that you're not doing it correctly. Although there are a variety of techniques and meditation philosophies, there probably is not any way a person could meditate incorrectly.

Getting Started

When beginning meditation practice, try to include the following:

1. Choose a quiet place where there will not be an interruption.
2. Silence all electronic devices.
3. Sit comfortably and close your eyes.
4. Breathe deeply and slowly, feeling the breath move into the body.
5. Relax each section of the body. It might help to contract each muscle and then relax it.
6. Quiet the mind. Notice mental chatter but do not judge it. Let it pass.
7. Aim for a "blank mind" state. Imagine a computer screen that is completely blank.
8. Notice the spaces between the thoughts and words and rest there.
9. After the meditation, thank your Higher Self for a good experience.

Meditation Tips

It is a pleasant experience to learn to meditate in a group, and even long-time meditators like being with others who meditate, as a different energy arises as individuals calm down and enter into a relaxed state of being together. A calm, focused leader with an attractive voice adds to the quality of the meditation. Some leaders offer a guided meditation with imagery that is very relaxing for the mind and body.

FACT

Scientific studies show that when a person meditates, alpha and theta waves increase in the brain. Electrodes attached to the head of the person who is meditating reveal these waves of relaxation and wakeful rest.

If you meditate at home, check that the room temperature is comfortable, possibly a little warmer than you might choose if you are physically active because the body temperature lowers somewhat during meditation. You might like to have a shawl or soft blanket nearby to wrap around yourself if you become too cool.

Start with a short meditation, perhaps ten minutes, and gradually add a few minutes as you become comfortable with the experience. Some people like to meditate for as long as an hour at a time, as there is a greater chance of experiencing visions, colorful flashes of light, and creative inspirations. It is possible, too, to divide the meditation practice with a portion in the morning and a portion in the evening.

First thing in the morning is a good time to meditate, as it quiets the mind, increasing the possibility for a peaceful day. Similarly, an evening meditation helps the individual become free of the business of the day, making it easier to invite peaceful sleep. It is beneficial to form a habit of meditating at the same time each day, in the same place, for the same length of time, as the body and mind become conditioned to welcome the quiet state of mind.

ESSENTIAL

Meditation is a spiritual oasis, available at all times. You can dip into your meditation practice in the midst of a stressful meeting at work, before an important phone call, and during family gatherings that are emotionally volatile. Your spiritual cushion is always there.

Any comfortable chair is satisfactory for meditation. Sometimes people assume that it is necessary to sit with crossed legs on the floor in order to meditate. This is a customary posture for people who come from cultures where it is common to sit on the floor. It is not a prerequisite for meditation, although floor sitting is common in many meditation groups.

Quiet music and a mat or pillow might add to your comfort. Some yoga studios or online suppliers offer special pillows and stools to complement the meditation experience.

Won't I Fall Asleep?

The meditative state is the state of consciousness that is almost, but not quite, asleep. Usually it is suggested that a person meditate sitting rather than lying down, as the reclining position does move a person into sleep rather quickly. In the sitting position, one has the quiet mind but still is aware of sounds and movement in the room, as if from a distance.

Walking Meditation

If you have tremendous difficulty sitting still during meditation, you might investigate groups that practice walking meditation. The technique is similar to the sitting meditation, but the practitioners quietly walk in a circle within a designated space during a specified length of time, usually forty-five minutes at a time, followed by a seated time of rest.

FACT

Labyrinths for walking meditation are situated in various places around the world, as well as in private locations. Some famous labyrinths include those at Grace Cathedral, San Francisco, California; Land's End Labyrinth, also in the Bay Area; and the labyrinth of Chartres Cathedral in France. Many mystics and seekers walk labyrinths as a type of pilgrimage.

Being Rather Than Doing

Perfectionists are so focused on doing so many things that the being aspect of humanness is lost. There is no harm in carving out blocks of time in a busy schedule to simply, quietly exist. This is an important time of relaxation for the mind and body to regenerate. Sit quietly with a cup of tea, watch the sunrise or sunset, listen to the sounds of the neighborhood, or just stare. This isn't the time to catch up on texting.

The first few times you attempt to do nothing, it can be jarring, as you are so accustomed to being in accomplishment mode. The intense feeling of needing to complete a task has to be reined in like a wild horse. Undoubtedly, you will feel discomfort and tremendous resistance, as if you have a plane to catch and it is taking off without you. This is the illusion of the importance of all those perfectionistic tasks that have ruled your life for a long period of time. There is freedom on the other side of that release.

Concept of a Higher Self

Most of the major world religions include ideas concerning a deity that the followers worship. It can be stimulating to learn about the beliefs of those religions, not only to understand those rich cultures, but also to inform one's own sense of a higher self.

Ultimately it is a solitary, individual process of figuring out a belief in a divine source. Many are available to teach you *their* way, but this important aspect of adult maturation cannot be borrowed from another. It is genuinely up to each person to work out a comfortable belief, one which provides a secure rudder in the maelstroms of life.

Questions for Myself

It might help to ask yourself some questions about what you believe or want to believe about a spiritual entity. The following can be a starting point for you to determine your values in this area:

1. Does my God have a gender?
2. Does my God reside in a specific place? Where?
3. Do I believe in angels?
4. Do I believe in animal totems or spirit guides?
5. What do I believe about life after death?
6. What do I think about heaven and hell?
7. Why would God bring me difficult challenges?
8. What is the difference between punishment and consequences?
9. Will I be an outcast if I reject my family's religion?
10. Does my God have form?

11. How does God indicate interest in various aspects of my life?
12. What are miracles and do I believe in them?

ALERT

> Persons who grow up in troubled families may have deep-seated resistance to any type of authority, finding it difficult to trust any entity of power. From this background, it is an important challenge to begin to trust a higher power, at first with small things, and later with larger, more important aspects of life. It is a gradual process.

Daily Routine to Counter Perfectionism

It can be a great comfort to create a spiritual practice that includes various specific rituals. These aspects of a daily routine counter the chaos of perfectionism and the painful memories of a difficult childhood background, bringing order and ease into daily life.

Some people like to start the day with a meditation. It is calming to decide on the various aspects of this practice and keep them somewhat the same each day, adjusting only if you have an appointment or travel plans that require a change for a day or two. The meditation can be followed by journaling.

Personal Journaling

Ira Progoff took the practice of journaling mainstream in the 1970s and 1980s with workshops across the United States. In more recent times it is common for people to journal, as it has become an accepted part of spiritual practice.

If you are unfamiliar with journaling, think about some ways you might begin. Set aside any belief that you have to do it right, as there is no set way to journal correctly. Perhaps select a notebook for the purpose of journaling. Your local bookstore or craft store will have a wide selection. Choose one that has a design, size, and weight that you like, as it will be a part of your life for many days. Think about whether you want lined or unlined pages. Many like to doodle and sketch as a part of the journaling process.

Each day, date the entry and simply let the words flow onto the page. Your writing might include important events of the previous day, strong emotions of the moment, or decisions weighing heavily. You can write down ideas and plans for the coming day or week. Half-baked ideas are welcome! The journal is a place to let seeds of new directions freely scatter on the page.

You can write prayers in your journal, prayers you know from a particular faith or your own spontaneous conversations with your spiritual Higher Self. It is a common practice to write blessings for those you worry about or those friends and family members who are experiencing trying times. Write out detailed blessings for people who annoy you! This will free you from the mental obsession of trying to change them.

ESSENTIAL

Sleepless nights or long waits in a reception room offer opportunities for prayer. Traffic jams, being on hold on the phone, and long check-out lines in a store offer further opportunities for prayer. A creative approach brings richness and depth to your spiritual life.

It is useful to write a daily gratitude list. Focusing on the good is a sure-fire way to move from tension and resentment to relaxation and appreciation. Let the gratitude flow into the journal, and over a period of days, you will find your perfectionism diminishing. If you like things the way they are, you are not so focused on making things perfectly some other way.

Think about the place of prayer in your life and how this can be a part of your daily routine. Some people talk with God while walking in nature or even along a busy urban thoroughfare. Some play a recorded prayer in the car while commuting. Others feel a sense of prayer when listening to certain types of music. It is completely up to the individual to work out a method of communicating with the spiritual guide. If you have a yoga practice, you might experiment with including prayer within some of the resting poses, such as Child's Pose. The physical ease is quite complementary with the spiritual openness that is conducive to prayer.

Overcoming Negative Associations

Perfectionists sometimes discover that the root of their difficulty is trying to please a harsh, punitive God—a bearded old man in the sky.

Part of the maturation process is developing an individual spirituality that is exactly in harmony with deeply held personal values. The result may be the same church as the childhood church, and perhaps not.

It helps greatly to thoroughly examine the nature of learned beliefs about a deity, death, sin, heaven, and hell, and see if they truly match what the adult prefers in the here and now. Sometimes childhood experiences with churches and those who worked in the churches or parochial schools leave a harmful residue of resentment, fear, and distrust of all authority figures, including God! It helps to tell the stories to a trusted friend, mentor, or therapist in order to become free of past associations.

For example, in one situation, a person remembered that the minister of the church in the individual's very young years had extramarital affairs with members in the church, causing chaos and confusion among the congregation. The child was too young to understand exactly what was going on, but could sense distrust in church gossip. The conclusion was that church leaders are dishonest and untrustworthy. They say all the good things, but their behavior is not so exemplary. Only through this conscious memory was the person able to let go of the old association and get to know other spiritual leaders on a case by case basis.

FACT

A December 2009 study of the Pew Research Center's forum on religion found that Americans' religious beliefs and practices do not easily fit into conventional categories. An earlier study revealed that 70 percent of Americans believe in the statement, "Many religions can lead to eternal life."

Adult Children's Spirituality

Adult children of alcoholics and other dysfunctional parents may have great difficulty accepting a loving God, as the old parental traits are projected onto the spiritual authority figure. It seems that the Higher Power is neglectful, abusive, tricky, too busy, misleading, and in general, downright cruel. This mindset is challenging to unravel because with that belief life's experiences tend to appear as a self-fulfilling prophecy. This can be most disconcerting, as it seems to prove that God is, in fact, rather cold and cruel.

Over time, however, the willingness to entertain the idea of a loving, generous God will gradually open the door to loving, generous experiences in life. Some, however, cling to bitterness to the end of their days, as it makes the childhood neglect and abuse quite real. Those embittered souls wear their difficulties like a badge of honor and suffering.

In recent decades the news has been full of instances of the abuses of power within some established churches. Sometimes adults remember instances of molestation that have been buried for decades. Along with the challenges of healing from such trauma, the survivors have to decide what they believe about the churches and those who work in the churches.

Women's Spirituality

Women have a process to go through in determining the place of their gender in a spiritual context. If one affiliates with a conventional church, where much of the power and control is held by men, it is difficult to feel comfortable with the growth process. It always seems that the men have to approve the direction and the women need permission. This subtle conditioning has to be faced. Some women opt out and seek spiritual centers with female leaders or fashion a personal, eclectic spiritual practice that does not depend upon any particular person. It might bring more of a sense of female spirituality to investigate the Tara figures of Tibetan Buddhism, the female saints of Catholicism, the Greek goddesses, and pagan beliefs concerning goddesses.

What Can You Do Instead?

A life with a spiritual connection is more peaceful and manageable than a life in which the individual tries to orchestrate everything alone. In fact, in some personal growth circles, living without a divine source of some kind is termed "edging God out," or living with too much emphasis on the ego.

Create an Altar

Having an altar in your home is a beneficial way to support your spiritual practice. You might find good ideas in your library or bookstore. A simple table can offer a beginning. Cover it with a cloth that is attractive and appealing to your spirit. Over a period of time gather objects and photographs that have meaning to you. It is not necessary to have a guru to have a spiritual life, but if someone has been especially inspiring to you, a photo of that person could be a nice addition to your altar.

You may have souvenirs of special times, places, and experiences that made you feel especially close to God. Group those objects in a way that is pleasing to your eye. Incense is an interesting sensory addition and can add to the ritual of spiritual centering. You might want to gather physical representations of material things that you want to manifest in your life, making your altar a sort of three-dimensional vision board.

Some cultures use candles, flowers, and grains to represent the abundance of the earth. You might enjoy putting a few ears of dried corn or a small bowl of rice on your altar to elicit a feeling of gratitude for the abundance of the earth.

Keep your altar clean, and change the arrangement from time to time to keep your response and interest fresh. You might want to include your vision board in your altar arrangement.

Browse in Bookstores and Libraries

It is invigorating and enjoyable to linger in the spiritual section of your favorite bookish place, tasting some of what is available from the wide range of spiritual disciplines and philosophies. You may find an author that you enjoy and read everything else that person has written. There is nothing to say that you have to accept a particular religion merely because you read books about it.

It can be interesting to explore Zen, Islam, Christian history, Native American shamanism, and Hinduism. Take a look at agnosticism and atheism and make up your own mind about what you believe. It might happen that you develop a personalized spiritual faith that draws bits and pieces from various cultures and various aspects of your own cultural background.

Listen to Lectures and Form New Friendships

It is stimulating to go to various spiritual centers and listen to speakers. Usually such places are quite welcoming to visitors, and you do not have to commit just because you are there. You might feel more secure visiting a very different kind of place with a friend who is a member.

Having friends from a variety of different spiritual orientations is a very enriching experience. One can learn firsthand the meaning of different rituals and practices and discern the effect in the person's life. Are they comforted by their beliefs? Do they seem confident in their lives?

ESSENTIAL

As you build your social network with new spiritual friends, search out those individuals who seem to welcome challenges, as they understand that a person's character flexes and grows with exercise. These people do not react with resentment when life throws them a curve ball. They dig in and put their spiritual practice to work and share what they learn with others along the way.

If you are not Buddhist, it can be very exciting to attend a temple on Buddhist's Day of Enlightenment. The lanterns, lights, feasts, and sense of celebration convey the joy of Buddha's experiences. Similarly, a non-Christian can attend a Christmas Eve candlelight service in a mainline Christian church and marvel at the candles, sense of new beginning, and the mere fact that every person in the congregation seems to know the words to the hymns, joining voices in song.

My Business, Your Business, or God's Business

Having a trusting relationship with a higher source clarifies areas of control for the perfectionist, and it becomes easier to discern what is really and truly your domain and what is not. When you have done all you can on a particular issue, it is time to release it to the spiritual ether. Meddling in others' business will no longer be as appealing as you learn the effects of your perfectionism. People generally do not like that in the long run, although some who are inclined to be dependent will bask in your solicitations. Such helpful diversions ultimately prevent you from flourishing in your own life as you are too busy living other lives.

Experiment for a set length of time. For example, it may be helpful to, for one week, make conscious contact with a spiritual source and give to that source all the parts of your life that are not working—the preoccupations, the perfectionist nature, difficult relationships, and challenging situations and decisions. Visualize the process of handing them over, again and again if necessary, and after the length of time has passed, determine whether you feel more peaceful. Is it better to have a spiritual partner? The perfectionist wants to do everything alone because nobody else's efforts really measure up, but a hand-in-hand relationship with a spiritual entity of your choice brings a higher-quality daily existence. It does take practice, especially after decades of trying to be perfect.

Dream Work

Many people work with their dreams as an important aspect of their spiritual practice. If you are a person who dreams frequently and remembers your dreams, this may be a way to attune yourself to a course that is informed by your subconscious mind.

There are many dream books available, and you may find them helpful; however, dreams are so laden with images that are specific to each individual that it can be useful to learn how to interpret dreams without running to a dream dictionary. Here are some suggestions for working with your dreams:

1. Keep a journal near your bed so you can write down dreams as you awaken.
2. Write down the dream as you remember it, like a scene or story.
3. Notice any strong emotions as you awaken and remember the dream and write those down.
4. Is the dream one that you have had repeatedly? Note that in your journal.
5. Use the margin of your journal to free associate from powerful images in your dream. Let the mind be very free in this process and completely true to your background. For example, if there is a woman named Dorothy in your dream, remember all the women you have known named Dorothy and write them down. Note their personalities and significance

in your life (including Dorothy from the *Wizard of Oz!*). Was there a spider in your dream? Make a list of your honest associations with spiders—fear, dislike of insects, *Charlotte's Web*, the world wide web of the Internet, whatever comes to mind.

QUESTION

What if I have persistent, repetitive nightmares?
The subconscious mind is very efficient in storing information about your experiences and beliefs. Nightmares can be a clearing out process that occurs after you achieve a place of security and strength. Sometimes nightmares can be a warning about danger in your waking life. Deeply hidden experiences from younger years sometimes come to light first in nightmares, then later in a more linear fashion. Persistent nightmares can be taken to a therapist for help, especially if they continue for months or years.

6. Look at the flow of the associations and determine what your deeper self is telling you. It may not be evident right away. It might help to set it aside for a day or so and see if something occurs to you later.

7. Look back over your dreams as you set aside each journal to see what trends are developing in your life.

8. If you have a relationship with a helpful therapist, ask if that person is comfortable helping you with your dream interpretation. Some professionals are well informed and sensitive. If you are comfortable working with a trusted counselor on your dreams, this can be a fruitful way to determine their meaning and what you might do with the information gleaned.

God Box

One way to fine-tune your trust in a higher source is to write down concerns on small pieces of paper and put them in a God box. Any box that you choose can be your God box, or you can buy or make one for this specific purpose. It is more enticing to get into the habit of giving concerns to God if the box is attractive and has some type of symbolism for you—perhaps shells or gems from nature, colors that you especially like, or the box was a gift from a treasured relative or friend.

Small Post-it notes are good for putting worries and issues into the God box. Simply jot down the essence of the situation and put it in the box. After a few weeks or months go by, spend some time reading the notes and see what really and truly has been resolved. This simple practice will help you to trust your Higher Power to a greater degree. If there are any concerns still pending, just keep putting them in the box.

Spiritual Retreats

Most religious and spiritual groups have periodic retreats where followers of a particular belief or practice come together for a focused time. Often the change in location from the demands of home and work is healing in and of itself. Some retreats have a specific purpose, and others are more open-ended. Some are tightly structured, and some have blocks of free time during which you can rest, meditate, enjoy a library, or socialize with others.

Some retreats offer days of silence, which can be an interesting discipline for perfectionists who like to talk a lot! The long periods of quiet inform a person of how much energy is used to express verbally and to listen to others' conversation. What a lot of effort! Silent retreats in the company of like-minded spiritual seekers are quite informative about the nature of the self and the relationship with a higher self.

Retreats are a good place to rest after traumatic happenings or major losses. The meals are usually prepared and served by the retreat organizers, and you are free to heal. Some retreat centers welcome visitors who are on a solo retreat without a structured program to follow. Sometimes professionals are on staff to assist a person individually if therapeutic conversations are desired. Often quiet times in a beautiful setting bring answers from within.

An Internet search for retreats of various types in your specific region will result in many possibilities for exploration. A retreat can be combined with a vacation, making the trip quite rejuvenating and purposeful. If there is a place around the country or world that you have always wanted to see, consider doing a retreat at that location.

Being in Nature

Time spent in the beautiful outdoors can be a part of your spiritual practice, bringing deep calm and reverence for the processes of life. There is nothing quite like the majesty of redwood trees, the power of the surf, or the delicacy of a finely manicured, formal rose garden. These settings take you away from the daily stresses of personal life and work, making it easier to become attuned to your spiritual nature.

If you like to camp, this is a way to be even closer to the rhythms of the earth, spending longer periods of time away from urban noise and demands. If possible, turn off all your electronic devices and enjoy some freedom from e-mails and texts. Most of those communications probably are not truly urgent.

FACT

The lotus flower has symbolic spiritual meaning in several cultures. In the Buddhist culture, it represents faith, purity, and growth, as the beautiful blossom emerges, seemingly impossibly, from murky mud, flourishing amidst the muddy background. For centuries, thousands of Buddhists have found hope in the shape, color, and mere existence of the miraculous lotus blossom.

If you cannot get away to a quiet place in nature, investigate what is available in your immediate vicinity. A museum might offer a lovely koi pond or herb garden. Even zoos sometimes have authentic areas that are almost like home for the animals.

When you are in nature, notice the sounds and smells of the environment. Thoughtfully go back to some of those basic questions on spiritual matters. What are the plant and animal forms in that place and how are they related to each other? What do the animals eat? How do the plants get their nutrients? What are the cycles of life for the flora and fauna that you are enjoying? Can you recreate some aspects of nature that you especially love in your home or office, perhaps as a part of an altar?

CHAPTER 20

The Discipline of Forgiveness

The state of perfectionism is inherently imbued with criticisms and resentments of various kinds. Some may be deeply historical, almost a part of the personality. You might feel that it is your role in life to constantly be railing at injustices, especially those directed at you. This can become a kind of identity—the angry person done wrong. Such deeply harbored anger can provide energy and direction, but it is not positive. It is useful to imagine life without those habitual angry resentments.

But Am I Condoning Terrible Wrongs?

It is an interesting mental feat to switch gears and imagine forgiveness toward those very people who made your life miserable. You might wonder if forgiveness means that you condone those terrible acts toward you. No, forgiveness does not mean condoning, and it does not mean that you have to let those people back into your life in any relationship involvement, although you might. All you intend to do is change your mental focus from resentment to acceptance.

ESSENTIAL

Some have said that harboring resentment is the same as drinking poison and expecting it to kill another person! Is this what you want to do?

Acceptance

Acceptance means that you 100 percent accept the reality of what occurred in the situation. Something happened that was unjust or was otherwise to your detriment. Another person may have been at fault, but that is not the issue at this juncture. Acceptance means that, yes, it happened; you embrace that as a part of your history and go on to other experiences.

In American society, forgiveness is often seen as an act of weakness. Within a competitive society, it is the exceptional person who is able to approach a difficult situation with compassion and caring toward the person who is guilty of a harmful act. Many do not want to relinquish the upper hand in a competitive situation, feeling somehow that they are losing.

Did You Have a Part in the Occurrence?

It can be helpful to examine your resentments to see if somehow you had a part in the occurrences that have been so troublesome. Again, as with other written exercises, it helps to write it all down and think with an open mind and heart whether there was something going on within you that precipitated the action of the other person. If so, you can make an agreement with yourself to handle things differently in the future.

Believing in Spiritual Forgiveness

Research shows that those who believe that God or some other spiritual deity is forgiving and benevolent experience life in a more relaxed, less stressful manner. They are less harsh toward themselves and others. This could be a clue to embracing less perfectionism, as perfectionism includes a harsh view toward the self and others, always expecting more or different behavior.

Humility is an aspect of forgiveness. One sees and accepts that there might be a larger picture, that things happen in context, and sometimes situations play out in a way that is beneficial to more people. Sometimes humility can be an act of just showing up to participate in something, even if the relationship was problematic in the past. One can hope for a new start and be the one to make the first move.

Remembering that forgiveness is available from God prevents a person from being too self-righteous about the act of forgiveness, lording it over the other person in a falsely magnanimous manner. Such a deceitful act of forgiveness does no one any good, as it is only a ruse to look good in the eyes of whoever might be around to witness it. True forgiveness happens first within the self, then with the spiritual source, and finally with the person one is forgiving. It is definitely not a quick fix, and it will undoubtedly take some time to go through all those stages.

Forgiveness as a Shift in Focus

The poison of resentment drains away when you shift your focus from a negative preoccupation toward the wrongdoer to other aspects of your life. Perhaps the negative obsession has been a major preoccupation for years, even decades. It can be quite refreshing to reclaim that energy for more beneficial aspects of your life. You may find that a persistent fatigue lifts, and you can finally approach life with hope and vigor.

ESSENTIAL

Forgiveness is an act of release—release of judgments, hurts, grudges, anger, perceived injuries, even memories of what occurred.

Redirect Your Focus

What you want to do is redirect your thinking to something or someone else. It's like unplugging an appliance and emphatically plugging it into a different outlet. This shift in focus requires tremendous mental strength and discipline, as it may have been a part of your identity for years to habitually be angry with particular people, situations, or institutions. This undue emphasis is a type of attachment, in the Buddhist sense. It is a trap that keeps you ensnared, even as you vow that one of these days you will invoke the proper revenge toward those who were mistaken!

The best revenge is to reclaim your mental freedom and use your emotions and intellectual faculties for your own purposes and to live out your interests, goals, and dreams. Those other people and situations will, undoubtedly, take care of themselves just fine and really do not need you to explain the error of their ways. Those who do wrong endure plenty of natural consequences within themselves, and it is not up to you to straighten them out. Somehow they will find their way, and life's circumstances will bring a measure of justice in the long run, sometimes in surprising ways. Your highest and best revenge is to live a very happy life, in spite of what happened to you. If you are in a position where it is necessary to interact regularly with the one who mistreated you, that person will be mystified by your peace, tranquility, and happiness. You can have some fun with this.

FACT

Forgiveness shifts the awareness from the past to the present. Whatever happened to cause the difficulty occurred at another time. It is over. Forgiveness allows you to think about now instead of then. Pain is replaced with peace, and joy replaces hurt.

The ability to forgive is a factor in long, successful marriages. It is as if there is a larger perspective held by both parties, an ability to forgive a variety of transgressions over a lengthy period of time. Forgiveness may take some time. It does not matter if it happens instantly or not. Sometimes the situations that take a while to figure out bring a deeper degree of forgiveness.

Change your Perspective

Sometimes you may shift your focus to such a degree that you are able to relate in a loving way with those persons who harmed you. Nothing special has to be said about the change in manner. You simply start acting in a loving, caring way toward the person that you resented in the past. This shift in focus changes the tone of the relationship, and the other person may learn to meet you halfway. Sometimes the person will not be aware of what has changed but become more comfortable in your presence, as he or she does not feel defensive or frightened, as was possibly the case before you decided to forgive.

It's as if you shed an old skin, like a rattlesnake crawls out of a skin that has become too small. Your larger self does not need the rigid beliefs and emotions about what was wrong with the person or situation. Your larger, evolved self is able to embrace a spiritual view of the situation, accepting other, flawed people who are doing the best they can, sometimes with a fairly small toolbox. Those limitations do not prevent you from loving others. Others cannot genuinely prevent you from enjoying the good that you deserve, and you begin to notice this more and more as you act and behave in a more mature manner in a wide variety of situations with a more diverse swath of human beings. Your repertoire has become broad and deep.

Relationship to Physical Health

Although research in regard to forgiveness is relatively new, findings point to a correlation between forgiveness and emotional, spiritual, and physical health. It appears that the benefits are greatest when the one who forgives hopes to restore goodwill in a relationship that had been close but became estranged.

Hostility is a component of not being able to forgive and also a symptom associated with cardiovascular disease. Researchers Woodruff and Farrow found that the locus of forgiveness activity in the brain is deep in the limbic system, the seat of the emotions. It does not lie in the cortex, the seat of judgment. This is a good clue to not dwell too heavily on the logic or illogic of a situation. It is more important to get to the emotional heart of the matter and release the wrong in an emotional and spiritual sense.

What Does Research Reveal?

A two year study concluding in 2002 at Hope College showed that when people are asked to think about a grudge held against a particular person, the body responds with changes in facial muscles, heart rate, and blood pressure. Sweat gland activity increased, and the subjects felt anxious. When researcher and psychologist Charlotte Witvliet asked her subjects to think of the begrudged person in a warm, compassionate manner, the bodily responses returned to normal. Sincere apologies relaxed the facial muscles, and frowns disappeared.

A study titled, "Forgivingness, relationship quality, stress while imagining relationship events, and physical and mental health," published in the *Journal of Counseling Psychology* in 2001, revealed that in romantic relationships, those relationships that are described as generally unhappy leave the persons involved with higher levels of cortisol, the chemical associated with the fight-or-flight response, possibly contributing stress to the body.

Research also implicates a relationship between the unwillingness to forgive and compromises to the immune system, making it easier for the body to succumb to viruses, bacteria, and infection, even dental disease.

Is Age a Factor?

In general, middle-aged and elderly persons are more forgiving, possibly because they find it more difficult to accommodate higher levels of stress that result from an aversion to forgiveness. People over forty-five who are generally forgiving have fewer psychological symptoms of anxiety and depression.

Forgive Your Body

In today's fast-paced society, many view their body as a machine that is always there, ready for whatever is required. It is easy to forget about maintenance, not to mention genuine caring and appreciation for the physical self. Then when illness occurs, it is a tremendous interruption in the frantic schedule, and one feels betrayed, even angry at the body.

Needless to say, these angry emotions toward the body do nothing to help the healing processes. Better to stop everything and let a long rest provide a haven for the body to do its natural healing. Anger releases the wrong hormones, making it difficult for the immune system to function and nutrition to find its way to the healthy cells so they may do their repair work. Many who have been interrupted by a major illness realize afterward that a long rest was indeed necessary.

Ideally one would not wait for an illness in order to rest, regenerate, and heal from the daily use of the body. Self-nurturing in a physical way is always a good thing—long baths, good nutrition, exercise, massage, and whatever other pampering your time and budget allow. Gratitude is in order when thinking about the miraculous processes of the human body. Instead of annoyance, think of the marvelous organs that take care of your daily needs and how beautifully coordinated all the systems are. Even with a bit of neglect, the body functions well most of the time. It is a refined, delicate instrument that deserves excellent care and appreciation.

Examples of Radical Forgiveness

Your forgiveness challenges may be many and seemingly insurmountable. You might find it inspiring to consider stories of others who have had quite difficult instances of forgiveness in their lives.

Forgiving Criminals

Writer Aba Gayle received news that her nineteen-year-old daughter had been shot, resulting in her death. The authorities found the murderer, and Ms. Gayle focused her life, for eight years, on the just punishment of the murderer. She felt no peace in the situation and decided instead to write to the person, who was housed in San Quentin. Ultimately she decided to make the journey to visit him in person. She found that her daughter's killer, as the others on death row, were not monsters. She spoke with the individual at length, and they cried together. The result of her act of radical forgiveness was the creation of a prison ministry that focused on prisoners with looming death sentences. She doesn't focus on their crimes. She focuses on their personal freedom and relationship with God. In this way, Ms. Gayle became free from the albatross of hatred resulting from the premature death of her precious child. Her soul became free.

Forgiveness opens the way to new possibilities. A closed heart and clenched fist cannot receive something new. An open heart and open hand are able to receive new insight and new experiences.

A ten-year-old child, Chris Carrier, of Florida, was stabbed and shot by an attacker in the swamps near his home. Miraculously he survived. In his adult years he learned from a law enforcement officer that his attacker was near death in prison. Carrier chose to visit the prisoner and spend those last moments together, forgiving him and bringing peace to both parties.

Forgiving Abusive and Neglectful Parents

Eventually one heals to the point that it is possible to see dysfunctional, limited parents as flawed beings who probably did the best they could with whatever capabilities they had. They quite possibly had difficult childhoods themselves and simply repeated patterns that were generational. Seeing these people as instruments of your biological existence lets you move to a point of forgiveness toward those who treated you badly during your formative years, setting in place the mold for perfectionism.

Forgiving parents for wrongdoing opens up floodgates of love, allowing a normal relationship to develop, even if the parents never change. It is unlikely that they will change, anyway, as the motivation has to come from within the person. Once you forgive your parents, other relationships become easier, warmer, and more alive. It is possible to live in the present, seeing each person and situation for what it actually is instead of projecting the parental template on every relationship that is similar to that of the father or mother.

Apologies from the wrongdoers are not necessary for you to become free. Those apologies may occur at some point in the future, and they may not. It really does not matter because the process of forgiveness most benefits the one who forgives.

What Can You Do Instead?

There are several ways to move from resentment to forgiveness. Whatever you choose will have to do with your personal style and preference.

Write Fourteen-Day Blessings

Some have found the practice of writing out blessings for those troublesome people and occurrences quite helpful. In your journal each morning, simply write out sentences, blessing each individual that is worrisome to you. Ask for blessings in each area of the person's life—health, love, career success, relationship happiness. It does not matter if you are sincere! You may be so angry that you actually wish terrible things for them, but this is not what you write on the page. Simply go through the motions of writing out positive blessings in each area of life, for each person that festers in your mind in a negative way.

FACT

Grace is an important component of forgiveness. The forgiving person experiences grace and generosity, and the recipient receives grace and release from guilt and punishment. Grace envelopes both forgiver and forgiven in hope and renewal.

Continue the blessing writing for fourteen days for each person that you harbor resentments against. Usually, after three or four days, the preoccupation lifts, and you are able to accept them in a more positive way. Sometimes this practice brings tremendous healing in deeply troubled relationships.

You might experiment with blessing your challenges, as there might be something in the situation that will provide tremendous learning or awakening. It has been said that the way out is through, and if you bless that problem, perhaps it will reveal its secrets and illuminate the path to the other side. The challenge adds to your story, and you will have more experience to offer others who might struggle with a similar task in the future. If you have a perfect life, there really isn't any colorful texture to contribute to your relationships.

Forgive Seventy Times Seven

The conventional Christian suggestion is to forgive each wrongdoer seventy times seven times. (See Matthew 18:22, though some translations say "seventy-seven" as opposed to "seventy times seven.") If you do the multiplication, you will see that this number (490) is quite large! If you are courageous enough to approach this task, you might make it a part of your morning journaling, but of course, you cannot expect to complete it all in one day. You might select some pieces of lined paper, and see how many pages it will take to write out 490 sentences of forgiveness for one person. There usually are about sixty lines on one page. You might complete the forgiveness writing for one person in about a week.

FACT

Forgiveness does not necessarily mean that you are forgetting the incident, and it does not necessarily mean that you have pardoned the offense.

Another way is to say the forgiveness sentences out loud, perhaps as you are driving. You can complete 490 forgiveness sentences verbally in about twenty minutes. Focus on one person and use your driving time in this beneficial way, perhaps for a week, and see if you feel a lightening of the spirit.

It might be interesting to organize a group of people who have similar goals in terms of forgiveness and chant forgiveness sentences together for twenty minutes at a time. Then shift to a different person for another twenty-minute interval. An hour of this work will allow each individual to forgive three people. It can be beneficial for a few people to share their experiences with this exercise while others in the group listen.

Forgive Yourself

Ultimately, the hope of the perfectionistic person is to achieve forgiveness of the self for not being perfect. This is a tall order, sometimes seemingly impossible. Any of the techniques mentioned in this chapter can be used to forgive the self. You are worth it! When you lift the judgment, blame, and self-criticism from yourself on a daily basis, you have an opportunity to enjoy a free and interesting life, full of creative expression and fulfillment.

ALERT

> The self-forgiveness process for the adult child involves acknowledging what occurred in the childhood home, grieving the loss of a normal upbringing, facing the self-hatred of perfectionism, and eventually healing the split between the disowned self and the loving mature self who is able to nurture the wounded child.

In order to achieve this, you will need a lot of courage to face the harsh self-talk directed at your own mind. This stage of awareness can be painful, but it is worth it to get to the other side. Those voices initially came from others in your life and you internalized them as your own. You can mentally reject them, just as you mentally adopted them during your formative years. You have that prerogative to decide what conversations take place in your own mind.

It is absolutely worth the effort to direct forgiveness activities inward—the fourteen-day blessings and the seventy-times-seven forgiveness work. You will definitely breathe easier at the end of such work, and you will like yourself a lot more, even if you are not perfect!

As much as possible, strive towards unconditional love and caring toward yourself. It might help to think of a small child or animal that you would want to handle with tender, gentle care. Approach yourself in a similar, forgiving, accepting way. You are doing the very best that you can, and kindness and love make your actions and endeavors much easier. No one is holding a stick over your head, although you may have felt that someone was! Remove those old critical images and embrace self-love.

Use Your God Box

If you find yourself constantly coming back to the mental preoccupation with perfectionistic demands on yourself or historical anger toward others, it is helpful to write out those instances and put them in your God box. You may need to do this more than once or even several days in a row. Forgiveness is a discipline, and you may need to face resentments and let them go multiple times. Keep in mind that you are aiming for freedom—freedom from old hurts, injustices, anger, disappointments, betrayals, and numerous situations that did not turn out as you had hoped. You can be free of it all.

If the Person Has Died

You might wonder how to manage the process of forgiveness if the person you are forgiving has died. You can write an honest letter and read it to a trusted friend or therapist. You can also go to the gravesite or place where his or her ashes were scattered, talk freely with the departed, and read a sincere letter to the person. Of course, it is impossible to know whether the person "hears" what you say. The important change takes place within you. The act of forgiveness is ultimately for you, although there are benefits for all concerned. You may find that when you forgive a parent who was neglectful or cruel, your relationships with your siblings improve.

Embrace Joy

Holding on to resentments, even if they seem justified based on the facts of what happened, locks a person into negative emotions. Releasing those old emotions with forgiveness opens up the possibility of joy in the here and now. Life and people (even with all their imperfections) add to the tapestry of your existence. An undue emphasis on everything that went wrong and continues to go wrong leaves no room for daily awareness and happiness.

As much as possible, on a daily basis, make room for joy in your life. Notice small things—a friendly exchanged greeting with a neighbor, an unexpected phone call, a beautiful flower, a song by your favorite performer, an unexpected conversation with a long-lost friend via social media. All these things are worthy of joy. Embrace it all and make a good day for yourself, however imperfect it might be.

CHAPTER 21

Moving Forward with Freedom

Perfectionism is like a veil, a shroud of gauze that hides the underpinnings and consequences of unbearably high standards. Once you have pulled those things aside, looked at the origins, and worked through the adjustments, you can confidently move into a different phase of your life. Like a birth or graduation, living and being without perfectionism, or at least claiming a lesser degree of perfectionism, requires new decisions. The old landmarks no longer apply. It is as if you see everything through a different lens.

What If Everything Turns Out Okay?

One can feel uneasy without the former mental paradigm of perfectionism. As uncomfortable as it was, the parameters were familiar. One gets used to a huge amount of tension, self-criticism, and a judgmental attitude toward external surroundings. Without all this, there is freedom, but it takes a while to adjust. Like jumping into the deep end of a swimming pool or visiting a foreign country, even after years of practice with the language, it takes a few strokes or several dozen conversations to feel truly at home in a different milieu.

If everything turns out okay, there will be no need for interminable suffering, constant complaining, and dread of the future. One can wake up in the morning and anticipate a good day instead of enduring fearful constrictions of the emotions and muscles while mentally going over lists of things that have to be done.

All will be well in the new terrain. The old map is unnecessary, and you can kiss it goodbye. Life always brings challenges and interesting problems to solve, but you have learned new techniques and approaches of self-acceptance and flexibility.

Setting Aside Former Identities

Letting go of perfectionism will likely require that you release old identities that lent themselves to trying to be perfect. This is possibly easier said than done. Perfectionists like to be right, and thinking about letting go of who you were means that your old self was wrong. This realization is uncomfortable. It doesn't mean that you were wrong as a person; it was merely a case of having many mistaken beliefs and ideas about yourself.

Who Were You?

It can be fascinating to explore those former selves. You might approach the task in a creative or artistic manner. Perhaps make a list of all the selves—scholar, career person, father, sister, coach, savior, fixer, quality control freak. Free-associate with your list and give your former selves silly names, if you feel like it. Were you Wonder Woman or Superman flying through the air with your cape? Were you Mr. Have-the-Last-Word no matter what? Honesty about your various selves will help you become free. It will be less painful if you can play with it.

ESSENTIAL

Writer Joseph Campbell said, "We must be willing to get rid of the life we've planned so as to have the life that is waiting for us." This requires some tolerance for ambiguity and the unknown.

If you like to draw or paint, it will be interesting to make pictures of your former selves, perhaps in a little cartoon booklet. If you are a storyteller or writer, jot down some essays about each of the selves and some of their more colorful escapades.

Spend some time on this exploration, as claiming the reality of the former selves, accepting their importance in your scheme of things for a number of years, and getting ready to let them go opens the way to new freedom. It is not a process that should rushed.

Say Goodbye

You may feel sadness and vulnerability as you release the old you with all the perfectionistic habits and strict structure. Whatever emotion you feel will be right for you. It might be relief, sorrow, anticipation, even love for those innovative personalities who allowed you to keep it all together for so many years.

FACT

Symptoms of withdrawal may surprise you. Nausea, anxiety, headaches, nervousness, fatigue, and the shakes are detox symptoms that are present when a substance abuser becomes clean. The process might be as profound for a person giving up a mental construct, such as perfectionism. Plenty of rest and a quiet, gentle environment will be helpful.

You might want to devise a ritual to signify the importance of the occasion. You could put them on your altar for a few days. You might make graduation caps and give each previous identity a diploma. You might create a scrapbook with a page for each one. These were important adaptations to very difficult circumstances and not to be scoffed at or treated too casually. Say goodbye, however, as the former selves have outlived their usefulness.

Is a New Career Choice in the Picture?

Releasing perfectionism may make you uncomfortable with your current or previous career choices. It is as if the perfectionism created a foggy web through which you viewed your interests and options. Circumstances change as you change, and this might include a yearning for a different direction.

ALERT

Adult children from difficult families go into the helping professions in large proportions. Some are motivated by a sincere, altruistic drive to serve others. Some are driven unconsciously to master the dynamic of the childhood home, to save others and make everything okay for someone somewhere. Such drives can be unhealthy and unrealistic. At this stage of coping with perfectionism it is helpful to take an honest look at your work life and determine whether it pleases you.

Write a Career Autobiography

It is helpful to write down your entire work history, from childhood up to the present time. Make it as detailed as you are able—whom you worked for, which aspects you liked and didn't like, how long you did that work, and why you left that work. Include the level of pay and whether you were satisfied. Try to remember tasks you did to earn money as a child and teenager.

If you attended college, how did you select your major? Think about whether someone influenced you in your choice. If that person had not had a voice, is there something else you might have enjoyed? Remember family attitudes toward various professions and honestly include those pressures in your work history.

Note especially important milestones in your work life—promotions, prizes, publications, raises, changes in professions, and geographic moves. Describe your academic programs of study and honors received. It is important to grasp the larger picture, the organic whole of your vocational life.

If there are very important hobbies or service responsibilities that are or were as important as your earning endeavors, describe those, too. Did someone nominate you to head a fundraising committee for a nonprofit organization, and you willingly spearheaded the effort? What were the satisfactions and frustrations? Did you enter your prize roses in a county competition and surprise yourself with the depth of your commitment to the task? Do you have a steady, ongoing presence in a church or community center that is pivotal to your weekly schedule? This is a part of your work life, even if it is unpaid.

Meditations and Dreams

Have new directions emerged in your meditations and dreams? Sometimes the first glimpses of something enticing can seem flitting and elusive. The perfectionistic self wants to reject anything purely joyful. As much as you are able, create a welcoming context for your subconscious mind to speak to you regarding deeply desired aims for your life. It might be important to set aside a particular journal for those visions, jotting them down in raw form so you can notice if something is taking shape over a period of weeks or months.

Dreams can sometimes seem obscure in their emotional or visual coding. Just do the best you can to write down anything that strikes you as important. As you face the fears of considering something new, the images will become clearer. The human mind has a way of protecting itself, and if you are too frightened to consider a change, your conscious mind will keep the idea away from you.

If you enjoy the vision board process, it would be possible to make miniature vision pages for aspects of a larger vision that seems to be taking shape. The form could be sleeved pages in a notebook or collaged pages in a journal.

Career Classes, Planning, and Testing

It can be very rewarding to take a career class where you are among others and can look at your values and preferences over a period of weeks. Having the companionship of other career seekers makes you feel more supported as you consider new options for your work life. Consider nonprofit career centers, counselors, coaches, and interest inventories in order to get a fresh look at the reality of who you are at this time and what your true preferences might be.

Approach this kind of study with an open mind, as your perfectionism may have skewed your studies and career choices in the past. Just think about it as someone else who did those things. A new person has shown up today, looking for joy and fulfillment in employment. Imagine you are an actor or actress, and you are ready for a new role.

Public libraries are a gold mine of helpful career resources—books, online, and free lectures. Some libraries offer weekly sessions with SCORE counselors, retired executives who are eager to help other businesspeople. Explore Internet communities for like-minded persons who are a little further along in their quest, sharing information and questions. Meetup.com (*www.meetup.com*) is active in some metropolitan areas, offering spontaneous get-togethers on a wide range of topics. Some of them might be perfect for you, enabling you to exchange tips with others on a similar path.

Create a Plan and Timeline

It is one thing to have a fantasy of doing something exotic and quite another to take action in a new direction. The fantasy might have been a convenient safe haven for a number of years, but your new career becomes quite real when you work to make it happen. Check in with yourself at every step of the way to see if you really like what you are doing. Sometimes those from perfectionistic or neglectful backgrounds need help to determine what is truly satisfying because the natural internal intuitive radar was blunted. A therapist, career coach, trusted mentor, or friend can assist with feedback and encouragement.

Create a timeline with realistic goals—perhaps six months, a year, and five years. Discuss this with others who will be a part of the change, especially a spouse or significant other. Examine the level of your prudent savings and other sources of income while you make a transition. Think about insurance and retirement and decide what you want to do in those areas.

Visualize, visualize, and visualize your target profession again! With a strong enough focus, the universe will respond.

Examining Your Relationships

With perfectionism as your daily companion, you may sense some restlessness and disquietude in your closest relationships. Did you choose a partner that you could dominate in hopes of getting perfect results? Did you hope to change that other person? Often those who come from alcoholic backgrounds choose a partner that needs serious reform, as that repeats the hope of the child with an alcoholic or substance-addicted parent. That type of relationship feels comfortable, or at least familiar. It can become considerably less comfortable when one realizes that the other person has so many issues that solving them all will take an entire lifetime. If you are considering making a major relationship change, consider joining support groups and enlisting the help of a professional who can guide you along the way. You may discover that the relationship is salvageable, if both parties are on a growth path.

FACT

Holding on to resentment is like holding your finger in a fire, even after you notice that it's burning and it hurts a lot! It probably makes sense to quickly release the cause of the pain.

In a similar manner, without perfectionism your social life may cry out for a tune-up. Do you have hanger-on friends who deluge you with woe-is-me litanies? Are they interested in you and your new directions? Do you have friends who share joy when you achieve what you have set out to do? As you let go of perfectionism, you may experience some attrition in your social life. Try not to be alarmed, as other, more appropriate friends will find you. You deserve friends who are able to relate to you in a loving, authentic manner.

Burying Perfectionism: Create a Ritual

Depending on your style and personality, you may want to create a specific ritual to let go of perfectionism. There are a variety of activities that can help you let go and move forward with freedom. Some of the following have been useful to others:

1. Write down something that represents perfectionism.
2. Make a visual representation of perfectionism.
3. Burn the representation of perfectionism and bury the ashes.
4. Make a miniature coffin and put perfectionism in the coffin.
5. Place the miniature coffin on your altar or near your God box.
6. Create affirmations of release and write them for several days.
7. Focus on release of perfectionism in your meditation and prayer practice.
8. Visualize yourself in your new life without perfectionism.
9. Create a vision board showing your life without perfectionism.

A sensitivity to your real beliefs and preferences as you create a ritual is important. You might want to do something that is very earthy, connected to the raw elements of life and death. Honor that. Perhaps words are more important to you. Scatter words about your altar or tape them on mirrors in your home. Movement might be an important aspect of how you engage in life. Burning a representation of your former perfectionism and vigorously scattering the ashes while you dance outdoors might be a good activity to connect your deeper cellular self to the changes you experience. Make it very real and authentic for yourself.

What Can You Do Instead?

Without perfectionism, life is wide open with a brand new range of possibilities. You are no longer hampered with the mistaken belief that whatever you do has to be perfect, and many more options are available.

Juggling Act

With so many tools at your fingertips to create a new start, without perfectionism, you may feel like a master juggler or aerial artist in Cirque du Soleil! Do what you are able to do, making fresh choices as they meet your needs. There is no right way to move through the process of diminishing perfectionism and creating a better life. You will discover your way with trial and error. When something doesn't seem to fit, try a different choice.

Never Too Late

It is never too late for you to undertake major improvements in your life. Some hardy people continue creative output far into their eighties and nineties, such as Louise Nevelson, Martha Graham, and Pablo Casals. Grandma Moses didn't start painting until she was in her seventies and worked well into her nineties, living to the age of 101.

Embrace Wonder

Regardless of your age and situation, without addictive emotional, mental, and behavioral tendencies, you are able to see the incredible wonder of life, partaking in pleasurable experiences in consistent ways that bring you happiness. The balance tips away from nervousness and sorrow, and you have longer series of truly good days. Each one is a creative entity that is fashioned by you and you only.

Dignity, Respect, a Slower Pace

Without perfectionism, you find yourself treating yourself and others with a higher degree of dignity and respect. Your relationship with yourself is more loving and wholesome, and you have more to offer to friends, family, and work associates. Cooperating with others is easier, and you are less afraid of disapproval from others.

As you drop obligations that are not essential, a slower pace of living becomes your norm. The slower pace allows your body to function more normally, and sometimes you are happy and relaxed, breathing deeply and truly enjoying life.

Become Like a Child

Painter Pablo Picasso said that it takes many years to become like a child. He constantly endeavored to keep a fresh perspective toward his work, eventually moving away from representation and fully embracing cubism. That childlike perspective is available to you, too!

Helpful Websites

Thirdworldpapa.com

An eclectic modern blog on many aspects of relationships.

www.thirdworldpapa.com

Davincidilemma.com

A website devoted to encouraging and helping multitalented people.

www.davincidilemma.com

Outofthefog.net

This site assists those who are coping with a friend or family member who has various psychological disorders.

www.outofthefog.net

Sober24.com

A blog devoted to issues surrounding sobriety from alcohol.

www.sober24.com

Us.mensa.org

Site for a social and networking organization for persons with a high IQ.

www.us.mensa.org

Additional Resources

Al-Anon Family Groups

757-563-1600

www.al-anonfamilygroups.org

For helping families recover from a family member's problem drinking.

Parents Anonymous

909-621-6184

www.parentsanonymous.org

For strengthening families, breaking the cycle of abuse, and helping parents create safe homes for their children.

Adult Children of Alcoholics

PO Box 3216

Torrance, CA 90510

562-595-7831

www.adultchildren.org

Twelve-step organization to help persons who come from alcoholic and other dysfunctional families.

Alcoholics Anonymous

PO Box 459

New York, NY 10163

212-870-3400

www.aa.org

Twelve-step organization that helps people stop drinking.

National Alliance on Mental Illness (NAMI)

3803 N. Fairfax Drive, Ste. 100

Arlington, VA 22203

703-524-9094

www.nami.org

This organization helps people with mental illness and family members of the mentally ill.

Overeaters Anonymous

PO Box 44020

Rio Rancho NM 87174

505-891-2664

www.oa.org

This twelve-step organization helps people who eat compulsively.

Debtors Anonymous

PO Box 920888

Needham, MA 02492

1-800-421-2383 (United States only)

www.debtorsanonymous.org

Twelve-step organization to assist persons who debt compulsively.

Gamblers Anonymous

PO Box 17173

Los Angeles CA 90017

626-960-3500

www.gamblersanonymous.org

This twelve-step organization helps people stop compulsive gambling.

Emotions Anonymous

PO Box 4245

St. Paul MN 55104

651-647-9712

www.emotionsanonymous.org

This twelve-step program helps people find emotional sobriety.

Families Anonymous

701 Lee Street

Des Plaines, IL 60016

1-800-736-9805 (United States only)

www.familiesanonymous.org

This twelve-step program assists family members who are coping with other family members who have behavioral or drug issues.

Obsessive Compulsive Anonymous

PO Box 215 New Hyde Park

New York NY 11040

516-739-0662

www.obsessivecompulsiveanonymous.org

This twelve-step program helps its members cope with symptoms of OCD.

Helpful Books and Pamphlets:

Adult Children of Alcoholics. *Newcomer* and *Identity Papers*, Torrance, California, 2004.

Alcoholics Anonymous World Service. *Alcoholics Anonymous, 4th Ed.*, New York, New York, 2001.

Beck, Martha. *The Joy Diet: Ten Daily Practices for a Happier Life.* Crown Publishers: New York, 2003.

Benjamin, Harold H. *From Victim to Victor: For Cancer Patients and Their Families.* Dell Publishing: New York, 1987.

Black, Claudia. *It Will Never Happen to Me: As Children, Adolescents, Adults*, 2002.

Bradshaw, John. *Bradshaw On the Family: A Revolutionary Way to Self-Discovery*, 1988

Bradshaw, John. *Healing the Shame That Binds You*, 2005.

Bradshaw, John. *Homecoming: Reclaiming and Championing Your Inner Child.* 1992

Camenson, Blythe. *McGraw-Hill's Careers for Perfectionists and Other Meticulous Types.* 2nd Ed. McGraw-Hill: New York, 2007.

Dolecki, Constance. *The Everything® Guide to Borderline Personality Disorder.* Adams Media: Avon, Massachusetts, 2012.

Domar, Alice D. *Be Happy without Being Perfect: How to Break Free from the Perfect Deception.* Crown Publishers: New York, 2008.

Forward, Susan. *Toxic Parents, Overcoming Their Hurtful Legacy and Reclaiming Your Life*, 2002.

Goldberg, Carey. "When perfectionism becomes a problem." The Boston Globe, March 2, 2009. Retrieved from Boston.com on June 5, 2012.

Goodman, Cynthia, and Barbara Leff. *The Everything® Guide to Narcissistic Personality Disorder.* Adams Media: Avon, Massachusetts, 2012.

Hyde, Michael J. *Perfection: Coming to Terms with Being Human.* Baylor University Press: Waco, Texas, 2010.

Norwood, Robin. *Women Who Love Too Much: When You Keep Wishing and Hoping He'll Change,* 2008.

Raiten-D'Antonio, Toni. *The Velveteen Principles for Women: Shatter the Myth of Perfection and Embrace All That You Really Are.* Health Communications, Inc.: Deerfield Beach, Florida, 2007.

Rubens, Jim. *OverSuccess: Healing the American Obsession with Wealth, Fame, Power, and Perfection.* Greenleaf Book Group Press, LCC: Austin, Texas, 2009.

Sher, Barbara. *Refuse to Choose: A Revolutionary Program for Doing Everything That You Love,* 2006.

Stoddard, Alexandra. *The Art of the Possible: The Path from Perfectionism to Balance and Freedom.* William Morrow and Company, Inc.: New York, 1995.

Whitfield, Charles L. *Healing the Child Within: Discovery and Recovery for Adult Children of Dysfunctional Families,* 1987.

Index

We Have

EVERYTHING®

on Anything!

With more than 19 million copies sold, the Everything® series has become one of America's favorite resources for solving problems, learning new skills, and organizing lives. Our brand is not only recognizable—it's also welcomed.

The series is a hand-in-hand partner for people who are ready to tackle new subjects—like you!

For more information on the Everything® series, please visit *www.adamsmedia.com*.

The Everything® list spans a wide range of subjects, with more than 500 titles covering 25 different categories:

Business	History	Reference
Careers	Home Improvement	Religion
Children's Storybooks	Everything Kids	Self-Help
Computers	Languages	Sports & Fitness
Cooking	Music	Travel
Crafts and Hobbies	New Age	Wedding
Education/Schools	Parenting	Writing
Games and Puzzles	Personal Finance	
Health	Pets	

Making Money in
a Health Service
Business on Your
Home-Based PC

Making Money in a Health Service Business on Your Home-Based PC

Second Edition

Rick Benzel

Paul and Sarah Edwards, Series Editors

McGraw-Hill
New York   San Francisco   Washington, D.C.   Auckland   Bogotá
Caracas   Lisbon   London   Madrid   Mexico City   Milan
Montreal   New Delhi   San Juan   Singapore
Sydney   Tokyo   Toronto

Library of Congress Cataloging-in-Publication Data

Benzel, Rick.
 [Making money in a health service business on your home-based PC]
Rick Benzel.—2nd ed.
    p.   cm.
 Formerly published under the title: Health service businesses on
your home-based PC
  Includes index.
  ISBN 0-07-913139-5 (p)
  1. Medical fees—Data processing—Vocational guidance.   2. Home-
based businesses—Vocational guidance.   3. Collecting of accounts—
Data processing—Vocational guidance.   4. Medical transcription—
Vocational guidance.   5. Insurance, Health—Adjustment of claims—
Vocational guidance.   I. Title.
R728.8.B46 1997
651'.961—dc20   96-29742
                                                           CIP

McGraw-Hill

A Division of The McGraw·Hill Companies

        5 6 7 8 9 0   DOC/DOC   9 0 2 1 0 9

P/N 0-07-006104-1
PART OF
ISBN 0-07-913139-5

*The sponsoring editor for this book was Scott Grillo, the editing supervisor was
Penny Linskey, and the production supervisor was Pamela Pelton. It was set in
Vendome by Renee Lipton of McGraw-Hill's Professional Book Group composition unit.*

Printed and bound by Donnelley/Crawfordsville.

This book is printed on acid-free paper.

To Terry, Rebecca, and Sarah

CONTENTS

Contents

PREFACE

When I wrote the first edition of this book, I did not anticipate the enormous interest it would generate among people seeking a new career. As I followed the sales of the book over several years, however, I became both proud and less surprised by its success because I realized that it was fulfilling a tremendous need for information and advice. I salute readers of the second edition of this book—by buying this book, you are already proving that you know how to approach a business or career decision as important as the one you may now face: by getting the best information available.

This second edition reflects an extensive amount of updating. Much has changed since the first edition of this book relative to the three businesses covered. The new material falls into the following categories:

Healthcare industry trends. New trends are occurring in healthcare that affect all three businesses. The foremost of these is managed care, which has had an impact on the medical billing profession, in particular.

Statistical and factual updates. One of the underpinnings in this book is to show some of the statistical data that indicate the growth and trends in healthcare. You will find many new charts and tables that businesspeople can use to plan their future.

Technological advancements. As always, there is a constant stream of new software, enormous improvement in hardware, and many other changes that can improve life for the small or home-based business. For example, the area of digital recording is beginning to alter the medical transcription field, opening up more opportunities for the home-based business. The maturation of the Internet also creates a fertile area for updating, as many companies and associations now have Web sites that you can visit for information and advice.

Case histories. Since the first edition, I have spoken to or interviewed hundreds of people who were either seeking to get into one of the businesses in this book or who were already successful at it. This new edition contains many of the best stories I heard that can serve as meaningful inspiration for you.

Business trends. In the first edition, I made many recommendations about how to get into each business; some of that information has had to be updated. I have focused especially in the chapter on medical billing to provide better, more reliable information about which business opportunity vendors to work with if you are interested in purchasing training and support along with the specialized medical billing software required for this profession.

CD-ROM capability. As you can see, the publisher has graciously agreed to include a CD-ROM with this book. This contains software demos for medical billing software.

According to an informal survey I conducted, the majority of people who bought the first edition of this book seemed to be interested in starting a medical billing service. For this reason, I have expanded the material on medical billing and made it the largest chapter in this book. This is not to suggest that the other two professions covered are slighted; there is truly an astonishing amount of information on CAP work and medical transcription, but I have tried to answer the many questions hundreds of people have asked me about medical billing. I apologize to those who may have wanted more information on the other two businesses, but I am sure you will not be disappointed with any chapter.

I probably don't need to convince you of the benefits of working for yourself. Self-employment *is* the wave of the future. It allows you the greatest freedom of choice, flexibility, and control of your life. Working for yourself provides an opportunity to make your own decisions and reap your own rewards. Indeed, self-employment can change your entire point of view on the meaning of life.

I know, because it has changed mine. After a 15-year career in publishing, working for several companies in Boston and Los Angeles, I made a transition in 1991 into my own home business as a professional writer and editor. Since that decision, I have not regretted once working for myself. In fact, I have never been more challenged or exhilarated in my professional life as I am now.

Part of my exhilaration comes from working on this book. Although I was not very familiar with the healthcare field when I wrote the first edition, I have truly become fascinated by all three businesses included here, and I have learned a great deal about each one. As a writer who focuses largely on small and home-based businesses, I sincerely believe that the three businesses in this book are among the best you can start if you enjoy the field of healthcare and you have either a background in it or an affinity for it.

Please note, however, that none of the businesses in this book is a get-rich-quick scheme. These are all businesses in which you must work hard.

I don't want to mince words about that. These are careers that require knowledge, effort, and marketing on your part.

I hope you find the information helpful if you are trying to decide on a new career. Let me add that the health field undergoes many changes on a frequent basis. The technology of medical billing and transcription changes, federal and state government rules and regulations about Medicare and Medicaid change, the insurance companies and HMOs that underwrite health insurance policies change, and even doctors and hospitals change. In short, while I believe this book to be as accurate and up-to-date as possible at the time of its writing, please be aware that you may learn slightly different information, rules, and regulations by the time this book reaches your hand or when you get into business. This only reflects how important it is to keep up with the profession you ultimately select.

Thank you for your time.

—RICK BENZEL

ACKNOWLEDGMENTS

As is the case with nearly every book published, many people contributed to the project in some form. I would like to thank especially the following pivotal people for their special role in helping me. First, I thank my wife Terry, and my daughters Rebecca and Sarah, for being there. I thank my personal friend L.F. for her invaluable guidance in my writing career. I express my gratitude to Paul and Sarah Edwards, who introduced me to these healthcare fields and the opportunity to work on this book. To Scott Grillo, my editor, many thanks for recognizing the value of enhancing the first edition of this book.

I am especially grateful to Randi Goldsmith, Director of McGraw-Hill Computing, for her leadership in developing the CD—Rom accompanying this book, and to Barry Kaplan of Mega Space, who worked endless hours to organize and program the CD—Rom into a clean, unified presentation.

I also thank my editing supervisor, Penny Linskey, for her excellent shepherding of the manuscript through final production.

In working on this second edition, I utilized many resources, particularly the knowledge and experience of many people in these businesses. I thank everyone who agreed to an interview, whose profiles you find in this book.

Special thanks go to the following individuals for spending hours of their time with me discussing their businesses and in some cases reading portions of the manuscript: my medical billing mentor Merry Schiff of Medical Management Software; Nancie Lee Cummins of Medical Management Billing; Richard Wunneburger, Ken Fisher, Cheryl Hamilton, and everyone at InfoHealth and Synaps Corporation; Jeff Ward, Darlene Pickron, and Will Crandell of Medisoft/The Computer Place; Gary Knox of AQC Resources; Norma Border of NACAP; my dear friends Tom and Nancy Koehler of In Home Medical Claims; Pat Forbis of AAMT; Linda Campbell of HPI; Ann Jacobsen of Medicode; author Donna Avila-Weil; Bernie Magoon of Lanier; and Scott Faulkner of Dictaphone.

Notices

- **Straight Talk**®, **Digital Express**® and **MVP**® are registered trademarks of Dictaphone Corporation. **Express Writer**™ is a trademark of Dictaphone Corporation.
- **Business Plan Pro**™ is a trademark of Palo Alto Software.
- **OneClaim Plus**® is a registered trademark of Santiago SDS, Inc.
- **Lytec Systems** is a division of National Data Corporation.

All other software is protected under copyright or trademark by its owner.

1

The Booming Healthcare Business

The healthcare professions are booming. Whether you are seeking to enter a completely new career or are branching out from an allied health field, now is a great time to consider starting your own business in healthcare. Today, and for many decades into the future, healthcare will remain a growing, thriving, recession-proof, profitable field for entrepreneurs and people seeking home-based businesses. Given the demographics of America's aging population with its growing need for medical attention, along with the new baby boom and a number of other factors, you have an irrefutable fact: the healthcare professions abound with opportunity. Healthcare has already become the second largest occupational sector in the United States, after the food industry. It is estimated that there were more than 10.5 million Americans employed in the health field in 1995, and projections for growth through the year 2000 are among the highest of all industries.

The upshot of this trend is a boon for the person interested in opening a small- or home-based business. With insurance companies, hospitals, labs, doctors' offices, and ancillary health businesses all looking to save money and lower costs, many opportunities exist for the home-based sole proprietor or small business entrepreneur. Smaller businesses can operate more efficiently, cut expenses, and be more productive. In fact, small businesses represent an important key to halting or at least slowing down the inflationary 8 percent to 10 percent annual growth rate in expenditures that has marked American healthcare for the past 15 years. New technologies and new ways of working are also changing the face of health careers and providing profitable opportunities for home-based and small business entrepreneurs.

Astounding Facts and Figures

A constant stream of statistics demonstrates the enormity of the American healthcare system and its projected nonstop growth. Unfortunately, it is difficult to put together a coherent snapshot of healthcare in America, because the significant time lag in collecting data and putting the statistics together makes the numbers appear to be outdated. There are also many statistics that are constantly being revised, so it is often impossible to compare facts from one month to the next and from one source of information to another, or even to determine which fact is reliable.

However, each year the Health Insurance Institute of America compiles an excellent guide to the healthcare industry, based on data collected by various government agencies and private associations. This guide, entitled *The Source Book of Health Insurance Data*, presents an impressive array of charts, tables, and text from which you can gather an astonishing knowledge about U.S. healthcare. Consider the following facts and tables as a general barometer of our healthcare industry and its opportunities:

- In 1995, the U.S. National Health Expenditure (NHE) broke the $1 trillion mark, and in 1996 (as this book was being written) it was projected to increase to $1.08 trillion. That's an 8 percent increase in healthcare spending over one year.

- Of the $1+ trillion spent in 1995, $987 billion was spent on personal healthcare (as opposed to research, construction of health facilities, and government public health programs that are not care related). Personal healthcare includes expenses for hospitalization and physician care, dental services, home health care, drugs and medications, vision products, and nursing home care. Figure 1-1 shows the breakdown of personal healthcare dollars in 1995.

■ The NHE has been slowly eating up the American economy. In 1995, the NHE was equal to more than 14 percent of the entire Gross Domestic Product (GDP), which means that healthcare consumes nearly one-eighth of all dollars produced in the United States. Even worse, it is projected that the NHE, which has been rising at a rate of 8 percent to 11 percent per year since the 1980s, will soon compose nearly one-fifth of the entire GDP. Table 1-1 projects the estimated increases in the NHE for 1996 through 2005. As you can see, within a decade, the NHE will exceed $2 trillion, nearly 18 percent of the GDP.

■ Of the $1 trillion spent for NHE in 1995, Medicare accounted for $190 billion to provide services to nearly 38 million people. The majority of Medicare money is spent on hospital and physician services. According to the Health Care Financing Administration (HCFA, pronounced Hick-fah), the federal agency that runs Medicare and is affiliated with the Department of Health and Human Services, nearly 30 percent of Medicare expenditures pay for the care of elderly people in the last years of their lives. Look again at Table 1-1 and notice how Medicare is expected to grow over the next decade. By 2050, HCFA projects there will be nearly 70 million Americans on Medicare, if the program survives that long.

■ In 1995, Medicaid—a combined HCFA and state government program—spent an additional $140 billion to cover more than 36 million

Figure 1-1
Breakdown of
personal health care
expenditures in 1995

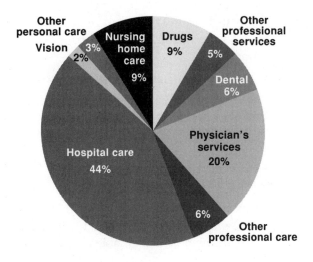

people (some people are covered by both Medicare and Medicaid). Combining Medicare and Medicaid, government subsidized insurance paid for nearly one-third of all healthcare in the country in 1995.

In addition to these figures, consider the following interesting demographic facts about the U.S. population and our healthcare needs:

- According to the latest available *complete* and *reliable* figures from the Health Insurance Association of America, in 1993, 220 million of 260 million Americans had some type of health insurance coverage, provided generally by private insurers, employer-run group plans, or government-sponsored programs.

- In 1993, there were 5,260 community hospitals in the United States with nearly 1 million hospital beds, and an average 65 percent occupancy rate. The number of hospitals has been decreasing over the past decade because of rising costs and increased use of outpatient services.

- In a typical year in America, there are about 25 million blood pressure checks, 90 million urinalyses, and 90 million blood tests performed.

- The number of doctors in the United States is mushrooming. According to figures from the American Medical Association (AMA), in 1993, a total of 653,000 physicians were distributed among many different specialties. The largest number, more than 100,000, were in internal medicine. In addition, according to HCFA, it is estimated that by the year 2000, there will be nearly 660,000 doctors, 161,000 dentists, and 40,000 osteopaths practicing in the United States, almost double the numbers in 1970. Furthermore, there are nearly 250,000 licensed pharmacists in the country. Table 1-2 (page 6) shows a breakdown by types of physicians.

- According to the latest figures from the National Center for Health Statistics, in 1993 there were more than 1.6 billion physician contacts between doctors and patients in the United States. This figure includes all contacts in person, via telephone, or at a hospital or facility. Women averaged 6.7 visits per year, while men averaged only 5.2 contacts per year. Table 1-3 (page 7) shows a breakdown by age and sex of physician contacts.

As you can see from the data, the healthcare industry is on a roller-coaster ride up, with no major downturns expected. Why is this so? The answer lies in a number of undeniable trends.

TABLE 1-1

Projected National Health Expenditures: 1996–2005

	1996	1997	1998	1999	2000	2001	2002	2003	2004	2005
Total National Health Expenditures	$1,087.1	$1,173.5	$1,269.3	$1,372.1	$1,481.7	$1,600.4	$1,728.8	$1,866.5	$2,014.2	$2,173.7
Private	594.7	641.3	693.7	749.4	807.9	871.8	940.1	1012.5	1089.3	1171.3
Public	492.4	532.2	575.6	622.8	673.7	728.7	788.7	854.0	924.9	1002.4
Medicare	208.9	227.8	247.8	269.9	293.5	319.1	347.4	378.5	412.8	450.9
Medicaid	150.2	163.8	179.2	195.9	214.5	234.6	256.5	280.1	305.7	333.4
Other	133.3	140.6	148.6	157.0	165.7	174.9	184.8	195.3	206.4	218.1
Average % increase from previous year		7.9%	8.2%	8.1%	8.0%	8.0%	8.0%	8.0%	7.9%	7.9%
Gross Domestic Product (GDP in $billions)	$7,506.6	$7,921.3	$8,360.9	$8,822.9	$9,301.1	$9,821.5	$1,0359.2	$10,926.0	$11,524.0	$12,155.5
National Health Expenditure as a % of GDP	14.5%	14.8%	15.2%	15.6%	15.9%	16.3%	16.7%	17.1%	17.5%	17.9%
U.S. Population	275.9	278.2	280.5	282.8	285.0	287.2	289.4	291..5	293.6	295.7
Per Capita Expenditures	$3,941	$4,218	$4,525	$4,852	$5,198	$5,572	$5,975	$6,404	$6,861	$7,352

Source: Health Care Financing Administration (HCFA), Office of Actuary: Data from Office of National Health Statistics.

DEMOGRAPHIC FACTS. The U.S. population is rapidly expanding. Whereas we were 190 million in 1960, we are now more than 270 million people and growing. Of special note is the fact that the distribution of the U.S. population has a high proportion of people who need regular health-care services: babies and new mothers, the middle aged, and the elderly. For example, in *each year* of the decade of the 1990s, nearly 4 million babies will be born. Also in each year of the 1990s, more than 20 million children will be below the age of 5, more than 4 million people will turn 45, and more than 2 million people will become 65. As you can readily imagine, these figures reflect a huge demand for healthcare services.

TABLE 1-2

Physicians
(Federal and
Nonfederal) by
Selected Specialty
and Activity, 1992

Specialty	Total Physicians	Patient Care	Office Based	Hospital Based
Anesthesiology	28,148	27,034	19,998	3,120
Cardiovascular diseases	16,478	14,709	11,460	1,407
Dermatology	7,912	7,550	6,318	371
Radiology	18,156	14,117	10,858	2,209
Emergency Medicine	15,470	14,813	9,373	3,796
Family Practice	50,969	49,269	40,479	2,555
Gastroenterology	7,964	7,121	5,724	538
General Practice	20,719	20,475	18,575	1,600
General Surgery	39,211	37,792	24,956	2,919
Internal Medicine	109,017	99,502	65,312	8,445
Neurology	9,742	8,559	6,330	917
Obstetrics/Gynecology	35,273	34,136	27,115	1,947
Pediatrics	44,881	41,482	29,110	3,851
Pathology	17,005	13,910	7,948	3,154
Ophthalmology	16,433	15,970	13,752	675
Orthopaedic surgery	20,640	20,244	15,832	1,277
Nuclear Medicine	1,372	1,181	736	307
Urology	9,452	9,214	7,688	573
Psychiatry	36,405	33,005	21,913	5,860
Totals	505,247	470,083	343,477	45,521

Note: There were 653,000 physicians in 1992. This table represents a selected group of this total. Excludes physicians in administration, medical teaching, and research. Figures in each row do not add up because of overlap.

Source: U.S. Department of Health and Human Services, Bureau of Health Professions.

INCREASED LIFE EXPECTANCY. Another demographic fact contributing to increased healthcare usage is a longer life. In fact, life expectancy in the United States has been on rise for a century. In just the last decade alone, the life expectancy for a male at birth has gone up more than 2 years, from 70 in 1980 to 72.1 in 1993. Similarly, a female's life expectancy at birth rose 1.5 years, from 77.4 to 78.9. These increases in longevity are due to advances in fighting the three leading causes of death

TABLE 1-3

Number of
Physician Contacts
per Year per
Person
(1990–1993)

	1990	1991	1992	1993
All persons	**5.5**	**5.6**	**5.9**	**6.0**
AGE				
Under 5 years	6.9	7.1	6.9	7.2
5—14 years	3.2	3.4	3.4	3.6
15—44 years	4.8	4.7	5	5
45—64	6.4	6.6	7.2	7.1
65—74 years	8.5	9.2	9.7	9.9
75 years +	10.1	12.3	12.1	12.3
SEX AND AGE				
Male				
Under 5	7.2	7.6	7.1	7.5
5—14	3.3	3.5	3.5	3.8
15—44	3.4	3.4	3.7	3.6
45—64	5.6	5.8	6.1	6.1
65—74	8	8.6	9.2	9.3
75 years +	10	11.6	12.2	11.7
Female				
Under 5	6.5	6.6	6.7	6.9
5—14	3.2	3.2	3.3	3.4
15—44	6	5.9	6.2	6.4
45—64	7.1	7.4	8.2	8.1
65—74	9	9.7	10.1	10.4
75 years +	10.2	12.7	12.1	12.8

ED: In all four faces
of Vendome the en
dash (—) and the em
dash (—) are very
close in size

We went over them
but we had en
dashes on this
galley page

Source: U.S. Department of Health and Human Services, 1994 National Health Interview Survey

in the United States—heart disease, cancer, and stroke—largely because new technology and pharmaceuticals have helped many people survive these formerly fatal diseases. Many more advances are likely to be discovered and implemented in the future as well, yet another sign that the demand for health services can only grow further.

INCREASED USE OF HEALTH INSURANCE.   The increasing use of health insurance is another factor in explaining the boom in healthcare, as more and more people have come to rely on some form of insurance from a commercial insurance company, an employer-sponsored plan, or a government source such as Medicare or Medicaid. Whereas in 1985 only 204 million Americans had public or private health insurance, the Bureau of Census estimated that nearly 230 million Americans were covered by health insurance in 1995. Because of this explosion, a staggering amount of money annually floods the economy to pay for health services such as physician fees, hospitalizations, lab fees, and so on.

For example, according to the latest figures available from 1993, private insurance paid $84 billion in claims benefits for physician services alone, while Medicare and Medicaid payments added another $58 billion. As Table 1-1 showed, the per capita expenditure for healthcare will rise from nearly $4,000 per year in 1996 to more than $7,000 per year by the year 2005.

HEALTH-CONSCIOUSNESS FEVER.   Over the past two decades, the American population has been growing more conscious of the value of health and fitness. On one hand, as members of the baby boom genera-tion age, they have become more sensitive than any previous generation to growing "older"—and fighting it every step of the way. On the other hand, a continuous flood of new research clearly demonstrates the link between taking care of one's body and longevity. As a result of both trends, more and more people are recognizing that a long and healthful life depends on their own efforts to eat properly, exercise, sleep well, and reduce stress.

The ramifications of this increasing pursuit of good health are actual-ly contradictory. On one hand, people are staying in better shape and practicing proactive and preventative medicine. But on the other hand, many people are also getting more frequent checkups as they age or whenever a slight health or dental problem occurs. This trend has undoubtedly played a role in increasing healthcare expenditures, as more and more worried people have demanded—"just to be sure"—office visits, lab tests, blood tests, and many other routines that may not have been done in the past.

THE MEDICAL TESTING CRAZE.   The demand for more and more medical testing does not originate solely with patients. According to the *Complete Guide to Medical Tests* by H. Winter Griffith, M.D., medical tests have become extremely important—if not a requirement—in nearly every healthcare situation. One benefit of tests is that our increasingly sophisticated technology allows doctors to make a more accurate diagnosis of a patient's problem. Whereas many types of ailments or problems may have gone undetected in the past, they can be caught much earlier today through the use of sophisticated blood or urine tests, as well as high-tech imaging techniques such as MRIs.

Needless to say, the other benefit of tests (and the one that truly drives up their usage more than any other factor) is that tests provide protection for doctors against the risks of a lawsuit for medical malpractice. In the past, a doctor may have forgone a test to save money if the chances of a patient having a certain disease were remote; today such tests are automatically done so that doctors can protect themselves against mistakes and errors in judgment. Doctors with two years of experience and doctors with twenty years of experience both recognize that testing protects them against the vagaries of distrustful patients, nuisance suits, and perhaps an occasional wrong decision. Tests become part of a permanent record for each patient, thus proving that the doctor has made every attempt to ascertain the underlying problem and to treat it accordingly.

Testing has become so prolific that there are now thousands of types of tests—such as the more than 900 analyses on blood alone—and one hundred or more new tests are invented each year. Dr. Griffith estimates that nearly 10 billion tests are ordered by doctors each year for their patients, costing between $100 billion and $150 billion annually—that's nearly 1 out of every 3 of our healthcare dollars!

GOVERNMENT AND PRIVATE INSURANCE REGULATIONS.
Another factor that points to continued growth in healthcare expenditures is the increase in medical regulations and rules from the federal and state governments, as well as from the thousands of commercial insurance companies. For example, Medicare and Medicaid laws now require many kinds of testing, second opinions, and record-keeping procedures—all aimed at limiting the skyrocketing costs of unnecessary medical care. Nevertheless, the overall effect of many regulations is that they end up adding to the costs they are trying to eliminate.

Many of these regulations are aimed at curbing abuse and fraud, both of which have unfortunately occurred in this otherwise respectable profession. Over the past decade, there have been many reports of doctors who falsely billed Medicare for services not rendered, as well as entire clinics such as one in a major metropolitan area that found people to file false worker's compensation claims supported by a doctor's fake diagnoses of injuries. Naturally, the doctors were keeping the insurance money for themselves until they were caught and prosecuted.

No matter how you look at these trends and figures, you will have a hard time not finding some niche to fill in the healthcare field if you so desire. Healthcare will most certainly continue to grow larger in the decades to come, with more and more services needed by a growing population of Americans, and supplied by an increasing number of healthcare providers. The savvy entrepreneur knows that for each doctor in the profession and each consumer, a corresponding array of service personnel is needed, and therein lies your opportunity!

Overview of Three Healthcare Businesses

Although there are many careers you can enter in the allied medical fields, this book focuses on three that can be run as home-based or small businesses, either on a full-time or part-time basis. Each business offers a moderate to high income potential, and all indications are that each business will remain a solid opportunity over the next decade. Here is an overview of the three businesses to help you understand the essential differences between them before you jump into the specific chapters.

MEDICAL BILLING. Many people have heard about medical billing but are not quite sure what business it is. In a nutshell, medical billing is the business of getting healthcare providers paid. Most of this work involves filing insurance claims on behalf of doctors, chiropractors, therapists, dentists, and other healthcare providers to commercial insurance companies and government agencies such as Medicare and Medicaid. Over the past few years, the most successful medical billing businesses have expanded their services to include what is called "full practice management," meaning that they handle all the bookkeeping and accounting functions for their doctor-clients, including patient statements, recording payments, preparing financial reports, and even advising the physicians on issues such as how to negotiate contracts with the growing number of managed care companies such as HMOs and PPOs that are trying to reign in doctors' fees.

Medical billing has become a "hot" business in the past few years, partially because of the advent and growth of electronic claims. Let's briefly explain this aspect of medical billing. Before computers, filing claims to insurance companies was a tedious and expensive process for doctors. A typical doctor who had several hundred patients, each with his or her own insurance company, was faced with a veritable quagmire in either letting patients file their own claims and waiting to get reimbursed before paying the doctor, or filling out the claims themselves to make sure they got done quickly and that the checks would be mailed directly to them. As a result, many doctors opted for the latter solution and filed the claims for their patients.

The problem was that each insurance company had its own rules and regulations, and, worse, the filing of claims had to be done using annoying paper forms with dozens of little boxes to fill in. Claims had to be either handwritten or typed, and many errors were made in filling out the claims. As a result, getting paid was a nightmare, and many healthcare providers who had agreed to handle claims for their patients simply gave up on collecting some of their money out of frustration or confusion. Some doctors literally lost thousands of dollars per month in unpaid claims.

The nightmare became even more critical for doctors in September 1990, when the federal government decided that Medicare recipients should not have to file their own claims. The government therefore legislated that it was the responsibility of *doctors* to file Medicare claims on behalf of their patients. Since the majority of people who see doctors are elderly, this meant that many doctors were literally swamped with Medicare claims to file, day in and day out.

Fortunately, over the course of the 1980s, more sophisticated software had brought about a new technology called "electronic claims processing" (often abbreviated ECP). With this technology, the doctor's office could use computers, special software, and a modem to handle the claims filing process. Electronic claims processing has many advantages, including simplifying the highly detailed record-keeping and accounting procedures used in medical offices. Most important, electronic claims substantially reduce the time it takes to prepare paper claims and the number of errors made—estimated to be as high as 30 percent—thereby speeding up the time it takes for doctors to receive reimbursements from the private insurance companies and government-run programs.

Unfortunately, many doctors' offices did not make the transition to electronic claims, usually because they did not have the computer equipment needed or the skilled personnel to use the software. In many cases, doctors simply did not understand the benefits of ECP. But in the late 1980s and early 1990s, as the cost of personal computers decreased and the benefits of ECP became more obvious, a new opportunity emerged for entrepreneurs to start independent medical billing businesses. The professional billing service takes over the filing of claims for doctors and moves them into the electronic twentieth century.

As mentioned earlier, handling electronic claims is just one side of running an independent medical billing service. Either right from the outset, or after getting a contract to handle just the claims, many billing services become involved with many other aspects of their clients' accounting needs.

The growth of managed care is the other key fueling independent billing agencies. Billers are literally becoming trusted financial advisors to their doctors, helping them decide the best ways to maintain their income in the face of severe reimbursement cutbacks from insurance companies and the dreaded monster of managed care plans.

Chapter 2 examines the details of starting your own independent medical billing service. You will find in this chapter a comprehensive explanation of how medical billing works, what knowledge and skills are required to run a billing service, and how to get started if you believe this business is for you. You will learn how health insurance works, how doctors' offices operate, and the steps to filing paper versus electronic claims and receiving payments. You will also get an introduction to the complex medical coding systems that you need to understand in processing claims for doctors.

The chapter especially emphasizes three issues that have been evolving since the early 1990s when the first edition of this book came out:

■ The impact of managed care on both doctors and medical billing services. The chapter discusses the growth of HMOs, PPOs, IPAs, POSs, and MSOs and explains how such managed care arrangements are reducing physicians' incomes *and* thus how they are increasing the need for and potential success of independent billing services.

■ The increasing level of sophistication and knowledge that it now takes to be successful in operating an independent medical billing service. Because of the growing complexity of running a doctor's office and the increased scrutiny of insurance companies to control costs, being successful in medical billing now requires a much higher level of insurance industry knowledge, computer skills, and marketing savvy to convince doctors to let you handle their financial affairs. The chapter therefore provides much advice about developing your industry knowledge as well as many inside tips on successful marketing strategies to get clients for your business.

■ How to get into the medical billing business. Because of the popularity of medical billing, many people have invested money to buy software and training without being fully aware of what it takes to be successful in this business. Since I wrote the first edition of this book, literally dozens of people have personally called me to get advice about buying a medical billing "business opportunity" that would train them to get into the business within a few days. This chapter therefore explains how to evaluate the "biz opps" you will probably find out there. Unfortunately, some vendors take advantage of people interested in this profession, leading them to believe that medical billing is a get-rich-quick occupation. They use high-pressure tactics to get people to buy their software and training at extremely high prices. My goal here is to provide some general information on how to evaluate and purchase a good business opportunity that will truly help you succeed. I provide recommendations for vendors to work with and give you warnings about how to recognize unscrupulous business opportunity companies.

You will find in this chapter a large number of personal stories from people who got into medical billing and succeeded. As their stories show, you must work hard to learn this business and become a "medical reimbursement expert." But it doesn't stop there. Even if you begin to be successful, you will need to continue working hard to stay abreast of changes because there are constant new insurance rules and regulations, new technologies that will affect the profession, and new trends in managed care that doctors will want you to explain to them.

CLAIMS ASSISTANCE PROFESSIONAL.   The inverse, or flip side, of a medical billing service is a *claims assistance professional* (often abbreviated CAP, and pronounced "cap" just like the hat). A CAP works with consumers—not doctors. If you are unfamiliar with this profession, it is common to confuse medical billing and claims assistance. The two professions share a large body of knowledge, such as how health insurance works, but they are oriented to different audiences and require very different skills.

CAPs help two types of consumers:

1. Those who must submit their own health insurance claims to their insurance company. Because some doctors do not file insurance claims on behalf of their patients (except in the case of Medicare claims, which, as stated earlier, physicians are required to file), many people must submit their own claims each time they see their doctor, dentist, chiropractor, or psychologist. However, these people are often confused by the filing procedures or they simply want someone to handle the claims for them.

2. Those who have already filed a claim and had it denied or incorrectly paid by their insurance company. This audience is the majority of the CAP market because, knowingly or not, insurance companies

and Medicare make many mistakes when they evaluate claims for payment. Claims are often lost, delayed, underpaid, or completely denied, leaving consumers angry and upset, but not knowing what to do. A CAP therefore reviews all medical invoices and bills and makes sure that the client is not being cheated out of money he or she deserves. The CAP may appeal a denied claim or contest an erroneous bill from a doctor.

In essence, CAPs help the confused, the forlorn, and the just plain busy through the complex maze of the health insurance world. A good CAP is like a skilled tax preparer who assists his or her clients to file tax returns with the goal of maximizing their refunds. In the same sense, a skilled CAP reviews medical bills and payments and tries to maximize both the coverage and the reimbursements each client can obtain from his or her insurance carrier—be it Medicare or a private company.

Today's CAPs must understand doctor's office procedures, managed care, Medicare and Medicaid regulations, and the intricate details of increasingly complex insurance policies that often seem to contain double-talk when it comes to spelling out basic issues such as copayments, deductibles, coordination of benefits, stop-loss limits, and prior authorizations. To be a CAP, you must be exceptionally detail oriented, have good math skills, have excellent negotiation and communication skills, and be able to work well with many kinds of people, from naïve consumers to hard-core naysaying insurance bureaucrats. You must also have an action-oriented, fighting personality that believes in justice for the little guy, as well as perseverance, stick-to-itiveness, and a strong belief in the rights of patients. While running a CAP business does not necessarily require you to become heavily computer literate, you should be familiar with basic computer software so you can use your PC to maintain a database of your clients and word process all your correspondence.

Chapter 3 explains the career of a medical claims assistance professional, including the background and skills you need to get started, and how to market and price your service. You will meet several CAPs who have become successful running their own businesses. As you will see, this is one profession in which the practitioners have a true love for their work that far exceeds the usual and customary dedication found in other professions. Of the three careers in this book, being a CAP is by far the most people oriented.

MEDICAL TRANSCRIPTION SERVICE. The third business covered in this book is medical transcription. In researching this field, hardly an interview went by in which I was not reminded that there is a serious shortage of transcriptionists in the United States. However, medical transcription is a rigorous and technical profession that requires extensive training and often a few years of experience before you can go off on your own. Medical transcriptionists are not just typists or secretaries; their skills are far more complex. They must have a good command of English grammar, *and* know thousands of words of highly technical medical vocabulary, *and* understand the garbled dictations of doctors who eat lunch while they dictate or doctors who have come from many parts of the world to practice in the United States, and for whom English is a second language, *and* be able to type 60 to 90 words per minute (or faster). As you can see, these are serious qualifications that are not easy to come by.

Because of these rigorous requirements though, medical transcription is an extremely valuable profession that is fast becoming a critical area of healthcare management. From routine patient visits and hospitalizations to complex surgeries and psychological exams, physicians are increasingly required by law and by ethics to prepare reports about their patients. In some cases also, such as accidents, lawsuits, and denied medical claims, doctors must prepare documents for insurance companies, police departments, employers, lawyers, and state-funded worker's compensation boards. Finally, in today's era of managed care, increasing numbers of doctors are also required to prepare authorization letters for patients who are referred to specialists outside of their network or HMO, as well as reports back to a primary care physician who is responsible for that patient within the network or HMO.

The transcriptionist's job is not easy. He or she must type up each report accurately from a dictated tape or digital recording, using proper English and the correct medical terminology, spelled correctly. In many cases, the transcriptionist must have reports back to the doctor or hospital within a quick turnaround time that may be as little as a few hours or perhaps one day.

Chapter 4 examines the world of medical transcription and shows you how to obtain training and preparation for this career. Note that, unlike the previous two businesses, which most people can start after just a few months of preparation, medical transcription requires more extensive preparation and education. Some people can enter the business with as little as six months of home study, but others may need one or more years of study if they do not have prior medical background.

Nevertheless, a career in medical transcription can be your ticket to independence, freedom, and financial self-sufficiency. You will meet several people in Chapter 4 who turned to a career in medical transcription with no previous medical background but who were able to achieve their goals within a reasonable time frame.

How to Use This Book

The next three chapters are the heart of this book and contain the essential information about the businesses profiled. Each chapter follows a roughly similar format and is divided into two major sections: **Background** and **Getting Started.**

In the Background section, you will find basic information about the business, including what the business does, how it works, the level of knowledge and skills you'll need, and information on the income and earnings potential. This section includes both the pros and cons of the business so you can truly understand what might await you if you decide to pursue this career. I have attempted to answer the question "Can I make a living doing this?" as well as "Will I enjoy this business?" The Background section ends with an informal 15-question checklist you can use to assess your feelings about the business and your chances of personal satisfaction and success.

In the second section of the chapter, Getting Started, you will find detailed information about how and where to find training, advice on hardware and software issues (as appropriate), tips for how to market your new business and determine your prices, and a final section on overcoming common start-up problems in that business. If after reading the first part of the chapter, you have decided that the business is not for you, you can probably skip or skim this second part of the chapter.

Scattered throughout each chapter are various "sidebar" features, based on interviews I conducted with people engaged in the business, or containing extra explanatory information. You will find many of these sidebars to contain the most valuable information in the chapter: personal stories of people who, just like you, decided to make that business their career. There is often no greater wisdom than that of someone who marched before you, although each person's experience will vary depending on his or her prior background, location, personal talent, and luck. Nevertheless, most of us can take inspiration from others who have made a success out of their own ventures.

The final chapter presents 10 steps to becoming an entrepreneur. To make remembering these steps easier, they are organized around a mnemonic device (a memory aid): DREAM BIG for $ & "smile face". Each letter or symbol in this acronym stands for one issue or activity you'll need to focus on as you get your business under way. This chapter is intended to serve as a reminder to seriously consider your decision, because many people think only about the income and earning potential without reflecting on whether they have the skills to be entrepreneurial or even whether they will truly enjoy the work they've chosen. I therefore urge you to read this last chapter where you'll find wisdom gleaned from many experts in the self-employment field.

A Note on the Choice of Businesses

I have chosen these three businesses for a variety of reasons. First, technically speaking, none requires a hard-core academic background prior to preparing for the business, such as a B.A. in biology, an R.N. degree, or an M.B.A. in health administration. Each business is more or less approachable by any hard-working, dedicated individual who has the entrepreneurial drive to operate his or her own business.

This is not to suggest that you can read this book today and be in business tomorrow. As in any profession or business, the more skills and background you have that relate to the business, the better off you are. If you have ever worked in a physician's office or an insurance company, or if you were a nurse or physician's assistant, or if you have had accounting or bookkeeping experience, or even computer consulting experience, you will have a leg up on those people who come into the healthcare field with absolutely no related background.

But I also want to convey that these skills are quite learnable. Most readers of this book should not have a problem learning about medical billing, claims assistance work, or medical transcription if they commit to studying the necessary subjects and make a sincere effort to run their business in a professional way.

Second, as mentioned earlier in this chapter, I also chose these three businesses because they appear to offer good potential for both personal satisfaction and a decent livelihood. While people are always reluctant to discuss their incomes, everyone interviewed for this book was optimistic and upbeat about what they were earning. Most answered affirmatively when asked if someone working full time at this profession could earn $30,000 to $60,000, or more.

None of these businesses is, however, a get-rich-quick operation (there are really none of those anyway). All require hard work, dedication, and even ambition, and there is still no guarantee. Running your own business is tough. You are the receptionist, marketing manager, sales agent, and professional running the shop. You *are* the business, and you will most likely need to work long hours to build up your company so that you are earning a decent income.

Last, I chose these businesses because I expect that they will be around for some time, and your initial investment of time and money to get into them will pay dividends for years. However, technology can change our world in the flash of an instant, and the medical field is particularly subject to technological advances. For example, voice recognition software is getting better and better and may change the medical transcription profession some day soon. Perhaps 5 or 10 years from now, doctors will be able to dictate their notes to a computer and specialized voice recognition software will automatically convert the speech into a perfect document. Politics too may change these professions. Perhaps our country will adopt a national healthcare plan that more or less abolishes health insurance claims, and both the medical billing and claims assistance businesses will fall by the wayside. Many changes are possible, but in reality, such changes are quite doubtful at this writing, so I feel confident in recommending these businesses to you.

Using Your PC

The title of this book suggests that these three businesses extensively utilize computers. However, the extent of computer usage varies greatly. In descending order of computerization, medical billing is very computer intensive and requires a fair knowledge of hardware and software. Medical transcription is less computer intensive and generally requires only a level of sophistication to operate basic word-processing software. Medical claims assistance turned out to be an industry that is only barely computerized, because, as you will see, insurance companies accept electronic claims only from doctors, not from individuals filing one claim at a time. A CAP must handle claims using the old tried-and-true paper forms.

In all, the computer skills necessary to be in these industries are not difficult to learn. Nevertheless, as you will see in each chapter, getting into one of these businesses means that you will likely need to do extensive marketing, so you can benefit from knowing how to use your PC to perform many general business functions. For example, if you can operate simple desktop publishing software, such as *Microsoft Publisher*, you can design your own brochures, newsletters, fliers, and other marketing documents. Developing such items yourself can often save you money because you can avoid hiring an outside designer or desktop publisher.

Similarly, knowing how to use contact management software, such as *Lotus Organizer* or *Symantec ACT!*, can help you keep better track of your appointments, schedules, meetings, and discussions with clients. If you bill by the hour, it helps to know how to use time management programs such as *Timeslips* to keep track of your productivity and to invoice your clients accurately.

Think of it this way: in today's market, if you are not using a computer to your best advantage, your competitor probably is, and that means you are likely losing opportunities or contracts that could be yours. So, regardless of which of the three businesses in this book you may start, you would be wise to use technology for all your important business functions. Throughout this book, I will refer you to a few such general business productivity programs that I believe to be the most useful.

Doing More Than One Businesses

Can you start more than one business? Most certainly. Several people I interviewed for this book practice two of these businesses at a time, particularly medical billing plus either CAP work or transcription.

For example, Linda Noel of Linda's Billing Service in Los Angeles does medical billing and medical transcription. As she explained, "I offer a personalized service which is the key to getting clients. It helps me be a full service agency, handling two areas of need for my clients." Linda's company is profiled in a sidebar in Chapter 2.

Lori A. Donnelly, founder of Donnelly Benefit Consultants in Bethlehem, Pennsylvania, likewise offers two businesses. Lori started out as a claims assistance professional and built that up as her primary business for six years. However, she eventually moved into medical billing when, quite by accident, an ambulance company saw one of Lori's advertisements in a newspaper and asked her to train someone to handle its claims processing. In thinking over the proposal, Lori realized that given how much she knew about insurance claims from her CAP business, she might as well do medical billing herself rather than train someone. So the ambulance company became her first client, and Lori continued from that point getting several more clients. She now has an ongoing medical billing practice that handles four doctors, and a CAP business that handles as many as 50 clients per month.

In general, it is wise to begin one business first and get it off the ground before expanding into another business. You don't want to confuse your clientele about which business you are really in. A doctor will be less likely to hire you if you walk into the office and say something like, "I am an expert in medical billing and would like to discuss how my company can improve your cash flow from insurance claims...but, oh, if you're not interested in that, I am also an expert transcriptionist." If you decide to offer more than one business, let it evolve over time.

As in any entrepreneurial venture, the sky is the limit for the ambitious, hardworking, and serious person. Whatever your goals, if you have an interest in the health professions, you will surely find something enticing for you in this book!

2

Medical Billing Services

Electronic medical billing services are riding a wave of change in U.S. healthcare. As the practice of medicine becomes more complex, and as insurance companies work overtime to figure out new ways to control costs, independent medical billing services are taking on even greater importance in the office operations of healthcare providers across the country.

In this chapter, we'll look at the basics of running a medical billing service, the pros and cons of getting into the business, and how to get started should you decide this field is for you. You'll learn about the complexities of the health insurance business, the increasing computerization of healthcare, and the advantages of electronic vs. paper claims. Most important, you'll get a sense of the emerging transition from traditional health insurance to managed care and how this revolution is affecting doctors professionally and financially. Through the sidebars in this chapter, you'll also meet many people who have started a home-based medical billing service. From their stories, you'll learn inside tips and advice on how to get your business off the ground and how to make it successful.

Medical billing is an excellent career or business opportunity for people with backgrounds in any of the following areas: accounting, law, computers (especially software), management, professional consulting, and general office administration. Of course, if you have experience working inside a doctor's office, you may already be quite familiar with this field, but it is not necessary to have this type of background to succeed. You'll learn why these backgrounds are so useful as you read the chapter.

Section I: Background

What Is a Medical Billing Service?

What exactly do medical billing services do? In simple terms, the main role of a medical billing service is to help healthcare providers of all kinds to get paid. Note that the term "healthcare provider" is the generic term commonly used to include medical doctors (M.Ds) of all types as well as chiropractors, physical therapists, dentists, psychologists, ambulance companies, suppliers of durable medical equipment (DME), and medical laboratories. (For simplicity in this chapter, the terms "doctor" and "physician" will sometimes be used interchangeably with "provider.")

A medical billing service essentially consists of two activities:

- Filing claims to the hundreds of private insurance companies and government-sponsored insurance programs (such as Medicare or Medicaid) in order to obtain reimbursement for medical services rendered to patients; and

- Sending statements to patients to obtain any necessary additional payments that their insurance has not covered.

In addition, a billing service that handles patient statements will often get involved in many other financial activities on behalf of its clients, such as managing the complete bookkeeping and accounting for the office, processing secondary insurance claims, following up on unpaid bills (soft collections), keeping track of accounts receivable owed to the doctor, producing reports to help a physician assess his or her financial status, and many other related tasks.

The distinction between these two types of activities is important to note. Some billing services just file claims and are often referred to as "just claims" businesses. In contrast, other billers handle the entire gamut of printing patient statements and maintaining all accounting and are therefore referred to as "full practice management" firms.

If you are interested in starting an independent medical billing service, you can choose to be either type of business; which one you choose depends on your background and skills, your goals, and your ability to get clients. This decision will be discussed in greater detail later in the chapter.

Why Is Medical Billing Attracting So Much Attention?

Medical billing services have actually been around for decades. As healthcare became more expensive in the United States between the 1940s and 1960s, and more people received health insurance plans from their employers, doctors had to resort to collecting from insurance companies and/or invoicing their patients. For this reason, there has long been a "cottage" industry of outside billing services that handled the bookkeeping for doctors and other types of healthcare providers. These billing services ranged from CPAs who specialized in medical practice management to women at home who did bookkeeping for a few doctors.

However, the medical billing profession has attracted a great deal of entrepreneurial attention in recent years for two reasons: (1) the growing feasibility and use of computers in "electronic data interchange" (EDI), which allows billing to be done from anywhere, and (2) the increasing complexity of healthcare that is driving doctors to seek help in managing their businesses. As part of the overview of this chapter, it is useful to look at each of these issues before going into the details about how to get started in your medical billing business. You cannot understand the medical billing industry without considering these two forces.

THE COMPUTERIZATION OF HEALTHCARE—THE EARLY YEARS Computers entered the health arena in the 1950s when more than 60 million Americans began receiving from their employers or buying their own health insurance to cover hospitalizations, surgical expenses, and physician care. To expedite the billing of health insurance claims, various data-processing companies with large mainframe computers made arrangements with hospitals and large medical practices to handle their claims. This was the beginning of computerized claims filing. Unfortunately, progress in expanding the number of claims filed by computer remained quite slow for the next 30 years, largely because of technological impediments in computer hardware and software, and a lack of vision of the role that computers could play in the process.

In the 1980s, several software companies began developing the capability to record claims using the new personal computers that were coming out at that time. This small step was largely focused on getting doctors to automate their offices. The manual typewriter could easily be replaced by a computer that could store patient records and invoices. Unfortunately, too many problems plagued the industry to allow it to take off: hardware limitations, bug-filled programs, slipshod software and hardware vendors, doctors who didn't understand the value of computerization, and dependence on floppy disks or magnetic tape that still had to be mailed to insurance companies.

In addition, one of the other major deterrents to computerization was that the format for computerizing claims was never standardized. This meant that doctors could not send a universal claim form to all insurance companies; each insurer had its own data format. A few software companies tried to resolve this problem by establishing themselves as "clearinghouses" or routing stations where claims of all kinds could be sent for "translation and editing," then forwarded to the appropriate insurer. Because of this problem, the conversion of the entire industry to a uniform "data interchange" standard remained a distant goal.

MEDICARE SPURS ON COMPUTERIZATION   The real impetus to continue computerizing the healthcare industry came from the skyrocketing costs of services from hospitals and doctors from the 1970s to the 1980s, especially in regard to medical care for the elderly. The major proponent of computerization turned out to be HCFA, the federal government agency responsible for administering Medicare, which is the program legislated under President Johnson to provide healthcare benefits for the elderly and certain others. The Medicare program took effect in 1966.

Between 1970 and 1980, HCFA realized that it would soon be faced with enormous growth in Medicare enrollment. By 1980, HCFA was already processing several hundred million claims on paper, and the task was clearly expensive and time consuming. In 1983, the agency began an aggressive campaign to shift hospitals and physicians to electronically transmitted claims to reduce costs and eliminate the backlog of paper claims. One of its smartest moves was to encourage the development of a standardized set of diagnosis codes and procedure codes so that doctors could easily list a patient's condition and what services they performed.

These codes replaced a hodge-podge system of coding that had previously blocked standardizing the electronic claims filing process.

As it turned out, HCFA's insight became the driving force for the industry. Its projections about future growth were right on target. By the end of the 1980s, Medicare was receiving nearly 500 million claims per year, 80 percent of which were from individual physicians, suppliers, and laboratories on behalf of their patients. Fortunately, Medicare's efforts to foster electronic claims processing began to pay off. By 1989, it was receiving 36 percent of its claims electronically; by 1991, this figure increased to 50 percent. In recent years, the percentage has been steadily rising, but it is still not 100 percent despite the easy availability of personal computers. At the time of this writing, HCFA was encouraging all insurance carriers (companies contracted by HCFA to process claims for Medicare Part B) to push for electronic filing from every doctor. Unfortunately, HCFA can only suggest this goal, because Congress has yet to pass a law requiring it. This means that hundreds of millions of Medicare claims still are done via paper claim forms mailed to the insurance intermediaries for processing.

COMMERCIAL INSURANCE COMPANIES SLOWLY JUMP ON BANDWAGON   Needless to say, millions of Americans are not part of Medicare and have their insurance through any of the hundreds of private insurance companies in the country or through a self-insured plan from their employer, often administered by a third party to whom the claims are sent. Although commercial and private insurance also generate hundreds of millions of claims per year, these insurance companies moved very slowly toward electronic claims. In fact, in the late 1970s and early 1980s, most private insurance companies resisted electronic claims, probably because of the expense to computerize their systems when the economic benefits were not clear.

The first significant support for electronic claims from commercial insurance companies came in 1981 when 11 of the biggest firms formed an association called the National Electronic Information Corp. (NEIC) to serve as a central clearinghouse for claims. By the late 1980s, NEIC began to play a stronger role and invited a larger segment of commercial insurers to join in taking claims electronically. Unfortunately, most commercial carriers still reacted cautiously. By 1990, although there were an estimated 3 billion claims filed annually to all insurers from hospitals, doctors, laboratories, and pharmacies, it was estimated that only 6 percent to 8 percent of commercial insurance claims from physicians were processed electronically, a mere drop in the bucket.

1990: WATERSHED YEAR FOR ELECTRONIC CLAIMS Electronic claims filing was given its most forceful push when Congress issued a directive that took effect in September 1990 requiring *all* physicians to file claims on behalf of their Medicare patients. Under the previous policy, doctors did not have to do so, and many left the paperwork to the patients to handle. Under the new policy, however, the burden for getting reimbursements from Medicare fell to the doctors.

Finding themselves suddenly deluged with claims that would not get reimbursed unless they did the filing themselves, many physicians were simply not prepared. In some cases, their offices were not computerized; and in other cases, they simply could not keep up with the volume of claims they had to file. Many physicians eagerly sought the services of outside billing experts.

This 1990 directive thus effectively started the revolution in medical billing, opening the door to many small and home-based businesses that foresaw an opportunity to provide a specialized service to doctors who could no longer manage their claims. Armed with more sophisticated hardware and software, some of these entrepreneurs began selling doctors the computers, software, and modems that would allow them to do claims filing on their own. More important, many other entrepreneurs saw an opportunity to sell claims filing, especially electronic claims filing, as a service they would perform for doctors. Thus originated the recent focus on independent medical billing services as a viable entrepreneurial endeavor.

ELECTRONIC VERSUS PAPER CLAIMS You are probably wondering at this point exactly what is involved in electronic claims filing. Let's describe how the process works and why it makes sense in today's health-care environment.

Before electronic claims, doctors and insurance companies used a slew of confusing paper forms to communicate with one other. Unfortunately, filing claims in this way was an enormously tedious process, usually performed by typing out and mailing paper forms to the various insurance companies covering the doctor's patients. The problem was, many insurance companies had their own paper forms, and filling them in often led to errors that would cause the claim to be rejected. This meant that doctors were not paid until the claim was corrected and sent back for processing. Even when a doctor's office purchased a computer and billing software, the office often simply recorded the patient information in the computer but printed the claims out on paper and mailed them to Medicare or the private insurance company. This process still did not ensure that the claims were error free, nor did it save much in the way of time and money.

With the advent of high-quality billing software and high-speed modems, the solution to this problem was clearly to make the process electronic. In simple terms, rather than fill out a paper form when a patient visits a doctor, electronic claims filing uses the computer throughout the entire process. All a biller needs to do is to type in the basic patient information, indicate date of service, place of service, diagnosis, and the procedures performed, then push a few buttons and send the claim via modem to the insurance company (sometimes via an intermediate routing station, which will be explained later) where it can be evaluated for payment.

The advantages of electronic claims over paper claims are significant. First, whereas a paper claim passes through many hands and is transferred from one location to the next via "snail mail," an electronic claim is keyboarded just once and can be sent from the doctor's or billing agency's office in seconds via modem to the insurance company. Paper claims also require a number of intermediary steps at the insurance company's office, because they need to be sorted, microfilmed, and keyboarded into the insurer's computer system. Electronic claims therefore save an enormous amount of time and labor.

Second, electronic claims save money in overhead costs in both preparation and processing time. Some estimates indicate that electronic filing saves from $3.00 to $12.00 per claim at the doctor's office, because of the speed at which they can be done and the reduction in errors. In essence, electronic claims save wasted salary that a billing clerk earns while filing claims by paper, claims that often contain errors and are rejected and returned. Meanwhile, at the other end, insurers are also recognizing that electronic claims save them money. HCFA estimates that it literally saves as much as $.50 per claim, amounting to hundreds of millions of dollars per year.

Third, electronic claims reduce the rejection rate because of fewer errors. Some estimates indicate that nearly one-third of paper claims contain errors and are rejected by insurers, because of either simple typing mistakes or coding errors made at the physician's office. Since a claim contains dozens of "fields" or units of information (name, address, policy number, diagnosis, procedures performed, etc.), it is easy to understand how such errors occur so frequently. Even worse, many rejected claims are never reprocessed at the doctor's office, because the billing clerk does not know what the mistake was or how to correct it. Some doctors have literally found entire desk drawers filled with rejected claims that were never resubmitted—amounting to tens of thousands of dollars in lost revenues.

In contrast, electronic claims cut down on rejected claims in a number of ways. Most billing software for electronic claims permanently stores a record for each patient a doctor has, so constant rekeying of this basic information is minimized, reducing the chances of mistakes and missing information. In addition, most high-quality medical billing software contains logical intelligence so that it can perform "error checking" on the claims. For example, the software can easily verify that all the blanks in the claim form are filled in, that the correct number of digits are used in each field (such as an ID #), and that a numeric code is not used where an alphabetic entry should be. Some software is also smart enough to catch illogical matches between diagnosis codes and procedure codes, such as a code indicating the doctor performed a hysterectomy on 10-year-old female. These kinds of mistakes really do happen!

Furthermore, as indicated earlier, many medical billers send their electronic claims first to a clearinghouse, whose software also checks them for errors and formats them according to the specifications of the insurance company to which they will be routed. Most clearinghouses provide an added service: If there is an error in the claim, the billing person can find out immediately—rather than weeks later by mail—because the clearinghouse electronically notifies him or her within hours or days that the claim contains a mistake. In this way, the claim can be corrected and resubmitted quickly.

All these advantages add up to a crucial benefit for healthcare providers: *electronic claims get processed more quickly at the insurance companies and are therefore paid much faster.* In other words, doctors can get paid sooner rather than later because the claims can be keyboarded more quickly, have fewer mistakes due to the editing and error checking they go through, and arrive earlier at the insurance companies. While paper claims often take 30 to 60 days to get paid, even if they are clean (i.e., without errors), electronic claims are usually paid within a few weeks, and sometimes in as little as 7 working days by commercial insurance companies. Medicare also gives priority status to electronic claims over paper claims. Since 1994, Medicare's policy has been that a clean claim that has been filed electronically may be paid in 14 days (but not before) and no later than 19 days, whereas paper claims must be held for a minimum of 27 days before they can be paid. (Note that, technically speaking, Medicare and insurance companies could pay electronic claims very fast, such as in just one or two days, but they intentionally sit on the claims for a minimum of 14 days to take advantage of the "float" on money. More will be said about this strategy later.)

The fast payment of electronic claims is critical to the financial survival of most doctors. Since a doctor usually gets as much as 80 percent of his or her gross earnings from Medicare or commercial insurance reimbursements, speeding up the payments can significantly improve cash flow. After all, wouldn't you rather wait just 20 to 25 days to get your insurance payments rather than 45 to 60 days?

Figures 2-1 and 2-2 contrast the process and timing for paper claims vs. electronic claims.

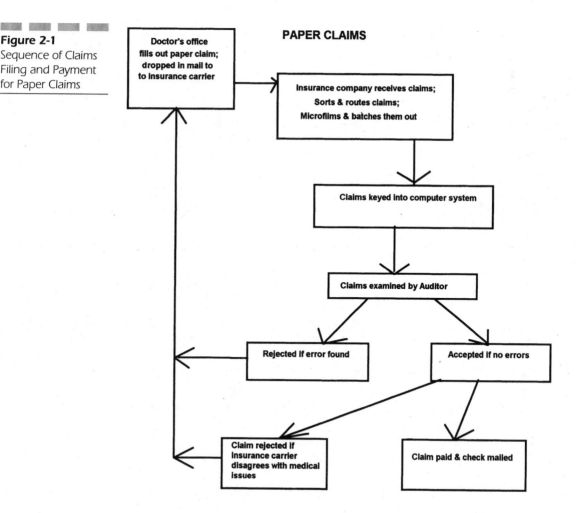

Figure 2-1

Sequence of Claims
Filing and Payment
for Paper Claims

PAPER CLAIMS

Doctor's office fills out paper claim; dropped in mail to to insurance carrier

Insurance company receives claims; Sorts & routes claims; Microfilms & batches them out

Claims keyed into computer system

Claims examined by Auditor

Rejected if error found

Accepted if no errors

Claim rejected if insurance carrier disagrees with medical issues

Claim paid & check mailed

Figure 2-2
Sequence of Claims
Filing and Payment
for Electronic Claims

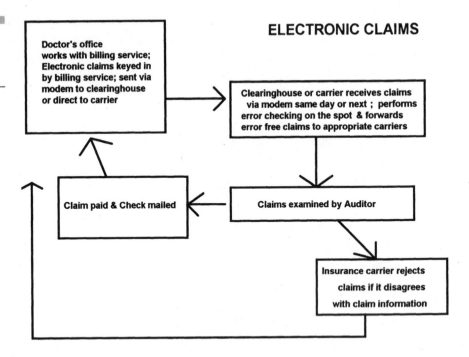

ELECTRONIC CLAIMS

Doctor's office works with billing service; Electronic claims keyed in by billing service; sent via modem to clearinghouse or direct to carrier

Clearinghouse or carrier receives claims via modem same day or next ; performs error checking on the spot & forwards error free claims to appropriate carriers

Claim paid & Check mailed

Claims examined by Auditor

Insurance carrier rejects claims if it disagrees with claim information

The Increasing Complexity of Healthcare

Electronic claims filing is only half the story behind the revolution in medical billing. The second factor driving the potential for independent medical billing services is the astonishing complexity of healthcare today, particularly in regard to the relationship between care and cost.

On one hand, the United States has long had the best medical care in the world and is capable of being the leader in taking care of its population. University and private research labs daily discover the secrets to conquering diseases of all kinds and invent new technologies to cure human ailments. Few doubt that U.S. doctors are the best trained and most sophisticated in the world. While some doctors go into business solely to make money, the vast majority love their work and eagerly want to take care of their patients to the best of their ability. For each patient seen with an illness or problem, they want to do whatever is necessary to cure the person and make sure he or she survives.

On the other hand, over the past 20 years, the cost of healthcare has skyrocketed far beyond belief, increasing at a rate ranging from 8 percent to 14 percent *per year* between 1980 and 1995. Worse, the projections for the

Business Profile: Jim Russell and Rich Russell

Jim Russell and Rich Russell are brothers who love music. Both have long been professional opera singers—but now they are also medical billers. They started their home-based billing business in 1995 after deciding that they needed to have a more consistent income to support their families, and more regular hours as well. They read the first edition of this book and decided to go into medical billing, purchasing a business opportunity from Medical Management Software, owned by Merry Schiff. Their firm, Hudson Valley Practice Management, is located in Rockland County, New York.

Getting their first client took some time (as it does for many people who enter the business). Jim explained to me:

> It took nearly five months to get the first client; I believe our approach was too soft; we did a direct mail campaign but did not follow up with calls.
> Then we began cold calling with a goal of just getting an appointment to see the doctor and give ourselves a chance to do a presentation about the advantages of electronic claims. Most of the doctors had heard about ECP, but had not thought of converting.

Their first client was an audiologist, and since then some of the doctors who had received their direct mail pieces have also come on board. They now have more than half-a-dozen clients, including a social worker, a podiatrist, a chiropractor, and an ambulance service. Jim points out that their clients saw immediate results: "Before we took over, Medicare was taking five weeks to two months to pay, but with electronic claims, my clients get paid within three weeks." Jim also says that a friend of his who works at one of the largest insurance companies in the area, MetroHealth, tells him that the claims examiners get pulled off paper claims anytime the electronic claims department has a backlog. This shows the priority given to electronic claims in that company.

Jim and Rich charge from $3.00 to $3.50 per claim, except for the ambulance service, for which they charge $15.00 per claim. Jim explained that there is a good market among rural volunteer ambulance services that typically don't bill for insurance reimbursement because they are community funded. Jim seeks them out and shows them how his service can at least earn them money so that their public funding is replenished. It's a win/win situation for them both.

If you are doing just claims on a per claim fee basis, Jim recommends that you give much thought to the nature of your client's business. For example, a therapist who can bill for up to six patient visits on one claim form (with each visit averaging $90 to $100) is happy to pay you $3.00 or even $5.00 to do the work. In contrast, Jim points out that an optometrist who gets only $6.00 for eyeglasses isn't going to give you half his income for filing the claim. In short, it is useful to think about what type of doctor you are approaching and how his or her fees are structured.

After one year, Jim and Rich are discovering that doing just claims is not sufficient. Several of their clients are smaller practices, such as a social worker who does not own a computer nor does she have an interest in learning to use one. As a result, Jim and Rich are now moving toward full practice management for her. They send out patient invoices and they produce special financial reports to help her see her cash flow. Jim and Rich expect their medical billing business to go from just claims to full practice management for most of their clients in the near future.

future continue to show advancing costs. As noted in Chapter 1, the National Health Expenditure is expected to rise an average of 8 percent per year between 1996 and 2005.

This dichotomy between what doctors are capable of doing versus the need to control costs cannot be underestimated. The conflict is causing profound changes in our healthcare system, from the way consumers choose their healthcare to the way even the best doctors practice medicine. We are no longer living in the 1950s when the good family doctor made housecalls, nor are we living in the 1980s when doctors would not hesitate to perform test after test to find out what might be wrong with a patient. The 1990s has created the dawning of a new era in healthcare!

Needless to say, the most critical change is that insurance companies and Medicare are seeking to contain costs as much as possible. Doctors are being squeezed more and more to cut corners wherever and whenever they can. When they get a new patient, doctors must verify what insurance benefits that person has so they won't perform a service the person is not entitled to receive. When they decide on a treatment, they must make absolutely sure the patient needs it before doing it, often submitting their diagnosis and treatment strategy to a review panel within the patient's insurance company or health maintenance organization, which has the final word. In some instances, doctors are even told to avoid the use of expensive medical technology until the final moment.

When it comes to handling their billing, doctors are being asked to produce more paperwork justifying their fees, and to be more rigorous in specifying their diagnosis. For example, the 1996 numeric coding system used to indicate the doctor's diagnosis breaks down each illness into many detailed subcategories. It is no longer sufficient for a doctor to indicate on a claim form that the patient has diabetes; the claim form must use a specific code that tells the insurance company if the patient has diabetes with renal manifestations or diabetes with ophthalmic manifestations, and each one of these codes has "modifiers" to even more specifically identify the manifestation. A doctor practically needs a master's degree in medical coding today to please the insurance companies!

It is not an understatement to suggest that the practice of medicine has become a schizophrenic profession. On one hand, most doctors want and need to focus on the art of medicine, staying constantly abreast of new cures, new drugs, new medical technology, new treatments plans, and new research that can benefit their patients. This takes time; most doctors would truly prefer to see patients, read research and case studies, and perhaps take an occasional day off at home. Unfortunately, most doctors are being forced to spend inordinate amounts of their time paying attention to the *business* of medicine, lest they lose money. They must stay current with the rules and regulations of Medicare and commercial insurance reimbursement. They must understand how to code their invoices properly. And they must make sure they don't perform a service that their patient's insurance company won't allow. In short, these are not always good times to be a doctor!

To make matters worse, many doctors are losing income. In the boom years of the 1980s, when healthcare was rising at 10 percent or more per year, it was not unusual for a general practitioner to make between $200,000 and $250,000 per year, while many specialists made from $300,000 to $500,000. Today, most doctors can no longer maintain these incomes—or even a reasonable income—because of declining insurance reimbursements and increasing amounts of lost fees because of denied claims.

Under the rubric of containing costs, many doctors are literally being forced to become part of a Health Maintenance Organization (HMO), a Preferred Provider Organization (PPO), or another of the many forms of "managed care" networks. We examine these types of arrangements in greater detail later, but for now suffice it to say that managed care organizations are trimming doctors' incomes to the bone. Some managed care groups simply buy out a doctor's practice and pay him or her a modest salary to work onsite; others allow doctors to remain independent in their own offices but force them to accept fees that amount to as little as 15 cents on the dollar compared to what they formerly charged.

The significance of today's revolution in U.S. healthcare is enormous for anyone interested in medical billing. As doctors continue to fall under the cost gun and lose control of their practices and their incomes, they are increasingly turning to "professional practice managers," people who have the expertise to help them run the business side of their practice. This is where a skilled medical billing professional has an opportunity. A medical billing professional who has in-depth knowledge of the health insurance industry and reimbursement issues, a high level of familiarity with medical coding, reasonable computer skills, and the ability to handle money and to do accurate financial record keeping and projections can be a true savior to increasing numbers of today's busy healthcare providers.

You may be asking why the doctor's office staff can't handle all this for the doctor. Isn't that what he or she is paying them for? The truth is that the complexity and bureaucracy of running a medical practice go far beyond the capabilities of most office personnel. Obviously, some doctors' offices have a skilled billing person who has been on staff for 5, 10, or more years and so may understand Medicare and private insurance reimbursement issues. This kind of person may have even helped the office become computerized and he or she has learned the software, gone to coding classes, and attended Medicare seminars to stay abreast of reimbursement rules and regulations.

However, it is far more common that doctors' offices are staffed by people who do not have such skills or backgrounds. They are not experts in coding, filing claims, insurance regulations, or the ins and outs of managed care. Many such people don't know how to use a computer in a sophisticated way, such as required by medical billing and practice management software. Doctors' offices typically have a constant turnover of personnel, so there is little opportunity for a billing clerk to master the complexities of billing and insurance reimbursement if he or she stays for only eight months or a year. In some cases, a low-paid billing staff person has little motivation to file claims correctly or to follow up on unpaid claims and mistakes. As pointed out earlier, many doctors literally have $10,000 to $50,000 in outstanding claims in a drawer that were once rejected and never reprocessed correctly. Doctors have to write off this lost income. (The term "write off" means that the money is removed from their projected income on the balance sheet, by crediting what had been debited. It does not mean that doctors get a tax write-off for the lost income.)

Dr. Richard Wunneburger, founder and president of InfoHealth (a division of Synaps Corporation), a Texas software firm that produces and sells medical claims and practice management software and training, knows firsthand the problems that have eroded the joy of practicing medicine in the past decade. Richard was himself a physician in a small multidoctor practice in Colorado when he realized that he and his partners could not keep up with getting their claims filed and paid correctly. Being technically inclined, Dr. Wunneburger therefore learned computer programming, wrote his own software, and eventually went on to found InfoHealth to sell his software to doctors and independent medical billing services.

But as Dr. Wunneburger points out, even the best software is not enough, because most physicians and office staffs are not equipped to keep up with the business of healthcare and the complexities of health insurance. As he told me,

The patient care side of medicine is changing dramatically and rapidly today; most doctors want to take care of their patients and learn new medical technology, but physicians today need to become very sophisticated about the business of healthcare. In fact, the need for business knowledge is almost outdistancing the doctor's time and ability to practice medicine. Much of the business knowledge required has become so complicated and technical that a typical office staff cannot keep up with that knowledge and take care of their patients at the same time. Today's doctors have to depend more and more on business professionals. In my software company, we get a tremendous amount of support calls not about our software, but about the business issues. The truth is, doctors have chosen to be doctors but it's difficult to be a doctor and a businessman.

WHITE KNIGHTS: PROFESSIONAL BILLING SERVICES As you can see, there are two significant forces driving medical billing: the increasing benefits of filing electronically, which most doctors are still not doing, and the growing complexities of managing a practice in the face of tremendous pressures from insurance companies and the government to control costs. This is truly a time of opportunity for the savvy entrepreneur who is willing to work hard to become a true medical billing professional. Let's examine in greater detail now what you need to learn if you want to get into the business.

How Billing Services Work

To understand the details of medical billing and what you need to know to get into the business, I have divided the information into five sections:

- The traditional private health insurance industry (commercial insurance, self-insured plans, the Blues)
- The increasing role of managed care plans (HMOs, IPAs, PPOs, POSs, MSOs, etc.)
- The public health insurance programs (Medicare, Medicaid, Champus, Worker's Comp.)
- The operation of a typical medical office: paper claims versus electronic claims
- Advanced practice management functions done by billing agencies

Whatever your background or previous experience, I suggest you read each of these sections to be sure you have a complete understanding of the issues you will invariably deal with if you enter medical billing. This information is critical to your success, and it may take some time to fully understand if you do not have a medical or insurance background. You

Business Profile: Dave Shipton

Dave Shipton is the perfect example of a white knight medical biller. Dave started in medical billing in 1992, after Defense Department cutbacks eliminated his job and he found himself in his mid-50s seeking a new career. Dave originally formed his company, Business Medical Services, with a partner who had a medical background as a respiratory therapist, while Dave had extensive computer skills from nearly 35 years in the Air Force and as a special operations trainer in the aircraft industry. After one year though, his partner decided to leave to take a "real" job. Dave quickly realized that he had to master both sides of the job if he was to succeed. He applied himself and learned everything he could about health insurance reimbursement, coding, and the operation of a medical practice. He had originally purchased software from a business opportunity vendor but was disappointed with its clearinghouse and eventually switched to the software produced by Synaps, the company owned by Dr. Richard Wunneburger, mentioned earlier.

In the course of the next four years, Dave proceeded to build his company to the point of handling full practice management for eight medical practices, most of which included multiple doctors. Over this time, Dave became a trusted advisor to nearly every one of his clients because of his expertise in understanding billing and the effects of managed care on their practices. Because of his knowledge, he handles all insurance reimbursement issues for them, from filing claims and recording payments, to comparing fee schedules to be sure they are being paid accurately, to advising them how to maximize their earnings with special reports he prepares for them.

In particular, Dave closely follows the trends set by the HMOs and PPOs that have moved into his area, seeking out doctors to become part of their networks. He even guides his clients into knowing which managed care organizations to join, and which to avoid. When I spoke with Dave, he was even helping one of his clients, a pain management clinic with several doctors, to prepare a presentation to obtain the contract from a major insurance company to handle all of their subscribers who had chronic pain. Dave had played a leading role in finding the contact for the presentation and in preparing the bid to get the business for his client.

Dave agrees that the billing business is definitely changing. He says,

> I started out doing just claims for my first few clients, charging strictly on a per claim basis. In fact, I still have one doctor for whom I just do claims filing at $3.00 per claim, but now all my other doctors want me to handle as much as I can for them. I literally train some of my clients who are new doctors how to manage their practice. From me, they learn how to verify insurance coverages, how to get patients to sign payment coverage sheets, and even how to prepare their superbills.

Dave adds that the key to the business is building trust. Doctors have to believe that you can truly help them. "I consider this business a partnership," Dave says. "If you don't have that kind of relationship, you are just another biller."

Dave's advice is, "If you don't like hard work, don't get into this business." He adheres to a credo used by Calvin Coolidge: "Nothing in this world can take the place of persistence." It seems as if Dave's philosophy has paid off for him.

may also want to consult other sources of information, as this material can only skim the surface of many of these issues. A list of additional references and resources is presented in the section on training later in the chapter (page 120) and in Appendix A.

The Private Health Insurance Industry

Although you are probably somewhat familiar with the healthcare industry as a consumer, as a billing professional, you must have a sophisticated knowledge of it, especially the relationship between doctors and insurance companies. With literally thousands of different insurance programs in this country, and a constant stream of new ones, developing expertise in insurance reimbursement is a critical factor in your success.

Health insurance can be divided into two general categories: private and public. Private health insurance is offered by hundreds of large commercial companies. Private insurance also includes Blue Cross and Blue Shield plans that are typically run on a not-for-profit basis. Another major form of private insurance are self-insured plans, a type of group coverage usually sponsored by an employer. Rather than pay premiums to an insurer who bears the risk, the employer sets aside money on its own to pay the claims of its employees. Because of the sheer amount of paperwork, many employers hire what is called a "third party administrator" (TPA) to administer their self-insured plan. The administrator is sometimes an insurance company but could also be a professional management firm. Such contractual arrangements are also known as administrative services only (ASOs). A variation of ASOs are MPPs, "minimum premium plans." These are plans in which the employer self-insures up to a certain amount but then pays a commercial insurance company to assume the risk for all claims beyond that amount.

The fastest growing type of private insurance are "prepayment" plans that fall under the general term of "managed care." Managed care includes primarily Health Maintenance Organizations (HMOs) but also many other networks and arrangements. Many private health insurance companies, self-insured plans, and Blue Cross/Blue Shield plans have moved toward managed care plans.

Here are some important details about each of these insurance forms.

COMMERCIAL INSURANCE   Many people obtain their insurance from policies offered by private, profit-making insurance carriers. Such policies come in the form of either *individual* or *group* plans, with group policies being the larger category. The term "group policy" refers to the fact that the insurance is underwritten to cover a large group, such as all employees of a company, or all members of an association or fraternal organization. Each person insured may be covered as an individual or as a family. The term "individual policy" does not mean that the policy covers only one person; instead, it refers to the fact that only one individual purchased the insurance, as opposed to an entire group. The policy itself, of course, can cover either a single person or a family.

Group plans have three advantages over individual policies:

- The cost of group plans per person is usually lower, because the risk is spread out over many people.

- No individual member of a group plan may be canceled separately. The entire group must be canceled.

- When employees who are covered under a group plan retire or otherwise leave their company (assuming it has more than 25 employees), they may make use of a special clause that allows them to convert their group coverage to individual coverage. This was made possible through the Consolidated Omnibus Budget Reconciliation Act (COBRA) in 1986. (As you might recall, some of the rationale for COBRA was eliminated in 1996 when Congress passed new legislation that allowed for complete portability of health insurance when employees change jobs, regardless of preexisting conditions. This rectified the problem formerly created when a person left one company but was often not eligible for insurance until after three months on a new job.)

Note that many group policies are actually self-insured plans administered by a commercial carrier. In fact, a 1994 study by the Health Insurance Association of America estimated that 81 million Americans were covered under group policies and 7.1 million carried individual or family policies from commercial insurance companies. Of the 81 million people covered under a group policy, nearly 60 percent were covered under ASO or MPP arrangements, in which employers hired a commercial carrier to administer their insurance plan or assume the risk for higher-than-average claims.

Some commercial policies are "indemnity" plans, meaning that they reimburse (indemnify) the patient for covered services up to a certain limit specified in the policy, leaving it up to the doctor or hospital to collect from the patient. Other commercial policies reimburse physicians directly according to what the insurance company considers "usual and

customary" fees. However, these types of plans ar[...]
into managed care arrangements, which will be dis[...]

Commercial health insurance policies vary grea[...]
not cover all illnesses or allow patients to see all [...]
providers, such as chiropractors. This is why doctors—[...]
son—are increasingly double-checking each patient's i[...] olicy, a
process called *insurance verification and eligibility.*

In a typical commercial policy, the insurance holder, called the *subscriber,* pays an annual *premium.* The insurance does not pay for any
healthcare until the subscriber's *deductible* is met. The deductible is the
amount the person or family must pay entirely in each calendar or policy year before the insurance company will pay any claims. Deductibles
usually range from $200 to $1,200 for an individual, and $600 to $3,600 for
a family. (A deductible for a family is generally three times the amount of
the deductible for an individual.)

Once the insurance company begins paying for claims, most policies
pay or reimburse for only 70 percent or 80 percent of what the insurance
company considers an appropriate fee. This is known as the *allowable*
amount. (See the sidebar on page 41, "Understanding Reimbursement-
Speak," for more details on this.) The other 20 percent or 30 percent paid
by the patient is known as the *copayment.* Fortunately, many commercial
policies cap the total copayment amounts that an individual or family
must pay per year; these limits range from $1000 to $10,000 beyond the
deductible. This is called a *stop-loss provision.* Once the subscriber reaches
that limit, the insurer pays 100 percent of all covered charges. On the other
hand, many commercial policies also have an annual and lifetime cap, limiting the charges that the insurer will pay. For instance, many dental policies limit the annual coverage to $1,000 and the lifetime coverage to
$25,000.

In general, commercial health insurance policies are one of three types:

1. *Basic Plans* pay for limited services performed in a hospital, X-rays, lab
   tests, drugs and medications, and sometimes but not usually outpatient doctor's visits. Basic plans typically have low or no deductibles,
   but also low levels of benefits.

2. *Major Medical Plans* are designed to pay large amounts in the event of
   major illnesses or injuries. These plans sometimes do not cover minor
   health problems and office visits.

3. *Comprehensive Medical Plans* combine coverages for both Basic and
   Major Medical, plus outpatient services such as doctor's office visits
   for illnesses. However, policies differ greatly; one policy may cover

psychiatric benefits up to $1,000 per year for outpatient visits, but not reimburse for chiropractic treatment or eye examinations as another policy does.

Finally, note that there are two distinguishing characteristics of traditional commercial health insurance policies:

1. Most such individual and group commercial policies pay healthcare providers on a fee-for-service basis. This means that the insurance company pays for each procedure after it is performed. (However, as indicated earlier, the insurer may only pay an amount that it determines to be appropriate, regardless of how much the doctor wants to charge.) Subscribers are responsible for any copayment, or in some cases the physician will accept what the carrier reimburses as his or her full payment.

2. Under most traditional plans, patients can choose any doctor they want, anywhere they want. They do not need any authorization to see specialists or to go to emergency rooms.

Because of these characteristics, traditional commercial insurance has long been the preferred type of health insurance for many Americans.

BLUE CROSS AND BLUE SHIELD PLANS   Blue Cross originated in 1929 when a group of teachers contracted with Baylor Hospital in Texas to provide hospital care at a fixed monthly cost. This type of arrangement was different from the indemnity plans of commercial insurance based on fee for service. Over the next decade, such Blue Cross plans became successful in many other parts of the country. Similarly, Blue Shield was devised in 1938 by the American Medical Association as an insurance method to cover doctors' services for a fixed prepaid amount per month.

Since their origins, separate Blue Cross and Blue Shield organizations were established in nearly every state in the United States. Each organization had a national association that had to approve the plans established in each state. The names Blue Cross and Blue Shield were licensed from the national associations. In 1986, the two associations merged to form the Blue Cross and Blue Shield Association to manage the various state insurers.

Over the past decade, the two Blues in most states have also merged to form one organization to compete directly with commercial carriers. In the past few years, there have also been some mergers of BC/BS organizations across state lines.

Most Blue Cross/Blue Shield plans were set up to be not-for-profit. In exchange for this status, they were forbidden by state laws from canceling

Understanding Reimbursement-Speak

In general, there are four methods by which insurers determine how to pay physicians and other healthcare providers:

1. *UCR (Usual, Customary, and Reasonable)*. This method has long been used to monitor and control costs in fee-for-service healthcare. Under UCR, insurance carriers choose the *lowest* of three amounts from the following:

   - Usual fee—this is the "usual" amount a physician charges for a service. Insurance companies determine this amount by keeping records on doctors over each year and averaging out the median (50th percentile) charge.
   - Customary fee—this fee is determined from insurance company profiles, based on the 90th percentile of fees charged by all providers within the same specialty area in the same geographic location for a specific service.
   - Reasonable fee—this fee is the lesser of the billed fee (the amount the doctor would like to charge), the usual fee, the customary fee, or another fee that might be justified under special circumstances.

   For example, assume Doctor A submits a fee for $220, while the customary fee in that area is $225; this doctor will receive only the reasonable fee, based on 80 percent of $220 (assuming that the insurance is an 80/20 plan). Meanwhile, Doctor B submits a bill for $250 as her usual fee; this fee is higher than the customary fee of $225, so she will receive the customary amount, based on 80 percent of $225.

   From an insurer's perspective, the flaw with UCR is that it actually creates inflationary pressure on fees, because the system encourages doctors to charge higher fees on a regular basis to make sure that their *usual* fees are higher than the *customary* range. For this reason, of course, many doctors prefer to be paid according to UCR rates.

2. *Schedule of Benefits Method*. In this method, the insurance company maintains a table of fees for all procedures and pays only these allowable amounts, regardless of what the physician charges. If the doctor wants to charge more, the patient may need to make up the difference.

3. *Maximum Fee Schedule*. In this method, the insurance company maintains a table of maximum payment amounts for all procedures; the doctor must agree to accept that payment as his or her total reimbursement.

4. *Capitation*. Capitation is generally used in prepaid plans under managed care. The term originates from the Latin word meaning "head." Under capitation, a doctor receives a set fee per month per person enrolled in the healthcare plan, whether or not the person sees the doctor. Capitation takes advantage of statistical probabilities that the majority of a physician's patients won't all get sick at the same time or use more healthcare than mathematically predicted for people in that age group. The capitation amounts vary based on geography, age, sex, and experience rating per population group.

   In addition to these four methods, the Harvard School of Public Health developed another method at the request of the federal government, largely to curtail the high cost of Medicare. This method is known as RBRVS, which stands for Resource-Based Relative Value Scale. The RBRVS system takes three factors into account in determining a doctor's fee: (1) the physician's actual amount of work, (2) the provider's expenses (except malpractice), and (3) the cost of malpractice. The system is not simple, however, because each of these factors is multiplied by an index based on geographic location, and the total is then multiplied again by a "conversion" factor determined by Congress to account for inflation. RBRVS was introduced in 1992 and has been phased in for Medicare bills since then. It was expected that many commercial insurance companies would eventually adopt RBRVS, but in general, they have not done so.

coverage for an individual because of illness. They were usually required to obtain approval for rate increases as well.

Blue Cross and Blue Shield were pioneers in the concept of prepaid plans that have become the foundation for managed care today. In addition to their standard individual and group policies, many Blues negotiated contracts with providers in an area to become part of a network. The providers had to accept payment according to a fee schedule determined by the Blue, often 10 percent lower than what the company paid other providers who were not participating. In exchange, the providers were paid directly rather than having to seek payment from the patients. In some contracts, the doctors were penalized if they referred patients to specialists who were not part of the Blue network.

MANAGED CARE ORGANIZATIONS As you undoubtedly know, traditional commercial health insurance plans, including self-insured and Blue Cross/Blue Shield plans, are largely viewed by insurance companies as the cause for skyrocketing costs of healthcare in the past two decades. As a result, more and more commercial insurance companies, self-insured plans, and Blue Cross/Blue Shield insurers have moved toward offering some type of managed care arrangement in addition to their traditional indemnity plans.

The most common term you will hear in the context of managed care is HMO, or Health Maintenance Organization. HMOs originated in the 1930s and were fostered by the federal government in the early 1970s as a way to cut costs. However, HMOs did not truly take off until the mid-1980s through the early 1990s. There are now roughly between 600 and 700 HMOs in the country, although the exact figure is difficult to determine because of the variety of HMO operations.

In general, the distinguishing characteristics of HMOs include five basic precepts:

1. Providers are prepaid on a capitation basis; they receive fees each month per subscriber, regardless of whether the provider sees the patient.

2. Patients typically pay only a small copayment, such as $10 per visit, or none at all.

3. Care is highly controlled; patients usually see a primary physician first who must authorize visits to specialists.

4. Patients are either forbidden to see providers outside the HMO network unless absolutely medically necessary, or they are subject to higher copayments or no reimbursement at all when they do.

5. The HMO tries to cut costs through preventative care; patients may see doctors at no additional cost for regular checkups to catch any serious illnesses before they become aggravated.

Despite these five common precepts, the term HMO has been used to refer to many different types of healthcare arrangements. Some people call any managed care organization an HMO, although there are other types of arrangements—such as Preferred Provider Organizations (PPOs)—that are not the same.

In addition, HMOs can be operated in many different ways. In some cases, the HMO is owned by an insurance company, so belonging to this type of HMO is synonymous with being insured. In the other cases, the HMO is an independent business with which several private insurers have contracted to serve its subscribers.

In some arrangements, doctors are literally staff employees of the HMO, and they work solely at the HMO facility; they cannot see other patients. In other HMO models, the affiliated doctors maintain an independent practice but become part of a network of physicians who agree to take patients from that HMO; these doctors can also take patients from other HMOs or other traditional fee-for-service insurance plans.

As mentioned, PPOs are a related type of organization, but they differ in that they generally follow looser rules. A PPO usually consists of a network of physicians who agree to see patients who are insured under a certain plan. In general, the patients in a PPO have more flexibility in choosing their own doctors from among an extensive list of candidates. In some PPOs, the patients can see specialists without a referral from a primary care physician first, although some PPOs charge people a higher copayment for seeing a doctor who is not a member of the network. Unlike HMOs, which usually pay doctors on a prepaid capitated basis, doctors affiliated with a PPO are usually paid according to fee-for-service, but they must accept a discounted rate compared to their usual fees. They may charge the patient a copayment based on 20 percent of the allowable fee or sometimes a fixed amount such as $10 per visit.

In the past few years, there has been a flood of new types of HMOs and PPOs as the need to create profitable managed care programs has heated up. There are now so many different models and methods of managed care that the average consumer (and doctor) needs a scorecard to keep track of all the different types of arrangements and their affiliated terms. Here is a short glossary of managed care terms you may encounter:

HMO, staff model: Under this arrangement, doctors are employed by the HMO and are paid a salary.

HMO, group model: The HMO pays a large group of physicians representing all specialties, usually on a capitation rate, to handle all its subscribers. In some group models, physicians work at an HMO facility, but in others, they work at their own offices. Some group models allow physicians to see only HMO patients; others do not.

HMO, network model: The HMO contracts with two or more groups of independent physicians who handle patients at their own offices. Physicians may see only HMO patients.

IPA (Independent Practice Association): Under this arrangement, the HMO contracts with individual independent physicians or associations to care for its subscribers. Many IPAs are prepaid plans on a capitation basis. Under most IPAs, physicians may see non-HMO patients on a fee-for-service basis. In some IPAs, the physicians organize the association themselves and approach the HMO for a contract, rather than waiting to be approached by the HMO.

PPO (Preferred Provider Organization): This is a loose network of doctors who agree to participate in an insurance plan, usually at a predetermined fee-for-service rate established by the insurer, which pays the providers significantly less than the usual and customary fee. (However, some PPOs now pay on a capitated basis.) Doctors in PPOs can usually see other nonmember patients in their own practices.

EPO (Exclusive Provider Organization): This is an extreme version of a PPO, almost like an HMO. Patients cannot see doctors who are outside the network selected by the insurer, or they must pay 100 percent of costs. Providers are reimbursed according to fee-for-service at a predetermined rate.

POS (Point of Service Plan): Also a hybrid between a PPO and an HMO, this type of plan requires patients to have a primary doctor who oversees their care and determines which specialists are necessary. If a patient seeks care from a participating provider, he or she pays little or nothing and may not file any claims. Care provided by out-of-network providers is reimbursed at a much lower rate (i.e., with higher copayments). The reimbursement to providers may be fee-for-service or capitation.

MSO (Managed Service Organization): The newest arrangement at this time, MSOs are managed care arrangements started by hospitals that form their own group of doctors. They want doctors to see patients in their own offices, but to use the hospital for lab work, X-rays, and so on.

All in all, understanding managed care can be very difficult for the neophyte, as the definitions of each type of arrangement change all the time. In fact, some medical professionals say that the powerful insurance companies proliferate many different types of plans to intentionally confuse consumers and take advantage of their inability to compare among health plans and be smart consumers. (Despite my own extensive experience as a researcher in healthcare and medical billing, I too find the diversity of managed care plans and the lack of standards so confusing that I agree with this conjecture.)

There is no doubt that managed care will continue to evolve over the next decade. According to recent surveys, in 1994, more than 50 million Americans—about 20 percent of the population—already belonged to some type of HMO and that number has risen by 1996 to almost 30 percent. California was the leader in HMOs, with 40 percent of its population enrolled in one, followed by Oregon (38%), Maryland (36%), and Arizona (35%). Meanwhile, surveys indicate that more than 45 million Americans belonged to PPOs in 1994.

See Table 2-1 for some interesting statistics on HMO and PPO enrollments in each state. See Table 2-2 for a list indicating HMO ownership in early 1995. See Figure 2-3 for a graph showing the breakdown of HMO models as of January 1995.

SUMMARY: PRIVATE INSURANCE VERSUS DOCTORS   From its modern beginnings in the early twentieth century, private insurance has been a boon for doctors. Because of the tremendous explosion in the American population, and the growth of corporations throughout the 1950s, 1960s, 1970s, and 1980s, group insurance became a standard benefit offered by most employers and demanded by employees. At the same time, most insurers created affordable individual policies for those people who did not have access to group coverage. As a result, doctors experienced several decades of consistent, patient growth, during most of which they were paid handsomely on a fee-for-service basis.

Table 2-3 shows the extent of this growth by indicating the increases in insurance payments among all types of private insurance between 1950 and 1993. Notice the sharp rise in payments between 1960 and 1980, and the steady rise each year from 1981 to 1989, after which the annual increases began to shrink substantially. This decrease marks the beginning of the effects of managed care.

As Table 2-3 makes clear, insurance companies have been trying to hold down costs, particularly physicians' fees, since 1990. Three factors had driven the cost of private insurance sky high in the 1980s: (1) consumers had

TABLE 2-1

Number of HMOs, PPOs, and POSs Per State—1994

	Number of HMOs[*]	Market Share[*]	Number of PPOs[**]	Market Share[**]	Number of POSs[***]
Alabama	8	10%	29	34.5%	2
Alaska	0	0	3	3.1	0
Arizona	20	35.8	30	16.5	1
Arkansas	6	3.8	9	2.5	2
California	36	38.3	84	23.4	5
Colorado	12	24.4	33	50.9	1
Connecticut	14	27.4	16	4.6	1
Delaware	6	20.5	6	1.2	1
District of Columbia	2	25.6	7	12.6	0
Florida	36	20.1	78	22.2	11
Georgia	11	8.8	39	13.3	4
Hawaii	7	23.2	6	40.7	0
Idaho	2	1.2	2	0.2	0
Illinois	27	16.9	50	24.4	2
Indiana	12	7.4	37	15.9	2
Iowa	3	4.1	13	8.9	0
Kansas	10	10.9	21	15.1	2
Kentucky	7	12.1	16	11.6	2
Louisiana	11	7.0	30	15.5	2
Maine	3	6.2	6	0.8	0
Maryland	16	36.2	21	21.1	3
Massachusetts	16	35.2	23	7.6	7
Michigan	17	20.2	28	7.7	5
Minnesota	9	26.6	14	32.9	1
Mississippi	1	0.3	10	22.8	1
Missouri	18	14.7	31	22.5	4
Montana	1	1.5	1	0.2	0
Nebraska	5	9.5	11	33.2	0

TABLE 2-1

Number of HMOs, PPOs, and POSs Per State—1994   (Continued)

	Number of HMOs*	Market Share*	Number of PPOs**	Market Share**	Number of POSs***
Nevada	7	14.7	20	18.5	1
New Hampshire	3	17.0	5	3.3	1
New Jersey	14	16.9	23	13.1	3
New Mexico	6	17.4	7	2.4	0
New York	33	24.3	23	3.8	4
North Carolina	12	8.3	24	11.2	3
North Dakota	2	1.1	0	0	0
Ohio	31	19.2	47	19.7	9
Oklahoma	6	7.3	20	12.9	4
Oregon	7	37.5	13	15.6	1
Pennsylvania	19	21.5	56	13.8	8
Rhode Island	3	28.8	3	9.6	0
South Carolina	4	4.2	18	11.6	2
South Dakota	1	2.9	3	1.6	0
Tennessee	17	16.2	37	31.8	4
Texas	31	9.7	67	28.7	9
Utah	8	19.2	11	8.6	1
Vermont	1	12.6	1	0.3	0
Virginia	13	8.4	19	7.9	4
Washington	11	16.4	21	24.1	2
West Virginia	0	0	7	4.2	1
Wisconsin	27	24.2	26	11.2	2
Wyoming	0	0	0	0	0
TOTAL	572		1105		118

*Source: Group Health Association of America, National Directory of HMOs

**Source: American Managed Care and Review Association (AMCRA) Foundation

***Source: American Managed Care and Review Association (AMCRA) Foundation

TABLE 2-2

HMO Ownership as of January 1, 1995

Total Plans	625
Insurance companies	154
National managed care chain	124
Blue Cross/Blue Shield	88
Independently owned	67
Hospital or hospital alliance	43
Corporation	26
Physician/hospital joint venture	19
Physician/medical group	18
Cooperative	10
University	10
County/state government	8
Private non-profit	8
Managed care company	7
Local non-profit	5
Health system joint venture	2
Hospital/university	2
Multiple owner types	2
National chain and physician group	2
Insurance company/hospital	1
National managed care chain/hospital	1
State medical association	1
Other	9
Unknown	18

Source: American Managed Care and Review Association (AMCRA) Foundation

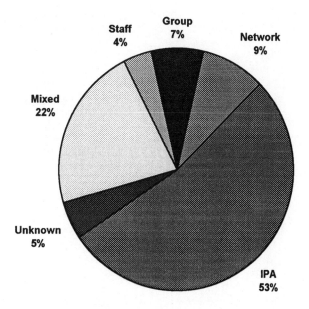

Figure 2-3
Breakdown of HMO
Model Types—
January 1995

great expectations of healthcare and demanded more services; (2) new technology created improvements in healthcare, but at increased costs; and (3) providers and consumers were not given incentives to contain costs. These factors have slowly prompted private insurers to rethink their policies and to devise new ways to constrain fees. In a sense, one might say that private insurers today are seeking retribution for the extravagances doctors enjoyed in past decades.

The significance of this transition for anyone wanting to get into medical billing can be seen in the confused eyes and smaller pocketbooks of most physicians today. Many of them can no longer afford to practice independently and "according to their own wits," the way they probably imagined it when they went to medical school. Instead, they are being forced to reduce their costs, kowtow to insurance companies, and join dozens of PPOs and HMOs in order to keep their patients (who themselves have been "encouraged" to switch to these types of plans by their employers to save money).

Mary Vandegrift, owner of a successful billing service called AccuMed Solutions, Inc., in Columbia, Maryland, notes that some of her doctors have signed up with as many as a dozen HMOs, and one of her doctors was a member of 17 managed care organizations. In terms of income, Mary also related to me that one of her clients, a specialist, used to make over $300,000 per year but has barely made more than $150,000 in the past few years and is now nearly broke because of her huge expenses.

TABLE 2-3

Private Health Insurance Claims Payments by Type of Insurer 1950–1993 (numbers are in billions)

Year	Total	Percentage Change from Previous Year(s)	Breakdown of Total*		
			Insurance Companies	Self-Insured and HMOs	Blue Cross/ Blue Shield
1950	$1.3		$0.8	NA	$0.6
1955	3.1	138	1.8	NA	1.4
1960	5.7	84	3.0	NA	2.6
1965	9.6	68	5.2	NA	4.5
1970	17.2	79	9.1	NA	8.1
1975	32.1	87	16.5	NA	16.9
1980	76.3	138	37.0	16.2	25.5
1981	85.9	13	41.6	18.9	29.2
1982	97.1	13	49.2	21.6	32.2
1983	104.1	7	51.7	24.1	34.4
1984	107.5	3	56.0	26.1	35.7
1985	117.6	9	60.0	32.5	37.5
1986	128.5	9	64.3	36.8	40.6
1987	151.7	18	72.5	56.5	44.5
1988	171.1	13	83.0	62.8	48.2
1989	194.5	14	89.4	79.8	50.7
1990	208.9	7	92.5	93.4	55.9
1991	223.0	7	97.6	112.0	60.0
1992	245.5	10	104.8	131.1	63.1
1993	253.5	3	103.6	144.7	62.0

*Numbers may not add up because of rounding.

Source: Health Insurance Association of America, Annual Survey of Health Insurance Companies; Blue Cross/Blue Shield Association, Group Health Association of America, Inc.

This is not to suggest that all HMOs or PPOs hurt doctors or restrict their income to the point of poverty. In many cases, doctors can continue to charge on a fee-for-service basis and earn decent incomes. For example, many specialists who are part of an HMO are allowed to charge fee-for-service; it is only the primary care physician who must accept capitation.

But, as Mary says, "There are some good HMOs out there...and some very bad ones!" She points to the financial risks many doctors unknowingly take when they agree to become part of a capitated prepayment HMO plan. For example, Mary told me about one of her doctors who is affiliated with an HMO plan and paid on a capitation basis. The rules of the HMO are quite complex, but the doctor effectively receives only a $5.00 capitation payment per month. This amount can end up being even less, due to what is called a "withhold." If the patient uses the services of the doctor more than statistically expected for that year, the insurer keeps some of the capitation payments as compensation. In Mary's analysis of this situation, some of her clients are "losing their shirts!"

Perhaps it is now becoming even clearer to you the many ways that a professional medical billing service can help its clients when it comes to private healthcare insurance reimbursement. First, the professional biller can attend to business while the doctor attends to medicine. This makes sense, because doctors typically don't learn business skills such as marketing, accounting, and financial analysis. Second, the billing service can make sure that reimbursements are expedited by using electronic claims filing, which usually obtains payments for the physician within a few weeks rather than months. Third, the professional biller can pay attention to the many different fee structures that a typical doctor today must track when he or she belongs to many different kinds of managed care plans. As indicated earlier, if a doctor belongs to a dozen or more HMOs and PPOs and each has its own fee structure, each claim must bill for the correct amount.

Fourth, the professional biller can keep track of the write-offs, the amounts above allowable fees that PPOs and HMOs do not let doctors charge their members. These amounts must be credited from the doctor's accounts receivable. Most doctors want to keep track of how much they have to write off each month, and the professional biller can provide this information. Finally, in cases of HMOs that pay by capitation, the professional biller can compare how much the doctor earns in monthly capitated fees versus how much he or she might have been able to bill if the claims had been charged on a fee-for-service basis. In this way, the professional biller can advise the client if it is worthwhile to continue to be a member of the HMO.

Some healthcare industry watchers predict that HMOs have had their heyday and will soon fall by the wayside. In 1995 and 1996, many HMOs reported unprofitable years, and several of the country's largest ones merged with others. More important though, many consumers have become leery of HMOs because of the reported poor quality of healthcare they provide. Many industry experts say there is an inherent conflict of interest that exists among doctors affiliated with HMOs: doctors are supposed to do what's best for their patients, but HMOs restrict their ability to do so because of their cost-saving rules and regulations. Ultimately, many people are predicting that, given the American love for independence and freedom of choice, PPO-type plans will eventually win out

Business Profile: Mary Vandegrift and Candis Ruiz

Mary Vandegrift started a medical billing business in 1993 after a long career with IBM. In the beginning, she tapped into her computer background to sell computer systems to medical offices, but she did not enjoy the sales aspect of her job. Mary eventually met a neighbor, Candis Ruiz, whose background in insurance sales seemed to be the perfect match. Together they formed a partnership that has taken off beyond their dreams. They eventually purchased software and additional training from Santiago SDS, Inc.

Mary and Candis now serve more than a dozen practices, for whom they mostly do full practice management. They are very involved with their clients, handling their billing and advising them on many financial issues arising out of the inherent problems of managed care. As discussed in the previous section, Mary has had several of her clients experience a notable shrinkage in income over the past two years, and so she has learned to make sophisticated financial projections to analyze the value of joining certain HMOs. As Mary says,

> Our job is almost like auditing; we have to keep track of the fees they are paid compared to how much they might have gotten. We try to stay on top of what HMOs are doing business-wise, and to become knowledgeable if not experts on every aspect of healthcare that we can. If it's a problem for the doctor, we consider it to be our problem. We take that headache off them so they can be doctors.

One of the most interesting strategies Mary has pursued is to recruit other professionals to be part of her team. She has introduced her clients to insurance people, accountants, lawyers, and others who can help the doctors improve their business. Mary realized this was a useful idea because, as she puts it, "Doctors don't have a sphere of influence outside of other doctors for business information. We go in and help them increase their patient load, improve their records management, verify that they are coding properly, and even take care of their office supply problems." At the moment, Mary and Candis use the experts to increase the professionalism of their service, but at some point in the future, they may organize this idea into a consortium of professionals that would work with all their clients as a group, while they share in their fees.

because they allow patients to choose their own physicians and make decisions based on their personal preferences, even if it costs them more to go outside the PPO network.

Public Health Insurance Programs

The two largest public health insurance programs are the federally run Medicare and the combined federal/state-run Medicaid programs. Public health insurance also includes CHAMPUS (the Civilian Health and Medical Program of the Uniformed Services), Veterans Medical Care, FEHBP (Federal Employees Health Benefits Program), and various other local government-run plans. Here are details about the major public health programs.

MEDICARE   The federal government began Medicare in 1966 to assist elderly and disabled citizens (typically on a fixed income) who faced rapidly rising costs in medical and hospital care. Medicare falls under the aegis of the Social Security Administration but is run by the Health Care Financing Administration (HCFA), an agency of the Department of Health and Human Services. Today roughly 37 million Americans are covered by Medicare. Table 2-4 shows the growth of Medicare in terms of enrollees and claims paid between 1983 and 1995 (the latest detailed information available).

Medicare coverage is divided into two parts, as follows:

1. **Part A** covers hospitalization, skilled nursing facilities, home health-care, and hospice care. Part A of Medicare is automatic and free of charge for almost every American over the age of 65 and the permanently disabled. It is financed through payroll taxes for Social Security. Each eligible subscriber pays a deductible ($760 in 1997, but it increases slightly every year) for each hospitalization, and then Medicare picks up the tab for 60 days of inpatient hospital care during the benefit period. In general, billing services are not involved with filing claims for Part A services, because hospitals process these claims through Medicare "intermediaries" in each state, which are sometimes insurance carriers or sometimes data-processing centers.

2. **Part B** of Medicare pays for inpatient or outpatient doctor's services performed in a hospital, clinic, doctor's office, or home. It also covers surgical services and supplies, diagnostic tests, laboratory tests, X-rays, ambulance transportation, physical and occupational therapy, blood (after 3 pints), outpatient mental health services, artificial limbs, and

durable medical equipment (DME). Part B of Medicare is voluntary, but most Americans sign up for it, paying a monthly premium ($43.80 in 1997, with increases each year) that is deducted from their Social Security checks. In general, Part B insurance covers the subscriber for 80 percent of what Medicare determines to be "allowable" charges in a given geographic area and specialty, according to its own fee schedule. The beneficiary is then responsible for an annual deductible ($100 in 1996), and for a copayment.

TABLE 2-4

Medical Enrollment and Benefit Payments (Parts A and B) (fiscal years 1967–1995)

	Hospital and/or Medical Insurance Part A + B		Hospital Insurance Part A		Supplementary Medical Insurance Part B	
	Number of enrolled persons (millions)	Benefit payments ($billions)	Number of enrolled persons (millions)	Benefit payments ($billions)	Number of enrolled persons (millions)	Benefit payments ($billions)
1967	19.5	$ 3.1	19.5	$ 2.5	17.9	$ 0.7
1970	20.5	6.8	20.4	4.8	19.6	1.9
1975	25.0	14.1	24.6	10.4	23.9	3.8
1980	28.5	33.9	28.1	23.8	27.4	10.1
1985	31.1	69.5	30.6	47.7	29.9	21.8
1986	31.8	74.1	31.2	48.9	30.6	25.2
1987	32.4	79.8	31.9	49.8	31.2	29.9
1988	32.9	85.5	32.4	51.9	31.6	33.7
1989	33.6	94.3	33.1	57.4	32.1	36.9
1990	34.2	108.7	33.7	66.2	32.6	42.5
1991	34.9	113.9	34.4	68.5	33.2	45.5
1992	35.6	129.2	36.2	80.6	35.4	48.6
1993	36.3	142.9	N/A	N/A	N/A	N/A
1994	36.9	159.3	N/A	N/A	N/A	N/A
1995	37.6	190.0	N/A	N/A	N/A	N/A

Source: U.S. Department of Health and Human Services, Health Care Financing Administration, Bureau of Data Management and Strategy.

One of the primary markets for professional independent billing services are physicians and other healthcare providers who have many Medicare patients, because, as indicated earlier, these doctors must file Part B claims for their patients. Part B claims are processed through insurance companies in each state that have been contracted to handle Medicare claims. In many states, these carriers are the Blue Cross/Blue Shield insurer, but this aspect of their business is separate from their commercial insurance. These contracted intermediary companies change from time to time, so I have not listed them in this book; you can find a current list of them in the official Medicare handbook published each year, available from the Social Security Administration or on the Internet at www.hcfa.gov. If you are just learning about medical billing, you need to know about the specific Medicare carriers in your state.

In addition to Medicare Parts A and B, many Medicare enrollees supplement their health insurance with an additional policy called Medicare Supplement Insurance, but usually referred to as *Medigap* because it fills in the gaps between Part A and B deductibles, copayments, and uncovered services. Medigap policies are purchased from commercial insurers, associations, and organizations such as the American Association of Retired Persons (AARP). When Medigap policies first appeared, insurance companies offered dozens of types of plans, causing a tremendous amount of confusion among Medicare enrollees. As a result, the federal government stepped in to regulate Medigap, standardizing the policies to just 10 choices, called Plans A to J. Every insurer that sells Medigap policies must sell the basic Plan A, plus a number of other plans. These plans differ in terms of what they cover and how much they pay for as a supplement to Medicare Parts A and B. For example, most of the plans will pay the Part A deductible and the copayments that Medicare normally requires for hospitalizations, skilled nursing facilities, and so on. Table 2-5 summarizes the 10 plans.

Understanding Medicare and Medigap is critical to a billing service. Doctors (and hence their billing service) must know a person's Medicare/Medigap coverage, and if any exceptions apply. For example, for most people over 65, Medicare is likely their primary coverage, with a Medigap policy providing "secondary" coverage. In many states, the claims for such individuals can be filed electronically: the Medicare carrier will pay its share and then automatically forward the claim electronically to the Medigap secondary insurer for payment. This means that the patient never has to hand over cash to the doctor, and the billing service needs to file the claim only once.

However, Medicare coverage can also be confusing. You must make sure that the person has only one Medigap plan, to avoid duplication of

TABLE 2-5

Standard Medigap Policies

Basic Benefits are included in all plans:

- Hospitalization—Part A coinsurance plus coverage for 365 additional days after Medicare benefits end
- Medical expenses—Part B coinsurance (generally 20% of Medicare-approved expenses)
- Blood: First three pints of blood each year.

Plan A	Plan B	Plan C	Plan D	Plan E	Plan F	Plan G	Plan H	Plan I	Plan J
Basic Benefits	Basic Benefits	Basic Benefits	Basic Benefits	Basic Benefits	Basic Benefits	Basic Benefits	Basic Benefits	Basic Benefits	Basic Benefits
		Skilled Nursing Coinsurance	Skilled Nursing Coinsurance	Skilled Nursing Coinsurance	Skilled Nursing Coinsurance	Skilled Nursing Coinsurance	Skilled Nursing Coinsurance	Skilled Nursing Coinsurance	Skilled Nursing Coinsurance
	Part A Deductible	Part A Deductible	Part A Deductible	Part A Deductible	Part A Deductible	Part A Deductible	Part A Deductible	Part A Deductible	Part A Deductible
		Part B Deductible			Part B Deductible				Part B Deductible
					Part B Excess (100%)	Part B Excess (100%)		Part B Excess (100%)	Part B Excess (100%)
		Foreign Emergency Travel	Foreign Emergency Travel	Foreign Emergency Travel	Foreign Emergency Travel	Foreign Emergency Travel	Foreign Emergency Travel	Foreign Emergency Travel	Foreign Emergency Travel
			At-Home Recovery			At-Home Recovery		At-Home Recovery	At-Home Recovery
							Basic Drugs ($1,250)	Basic Drugs ($1,250)	Basic Drugs ($1,250)
				Preventive Care					Preventive Care

Note: All plans may not be available in every state.

benefits. (Before the new law restricting Mediga[...]
icy, some people actually made money on their[...]
several policies that would pay their deducti[...]
would thus pocket the excess as profit.)

Another glitch can be finding out that for [...]
Medicare is not their primary insurer. This can happen when [...]
is still employed and has health coverage from his or her company. In this
case, the employer policy is primary to Medicare. Similarly, Medicare is a
second payer whenever the claim involves a work-related injury, an automobile or other accident, and in a few other circumstances.

Another vital aspect of Medicare reimbursement that a professional
biller must understand is the distinction between *participating* and *non-participating* providers. Similar to the way that many old Blue Shield plans
worked, doctors may or may not accept Medicare's fee schedule. There are
pros and cons to each side.

Once per year, doctors must decide either to participate in Medicare,
thus becoming a PAR (participating) physician by "taking assignment," or
to not participate, called a NON-PAR.

- PAR—Taking assignment means that the doctor accepts the allowable
  fee determined by Medicare as his or her full payment for services
  rendered to the Medicare patient. This means that he or she cannot
  charge the patient the difference between the standard fee and the
  allowable amount. In return for this cooperation, Medicare will mail
  its check directly to the doctor, saving the physician the risk of collecting from the patient. Note: remember that Medicare will then pay
  the physician only 80 percent of the allowable amount, and the
  patient *must* be billed for the remaining 20 percent copayment.

- NON-PAR—In contrast, doctors can choose not to participate in
  Medicare. They must file claims for patients, but they can charge
  patients up to 115 percent more than Medicare allows (this is called
  the *limiting charge*). However, there is a major penalty for not participating: Medicare will mail the check to the patient, so the physician
  must collect his or her fees directly from the patient—a potentially
  risky venture.

Table 2-6 compares one patient who sees Dr. Smith, a participating
provider, with a patient who sees Dr. Jones, a non-participating provider.
Assume that both patients are treated for the exact same problem and
both doctors practice in the same geographic area.

2-6

ple of Difference in Charges Between a Participating Provider and a Non-Participating
vider Under Medicare

	Customary Charge	Limiting Charge	Medicare Allowable Amount	Paid by Medicare	Balance Due from Patient	Write-off
Dr. Smith (PAR)	$300.00 (disallowed)	N/A	$159.52	$127.62 directly to doctor	$31.90	$140.48
Dr. Jones (NON-PAR)	$300.00	$183.44	$159.52	$127.62 directly to patient	$55.82	$116.56

Explanation

Dr. Smith has agreed to be a PAR provider and so is willing to accept the Medicare allowable amount as total payment. His patient owes only $31.90 because Dr. Smith accepts $159.52 as the full fee rather than his usual fee of $300. Dr. Smith receives 80% of $159.52, hence $127.62, and so must collect $31.90 from the patient either at the time of visit or after Medicare pays him. He receives the check directly from Medicare. He must also write off the $140.48 difference between his usual fee and the Medicare approved amount.

Dr. Jones is a NON-PAR provider. She is able to collect $183.44 because she is allowed to charge 15% more than the Medicare allowable amount. Medicare pays 80% of the allowable amount, hence $127.62 to the patient, so the patient must pay the $55.82 difference to Dr. Jones. Note that Dr. Jones can ask the patient to pay the entire $183.44 up front since Medicare will reimburse the patient later.

As mentioned in the sidebar on page 41, "Understanding Reimbursement-Speak," Medicare has been phasing in a new fee schedule called RBRVS to replace the UCR method. A billing service that offers full practice management will need to understand this new fee schedule, the distinction between PARs and NON-PARs, and the differences between billed amounts, allowable amounts, limiting charges, Medicare-paid amounts (80 percent), copayment amounts (20 percent), and write-off amounts. Got it?

A NOTE ON MEDICARE HMOS In recent years, Medicare has endorsed the HMO concept as a way to cut its own costs and has therefore contracted with a variety of HMO facilities to take over the care of Medicare members. Under these Medicare-HMO models, the subscriber must continue to pay the Medicare Part B premium to HCFA, but the person will generally not pay any deductibles for Part A services or any 20 percent copayments for Part B services, thus potentially saving a lot of money, especially if the person does not have Medigap coverage or is very ill.

Some Medicare HMOs are of the pure type, in which the person cannot see doctors outside the network. These plans, called "lock-ins," require patients to obtain all covered care through a primary care physician and referrals to specialists. Other Medicare HMO plans operate with more flexibility. If the patient goes outside the network, the HMO will not pay, but Medicare will (in which case the patient will usually need to pay any deductibles plus the 20 percent copayments). These types of plans are good for seniors who live in different states at different times of the year or who want to continue using a particular physician.

Certain extra benefits make Medicare HMOs more attractive than "regular" Medicare. Many HMOs provide routine preventative checkups, eye examinations and glasses, hearing aids, and discounted prescription drugs. Because of the lower costs to patients and the extra benefits, it is now estimated that millions of Medicare enrollees have opted to join a Medicare approved HMO rather than continuing to see independent physicians on a fee-for-service basis.

However, as I write this book, there have been many reports from dissatisfied consumers in Medicare HMOs. Many people have complained that their HMOs do not give them quality care, that their primary physician refuses to let them see a specialist, and so on. In each state, there is a "peer review organization" (PRO), a panel of doctors who are paid by the federal government to monitor problems in Medicare. However, filing complaints to PROs is slow and time consuming.

Again, you will need to be familiar with these issues should you get into the medical billing business.

MEDICAID   Medicaid is administered jointly by HCFA and each state government, according to general guidelines established by federal law. Medicaid assists those whose incomes are below certain levels. In 1995, an estimated 36.2 million people utilized Medicaid, of which more than 17 million were dependent children. Note also that many Medicare members who cannot afford Medigap secondary insurance can be covered by Medicaid, which pays deductibles and copayments for them. These people are often called *Medi-Medi* crossovers. (Note if you are doing electronic claims filing: just as Medicare can send secondary claims electronically to many Medigap insurers, it can also forward the claims electronically to the appropriate Medicaid carrier. This relatively new process has facilitated the electronic filing of millions of Medicare claims that also require secondary payers.)

Many physicians do not accept Medicaid patients because the allowable amounts for billed charges are typically as low as 30 percent to 35 percent of the usual and customary fees the physician charges. For many physicians, this makes treating Medicaid patients almost a losing proposition.

Medicaid claims are processed differently in each state, either through an insurance carrier such as a Blue or a computer service company that handles the claims for HCFA. Medicaid regulations are very strict regarding what kinds of medical services are covered, and what the allowable fees are.

CHAMPUS   CHAMPUS is the Civilian Health and Medical Program of the Uniformed Services, a healthcare program for dependents of active military personnel, as well as retired military personnel and their families. Under CHAMPUS, covered persons can use civilian doctors for medical care and have a portion of the care paid for by the federal government. At age 65, CHAMPUS beneficiaries are transferred to the Medicare program.

WORKER'S COMPENSATION   Worker's compensation covers medical expenses and disability benefits when an illness or injury results directly from work. Employers with more than a certain number of employees are required to carry this insurance from a carrier of their choice.

Worker's comp. claims are more complex than standard claims, as they require second opinion reviews and many kinds of reports filed by doctors to verify the injuries. If you do billing for worker's comp. claims, it is recommended that you charge more because they take longer.

How a Doctor's Office Works

How a billing service works is directly tied into how a doctor's office works. If you have no background working in a doctor's office, you will be surprised by how many elements are involved. For this reason, this section reviews the operation of a typical physician's office.

To begin, most healthcare practitioners have one or more office personnel who handle the reception work; provide some patient support; and perhaps work on the claims filing, billing, and accounting functions. The person may be called "office manager," "receptionist," "business assistant," or there may be one of each. These office personnel may be a major impediment to your signing on a doctor—or they may be your allies. We discuss this issue in the "Marketing Guidelines" section later in the chapter.

Business Profile: Heidi Kollmorgen and Susan Kruger

Heidi Kollmorgen and Susan Kruger are partners in H/D Medical Receivables, Inc., in Cleveland, Ohio. Heidi started the business after doing billing for a doctor's office in-house for eight years; little by little, she realized that she preferred to be her own boss. Like many parents today, she also wanted to be available at home for her two children, Haley and Dylan. Through careful planning, she left her job and opened up her own company to handle "just claims," purchasing software from Medical Management Software and Merry Schiff. Her first client turned out to be her former employer, who had not found someone to replace her. While getting that contract was a cinch, Heidi told me that getting additional contracts with doctors has not been easy, as few physicians in her city have been willing to outsource billing.

Heidi therefore jumped at the chance to work with Susan when they met at their community club. Susan had worked as a hospital administrator and at a bank in marketing, so she had excellent skills in making appointments to see doctors and presenting their sales pitch. Her primary strategy is to become friendly with the office staff, as they are the gatekeepers to the doctor. Even when the office tells Susan it is not interested in hiring out its billing, Susan continues to drop in and make small talk about the newest medical coding procedures and what might be happening in healthcare at the time. As Susan says, "It's all in your manner; if you don't present yourself as a know it all, you can truly build a rapport with the office staff, and when the time is ripe, they even get behind you because you make their life easier."

Heidi and Susan say that after a few years, they were fortunate in finding several doctors who were in desperate need of their services for full practice management. They cite a major reason for this: the fact that as HMOs have become more and more common in the Cleveland area, doctors have to spend much of their time arranging referrals for their patients to specialists. Referrals require dictating medical reports and making many phone calls, functions for which the doctor relies on the office staff for support. This is why outsourcing the billing ultimately improves the conditions in a doctor's office for the office staff. Their time becomes free to help the doctor, instead of doing the billing and handling calls from patients asking about their invoices. Only in one case when Susan and Heidi took over the billing did an office staff person lose her job; in all the other cases, the office staff have been reassigned to patient relations and other office work.

Heidi and Susan now focus on full practice management. They file claims electronically and track each client's receivables, including comparing what the doctor receives from capitated payments versus fee-for-service payments. Heidi was also working with a group of doctors to help them organize and negotiate proactively with an HMO before being swallowed up by one. In building her business, Heidi believes that experience makes a difference: "The more you learn about practice management and gain experience, the better living you will earn."

THE BACKGROUND WORK   Assuming the doctor's office is independently run (not a staff HMO model), the following background events typically occur just to log the patient in.

1. When a patient first sees the physician (or dentist), he or she is asked to complete a *patient registration form*. This form includes the patient's vital statistics: name, address, sex, phone number, employer, primary insurer, member number, secondary insurer if any, and so on. The patient also usually signs a *release and assignment of benefits form* that allows the doctor to release information about the diagnosis and treatment to the insurance company so that he or she may bill the insurer directly and receive the payment. This form may be part of the registration form or it might be a separate form. Figure 2-4 shows a typical patient registration form.

2. If necessary, the patient fills out a *pre-authorization form* (also called a *pre-certification form*), which is used to specify information about a planned procedure or service that requires approval in advance by the insurance carrier, Medicare, or Medicaid. If the physician fails to obtain this approval, he or she may be denied payment by the insurance carrier or Medicare. Many insurance companies now have 800 phone numbers for physicians to use in emergencies when immediate authorization is necessary.

In the coming years, the process of checking eligibility and pre-authorizing treatments may be done via computer. Several software companies are developing systems that would allow the doctor's office or the outside billing service to use a modem to check the patient's insurance coverage and/or obtain approval for a service. Such new technology is an important step toward computerizing the medical industry and speeding up the doctor's ability to treat patients. It may also be likely that an independent billing service can either sell this software as part of its service, or do the work for doctors by phone whenever the physician gets a new patient.

3. The next form, usually called the *superbill* (also referred to as the fee ticket, visit slip, or encounter form) is used to record the purpose of the patient visit and billing information. The form contains blanks for the patient's name and other information and then lists the most common diagnostic and procedure codes used by that doctor. These codes are now required by all insurance carriers to demarcate why the patient saw the doctor and what services the doctor performed (more details about these coding systems appear later in the chapter). Since there are thousands of possible diagnosis codes and procedure codes, each office usually designs and prints its own superbills listing only the codes the doctor most commonly uses in his or her specialty. The superbill also serves as a payment receipt if the patient has to file his or her own claims.

Figures 2-5A and 2-5B show typical superbills.

▓▓ ▓▓ ▓▓ ▓▓
Figure 2-4
Patient Registration
Form (Courtesy of
Dave Shipton)

NAME:_____, SOCIAL SECURITY: _____

ADDRESS:_____
            (Street)   (City)   (State) (Zip Code)
PHONE:(___) ___-_____, BIRTHDATE:___/___/___(Month, Day, Year), AGE:_____, SEX_____

STATUS: Married___, Single___, Other___, EMPLOYED: Yes___, No___, Full Time___, Part Time___,

EMPLOYER:_____ PHONE:(___) ___-_____

ADDRESS:_____
            (Street)   (City)   (State) (Zip Code)

PRIMARY INSURANCE INFORMATION

NAME:_____, SOCIALSECURITY#:_____
(Policy Holder) (the primary person the insurance policy is assigned to) (If same as line 1, PRINT "SAME")

ADDRESS:_____
            (Street)   (City)   (State) (Zip Code)
PHONE:(___) ___-_____, BIRTHDATE:___/___/___(Month, Day, Year), AGE:_____, SEX_____

PATIENT'S RELATIONSHIP TO INSURED: Self___, Spouse___, Child___, Other___,

INSURANCE COMPANY:_____, POLICY NUMBER_____

GROUP NUMBER:_____, PLAN:_____, CERTIFICATE NUMBER:_____

ADDRESS_____
           (Street)   (City)   (State) (Zip Code)

SECONDARY INSURANCE INFORMATION

NAME:_____, SOCIAL SECURITY #:_____
(Secondary Policy, another person who may be responsible for payment) (If same as line 1, PRINT "SAME")

ADDRESS:_____
            (Street)   (City)   (State) (Zip Code)
PHONE:(___) ___-_____, BIRTHDATE:___/___/___(Month, Day, Year), AGE:_____, SEX_____

**Corrected
art to come**

INSUREDS RELATIONSHIP TO PATIENT: Self___, Spouse___, Child___, Other___,

INSURANCE COMPANY:_____, POLICY NUMBER_____

GROUP NUMBER:_____, PLAN:_____, CERTIFICATE NUMBER:_____

ADDRESS_____
           (Street)   (City)   (State) (Zip Code)

PLEASE READ AND SIGN THE FOLLOWING STATEMENT

I authorize the release of any medical or other information necessary to process insurance claims. I authorize
payment of medical benefits to the physician or supplier for services described in the insurance claim. I understand
that some Commercial Insurance plans (Metropolitian, Prudential, Aetna, PPO, HMO, etc.) may not cover the total cost
of treatment (due to the nature of the insurance plan or that some treatment(s) may be considered medically
unnecessary by the insurance company) and that I am responsible for any copayment, deductable and other charges
not covered by my primary or secondary insurance plan(s). Medicare Patients, I understand that I am responsible
for the deductable and copayment applied to my Medicare Insurance coverage.

SIGNATURE_____DATE_____

ALL INFORMATION IS KEPT STRICTLY CONFIDENTIAL

Anytown Cardiology

Pt. Name (LAST)	(FIRST)	Date of Birth	Insurance Type	Date of Service	Doctor's Name

DIAGNOSIS CODES

Angina Pectoris (NOS)	413.9
Aortic Stenosis	747.22
Aortic Valve Prolapse	424.1
Atrial Fibrillation	427.31
Atrial Flutter	427.32
Cardiac Dysrhythmia (NOS)	427.9
Cardiomyopathy, Idiopathic	425.4
CV Insufficiency (Carotid, WO CVA)	433.10
CV Insufficiency (NOS)	437.1
Cong. Heart Disease (NOS)	746.9
Congestive Heart Failure	428.0
COPD (NOS)	496
Coronary Atherosclerosis, unsp.	414.00
Diabetes W/ Insulin Depend.	250.01
Diabetes Wo/ Insulin Depend.	250.00
Emphysema	492.8
Fistula, Arteriovenous	414.19
Heart/Renal Failure (NOS)	404.90
Hyperlipidemia (NOS)	272.4
Hypertension, Uncontr (NOS)	401.9
Hypertensive Cardiomyopathy	402.91
Ischemic Heart Disease	414.8
Mitral Insufficiency /Prolapse	424.0
Mitral Valve Stenosis	394.0
Mitral/Aortic Valve Insuff.	396.3
Myocardial Infarction	411.89
Myocarditis, Viral	422.91
Post CV Disease	438
Pulmonary Artery Stenosis	747.3
Rheumatic Heart Disease	391.9
Supraventricular Tach.	427.0
Tricuspid Insufficiency	397.0

Consultations

Office Cons. prob. focused 15 min	99241
Office Cons. expanded 30 min	99242
Office Cons. detailed 40 min	99243
Office Cons. compreh, mod. 60 min	99244
Office Cons. compreh, high 80 min	99245

Follow-up Office Visits

Minimal 5 min	99211
Focused 10 min	99212
Expanded, low complex, 15 min	99213
Detailed, mod. complex, 25 min	99214
Comprehen, high complex, 40 min	99215

Referring Physician

September 27, 1996 © Priority Medical Management

PROCEDURES
Electrocardiography

EKG	93000
CV stress, test & report	93015
CV stress, report only	93018
Holter	93224
Holter removal	93225
Holter (with printout)	93230
Holter (with printout) removal	93231

Ultrasound

Abdominal aorta	76700
Duplex scan of aorta	93978

Echocardiography

2D complete	93307
Doppler complete	93320
Echo stress	93350

Abdominal aorta	76705
Duplex scan, carotid bilateral	93880
Carotid flow scan	93875

PVP

Duplex scan of lower aorta	93925
Duplex scan of extremity veins	93970

Pulmonary Function Tests

Spirometry	94060
Membrane diffusion capacity	94725
Residual capacity	94240
Breathing response to CO2	94400
Maldistribution of inspired gas	94350
Airway closing volume	94370
CO diffusing capacity	94720
Thoracic gas volume	94260
All of the above	PFT

Vascular Studies

CV arterial, bilateral	93875
Venous study, bilateral	93965
Extremity arteries, single level	93922
Extremity arteries, multi-level	93923
Extremity arteries, lower, with stress	93924

Other

Routine venipuncture	36415
Handling fee	99000

Notes

Figure 2-5A   Superbill for a typical cardiology practice (Courtesy of Neal A. Kling, Priority Medical Management, Poway, CA)

Peachblossom Family Practice

Name: *Last*		First		Date of Birth		Account Type	Date of Service		Dr's Name	

NEW		X-RAY		PROCEDURES		SUTURES/CASTING	
Focused	99201	Abdomen	74020	Audiometry	92552	*Requires Accident Report!*	
Expanded	99202	Abdomen (KUB)	74000	Colonoscopy	45378	Simple? Intermediate?	S I
Detailed	99203	Ankle	73610	CV stress test	93015	Enter *length* and *location*	
Comp. (45 Mins)	99204	Cervical spine	72040	EKG	93000		
Initial OB	Z1032	Chest (2 views)	71020	Endoscopy, upper	43235		
		Elbow	73080	Holter monitor	93230		
ESTABLISHED		Face	70150	Holter removal	93231		
Minimal	99211	Femur	73550	IV therapy	90780	Casting supplies	A4580
Focused	99212	Finger	73140	Nerve study	95904		
Expanded	99213	Foot	73630	Pulmo aide	94640		
Detailed	99214	Forearm	73090	Spirometry P&P	SPIRO		
Comp. (45 Mins)	99215	Hand	73130	LAB (IN OFFICE)			
OB Prenatal	Z1034	Hips, bilateral	73520	Glucose	82947		
OB Postpartum	Z1038	Hip	73510	Hemoglobin	85018		
		Knee	73562	Hemoccult stool	82270		
INJECTIONS		Lumbosacral	72110	Pregnancy, urine	81025		
Ancef	J0690	Neck, soft tissue	70360	Urine dipstick	81002		
B12 Complex	J3500	Pelvis	72190	Venipuncture	36415		
Demerol	J2175	Ribs, bilateral	71111				
Depoprovera	J1055	Ribs, unilateral	71101				
Dexamethasone	J1100	Sacro-iliac	72202			SUPPLIES	
Diphenhydramine 50mg	J1200	Sacrum & Coccyx	72220	LAB (OUTSIDE)		Ace bandage	A4460
Droperidol	J1790	Shoulder	73030	Afetoprotein	82105	Gauze pads	A4200
Epinephrine	J0170	Sinus series	70220	Arthritis panel	ARTH	4" roller bandage	A4202
Estradiol Valerate 40mg	J0970	Skull series	70260	Blood lipoprotein assay	83718	Electrodes	A4556
Furosemide 20mg	J1940	Thoracic Spine	72070	CBC	85025	Irrigation tray	A4320
Gentamicin 80mg	J1580	Tibia/fibula	73590	Culture, throat	87060	Surgical tray	A4550
Glycophyrolate 0.2	X6258	Toes	73660	Culture, urine	87086		
Keflin 1gr	J1890	Wrist	73110	Culture, vaginal	87070	SURGICAL	
Lidocaine 1%	J2000	ULTRASOUND		Estrogens, total	82672	Biopsy, skin	11100
Lincocin 300mg	J2010	Abdominal	76700	GC & Chlamydia	87110	Cryotherapy	17340
Marcaine HCL 0.25%	J0670	Breast(s)	76645	Hepatitis panel	80059	Debridement, burn	16020
Methylprednisolone 40	J1030	OB	76805	HTLV or HIV test	86689	Debridement, skin	11041
Methylprednisolone 80	J1040	Pelvic (Non-OB)	76856	Lipids profile	80061	Destr. les., face	17000
Penicillin 600,000	J0560	Prostate	76856	Liver function screen	LIVER	Destr. les. - nonfacial	17100
Penicillin 1.2 Mil	J0570	Renal	76770	Mono test	86317	Excision of nail	11750
Penicillin 2.4 Mil	J0580	Scrotum	76870	O&P, stool	87177	I&D, seb. cyst	10060
Phenergan	J2550	Thyroid	76536	Older adult profile	OLD	I&D, hematoma	10140
Progesterone 50mg	J2675	PVP		Pap smear	88150	Inj. trigger pts.	20550
Rocephin	J0696	Dup. scan lower aorta	93925	Pap smear, abnormal	88151	Removal, cerumen	69210
Triamcinolone	J3301	Sup. scan extrem. veins	93970	PAP test (prostate)	84066	Rem. for. obj., eye	65205
Toradol	J1885	VASCULAR STUDIES		Pregnancy, serum	84703	Rem. FO eye embedded	65210
Valium	J3360	Abdominal aorta	76705	Prenatal panel	80055	Removal FO, nose	30300
Versed	90782	Carotid, duplex	93880	Prolactin assay	84146	Removal, skin tags	11200
Vistaril	J3410	Extr. arter. upper	93922	Protein electroph.	84165	Removal, warts	17110
		Extr. arter. lower	93923	PSA	84153	NORPLANT	
IMMUNIZATIONS		Extr. art. low w/stress	93924	RPR	86592	Insertion	11975
DTP	90701	Cerebrovascular	93875	Rubella	86762	Norplant kit	X1520
DT	90702	Venous, lower	93965	Sedimentation rate	85651	Surgical tray	A4550
Gamma Globulin	J1470	OTHER DRUGS		SMAC	80018	Anesthesia	J2000
Hepatitis B	9074?	Acet. w/Cod 300mg	99070	T4 test	84436	Removal	11976
HIB	90737	Chlorzoxazone 500mg		T7 (Thyroid panel)	80091	PHYSICAL THERAPY	
Influenza	90724	Diphenhydramine		Toxoplasma	80090	Hot/Cold packs	97010
Mantoux Test	86580	Elavil Amitriptyline 10mg		Urinalysis, micro	81000	TENS unit	64550
MMR	90707	Ibuprophen 200mg #30				TENS unit leads	E0730
Polio	90712	Naprosyn 500mg #20		ECHOCARDIO		Ultrasound	UL95
Tetanus Toxoid	90703	Pediazol 600mg		2D, comp	93307		
STEROID INJECTIONS		Podophilin		Doppler, comp	93320		
Small joint	20600	Robaxin 750mg #20		Echo stress	93350		
Medium joint	20605	Seldane 60mg					
Large joint	20610	Tylenol 500mg #30					
		Valium 5mg #30					

	ICD9 Code		ICD9 Code		ICD9 Code	Ded.Remain	Payments
1		3		5			
2		4		6			

September 27, 1996 © Priority Medical Management, Poway, CA

Figure 2-5B Superbill for a typical family practice physician (Courtesy of Neal A. Kling, Priority Medical Management, Poway, CA)

It may be that in several years, the paper superbill will be replaced by some form of computerized record that the doctor or office staff keys in, perhaps on a portable or laptop computer device specially made for this purpose. If you become a billing service, you should pay attention to such technological developments, as they may bring in further opportunities for services you can offer your clients in helping them computerize many current paper-based operations.

After the patient visit, the doctor passes the superbill to the front office staff, and the insurance process and patient billing get under way. In some cases, the billing person will ask the patient to pay the fee at the time the service is rendered, and it is then up to the patient to obtain reimbursement from his or her insurance. In the case of Medicare, the doctor's office must file the claim on behalf of the patient. If the physician is a PAR provider, the patient usually makes no payment at this time or only the 20 percent copayment (unless he or she has Medicaid or Medigap insurance as the secondary payer).

Next, processing the superbill depends on whether the office still uses a paper-based method of accounting and claim filing, or is computerized and does its own claim filing, or uses an outside billing service. Here's a comparison of paper accounting systems versus electronic accounting systems including electronic claims, regardless of whether the electronic accounting is done at the doctor's office or by an independent billing service.

PAPER CLAIMS AND ACCOUNTING

Step 1—Paper. If the office is paper based, the billing clerk refers to the superbill and types out a preprinted paper claim form, called the HCFA 1500 (pronounced Hick-fah fifteen hundred). This is now the universal claim form required and accepted by every insurance company and Medicare for filing medical claims other than hospitalizations. (Hospitals, emergency care clinics, and certain other types of healthcare providers use a different form, called the UB92.) Dentists use another form, called the ADA form that, like the HCFA 1500, indicates the diagnosis and procedures the dentist performed.

The HCFA 1500 and ADA form are shown in Figures 2-6 and 2-7. The accompanying sidebar explains how the HCFA 1500 form came about.

Step 2—Paper. Depending on the doctor's office, the claim form may get typed out the same day as the patient's visit or the clerk may wait several days before completing many forms all at once. As noted earlier in the chapter, paper claim forms are then mailed to the insurance carriers

The HCFA 1500

The story behind the HCFA 1500 is important to know. It familiarizes you with some terminology and sheds light on why the healthcare industry has been slow to implement efficient procedures in the health insurance arena.

In the past, claims filing was a nightmare. Nearly every commercial insurance company, as well as Medicare, Medicaid, and Blue Cross/Blue Shield, had its own unique paper claim form. Keeping track of which form was to be used for which carrier was a major job. Every form had its particular requirements for reporting the doctor's diagnosis, the procedures performed, and the fee.

In the early 1980s, the American Medical Association established a task force to develop a standardized form that would be acceptable to the various government agencies and to the commercial carriers. The result of its work was the Uniform Health Insurance Claim Form, called the HCFA 1500, issued originally in 1984. In 1990, the form was revised to eliminate the spaces in which doctors would write an explanation of unusual services or circumstances to justify their fee. The new version, called the Red Form (since it is printed in red ink), allows spaces only for standard codes representing the diagnosis and the procedure performed. The Red Form also requires patients to provide information about any secondary insurance carrier so that the primary carrier will not duplicate any benefits paid.

Most medical billing software programs print HCFA 1500 claim forms. Of course, the goal is to file electronically and completely abandon the paper form.

via U.S. mail. Meanwhile, to track the patient's account, the billing clerk also writes the charges for the visit in a daily log (often called a "pegboard system") or on a patient ledger card that serves as a record of that person's accounts. Figure 2-8 shows an example of a patient ledger card.

Step 3—Paper. The mailed claim form eventually arrives at the insurer's office, where it is opened, screened, assigned a control number, microfilmed for record keeping, and then manually entered into a computer by a claims examiner. If it contains no errors, the physician receives payment for the claim in 30 to 90 days. However, if the claim contains errors, such as missing information or an incorrect or unacceptable diagnosis or procedure code, it is denied and returned to the doctor's office for correction. It may take several months before the claim can be corrected and resubmitted.

Many people with inside knowledge of how insurance companies work point out that many insurers "lose" claims and take months to "find" them (or never do). In fact, it is common knowledge in the business that commercial insurers took advantage of the perception of many errors in paper claim forms so as to delay paying claims as long as possible. Each day a provider was not paid was money in the bank for the insurers, on which they earned interest. It was also com-

PLEASE
DO NOT
STAPLE
IN THIS
AREA

TOPFORM DATA, INC. (800) 814-7470

REORDER ITEM #1117

HEALTH INSURANCE CLAIM FORM

PICA		PICA	

1. MEDICARE	MEDICAID	CHAMPUS	CHAMPVA	GROUP HEALTH PLAN	FECA BLK LUNG	OTHER	1a. INSURED'S I.D. NUMBER	(FOR PROGRAM IN ITEM 1)
(Medicare #)	(Medicaid #)	(Sponsor's SSN)	(VA File #)	(SSN or ID)	(SSN)	(ID)		

2. PATIENT'S NAME (Last Name, First Name, Middle Initial)

3. PATIENT'S BIRTH DATE MM DD YY   SEX M F

4. INSURED'S NAME (Last Name, First Name, Middle Initial)

5. PATIENT'S ADDRESS (No., Street)

6. PATIENT RELATIONSHIP TO INSURED
Self ☐ Spouse ☐ Child ☐ Other ☐

7. INSURED'S ADDRESS (No., Street)

CITY   STATE

8. PATIENT STATUS
Single ☐ Married ☐ Other ☐

CITY   STATE

ZIP CODE   TELEPHONE (Include Area Code) (   )

Employed ☐ Full-Time Student ☐ Part-Time Student ☐

ZIP CODE   TELEPHONE (Include Area Code) (   )

9. OTHER INSURED'S NAME (Last Name, First Name, Middle Initial)

10. IS PATIENT'S CONDITION RELATED TO:

11. INSURED'S POLICY GROUP OR FECA NUMBER

a. OTHER INSURED'S POLICY OR GROUP NUMBER

a. EMPLOYMENT? (CURRENT OR PREVIOUS)
☐ YES ☐ NO

a. INSURED'S DATE OF BIRTH MM DD YY   SEX M F

b. OTHER INSURED'S DATE OF BIRTH MM DD YY   SEX M F

b. AUTO ACCIDENT?   PLACE (State)
☐ YES ☐ NO

b. EMPLOYER'S NAME OR SCHOOL NAME

c. EMPLOYER'S NAME OR SCHOOL NAME

c. OTHER ACCIDENT?
☐ YES ☐ NO

c. INSURANCE PLAN NAME OR PROGRAM NAME

d. INSURANCE PLAN NAME OR PROGRAM NAME

10d. RESERVED FOR LOCAL USE

d. IS THERE ANOTHER HEALTH BENEFIT PLAN?
☐ YES ☐ NO   If yes, return to and complete item 9 a-d.

READ BACK OF FORM BEFORE COMPLETING & SIGNING THIS FORM.
12. PATIENT'S OR AUTHORIZED PERSON'S SIGNATURE I authorize the release of any medical or other information necessary to process this claim. I also request payment of government benefits either to myself or to the party who accepts assignment below.

SIGNED _____   DATE _____

13. INSURED'S OR AUTHORIZED PERSON'S SIGNATURE I authorize payment of medical benefits to the undersigned physician or supplier for services described below.

SIGNED _____

14. DATE OF CURRENT: MM DD YY   ILLNESS (First symptom) OR INJURY (Accident) OR PREGNANCY (LMP)

15. IF PATIENT HAS HAD SAME OR SIMILAR ILLNESS. GIVE FIRST DATE MM DD YY

16. DATES PATIENT UNABLE TO WORK IN CURRENT OCCUPATION MM DD YY   MM DD YY
FROM   TO

17. NAME OF REFERRING PHYSICIAN OR OTHER SOURCE

17a. I.D. NUMBER OF REFERRING PHYSICIAN

18. HOSPITALIZATION DATES RELATED TO CURRENT SERVICES MM DD YY   MM DD YY
FROM   TO

19. RESERVED FOR LOCAL USE

20. OUTSIDE LAB? $ CHARGES
☐ YES ☐ NO

21. DIAGNOSIS OR NATURE OF ILLNESS OR INJURY. (RELATE ITEMS 1,2,3, OR 4 TO ITEM 24E BY LINE)

1. |_____._____   3. |_____._____

2. |_____._____   4. |_____._____

22. MEDICAID RESUBMISSION CODE   ORIGINAL REF. NO.

23. PRIOR AUTHORIZATION NUMBER

24.	A				B	C	D		E	F	G	H	I	J	K
	DATE(S) OF SERVICE				Place of Service	Type of Service	PROCEDURES, SERVICES, OR SUPPLIES (Explain Unusual Circumstances)		DIAGNOSIS CODE	$ CHARGES	DAYS OR UNITS	EPSDT Family Plan	EMG	COB	RESERVED FOR LOCAL USE
	From MM DD YY		To MM DD YY				CPT/HCPCS	MODIFIER							
1															
2															
3															
4															
5															
6															

25. FEDERAL TAX I.D. NUMBER   SSN ☐ EIN ☐

26. PATIENT'S ACCOUNT NO.

27. ACCEPT ASSIGNMENT? (For govt. claims, see back)
☐ YES ☐ NO

28. TOTAL CHARGE $

29. AMOUNT PAID $

30. BALANCE DUE $

31. SIGNATURE OF PHYSICIAN OR SUPPLIER INCLUDING DEGREES OR CREDENTIALS (I certify that the statements on the reverse apply to this bill and are made a part thereof.)

SIGNED _____   DATE _____

32. NAME AND ADDRESS OF FACILITY WHERE SERVICES WERE RENDERED (If other than home or office)

33. PHYSICIAN'S, SUPPLIER'S BILLING NAME, ADDRESS, ZIP CODE & PHONE #

PIN#   GRP#

(APPROVED BY AMA COUNCIL ON MEDICAL SERVICE 8/88)
APPROVED OMB-0938-0008

PLEASE PRINT OR TYPE

FORM HCFA-1500 (12-90)
FORM OWCP-1500   FORM RRB-1500

CARRIER — PATIENT AND INSURED INFORMATION — PHYSICIAN OR SUPPLIER INFORMATION

Figure 2-6   HCFA 1500 Claim Form

ATTENDING DENTIST'S STATEMENT

CARRIER NAME AND ADDRESS

CHECK ONE:

_____ DENTIST'S PRE-TREATMENT ESTIMATE

_____ DENTIST'S STATEMENT OF ACTUAL SERVICES

PATIENT COVERAGE INFORMATION

1. PATIENT NAME — FIRST — M.I. — LAST
2. RELATIONSHIP TO INSURED — SELF — CHILD — SPOUSE — OTHER
3. SEX — M / F
4. PATIENT BIRTHDATE — MO. / DAY / YEAR
5. IF FULL TIME STUDENT — SCHOOL — CITY

6. EMPLOYEE/SUBSCRIBER NAME AND MAILING ADDRESS
7. EMPLOYEE/SUBSCRIBER SOC. SEC. OR I.D. NUMBER
8. EMPLOYEE/SUBSCRIBER BIRTHDATE — MO. / DAY / YEAR
9. EMPLOYER (COMPANY) NAME AND ADDRESS
10. GROUP NUMBER

11. IS PATIENT COVERED BY ANOTHER PLAN OF BENEFITS? — DENTAL — MEDICAL
12-A. NAME AND ADDRESS OF CARRIER(S)
12-B. GROUP NO.(S)
13. NAME AND ADDRESS OF EMPLOYER

14-A. EMPLOYEE/SUBSCRIBER NAME (IF DIFFERENT THAN PATIENT'S)
14-B. EMPLOYEE/SUBSCRIBER SOC. SEC. OR I.D. NUMBER
14-C. EMPLOYEE/SUBSCRIBER BIRTHDATE — MO. / DAY / YEAR
15. RELATIONSHIP TO INSURED — SELF — PARENT — SPOUSE — OTHER

I HAVE REVIEWED THE FOLLOWING TREATMENT PLAN. I AUTHORIZE RELEASE OF ANY INFORMATION RELATING TO THIS CLAIM. I UNDERSTAND THAT I AM RESPONSIBLE FOR ALL COSTS OF DENTAL TREATMENT.

I HEREBY AUTHORIZE PAYMENT OF THE DENTAL BENEFITS OTHERWISE PAYABLE TO ME DIRECTLY TO THE BELOW NAMED DENTAL ENTITY.

▶ SIGNED (PATIENT, OR PARENT IF MINOR) — DATE

▶ SIGNED (INSURED PERSON) — DATE

BILLING DENTIST

16. NAME OF BILLING DENTIST OR DENTAL ENTITY
24. IS TREATMENT RESULT OF OCCUPATIONAL ILLNESS OR INJURY? — NO — YES — IF YES, ENTER BRIEF DESCRIPTION AND DATES.

17. ADDRESS WHERE PAYMENT SHOULD BE REMITTED
25. IS TREATMENT RESULT OF AUTO ACCIDENT?
26. OTHER ACCIDENT?

CITY, STATE, ZIP
27. ARE ANY SERVICES COVERED BY ANOTHER PLAN?

18. DENTIST SOC. SEC. OR T.I.N.
19. DENTIST LICENSE NO.
20. DENTIST PHONE NO.
28. IF PROSTHESIS, IS THIS INITIAL PLACEMENT? — (IF NO, REASON FOR REPLACEMENT)
29. DATE OF PRIOR PLACEMENT

21. FIRST VISIT DATE CURRENT SERIES
22. PLACE OF TREATMENT — OFFICE / HOSP. / ECF / OTHER
23. RADIOGRAPHS OR MODELS ENCLOSED? — NO — YES — HOW MANY?
30. IS TREATMENT FOR ORTHODONTICS? — IF SERVICES ALREADY COMMENCED, ENTER: — DATE APPLIANCES PLACED — MOS. TREATMENT REMAINING

IDENTIFY MISSING TEETH WITH "X"

FACIAL — LINGUAL — RIGHT — UPPER — LEFT — PERMANENT — PRIMARY — LOWER — LINGUAL — FACIAL

31. EXAMINATION AND TREATMENT PLAN - LIST IN ORDER FROM TOOTH NO. 1 THROUGH TOOTH NO. 32 - USE CHARTING SYSTEM SHOWN.

TOOTH # OR LETTER	SURFACE	DESCRIPTION OF SERVICE (INCLUDING X-RAYS, PROPHYLAXIS, MATERIALS USED, ETC.)	DATE SERVICES PERFORMED MO. DAY YEAR	PROCEDURE NUMBER	FEE	FOR ADMINISTRATIVE USE ONLY

32. REMARKS FOR UNUSUAL SERVICES

I HEREBY CERTIFY THAT THE PROCEDURES AS INDICATED BY DATE HAVE BEEN COMPLETED AND THAT THE FEES SUBMITTED ARE THE ACTUAL FEES I HAVE CHARGED AND INTEND TO COLLECT FOR THOSE PROCEDURES.

SIGNED (TREATING DENTIST) — LICENSE NUMBER — DATE

TOTAL FEE CHARGED / MAX ALLOWABLE / DEDUCTIBLE / CARRIER % / CARRIER PAYS / PATIENT PAYS

Form Approved by the
AMERICAN DENTAL ASSOCIATION
1990

TOPFORM DATA, INC. • (800) 854-7470   Reorder Item #1116

Figure 2-7   ADA Dental Claim Forms

Figure 2-8
Patient Ledger Card

Statement

John Doe Patient
1234 Main Street
Springfield, IL

				Credits		
Date	Code	Description	Charge	Payments	Adjustments	Current Balance

OV - Office Visit   HOSP - Hospital Visit   ROA - Received on Account
OS - Office Surgery   HS – Hospital Surgery   NC - No Charge
TC - Telephone Consultation SA - Surgical Assistant   INS - Insurance payment
FA - Failed Appointment   ER - Emergency Room
RP - Report

mon knowledge that claims examiners at insurance companies would never check claims and correct minor errors if they found some. Claims with even the slightest error, such as no check mark in the male/female box for a patient named Edward, would be rejected. (I guess there are female Edwards; one never knows!) The result was a very high rate of rejection.

Step 4—Paper. When a claim has no errors and is approved, the insurer sends out a document called an Explanation of Benefits (EOB) to the patient and a copy of it to the physician. For Medicare, the patient is mailed an Explanation of Medicare Benefits (EOMB), while the physician receives a computerized report.

The EOB or EOMB shows the amount charged, the amount allowed, and the amount paid for each procedure. Remember that Medicare and most commercial insurance policies pay only 80 percent of the allowable fee for physician services, leaving the patient responsible for the 20 percent coinsurance. If the physician has accepted assignment, he or she receives the check directly. If not, the patient receives the check.

Next, in a traditional paper accounting system, the billing clerk must log payments onto each patient's ledger, and to a daily accounts receivable journal that keeps track of the day's cash flow. To remind patients about their due balances and copayments, the clerk also sends out a monthly statement to each patient, often by simply photocopying the ledger cards showing the balance due—a time-consuming task that can take a billing clerk hours.

Step 5—Paper. If the patient has secondary insurance, another paper HCFA 1500 form must now be filed. This form must be accompanied by a copy of the EOB from the primary insurer showing how much it paid, so the secondary insurer does not duplicate any payments. It might take another 30 days to receive the remainder due from a secondary insurer.

These steps describe the billing and accounting operation of many medical offices that continue to operate manually or are only partially computerized. As mentioned earlier, some offices use computers to do their accounting but print out the HCFA 1500 forms and mail them on paper for insurance reimbursement rather than doing electronic claims processing using communications software and a modem.

However, filing paper claims is a risky business. Between the expense and effort required to fill them out, and the lengthy time delay to get them reimbursed, combined with the anxiety of dealing with our unpredictable postal service and insurance companies that love to deny claims, continuing to use paper claims is like throwing money away. Few people doubt that the days of paper claims are numbered.

ELECTRONIC CLAIMS AND ACCOUNTING   In an office that utilizes computerized accounting systems and electronic claims processing, patients still fill out a registration form and doctors still use paper superbills (although, as pointed out, these paper forms may also become computerized very shortly). The procedure differs in the steps that occur after the superbill is prepared. A clerk in the office or the independent medical billing service does the following:

Step 1—Electronic. The first step in an electronic office is to set up the software. The setup work is perhaps the most time-consuming phase for a medical billing service, but once it is done, electronic claims processing and accounting take considerably less time than handling paper forms and are virtually error free.

Most medical billing software programs today are easy to use. They may be DOS-based or Windows-based. In either type, there is usually a "main menu" of basic functions from which you select your commands. Each main menu command then leads to "submenus" with more detailed commands, just like programs such as *Microsoft Word for Windows* with the commands across the top that you access by pointing at and clicking your mouse, or in the popular DOS-based *WordPerfect 5.1* with its many function key commands.

To help visualize these programs, look at Figures 2-9 and 2-10. Included with this book is a CD-ROM that contains demonstration software from a selection of vendors.

- Figure 2-9 shows a few screen shots from the program *Claims Manager* produced by InfoHealth. This program is a full practice management software package that handles all basic accounting functions as well as electronic claims filing.

- Figure 2-10 shows a few screen shots from the program *Lytec Medical for Windows*, produced by Lytec Systems (and resold by several business opportunity vendors). This software is also a full practice management program that handles accounting functions and electronic filing.

Whichever software you use, the setup procedures are quite similar because you need to store the same type of information. All software involves creating database "records" for each patient, doctor in the practice, and insurance company to be billed by the practice. You usually can also create a database of the commonly used diagnostic and procedure codes (or the software may already have the procedure codes stored in it from the AMA, which owns the copyright on these codes). If the software you are using performs accounting and practice management functions, the setup also includes entering the existing account balances for each established patient.

For example, when you first get a client, you will need to enter all current patients, including their name, address, Social Security number, the primary and secondary insurance company, the plan ID number and the group number, the employer, and a variety of other data. Table 2-7 shows a list of the patient fields that are typically required in a software package for patient data.

Similarly, you need to create a database record for every provider in the practice, including his or her address, tax ID number, and other special ID numbers sometimes assigned by Medicare and Medicaid.

■■■ ■■■ ■■■ ■■■
Figure 2-9
Sample Screens from
InfoHealth Claims
Manager Software

```
                        SYSTEM MENU
          ─────────────────────────────────────
             D - Daily Functions
             E - End of Day Reports
             R - Reports & Forms
             C - Claims Processing
             M - Month End Processing
             P - Practice Analysis
             L - Login Options
             S - System Services


        [Esc] - Exit                [F1] - Help
```

```
Account Frederick Morgan          Patient Number 00002-00000 │ 05/31/96
Patient Frederick Morgan          Doctor 02    Billcode 21   │ 08/19/96
                                  InsCo  0003  Codeset  A04I │ 14:25:20
── Code ──── Diagnosis ──────────
1. *  246.8  Thyroid Disease                  Insurance amount:    30.00
2.                                                                  0.00
3.          ┌──────────────────────────────────────────┐          30.00
4.          │         Reimbursement Calculator          │          30.00
            │──────────────────────────────────────────│
── Code ─── │ Insurance charges #        =====>   30.00 │ Pos  Tos  DxRf
1. *99213.00.│ Insurance allowed ===============>  22.80 │ OF   1I   1
            │ Primary pmt (02P) #        18.24          │
2.          │ Other pmts  (02P) #                       │
            │ Deductible remaining                      │
3.          │ Insurance write off (02C) =========>  7.20 │
            │──────────────────────────────────────────│
4.          │ Amount insurance remaining (07C) ===>  4.56 │
            │ Amount patient responsible (01D) ===>       │
5.          │──────────────────────────────────────────│
            │ [F2]=Store                    [Esc]=Exit  │
6.          └──────────────────────────────────────────┘

7.

[Esc]=Exit   [F1]=Help   [F2]=Store
```

As mentioned earlier, one advantage of today's sophisticated medical billing software is that keying information involves error checking. For example, the software will block you from keying in an alphabetic character if the field accepts only numeric characters, or it may beep if you have keyed in only nine digits where ten are expected.

Assuming that the setup has been done correctly at this point, you are ready to begin taking superbills from your clients and turning them into electronic claims.

Step 2—Electronic. This step involves getting the superbill document from the physician. Some billing services pick up the documents from their clients on a daily or weekly basis; others have the doctor fax them.

Note: several vendors sell programs that allow you to "download" superbill information from the computer in the doctor's office, assuming the staff has keyboarded it. For example, the best program of this kind is called *Data-Link,* available from ClaimTek Systems, a

Patients

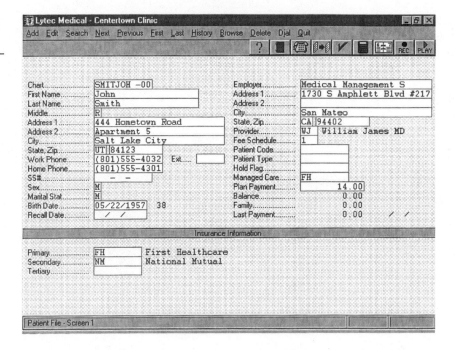

Figure 2-10
Sample Screens
from Lytec Medical
for Windows

Patients - (Insurance Information) - Zoom

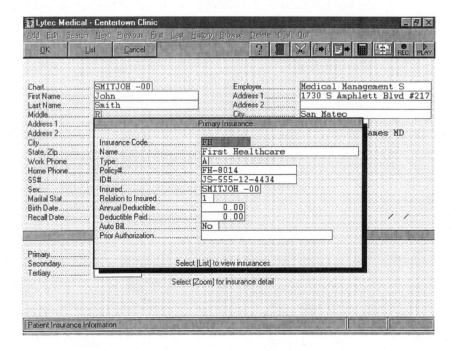

Figure 2-10
Sample Screens
from Lytec Medical
for Windows
(Continued)

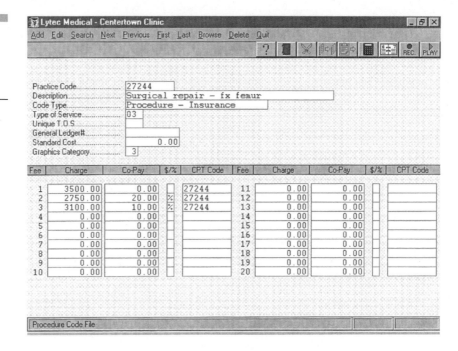

business opportunity vendor in Portland, Oregon. *Data-Link* allows the doctor's office to key in some of the data; the outside billing service then uses *PCAnywhere!* software to tap into the doctor's computer and retrieve the data; the service can then process all the claims and do the accounting at night, delivering updated data back to the doctor's computer in the morning. While some people question the logic of these types of arrangements (why would the doctor pay you when his or her staff is still doing some of the work?), you should consider such linking software in the context of how it might serve your business. In other words, some billing service owners believe it will help them get clients; others think that it will not.

Step 3—Electronic. The next step for a billing service is to key in the data for all the superbills collected. Every billing service I have interviewed estimates that data entry takes less than one minute per patient, because today's software is so easy to use and prompts for the fields of information needed to complete the claim. (The exception is new patients, when you need to go through the setup routine, which takes longer.) For the standard claim, you simply need to key in the patient code or name, the diagnosis codes, procedure codes, fees, date

TABLE 2-7

Fields to Keyboard for a Typical Patient Record

Last name

First name

Middle initial

Address 1

Address 2

City

State

Zip code

Home phone

Work phone

Date of birth

Sex

Patient category (private, insurance, Medicare, Medicaid, worker's comp.)

Primary physician's code

Location of service (office = 1, hospital = 2, branch office = 3, home = 4, etc.)

Referring physician

Facility of services

Is the condition related to employment? (Y/N)

Is the condition related to an accident? (Y/N)

Date of accident

State in which accident occurred

Date of illness/injury/or pregnancy

Date first consulted doctor

Date of similar previous injury

Date of admission to hospital

Date of discharge from hospital

Disability from date

TABLE 2-7

Fields to Keyboard for a Typical Patient Record (Continued)

Disability to date

First insurance carrier

Insured person's ID #

Is the insured person related to the patient? (Y/N)

Accepts assignment (Y/N)

Bill the carrier (Y/N)

Patient's signature on file (Y/N)

Pay benefits to patient (Y/N)

Insured person's name (if different from patient)

Medicare coverage

Secondary insurance company

Second insurance related to insured

Accept assignment from second insured (Y/N)

Bill other carrier (Y/N)

Medicare other policy prefix

Marital status

Employment status (full-time, part-time, retired, no)

Student status (full, part, no)

Prior authorization #

Recall date/time

First diagnosis

Second diagnosis

Third diagnosis

Fourth diagnosis

Primary responsible party (name)

Secondary responsible party

of service, location of service, and a few additional fields. Many software programs store the data, so all you need to do is press a Function key or click on the mouse and a list pops up, from which you can highlight the entry rather than typing it.

Step 4—Electronic. After you have keyboarded the day's claims, you usually go back to your main menu and select the function for "batch" electronic claims filing. This allows you to send an entire group of claims all at one time. The software may first prepare a summary printout of the claims to transmit so that you can verify the report before going online; this also serves as a record for you. Some software also compresses the data file to increase transmission speed.

Step 5—Electronic. The next step is the actual transmission of the claims to the insurance companies over the phone lines using a communications component of your billing software and a modem. Note that most billing services do not transmit directly to each and every insurance company, but rather to a central clearinghouse that acts as a routing station between the billing service and the insurers. One reason for this is that the data format standards among insurance companies still differ, just as they do with paper claims. Where one company wants a ten-digit number with trailing zeros, another wants leading zeros. (Medicare has recently implemented a standard electronic data format policy that will apply to all Medicare intermediaries throughout the country.)

Clearinghouses rectify the discrepancies among insurance company data preferences by translating from the language of your software to the language required by each insurer in a matter of seconds. Claims for your local Medicare are translated one way, while claims for Aetna or another commercial carrier are translated into its respective data format.

Do you need a clearinghouse? In some cases, no. A billing service can transmit directly to a local carrier such as Blue Cross or a regional Medicare carrier. In fact, many Medicare intermediaries give away free software to facilitate filing electronic claims directly to them. However, in the long run, most billing services that handle many claims from a variety of doctors choose to use a clearinghouse because it saves them time and confusion. By going through a single clearinghouse, you do not need to work with more than one medical billing software package, and all your data are stored in one program.

Furthermore, clearinghouses serve another vital purpose as well: *online* error checking. As pointed out earlier, the quality and comprehensiveness of error checking at the clearinghouse significantly reduces the error rate on incomplete or inaccurate claims to practically zero.

However, clearinghouses are not free. Most charge between $0.35 and $0.50 per claim, and some also have an annual registration fee plus a per doctor fee. Also, to make sure you know how to use the software and dial them up, they usually require that you take a simple test by sending in 20 or so claims to prove that you can code and transmit correctly. See the sidebar "Clearing the Air About Clearinghouses" on page 80 for more information.

Step 6—Electronic. After receiving the claims, the clearinghouse notifies you (usually within minutes while online) about the claims received and processed to each insurance carrier, and those rejected because of errors. You can then make a paper copy of this report, called an Audit/Edit Report or Sender Log, for your records. In many cases, you can make an immediate correction on certain rejected claims and resubmit them the same day. However, if an error is due to coding, you are best advised to confer with your doctor's office before resubmitting the claim.

Insurers process clean electronic claims within 7 to 15 days, and clean Medicare claims are reimbursed in 14 to 19 days for PAR providers. Because of the error checking that occurs in both the keying-in phase and when you are online with the clearinghouse, filing claims electronically is significantly faster and less prone to mistakes than filing paper claims.

Practice Management Functions

If you perform practice management for your clients, your software will invariably make all the other functions you need to do more efficient. Let's examine the additional functions you might perform in the way of full practice management.

Whenever a claim is paid and the physician receives the EOB and a check, you will continue to track each patient's account. Many billing services do this by arranging for the office staff to forward them copies of all EOBs that come in each day, so they can key in the payments and adjust the accounts. This may be done through the mail or by fax. To simplify the process, some doctors even agree to have the insurance companies send the EOBs and checks directly to their billing service. Of course, you must establish a significant amount of trust for this to occur.

Clearing the Air About Clearinghouses

Clearinghouses are confusing to most people new to medical billing. One way to understand them is to realize that although the HCFA 1500 standardized the paper claim, electronic claims are still not universally formatted. Clearinghouses are the solution to the chaos that would occur if doctors had to send electronic claims to each different insurance company their patients had. Another way to think about clearinghouses is the purpose they serve for the insurance companies themselves. Given that there are hundreds of insurers in the country, and each one has its own proprietary computer system and data demands, a clearinghouse is the only way that doctors and billing services can communicate with them.

When electronic claims are sent, the data are "formatted" a certain way according to the insurance company's needs. Here's an example from Frank Haraksin, president and founder of Electronic Translations and Transmittals Corporation (commonly known as ET&T). As Frank told me, "Some insurers take a data field and do what they need with it. In one case, a Blue I worked with wanted a plan code to occupy a certain field in its system. That was fine, but another insurer wanted a blank space there."

In order to be useful, a clearinghouse needs to make contracts with as many insurance companies as it can if it wants to accept claims from billers and doctors throughout the country. This means that a lot of programming goes into making a clearinghouse successful. In return, clearinghouses make money from both sides of the fence. Insurance companies pay them a per claim fee for transmitting the claims electronically to them, saving the insurers money on processing paper claims. Doctors and independent billing agencies usually pay a per claim fee as well to compensate the clearinghouse for taking their claims and transmitting them to the insurance companies.

The competition among clearinghouses for customers (like you) has heated up in recent years. Frank Haraksin estimates that there are now about 30 clearinghouses battling for your business, and the industry may be due for a shakedown. In fact, in the most recent years, several clearinghouses have been purchased by other companies. The company formerly called ETS in Atlanta was purchased by Equifax, Inc., which, in turn, was purchased by National Data Corporation, a large conglomerate of information service companies. As Chris Heller, Account Manager for National Data Corporation's Health EDI Services reminds readers, "The advantage of a clearinghouse is the edits that it can perform to increase the chances of being paid to nearly 100 percent. When you send a claim to a clearinghouse, you get immediate online information about the claim; you know if it was accepted or rejected."

When you buy your medical billing software, you may be told to work with a certain clearinghouse that has contracted with your software company to handle its claims. Note that you may not need to work with that particular clearinghouse. In most cases, you can shop around to find a clearinghouse that might offer a better deal. For example, Frank Haraksin points out that his company ET&T is very competitive with other clearinghouses. Frank indicates that ET&T has no annual sign up fee and no per doctor fees; its only charges are per claim (and there is no fee if your claim is rejected at the clearinghouse for incompleteness). Frank also indicates that because his company is small, it can get you online more quickly than some other clearinghouses. His company accepts any billing software format, such as *Medisoft* or *Lytec*. See Appendix A for information about clearinghouses.

PERF PROV	SERV DATE	POS	MOS	PROC	BILLED	ALLOWED	DEDUCT	COINS	PROV. PD.	RC-AMT	
NAME		31	HIC 123-432-000A						ASG	Y	
0PL1234B0			1 908456z9								
	052496		1	96115	300.00	159.52	0.00	31.90	127.62	CO-42	140.48
PT RESP	31.90		CLAIM TOTALS		300.00	159.52	0.00	31.90	127.62		127.62 NET

CLAIM INFORMATION FORWARDED TO: MEDI-CAL

NAME		31	HIC 123-432-000A						ASG	Y	
0PL1234B0			1 908456z9								
	052696		1	90820	150.00	98.14	0.00	19.63	78.51	CO-42	51.86
PT RESP	19.63		CLAIM TOTALS		150.00	98.14	0.00	19.63	78.51		78.51 NET

CLAIM INFORMATION FORWARDED TO: MEDI-CAL

NAME		31	HIC 123-432-000A						ASG	Y	
0PL1234B0			1 908456z9								
	052796		1	96115	300.00	159.52	0.00	31.90	127.62	CO-42	140.48
PT RESP	31.90		CLAIM TOTALS		300.00	159.52	0.00	31.90	127.62		127.62 NET

CLAIM INFORMATION FORWARDED TO: BLUE CROSS OF CALIFORNIA

TOTALS	TOTAL CLAIMS				TOTAL BILLED	TOTAL ALLOWED	TOTAL DEDUCT	TOTAL COINS	TOTAL PROV. PD.	AMOUNT OF CHECK
	3				750.00	417.18	0.00	83.43	333.75	333.75

Figure 2-11   Example of Medicare Remittance Notice

In the case of Medicare, the local carrier for Medicare sends doctors a long list showing all claims processed in the most recent batch. The list summarizes each claim, including the original fee billed, the allowable amount, the amount paid, the coinsurance, and the required write-off. This is called a remittance notice. Figure 2-11 shows what this report looks like.

Your first step is therefore to key in all the data from the EOBs and any Medicare remittance lists. This is done in the accounts receivable module that full practice management software contains. You begin by looking up each patient's record and keying in the amount paid based on the EOB or the Medicare remittance notice. Most medical billing software automates a portion of this record-keeping function, such as calculating the 20 percent coinsurance payment and the write-off once you enter the amount paid.

If the patient is a managed care patient on a capitated payment, the EOB will so indicate and show that the original fee is denied. You therefore need to go into the accounts receivable module and record a write-off for the fee-for-service charge that was originally posted. These postings eventually allow you to compare how much the doctor would have earned if the patients had been fee-for-service versus the amount of capitated payments you received from that HMO. Obviously, the doctor may come out ahead with some patients and behind on others, so you must calculate profitability by taking into account many patients over months of time. Some software, such as *Lytec Medical for Windows,* has a specific module for managed care patients. As Lytec points out in its manual:

> Please be aware that insurance companies making capitated payments as part of a managed care plan need to be billed just like any other insurance company. These insurance companies still need to know how often and why a patient is getting healthcare treatment. Before entering transactions into the Changes and Payment screen, you will need to add a managed care adjustment code in the procedure code file and also modify the existing procedure codes.

Many industry experts expect that electronic funds transfer from insurance companies right into providers' bank accounts will become more common. If so, this improvement may substantially automate the posting of payments and write-offs. You may not even need to key in the amounts; updating the accounts receivable records will be done automatically when you log on to capture the notification of payments to your doctor's bank.

As discussed throughout this chapter, a billing service offering complete practice management will likely become involved in many additional functions related to the doctor's business. These can include

- Printing out monthly statements for patients showing their past payments and balances due. Most medical billing programs make this process fast and easy. You can often add a customized comment, such as "Balance due over 60 days; please remit today." (My dentist adds a "quote of the day" from a famous philosopher.)

- Preparing financial reports for doctors showing the status of their cash flow and analyzing the major factors of their business, including aged balances (showing which patients are delinquent in their payments for 30, 60, and 90 days or more), and insurance aged balances (showing which insurance companies are delinquent for 30, 60, and 90 days or more). Many doctors also like to get reports showing which procedures generate the most income, which clients see them most frequently, what percentage of their fees is generated from referrals, and so on. Most current state-of-the art billing software allows you to provide a variety of sophisticated financial summaries, as well as visual data in the form of pie graphs, bar graphs, and so on. Figures 2-12 through 2-14 show samples of two reports and a graph that many practice management software packages can produce.

- Advising the doctor about the correct use of diagnostic and procedure codes that determine how much reimbursement the physician receives. Many doctors code incorrectly or unintentionally "down-code," meaning that they use a code that pays less than they could receive for a service. In addition, doctors do not have the time to keep up with the changes in coding that Medicare and other insurance firms regularly implement; and in many cases, the doctor's staff also does not stay abreast of new coding requirements. The professional billing service that is current with coding procedures can therefore play an important role in ensuring that doctors are properly reimbursed for services rendered.

- As stated throughout this chapter, another important practice management function for a billing service is analyzing the doctor's practice and making recommendations about managed care options, such as whether to join certain HMOs and PPOs. As you have seen in several of the business profiles in this chapter, some billing services even become involved in preparing proposals on behalf of their clients to handle the patients of a certain HMO. Most qualified billing services will prepare financial analysis reports showing their client patient usage under capitated fees as well as comparisons of capitated fees received versus fee-for-service fees written off.

As you can readily see, a professional billing service offering electronic claims filing and full practice management can alleviate many problems for a medical practice. Working hand in hand with the doctor's office staff, a good billing service can serve the interests of the doctor and the patients. This explains why billing services are increasingly able to sign on a growing number of healthcare providers who are no longer able to pay attention to their business.

Page 1 DIAGNOSIS STATISTICS for Month 7 Ending July 31, 1996
        Order:NAME Range:ALL RECORDS

CODE	DESCRIPTION	DEPT	********* MONTH TOTALS *********		********** YTD TOTALS **********		
			FREQ / RATIO	CHARGE / RATIO	FREQ / RATIO	CHARGE / RATIO	NUM

Physician 01 - Anderson, Robert H., M.D.

CODE	DESCRIPTION	DEPT	FREQ / RATIO	CHARGE / RATIO	FREQ / RATIO	CHARGE / RATIO	NUM
491.0	BRONCHITIS	2	3 / 37.50%	147.00 / 42.73%	5 / 8.06%	192.00 / 9.55%	44
382.9	OTITIS MEDIA	2	1 / 12.50%	0.00 / 0.00%	3 / 4.84%	0.00 / 0.00%	4
844.9	SPRAIN, KNEE	2	2 / 25.00%	130.00 / 37.79%	2 / 3.23%	130.00 / 6.47%	13
463	TONSILLITIS	2	1 / 12.50%	32.00 / 9.30%	5 / 8.06%	132.00 / 6.57%	1
***** TOTAL CHARGES			8 /100.00%	344.00 /100.00%	62 /100.00%	2010.35 /100.00%	

Physician 02 - Barr, John S., M.D.

CODE	DESCRIPTION	DEPT	FREQ / RATIO	CHARGE / RATIO	FREQ / RATIO	CHARGE / RATIO	NUM
493.9	ASTHMA, ALLERGIC NOS	2	1 / 11.11%	127.00 / 28.05%	1 / 3.03%	127.00 / 12.60%	45
276.5	DEHYDRATION	2	2 / 22.22%	0.00 / 0.00%	2 / 6.06%	0.00 / 0.00%	34
276.9	ELECTROLYTE IMBAL.	2	1 / 11.11%	0.00 / 0.00%	1 / 3.03%	0.00 / 0.00%	28
401.9	HYPERTENSION	2	2 / 22.22%	136.80 / 30.21%	2 / 6.06%	136.80 / 13.57%	15
844.9	SPRAIN, KNEE	2	1 / 11.11%	45.00 / 9.94%	4 / 12.12%	121.40 / 12.05%	13
435.9	TIA	2	2 / 22.22%	144.00 / 31.80%	2 / 6.06%	144.00 / 14.29%	12
***** TOTAL CHARGES			9 /100.00%	452.80 /100.00%	33 /100.00%	1007.80 /100.00%	

Physician 03 - Martin, J. F., M.D.

CODE	DESCRIPTION	DEPT	FREQ / RATIO	CHARGE / RATIO	FREQ / RATIO	CHARGE / RATIO	NUM
311	DEPRESSION	2	2 / 66.67%	125.00 / 69.25%	2 / 8.33%	125.00 / 10.11%	27
044.9	SPRAIN, KNEE	2	1 / 33.33%	55.50 / 30.75%	1 / 4.17%	55.50 / 4.49%	52
***** TOTAL CHARGES			3 /100.00%	180.50 /100.00%	24 /100.00%	1236.45 /100.00%	

Practice totals

CODE	DESCRIPTION	DEPT	FREQ / RATIO	CHARGE / RATIO	FREQ / RATIO	CHARGE / RATIO	NUM
493.9	ASTHMA, ALLERGIC NOS	2	1 / 5.00%	127.00 / 12.99%	1 / 0.73%	127.00 / 2.30%	45
491.0	BRONCHITIS	2	3 / 15.00%	147.00 / 15.04%	5 / 3.65%	192.00 / 3.47%	44
276.5	DEHYDRATION	2	2 / 10.00%	0.00 / 0.00%	3 / 2.19%	0.00 / 0.00%	34
311	DEPRESSION	2	2 / 10.00%	125.00 / 12.79%	3 / 2.19%	175.00 / 3.16%	27
276.9	ELECTROLYTE IMBAL.	2	1 / 5.00%	0.00 / 0.00%	2 / 1.46%	0.00 / 0.00%	28
401.9	HYPERTENSION	2	2 / 10.00%	136.80 / 14.00%	9 / 6.57%	439.30 / 7.94%	15
382.9	OTITIS MEDIA	2	1 / 5.00%	0.00 / 0.00%	3 / 2.19%	0.00 / 0.00%	4
844.9	SPRAIN, KNEE	2	3 / 15.00%	175.00 / 17.91%	6 / 4.38%	251.40 / 4.54%	13
044.9	SPRAIN, KNEE	2	1 / 5.00%	55.50 / 5.68%	2 / 1.46%	78.30 / 1.41%	52
435.9	TIA	2	2 / 10.00%	144.00 / 14.73%	4 / 2.92%	209.00 / 3.78%	12
463	TONSILLITIS	2	1 / 5.00%	32.00 / 3.27%	15 / 10.95%	704.45 / 12.73%	1
***** TOTAL CHARGES			20 /100.00%	977.30 /100.00%	137 /100.00%	5533.60 /100.00%	

Figure 2-12 Example of a Tabular Report—Practice Analysis by Diagnosis Frequency

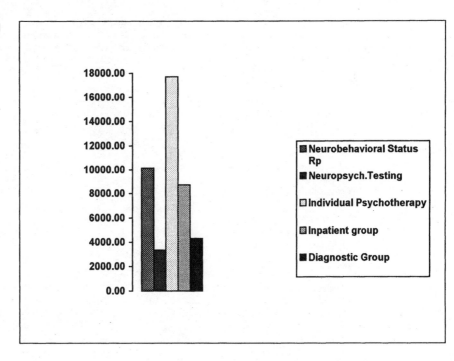

Aging Report Summary

Type	Past due -> 0 - 30	-> -> -> 31-60	-> -> -> 61-90	-> 91+
Patient Accnt's	2524.00	652.00	829.00	332.00
%	58%	15%	19%	08%
Insurance	7924.00	879.00	321.00	212.00
%	85%	09%	03%	02%
Totals	10,448.00	1,531.00	1,150.00	544.00

Total patient receivables: $ 4337.00
Total insurance receivables: $ 9336.00
Total receivables: $13,673.00

Corrected art tk

Figure 2-13   Example of a Tabular Report—Aging Report Summary

Figure 2-14
Examples of a Graph
Report—Bar Graph
Analysis by
Procedure

■ Neurobehavioral Status Rp
■ Neuropsych.Testing
☐ Individual Psychotherapy
▨ Inpatient group
■ Diagnostic Group

Business Profile: Sheryl Telles and Kathy Allocco

Sheryl Telles and Kathy Allocco worked for a local physician for many years; between them, they had more than 35 years of experience in medical management. The day came, however, when they saw opportunity knocking at their door. Prompted by the increasing use of managed care arrangements in Arizona, the two set up their company, Arizona MedLink Provider Resources, in Scottsdale to help doctors preserve their independence. Fortunately, they were able to tap into their combined skills: Sheryl has a medical coding background while Kathy knows billing and insurance. Sheryl also does medical transcription as part of their business, subcontracting out the work. The software they use is from Medisoft.

At first, they had no clients and a lot of apprehension about the future; but keeping focused on their skills, their friendship, their dream, the firm got its first client in seven weeks, after doing a brochure and targeted marketing letter. They also arranged for an interview in a local business journal that helped them get free publicity. Within one year, it seemed that they were well on the way to success. Kathy and Sheryl now handle full practice management functions for 13 practices (many of which involve multiple doctors), and their goal is to pick up an additional practice per month. They service a variety of clients, including podiatrists, family practitioners, psychiatrists, orthopedic surgeons, and chiropractors. For their work, Kathy and Sheryl charge a percentage of everything they collect, which is common for full practice management billing services. They also have two employees and moved from Sheryl's home office to a 3000-square-foot office.

Kathy and Sheryl speak about medical billing from the heart. As they related to me, "In Arizona, the choice for doctors about how to practice is being taken out of their hands. Doctors are being told what to do and how to do it. They are being forced to join dozens of different HMOs and MSOs. There are even some sneaky insurance companies that establish lucrative fee-for-service PPO plans that doctors want to join, but the insurer then makes the doctor join their HMO too, in which the doctor is paid at a *very low* capitated rate, as little as $3 per patient. This is also bad for consumers, because the patients who are on that $3 capitated plan often get treated by phone. The doctor literally can't afford to see them."

Kathy and Sheryl point out that doctors need to keep careful track of whatever they do today, because insurers will question everything and frequently deny payments. Because of the proliferation of insurance plans, doctors can get confused; they can do X in the office and get paid, but they can't do Y.

Kathy and Sheryl have a formal partnership agreement, created for them by a lawyer. When asked why each didn't go into business for herself instead of working together, Kathy told me, "You can always hire employees who have the skills you lack, but for us, the question was, did we want to do it alone? We decided that we would rather work together and reap the rewards."

One key to their success is that they function exceptionally well together. They admit to having experienced an occasional disagreement over business strategy, but they are able to resolve their differences through discussion and negotiation. They also highly value their long-standing friendship, which prevents them from ruining their relationship over a business squabble.

When I interviewed them, Kathy and Sheryl were in the midst of developing a new clearinghouse that would handle eligibility requests on a nationwide basis. Whenever a doctor needs to verify a patient's insurance and its coverages (deductibles, copayments, procedures covered, etc.), the information can be requested via modem through Sheryl and Kathy's clearinghouse to insurance companies nationwide. Their new company is called EDI Pathway, and their partner in that business is Noreen Sachs. Information about reaching them is found under "Clearinghouses" in Appendix A.

Knowledge and Skills Needed to Run a Medical Billing Business

Some home businesses are easy to start, while others require an extensive range of skills and knowledge. On a scale of 1 to 10, with 10 being the measure of highest difficulty, medical billing is now probably between 7 and 10, depending on your background and personal style. In researching this book, I met billing service owners who were able to jump right in, although they had no medical experience or knowledge. The most successful people I interviewed usually had a professional background involving one of the following: healthcare, nursing, banking, insurance, finance, administrative work, computer consulting, or marketing.

Regardless of your background, to be successful in medical billing, you will need to learn three areas to develop your knowledge and skills. You need

- A moderate knowledge of medical coding procedures
- A moderate to high level of knowledge and skills with computers and software
- A high level of knowledge and skills in marketing and sales to get clients

Each of these areas can be mastered in a few months, but the greater the slope of your learning curve, the longer it will take you to get your business off and running.

Of course, dedication, persistence, and personal outlook have much to do with your ability to traverse the hurdles. If you enter your new business venture thinking you cannot learn what it takes to succeed, or that you can handle only half the task, you will almost certainly fulfill only that limited vision of yourself. You may find that you have to s-t-r-e-t-c-h your thinking and your commitment if you are to succeed.

After reading the following sections, which cover the various areas of knowledge and skills needed for medical billing (except for the insurance business and the business of medicine, which this chapter has already covered), try the following informal method of charting your challenge. First, choose a unit of time with which you feel comfortable learning something new; perhaps it's one month, three months, or six months. Then, for each skill/knowledge area, plot your starting point on a scale of 1 to 10.

For example, if you have a medical background and some computer skills, but no marketing or selling experience, you might give yourself an 8 for Medical Knowledge, a 4 for Computer Knowledge, and a 2 for Business Knowledge. Then, using those numbers as your starting points, plot your learning curve for each area over the course of time you have allocated. Figure 2-15 shows how the learning curves might differ for a person with a nursing or medical front office background versus a person with sales experience but no medical background.

The purpose of this informal exercise is to help you become conscious of your strengths as well as those areas in which you will need to concentrate some effort. If you find that you have a low learning curve in only one area, you may be more inclined to move your business plans along quickly. On the other hand, if you find that you have two or three very steep curves, it may be better for you to improve your knowledge and skills in those areas before moving ahead in your business or investing in software or a business opportunity. Remember, do this exercise after you have read the following sections that present a brief preview of each knowledge or skill base you need.

Figure 2-15
Plotting Your
Learning Curve

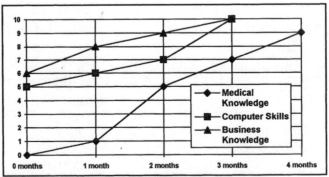

Graph for   entrepreneur with previous experience in business

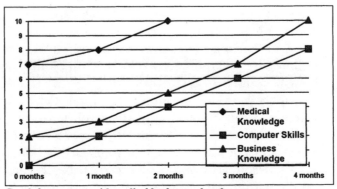

Graph for a person with medical background such as a nurse

Area 1: Knowledge of Medical Coding

Earlier in this chapter, I referred to two sets of codes used by insurance carriers and the medical community. These codes are a kind of shorthand for the doctor's diagnosis of the patient's problems and for the services he or she performs. These coding systems have come to the foreground of the health insurance industry in recent years because of increased computerization. Being familiar with them—and even becoming an expert in coding—is critical to your ability to get clients. Rising healthcare costs and a growing reluctance on the part of insurance companies to overpay for services or to pay for needless procedures have created a greater emphasis on identifying the precise diagnosis and procedures.

Here is a brief review of the two coding systems.

ICD-9-CM DIAGNOSIS CODES   Prior to 1988, healthcare professionals described the reason for their encounter with a patient by writing out longhand the patient's complaints, condition, injury, symptoms, and diagnosis. However, the 1988 Medicare Catastrophic Coverage Act instituted the ICD-9-CM coding system, which had to that point been in only limited usage. The ICD-9-CM stands for International Classification of Diseases, 9th Revision, Clinical Modification. ICD-9-CM is now mandated for all Medicare and Medicaid claims and nearly all commercial insurance claims.

Originally devised to improve statistical recordkeeping on the spread of diseases by the World Health Organization (WHO), the ICD-9-CM codes have been tailored for clinical use in the United States. (WHO updates the codes every 10 years, but HCFA and the U.S. Public Health Service issue annual changes and addenda.) The codes are usually printed in two volumes. The first volume is a "tabular" list; it contains the numerical listings of disease codes from 001.0 through 999.9 (plus some additional "V" codes for vaccinations, some types of exams, treatments and other issues, as well as a section of "E" codes for causes of external injuries such as traffic and boating accidents). The second volume is an alphabetic listing of diseases. Physicians and billers often need to use one or the other volume to look up a code.

Figures 2-16 and 2-17 show a page from each of these volumes.

The ICD-9 codes are used to facilitate automation of the claims process and payments. Doctors must follow strict requirements in utilizing the ICD-9-CM codes to supply proof that the services performed (which are the basis for the insurance paid) are backed up by an appropriate and cor-

◆ ● **800.3** Closed with other and unspecified intracranial hemorrhage
◆ ● **800.4** Closed with intracranial injury of other and unspecified nature
● **800.5** Open without mention of intracranial injury
● **800.6** Open with cerebral laceration and contusion
● **800.7** Open with subarachnoid, subdural, and extradural hemorrhage
◆ ● **800.8** Open with other and unspecified intracranial hemorrhage
◆ ● **800.9** Open with intracranial injury of other and unspecified nature
● **801 Fracture of base of skull**
     Requires fifth-digit. See beginning of section 800-804 for codes and definitions. 🏛

INCLUDES	fossa:	sinus:
	anterior	ethmoid
	middle	frontal
	posterior	sphenoid bone
	occiput bone	temporal bone
	orbital roof	

● **801.0** Closed without mention of intracranial injury
● **801.1** Closed with cerebral laceration and contusion
● **801.2** Closed with subarachnoid, subdural, and extradural hemorrhage
◆ ● **801.3** Closed with other and unspecified intracranial hemorrhage
◆ ● **801.4** Closed with intracranial injury of other and unspecified nature
● **801.5** Open without mention of intracranial injury
● **801.6** Open with cerebral laceration and contusion
● **801.7** Open with subarachnoid, subdural, and extradural hemorrhage
◆ ● **801.8** Open with other and unspecified intracranial hemorrhage
◆ ● **801.9** Open with intracranial injury of other and unspecified nature
● **802 Fracture of face bones**
     Requires fifth-digit. See beginning of section 800-804 for codes and definitions. 🏛
     802.0 Nasal bones, closed
     802.1 Nasal bones, open
● **802.2** Mandible, closed
     Inferior maxilla   Lower jaw (bone)
  ◆ **802.20** Unspecified site
     802.21 Condylar process
     802.22 Subcondylar
     802.23 Coronoid process
  ◆ **802.24** Ramus, unspecified
     802.25 Angle of jaw
     802.26 Symphysis of body
     802.27 Alveolar border of body
  ◆ **802.28** Body, other and unspecified
  ◆ **802.29** Multiple sites
● **802.3** Mandible, open
  ◆ **802.30** Unspecified site
     802.31 Condylar process
     802.32 Subcondylar
     802.33 Coronoid process
  ◆ **802.34** Ramus, unspecified

     802.35 Angle of jaw
     802.36 Symphysis of body
     802.37 Alveolar border of body
  ◆ **802.38** Body, other and unspecified
  ◆ **802.39** Multiple sites
     802.4 Malar and maxillary bones, closed
       Superior maxilla   Zygoma
       Upper jaw (bone)   Zygomatic arch
     802.5 Malar and maxillary bones, open
     802.6 Orbital floor (blow-out), closed
     802.7 Orbital floor (blow-out), open
◆ **802.8** Other facial bones, closed
       Alveolus   Palate
       Orbit:
         NOS
         part other than roof or floor
       EXCLUDES   orbital:
         floor (802.6)
         roof (801.0-801.9)
◆ **802.9** Other facial bones, open
● **803 Other and unqualified skull fractures**
     Requires fifth-digit. See beginning of section 800-804 for codes and definitions. 🏛
     INCLUDES   skull NOS   skull multiple NOS
● **803.0** Closed without mention of intracranial injury
● **803.1** Closed with cerebral laceration and contusion
● **803.2** Closed with subarachnoid, subdural, and extradural hemorrhage
◆ ● **803.3** Closed with other and unspecified intracranial hemorrhage
◆ ● **803.4** Closed with intracranial injury of other and unspecified nature
● **803.5** Open without mention of intracranial injury
● **803.6** Open with cerebral laceration and contusion
● **803.7** Open with subarachnoid, subdural, and extradural hemorrhage
◆ ● **803.8** Open with other and unspecified intracranial hemorrhage
◆ ● **803.9** Open with intracranial injury of other and unspecified nature
● **804 Multiple fractures involving skull or face with other bones**
     Requires fifth-digit. See beginning of section 800-804 for codes and definitions. 🏛
● **804.0** Closed without mention of intracranial injury
● **804.1** Closed with cerebral laceration and contusion
● **804.2** Closed with subarachnoid, subdural, and extradural hemorrhage
◆ ● **804.3** Closed with other and unspecified intracranial hemorrhage
◆ ● **804.4** Closed with intracranial injury of other and unspecified nature
● **804.5** Open without mention of intracranial injury
● **804.6** Open with cerebral laceration and contusion
● **804.7** Open with subarachnoid, subdural, and extradural hemorrage
◆ ● **804.8** Open with other and unspecified intracranial hemorrhage
◆ ● **804.9** Open with intracranial injury of other and unspecified nature

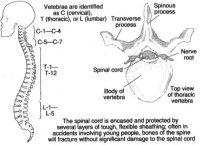

LeFort fracture types
Frontal bone
Lacrimal bone
Ethmoid bone
Nasal bone
Orbital floor
Type III
Zygomatic bone (malar) and arch
Type II
Maxilla
Type I
Subcondylar
Parasymphysis   Body
Symphysis
Angle
Common fracture sites of mandible

Vetebrae are identified as C (cervical), T (thoracic), or L (lumbar)
Spinous process
Transverse process
C-1—C-4
C-5—C-7
T-1—T-12
Spinal cord
Nerve root
Body of vertebra
Top view of thoracic vertebra
L-1—L-5
The spinal cord is encased and protected by several layers of tough, flexible sheathing; often in accidents involving young people, bones of the spine will fracture without significant damage to the spinal cord

🏛 Unpublicized government change   ● Additional digit(s) required   ◆ Nonspecific code   ■ Not a primary diagnosis   **Volume 1 — 161**

Figure 2-16   ICD-9-CM Tabular Listing

History — continued
  irradiation V15.3
  leukemia V10.60
    lymphoid V10.61
    monocytic V10.63
    myeloid V10.62
    specified type NEC V10.69
  little or no prenatal care V23.7
  lymphosarcoma V10.71
  malaria V12.03
  malignant neoplasm (of) V10.9
    accessory sinus V10.22
    adrenal V10.88
    anus V10.06
    bile duct V10.09
    bladder V10.51
    bone V10.81
    brain V10.85
    breast V10.3
    bronchus V10.11
    cervix uteri V10.41
    colon V10.05
    connective tissue NEC V10.89
    corpus uteri V10.42
    digestive system V10.00
      specified part NEC V10.09
    duodenum V10.09
    endocrine gland NEC V10.88
    esophagus V10.03
    eye V10.84
    fallopian tube V10.44
    female genital organ V10.40
      specified site NEC V10.44
    gallbladder V10.09
    gastrointestinal tract V10.00
    gum V10.02
    hematopoietic NEC V10.79
    hypopharynx V10.02
    ileum V10.09
    intrathoracic organs NEC V10.20
    jejunum V10.09
    kidney V10.52
    large intestine V10.05
    larynx V10.21
    lip V10.02
    liver V10.07
    lung V10.11
    lymphatic NEC V10.79
    lymph glands or nodes NEC V10.79
    male genital organ V10.45
      specified site NEC V10.49
    mediastinum V10.29
    melanoma (of skin) V10.82
    middle ear V10.22
    mouth V10.02
      specified part NEC V10.02
    nasal cavities V10.22
    nasopharynx V10.02
    nervous system NEC V10.86
    nose V10.22
    oropharynx V10.02
    ovary V10.43
    pancreas V10.09
    parathyroid V10.88
    penis V10.49
    pharynx V10.02
    pineal V10.88
    pituitary V10.88
    placenta V10.44
    pleura V10.29
    prostate V10.46
    rectosigmoid junction V10.06
    rectum V10.06
    respiratory organs NEC V10.20
    salivary gland V10.02
    skin V10.83
      melanoma V10.82
    small intestine NEC V10.09
    soft tissue NEC V10.89
    specified site NEC V10.89
    stomach V10.04
    testis V10.47
    thymus V10.29
    thyroid V10.87
    tongue V10.01
    trachea V10.12
    ureter V10.59

History — continued
  malignant neoplasm — continued
    urethra V10.59
    urinary organ V10.50
    uterine adnexa V10.44
    uterus V10.42
    vagina V10.44
    vulva V10.44
  manic-depressive psychosis V11.1
  mental disorder V11.9
    affective type V11.1
    manic-depressive V11.1
    neurosis V11.2
    schizophrenia V11.0
    specified type NEC V11.8
  metabolic disorder V12.1
  musculoskeletal disorder NEC V13.5
  myocardial infarction 412
  neglect (emotional) V15.42   ◆
  nervous system disorder V12.4
  neurosis V11.2
  noncompliance with medical treatment V15.81
  nutritional deficiency V12.1
  obstetric disorder V13.2
    affecting management of current pregnancy
      V23.4
  parasitic disease V12.00
    specified NEC V12.09
  perinatal problems V13.7
  physical abuse V15.41   ◆
  poisoning V15.6
  poliomyelitis V12.02
  polyps, colonic V12.72
  poor obstetric V23.4
  psychiatric disorder V11.9
    affective type V11.1
      manic-depressive V11.1
    neurosis V11.2
    schizophrenia V11.0
    specified type NEC V11.8
  psychological trauma V15.49   ◇
    emotional abuse V15.42   ▼
    neglect V15.42
    physical abuse V15.41
    rape V15.41   ▲
  psychoneurosis V11.2
  radiation therapy V15.3
  rape V15.41   ◆
  respiratory system disease V12.6
  reticulosarcoma V10.71
  schizophrenia V11.0
  skin disease V13.3
  smoking (tobacco) V15.82
  subcutaneous tissue disease V13.3
  surgery (major) to
    great vessels V15.1
    heart V15.1
    major organs NEC V15.2
  thrombophlebitis V12.52
  thrombosis V12.51
  tobacco use V15.82
  trophoblastic disease V13.1
    affecting management of pregnancy V23.1
  tuberculosis V12.01
  ulcer, peptic V12.71
  urinary system disorder V13.00
    calculi V13.01
    specified NEC V13.09
HIV infection (disease) (illness) — see Human
  immunodeficiency virus (disease) (illness)
  (infection)
Hives (bold) (see also Urticaria) 708.9
Hoarseness 784.49
Hobnail liver — see Cirrhosis, portal
Hobo, hoboism V60.0
Hodgkins
  disease (M9650/3) 201.9
    lymphocytic
      depletion (M9653/3) 201.7
        diffuse fibrosis (M9654/3) 201.7
        reticular type (M9655/3) 201.7
      predominance (M9651/3) 201.4
    lymphocytic-histiocytic predominance
      (M9651/3) 201.4
    mixed cellularity (M9652/3) 201.6
    nodular sclerosis (M9656/3) 201.5
      cellular phase (M9657/3) 201.5

Hodgkins — continued
  granuloma (M9661/3) 201.1
  lymphogranulomatosis (M9650/3) 201.9
  lymphoma (M9650/3) 201.9
  lymphosarcoma (M9650/3) 201.9
  paragranuloma (M9660/3) 201.0
  sarcoma (M9662/3) 201.2
Hodgson's disease (aneurysmal dilatation of
  aorta) 441.9
  ruptured 441.5
Hodi-potsy 111.0
Hoffa (-Kastert) disease or syndrome
  (liposynovitis prepatellaris) 272.8
Hoffman's syndrome 244.9 [359.5]
Hoffmann-Bouveret syndrome (paroxysmal
  tachycardia) 427.2
Hole
  macula 362.54
  optic disc, crater-like 377.22
  retina (macula) 362.54
    round 361.31
      with detachment 361.01
Holla disease (see also Spherocytosis) 282.0
Holländer-Simons syndrome (progressive
  lipodystrophy) 272.6
Hollow foot (congenital) 754.71
  acquired 736.73
Holmes' syndrome (visual disorientation) 368.16
Holoprosencephaly 742.2
  due to
    trisomy 13 758.1
    trisomy 18 758.2
Holthouse's hernia — see Hernia, inguinal
Homesickness 309.89
Homocystinemia 270.4
Homocystinuria 270.4
Homologous serum jaundice (prophylactic)
  (therapeutic) — see Hepatitis, viral
Homosexuality — omit code
  ego-dystonic 302.0
  pedophilic 302.2
  problems with 302.0
Homozygous Hb-S disease 282.61
Honeycomb lung 518.89
  congenital 748.4
Hong Kong ear 117.3
HOOD (hereditary osteo-onychodysplasia) 756.89
Hooded
  clitoris 752.49
  penis 752.69   ◇
Hookworm (anemia) (disease) (infestation) — see
  Ancylostomiasis
Hoppe-Goldflam syndrome 358.0
Hordeolum (external) (eyelid) 373.11
  internal 373.12
Horn
  cutaneous 702.8
    cheek 702.8
    eyelid 702.8
    penis 702.8
  iliac 756.89
  nail 703.8
    congenital 757.5
  papillary 700
Horner's
  syndrome (see also Neuropathy, peripheral,
    autonomic) 337.9
    traumatic 954.0
  teeth 520.4
Horseshoe kidney (congenital) 753.3
Horton's
  disease (temporal arteritis) 446.5
  headache or neuralgia 346.2
Hospice care V66.7   ◆
Hospitalism (in children) NEC 309.83
Hourglass contraction, contracture
  bladder 596.8
  gallbladder 575.2
    congenital 751.69
  stomach 536.8
    congenital 750.7
    psychogenic 306.4

Figure 2-17   ICD-9-CM Alphabetic Listing

responding diagnosis. Physicians must use the most specific level of coding possible. This generally means using a four- or five-digit code rather than a three-digit code. As the ICD-9-CM warns, "Claims submitted with three- or four-digit codes where four- and five-digit codes are available may be returned to you by the Medicare carrier for proper coding It is recognized that a very specific diagnosis may not be known at the time of the initial encounter. However, that is not an acceptable reason to submit a three-digit code when four or five digits are available.."

Physicians are also not supposed to choose codes based on "probable," "suspected," or "questionable" hypotheses. When a physician does not know the diagnosis, codes that represent a description of the symptoms or a "family history of" classification must be used. There are also rules about which codes must come first (e.g., the primary diagnosis), how many codes are allowed (e.g., up to four), how to code late effects (effects that appear before a no-longer acute cause), as well codes that apply to where the service was performed, the frequency of the service, and level of service provided.

As you can imagine, understanding and working with the ICD-9 diagnosis codes require some knowledge of medical terminology. Although billing services are not responsible for the original coding itself (the doctor is), your professionalism is enhanced when you know the codes of the specialties you hope to service. (In other words, don't walk into a specialist's office without first learning which codes are commonly used in that specialty.)

Remember: knowing the coding can also pay off by giving you an additional service to offer. Many billing services that know coding well can offer to review a doctor's superbill to make sure it is up to date and that the doctor is getting reimbursed at the highest level. This increases your value to physicians. Caution: don't attempt to formally advise physicians about coding or to change codes yourself; it could open you up to malpractice suits. However, if you discuss the coding with your client and tell him or her what you believe to be a better code to use, the physician can consider your opinion and make the decision.

PROCEDURES CODES   Procedure codes are similar to diagnosis codes, in that they are a shorthand for the services performed by the doctor. Prior to 1983, there were more than 120 different procedure coding systems in the United States. For each of the insurance companies they dealt with, doctors had to be familiar with the codes currently in use. This is one reason that doctors began giving their patients the responsibility for filing claims themselves.

Medicare and HCFA established the current coding system in 1983, largely based on codes recommended by the American Medical Association. Most commercial insurance companies now use this same coding system. The codes are complex and are updated each year. For example, in 1992, there was a major change in the way physicians were instructed to code the nature of the patient/doctor contact when reporting to Medicare; many insurance companies have also adopted this same system.

The coding system is divided into three levels, with the top level being the most utilized. This level is called the CPT-4, which stands for Current Procedural Terminology, Fourth Edition. The CPT is a listing of more than 7,000 codes representing services performed by medical personnel of all kinds. Updated and published each year by the American Medical Association, the CPT keeps track of all currently accepted medical procedures.

The main body of the CPT codes is divided into six sections; each section represents a broad field of medicine, such as shown in the following list. Each of these sections contains hundreds of specific procedures, each with a unique five-digit *numeric* code:

Evaluation and Management	99200 to 99499
Anesthesiology	00100 to 01999
Surgery	10000 to 69999
Radiology, Nuclear Medicine, and Diagnostic Ultrasound	70000 to 79999
Pathology and Laboratory	80000 to 89999
Medicine	90000 to 99199

Remember that most healthcare providers do not use all these codes, because they typically specialize. Most physicians commonly work with about 100 codes on a daily basis; these are the codes that they preprint on their superbill.

Although using the procedural codes is straightforward, several areas often cause confusion for doctors and billing specialists. One area in particular is the Evaluation and Management Codes (E/M). These codes were completely revised in 1992 for Medicare, but now commercial carriers have adopted them as well. The E/M codes are complex, with dozens of different codes that apply either to new or established patients. ("New" patients are those whom the doctor has not seen in at least three years.) The codes also take into account the location of the visit (e.g., office, home, hospital, clinic) and many other specific issues. There are also a variety of two-digit supplemental codes, called modifiers, that the physician must append to a

Evaluation and Management Codes

The Evaluation and Management Codes (E/M) define the physician/patient contact in terms of the time, depth of diagnosis, and level of decision making and thinking required for that meeting. Naturally, a 5-minute visit to diagnose a sore throat and take a throat culture does not cost as much as a 45-minute visit to suture a wound. The technical and intellectual requirements are substantially different.

The E/M codes were devised and went into effect in 1992 to classify the work of doctors for Medicare billing. Commercial carriers require these codes now as well. The new codes replace the old six-level "Visit" codes for reporting service using the nomenclature of *brief, limited, intermediate,* and *comprehensive* with a more complex hierarchical system divided into many categories and subcategories. For example, there are categories, such as office visits, hospital inpatient visits, consultations, emergency department services, critical care services, nursing facility services, rest home services, home services, case management services, preventive care services, and newborn care. These categories are further divided into two or more subcategories, such as office visit—New Patient vs. Established Patient, or Hospital Inpatient Visits—Initial Visit versus Subsequent Visit.

These subcategories are then further divided into levels of services, selected according to seven components, as follows:

Key Components (these carry the most weight)
- History (4 types: problem focused, expanded problem focused, detailed, comprehensive)
- Examination (4 types: problem focused, expanded problem focused, detailed, comprehensive)
- Medical Decision Making (4 subcategories: straightforward, low complexity, moderate complexity, and high complexity)

Contributory Factors
- Counseling (discussions with family/patient over diagnosis, prognosis, risks of treatment, importance of compliance with treatment, risk factor reduction, and patient/family education)
- Coordination of Care (a patient encounter with other providers or agencies)
- Nature of Presenting Problem (5 levels: minimal, self-limited or minor, low severity, moderate severity, and high severity)

Additional Factor
- Time (face-to-face time versus unit/floor time)

As you can imagine, for a doctor to arrive at a decision combining all these factors to convey which type of service he or she provided is not a simple issue. The Medical Decision Making subcategory alone requires an entire table to determine which level of decision making was used, as shown in Table 2-8.

Despite the effort that doctors must exert to properly select an E/M code, insurance carriers have also developed their own standards, so in some cases, the coding is an exercise in futility.

primary code to indicate extra services, such as special prolonged time, concurrent care (more than one doctor attending), repetitive service for chronic care, and so on. The sidebar on "Evaluation and Management Codes" will give you some idea of CPT coding.

These coding complexities can make the work of a neophyte billing service quite confusing, yet they are extremely important. Just as with diagnosis codes, if a doctor has chosen the wrong code or reports a procedure that does not correspond to a diagnosis, the claim will be rejected, delayed, or downcoded.

LEVEL II AND III CODES.   As stated earlier, the CPT codes are just the top level of the procedural codes. Below CPT are two additional sets. The entire system is referred to as HCPCS (pronounced HicPics), which stands for HCFA Common Procedure Coding System. The Level II codes, called the National Codes, are used to bill Medicare for many items not listed in the CPT codes, such as medical supplies. CPT has only a few dozen codes to bill for supplies while there are several thousand codes in the Level II book for items such as gauze pads and syringes, as well as drugs, injections, and durable medical equipment (DME) that may be sold or rented to patients. All these items must be coded as part of a physician's services.

The Level II codes are five-digit alphanumerics, ranging from A0000 to V5999. These codes are revised each year, and there are usually hundreds of additions, deletions, and changes that billers must learn by purchasing

TABLE 2-8

Decision-Making Factors Influencing E/M Codes

Number of Diagnoses or Management Options	Amount and/or Complexity of Data to be Reviewed	Risk of Complications and/or Morbidity or Mortality	Type of Decision Making
Minimal	Minimal or none	Minimal	Straightforward
Limited	Limited	Low	Low complexity
Multiple	Moderate	Moderate	Moderate complexity
Extensive	Extensive	High	High complexity

a new edition of the HCPCS book and by reading Medicare bulletins and books on coding. A list of Level II codes follows:

Transportation Services	A0000—A0999
Chiropractic Services	A2000
Medical and Surgical Supplies	A4000—A5500
Miscellaneous and Experimental	A9000—A9300
Enteral and Parenteral Therapy	B4000—B9999
Dental Procedures	D0000—D9999
Durable Medical Equipment (DME)	E0000—E1830
G Codes for Procedures	G0001—G0062
Drugs Administered Other Than Oral Method	J0000—J8999
Chemotherapy	J9000—J9999
Orthotic Procedures	L0000—L4999
Prosthetic Procedures	L5000—L9999
Medical Services	M0000—M9999
Pathology and Laboratory	P0000—P9999
Temporary Codes	Q0000—Q9999
Diagnostic Radiology	R0000—R5999
Vision Services	V0000—V2799
Hearing Services	V5000—V5900

The lowest level of procedure coding is called the HCPCS Local Level 3. These codes are alphanumeric, ranging from W0000 to Z0000. They are established by the local Medicare office in each state and vary greatly. Local codes are used to describe new procedures that one Medicare office may recognize. Local codes will likely be used less and less, because Medicare is trying to standardize its benefits for all citizens.

While this three-tier program of coding makes it easy to identify exactly what transpired between doctor and patient, it takes time to master and may be confusing to all but the most experienced coders. With hundreds of coding changes each year, it goes without saying that the entire CPT/HCPCS system is hard to keep up with. As a result, there are many professional books intended for teaching doctors how to use the codes.

A billing service that knows coding has a significant advantage in the market. This is not to suggest that you need to memorize codes; becom-

Business Profile: Nancie Lee Cummins; Medical Management Billing

Nancie Lee Cummins got into medical billing from a background selling group health and life insurance to employers. With her knowledge of the healthcare industry, she felt that medical billing was the right business for her. To purchase her software and learn the details of the business, she went to a trade show for business opportunities and evaluated several offers, finally selecting Medical Management Software from Merry Schiff.

After her training, she immediately began marketing—and it paid off. She sent out 25 letters, from which one doctor responded and hired her. That client eventually referred another doctor to Nancie, and now all her clients have come from referrals.

Nancie now has six practices and is expecting to sign a 10-provider IPA outpatient mental healthcare facility. She attributes her success to the excellent training and support she received from Merry Schiff and to the referrals she has gotten. She also believes that specializing in billing for mental health practitioners, such as clinical psychologists and social workers, has been effective for her business.

In Nancie's view, medical billing is a professional business that must be treated with integrity. She says,

> If you get into this business, you have to work hard at it. You have to constantly read and educate yourself. Your knowledge is what makes the difference for your clients. For example, let's say you are coding a depression, and the doctor gives you a code for "general" depression, you need to know that this code will kick out (get denied) because it is not specific enough. The insurance company wants to know if it's single incident or multiple, what type, and so on. It may be that the doctor coded it incorrectly. While a worker's comp insurance might have taken the code, if it's a Medicare patient, the code should have one or two more digits to make it work. Many doctors simply don't know this; they give wrong codes, or they use old coding books.

To keep up on her training, Nancie goes to Medicare workshops whenever they are available. She also doesn't hesitate to call Medicare and ask questions when necessary. She finds the Medicare staff quite willing to help her, and in fact, she gets even better service when she says that she's a biller.

For most of her clients, Nancie performs full practice management. She files claims electronically, prints out and mails patient invoices, and prepares many financial reports. Because of managed care, she finds her responsibilities growing. For example, she has helped her doctors prepare proposals for HMOs and PPOs, and when we spoke, she was working with another potential client as he set up an MSO.

Nancie's expertise once prevented one of her doctors from making a costly error. The doctor was part of several clinics and believed that he was losing money in one of them. Nancie produced a report for him that proved that he was actually making more money in that clinic in less time than he was making at the clinic he had thought was his best choice. He decided to continue seeing patients in the first clinic, thanks to Nancie.

ing familiar with them is sufficient. Your goal is to appear professional when you speak with any potential client. Be sure to review the codes in that doctor's specialty before trying to sell your billing expertise. Be sure you stay up to date with Medicare especially. The agency is an ever-changing operation, and its need to control costs results in more and more documentation to justify medical procedures. A billing service must therefore maintain an ongoing knowledge of Medicare, not just learn about it once. As you operate your business, be sure to read the Medicare bulletins and attend the Medicare and Medicaid conferences.

Area 2: Computer Software and Hardware Issues

The level of computer knowledge you will need to be successful in medical billing is growing. As in all professions, more and more tasks are computerized, and the future predicts a constant stream of new technology you will need to keep up with. You also need to prove to prospective clients that you are as computer literate as—if not more than—they are. So, if you don't have a technical background in computers and software, you may be at a disadvantage in this field. However, Nancie Cummins, profiled earlier, is proof that you don't need to be a computer wizard; you simply need to master whichever medical billing software package you purchase to the point that you can do what your clients need better than they can.

Here's a brief explanation of some of the issues you need to understand.

HARDWARE   In most cases, the level of your hardware knowledge will pertain only to your own computer. You must obviously know how to use and care for your own PC to keep it healthy and running without problems or memory lapses. The worst thing you could do to your business would be to tell clients that your computer is down and their billing will be delayed.

However, because you may also get involved in the "bigger picture" for a client, you may be asked to help the doctor's office update its computer system and/or automate its own procedures. This means that the more you know about hardware, the better. It therefore helps to keep up on the options and prices of new PCs, where to buy equipment (new and used), and other issues such as local area networks, computer-to-computer remote accessing via phone lines, and how to use a modem. Of course, you can subcontract to a computer consultant should the occasion arise when a doctor needs you to consult on hardware issues. For the most part, as an independent billing service, your hardware knowledge goes only to the level of taking care of your own setup.

MEDICAL BILLING SOFTWARE Today's medical billing software has improved to the point that most people can learn what they need to know in a few days. The old days of complex nonintuitive commands and ugly, confusing interfaces are gone. Most billing software does what you want it to do "transparently," meaning that you don't need to get involved in the behind-the-scenes actions the software performs; you can tab through simple menu commands or point with your mouse to an icon to open a file, find a patient record, or post a payment.

It is worthwhile to learn to use your medical billing software before you go into business. In fact, some software companies will give you hypothetical physicians and patients with which you can practice so that you can develop your efficiency in keying in claims. Now is the time to learn your software, not when you are already up and running.

Which software to purchase is covered later in the chapter.

OTHER SOFTWARE. Once you are in business, much of your time is devoted to keying and transmitting claims using your medical billing software. Since many of these software programs are comprehensive, fully integrated practice management software packages, you have little or no need to learn how to use separate stand-alone accounting programs or database programs.

A medical billing service is a business, however, and you may wish to become proficient in using other types of business software, such as word-processing programs or database managers that allow you to create mail-merged letters and to print mailing labels for your marketing materials. Desktop publishing software will also enable you to design and print your own brochures, advertisements, and direct mail marketing pieces. Knowing how to use presentation software can help you prepare charts, graphs, slides, and other printouts when you give presentations to potential clients. Finally, using a bookkeeping or accounting programs is useful to invoice and bill your clients, and contact management programs can help you keep track of your business leads. Each of these categories has dozens of programs available, ranging from simple-to-use inexpensive software to complex and costly programs. To save yourself money and time, consider integrated software programs that combine several of these types of software, such as programs that offer word-processing, database management, and spreadsheet accounting all in one package.

If you have no background in computers, you may start to feel overwhelmed with how much computer work you have in front of you while trying to learn, at the same time, about the medical billing field. Take your time; you can learn it if you have the right attitude. Allow yourself an extra month to get acquainted with your software before you begin your billing service.

My view of the computer hardware and software industry is reminiscent of the ancient Greek mythological king Sisyphus, who was condemned to roll a stone uphill, only to watch it fall again when it reached the top. However, the difference is that our task is not a punishment, but a learning treat! So enjoy your challenge of learning and using new software and hardware. It's only going to get better!

Area 3: Business Knowledge and Skills

Paul and Sarah Edwards wrote in their book *Getting Business to Come to You,* "You are not in business until you **have** business." Their point is especially true in organizing a medical billing business. You can set up the best home office, purchase the most sophisticated software, and study the ICD-9 and CPT books till you have mastered them cold, but unless you have a doctor paying you for services, you are out of business.

Getting clients and keeping them require hard work, knowledge, and business acumen. Nearly everyone I interviewed for this book told me that the first few months of marketing their business were difficult and frustrating. Even worse was closing the first sale. They pointed out many reasons for this:

- Difficulty in getting busy doctors to pay attention to you or allowing you to give a presentation. (Imagine yourself walking into a crowded doctor's office with a waiting room full of ill people and leaning your head over the counter to ask the front office manager, "Excuse me. Is the doctor available?" Do you really think the doctor will interrupt what he or she is doing to meet you?)

- Financial and emotional barriers that prevent many doctors from wanting to hand over their cash flow to anyone. (Imagine a doctor who is already losing income from insurance companies and feeling frightened about his or her future. Will this be a trusting person?)

- Time it takes for doctors and their staff to make a decision to outsource this work. (Imagine a busy doctor trying to make up his or her mind about whether or not to outsource and how much to pay you.

Next imagine the office politics behind the decision to outsource; is anyone threatened?)

■ Concern over the potential for errors when outsourcing this work. (Imagine a doctor's face when her billing clerk tells her that they have $3,000 in unpaid claims; will that doctor believe you can do it better?)

All these barriers add up to a single truth: you must have or be able to develop excellent business skills, especially marketing and sales abilities. Let's examine each of these briefly.

MARKETING Marketing is the skill of letting people know about your products or services, so they can decide whether or not to buy. Marketing is actually a combination of fields and activities: cold calling, direct mail, advertising, premiums, special promotions, and public relations. Each of these requires different talents and skills, and each has its pros and cons. Which of the marketing strategies you use depends on many factors: your personal preferences, your budget, and your audience. Some people are effective at cold calling, while others are not. Some locales are more receptive than others to direct sales. There are many variables, so you must analyze your particular situation and determine what's best for you.

In medical billing, marketing is especially vital because, as just mentioned, getting a doctor to give you responsibility for managing his or her accounts can be quite challenging. Many people I interviewed for this book swear that cold calling works best for them; others stopped cold calling and found success through direct mail campaigns using a persuasive letter or brochure. We'll examine the various techniques in greater detail in the "Getting Started" section of this chapter, but for now, suffice it to say that you cannot succeed in medical billing unless you are willing to market yourself aggressively.

SALES Marketing is useless without sales. You could have the most attractive brochure when you call on the front office manager, or make the most persuasive sales pitch to the doctor, but unless you **close** the deal, you don't have business.

Unfortunately, many people immediately think of sales as a crass profession. They hate the thought of doing sales, and they shudder to think that someday, they might "force" somebody to buy something from them. Indeed, to many people, sales means pressure tactics, deceit, and manipulation. None of these need describe a good salesperson. A more positive way to think of sales is that it is the natural conclusion to a good marketing plan.

Successful selling require three skills:

1. Identifying the customer's motivations. The foremost skill is knowing how to go beneath the surface to identify your customer's true motivations. One of the first rules in sales is making sure you can answer your customer's silent question, "What's in it for me?" Customers know what's in it for you; they need to know how you can help them. According to Jackie Hall, president of the Hall Group, a corporate consulting firm that works with InfoHealth Corporation (the medical billing software company mentioned earlier),

> Salespeople need to ask about the doctor's aspirations and dreams for his or her business. This is the heart of the matter. If you focus on technical jargon about insurance and claims that doctors know nothing about, they will try to ask you questions to test your knowledge and make sure you know more than they do! Instead, ask them about their hopes and dreams for their business.

This advice is sound. In today's healthcare environment, you will likely hear many similar answers from doctors when you ask about their aspirations and dreams. Many will tell you that they want to preserve their independence and income security in the face of managed care. Many will also tell you that they want to practice medicine, not business. They are frustrated by Medicare, Medicaid, and private health insurance rules and regulations. Your ability to sell is therefore strongest when you can address these issues persuasively and convincingly. You need to show your commitment to be a strong advocate for the doctor and to expertly handle his or her practice management problems.

2. Persistence. The second sales skill is persistence. You must be persistent enough to know when you are into a worthwhile negotiation, yet astute enough to know when you are probably wasting your time. Many people who dislike sales actually dislike the idea of having to ask someone (often repeatedly) to buy their service. They also hate rejection. However, thoughtful persistence is needed, because few people buy right away and you cannot afford to lose a potential client by giving up too early.

3. Negotiation skill. The third sales skill is the ability to negotiate for a win/win close. Negotiation is both a skill and an art. You need to know when and how much to compromise, when and how to yield your ground as much as when and how to hold it. Often, people without sales experience dislike negotiating because they believe they must throw themselves at the customer's feet in order to get the business. On the contrary, good negotiation should convey that you respect yourself and expect others to pay you fairly and treat you appropriately. Ask yourself when was the last time you met a doctor who worked for free. If you are like most people, this humorous prodding illustrates how important confident negotiation is to your business success.

Charting Your Challenge

The foregoing sections have presented three areas for you to assess your current knowledge base and skills. Take a moment and reflect on your knowledge of them. How much about medical coding and insurance regulations do you need to learn? How computer literate are you? What is the level of your business skills? If you haven't already, you may now want to complete the chart suggested on page 88, in which you plot your learning curve.

If you are going into business with a spouse or partner, don't forget to examine his or her skills and see if combined, the two of you complement each other. It often happens that one person has one set of skills, such as excellent marketing intuition, while the other has a solid background in another set of skills, such as in computers or medicine. The sidebar on DAPA Medical Billing Services illustrates a husband/wife team whose complementary skills turned their venture into a true success.

Income and Earning Potential

There have been many claims about the potential of a medical billing business, but earning potential is one area to evaluate carefully if you are considering this profession. The difficulty with calculating your earning potential is that until you are in the business, you often can't determine how to charge your clients. Much depends on whether you are able to do claims only or full practice management. Of course, it also depends on how many doctors you have as clients, and how busy they keep you.

In general, there are four methods of pricing in a medical billing business. The following sections explain these methods. I have tried to show each method in an average light, without pretending that medical billing is a get-rich-quick scheme. For most people, it is not. For this reason, I highly recommend that you scrutinize any earnings projections anyone shows you outside of this book. You will frequently find brochures from medical billing opportunity vendors that list income projections, but please take these as strictly hypothetical (and optimistic) projections until you know more about your specific market potential.

Daniel F. Lehmann and Patricia Bartello—DAPA Medical Billing Services

The saying "two heads are better than one" is an apt assessment of the complementary business partnership of these two individuals.

Dan Lehmann entered medical billing after 25 years in management and manufacturing, working into high-tech automotive and robotics industries. He also taught college business courses for a few years, but like many people who grow tired of working for others, Dan yearned for his own business enterprise. His wife, Pat Bartello, had a strong medical background with a master's degree in educational psychology. She had also worked in a hospital in collections and had operated a successful medical transcription business. When they decided to follow their dream, they carefully evaluated many types of businesses and selected medical billing as their best option.

Dan and Pat agree that it takes a combination of skills to be in this business. One skill that Dan contributed was a strong business background. He prepared a business plan for their operation when they first began and does monthly updates to track their progress. Dan was also quite versed in computer hardware and software. As for Pat, she knew medical terminology and was comfortable speaking to doctors and doing presentations. As Pat told me, "Doctors are very suspicious, and so you have to come across credibly. When you first call on them, they may throw out some jargon just to test you, and if you respond accurately, you've got their ear."

Dan and Pat offer complete reimbursement management and they specialize in working with physicians in geriatrics and geriatric psychiatry. Because they live on the borders of Virginia, Maryland, and Washington D.C., they've ended up with clients in all three areas, which complicates their work to some extent. They file a large number of Medicare claims, many of which go to different Medicare carriers. (Note: the Medicare carrier to whom you file claims depends on the location of the doctor's office, not where the patient lives. Pat and Dan have doctors who have multiple offices in different counties, so their claims must be filed to different Medicare carriers.)

Just as with every biller profiled in this chapter, Dan and Pat have noticed a change in the business over the past several years. As Pat told me,

> Things are growing worse. There's a huge increase in managed care today, requiring patients to have authorization to see a specialist. We have many cases where there hasn't been a valid referral, so the claim gets denied. Ultimately, this situation puts a lot of pressure on both doctors and billing offices. Without a valid referral, the doctor doesn't get paid. But it also affects us. We don't want to put effort into filing a claim when there was no authorization, because we don't get paid either. We therefore end up doing a lot of verification to make sure the referral has been made before we file a claim. For example, let's say a patient has been authorized to have ten visits with a psychologist. We plug that information into our computer so that as the patient uses up the visits, our system counts them down.

Dan and Pat believe that medical billing in their area is still an excellent business opportunity, but it has become more competitive. They find doctors more open to outsourcing, but at the same time, more concerned about the costs of doing so:

> Doctors hear that Medicare provides free software, and they think "why should I pay to outsource when I can have my clerk do it more cheaply?" But we show doctors that we can handle their practice with more accuracy and a

better return-on-investment because we do everything: insurance verification for managed care, primary billing, secondary billing, patient statements, and so on. We also do it better, and less expensively than they can do it in their office because we work on volume.

Since I interviewed them for the first edition of this book, Dan and Pat have grown their business to the point at which they can no longer use DOS or Windows-based software. Dan recently invested in an extensive UNIX system for their home office that provides him with many sophisticated features plus simultaneous usage because they have employees who work off-site and need to tie into the system. As Dan told me years ago, "The important thing as a service agency is to respond quickly and accurately." Seems like Dan and Pat are doing just that.

PER CLAIM FEE BASIS In the per claim fee method, you would charge your clients a set fee for each claim you process, whether or not the claim is ultimately paid by the insurance carrier (except if you are at fault for a rejected claim because of a typographical error you committed). The per claim fee varies around the country from $2.00 to $6.00, but the majority of people I interviewed say they are able to charge $3.00 to $4.00 per claim.

Let's use the $4.00 figure to work through an example of a billing service and to calculate its earnings. In this case, let's assume that the billing service uses a clearinghouse that charges a $300.00 annual fee, plus a $50.00 annual setup fee per physician, plus $0.50 per claim. (Note: the per claim clearinghouse fee can range from $0.35 to $0.60, depending on the deal you are able to strike with your clearinghouse.) We will exclude from this projection that some clearinghouses also charge a fee for rejected claims, and a postage fee when they cannot transmit your claim electronically but must "drop it" to paper and mail it.

To be conservative about this projection, assume that you have only two clients for your first two months of operation, and you add a new client every few months, for a total of five physicians over the first year of operation. Each physician sees 3 to 4 patients per hour (some physicians see many more, of course, but some see far fewer). Assume therefore that each doctor averages 15 claims per day for 20 billable days per month. This equals 300 claims per month @ $4.00, hence $1,200 per month per physician. Table 2-9 shows how your income and expense chart would look under this scenario.

From this table, you can see that a "just claims" billing service might generate $47,000 in income with five doctors each supplying 300 claims per month. Remember that this income excludes marketing costs, which could

TABLE 2-9

Income and Expense Projections for a Typical Billing Service Charging on a Per Claim Basis

Month	1st	2nd	3rd	4th	5th	6th	7th	8th	9th	10th	11th	12th	Total
# of clients	2	2	3	3	3	4	4	4	5	5	5	5	5
# of claims @$4.00 per claim	600	600	900	900	900	1200	1200	1200	1500	1500	1500	1500	13,500
Gross Income	$2400	$2400	$3600	$3600	$3600	$4800	$4800	$4800	$6000	$6000	$6000	$6000	$54,000
Expenses @$0.50 per claim + $50.00 per client registration fees	$300 plus $100 new reg fee	$300	$450 plus $50 new reg fee	$450	$450	$600 plus $50 new reg fee	$600	$600	$750 plus $50 new reg fee	$750	$750	$750	
Total Expenses	$400	$300	$500	$450	$450	$650	$600	$600	$800	$750	$750	$750	$7000
Net Income (Gross less Total expenses)	$2000	$2100	$3100	$3150	$3150	$4150	$4200	$4200	$5200	$5250	$5250	$5250	$47,000

Notes:

1. Excludes income from additional fees such as setup charges or fees for sending patient statements
2. Excludes expenses for marketing, cost of software, and overhead

easily amount to $2,000 or more for brochures, letters, direct mail postage, business cards, stationery, and other items.

On the other hand, this projection does not include additional fees you can charge for setting up new accounts for each physician, or doing any practice management functions such as preparing and mailing patient invoices. Many billing services charge $2.00 or $3.00 per patient when they do the setup. If a doctor has 250 to 500 active patients, this could generate an additional $400 to $1,500. In our hypothetical example, the billing service could increase its net income to $52,000.

A variation on the per unit fee basis is to use a sliding scale, as did one of the people I interviewed. He charges each of his clients according to how many claims per week he receives from them, as shown here:

Claims per Week	Charge per Claim
1—99	$6.00
100—199	$5.00
200—299	$4.50
300—399	$4.00
400—499	$3.50
500 or more	$3.00

The owner chose this method because he had several clients who wanted his services but processed only a limited number of claims per week. Because they needed his services, they agreed to pay a much higher fee per claim to compensate him for the lower volume.

Doing full practice management results in much higher fees. The going rate to send out monthly statements to patients is $2.00 per statement (plus postage). If a physician has 200 active clients to whom he or she must send a monthly statement, you can add another $400.00 per physician per month to your income. That means an additional $3,600 per year per physician × five doctors: an additional $18,000 along with your $47,000 income. As you can readily see, adding services can significantly increase your income potential.

HOURLY BASIS Another method of charging is to set an hourly fee for your work. However, this method is one of the least used in the medical billing profession. The sidebar on Linda Noel exemplifies one such owner who charges by the hour because she has several clients who process only a small number of claims per week. Charging by the hour, in quarter hour increments, allows Linda to account for the time she spends getting files ready, transmitting them, and doing patient billing and fol-low-up phone calls.

The hourly fee you set will depend on your geographic location, the competition, and whether or not doctors perceive you as a professional biller or just a clerk. If your client is a doctor who has had an in-house billing person for years, there may be an unfortunate tendency to corre-late your work with this hourly paid employee. Beware of this situation.

Try to make your hourly fee as high as you can get it right away, per-haps $20 to $35 per hour, because changing an hourly fee once you sign a contract is difficult. While employees get annual raises, outside services such as free-lancers and consultants usually cannot increase their fees until they have had the contract for several years.

Your annual income based on an hourly fee basis depends on how much you work. If you can work 20 to 30 hours per week at $25.00 per hour × 50 weeks per year, your income will range between $25,000 and $37,500.

PERCENTAGE BASIS   The third method of pricing your service is to charge clients a percentage of every dollar you bring in, including all elec-tronic claims and all patient billing you do. This method of charging is by far the most popular and offers the best potential. Of dozens of people I

Business Profile: Linda Noel

Linda Noel was managing a psychiatric clinic in West Los Angeles when she and her husband decided to start their family. Not wanting to give up her career, she opted for the only logical choice: a home business utilizing her medical experience. Not only did she get the support of her former employer, but he helped her by spread-ing the word to attract other clients who soon signed on with Linda.

Today, Linda has nine clients, enough to keep her working a comfortable 30 hours per week, leaving her time to be with her children. For simplicity, she works only with single physician practices and bills most of them on a straightforward basis of $15 to $21 per hour. For a few, she adds a small percentage fee for collections if the billables are hard to collect. "In my practice," Linda told me, "I do everything from billing to accounts receivable; I function just as someone who works in their office would, including occasionally scheduling appointments. I do transcription and billing (both electronic and paper)."

Linda doesn't believe that you must absolutely have a strong medical background to get into the business, but she knows that working in a physician's office helped her. She points out that the constantly changing Medicare regulations are hard to keep up with, so she seriously recommends taking courses offered by Medicare.

"Running a personalized service is a key to getting and keeping clients," Linda says. "You've got to have doctors who like you and are willing to refer you to others."

interviewed, nearly all were charging from 6 percent to 8 percent of net collectible amounts.

In using the percentage method, note that you need to clarify with your client which items you will get paid on. For example, if a patient pays cash to cover the 20 percent coinsurance or a $15 copayment fee, at the time of the visit will you get a portion of this money? In most cases, no. Most doctors want to pay billers only for the claims and patient statements for which they bill out. However, if you have to update the account, you should rightly get your percentage.

As you might imagine, it is far more difficult to convince a doctor to agree to pay you 6 percent or 8 percent of the practice's total collectibles than it is to charge $3.00 per claim. The key to winning this argument is to show your client the advantages of using your services, particularly that you can significantly increase the "collection efficiency" of the office. This is the level at which the physician is able to collect on billables.

For example, consider a physician who bills $1 million per year and pays 1.5 staff people to do billing in-house at a combined salary of $35,000. Assume this doctor is able to collect at only a 75 percent efficiency (hence, $750,000) because his staff does not have time to follow up on denied claims, rejected claims, lost claims, and patients who don't pay. Contrast that situation with what you can offer: if you commit to collecting on 85 percent of collections (hence, $850,000), the doctor can benefit by more than $50,000. Table 2-10 shows the calculation for this.

TABLE 2-10

Comparison of Collection Efficiency: In-House Staff vs. Outside Service

	Physician Using Salaried In-House Staff	Physician Hiring an Outside Billing Service at 8%
Billables	$1,000,000	$1,000,000
Collection efficiency	×75%	×85%
Collections	$750,000	$850,000
Cost of collections	($35,000)	($68,000)
Net income	$715,000	$782,000

As Dan Lehmann remarked about the percentage method,

> We charge 8 percent or more, but we do everything for the doctors: patient registrations (we even supply the forms), daily charges, electronic filing twice or three times per week, insurance verification. In some cases, we eliminate the need to have an in-office clerk even part time. Their wage plus benefits, which may amount to $20,000 to $30,000, is less than ours, but we can collect far more than they can.

The percentage method is your best choice if you are offering full practice management services. This method compensates you for the efforts you make to follow through on all accounts receivable and make sure they are collected. Of course, any errors or mistakes you make may reduce your income under this method. Doctors will also be much more suspicious if they believe you are doing sloppy work and not collecting as much as you could.

Projecting an annual income under the percentage method is difficult. Whereas with the per claim method, you can estimate how many claims the doctor will have, with the percentage method, you have less control over how much insurance companies will reimburse, how many bad claims you may get stuck with, and what type of patients the doctor may treat. If you are planning to charge a percentage, you need to openly discuss with your client the facts about his or her practice before you commit to this method.

MIXED METHOD   The last method of charging for your services is the mixed method. As the name implies, you can mix any of the methods discussed earlier, depending on your clientele. If you have a client who wants only claims, you will obviously need to charge on a per claim or hourly basis. With another client though, perhaps you might start out on a per claim basis and slowly work your way to percentage as you increase your role in handling full practice management.

Whichever method you choose, don't forget to counterbalance your income projections with an accurate estimate of your expenses, including costs for marketing materials, printing, postage, phone bills, and other overhead (stationery, furniture, mileage, etc.). Projecting your income for a new business in the first year can often be enhanced by making more than one calculation—for example, best-case and worst-case scenarios—and revising your projections as each month of operation passes.

Again, take whatever projections you hear from others with a grain of salt. Your income will depend on your area and on the kind of customers *you* find. While I used 300 claims per month in the earlier example, no one can guarantee that you will achieve any particular number of claims.

Deciding If This Business Is for You

The first part of this chapter presented the background for understanding medical billing services. Armed with this brief sketch, the following checklist can help you decide if this business is for you. Take a moment now to do this 15-question checklist before reading the remainder of the chapter.

- Does the business of medical insurance and computer coding appeal to me?
- Do I have the drive to grasp complex medical terminology and coding matters?
- Can I work comfortably with doctors and their office personnel?
- Do I have enough computer skills and an interest in learning new software?
- Do I enjoy detailed work, such as keying in medical records?
- Can I sell my services face to face and close a deal?
- Do I have the drive and persistence to close several clients?
- Do I understand direct mail marketing and other forms of marketing?
- Do I negotiate well?
- Do I want to assume financial responsibility for ensuring my clients get paid?
- Do I have two to three months to get my business started?
- Do I have from $500 to $7,000 to purchase medical billing software or a business opportunity package that includes training and marketing support?
- Do I have the talents, skills, knowledge, and abilities that can help me succeed in the healthcare business?
- Does my partner (if I have one) provide complementary skills to my own so that we can work together to succeed?
- Do I have a suitable location from which I can conduct this business?

If you answered yes to most of these questions, the next section provides brief guidelines on how to get started in your own medical billing business. The section is organized according to the sequence of steps you need to take: choosing your software and hardware (including whether or not to buy a business opportunity); obtaining training; learning how to price your services; guidelines for marketing your business and getting a first client; and overcoming common start-up problems.

Section II: Getting Started

Choosing Your Software

Many medical billing software firms and business opportunity vendors are competing to sell you software. If you read business magazines such as *Home Office Computing, Entrepreneur, Success,* and others, you'll find a variety of advertisements for medical billing software and/or training. There are literally dozens of companies involved in selling practice management programs; some sell only to doctors' offices, but as the business changes and there is greater recognition of the need for independent medical billing companies, you will find more and more companies eager to sell software and training to entrepreneurs who want to set up their own businesses. (See the next section, "Should I Buy a Business Opportunity.")

How do you decide which software to buy? Unfortunately, there is no one answer to this question. Each person has his or her own needs, and each program has its unique design that creates both advantages and disadvantages. Additionally, software is an ever-changing product, with new bells and whistles constantly added each year. If I were to recommend one software program today or critique another, my recommendations will become flawed quickly because they will be outdated within months or years. Thus, it is impossible to provide specific software recommendations.

Nevertheless, here are some guidelines about what to look for:

1. There are differences in software. Some software programs are DOS-based while others are Windows-based. That choice depends on your preferences and your computer system. Needless to say, the Windows environment has become nearly the dominant software platform in recent years, so most software firms will move their DOS-based software to Windows in the coming years if they haven't already.

2. Most software products are designed to make the medical billing process efficient, but among the products I reviewed, enough signifi-

cant differences exist that I urge you to evaluate for yourself *more than one product*. Don't try out just one software demo copy and make a decision based on that. Judge for yourself which of several software programs makes you feel comfortable and which one is easiest for you to use.

3. Don't buy a software program without seeing a demonstration of how it performs. Most companies are willing to send you a free demo copy, or you can visit someone who uses it.

4. Look for professional features in the software. For example, make sure your software allows you to do the following:

- True billing service capability. Because you'll probably aim to do full practice management, you want to be sure your software allows you to keep track of many different providers. Some software is intended to handle a single practice only and is not appropriate for a professional billing service.

- Claims only versus practice management software. Some software allows you to submit electronic claims, but it doesn't contain the accounting operations you need to do full practice management.

- Open item accounting. Because Medicare and other insurers sometimes approve only some of the charges on a claim, you must be able to record payments and link them to the charges billed. That way, if you need to question a denied claim, or bill the patient for the difference, you can tell which charges were not paid.

- Multiple fee schedules. With the growth of managed care plans, doctors need to be able to have multiple fee schedules. They are required to accept one set of fees for Medicare patients, another set of fees for patients under HMO Plan A, and another set of fees under PPO Plan B. This means that your software should be able to store up to several dozen fee schedules. As mentioned earlier, some software also has special modules for managed care patients who fall under a capitated plan, because you need to log their reimbursements differently.

- Pop up windows for common data sets. Some data sets, such as insurance companies, procedure and diagnostic codes, and fees are annoying to have to retype over and over again. To facilitate this, many software products provide pop-up windows that store the data sets, so all you need to do is point and click on the item you want instead of typing it.

- Clearinghouse flexibility. Does the software allow you to work with any clearinghouse you want, or must you use the clearinghouse recommended by the software vendor?

The CD-ROM disk accompanying this book includes several samples of medical billing software. These programs are demonstration copies; some are self-running demos and others are real working versions of the software, albeit "disabled" or "limited" in their scope (i.e., don't try to use them to get into business because they won't allow you to input many patients or claims; they are sample copies only). The vendors of these software products invite you to contact them directly or, in the case of Lytec and Medisoft, to contact any of the several business opportunity vendors who resell the software along with training. You can contact InfoHealth and Santiago SDS directly about purchasing their software plus training. See Appendix E for more information.

Should I Buy a Business Opportunity?

Because of the complexity of learning about the medical billing business, many software companies do not offer training to entrepreneurs. They prefer to focus on selling their software directly to medical providers' offices. Other software companies will sell to entrepreneurs, but they don't provide the level of training you need to market and succeed in this field.

As a result, many "business opportunity" companies have appeared that follow the model of software VARs (valued-added resellers). These people package the software from respected medical billing software houses, along with their own materials and training programs. They charge you a much higher fee than you would pay for just buying the software directly from the software company, but in general, they provide far more training and support.

However, because of their nature, business opportunities are regulated by many states almost like franchises, to help prevent consumers from investing in bogus deals. Business opportunities are known as "seller-assisted marketing plans" (SAMPs). They differ from franchises in that you are not required to pay continuing royalties or a percentage of your profits year in and year out. You are also not allowed to use their company name nor do you need to adhere to strict rules about how you run your business, such as franchise laws impose. When you buy a business opportunity, you are simply paying someone to sell you (you hope) good information about what's required to operate the business, often along with software and collateral materials.

If you are considering buying a business opportunity, it is wise to scrutinize the vendors closely to be sure you are dealing with an honest and qualified company that truly knows the business and can train you. Unfortunately, ever since medical billing became a popular business in the 1990s, a number of the business opportunity vendors selling software and training did not truly know the medical profession. Several of these companies enticed hundreds of entrepreneurs to purchase their opportunity, and then these firms went out of business after cashing the checks, leaving their customers with no support. Worse, several of these same companies then reopened under a different name in another state and repeated the ruse. Much to our dismay, several of these companies are still around, preying on people who are seriously exploring new careers and livelihoods. Some of these companies have been charged by the Federal Trade Commission (FTC), which also regulates business opportunities, but they continue to stay in business.

Here are some tips to assess whether you are dealing with a good business opportunity vendor:

1. If you experience high-pressure sales tactics, it is likely not a company with which you want to do business. Many people have called me to complain about high-pressure tactics from companies, such as offering a special price that is "good only if you buy it today." Don't fall for such maneuvers and tactics. If a company offers you a deal to buy today, you can be sure it is not interested in working with you over the long term. It only wants your money.

2. Find out if the vendor has any complaints lodged against it with the attorney general's office in your state. If any prior customers have had difficulty with the unscrupulous vendor, they may have filed a lawsuit or notified the state attorney general's office. If so, you can find out about these complaints. You should also check with the Better Business Bureau in your state as well as with those of surrounding states. If there are numerous complaints about the company, this is certainly a red warning flag for you. Don't underestimate it.

3. Find out if your state is one of those that regulates business opportunities or SAMPs. At this time, the following states have such laws: Alabama, California, Connecticut, Florida, Georgia, Illinois, Indiana, Iowa, Kentucky, Louisiana, Maine, Maryland, Michigan, Minnesota, Nebraska, New Hampshire, North Carolina, Ohio, Oklahoma, South Carolina, South Dakota, Texas, Utah, Virginia, and Washington. Other states may have similar regulatory programs over SAMPs by the time this book comes out. If your state regulates SAMPs, make sure your vendor adheres to the regulations. Request a document from the vendor indicating that it is registered to sell in your state. (The registration must reflect the state in which you live, not the state in which the vendor resides.) If it is not registered, it is up to you to decide whether you want to buy from it. If you do purchase and change your mind or find that you have been seriously shortchanged in the level of support you were promised, you have little chance of getting your money back.

4. Note also that under most SAMP laws, business opportunity vendors are not supposed to make representations about how much income you can earn in medical billing, or if they try to do so, they must report names, addresses, and phone numbers of those people who have made the income level they contend. Watch out for exaggerated income projections, such as people earning $70,000 or $100,000 within one year. It takes time to get this business going, and even the most successful people say that the first year was a financial struggle.

5. Get at least three references from the vendor and check them out. Unfortunately, some vendors use "plants" (also called "singers") who are paid to confirm how wonderful the vendor was; you have no way to know this. However, make every effort to assure yourself that these references are truly in the medical billing business.

6. Be precise in identifying exactly what type of support the vendor is supposed to give you for the price you pay. Does it consist of live training? Phone support? Manuals? Technical training? Marketing training? Several people have told me terrible stories of vendors who spend all day teaching the basics of software, which can be learned from a manual, with no time spent on teaching how to market to doctors. Marketing is the hard part, and if the vendor cannot help you with marketing, you may not be successful in getting a client.

7. In addition, be clear in your own mind how much support you need. If you have experience as a bookkeeper, administrative assistant, or a computer consultant, for example, you might feel that you don't need as much training. However, for all but the most experienced people with medical backgrounds, it is very likely that buying training from a qualified business opportunity vendor can make the difference between success and failure.

LIST OF RECOMMENDED VENDORS OF BUSINESS OPPORTU-NITIES If you agree that it is in your best interest to purchase training and support along with your software, here is a short list of the most reputable and reliable business opportunity vendors that I recommend:

- Medical Management Software—Merry Schiff—800-759-8419
- ClaimTek Systems—Kahil Farhat—800-224-7450 or 503-239-8316
- Santiago SDS Inc.—Tom Banks/Mary Lee Hyatt—800-652-3500
- Electronic Filing Associates—Ed Epstein—800-596-9962

Appendix A contains details about each of these vendors. These business opportunity vendors are all companies that I have come to respect from their track record in this industry for honesty, integrity, and verifiably *high-quality* training and support. You may find other companies to work with on your own, but I am confident that these business opportunity vendors will work with you in an honest, forthright manner. No one can guarantee your success, but these vendors will at least give you the training and support that you expected to get as part of your package.

If you believe that you have the background and work experience to jump right into the medical billing business without special training, you might want to consider purchasing software directly from a software house. I recommend the following: MediSoft, Lytec, and Oxford Medical Systems. You can find details about these software firms in Appendix A.

A Note on Starting Out

Be prepared for a delay in doing electronic claims filing when you first start. If you are working through a clearinghouse, you may need to fill out several agreement forms, one of which can only be done when you get your first client. Your doctors must also sign agreements with the clearinghouse. All this takes a few weeks to complete. The clearinghouse will probably ask you to process 20 or so claims to make sure you know what you are doing. This also adds time. Meanwhile, if you are already taking claims from a client, you will have to print them on HCFA 1500 paper forms for these first few weeks. Don't try to fool your client; be honest and make sure he or she understands that it takes time before the fast results of electronic claims processing can be observed.

Choosing Hardware and Other Equipment

If you don't have a PC yet, you should choose your hardware based on the software you decide to purchase. As indicated earlier, however, most software is moving toward a Windows platform, so purchasing the most cost-effective yet powerful PC you can afford is your goal. In general, this means buying a PC with a Pentium chip with 16 or more Mb of RAM. You can get by with a 486 personal computer and 8 Mb of RAM, but prices are going down so fast that it usually costs little more to buy a Pentium PC now. You may also be able to use a 386 computer, but your software will run much more slowly.

You will need at least a 500 megabyte hard drive. Fortunately, most PCs sold in retail stores or via mail order (such as Gateway, Dell, or Micron) are now sold with hard drives that have ample space; today's new computer generally comes equipped with anywhere from 1.2 to 2.5 gigabytes of hard disk space. Remember that it helps to have this extra disk space to store all the other software you will want to own to perform many general business functions. Software such as desktop publishing or database programs usually require 10 to 20 Mb of hard drive space for the program alone, and your data will usually occupy another 50 Mb. This means that for each program you load into your computer, you probably want to reserve space for 60 to 100 Mb. Five or more programs, including a desktop publishing package, a database, a spreadsheet, and you are approaching $\frac{1}{2}$ gigabyte.

Whether you are purchasing new hardware or upgrading what you already own, I recommend thinking long term. With prices dropping quickly, you can often spend as little as $1,000 to $1,500 to equip yourself with a professional computer system.

As far as other equipment goes, you will need the following:

- *Monitor.* A color monitor (VGA or SVGA) eases strain on your eyes and helps you work more productively. The colors help distinguish menus and screen entry fields. If you can afford it, consider purchasing at least a 15" monitor instead of a 14" model as visual studies have shown that people are more productive when their screen area is larger.

- *Fax machine.* One of the most common ways to conduct your business is to have providers fax you their superbills. As a result, a good fax machine is critical. You need to keep the faxes as your permanent records, so do purchase a plain paper fax rather than a thermal paper machine. Reliable plain paper fax machines cost as little as $400 at office supply stores and through computer/technology catalogues.

Note: you cannot use an internal fax/modem for this purpose. You need a paper copy of faxed superbills to place in your records.

- *Modem.* Most software and clearinghouses support 9,600, 14,400, and 28,800 baud modems. Obviously, the higher the baud rate, the faster your transmission, so 28,800 or higher is your best bet.

- *Backup Devices.* You should be able to keep backups of your files for security purposes. Do not risk a hard drive crash with your client's data. A tape drive backup is less than $200 and well worth the expense. If you prefer, use one of the portable or removable hard drive backup devices, which sell for just slightly more than tape drives.

- *Printer.* Even if you are doing electronic filing, it is worthwhile purchasing a laser or inkjet printer to use for all your other practice management functions, such as patient invoices, reports, and graphs. Having a laser or inkjet printer also allows you to prepare your own marketing materials such as brochures, fliers, and direct mail letters. You can also use a laser printer to print the occasional HCFA 1500 you may need if your clearinghouse does not send to a small insurance company, although these days, the clearinghouse will probably drop it to paper for you.

- *Office Furniture.* Processing claims and setting up patient files is tedious work. To prevent neck and back strain, or problems such as carpal tunnel syndrome in your wrists and fingers, buy yourself an ergonomically designed chair with arm rests.

- *Phone Lines.* As a professional businessperson, you must have a business phone distinct from your family phone. You do not want a client to speak to your child, a relative, or the baby-sitter. You can order either a regular personal phone line or a business line, which costs more. Some phone companies now offer special pricing for home-based businesses. A home-business line or regular business line usually entitles your business to a listing in the *Yellow Pages.* This can be useful for marketing; several medical billing companies have told me they did receive calls from their *Yellow Pages* ads. While the phone company is installing your second line (your home line is the first), consider having a third one installed at the same time to use for your fax machine and modem. A third line allows your clients to fax you at any time instead of having to interrupt you on the second line if you are on the phone. You also do all your electronic transmissions via modem over the third phone line, so you can take business calls on your second line at the same time.

■ *Postage Meter.* If you handle patient statements, it is also well worth the slight expense to lease a postage meter, thus saving many trips to the post office. Meter rentals are not expensive today, particularly if you compare the cost to the time you lose going to the post office and the price of gas.

Resources and Training

Preparing yourself to run a medical billing service is perhaps the most valuable action you can take before starting your business. As indicated throughout the chapter, this business has become a real profession, requiring increasingly sophisticated knowledge and skills. Without adequate training, you will take much longer to get your business under way—or you will become so frustrated that you will quit before you get your first client. Here are some suggestions for educating yourself.

INDUSTRY ASSOCIATIONS   One of the first steps you can take is to contact the association that serves people in the medical billing industry.

NATIONAL ELECTRONIC BILLER'S ALLIANCE (NEBA).   This association was founded by Merry Schiff (owner of Medical Management Software, Inc., one of the software and business opportunity vendors listed earlier). NEBA provides an extensive array of training and marketing support materials, including books, audiotapes, and a newsletter.

If you are interested in learning more about medical billing in a home-study course, NEBA has a comprehensive program that contains details on every aspect of the business. NEBA also offers a certification exam for billers who would like a credential. The organization currently includes several hundred members, ranging from people who are new to medical billing to experienced billers. NEBA also provides a World Wide Web site with information and advice to improve marketing skills and develop expertise of reimbursement issues. You can contact NEBA at 415-577-1190 or fax at 415-577-1290 to request information. The Web site address is www.nebazone.com.

COURSES Many community college and adult education schools have courses or workshops in medical billing and coding. In some cases, these courses are intended to train people who want to work in the front office of a physician's practice, but other courses are specifically targeted to entrepreneurs. For example, the Learning Annex in Los Angeles has several popular courses on running a home-based medical billing service. If you enjoy a classroom atmosphere, this type of training may be for you. These courses are most often inexpensive, but they are typically quite limited in scope. If you are eager to get your business under way, taking college courses one at a time may prolong the amount of time it takes to learn what you need to know.

As indicated earlier, NEBA has a home-study course that goes into extensive detail on insurance, medical office procedures, coding, and marketing/sales.

Another home-study medical billing course is offered by At-Home Professions, a Colorado-based home-study company that has courses in many disciplines. See Appendix A for more information about its courses.

BOOKS AND NEWSLETTERS There are many books you can read to learn more about billing, coding, and other aspects of medical billing. Look for a medical bookstore in your city where you can purchase coding manuals and other reference books. One excellent book is *Understanding Medical Insurance: A Step-by-Step Guide* by JoAnn C. Rowell, available in many medical bookstores and from medical suppliers such as Medicode (see following).

The ICD-9 is available from the U.S. Government Printing Office, and the CPT coding book can be purchased directly from the American Medical Association. You can also obtain both these books from several private companies that republish them under license in special easy-to-use formats. One such supplier is Medicode, which offers the most recent CPT edition and a large assortment of medical coding "how-to" guides, including the following titles:

■ Reimbursement Manual for the Medical Office: A Comprehensive Guide to Coding, Billing, and Fee Management

- CPT Coding Made Easy!: Technical Guide (2 vols.)
- Insurance Directory
- Coder's Desk Reference
- CPT Billing Guide
- Code It Right!
- Reimbursement Strategies

Medicode can be reached at 800-678-8398 in Salt Lake City, Utah. Ask for Ann Jacobsen. See Appendix A for details about special discounts that Medicode offers readers of this book.

Another source of excellent information on medical billing is Gary Knox, of AQC Resources, a consulting company in San Jose, California. Gary has been studying medical software and business opportunity companies for many years. As Gary has noticed, the field has matured. He says,

> Medical billing today is a better industry than it was a few years ago. There is more acceptance to outsourcing billing now. Unfortunately, many people are not taught the skills to market themselves; even if they get one or two offices, they're not trained well enough and they fail.
>
> I would like people to know that success in this industry is 75 percent marketing. It's no longer a "just claims" business that physicians will consider. If they are going to outsource, they want more than that. They want a full service agency, especially with HMOs dictating to them what to do. They want someone who can help them with eligibility verifications, authorizations, and so on. So you need to have a broad experience today; it isn't "just claims" anymore.

Gary publishes an informative bi-monthly newsletter on the medical billing industry for $59 per year. Gary can be reached at 408-295-4102. See Appendix A for more information on AQC resources.

ONLINE FORUMS In addition to the Web site for NEBA, there are two public online boards that many people in medical billing find useful.

- **CompuServe.** In the Work from Home forum of CompuServe, there is a subsection for people interested in medical billing. (This section also covers medical transcription.) You will find here "libraries" of files that can assist your research. For example, the forum periodically hosts a "live" chat night in which many people get together to discuss medical billing online, and these written conversations are eventually compiled into a file you can download and read at your leisure. There are also files that other people (including myself) have uploaded for anyone to read and comment on. If you are already a subscriber to CompuServe, just enter the command in the Go menu, "Work from Home" and you will be transferred to that forum. Then go to the Libraries menu, and select "Medical Billing and Transcription." If you are not yet a member of CompuServe, you can easily join by installing its software in your computer and dialing up the pre-arranged number. You can find CompuServe software for free in many computer magazines sold on newsstands, or call 800-487-0453.

■ **America Online.** Like CompuServe, there is an area on AOL that serves as a forum for people interested in medical billing. You can find this section by entering the key word "Business Strategies," then go to the "Home Business Message Board." Then enter "New" and "Medical Claims Processing." You can obtain free AOL sign-on software in nearly any computer magazine sold on newsstands, or call AOL at 800-827-3338.

GENERAL BUSINESS TRAINING Because medical billing is very marketing intensive, you may want to expand your entrepreneurial skills with courses in marketing, sales, publicity, and business planning. Many extension schools and local colleges offer courses or workshops on these business topics. You will likely find many kindred souls at such courses, since many people today are interested in learning to run their own home-based business.

There are also dozens of business books that teach the skills of marketing and sales. Browse through your local bookstore for books such as those from Paul and Sarah Edwards: *Working from Home, The Secrets of Self-Employment,* and *Getting Business to Come to You* (co-authored with Laura Clampitt Douglas). Read magazines such as *Home Office Computing* and *Success.* Given the political nature of healthcare in this country, it is also worthwhile to read newspapers such as the *Wall Street Journal,* the *New York Times,* and even *U.S.A. Today,* so you can stay abreast of new legislation affecting the healthcare field as well as profiles of successful businesspeople who might inspire you.

Contact your department of commerce or local chamber of commerce for booklets they publish about starting a business. SCORE (Service Corps of Retired Executives) and other associations of businesspeople and networking organizations can also be helpful. You will be surprised by how many people are willing to share their expertise and knowledge with you. Start by making a chart of people you know, and ask each one if he or she has any friends in the medical field with whom you could chat to get advice and information about your new venture. Many of the successful medical billing owners I interviewed got advice from their own doctors about the business and their marketing ideas.

Whatever you do, make time each week for learning more about medical billing and operating a business as a home-based entrepreneur. Chapter 5 addresses general business self-improvement issues in more detail.

Tips for Pricing Your Service

Choosing your pricing strategy is always a difficult task. If you price too low, you will not maximize your earnings, and you may even lose money. For example, one medical billing service I interviewed that was doing "just claims" began its pricing at $2.00 per claim and quickly found that it had no profits. On the other hand, if you price your service too high, you may drive away potential clients, or lose them quickly to lower priced competitors. Because this is a service business, your prices need to reflect the quality and level of service you are delivering. Will you process 50, 100, or 150 claims a week for a given doctor? Will you also do regular patient invoicing? Send out late notices? Key in checks and cash payments to complete accounts receivable? Will you be providing your clients with monthly reports such as aged balances and practice activity analysis graphs?

In short, you cannot price your service until you know your clients' needs. It is advisable not to put any printed notice showing your fees in your advertising or direct mail brochures. You need first to find out about each practice that expresses an interest in your services, so you can return later with an accurate proposal reflecting what you can do for it. Only when you know what services you will provide can you decide how much to charge. Some guidelines for all these decisions follow.

LOCATION Location is always an important consideration in pricing. Living costs are greater in large metropolitan areas than in small cities and towns in most parts of the country. You need to get some sense of the fee structures in your community. If you are doing just claims, you might be able to charge $4.00 to $6.00 per claim in some cities. However, in many smaller areas, you'll be limited to $2.50 or less. If you are handling full practice management, you may be able to charge from 8 percent to 12 percent of all collections if there is a lot of overhead work for you to do, such as many secondary claims, appeals, patient statements, and soft collections. However, in other locations, you may be able to get only 6 percent at best. Whatever your fee, negotiate for the highest rate you can right at the outset, because it is difficult to raise your rates after you have started. If you go back in six months to ask for a higher fee, you risk losing your customer(s).

ESTIMATE OVERALL AMOUNT OF WORK   Like any business, doctors have good days and bad days, so try to estimate how much work and how many claims your client has in one month. Use a full month as your measure of business, not a day or week. Set your fee structure at a higher rate if you will be handling fewer claims per month, and lower your rate if the client will be giving you many claims. This will give your clients the sense that you discount your fees for volume work. Alternatively, you could offer a sliding fee schedule for each month, depending on how many claims and/or patient statements are ultimately processed.

COMPARE PER CLAIM METHOD WITH PERCENTAGE METHOD
To compare these two measures, you need to have a frank discussion with your client to learn how many claims per month are filed versus their dollar value. Many doctors will not want to divulge such personal financial information to you. However, if you can focus the doctor on how well you will increase his or her collection efficiency, you may be able to obtain a ballpark figure that allows you to estimate the doctor's annual income. You can then do your own comparison of per claim versus percentage methods to see which way you come out ahead. In general, most people who do full practice management find that charging according to the percentage method generates the higher income.

BE REASONABLE   When you set your fees, don't think that doctors make so much money that they have enough to share generously with you. As discussed earlier, today's doctors are feeling many cutbacks in income because of managed care. You will encounter doctors who want to penny pinch everything you do. Nancie Cummins suggests a good line to use when you find yourself in this position. Tell the doctor that you will not nickel and dime him or her when you do your work; you will not charge for long distance phone calls or for special trips to their office to pick up superbills, and so on. In return, tell the client that you believe you deserve not to be nickled and dimed either. As Nancie says, "Let the doctor know you are worth that extra 1 percent and that you take pride in what you can do for his or her practice." In addition, remember that each practice you service doesn't need to know about your other clients or what you charge them.

Marketing Guidelines

Nearly every person I interviewed for this book told me, "Getting clients is the hardest part of this business." *Do not forget this* and certainly don't think that it won't be true for you. Although many other people or vendors may tell you that medical billing is a great business opportunity in which you can become "rich" quickly, remember that you *will* have difficulty getting customers unless you can convince doctors that you have the skills and expertise to get their claims filed more quickly, increase their cash flow, and help them manage their practice.

One reason for doctors' reluctance to outsource billing is that this portion of client contact has traditionally been thought of as easy and unimportant. In a doctor's eyes, the emphasis has always been on treating the patient. Filling out claims was a secretarial function.

But as indicated throughout this chapter, today's healthcare environment has completely changed this perspective. Cost is now as important as treatment. Doctors and insurance companies are no longer simply on opposite sides of the fence; they are on opposite sides of the universe! For the most part, their financial interests are diametrically opposed. Doctors would prefer to do and spend whatever it takes to keep their patients alive and healthy; insurance companies would prefer to spend as little as possible, regardless of what happens to the patient. Doctors also believe they should be paid commensurate with their extensive educational background and the risks they take. Insurance companies believe doctors' incomes should be pared way down.

Despite the new environment, you will face an uphill battle convincing doctors to (a) hire an outside billing service to take care of their accounts and (b) hire *your* billing service as opposed to someone else's. This means that you must apply nearly all of your initial efforts to marketing and sales. Many doctors are still adverse to outsourcing their billing and practice management; they believe that their staff can handle these functions, or they are simply reluctant to make a change.

Here are some tips for conducting a successful marketing campaign. Note that there is simply not enough room in this book to provide a comprehensive medical billing marketing course that ensures that you will get some clients. If you do not have a background in marketing or feel anxious about selling to doctors and other healthcare providers, I recommend that you purchase a business opportunity from one of the vendors listed in Appendix A, who can provide the extensive training and support in marketing that you truly need. Also contact the two associations already mentioned, NEBA and NACAP; each one has a library of specific marketing materials, such as sample direct mail letters and brochures, presentation materials, and audiotapes that provide in-depth guidance in this complicated subject.

SPECIALIZE YOUR SERVICE   Several successful medical billing owners I interviewed ended up focusing their business on doctors in a certain specialty. In some cases, it happened by chance, such as Nancie Lee Cummins, who found herself working largely with psychologists, social workers, and mental health clinics. Dan Lehmann and Pat Bartello work extensively with physicians in areas related to gerontology. The value of specializing your business is that you become as much an expert in that field as the doctors, at least when it comes to coding and insurance reimbursement. Through practice, you start to master the ICD-9 and CPT coding, and you know even the uncommon situations. You also become familiar with the fee schedules in that field, and if you have several clients in a specialty, you can compare how they each run their businesses. In short, specializing often adds a dimension to your knowledge that impresses potential new clients, so you can build your business faster.

Table 2-11 shows a list of medical specialties you might want to consider.

DETERMINE WHICH MARKETING TECHNIQUES YOU ARE MOST COMFORTABLE USING   The best way to approach marketing is to first determine your own special talents and interests. After all, there is no point pursuing a marketing approach that you cannot bring yourself to do.

Start by examining yourself. Each of us has some natural marketing talent that simply needs to be discovered. Consider your previous business experience and see what marketing tools you've already developed Ask yourself, "Have I done direct mail? Have I written catalogue copy or product specifications? Called on clients, patients, or doctors and put them at ease during a first meeting?" Perhaps you have a flair for design and copywriting, so developing a powerfully persuasive flier or brochure will be your lead into the office. Or perhaps you have the gift of a charming personality and easy conversation that enables you to approach the most abrasive receptionist and quickly smooth over relations.

If you feel uncomfortable about your ability to do marketing, take a course at a local college or business school, and read some books about it. You will need to learn about "marketing mix" (the proportion of the four major marketing methods you can use: advertising, public relations, direct

TABLE 2-11

Medical Specialties in Medical Billing

- acupuncturists*
- allergists
- ambulance services
- anesthesiologists
- cardiovascular physicians
- chiropractors
- dentists and dental hygienists***
- dermatologists
- durable medical equipment suppliers (DMEs)**
- endocrinologists
- gastroenterologists
- general practice doctors
- general surgeons
- geriatric doctors

- gynecologists
- hematologists
- immunologists
- internal medicine physicians
- medical laboratories
- nephrologists
- neurologists
- obstetric physicians
- occupational therapists
- oncologists
- ophthalmologists
- optometrists
- oral surgeons***
- orthodontics specialists**
- orthopedic surgeons

- osteopaths
- pathologists
- pediatricians
- physical therapists
- plastic surgeons
- podiatrists
- proctologists
- psychiatrists
- psychologists
- radiation therapists
- radiologists
- rehabilitation specialists
- rheumatologists
- thoracic surgeons
- urologists

Notes:

*Medicare will not accept claims electronically or on paper.

**Claims may require a special format of the HCFA 1500.

***Requires American Dental Association format and dental software for some procedures not billable on an HCFA 1500 form.

selling, and sales promotions), direct mail campaigns, copywriting, market segmentation, niche marketing, and a host of other topics.

If you prefer, hire a marketing consultant to help you in those areas with which you are unfamiliar if you are willing to pay for help. Specialists can sometimes make the difference between success and failure.

Note: Some business opportunity vendors will promise to do cold calling and other marketing on your behalf to set up appointments with providers. While this may seem useful, unless you are ultimately willing to do marketing on your own, such promises of getting you appointments are hollow. You must be able to do some portion of your own marketing and you must be able to give a good presentation (unless you intend to work with a partner who can do the sales presentations for you).

LET PEOPLE KNOW YOU ARE IN BUSINESS You cannot simply take an ad out in the *Yellow Pages* and wait for customers to come to you. That is unrealistic. You must do one or more marketing activities, such as networking, direct mail, cold calling, publicity, or workshops, to let people know you are in business. In other words, you must take action in one form or another. In general, most billers seem to be the most successful using networking, cold calling, and direct mail (followed up with calls).

On the other hand, I have received reports of people who purchased their medical billing software and made a few phone calls to doctors, thinking that this was "marketing." When they were rejected after two or three "not interested responses," they gave up and concluded that they were never going to succeed. Such trivial first steps do not make a marketing campaign. You must be willing to follow through with a well-thought-out and continuous attack for several months.

KEEP YOUR DIRECT MAIL SIMPLE Direct mail letters or solicitations were one of the most common marketing techniques among people I have interviewed. Direct mail is useful because it reaches a large audience of doctors to announce your business and seek appointments.

When you write and design your first direct mail letter, remember that a busy doctor has little time to read. Keep your letter short, succinct, and to the point. See the sample direct mail letters shown in Figures 2-18 and 2-19. (Note: these are intended to be samples only; it is recommended that you adapt and customize them to your market, depending on whether you are doing just claims or full practice management.)

Mailing out a few hundred letters per week is expensive, so be sure to allocate enough of your financial resources for this type of marketing, at least for the first few months. Many new billing professionals mail out 25 to 50 letters to healthcare providers in their area each week. Of course, they also follow up on letters sent out in previous weeks too. Direct mail is not useful without follow-through.

Another popular direct mail piece is a three-fold brochure. Brochures give you more space to write about the merits of your electronic claims processing, and your expertise in practice management. However, they are more expensive to produce, so you may want to use brochures only for your most important prospective clients.

Where do you get names for your mailings? Some business opportunity vendors will supply you with a list of 1,000 names of doctors who do not bill electronically. Such lists are often generated through Medicare. NEBA can also supply you with such lists; see Appendix A.

> Your Letterhead Stationery
> Address
> City, State, Zip
>
> Date
>
> Dear Dr. (insert name),
>
> Are you dissatisfied with the amount of time it takes your insurance claims to be processed? Are you waiting 60 or more days to obtain reimbursements?
>
> If so, my company can significantly improve your claim-to-check turnaround time. We can literally cut in half the amount of time it takes you to receive insurance reimbursements.
>
> We are also experts in helping doctors in your specialty manage their practice, from improving your patient reimbursement ratio to working with you to develop effective business strategies in today's managed care environment.
>
> I will call your office within the next few days to arrange an appointment during which I would like to personally show you the specifics on how my company can benefit you. I look forward to speaking with you then.
>
> Sincerely,
>
>
> (Your Name)
> (Your Title)

One problem with direct mail is that you must send out a generic letter to a large client base, but you do not know what their specific problems are. One physician may be more concerned with staff turnover, while another is worried about lost claims. This is why you must follow up on each mailing you do and try to speak directly with the physician so you can learn the specifics of his or her situation.

DEVELOP A PROFESSIONAL APPEARANCE Yes, a good marketing campaign costs money, but you can't expect to compete or attract attention without high-quality brochures, business cards, stationery, and a company logo. I'm not suggesting that you must buy the services of the best professional designers and printers in your area, but simply that you not be penny wise and pound foolish. Your marketing materials announce that you are a professional businessperson.

If your printer tells you to use a higher quality business card stock that costs an extra $30.00 per thousand, it may well make the difference in a

Figure 2-19
Sample Direct Mail
Letter #2

Your Letterhead Stationery
Address
City, State, Zip

Dear Dr. (insert name),

Try out our electronic claims processing and billing service for two weeks free!

The only way to know whether or not something is right for your practice is to try it out. We are so convinced that our medical billing service will reduce your office paperwork, eliminate suspended claims, and reduce delays in insurance reimbursement that we'd like to make it easy for you to try us out.

We know that you and your staff would rather concentrate your efforts on caring for your patients than worrying about insurance payments and denied claims. We at (*Your Company Name*) are experts in electronic claims filing and physician practice management.

Your claims will be processed faster, and you'll notice an immediate reduction in rejections. Your billing costs will be lowered, and your billing headaches will disappear.

Now is the time to take advantage of our expertise. In today's managed care environment of greater cost containment, we can help you regain control of your practice and your income security.

This is a risk-free, no-obligation opportunity. If at the end of the two-week trial period, you are not completely satisfied, you owe nothing. So take the first step and call us at 444-1234 today to ask whatever questions you have and arrange for us to start.

Sincerely,

Your Name
Your Title

prospect keeping your card and calling you a few months later. For example, Nancie Cummins had her stationery letterhead printed in silver foil; she used this stationery to write a direct mail letter that she sent to just 25 prospects. One of them was so impressed with her letter that he hired her right away, so she actually landed her first client within weeks of starting out.

Spending time on developing your marketing materials is important too. Don't rush through the writing process as you compose direct mail letters and brochures. Once you've written a draft, let it sit for a few days, and then review your writing to see if you might find a better way to convey your message. Be detailed oriented in all your correspondence and written materials. I have seen cover letters with grammatical errors and misspellings, suggesting that they were written by a person who did not pay attention to details. Would a doctor hire that person? Certainly not.

In addition, get feedback from others on your marketing materials. Ask the opinion of your spouse, business partners, friends, and even a few doctors on any letters or brochures you produce. You may find what you have written to be perfect, but don't be defensive if someone suggests different wording. If you are in doubt, hire a professional copywriter to revise your brochures and direct mail pieces.

FOCUS ON SERVICE AND BENEFITS In all your marketing materials, focus on the benefits to the customer you can provide, such as improving cash flow, increasing the reimbursement ratio, and stabilizing the physician's income security. Avoid wasting words touting your credentials or on details about the technology of electronic claims. Aim to answer the doctor's question, "How does this person make operating my healthcare practice better?"

If you are doing just claims, let the client know that you can simplify the claims filing process, reduce office paperwork, accelerate the speed at which he or she is reimbursed, and increase collection efficiency. If you offer full practice management services, add to the list that you can improve the doctor's income by thoroughly tracking and collecting on all accounts receivable.

THE PROS AND CONS OF COLD CALLING The verdict on the effectiveness of cold calling is still out. I interviewed many people who told me that cold calling was a complete waste of their time. They indicated that they were never able to see a doctor or set up an appointment by just visiting a doctor's office off the street. However, other people told me that cold calling worked for them, and even that they made cold calling their #1 marketing strategy. Ultimately, the use of cold calling always seemed to reflect more the individual's special talents in this area than a true indication of an easy marketing technique. So, try cold calling if you feel comfortable doing it; otherwise, don't bother.

However, if you use cold calling, here are some tips to improve it:

■ Don't aim to make a sale during the first cold call. Most people indicated that cold calling works best when your objective is simply to make an appointment to come in and see the prospective client to make a larger, more coherent presentation. You can either make a cold phone call or visit the doctor's office, but don't expect to be invited right then and there to close the deal.

- Send printed materials in advance of cold calling. Send out a direct mail piece first, so that when you cold call, it's really more of a warm call. The doctor or office manager may recognize your name from the mailing you recently sent.

- Make use of any networking contacts you have before you make a cold call. Remember, doctors have a constant stream of sales representatives calling on them day in and day out from pharmaceutical companies, equipment manufacturers, office supply people, and temporary agencies. Your business may be important to you, but to a busy front office person, you are just another salesperson.

- Be prepared for rejections, but don't let them interfere with your professionalism. Always leave your name and business card—and leave on good terms. You never know when a staff billing person might quit, or when the doctor realizes that it is time-consuming to train a new person every few months. Several successful billers told me that they heard back from a doctor months after their initial call—and the doctor eventually became their client.

GET TO THE DECISION MAKER Medical practices vary greatly in terms of who is actually in a position to give you their business. In some practices, the doctor is the only one who can make a decision, but in others, it may be the physician's spouse, or an office manager, or a staff billing person. You need to find out who might be involved in the decision making to do billing offsite, and then convince that person that you can benefit the office in many ways. You may also find that a staff person feels threatened by you and believes you will eliminate his or her job. However, as indicated earlier, many billing service owners I interviewed, such as Mary Vandegrift, told me that staff people often feel relieved when they are no longer assigned to do the billing. There are usually many other tasks they can do around the office.

Whoever the decision maker is, your goal is to find that person and get a face-to-face interview for at least 20 minutes during which you should have a well-prepared presentation. Many professionals use flip charts or have a self-running computer demo that uses graphics to help them cover the issues.

Note: Several business opportunity vendors and others sell a software program you can use during your presentation to compare how much it costs a doctor to file paper claims versus electronic claims. The software lets you key in salary information for office personnel, overhead costs, claim rejection rates, and so on. From this information, the program calculates the cost per paper claim and contrasts this cost with how much an electronic claim will cost to process. From all reports, the software is generally impressive and effective. You can purchase this software, *ClaimsWizard,* from NEBA. See Appendix A for information.

If you have an opportunity to do a presentation, aim to make personal contact with the doctor to find out what problems he or she is experiencing in the office—and how he or she is impacted by managed care in your area. Explore as deeply as you can what the physician's situation is: Has his or her income been falling? Has he or she been at odds with HMOs and PPOs that have put pressure on him or her to join? Seek to get the doctor to feel that you are trustworthy. Trust is perhaps the most essential element in your relationship with a medical practice that is handing you its financial survival.

After your presentation, ask for details about the number of patients, claims, and billables that allow you to prepare a proposal to present at a follow-up meeting within a week. In general, don't negotiate for closure that day; let the doctor know that you would like his or her business and that you need time to create a truly customized bid that reflects how your service can help that office.

Once you get to the second appointment, seek out any objections and try to answer them one by one that day. Look for a way to begin closure: Is the doctor showing approval of your ideas? Does he or she admit to having a falling income? Is he or she asking you more and more questions? These are often clues that you can begin to funnel your discussion down to brass tacks, such as when you might begin the work.

OFFER A FREE TRIAL PERIOD One of the most effective ways to boost the closing process is to offer a free trial period so you can show the physician how your service can help. This advantage of a trial period is that it provides you with a way to get your foot in the door. You can then size up the practice, determine how many claims it may get per week, and modify your bid accordingly. For instance, the average family practice doctor has about 400 claims per month. (He or she sees approximately 30 patients each day, with 10 paying cash and 20 having insurance claims to file. Hence, 20 claims per day times 20 working days per month = 400 claims.) This also means that when you work with a family practice doctor, you will probably need to pick up the superbills daily or have them faxed to you for processing once per day or at least every other day. This increases your time. On the other hand, the number of claims you receive from many specialists may be small, so that you need to pick up superbills only once a week. This reduces your commuting time, and perhaps your processing time.

In sum, you get a chance to evaluate the complexity of your work when you offer a free trial period. You can decide if this practice requires extra time, if the staff is well organized and efficient, giving you complete data immediately, or if the work is going to be chaotic. Each practice's claim volume will differ as well, affecting how you retrieve the superbills.

A free trial period is also valuable because you can increase your knowledge of many different practices. For example, some specialties such as chiropractors, psychologists, and physical therapists have many repeat patient visits, so it is easy for you to do the claims. In contrast, surgical offices usually do not have repeat patients, so the amount of work you need to do for such offices is greater. Similarly, some practices, including psychologists, record several office visits on one claim form, so this work is easy. Other practices want only one office visit per claim, so again, you will have a lot of keyboarding to do.

Some billing agencies offer to do a trial period limited to one week or a specific number of claims such as 50, while charging for anything above that number. This strategy allows them to sign a contract immediately for a period of one or two months, because you convince the doctor that he or she can save money by taking some free claims right now in exchange for signing a longer-term contract that can be canceled if he or she is dissatisfied. As in many types of businesses, people tend not to annul contracts once they are written.

Overcoming Common Start-up Problems

It isn't surprising that every business has some common start-up problems that can prevent you from succeeding if you don't resolve them within six months. Following is a brief review of those problems that seem to plague medical billing businesses. By reading about them now, before you are in business, you can take steps to avoid them lest they happen to you.

COMPUTER GLITCHES AND SOFTWARE PROBLEMS Don't wait until you are in business to discover computer or software problems. Make sure you know what you are doing before a doctor is relying on you to process claims and track his or her accounts receivable. However, don't focus on learning your medical software to get into the business; you must also learn the medical industry basics and marketing principles discussed in this chapter. Knowing how to use software doesn't get you clients.

LOW DIRECT MAIL RESPONSE RATES Many people have high expectations when they send out direct mail, but typically a 1 percent to 3 percent response rate is about all you can expect. This means if you send out 500 letters, don't expect more than about 15 call-backs. However, if you get fewer responses, consider redesigning your brochure or letter. Get someone to help you, and test it before another mailing by showing it to at least six people for reactions.

SLOW BUILD-UP OF CLIENTELE Many of the billing services I spoke with told me that getting their first client took as many as six months, but after signing their first doctor, they quickly signed another few and more over time. You should definitely have enough savings to keep going at least 12 months. As this chapter has warned, marketing is the toughest part of this business.

MARKET RESISTANCE You may find resistance to your services for a variety of reasons. If so, assess if you have tried a wide enough variety of doctors, and are you doing everything you can to build trust with your customers?

One point of resistance is that doctors may tell you that they already have computers in house; if you hear this response, don't fail to ask, "Yes, but are you doing electronic billing, including Medicare and commercial carriers?" Also ask whether the prospective client has a high turnover rate among staff so that he or she is training people frequently and losing money on lost claims. These questions point to issues frequently neglected by physicians—and they help reinforce the service you can provide.

As you can see, you should be prepared to allay many concerns that physicians read about and hear every day from colleagues. Convincing a physician to use your outside service is possible if you focus on the four Cs:

■ **Complexity.** Since insurance reimbursement and medical coding change frequently, why burden a staff person with keeping up on this never-ending struggle when *you* are an expert in it? You can stay abreast of changes and reduce errors and mistakes.

■ **Cost.** In the long run, it almost always costs more to have a salaried worker do billing than an outside expert agency that can increase reimbursement efficiency.

■ **Consistency.** You can provide round-the-clock coverage in a more consistent manner than a staff that is subject to constant turnover or is occupied with other office duties.

■ **Competition.** In today's competitive managed care world, everyone in the medical profession is feeling the pinch. Because of your expertise, you can help doctors compete more effectively against HMOs and other arrangements that are cutting physician salaries and independence.

If you take the four Cs and put them together with the four Ps of marketing (price, product, place, and promotion), you get the four PCs, a good mnemonic device to remember the basic guidelines in marketing for a medical billing business.

LOW PROFITABILITY   If low profitability is your problem, you may not have done enough homework to calculate your fees in your favor. As mentioned earlier, it is better not to face this problem, but if you do have it, you need to find new clients immediately, with whom you can charge a higher rate. Although getting your first client by offering a low rate may have worked at that time, you cannot make a living by charging too little.

Alternatively, try to sign these current clients into purchasing additional services from you at higher fees, such as having you work into full practice management so you can move into charging on a percentage basis.

TURNOVER IN CLIENTELE   It is wise to ask clients to sign a contract with you for a year at a time. This minimizes client turnover and gives you 12 months to prove yourself. Even if you make one mistake, you have time to correct it, apologize, and perhaps do something special for the client to convey that you value his or her business and want to keep it.

Building Your Business

Several business opportunity companies I interviewed told me that they see many people purchase the medical billing software package and months later, they have done nothing with it. For such people, the idea of purchasing a business venture was promising, but they did not have the motivation and knowledge to get the business off the ground.

Remember this as you consider medical billing. As in romance, there is a thrill in the chase, but if you spend the time and money to get into the business, you should be prepared to live with your business for a few years. One common mistake made by too many entrepreneurs is thinking and acting for the short term.

Medical billing services are here to stay, though the business may change as new technologies come to fruition and as new managed care arrangements and Medicare regulations move the industry in increasingly cost-saving directions. But if you are getting into this business, stay abreast of these changes and look to a bright future!

Claims Assistance Professional

Do you believe in helping the little guy? Does your hair stand on end when you hear about undue and unfair hardships and corporate injustice? Do you enjoy verbal sparring with a worthy opponent? Do you like to nitpick and find mistakes? Do you feel drawn to helping others fight "the system"?

If your answer is Yes to these questions, then being a medical claims assistance professional (CAP) may be the right career for you. As mentioned earlier, claims assistance professionals work for people (not doctors) who are consumers of medical services. Their primary role is to help people organize, file, and negotiate health claims of all kinds. Like tax assistants or personal business consultants, their job is to ensure that the consumers get the maximum benefits and the best possible services from their medical providers and from their insurance companies.

This chapter explores the business of a claims professional, explains the necessary background and preparation for this career, and details the many ways you can conduct and market this valuable service. (Note: if you didn't read Chapter 2 on medical billing, it may be useful to do so now, since that chapter covers many basic issues that are pertinent here, especially the sections on the health insurance industry, Medicare, and Medicaid.)

Section I: Background

What Is a Claims Assistance Professional?

Anyone who has ever read a health insurance policy or who has waited months for a reimbursement check to come through knows firsthand the frustration and confusion that can overwhelm even the brightest individual when it comes to dealing with our complex healthcare system. With thousands of different health insurance carriers in the United States offering nearly 10,000 different types of plans, it's easy to see how consumers can feel totally baffled whenever they have to deal with health insurance claims.

Today's world is especially complicated when it comes to healthcare. First, there are millions of people who have joined or been assigned to a managed care program, but they cannot figure out how much to pay and to whom to pay it. There are many cases of spouses who both work but each has a different health plan. There are situations in which one spouse is retired and on Medicare while the other still works and is covered by an employer health plan. These scenarios depict the complexity of health coverage for millions of people when it comes to filing health insurance claims.

Enter, however, the claims assistance professional who knows health insurance rules and policies inside out, who has the exact phone numbers for all the local Medicare and insurance company offices right at the tip of his or her tongue or Rolodex, and who fears not when it comes to arguing with doctors or insurance claims adjusters. Such people are, in effect, a combination of professional consultant, personal advisor and representative, and hard-core negotiator, wearing each of these hats in turn as they help ordinary mortals through the thick and thin of dealing with their health insurance nightmares.

The CAP profession seems to have actually come into its maturity just in the past few years. Much of the impetus for its rise is due to the burgeoning enrollments in Medicare and the growing complexity of the program, as you saw in Chapter 1. A major indication of the growth of the CAP career is the fact that a national association was formed in 1991 to formalize the profession and give it some respect and clout. Called the National Association of Claims Assistance Professionals, Inc. (NACAP), the organization helped to solidify the industry and bring together over 1000 claims assistance professionals from across the country. Unfortunately, just as this new edition of this book was going to press, the two leaders of this private association withdrew and it went out of business until new leadership emerges. At this time, Lori A. Donnelly, a CAP in Bethlehem, Pennsylvania, has agreed to help develop a new association from interested parties. You will find information on contacting her later in this chapter.

Despite the temporary loss of an official NACAP organization, the CAP profession still stands strong. As the former NACAP National Director Norma Border told me, the need for claims assistance professionals doesn't appear to be changing.

The success of NACAP speaks strongly for the growing importance of this profession. Border pointed out, for example, that insurance regulations are constantly changing, and so some part of her job is to stay abreast of the political happenings in Washington, D.C., so that the association can keep tabs on congressional hearings dealing with the insurance industry—and even lobby when necessary to support its interests. In addition, one might surmise that the growth of the profession reflects serious social and political healthcare policy issues in this country, because so much is at stake when it comes to health insurance. For example, at this writing, Congress and President Clinton were implementing the new legislation that will take effect in 1997 that allows for "portability" of health insurance to protect people who change jobs.

Border completely supported the idea presented in Chapter 2 that today's managed care environment is changing a great deal in the healthcare industry, not just for doctors, but for consumers, too. She told me,

> The newest thing for CAPs is managed care. Some CAPs ask me, "If we are moving to a managed care environment, or what seems to be a claimless environment, is there anything left for a CAP to do?" The answer is most definitely *yes*. Anytime the insurance industry establishes a gatekeeper and sets up procedures for consumers to get care, there's a need for CAPs. The consumer needs an advocate to make sure that the paperwork is processed properly and that the physician services are provided at an optimal level.

Border added, for example, that her mother recently had a knee replacement, and her orthopedic surgeon never completed the insurance form, leaving her mother with a bill for $16,000. This is the type of situation that calls for a CAP.

It is now absolutely certain that becoming a claims assistance professional is a viable career. As Harvey Matoren, owner of Claims Security of America (formerly Health Claims of Jacksonville, Inc.) and, ironically, a former insurance company senior executive himself, explained to me,

> Nobody is out there to fend for the average [health insurance] consumer. There are lots of people to protect the interests of the insurance companies, hospitals, physicians, and other healthcare providers, but when it comes to recovering what is due to the average person, most people can't maximize their reimbursements and so they live under tremendous frustration and stress.

Let's turn our attention now to see how the claims assistance professional can help, and what people in this profession do day by day.

Whom Do CAPs Help?

CAPs may help anyone and everyone who has health insurance and files claims. As Chapter 1 pointed out, this means that your client base includes more than 220 million people who are covered by private or public health insurance. More important, each one of these people sees a doctor an average of six times per year. In fact, in 1993 (the latest statistic available) there were more than 1.6 billion physician contacts in the United States. Go back and review Table 1-3 on page 7, which breaks down physician contacts by age and sex. Notice that women see doctors more frequently than men in most age categories, except over age 65, when men—probably because they failed to see doctors more often at younger ages—surpass women!

Another interesting set of statistics is shown in Table 3-1. While the data are from 1991 and are the most recent available, the table demonstrates the huge number of office visits that Americans make to physicians each year: a total of nearly 670 million.

But why does this cause a need for claims assistance professionals? The answer is, processing health insurance claims is prone to a significantly high error rate. Errors can be made at the insurance company, at the doctor's office, or at the hospital—and these errors create havoc for consumers. Claims to insurance companies can be erroneously denied, delayed, or underpaid, leaving the consumer with an incorrect balance due the physi-

TABLE 3-1

Number of Office Visits by Physician Specialty—1991

Specialty	Number of Visits (in millions)
All visits	669,689
General and family practice	164,857
Internal medicine	102,923
Pediatrics	74,646
Obstetrics and gynecology	56,834
Ophthalmology	41,207
Orthopedic surgery	35,932
Dermatology	29,659
General surgery	21,285
Otolaryngology	19,101
Psychiatry	15,720
Urological surgery	12,758
Cardiovascular diseases	11,629
Neurology	6,798
All other specialties	76,341

Source: U.S. Department of Health and Human Services, National Center for Health Statistics, Advance Data, 1993.

cian. Although they write the policies and program the computers, insurance companies often make mistakes in the amount of a patient's deductible, copayments, or stop-loss limit. Physicians too make mistakes. They may bill patients for amounts that the primary insurance carrier should have paid. They may bill patients for amounts that secondary insurance coverage should have paid. They may even double bill patients for amounts that a primary or secondary insurance carrier already paid. As a result, consumers must be ever-watchful of each and every claim they generate.

There are also many people who want nothing to do with their insurance claims. Such people know they cannot possibly keep up with the "fine print" in their health insurance policy. They hire CAPs to avoid the dirty work of checking claims and arguing with doctors, insurance adjusters, and hospital administrative staff.

To categorize the types of people or situations a CAP can help, I have developed the following profiles.

THE LAZY SELF-FILER Many doctors simply refuse to file non-Medicare claims, and so millions of patients end up filing themselves—after they've paid their doctor or dentist—using traditional paper forms and receipts. When they sit down to do this though, many people are simply put off by the technicality of the work and would prefer to have someone do it for them. Particularly if they have an extended illness and end up with many bills over time, these people suddenly realize that they have paid hundreds or thousands of dollars out-of-pocket, and so they look to a claims assistance professional to get them out of the jam.

THE MANAGED CARE PATIENT A growing problem in today's managed care environment is that many HMOs are newly established, and they literally don't know what they are doing. According to Lori Donnelly, a CAP in Pennsylvania, many HMOs are so new that they haven't worked through their own procedures and are not able to provide the consumer with consistent explanations of what's approved and what's not. Remember also that an HMO or PPO may be comprised of many affiliated doctors, and the coverages can vary from policy to policy. In short, despite its supposed simplicity, managed care generates its share of billing mistakes.

THE "NOT-AUTHORIZED" CLAIM Sarah Bissel went to her primary care physician for a stomach problem. He recommended that she see a gastrointestinal specialist if her pain persisted for more than another day. However, Sarah forgot to call the primary care physician to approve the referral when she went to the specialist the next day. When the claim was filed, the insurance company refused to pay it, claiming that approval had not been given. Sarah hired a CAP who was able to straighten out the situation with a few phone calls.

THE SHIRKING DOCTOR PASSES THE BUCK Kyle Assad recently saw his physician for a strep culture. The physician's billing clerk told Kyle that his office would handle the insurance claim. However, two weeks later, Kyle received a bill in the mail. He called the doctor's office and they assured him they would take care of the insurance claim. A few more weeks went by, and Kyle received another bill. Finally, he contacted his CAP who called the doctor's office and reminded them that they had agreed to take responsibility for processing the claim. Kyle was finally left in peace.

THE FLUSTERED VICTIM OF LEGALESE   Roberta Stevenson can't stand paperwork. Give her a contract or any document with legal jargon and her mind turns right off. It's not that Roberta isn't bright; she simply can't follow the formal legal terminology and sentence structure typically used in insurance documents. Roberta would simply prefer to hand over her claims to a CAP, who has the expertise needed to understand the policy and know what is and is not covered.

THE BUSY FAMILY   John and Jane Adams and their two teenagers never have any leisure time. The Adamses, who both work, come home from the office early in the evening and immediately get involved in dozens of projects, from shuttling the kids to ballet rehearsals and baseball games to fixing the kitchen sink and planting the spring garden. The result of their busy lifestyle is that whenever a member of the family visits the doctor, Mr. and Mrs. Adams have no time left to fill in the claims and file them. When there is a problem on a claim, they also don't have a moment to spare to make phone calls back and forth to their doctor's office and insurance company to clarify the issue. For many families like the Adamses, paying a small fee to have a professional handle claims work simply makes life more enjoyable.

THE MIXED INSURANCE FAMILY   Al Smith works for a local manufacturer and has a family health insurance policy through his employer. His wife Sally also works, and her health insurance plan, which acts as her secondary coverage, is supposed to pay any copayments she owes after her husband's family plan pays out the primary benefits. However, some recent medical bills have totally confused the family about which insurance company is going to pay for what—and why neither wants to pay one of the charges. The mixed insurance family is an excellent candidate for a claims assistance professional.

THE MULTIPLE INSURANCE INDIVIDUAL   Arnold Pimler believes in health insurance. Over the years, he has collected and/or purchased five different policies. When he finally became ill with cancer and had an extended hospitalization, he left it to a CAP to figure out who should pay what to whom.

THE RETIRED LIFERS   Jack and Bobbie Mormin recently retired to a Sun Belt state to enjoy some peace and quiet, and a bit of golf. While they do not have any major medical ailments, they prefer to spend not a drop of their time thinking about their health insurance policies. So they hire a CAP service to handle whatever comes their way each year for a small fee.

THE CHILD OF AN AGING PARENT   Maggie O'Brien's 78-year old mother recently had surgery and required several thousands of dollars in follow-up treatment and physical therapy. Little did the mother know that her Medicare and Medigap insurance policies did not cover all the procedures, and now Maggie is stuck with trying to figure out how to maximize their reimbursements and minimize their out-of-pocket payments. Unfortunately, Maggie works at a demanding job and has little time to make phone calls to the insurance company or to Medicare. She loves her mother but does not really want this problem dumped in her lap, so she hires a claims assistance professional.

THE CRISIS FAMILY   Tragically, 52-year-old Alan Roberts has a terminal illness, and his family is spending every waking minute trying to comfort their loved one through the ordeal. Meanwhile, the medical bills keep mounting, and some health claims sent to Mr. Roberts's insurance company are being denied or rejected for unexplained reasons. This family realizes that there are more important things in life at the moment, and so they hear through word of mouth about a claims assistance professional in their area who can handle their problems. The family can now live in peace and be with their loved one, while the CAP ensures they get what they deserve from their insurance policy.

THE CAUGHT-IN-THE-MIDDLE SITUATION   Mike Loring recently went to his doctor twice in one week for a bad cold, and while he was there, he also received a chest X-ray and blood test from the lab next door. He paid all four charges (two doctors' visits and two tests) in cash, since the physician and lab preferred to have the money immediately and insisted that Mike deal with his own insurance company. However, when Mike filed the claims amounting to $300, his insurance company said that the diagnostic codes were missing from his receipts, and that the procedures didn't match. Mike started to make the phone calls to straighten out the situation, but eventually he became fed up with the runaround he was getting; he simply wanted his 80 percent of $300 back. He called a local CAP and signed up immediately to have the claims pursued on his behalf.

THE MEDICARE SQUEEZE   Norman Fields, a 72-year-old retired teacher, recently fell off a ladder while painting his house one summer day. He suffered a broken arm and numerous minor injuries that required a brief hospitalization followed by repeated physical therapy treatments. Unfortunately, his slew of claims was only partially paid by Medicare, with many claims being downcoded from what the doctors had billed. He also began receiving invoices from his doctor for amounts of money that he thought were greater than the allowable amounts. When Norman contacted a CAP, he learned that the doctor was erroneously billing him for amounts beyond the "allowable"—amounts that he was not supposed to charge patients.

THE COBRA LURCH (COBRA is a nationally mandated law that became effective in 1986 to cover certain qualified people who had group insurance but lost their coverage through job loss, divorce, death of a spouse, unemployment, or reduction in working hours. When such situations occur, a qualified person is allowed to convert his or her group insurance into an individual policy, paying monthly premiums for up to 18 months. This situation, however, sometimes engenders the following circumstance.)

Rochelle Williams was covered by a COBRA policy. She dutifully mailed her monthly premium check to the insurance company so that her account would remain current. One month, however, after she had seen her doctor, she began receiving calls from the doctor's office to pay the bill because her insurance had been rejected. After hiring a CAP to check the situation for her, it turned out that the insurance company was taking several weeks to credit her COBRA insurance with her monthly checks. It refused to pay Rochelle's claims because the computer showed her as being canceled from the group policy and delinquent in her COBRA payments. The problem was entirely the fault of the insurance company.

THE EXPERIMENTAL PROCEDURE CLAIM Ruth Kress was diagnosed with a rare blood disease in the early part of the year. Fortunately, her best friend recommended a wonderful doctor who was using a somewhat new treatment for this blood disease; this treatment was, however, an accepted treatment for another disease. Ruth was miraculously cured, but now her insurance company denied the $25,000 in claims, claiming that the treatments were "experimental" and were therefore not covered under her policy. Ruth used a CAP to negotiate the case and was able to get the majority of the claims paid.

THE BUREAUCRATIC RUNAROUND Glenda Peterson incurred $30,000 in medical bills over the past year due to a serious illness. They were all rejected by her insurance company, and in frustration she hired a claims assistance company to work on her behalf. When the company took over, it learned that several simple errors had been made and that by resubmitting the claims with new diagnostic codes, the claims would be paid. The problem was that no one at the insurance company had the courtesy to tell Glenda that all she had to do was to reprocess the claims with the errors corrected.

THE INTIMIDATED VICTIM Randy Bern hates to argue. Although he knows that his insurance company made a simple and obvious mistake on a recently submitted claim for $860, he feels that he must "convince" the person with whom he spoke about this error. Unfortunately, Randy was speaking with a supervisor, who growled and howled at him. The supervisor insisted that "Mr. Bern doesn't understand company policy." Mr. Bern felt burned, and so he contacted a claims professional who wasn't afraid to put the supervisor into her proper place.

Saving Your Clients More Than Just Money

The preceding scenarios are indicative of the kinds of situations people get into when dealing with our health insurance system. In each case, an experienced, knowledgeable, efficient medical claims assistance professional can provide valuable services. Foremost is getting the reimbursement money from the insurance company for fees the client may have already paid to a doctor, or which the client owes the doctor who graciously awaits the reimbursement. But more than this financial role, claims assistance professionals also provide the following important services:

■ **Eliminate stress.** CAPs remove a tremendous amount of stress most people experience when dealing with intimidating bureaucratic organizations. From the lunch-hour calls when the insurance clerk puts you on hold for 20 minutes, to the frantic trips to the doctor's office to get your claim form signed, most people feel like they are unwitting victims in a Kafka-esque nightmare over which they have no control. And worse, the stress can be unhealthy for some people, particularly the elderly. As Mary Ellen Fitzgibbons, a CAP in Chicago related to me, "I have one client who says she feels like she's going to have a heart attack whenever she speaks with her insurance company. She gets so emotionally upset, she just can't do it by herself."

- **Save people money.** Many people mistakenly pay providers before Medicare or their insurance company reimburses the provider, and so the burden is on the patient to recover his or her money, which can take weeks. Even when a physician or hospital provides assistance to patients for their health claims, it is a self-interested service, usually limited in scope to reviewing claims for services only it has provided. For example, some hospitals offer clinics to senior citizens to teach them how to handle their own health insurance claims, but these people are often too old or too sick to handle the balance of the required work.

- **Save people time.** The average consumer knows little about navigating through the channels of the insurance industry and can spend hours and hours to take care of a situation that a claims professional could handle in 30 minutes. But time is money today; many people would rather pay someone $20 or $50 if it saves them a few hundred dollars and their valuable time.

- **Save people embarrassment.** When a foul-up occurs, many doctors' offices will turn a bill over to a collection agency. Suddenly, the consumer finds himself or herself getting dunning notices, and perhaps even has a negative report made to his or her credit record. I had this happen to my family recently. My wife had a series of about six charges, each for $80.00, for blood tests from a laboratory to which she was sent by her allergy clinic. We thought we had paid all 6 bills; none ever came in the mail. One day, we started getting dunning notices from a collection agency for $80.00. We called the lab and were told everything was paid. Eventually though, as we continued to get dunning notices, we discovered that one of the payments was erroneously recorded to another doctor in the allergy clinic, and that the laboratory had also misdated the invoice, calling it a "post-test" result instead of a "pre-test" result, thereby confusing two claims. In the end, I had no way of knowing that all the confusion was happening behind the scenes, and that we did owe one bill for $80.00, but my credit received a black mark. I would have gladly handed this problem over to a claims professional!

- **Help people in time of crisis.** CAPs preserve family priorities and help people in times of need and crisis. Many families today find themselves responsible for the healthcare of their aging parents. For them, spending a few dollars is much less important than being with their family and being sure they can devote their attention where it is most needed. CAP Lori Donnelly also notes that many times people going through a divorce utilize a claims professional to avoid seeing the ex-spouse and to help deal with the sticky financial arrangements that their divorce engendered.

■ **Maximize investment in health insurance.** The majority of people don't know what to expect when it comes to health insurance reimbursements. Consequently, they have no protection against mistakes, errors, delays, and even intentional malfeasance on the part of an insurance company. In fact, among health insurance insiders, few doubt that most insurance companies intentionally delay claims payments, or give people the runaround when they don't want to pay a claim to preserve their own cash flow. Every CAP I spoke with had quite a few horror stories to tell about people who had lost money because of a minor error or a simple mistake on their claims. Harvey Matoren of Claims Security of America had one client who had more than $60,000 of bills rejected by her insurance company. When Harvey looked into it, he discovered that the claims had been submitted under the wrong component of her insurance policy, but no one at the insurance office had bothered to tell the woman to send the claims in the name of the other component—Major Medical—under which they would have been accepted and paid. Harvey easily got 90 percent ($54,000) back for the client. As ludicrous as this sounds, Harvey and many others I spoke to indicated that such intentional mistakes happen all the time.

■ **Advise about health insurance matters.** CAPs often informally consult with people to help them decide which health insurance policies to purchase, especially when it comes to Medigap policies. Note: in some states, this will be considered insurance brokering, and since claims professionals are not technically allowed to do this, you need to be careful about how you phrase your recommendations. Many CAPs therefore discuss insurance with their clients only by offering to give a "personal opinion" rather than a "professional" one. But their suggestions do help the average consumer understand health insurance.

■ **Provide a service to physicians and hospitals.** Many CAPs help doctors and hospitals in a very concrete way. This occurs when a patient owes money to a physician or hospital, but the person expects it to be magically paid by the insurance company, forgetting that he or she also owes a copayment or a deductible. The CAP can therefore clarify the billing for such patients, allowing doctors and hospital billing departments to get their money faster.

Business Profile: Barbara Melman

Barbara Melman is perhaps one of the originators of the CAP business. Her company Claim Relief, Inc., in Chicago has been operating since 1984. Barbara spent many years as an insurance adjuster and noticed the need for this service in the early 1980s when she realized that people did not know how to submit claims to her company.

Since that time, Barbara has turned her CAP business into a well-known Chicago story. She writes a weekly Sunday column for the *Chicago Sun-Times* to answer questions people send her about their health insurance problems. (See Figure 3-1 for a sample column.) Barbara believes that the health insurance problems of yesteryear pale in comparison to today's problems. As she sarcastically points out,

> Before, you could submit a claim and if it was done correctly, an insurance company would pay. Today, however, even if a claim is correct, you have to argue about everything with insurers. In my view, insurance companies simply do not want to pay most claims, especially those that are expensive or are ongoing.

Barbara gave an example. She was working with the family of a four-year-old child who was born with many birth defects. She was hired because the insurance company stopped paying the child's claims. In the child's early years, the insurer paid most of the child's therapies; one day, however, it simply stopped paying the claims, demanding more documentation as if the situation were a new one. The family became annoyed: the more details that were sent in, the more the insurer demanded. That's when the family contacted Barbara, who was able to straighten out the situation and get the claims paid again.

Because of Barbara's reputation, most of her clients come from word of mouth, although she also maintains good relations with financial advisors who hire her on behalf of their clients. Barbara now has hundreds of active clients, and she can count total clients in the thousands. She employs two people to help her with the claims. Nevertheless, Barbara is still home-based. She charges clients on an hourly basis (currently $45 per hour) but she bills in half-hour increments. Much of her work is focused on appeals of denied claims, but she also handles the filing of many secondary claims that are not done electronically, and claims for catastrophic coverage. Her clientele is mixed, although Barbara sees it changing. It used to be mostly seniors but she now has more and more people with private insurance who she says have it the worst because commercial insurers are not paying.

Barbara's advice for people thinking about the CAP business is: "You need a good grounding in insurance and how it works. You also need to be willing to do whatever it takes to get claims paid that are being denied."

HEALTH & FITNESS

Insurance Co. Claims It Just Doesn't Get It

Q. *I have submitted my insurance claim two times to my insurance company and for the second time they have told me they do not have it. What should I do at this point to get my claims paid?*

A. Unfortunately this happens all too often. Let me give you a couple of options. Call your insurance company and ask for a supervisor and explain the situation. Ask if you can fax or send the claims directly to him or her marked "personal and confidential." Another option is to send your claims via registered mail with a return receipt requested. Always make copies of your claims.

Q. *I will be turning 65 shortly and have been flooded with Medicare supplement information. How can I be sure I am making the right decision when all the plans appear to be the same?*

A. It is very confusing because all of the companies must offer you the same plans (A through J). However, not all companies offer all of the plans to you. If you want a prescription drug benefit, you must choose the companies that make this benefit available (plans H, I or J). If you do not think you need a drug benefit, look at plans A thru G and choose the company with the most affordable premium, as the benefits are all the same. Also, be aware that if you are unsatisfied or next year another company offers a lower premium you can switch with no penalty of any kind.

Q. *My father passed away in January, and his insurance was paid up until March. Do I have to wait until all of his bills are paid before we can advise the company of his death?*

A. Your father's insurance was active until the date of his death. You are entitled to a premium refund for any premium paid after that date. Send the insurance company a copy of the death certificate and a short note advising where to return the excess premium. All of his claims will continue to be processed until they are concluded.

Q. *I am three months pregnant with my first child, and some* of my friends tell me their medical insurance covers their well baby care, and others have said theirs does not. Can you explain the discrepancy?

A. I have never understood why insurance carriers would not cover well baby care when it makes sense to protect against a condition before it starts. It certainly would seem cost-efficient. Many companies cover these services, many still do not. If you will be obtaining new insurance after the baby's birth, try to find a plan that does provide this benefit as checkups and shots can be very costly. Check with your current carrier to see if this is a benefit of the plan you now carry.

Q. *I am very upset over a denial of a medically necessary surgical procedure I had done a few months ago. I have submitted additional information to my company, but they denied the claim again. What recourse, if any, do I have?*

A. You sound like a fighter, and that's a very important factor. Write the insurance commission of your state (in Illinois the address is Illinois Department of Insurance, 320 W. Washington, Springfield, Ill. 62767) and send it all the data pertaining to your claim and the denial. The commission will conduct a review with your insurance company and contact you.

An exception is if your coverage is carried through a self-insured group; then you would go directly to your employer for the review.

Barbara Melman is president of Claim Relief, a Chicago company that helps people with health insurance problems. Write to her at the Chicago Sun-Times, Sunday Health & Fitness, 401 N. Wabash, Suite 400, Chicago 60611.

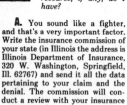

INSURANCE Q&A
BARBARA MELMAN

The Life of a CAP

The day-to-day life of many CAPs I interviewed was invariably hectic. These claims assistance professionals operated full time and indicated that they had 300 or more active customers (i.e., people who contacted them at least once over the course of a year). It was not surprising to hear of 10-hour days, spent doing the following:

Typical Duties	Time Spent (hours)
Taking phone calls or in-person meetings from current customers	3.5
Making phone calls to insurance carriers and doctors	1.5
Filling out claims forms and writing appeals	2
Reading professional materials and insurance policies	1
Marketing (phone calls or in-person meetings with potential new clients)	1
Opening mail and filing	1

As you can see, much of the time is taken up by phone calls or in-person contact with clients and insurance companies.

For simplicity, the actual claims work a CAP performs can be divided into five common types of activities:

- Filing primary claims to insurers
- Filing secondary claims to insurers
- Reviewing Explanation of Benefits (EOBs) letters for clients
- Filing appeals of disputed or denied claims to insurers
- Filing appeals of disputed bills to a doctor's office

FILING PRIMARY CLAIMS Because many patients must file their own claims, the CAP obtains a copy of the superbill or receipt that the patient has from the doctor's office, indicating the diagnosis and the fees charged. The CAP must then fill out a paper HCFA 1500 claim form, photocopy the superbill, and send it via mail to the insurer. If all works well, the claim will be paid by the insurer.

FILING SECONDARY CLAIMS Many people purchase a private secondary insurance policy to pay their deductibles, copayments, and any noncovered healthcare services. However, most such private secondary insurance claims must be filed on paper because the secondary insurer needs to see a copy of the EOB showing how much the primary carrier paid. (This is becoming less true for Medigap secondary insurance, which is increasingly handled electronically directly from Medicare after the primary Medicare claim is filed and paid. However, in general, it is still common for private secondary insurance not to be processed electronically; a paper claim is generally required.)

In such secondary situations, the CAP must therefore obtain from the patient a copy of the original superbill plus the primary insurer's EOB. The CAP must then file a paper HCFA 1500 via mail to the secondary insurance company along with the photocopies. If all works well, the claim will be paid by the insurer.

REVIEWING EOBs   For each claim filed, Medicare or the private insurance carrier issues an EOB to the patient listing the amount charged by the doctor, the amount approved, and the amount paid. Despite computerization, a CAP reviews all the EOBs for each client to make sure that the claim was processed correctly and contains no errors that can cost the patient.

FILING APPEALS   This step derives directly from the review of EOBs. As indicated earlier, insurance companies and Medicare process many claims incorrectly, resulting in a mistake that can cost the patient. The claim may be denied, underpaid, overpaid, or delayed. A large portion of a CAP business therefore involves detecting the errors and filing an appeal to the insurer to get the claim reconsidered and paid.

FILING APPEALS TO DOCTORS   Errors can also occur in bills that patients receive from their doctors. A CAP must therefore review every doctor's bill and make sure that any amounts charged match up with real charges as well as any payments that have been made. It often happens that a doctor's bill has not credited the patient for an insurance payment made, or has double billed the patient although the insurance company has paid.

We'll review more details about how to detect errors in EOBs and file appeals later in the chapter.

Business Profile: Tom and Nancy Koehler

When Nancy Koehler, a social worker with a variety of work experiences, met a woman in 1986 who was doing medical claims assistance, she was curious about the profession but didn't do anything about it. A year later, when her friend showed up one morning, excited about her upcoming retirement, but worried about the capabilities of the person to whom she was thinking of selling her business, Nancy suddenly realized that an opportunity was knocking at her door. Her friend agreed to cancel the other sale, and Nancy found herself with a new venture in life: In Home Medical Claims, of Poway, California.

Business was slow at first, but Nancy loved the job and the feeling of helping others. Her enthusiasm was so unbounding, in fact, that her husband Tom, a former Navy fighter pilot for 20 years, came home one day and decided to quit his job as a project manager for a Defense Department manufacturer of navigation systems. Never imagining that one day they would find themselves working together, Tom and Nancy slowly recognized they had the perfect complement of skills to make their business work. With her medical background, Nancy brings a solid understanding of Medicare and the claims business, which Tom has now learned too. With his project management background, Tom takes charge of their business planning and handles what he aptly calls the P&L responsibility for their business. He uses a Casio digital diary to keep track of their daily appointments, and an "oldish" personal computer with various programs such as *Timeslips* to keep track of their clients and do their monthly invoicing.

In business now for 10 years, Nancy and Tom have several hundred clients for whom they regularly handle medical claims assistance, mostly focusing on the elderly Medicare subscribers who live in their upper-middle-class southern California region. Tom and Nancy were fortunate to get their first client at a large apartment complex. That person then referred many others to them, and today, nearly every one of their clients comes from referrals. Tom and Nancy do practically no marketing, except for occasional speaking engagements Nancy takes on as a noted Medicare expert.

Tom admits,

> What makes our business great is the demographics here. But we also did our homework. We took several workshops from the Small Business Administration (SBA) on marketing and business planning, and Nancy also went to SCORE (Service Corps of Retired Executives) for some advice and managed to get a former Blue Cross executive from Michigan who had retired here as her mentor. Our operation is sophisticated but simple. We limit the number of clients we cover so we can maintain a quality service and trust, which is one of the most important aspects of this business.

There are two factors that distinguish their CAP business from most others, however. First, as the name of their company, In Home Medical Claims, implies, Tom and Nancy go to their clients, not the other way around. This is a major factor for them, since many of their clients cannot leave their homes easily. Second, Tom and Nancy have naturally evolved their business into handling many financial and personal matters for their elderly clients. The level of trust that their clients have come to place in Tom and Nancy is so great that they have accepted whatever tasks are

(Continued)

required, including balancing checkbooks, paying bills, making appointments with lawyers and doctors, and even assuming power of attorney for a few clients who could no longer act in their own behalf.

Because of her expertise in insurance, and the increasing conflicts between Medicare HMOs and patients, Nancy also gets pulled in occasionally to attend meetings on behalf of her elderly clients to protest many new types of healthcare service problems. When I recently met them for an interview, Nancy recounted several long stories about complications that regularly occur among Medicare HMO patients who are denied coverage for services to which they are entitled. In one angry meeting with Medicare officials, Nancy pulled in several professional colleagues to argue in favor of a 90-year-old man who was being threatened with loss of insurance because his doctor wanted him to move to a facility closer to his practice. Nancy helped win the argument, probably preserving the man's life for several years.

Tom and Nancy have become well known in the CAP field and are active members of NACAP. They are excellent models for anyone interested in this profession. Meeting them in person leaves no doubt that here is a couple who have truly found their niche in life: helping other people in any and every way they can.

Knowledge and Skills Needed

Like medical billing services, a CAP deals in depth with the complex rules, vocabulary, and procedures of the health insurance industry and doctors' offices. Also, like medical billers, a CAP must spend enormous time and energy setting up the business and getting clients. Many of the same skills and knowledge base therefore apply to this profession as well. The next part of the chapter is therefore divided into the following five sections:

- Knowledge of health insurance and the claims process
- Knowledge of EOBs and appeals
- Organizational skills
- Knowledge of business, including marketing and sales
- Knowledge of computers and business software

As with medical billing, the more experience you have in any of these areas, particularly in the insurance industry, the easier building your business will be if you are just starting out. For example, if you have worked in a physician's office doing billing, or as an adjuster in a health insurance company, or in a corporate personnel department doing benefits, you will probably have a much easier time getting your business off the ground.

All of the needed skills are learnable, however. The novice will simply need more time or a different entry path into the business, such as working first in a medical office or with an established claims service to build up your background. After reading the following sections and exploring these areas in detail, you might want to do the activity suggested in the previous chapter in which you informally plot your learning curve across the three principal areas of this business: insurance industry knowledge, business skills, and computer literacy. See Chapter 2 for more information about this planning activity.

Knowledge of Insurance and the Claims Process

First and foremost, a claims professional must have a complete understanding of the health insurance business—who the players are; how doctors, hospitals, and insurance companies interact; how claims are processed; and how to read EOBs. Without a sound grounding in these areas, one simply cannot be a "professional." As Tom Koehler of In Home Medical Claims characterizes it, "This profession requires integrative skills; you have to look at EOBs, at the physician's bill, and at all the insurance policies a client has, and put it all together to come out with one conclusion: did the person get paid the right amount?"

As a result, you need to know about items such as the following:

- How to read a health insurance policy (see the sidebar, "Reading an Insurance Policy")
- The terminology commonly used in the health insurance business, such as deductible, out-of-pocket limit, stop-loss limit, coinsurance, allowable amount, limiting charge, excess charge, and so on
- The differences among types of healthcare coverage offered (i.e., basic, major medical, wraparound, catastrophic, cancer)
- The specialized rules covering coordination of benefits (i.e., when a subscriber has more than one policy, such as two working spouses with policies, or children of divorced parents. When this occurs, you must know which policy is considered primary and which is secondary. It depends on whether the insurance company follows the *gender rule* or the *birthday rule*).

- The rules and regulations governing Medicare Parts A and B and Medigap policies
- The major-medical coding systems: ICD-9-CM, CPT, HCPCS, and so on
- The procedures followed by doctors' offices and other types of healthcare providers in billing and accounting for patient charges
- The trends toward managed care and Medicare HMOs, and how they affect consumers
- The various types of fee schedules used to pay physicians, including UCR, capitation, and RBRVS

Much of this information was presented in Chapter 2, so if you have not read it by now, you may wish to review that chapter, particularly the sections on health insurance and Medicare.

Please note especially that understanding medical coding is almost as important for a claims professional as it is for a medical billing service. A claims professional must have an excellent command of these codes (although you won't need to memorize them, since there are thousands) because many claims are rejected or downcoded (i.e., reimbursed at a lower amount) because of incorrect coding, missing modifiers, and wrong location codes. This means that your client may not be reimbursed, or may receive a lower amount than he or she deserves. As you may recall from the previous chapter, there is little doubt that insurance companies, which have a vested interest in minimizing their payouts, are not bending over backward to make sure the patient is properly paid. In short, if you don't know your coding, you cannot protect the interests of your clients.

In addition, staying abreast of Medicare rules and regulations is vital, since a large number of your clients will be the elderly. For example, Medicare has specific exclusions for certain procedures, as well as many limitations on payments. Many Medicare subscribers don't even understand the basic difference between a PAR and NON-PAR provider, so the CAP may need to explain this to help them avoid going to a more expensive doctor or overpaying a disallowed fee. You also need to know the rules to follow when Medicare is not the primary insurance carrier, even for an elderly person. This situation is referred to as MSP—Medicare as Secondary Payer—and can occur when a person over 65 is still working and has an employer group insurance plan. (It can also occur if the person's spouse is still working and the family is covered by that employer, or if the medical services were related to a work injury or automobile accident, in which case Medicare will not pay as primary insurance.) You must also know the changes in Medicare fees each year: the amount of the deductible and copayments for Part A and Part B, as well as the dollar limitations placed on certain services and hospitalizations. And finally, you must also understand the somewhat complex realm of Medigap insurance policies, which many consumers are still confused about, despite the recent federal government regulation that limits them to 10 standard policies.

As you can see, there is quite an extensive array of insurance industry knowledge and inside information that a claims professional must have under his or her belt. If you approach the field as if it were a puzzle though, you will feel challenged by learning it all, rather than frustrated and confused. One piece at a time does it!

Reading an Insurance Policy

As a CAP, you need to become familiar with reading commercial (private) insurance policies. The typical outline for these policies is as shown in Figure 3-2.

Because of space limitations, it is not possible to reproduce a full policy in this book. It is highly recommended that you examine your own policy or one belonging to a friend or relative to gain experience in reading such documents.

Figure 3-2
Outline of a Typical
Insurance Policy

OUTLINE OF A TYPICAL INSURANCE POLICY

I. Schedule of Benefits

II. Eligibility Requirements

    A. Dependent requirements

    B. Termination of coverage

III. Definitions

IV. Covered Expenses

    A. Hospital Expenses

        1. Precertification requirements

    B. Major Medical Expenses

V. Limitations and Exclusions

VI. Coordination of Benefits

    A. Effect of Other Coverage

    B. Effect of Medicare

    C. Effect of Automobile coverage

VII. Continuation of Coverage

    A. COBRA

    B. Conversion

VIII. Claiming Benefits

    A. Time to File Limitations

    B. How to Appeal

    C. ERISA Rights

Knowledge of EOBs and Appeals

Another key skill of a CAP is the ability to look at an EOB (or an EOMB from Medicare) and determine if it contains any errors. Figures 3-3 through 3-6 show samples of a commercial EOB and the three types of Medicare EOMBs.

The fact is, simple errors and screwups occur constantly, and if you are unable to detect them, you cannot do your job.

The types of errors made are truly amazing and include errors due to

- Miscoding of physician services
- Missing information
- Incorrect policy numbers
- Incorrect allowable amounts
- Services never rendered
- Services rendered but not charged
- Downcoding of services
- Denied payments due to lack of authorization

Most people are simply not aware of the errors that may be contained in their EOBs. For example, in researching this book, one elderly woman in a senior center related to me that she once received from Medicare an EOMB indicating that her account was being charged for a hip operation—but she had never had one! It seemed that the wrong Medicare ID number had been used.

Nancy and Tom Koehler related many stories affirming the simplest of errors:

> We've seen all types of mistakes. One hospital in this area billed a client for outpatient services, and when we called to ask if it had billed Medicare first, it turned out it hadn't. Another client received a bill for the copayment amount on a Medicare Part B outpatient service, but because he had neglected to tell the hospital that he had supplemental (secondary) insurance, he thought he had to pay the bill himself. We simply told the hospital to forward the bill to the secondary insurance, and it was taken care of. In another case, the doctor billed both our client and the secondary insurance company, and so we made sure the doctor didn't get paid twice. We also have a client who retired from a company in Tennessee that was self-insured, and for some reason, the hospital didn't want to send the bill there. So we helped the client get it taken care of: he paid the 20 percent

copayment, and then we made sure the company received the bill and paid it. The client was happy and it saved him a lot of time and stress.

Some situations are much more complex. CAP Mary Ellen Fitzgibbons of Chicago recounted one incident to me in which a hospital made several serious errors in billing Medicare for services rendered for a woman. The problem was, the woman had died, and the secondary insurance

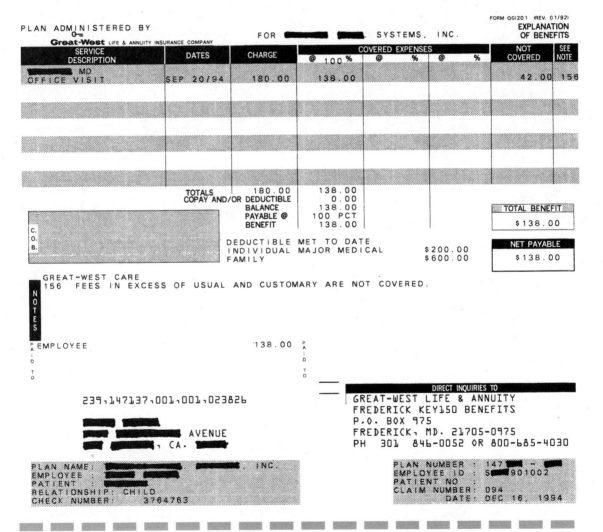

Figure 3-3 A Typical EOB from a Commercial Insurance Company. The doctor's charge was $180, but the insurance company determined that the usual and customary fee should be only $138. That leaves $42 not covered. In this case, the insurance company paid 100% of $138.

19616212474604

U.S DEPARTMENT OF HEALTH AND HUMAN SERVICES/HEALTH CARE FINANCING ADMINISTRATION

MEDICARE BENEFIT NOTICE

DATE 06/24/96

HEALTH INSURANCE CLAIM NUMBER

◄

**Always use this number
when writing about your claim**

This notice shows what benefits were used by you and the covered services not paid by Medicare for the period shown in Item 1. See other side of this form for additional information which may apply to your claim.

1 **SERVICES FURNISHED BY**	**DATE(S)**	**BENEFITS USED**
HOSPITAL	05/24/96 THRU 06/04/96	11 INPATIENT

2 **PAYMENT STATUS**

$736.00 WAS APPLIED TO YOUR INPATIENT DEDUCTIBLE.

MEDICARE PAID ALL COVERED SERVICES EXCEPT:
    $736.00 FOR THE INPATIENT DEDUCTIBLE.

IF NO-FAULT INSURANCE, LIABILITY INSURANCE, WORKERS' COMPENSATION,
DEPARTMENT OF VETERANS AFFAIRS, OR, IN SOME CASES, A GROUP HEALTH
PLAN FOR EMPLOYEES ALSO COVERS THESE SERVICES, A REFUND MAY BE DUE
THE MEDICARE PROGRAM. PLEASE CONTACT US IF YOU ARE COVERED BY ANY
OF THESE SOURCES. YOU DO NOT HAVE TO CONTACT US TO REPORT A MEDI –
CARE SUPPLEMENTAL (MEDIGAP) POLICY.

BLUE CROSS OF CALIFORNIA – MEDICARE
P. O. BOX 70000
VAN NUYS   CA   91470
                  (818)-593-2006   △

**If you have any questions
about this record, call
or write**

TELEPHONE NUMBER

FORM HCFA-1533 (3-92)

Figure 3-4 A Medicare Part A EOMB

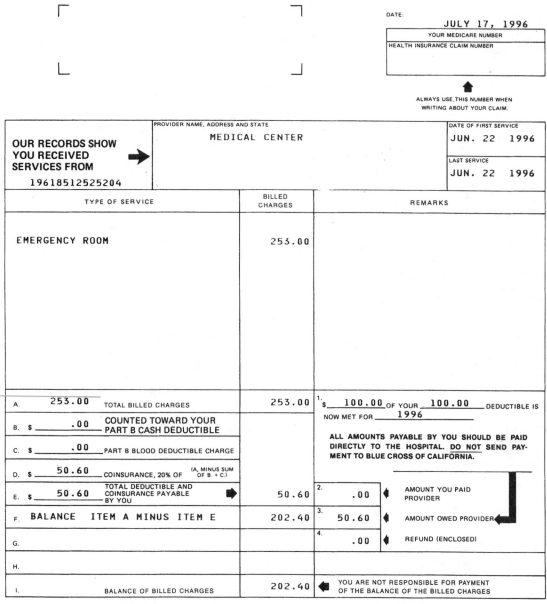

THIS IS NOT A BILL

DATE:

JULY 17, 1996

YOUR MEDICARE NUMBER

HEALTH INSURANCE CLAIM NUMBER

ALWAYS USE THIS NUMBER WHEN
WRITING ABOUT YOUR CLAIM.

OUR RECORDS SHOW YOU RECEIVED SERVICES FROM	PROVIDER NAME, ADDRESS AND STATE
	MEDICAL CENTER
19618512525204	

DATE OF FIRST SERVICE
JUN. 22 1996

LAST SERVICE
JUN. 22 1996

TYPE OF SERVICE	BILLED CHARGES	REMARKS
EMERGENCY ROOM	253.00	

A. 253.00 TOTAL BILLED CHARGES	253.00	1. $ 100.00 OF YOUR 100.00 DEDUCTIBLE IS NOW MET FOR 1996	
B. $ .00 COUNTED TOWARD YOUR PART B CASH DEDUCTIBLE		ALL AMOUNTS PAYABLE BY YOU SHOULD BE PAID DIRECTLY TO THE HOSPITAL. DO NOT SEND PAYMENT TO BLUE CROSS OF CALIFORNIA.	
C. $ .00 PART B BLOOD DEDUCTIBLE CHARGE			
D. $ 50.60 COINSURANCE, 20% OF (A, MINUS SUM OF B. + C.)			
E. $ 50.60 TOTAL DEDUCTIBLE AND COINSURANCE PAYABLE BY YOU	50.60	2. .00 AMOUNT YOU PAID PROVIDER	
F. BALANCE ITEM A MINUS ITEM E	202.40	3. 50.60 AMOUNT OWED PROVIDER	
G.		4. .00 REFUND (ENCLOSED)	
H.			
I. BALANCE OF BILLED CHARGES	202.40	YOU ARE NOT RESPONSIBLE FOR PAYMENT OF THE BALANCE OF THE BILLED CHARGES	

556 6/95

Figure 3-5 Medicare Part B, Hospital EOMB

Summary of this notice dated **February 2, 1996**		
Total charges:	$	72.00
Total Medicare approved:	$	53.81
We paid your provider:	$	0.00
Your total responsibility:	$	53.81

Your Medicare Number is:

YOUR PROVIDER ACCEPTED ASSIGNMENT

Details about this notice (See the back for more information.)

BILL SUBMITTED BY: MED CORP
Mailing address:

Dates	Services and Service Codes Control Number 96017-4139-12-000	Charges	Medicare Approved	See Notes Below
Jan. 2, 1996	1 Office/outpatient visit, est (99214)	$ 72.00	$ 53.81	a

Notes:

a The approved amount is based on the fee schedule.

Here's an explanation of this notice:

Of the total charges, Medicare approved	$ 53.81	The provider agreed to accept this amount. See #4 on the back.
Less the deductible applied	- 53.81	**You have now met $53.81 of your $100.00 deductible for 1996.**
Medicare pays 80% of this total	$ 0.00	
Medicare owes	$ 0.00	
We are paying the provider	$ 0.00	
Of the approved amount	$ 53.81	
Your total responsibility	$ 53.81	The provider may bill you for this amount. If you have other insurance, the other insurance may pay this amount.

IMPORTANT: If you have questions about this notice, call us at 1-800-675-2266. If you reside in area codes 213 or parts of 310 or 818, call 213-748-2311. Or visit us at 1149 S. Broadway, Los Angeles. Please have this notice with you.

To appeal our decision, you must WRITE to us before AUG. 2, 1996 at Transamerica Occidental Life Insurance Co., P.O. Box 30540, Los Angeles, CA 90030. See 2 on the back.   (000-0467641)

Figure 3-6 Medicare Part B, Provider EOMB

company wouldn't figure out the difference between the Medicare allowable amounts and the amounts paid because of the mistakes made by the hospital. Meanwhile, the family was being held liable by the hospital for the deceased woman's bill of $20,000. The family was receiving collection notices, although the hospital refused to correct its own mistakes. As Mary Ellen said, "The average person pays the collection notices without question, but in many cases there's been a serious misunderstanding or error made that must get rectified."

Figures 3-7 and 3-8 illustrate one situation that contained an error. Figure 3-7 shows the actual EOB from Pennsylvania Blue Shield dated 3/11/95 and Figure 3-8 shows the doctor's bill sent to the patient on 4/17/95. See if you can guess what is wrong, then read the caption. (These are real EOBs; the names of the patients and doctors involved have been deleted to protect their privacy.)

This case is just a sample of what you need to learn as a CAP. Unfortunately, space limitations preclude showing you more practice EOBs here.

EXPLANATION OF BENEFITS

Pennsylvania BlueShield
An Independent Licensee of the Blue Cross and Blue Shield Association

Camp Hill, PA 17089

KEEP FOR YOUR RECORDS

PENNSYLVANIA BLUE SHIELD
CUSTOMER SERVICE
PO BOX 890036
CAMP HILL PA 17089-0036

Subscriber: ELIZABETH ▟▟▟▟▟

Patient: ELIZABETH ▟▟▟▟▟

Provider: UNIVERSITY OF ▟▟▟▟▟▟▟
(000▟▟038)

ID Number: ▟▟▟470

Claim Number: 65065033550

Page: 1 of 1

Date: 03/11/▟▟

PROCEDURE DESCRIPTION PROCEDURE CODE (NUMBER OF SERVICES)		SERVICE DATE(S)	PROVIDER'S CHARGE	ALLOWANCE	AMOUNT PAID	AMOUNT NOT PAID	REMARKS
DIAGNOSTIC TEST/EEG 95816	(001)	02/03/95	180.00	84.00	84.00	96.00	Q1010
	TOTALS		180.00	84.00	84.00		

Q1010   These services were provided by a Pennsylvania Blue Shield Participating Provider. Blue Shield's ALLOWANCE will be accepted by the provider as full payment for covered services. You do not owe the Provider any balances for the covered services listed above.

Pennsylvania Blue Shield has paid the Provider the amount shown in the AMOUNT PAID column.

Figure 3-7 Example of EOB from a commercial insurer. Note that the doctor's original charge was $180, but the allowable amount was only $84. The doctor must write off the $96 excess. The statement printed on the EOB specifically says that this amount is supposed to be "full payment." Now look at Figure 3-8.

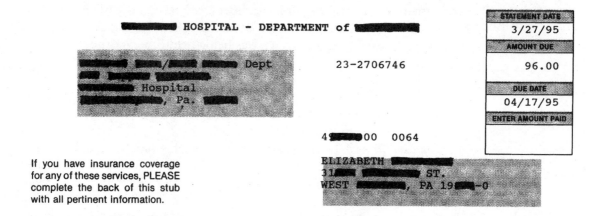

████████ HOSPITAL - DEPARTMENT of ████████		STATEMENT DATE
		3/27/95
		AMOUNT DUE
████████ ███/███ █████ Dept	23-2706746	96.00
████████ Hospital		DUE DATE
████████, Pa. ███		04/17/95
		ENTER AMOUNT PAID

4█████00 0064

If you have insurance coverage
for any of these services, PLEASE
complete the back of this stub
with all pertinent information.

ELIZABETH ████████
31███ ████████ ST.
WEST ████████, PA 19██-0

DETACH AND RETURN TOP PORTION WITH YOUR PAYMENT

RETAIN BOTTOM PORTION FOR YOUR RECORDS

ACCOUNT NO.	PATIENT NAME				STATEMENT DATE
49████00 ████	ELIZABETH S				3/27/95

DATE OF SERVICE		CPT	DESCRIPTION OF SERVICE	CHARGE	CREDITS	BALANCE
2/03/██	JL	95816	Routine EEG	180.00	84.00	96.00

This statement represents current amounts due and may not be your
total account balance. Billing Questions - Call (215) ████████

PLEASE PAY THIS AMOUNT	96.00

Figure 3-8 Example of a Doctor's statement to a patient containing an error. In Figure 3-7, the EOB indicated that the doctor must accept $84 as the full payment and write off $96. However, this invoice was erroneously sent to patient a few weeks later, demanding the remaining $96. A trained CAP will catch errors of this type and save their clients money.

Obviously, when errors are found, the CAP must take action to rectify them. A claims professional must therefore know the protocol for appealing claims. In some cases, the CAP can try a quick phone call to get the claim reviewed by either the physician or the insurance company, without sending anything in writing. However, in most cases, the first level of a formal appeal will involve writing a letter to the insurance company, Medicare, or the doctor's office pointing out the mistake and how it needs to be corrected. Medicare has an official form to be used—Form 1964—but most CAPs indicate that they write all their appeal letters, even those to Medicare, on their company letterhead without problems. Similarly, when the mistake has been made at the doctor's office, the CAP must phone or send a letter with copies of any necessary documents, such as the EOB.

For any appeal, knowing whom to contact via phone or by mail can be critical. As Tom Koehler points out, "Knowing exactly the right person to call or write is often what makes the difference between falling into claims limbo or getting action." Some CAPs even resort to having a friend who works at one doctor's office call another physician's office to discuss the situation "from the inside."

Figures 3-9 and 3-10 show simple template forms that CAP Lori Donnelly uses to submit appeals for her clients. As you can see, all that is needed is to write in clear English the errors you have discovered, why they are mistakes, and how they should be corrected.

Getting Authorized to Represent Your Client

Because the CAP profession is still relatively new, many doctor's offices and insurance companies are not familiar with the fact that a third party can call or write them to discuss the status of a patient's claims. Medical information and claims are often considered private and confidential information that no one but the patient has a right to know. If a CAP finds an error on a physician's bill and calls the insurance company or doctor's office to query the matter, he or she often gets the following response: "Who did you say you are? Are you related to the patient? Oh, no, we can't discuss such information with anyone but the patient himself (herself)."

To get around this, some CAPs simply tell insurance adjusters and doctors that they are a "friend" of the patient, or that they are related to the patient, or that they are "helping" the patient straighten out the problem. One CAP told me that she can usually get around the situation by simply saying, "I'm a friend of Mr. (Mrs.) So and So," and then moving on quickly to the issue without giving the person time to react.

However, to avoid the appearance of unethical behavior, many CAPs now have resorted to asking all clients to sign a formal document that authorizes them to act on the client's behalf in related healthcare matters, such as reviewing doctor's bills, insurance claims, and filing appeals. In general, this document appears to work in most cases, even with Medicare. Figure 3-11 shows an example of this type of authorization document.

(Print on your Letterhead)

REQUEST FOR REVIEW

Date: _____

Appeal #_____

Please be advised that we request a review of your denial of
claim # _____ , based on the information stated below.
Please advise us of the result of this review as soon as
possible.

_____

_____

_____

_____

_____

_____

_____

_____

Patient _____Service Date _____

Provider _____Total Charge _____

Please note that this company, {name of your company}, is
acting on behalf of your insured with regard to the submission
and payment of all medical claims. All inquiries should be made
to {name of your company}. The insured's written authorization
is attached.

Figure 3-9 Insurance Appeal Letter

(Print on your Letterhead)
Your Name
Your Address
Today's Date

Doctor's Name
Doctor's Address

Dear Dr. {......},

I am a claims assistance professional representing {*name of client*}. I am authorized to act on behalf of Mr./Ms./Mrs. {name} with regard to the submission and payment of all claims. The insured's written authorization is attached.

My client recently received your bill for {*amount*} for {*name of service provided*} which you rendered on {*date of service*}.

As you can see from the enclosed copy of my client's Explanation of Benefits, the insurance company {Medicare} has
- rejected the claim because {*enter the reason in your own words*}

  _____

- indicated that the allowable fee is only _____
- {other} _____

  _____

We therefore respectfully submit that you review and/or correct the charges as follows:

_____
_____

Sincerely,

{*Your name*}

Figure 3-10 *Provider Appeal Letter*

[Print on Your Company Letterhead]

AUTHORIZATION TO REPRESENT

I hereby appoint {*name of your company*} as my agent to file all claims for benefits on my behalf, for myself, and all dependents covered under my benefit plan(s).

I authorize my insurance carrier(s) to speak to or correspond with an agent of {*name of your company*} in connection with claims filed by them on my behalf.

I hereby authorize any Physician, Dentist, Hospital, Pharmacy, Insurance Company, Employer, Third Party Administrator, or Organization to release any information regarding the medical, dental, mental, alcohol or disability or employment related information concerning this claim to {*name of your company*} for the purpose of validating and determining the benefit(s) payable in connection with this claim. A copy of this signature will be valid.

Insured's Signature _____

Spouse's Signature _____

Date _____

Figure 3-11 Authorization to Represent

Organizational Skills

Although Chapter 2 pointed out the growing computerization of claims processing between doctors' offices and insurance companies, at the consumer level, claims are still a paper-intensive business. This means that a CAP must have excellent organizational skills, including the ability to categorize priorities, organize paperwork, remember to make copies, and color code the filing system.

For instance, assume you have 100 clients, and each client has 20 EOBs and 20 doctor bills for you to review over the course of 2 months. That equals 4,000 pieces of paper that will likely pass by your desk at least once in 60 days! Since most claims take several days to settle, it is actually more likely that you will need to look at each document two or three times, which means that those 4,000 pieces of paper go by your eyes more like 8,000 or 12,000 times. So if you are the type of person who stacks paper in random piles on a desk, this job is not for you (or if you insist it is, your clients will probably fire you for losing their paperwork).

In short, being a CAP requires that you have an intuitive sense of organizing information. While a personal computer will help you do this, much of the business is not yet highly computerized, because of the sheer number of paper documents (EOBs, doctor's invoices, appeals letters) that must be physically generated and stored. I will address the growing use of computers in the CAP business in greater detail later, but for now, suffice it to say that the mountain of paperwork you will get in this job is far more than most people realize. Many CAPs have not computerized extensively, preferring to develop a fool-proof tracking scheme that they can use for each client.

For example, some CAPs adhere to a multifolder system such as a 3-level color-coded folder system for each client. This might be something like red = active claims, yellow = recently completed claims, and blue = old claims. If a client has active claims being filed or appealed, his or her red folder is kept on your desktop as a reminder of what needs to be done. Any time a completed claim or appeal is mailed out, a copy is made and stored in the red folder. Then, when claims are eventually settled, the corresponding documents are moved to the yellow folder. The yellow folder is occasionally cleaned out and older documents are shifted to the blue folder. And so on.

To make sure that proper records are kept, CAP Lori Donnelly uses a one-page "tracking form" in each client's red folder. This tracking form, shown in Figure 3-12, gives her the ability to log the status of each claim when it is first filed. If a claim must be appealed, she then has a separate appeals tracking form for each client (this form is not shown; it looks similar to the tracking form in Figure 3-12).

Of course, CAPs also have to generate invoices for their clients, so that's even more paperwork! As you can see, this is not a career for the type of person who stacks tax documents in a shoe box and expects to find everything at the end of the year.

Knowledge of Business

Earlier in the chapter, I mentioned that the claims professionals I spoke with indicated that they had 200 to 300 clients and more. As you might

CLAIMS TRACKING FORM -- PRIMARY INSURERS

Client: Client #:

Patient: Batch #:

Sent to: Date:

1	2	3	4	5	6a	6b	6c	7
Date of Service	Identify Service	Provider (name of doctor)	Actual Charge	Allowable Fee per Insurer or Medicare	Payment made	Date	Balance due	Appealed? (if appealed, mark Appeals Tracking Form #)

Figure 3-12 Claims Tracking Form. 1) Fill in top portion. 2) Fill in columns 1-4 on submission of original claim. 3) Fill in columns 5-6a, 6b, and 6c after the EOB is received. 4) Indicate in column 7 if claim needs to be appealed.

imagine, it takes time to build up such a large clientele, and marketing and selling your services are critical skills if you want to stay in business. Although you might think that many of the same marketing concepts discussed in Chapter 2 apply here, remember that the CAP profession deals with the public at large as its potential customers, not with doctors. This means that getting customers is accomplished very differently.

MARKETING Unlike medical billing services, your market is broad, unfocused, and seldom knows about the CAP profession. In general, consumers have little comprehension of what you can do for them. Doctors at least know about medical billing and electronic claims, so they are often a much easier target for the entrepreneur seeking a business.

In contrast, a CAP must have a good sense of how to market "services" to the general public. Because your audience is so vast, cold calling as the primary method of getting customers is useless. It would be highly unproductive to spend your time knocking on doors or making dozens of phone calls to find one client at a time.

In the CAP business, your best bet for marketing is to learn how to get people to come to you. You need to learn about *marketing mix,* that is, how to select from four major marketing methods to bring clients to you: advertising, public relations, direct mail, and sales promotions.

ADVERTISING. Some CAPS advertise in local newspapers, or on a mid-day talk show on the local radio, or even on the back of cash register receipts. To do this, you must understand advertising rates and how to design effective print and/or spoken advertising. You will need to calculate your budget and what the payoff might be in comparison to the costs of such advertising. You might consider local newspapers and other less expensive or free sources for advertising. You may also want to design unique brochures to leave at bus stops, stores, or parking lots, or any number of methods that are used when you need to reach thousands of people. This all means that your copywriting and graphic design capabilities need to be developed.

PUBLIC RELATIONS. Every claims professional I spoke with indicated that public relations was one of the best forms of marketing. Writing articles or getting them written about you and your business is an extremely cost-effective method of getting your company name in front of tens of thousands of people. See the sidebar on Harvey Matoren, whose company Claims Security of America has been written up in numerous newspapers including the prestigious *Kiplinger's Personal Finance Magazine,* for an example of the value of PR.

DIRECT MAIL. The third area of your promotional mix, direct mail, is of course a major undertaking and probably worth studying if you are inexperienced at it. It costs money and takes time to print thousands of letters, find a good mailing list, and get your mail out properly. Learning from others or simply hiring a direct mail consultant could prove useful. Visit a bookstore and find some books on doing direct mail, such as *Direct Mail Copy that Sells* by Herschell Gordon Lewis (Prentice Hall).

SALES PROMOTIONS. This fourth aspect of your marketing mix can actually be quite valuable. Because people don't often know about the

Business Profile: Harvey Matoren

How would you like to have your company written up, at no expense to you, and paraded in front of millions of people who are your potential customers? Sound too good to be true? It's not, and that's exactly what happened to Harvey Matoren and his wife Carol. Their company (formerly called Health Claims of Jacksonville, Inc., but now titled Claims Security of America to reflect their growing nationwide clientele) was covered in a variety of local Florida newspapers and in the prestigious *Kiplinger's Personal Finance Magazine* as well as in *Business Week, Cosmopolitan,* and *Working Woman* magazines a few years ago—and from that point on, their business has skyrocketed.

Ironically, Harvey and Carol left excellent positions in the insurance industry in Florida to start their own business as claims assistance professionals from their home in 1989. Harvey had been a senior vice president with Blue Cross and Blue Shield, and president of its HMO subsidiary. Carol was a senior health industry analyst and a registered nurse. But they had dreams of forming their own business, and they felt drawn toward helping the average person navigate through what they knew firsthand was a tough world in the insurance business. As Harvey told me, "We were already in our middle years and we looked at this as an opportunity to grow a business that had lots of potential and that we felt was much needed in our country. We know how difficult it is for the average person to get through the insurance system, and we wanted to make a difference."

After eight years in business, Harvey is more than upbeat about the future of the profession. As he told me,

> My feeling is that we have hardly scratched the surface of clients for this business. Anyone and everyone needs this type of service, from Medicare recipients to individuals, couples, and families who just don't have time. Even with healthcare reform, we see that there is a continuing need for claims assistance with all the paperwork that has to get done.

Harvey continued, buoyant about the need for qualified CAPs,

> In fact, regardless of what happens with healthcare reform—or shall I say, even more so *because* of it—with more managed care, there is an even greater need for CAPs. Anytime there is a change, people have trouble. For instance, there are a lot of issues in managed care to contend with right here in Florida. We have many patients who have joined managed care programs, but they don't understand the rules of the game. When their claims are denied, they encounter lines like, "Sorry we're not going to cover this because you went out of the network." This is why my business exists.

Harvey then related a specific incident in which he took part,

> We had a client in a managed care system. The gentleman went to his closest emergency room one night at 3 A.M. suffering from chest pains. Fortunately, he did not have a heart attack, just chest pains. But it turned out that this hospital was not his HMO hospital, so the HMO denied payment, saying it was not an emergency since he didn't actually have a heart attack. This has turned out to be a major issue in healthcare: HMOs are making decisions based on "diagnosis," not "symptoms presented." The problem has gotten so bad that in some states, they have made laws that HMOs must base their decisions on symptoms.

Harvey believes that the key to success in the CAP business is to make it an intervention business. He points out that some CAPs just file a claim and make sure it gets submitted; on the other hand, he points out, "My company goes the extra mile to maximize the reimbursement and make sure the client pays only those bills he has to pay."

While Harvey isn't sure how many clients he's received from publicity over the years, there's no doubt that the PR has contributed to his prestige and credibility in the public's eye. Thanks to hard work, exceptional knowledge of the insurance industry, and lots of publicity, Harvey and Carol now have a large suite in an office complex, several employees, and clients stretching all across the country.

Harvey is willing to speak with prospective CAPs and conducts workshops and training seminars. He is also distributing a CAP business opportunity for those unable to attend the workshops. Harvey also has specialized software for your CAP business. For details on his training, business opportunity package, and software, contact him at 904-733-2525, or by writing to Claims Security of America, 3926 San Jose Park Drive, Jacksonville, FL 32217.

CAP business, you could offer a special promotion such as working on one claim for each new client for free, or reducing your fee by one-half to every new client in the month of June. Special promotions are often helpful to get new customers to sign up with you; many people can be enticed to try out your service and then will stay if they like it.

One additional aspect of any marketing campaign—no matter what the business—is networking and getting word-of-mouth referrals. Nearly every CAP I interviewed said that getting current customers to recommend you to other clients is the surest way to generate new business. Whether it's relatives, professionals you know, or current clients, you want to encourage everyone in your sphere of daily contacts to talk about your business with others and spread the word. Many entrepreneurs assume that their customers know that referrals are appreciated, but they don't end up with new business. It therefore helps to let your friends and clients know that you would like referrals. You might even offer a discount to those clients who refer new customers to you.

To learn more about all these areas of marketing, one of the best books is *Getting Business to Come to You* by Paul and Sarah Edwards (Jeremy P. Tarcher). I also recommend *Selling Your Services* by Robert W. Bly (Holt), but you can find literally dozens of other titles in bookstores. This is a business area in which you can easily build a library, consulting it regularly for ideas, tips, and brainstorming tools.

SALES   As a claims assistance professional, you will deal extensively with the general public. This means that you must remember that each person is different and that the customer is always right. Whoever your clients are, you need to think in terms of preserving your integrity and reputation in the business, as Tom and Nancy Koehler have done.

Also keep in mind that many people may not fully understand what you do and so getting your first clients to sign on with you is often frustrating and time-consuming. I interviewed one CAP in the Los Angeles area who had tried for six months to get clients, but unfortunately she could not even sign a single individual, despite what appeared to be reasonably good marketing literature.

Being a CAP was unanimously described as a people-oriented business, in which you are like a public defender protecting the innocent victims of our nightmarish health system against the penurious corporate giants of the insurance industry. All of the individuals I spoke with loved their work, especially the thrill of winning a claim for their clients. As Rikki Horne, founder of Medical Claims Management in Newbury Park, California, proudly announced, "I like providing a real service. People come to me and they are vulnerable. You need to care about the people you work for. When your client gets a check for $1,200, you feel as if you did it for yourself."

Knowledge of Computers and Software

The claims assistance professional does not work with electronic claims; these can be filed only on behalf of physicians and healthcare providers to insurance companies. A CAP therefore does not need to purchase medical billing and electronic claims software, such as those described in Chapter 2.

In addition, as mentioned earlier, most CAPs continue to do their work manually, without a heavy usage of computers and software to record the claims they file on behalf of their clients or to track the appeals they may submit. A few CAPs use a standard off-the-shelf database program to create records for each client and each claim, but most simply record these tasks using paper documents and standard office filing procedures. When a CAP uses a computer, it is simply to word process letters and appeals.

Nevertheless, it is expected that we will see an increasing computerization of the field in the future. NACAP reported to me that it was aware of several developers who were creating CAP software. As indicated in the sidebar on page 174, Harvey Matoren has also created specialized CAP software for his own company and is considering making it available for the general market. If you are interested in examining such programs, contact NACAP and Harvey Matoren.

As with any business though, you will still find that computerizing your general business functions will add to your efficiency. For example, since you will likely deal with hundreds of people, you can benefit by using contact management software to track the status of your marketing efforts and record your appointments and daily schedule. Like many salespeople, you may find software such as Symantec's *ACT!, Lotus Organizer,* or *The Maximizer* to improve your efficiency and productivity. Be sure to get a program that matches your hardware capability, as some of the programs are DOS-based while others are Windows 3.x or Windows 95. Visit a retail software store such as CompUSA where you can usually try out hundreds of software programs to see if one appeals to you.

If you are not familiar with such programs, you should not fear their highly technical-sounding names, as they are really only software versions of filing cabinets and Rolodex indexes, although they are much more powerful and can help you organize more information quickly. Database software and contact management software are merging into the same product, in that both serve what is often called a *personal information management* function. These programs contain electronic record-keeping systems in which you get either preformatted screens or ones that you design yourself to keep track of your contacts. Each screen contains fill-in "fields," such as name, address, phone number, fax number, date of last meeting, action plan, and so on. Each screen (or perhaps two tied together) is called a record and is similar to an index card or file you might keep on a person or company you wanted to track. A group of records composes a database. The advantage of this software is that you can browse through a database very quickly to find the information you want. Even better, you can have multiple databases, such as one for all your insurance companies, and another for your clients, one for your prospects, one for your daily appointments, and so on. The power of the database is that you can link records in an interrelated fashion (called a relational database) so that you can jump from one record in one database to another record in another database.

Database management programs effectively allow you to keep tabs on all your clients, which claims you've filed for them, how often you see them, how much time you spent on their project, and what results you achieved. Most also let you produce weekly schedule listings and customizable calendars.

Other programs, such as *Timeslips* from Timeslips Corporation, consistently a best-seller, allow you to accurately track your time if you bill clients on a per hour basis. The software, available in both Windows and DOS versions, automatically logs the time you spend on a project and then allows you to generate reports and invoices that incorporate any of several fee schedules you have stored. For example, you can bill one client at $50/hour, and another at $35/hour if you so desire. (You can use this software even if you charge on a flat-fee basis. By keeping track of your time, the software allows you to compare how many hours you have spent on a project so you can judge if you have been charging too little or too much.)

Database and contact management programs are quite powerful, but they generally require time to learn to use. However, such productivity software can assist you enormously by making you more efficient. Given the number of programs on the market, be sure to experiment and read reviews so that you can find the right software program for your needs.

Income and Earning Potential

Projecting your potential income in a CAP business is difficult. First, every claims professional I spoke to mentioned that it took at least half a year to a year to build up his or her business to a level that could even be classified as income. Second, CAPs use four different methods of pricing their service. As a result, the best way to discuss income potential is to evaluate the four basic pricing strategies and extrapolate from there.

FLAT-FEE PRICING   Using the flat-fee method, the claims service simply charges a single annual fee to a client for however many claims that person has during the year. One business, Claims Security of America, charges $250 per year for a single person, $450 per year for a couple, and $550 per year for a family of four, plus a one-time registration fee of $35 to set up the account for an individual or $70 for a family. For these prices, Matoren and his staff will work on as many current claims as a client has. (They also charge additional fees based on a percentage of what they recover for any old claims that they take over and appeal.)

The advantage of this method is that you can obtain your money up front (or in a few installments); the disadvantage is that you could end up with some clients who have far more claims than the average person, and for whom you could spend dozens of hours working while getting a very low payback. In general, claims professionals who use this method told me that they felt it all averaged out, because many people who pay the one-time fee have only a few claims per year.

To illustrate earning potential, Table 3-2 shows what your income might look like over one year with the following assumptions: you are just starting out; and over the course of the year, you get 144 clients joining your

TABLE 3-2

Income Projections for a Claims Service Charging on a Flat Annual Fee Basis

Month	1st	2nd	3rd	4th	5th	6th	7th	8th	9th	10th	11th	12th	Total
Number of Single Clients @ $200 per Year	5	5	5	5	5	5	5	5	5	5	5	5	60
Income	$1000	$1000	$1000	$1000	$1000	$1000	$1000	$1000	$1000	$1000	$1000	$1000	$12,000
Number of Couples @ $350 per Year	4	4	4	4	4	4	4	4	4	4	4	4	48
Income	$1400	$1400	$1400	$1400	$1400	$1400	$1400	$1400	$1400	$1400	$1400	$1400	$16,800
Number of families @ $450 per Year	3	3	3	3	3	3	3	3	3	3	3	3	36
Income	$1350	$1350	$1350	$1350	$1350	$1350	$1350	$1350	$1350	$1350	$1350	$1350	$16,200
Total Number of Clients	12	12	12	12	12	12	12	12	12	12	12	12	144
Plus $35 Registration Fee for Each Client or Family	$420	$420	$420	$420	$420	$420	$420	$420	$420	$420	$420	$420	$5,040
Total Monthly Income	$4170	$4170	$4170	$4170	$4170	$4170	$4170	$4170	$4170	$4170	$4170	$4170	$50,040

service at the hypothetical rate of 5 singles, 4 couples, and 3 families per month. To be conservative vs. the rates charged by Claims Security of America, assume your clients pay $200, $350, and $450 respectively for their annual fees, plus a $35 registration fee.

As you can see, this scenario can lead to more than $50,000 in gross income in a year. Remember though that this is based on an optimistic estimate; it is only a projection and your monthly growth in paying customers may be much lower, depending on how successful your marketing is and the size of your client base. You could end up with only 50 or 75 clients in the first year, rather than 144, and so your earnings would be much lower. This projection also does not account for any expenses, such as marketing, phone service, gas, overhead—which could consume up to 40 percent of your income in that first year. Be sure also to calculate your overhead and direct expenses. If you work from home for a while, you can probably keep your overhead low, spending only a few thousand dollars for brochures, business cards, stationery, and computer supplies, without paying for office space or secretarial help.

HOURLY PRICING   Several of the companies I interviewed tried the flat-fee structure and decided they weren't earning enough for their needs so they switched to an hourly fee basis. As one owner said to me, "I think an hourly fee is more fair to the client, and they know what they are getting." On the other hand, one company thought that charging an hourly fee made the public compare the CAP to an attorney or a tax accountant, but that the CAP didn't deserve to make as much as those professionals.

Nevertheless, in many areas, an hourly fee makes sense. It might be difficult to get people to pay a flat fee up front, because they are not sure whether they want to use you for an entire year. People are often more willing to pay a small amount until they know you can handle their needs.

As you might guess though, there was no uniformity among the hourly fee charged. It depends on location, clientele, and competition. The lowest rate I found was $24 per hour, with $40 being an average rate, and $80 being the highest. Note that even if you charge an hourly rate, you still should always bill in at least 10- or 15-minute increments, just as lawyers or accountants do. This is fair to you because you might spend 15 minutes on a few phone calls and still want to get paid. It is also fair to the client who wouldn't want to pay you for two hours work when you put in only 1.5 hours.

Table 3-3 illustrates one income projection based on billing at $40.00 per hour and starting out very slowly. In this conservative scenario, you bill

TABLE 3-3

Income Projection for a Claims Service Using a $40.00 Hourly Fee

Month	1st	2nd	3rd	4th	5th	6th	7th	8th	9th	10th	11th	12th	Total
Number of Billable Hours per Month @ $40/hour	20	25	30	40	50	60	70	80	90	100	110	120	795 hours
Income	$800	$1000	$1200	$1600	$2000	$2400	$2800	$3200	$3600	$4000	$4400	$4800	$31,800

only 20 hours in your entire first month of operation, then build up your monthly billing hours every consecutive month by adding an additional 5 or 10 hours.

As you can see, even under conservative circumstances, if you build your business slowly over 8 or 10 months, you can still arrive at a reasonable $30,000+ income per year. If you begin your business more quickly, you can easily outpace this projection. Don't forget that handling one claim may not take an hour's work, so in this scenario of 795 billable hours over the course of a year, you actually need several hundred clients to bill at this monthly work rate (and even more to bill at a higher work rate).

THE PERCENTAGE METHOD Few companies use the percentage method, but it was implemented by at least one firm. In this method, you take a percentage of any claim you appeal for your clients. The percentage varied, starting at 10 percent of any reimbursement greater than $300 to 15 percent of any reimbursement less than $300.

Estimating annual income under this method is by far the hardest to do. Without any experience in the field, you have no way of knowing how many claims you might handle, or how much they might be worth. Even with experience, you cannot count on getting claims with high-dollar values. You also need to track your claims in great detail, probably using a computer.

On the other hand, this method probably has the greatest potential earnings. All you need are a few hospital claims, for example, in which you find errors worth $10,000 or more.

As you can see, this method is geared toward handling appeals and counts on finding large errors. This method is often used in a business related to CAP work, hospital bill auditing. See the sidebar on page 183 for more information about this related profession.

Business Profile: Rikki Horne

Rikki Horne got into CAP work from a mixed background as a reference librarian at Northwestern University Medical School and a professional career in marketing for a greeting card company after she got her M.B.A. Never one to sit still, Rikki decided that she wanted to have her own business, but which one?

The answer came providentially. With her own mother sick, Rikki ended up handling all the claims that were generated from the illness. When a friend commented that Rikki was quite gifted in ferreting out the errors on her mother's claims, her business was born. Her company officially started in Chicago in 1983, and her first niche was Medicare patients (because they had to file all their own claims until the 1990 law required doctors to file for them). Rikki also discovered an excellent source of clients: trust departments of banks that supervised the estates of wealthy individuals. Rikki got a couple of big banks in Chicago to give her the claims for these clients.

Rikki eventually moved to Los Angeles, but her clientele was so enamored of her work that they continued using her services, despite the distance. To continue building her business, Rikki made another smart move. She did a direct mailing to all people in a high-income zip code area and one letter fell on wise ears. The recipient was a wealthy individual, who took Rikki's letter to his personal business manager. That manager also turned out to work for a variety of Hollywood celebrities, and soon Rikki was invited to handle the claims and appeals for an assortment of stars. As she told me, "This turned out to be a great pitch letter. From one lead, I ended up with 20 or 30 clients." She also explained why she was hired: "The business managers don't have the expertise to review claims, and they have other priorities. I or my staff go to the agent's office about once a week, or perhaps twice a month. The only problem with this is that confidentiality is an important issue for them; and only recently have they started letting me bring some of the paperwork back to my office."

Since moving to L.A. in the late 1980s, Rikki has built a solid business. She currently has two full-time employees to handle hundreds of clients. Rikki charges by the hour at a rate of $60/ hour; and she bills in 10ths of an hour. She says that most of their work is straightforward bookkeeping; they keep track of payments and make sure that the insurance companies are paying correctly. In addition to her "celebs," she also has other clients, such as retired schoolteachers and middle-class working families.

Rikki agrees that CAP work continues to be needed. She pointed to one area that seems to be growing: appealing denied claims for private nursing at home. Many insurance companies are now refusing to pay for home care, although the policy covers it. The insurers are turning around and claiming that the home care was not "medically necessary." As Rikki says, "There's ways around this. You have to know how to read an insurance policy; there are a lot of gray areas in which a good CAP can help a client."

THE MIXED METHOD   The last pricing structure involves mixing and matching the methods according to your risk tolerance, clientele, location, and needs. You might, for example, charge a lower annual fee for up to 10 claims per person, and then an hourly rate for additional claims. Or you might charge a flat fee for new claims, and an hourly rate or a percentage for old claims that a client brings in when they first sign up.

The mixed method makes predicting your income difficult, and it may confuse clients—especially the elderly—if your fee schedule has too many scenarios. Nevertheless, the mixed method can be a good way to start your business and make people feel that you are offering a special promotion. For example, you might offer a low annual fee for the first year to cover a client's first 10 claims, followed by an additional fee or

Hospital Bill Auditing

A closely related business to CAP work is hospital bill auditing. Many experienced CAPs, such as Harvey Matoren, include hospital bill auditing in their services without any special distinction from doctor bills and EOB auditing, but some people consider hospital bill auditing as more specialized. One reason for this is that hospital bills can be much more complex than bills for outpatient physician services and office visits. Hospital bills may include charges for supplies, equipment, lab tests, doctor's visits, room fees, and an assortment of items that can go on for pages. In addition, most hospital billing is done according to entirely different fee structures than those a CAP sees for physician billing. For example, under Medicare rules, hospitals usually bill according to DRGs (diagnosis-related groups) rather than individual procedures and supplies. A DRG might be compared to a "price fixed menu" in that it includes everything. For instance, rather than billing separately for all procedures and supplies needed for a gall bladder surgery, only one inclusive charge is billed. Medicare implemented DRGs in an effort to curtail excessive billing, and many commercial insurance companies and managed care organizations are now contracting with hospitals to use such grouped fees as well.

It is often stated that hospital bills contain far more errors than standard outpatient physician bills, and that these errors can amount to large sums of money. In *Understanding Your Hospital Bill*, an independent nurse auditor hired by authors Nancy Collins and Jan Sedoris did 1,144 audits of hospital bills between 1992 and 1994. She found 859 bills with overcharges, totaling nearly $900,000. In other words, 75 percent of the bills audited contained errors.

The complexity of hospital billing and the chance for errors explain why some people have taken to specializing in hospital bill auditing. Such entrepreneurs typically seek clients with large hospital bills, such as people who have had surgeries or extended care. Some auditors even obtain contracts with insurance companies and large companies who want to be sure they are not being overcharged for hospital services. In exchange for their auditing services, many hospital bill auditors expect to receive 50 percent of any errors they find that result in a refund.

If you decide to enter the CAP business, you may wish to learn more about this specialized area of hospital bill auditing. One company, Healthcare Data Management, Inc., operated by William Conlan, sells software and a training package for this profession. (A self-running presentation demo of the business opportunity is included in the CD-ROM that accompanies this book. Note: this presentation does not include an actual demonstration of the Windows-based software Mr. Conlan includes in his business opportunity package; be sure to ask him for a copy.) Mr. Conlan can be contacted at 800-859-5119 or 610-341-8608 or at his Web site http://www.healthserve.com. See Appendix B for more information about Healthcare Data Management.

hourly rate or percentage commission for all claims thereafter. Then in the second year of each client's term with your service, you might simplify the rate and offer an hourly fee or annual charge.

Estimating Your Expenses

The start-up costs for becoming a CAP are generally low compared to most businesses. Most CAPs I interviewed began by working out of their home, although some like Rikki Horne and Harvey Matoren eventually moved to a small office in an effort to enhance their credibility and increase their storage space.

Your investment in office equipment (computer, printer, phones) and supplies is fairly minimal, from $2,000 to $5,000 on average, and you might even get by with less if you already have a computer, a furnished home office, and other general business equipment. Your expenses might amount to

Office equipment (computer, printer, software)	$1,500—$3,500
Business cards, letterhead, envelopes	200— 500
Brochure	500— 1,000
Office furniture	600— 1,000
Photocopier	400— 1,000
Phone (including installation)	300— 500
TOTAL	$3,500—$7,500

Deciding If This Is for You

Now that you've reviewed the first part of this chapter about the claims profession in general, you may be ready to decide if this is a business for you. The following checklist will help with your decision or prompt you to think about the conclusions you may have already drawn. Take a moment now to do this 15-question checklist before reading the remainder of the chapter.

- Am I organized, logical, punctilious, attentive, and patient? _____
- Can I track many projects at a time without getting confused or forgetful? _____

- Do I have a business background or medical background that can serve me in this business? _____

- Do I enjoy working with the public? _____

- Do I enjoy office work, filling in paper forms, filing, and managing information? _____

- Do I enjoy or am I willing to spend much of the day inside an office on the phone? _____

- Do I enjoy being a detective and working with numbers and details? _____

- Do I understand or am I willing to learn about health insurance procedures and claims? _____

- Do I find it easy to read a long, legalese document, such as an insurance policy, and understand what it says? _____

- Can I tolerate the bureaucratic snafus and snarls that invariably happen in this business? Will I persist when necessary, such as calling Medicare eight times if I have to help one of my clients? _____

- Am I articulate and able to convince other people to listen to my argument? _____

- Do I feel comfortable disagreeing and negotiating with intimidating people in positions of authority at insurance companies or Medicare? _____

- Do I enjoy marketing, networking, and putting my face out in the public in order to drum up business? _____

- Do I like working with elderly people who may be a large percentage of my clientele? _____

- Are people drawn to me because I give them a feeling that I am trustworthy and confident? _____

If you answered the majority of these questions affirmatively, or if you have any doubts but want to proceed, the next section provides brief guidelines for how to get started in your business. The section is organized according to a sequence of steps you might wish to take: setting up your office; resources for training and learning; tips for pricing your service; marketing your business; and overcoming common start-up problems.

Section II: Getting Started

Setting Up Shop

One of the first items of business in getting started is to make sure you can legally practice as a CAP in your state. Norma Border of NACAP reminds anyone who is contemplating this business that in at least 14 states, a claims assistance professional must be licensed and/or bonded in ways similar to insurance brokers or what are called "public adjusters." These states include

■ Alabama	■ Minnesota
■ Alaska	■ Nebraska
■ Arizona	■ New Hampshire
■ Connecticut	■ New Mexico
■ Florida	■ Oregon
■ Hawaii	■ Rhode Island
■ Kentucky	■ Vermont

This list may change, so Border suggests that you check with your state's insurance commissioner to make sure you are adhering to any licensing requirements that have occurred since the publication of this book.

If your state is one that requires a license, contact your state's insurance commissioner to find out about the appropriate rules and requirements. You may need to take an exam. If so, the commissioner will likely have a manual to help you prepare for the exam, such as the Florida Adjuster's Study Manual that contains general information about health insurance, types of policies, Medicare information, and so on. Even if you don't live in a state that requires an exam, you might ask a friend who lives in an exam state to request a study manual for you. This will improve your general knowledge.

The purpose of licensing is to protect consumers. Claims professionals deal with the public and must be knowledgeable and skilled; they cannot mislead people or unknowingly advise them about insurance matters. As you might guess, such regulations suggest that the states and insurance companies have a great deal of influence over the average consumer of health insurance.

Setting Up Your Office

Most CAPs begin their business in their home, and only over time and with a growing practice do they move into an office. A home office will obviously save you much money in overhead expenses, but you will need to make sure you set up a professional home office where clients can meet you and spend time reviewing their health claims and discussing their needs.

You must carefully evaluate your home office situation. Do you have a separate location away from the rest of your house? Is it soundproof, so that you will be undisturbed by children, pets, and neighborhood noises? Can you make a separate entryway so that clients will not disturb your family? Will people need to climb stairs to get to it (not a good idea if your clients are elderly people)? Do you have a professional-looking desk and comfortable chairs for yourself and your clients? Do you have enough space in this area for at least three people to sit comfortably (many couples may visit you)?

First, consider all of these issues in designing your space, or hire a space planner or an interior designer to help you make the best use of the space you have. Look into the modern office designs that are frequently described in computer and home business magazines, and check out ergonomic furniture at office stores. Furniture products from companies such as Herman Miller and Steelcase have received good reviews for comfort and health. Plan ahead so that your filing systems, in-boxes, and wall charts all work together.

Second, as pointed out earlier in the chapter, it is not an absolute requirement that you computerize your office in this business, but you will greatly enhance your image and your productivity if you have a computer and the right software, such as a contact management program and a time-keeping and invoicing program. The right software will allow you to do your own project management, word processing, and graphic design, saving money on marketing, typesetting, bookkeeping, and other traditional business expenses.

If you intend to purchase a computer, or if you are upgrading the hardware you own, consider the long-term consequences of your purchase. If you can afford it, splurge and buy a high-quality personal computer (Pentium or above) system that gives you faster speeds and more computing power.

If you intend to offer your services at your clients' homes, as Tom and Nancy Koehler do, it is useful to purchase a laptop computer that you can take with you on appointments. This will allow you to take notes and examine your computerized records. A laptop may actually be a worthwhile investment if many of your clients will expect you to come to them.

For software, find a database manager or contact management program that fits your computer experience and budget. Many programs are available in a wide array of prices. Another choice is to use an integrated program that includes word processing, a spreadsheet, and a database, such as *Microsoft Office.*

HARDWARE

- Printer. A laser printer will give you clean, crisp documents that enhance your professional image on letters you write to clients, doctors, and insurance companies. Laser printers can be purchased for very little today and will make the difference in having your company perceived as a professional business.

- Label printer and postage meter. Since you will do extensive correspondence via mail, you might wish to invest in a dedicated label printer, a special narrow gauge printer that handles a long line of stick-on mailing labels. Similarly, a postage meter can be rented for a small amount, saving you many trips to the post office.

- Phone system. Much of your business is done by phone, so spending your money on the best equipment you can buy makes sense. Invest in a business phone that is separate from your family phone; consider also the use of a two- or three-line phone so that you can take more than one business call at a time, rather than using call waiting. If you find yourself spending many hours on the line, get a headphone set to alleviate the strain on your neck and arms.

  Be sure to have a high-quality answering machine or voice mail, so that you never risk losing messages. Finally, you may wish to pay the extra fee to your phone company to categorize your phone calls and organize them on your bills according to phone numbers. This will facilitate tracking your calls if you want to bill your clients for long-distance charges.

- Car phone. With the rapid decrease in the price of a car phone, consider investing in one, particularly if you travel to your clients' homes. You can use the phone to take other calls, do business while you drive, or let clients know you are on the way.

- Modem. You will probably not need a modem, except for logging on to online services and the Internet. Norma Border of NACAP indicates, however, that in the near future claims assistance professionals may be able to access their clients' records through a network or clearinghouse connected with the Medicare carriers, so stay abreast of this situation.

- Photocopier. A personal copier will be a time-saving and valuable investment in this business. In general, you must make copies of anything you mail out to insurance companies and doctors' offices. Keeping good records of your clients' claim forms, receipts, and correspondence is critical to this job, so get the best personal copy machine you can afford.

- Fax machine. Faxes are becoming more and more useful in any business. Some CAPs receive copies of EOBs from their clients by fax, so consider this piece of equipment as a necessary purchase.

Resources and Training

ASSOCIATIONS As indicated earlier, the old NACAP organization folded just as this new edition of this book was going to press. Several former members of NACAP are eagerly working to establish a new organization, which will include individuals who have been practicing CAPs for many years as well as any people new to the industry who are seeking assistance in getting their business off the ground. At this time, CAP Lori Donnelly from Bethlehem, Pennsylvania, is willing to hear from anyone interested in developing a new association for CAPs. As Lori states, "there is a clear need for an organization in this field where members can help each other with difficult cases, exchange information and marketing ideas, and even meet on an annual basis to renew their friendships and professional credentials."

One of the items that a new association might undertake, similar to the old NACAP, is a certification process that provides members with a credential to use in their marketing. The certification shows the public that, as a CAP, you understand the insurance industry and all its details, and that you are qualified to represent clients and handle their claims.

Lori Donnelly can be contacted by e-mail at dbclad@aol.com or by fax at 610-974-8271. She will be pleased to hear from people who are new to the CAP business and would like to participate in developing a new association for professionals. The new association will offer many opportunities for networking, training, and marketing support.

Figure 3-13 Brochures and Newsletters from NACAP

COURSES/TRAINING MATERIALS Here are a few additional ways to prepare for becoming a CAP.

- Contact the Institute of Consulting Careers (ICC) at 800-829-9473. This company publishes an extensive CAP training course developed by CAP Lori Donnelly and myself. The course includes two manuals, two videos, and a diskette. See Appendix B for more information about ICC.

- Contact Harvey Matoren of Claims Security of America. Mr. Matoren provides workshops and seminars to train new CAPs. For information, call 904-733-2525 or 800-400-4066.

- Take a course in medical billing and health insurance in a community college or extension school. Such courses can help you develop some of the background you need in medical coding and various kinds of insurance regulations and policies.

BOOKS To begin, you must have a copy of the current annual edition of the *Medicare Handbook*. This guide is invaluable in helping you understand Medicare's complex policies, the yearly amounts for deductibles and copayments, and the health coverage provided under Parts A and B. The book is updated each year, so be sure to get a current copy from your local Medicare office. You can download the annual *Handbook* from the Medicare Web site: www.hcfa.gov. See Appendix B for more details.

You can also browse a Government Printing Office (GPO) store; there's one located in 21 cities or call the order desk at the Superintendent of Documents in Washington, D.C., at 202-783-3238. The GPO publishes additional information on Medicare as well as on various congressional hearings and laws regarding the insurance industry and other topics of interest to people in the medical professions. Your public library may also have a copy of the GPO Monthly Catalog and GPO Sales Publications Reference File.

For information on medical coding books, contact a medical supply company such as Medicode or go to a medical book store in your area. As indicated in Chapter 2, Medicode sells a full supply of health industry reference books, such as the ICD-9 and CPT coding books, the *Insurance Industry Directory,* the *DRG Guide,* and many other titles. Medicode can be reached at 800-678-TEXT.

GENERAL BUSINESS DEVELOPMENT Many local chapters of the Small Business Administration offer courses on starting a new enterprise, business planning, and marketing. The Service Corps of Retired Executives (SCORE) likewise can prove valuable. When she was starting her new business, CAP Nancy Koehler contacted SCORE and was assigned a mentor who by chance was a former executive with Blue Cross. This helped her gain a strong knowledge of the insurance industry.

For improving your knowledge of marketing, consulting, sales, or running your own business, browse your local bookstores for the latest books on entrepreneuring and running a home-based business. You should definitely read three books from Paul and Sarah Edwards, *Working from Home, The Secrets of Self-Employment,* and *Getting Business to Come to You* (all published by Jeremy P. Tarcher/Putnam). Try also *Selling Your Services* and *How to Promote Your Own Business* by Robert W. Bly (Holt).

If you find yourself with little time to read, I recommend subscribing to a few business magazines and high-quality business newspapers. In this way, you can read shorter articles and still manage to get good information about new software and new business ideas. You may also wish to subscribe to *Medical Economics,* a magazine for the medical profession that covers matters of financial interest to doctors and healthcare providers. The magazine can be reached at 201-358-7200.

Pricing Your Service

You can choose from among four methods to price your service, but you need to consider several factors to determine which method makes the most amount of sense (and cents) for you. Your choice will be influenced by the following:

- *Your clientele.* If you expect to serve a largely elderly population, consider that some may balk at paying a flat fee if they do not know you or your service. They may be more willing to pay an hourly fee. On the other hand, those with many claims may prefer a flat rate, because they will think they are saving money. If you expect to sign up many families and younger couples, you may find that they prefer a fixed rate, because they may not want to pay a high-priced hourly fee.

- *Your competition.* There may be competing services in your area, so do find out how much they charge and by which method. Another agency charging a lower price doesn't prevent you from charging whatever you want, but it is usually difficult to price higher than competitors because consumers today are price sensitive. You should also give some thought to future competitors. If you start at a high price and a competitor opens up a few months after you, you need to protect your territory.

- *Your locale.* Major metropolitan areas may tolerate a $300 per year annual fee or $60 per hour, but many other areas with a lower cost of living will force you to charge much lower annual or hourly fees. If you intend to charge an hourly fee, it helps to know the going rate for similar professionals in your area, such as accountants.

- *Your reputation and experience.* It may be difficult charging $60 per hour if you have little experience in this field, but if you have a background in the insurance industry, many people will think you are a professional and would be willing to pay your fees. On the other hand, if you have very little experience, you do not want to be in the position of defending your fees if a client wonders why it took you three hours to do something that an experienced person would have accomplished in one hour.

- *Your cash flow needs.* Some people have to start out using borrowed money to finance their venture. If that is true for you, the annual membership fee method allows you to bring in large amounts of money more quickly to pay back your debt. However, you need to remember that once you receive up-front money from clients, you must spend a year working on their claims without further payment for your time. As the months go by, you must remain as courteous and helpful to those clients as you are to new ones.

- *Your other policies.* Are you going to charge for phone calls, postage, or mileage? In determining your pricing, don't forget to allocate enough to cover your direct expenses per client. If you intend to charge $25.00 per hour, you may want to see if you can get $28 or $30 to be sure you cover your expenses.

- *Your projected number of clients and claims.* You may believe that your area has great potential and that given your contacts and reputation, you will be able to bring in many clients quickly. If so, you might want to charge on a percentage basis, since this method is by far the most lucrative.

- *Your perception of value.* You have probably heard that when you charge too little, many people don't think you're offering a service of value. This suggests that it is important to be careful that you don't underprice your service.

In sum, your best plan of action is to spend some time with a spreadsheet and calculate a number of different scenarios. Compare and contrast your income opportunity using the flat-fee method, an hourly method, and the percentage method. Be as specific as possible: have your plan estimate income for each week of your first year, showing your growth in clients multiplied by billable hours, annual fees, or percentage. Then examine which method maximizes your income while offering the most reasonable pricing terms for your location, competition, clientele, and reputation/experience. If you find that you can earn the most with an annual fee, you may nevertheless need to operate on an hourly basis if a sizable portion of your potential clients would balk at paying you $200 to $400 all at once. (Note that offering clients the choice of paying an annual fee on a monthly basis through their credit card is often more acceptable to them.)

Whichever pricing method you choose, the CAPs I interviewed suggest that you also charge a registration fee in the first year for each client. It takes time to set up accounts, call insurance companies to obtain information about policies, set up files, and take care of all the initial prep work. Many CAPs charge from $30 to $50 as a registration fee.

In addition, consider if you are going to offer other services, such as those performed by Nancy and Tom Koehler of In Home Medical Claims, who pay bills for their clients, keep financial records, and make appointments with attorneys and accountants for their elderly clients during tax season. If so, you need to either add a surcharge to your annual fee or choose to go by the hourly method. Above all, keep your pricing simple and clear so that your clients can understand what they are paying for.

Finally, consider the reality of this business that many CAPs remark on: whichever pricing method you use, you need to account for losing some number of clients each year. People do die, and if you have an elderly clientele, you might lose from 5 percent to 10 percent or more of your clients each year.

Marketing Tips

The biggest challenge facing CAPs is to let the public know about the business. Your start-up efforts must be directed at informing the public about both the profession in general and your new business in particular. Most Americans still don't believe that they need a professional to help them with their health insurance, because they don't realize that so many errors are made. As Norma Border of NACAP phrased it,

> People with no acute or chronic illness don't need a CAP, but as soon as you have a chronic illness or a traumatic incident such as an accident, consumers need a CAP to make sure they get full coverage. People also don't

realize that many insurance programs have been upgraded, such that their insurance may cover specialized services they didn't know about. That's the value of using a CAP.

If you intend to operate your claims service full time, remember that this is business in which the size of your customer base is critical. Unlike an accountant or attorney who might have some clients from whom they can earn tremendous amounts of money, you will need many clients to generate enough income. Your goal is growth; you need to increase your client base and never let up. Most claims professionals have 200, 300, or more clients, and some serve over 1,000 clients coast to coast. If your marketing is so successful that you get too many clients to handle yourself, hire an employee to do the filing, typing, invoicing, and other administrative tasks, or find a partner to share in both CAP work and the perpetual marketing.

Nearly every CAP agrees that this business can be slow to start. You therefore need to be prepared for a few months of intensive marketing. The following guidelines address what you can do to respond to your challenges.

KNOW YOUR MARKET   Get the demographic data on the area in which you intend to conduct your business. Know how many citizens in each age group and sex there are, where they live, and what their income levels are. After all, you are a service business catering to the general public, so being sure you know your clientele is vital. It helps to live in an area with a heavy concentration of elderly people, mixed with professional families with two working spouses and working singles.

USE WORD-OF-MOUTH POWER   Word of mouth is by far the most important marketing method in this business. Because people are putting their faith in your service, you want customers who can trust you with their personal medical information and financial situation and will then refer you to others. Just as people frequently obtain their accountant, tax preparer, or attorney based on recommendations from others, you want to have clients who can recommend the quality of your work to others.

Begin by making a contact tree of everyone you know: friends, relatives, former colleagues, employers, neighbors, and so on. Send everyone of them a flier with a personal note to make sure they know you are now in the CAP business. Ask them to sign up with you for a year, and to tell their friends about you. If every client generates 10 leads for you, you could move from zero to 100 clients in just a few months. The sidebar on Fitzgibbons & Associates illustrates the power of word-of-mouth.

Business Profile: Mary Ellen Fitzgibbons

Mary Ellen Fitzgibbons of Fitzgibbons & Associates runs her claims practice about 20 hours a week, without doing a shred of marketing. Each and every one of her clients comes to her through word of mouth. Some of her clients are elderly people who have seen Mary Ellen save them thousands of dollars and so refer their friends to her. Other clients come from Mary Ellen's own friends. She even once had an attorney who heard of her and subcontracted to her for a problematic case he was handling. As Mary Ellen says, "I am not just a claims submitter: I am a heath claims management service. Clients send me their paperwork, and I clean up all the problems they have had."

Mary Ellen got into the business from a varied background that included working in the personnel department of a major food manufacturer, a nursing degree with experience in a hospital, and working as an insurance administrator for a consulting company where she monitored insurance claims to protect the retired employees of the company. She says,

> This job demands toughness and negotiation skills. Sometime people at the insurance companies tell you, "Oh this is not possible," so you need to ask to speak to the manager or someone higher up in the organization. Otherwise you can't get the job done. Trust is also really essential. You want people to know how you do the job, so that they trust you and don't think you're a maverick.

Mary Ellen believes that her success speaks for itself. She adds, "I've never had a case where I didn't find a mistake, and in a few cases, I've found mistakes as high as $40,000."

USE FLYERS AND BROCHURES To get your information to the public, don't be surprised by the recommendation that you print 5,000, 10,000, even 20,000 one-sided, one-page flyers to put in stores or on cars in parking lots or even going door to door in high-density neighborhoods. Keep the flyers simple, clear, and to the point, focusing on the benefits you can provide. Include wording that shows how anyone can gain from your services, not just elderly or people with health problems. To heighten the effect of the flyer, get an artist to do a small illustration that dramatizes the issue, such as showing a concerned looking couple eyeing their doctor's bill, or a perplexed looking person with a stack of bills next to him. Quote testimonials from some of your clients indicating how much money, stress, and time you saved them. In your flier, offer a promotion, such as a free consultation, and include your business phone number.

Regarding brochures, you may wish to print 500 to 1,000 copies of a trial brochure because these are more expensive. Choose a high-quality paper stock and print in two colors. To increase its power, hire a designer to work on the brochure with you, or use your laser printer and desktop publishing program to design one yourself. This brochure should be an $8\frac{1}{2} \times 11$ sheet of paper, single or double folded to end up with four or six surfaces on which to present your message. The folds add drama to the brochure. Figure 3-14 shows the brochures used by Claims Security of America (Harvey Matoren), In Home Medical Claims (Tom and Nancy Koehler), and a brochure produced by NACAP that you can purchase and customize with your business name. You might make one page of your brochure into a business reply return card that the reader can mail back to you for more information, as does the brochure from Claims Security of America in which the righthand fold is a perforated tear-off card. Give out your brochures wisely, because they are expensive. Bring them with you to meetings and public speaking engagements or put them into stores, such as pharmacies, that agree to let you exhibit them.

OFFER A PROMOTION   When you are just starting out, consider offering a promotion to induce people to join your service. Everyone likes to feel that he or she is getting a good bargain, so offer 10 percent to 15 percent off the first year's fees if you charge on the annual basis, or one hour of free claims consulting if you charge on an hourly basis. The key is get people to call you, giving you an opportunity to explain how much you can help them so you can close the sale. Once they sign on with you, you have a good chance that they will become repeat business over the years. In a service business, especially when people don't think they need your service, a promotion is often the single most powerful draw to get people to make up their minds.

GET PUBLICITY   Make your goal the following: each month or week, inform thousands of potential clients about your business. You can try to get publicity in local newspapers, community bulletin boards, cable television, local radio shows—wherever you can find it. You are performing an intriguing service and many reporters and radio show hosts would love to have you relate some of your most interesting successes for the public. After all, consumers always enjoy a moralistic victory in which the little guy defeats the corporate giant and proves that persistence pays off. Once you get a story into the media, you can use copies of it in a press kit to generate more interviews with other writers or shows.

USE SELECTIVE ADVERTISING   Most CAPs I interviewed indicated that display advertising did not help them get clients. Although some

Figure 3-14   Examples of brochures for a CAP business

CAPs advertise in the Yellow Pages, most people aren't aware that they can look up this profession in the phone book. The ads in newspapers are usually too expensive for the results they generate. Spending a few hundred or thousand dollars for a week-long advertisement that brings you only one or two customers is money wasted.

The most successful ads were those in media targeted to the elderly, such as local community newspapers. CAP Lori Donnelly found that advertising on the placemats at a popular restaurant that is frequented by seniors was effective for her.

DIRECT MAIL Direct mail is not generally used by CAPs, although Rikki Horne had tremendous success using a targeted direct mail piece to residents in a high-class zip code area (Beverly Hills, California). Her direct mail paid off because one of the recipients showed it to a business manager for celebrities, and that manager hired her to handle the claims for all his clients.

You may wish to experiment with a short mailing list of targeted individuals in a certain area of your town, or of a certain age range or income bracket. Another option is "card decks," groups of small direct response cards you receive in the mail. In many communities, you can find publishers of these card decks or coupon books whose prices may allow you to try a few test ads.

NETWORKING While many people believe that networking is glad-handing or being immodest about themselves, it is really a highly appropriate and successful way to get business. At any meeting you attend, let people know what you do. You will be surprised at how many people respond with a horror story about a relative or friend who just experienced difficulty with a claim. Remember, errors and mistakes on claims happen far more than you might think. Be sure to bring your business cards to such meetings.

Look also to meet other people in the health professions: nurses, home care agency staffs, nursing registry members, and hospital and retirement home personnel. Each of these contacts may be able to refer business directly to you, or at least refer you to other people who can help you find customers. Some hospitals have volunteers who provide advice about claims to patients, but these people cannot handle complex or difficult claims. If you can befriend the staff at a local hospital, you may find yourself with plenty of referrals.

Another venue for networking are accountants, lawyers, and corporate executives in your area who understand that their clients or their company may not be getting the best treatment from an insurance carrier. You may find that you can get yourself hired to work on claims for their clients or employees on a contract basis to be sure that both the firm and the individuals get the proper reimbursements on their medical policies. Several CAPs spoke to me about getting contracts from the trust department at banks to handle the claims for their customers.

PUBLIC SPEAKING As part of your informational campaign, an important aspect of your marketing is to conduct workshops about the business. Find opportunities to speak to groups, associations, or boards containing senior citizens. Go to senior centers, retirement living homes, and community centers where you can offer to give a talk about the health insurance industry, Medicare, and errors on medical claims. Use any previous expertise you have to develop an interesting, informative talk that people will enjoy. Try out different approaches to see which works best, such as a professional and serious title such as "Maximizing Your Returns on Health Insurance" or a controversial approach such as "Are You Being Cheated by Your Insurance Company?"

Be sure that any time you speak to a group, you are allowed to hand out your brochures or leave them for people on a back table.

Overcoming Common Start-Up Problems

Although a medical claims business is a great entrepreneurial opportunity for people who have the right mix of personal experience, medical and business knowledge, and a love for this kind of work, take the advice of those already in the business, "It takes time to build the business." You will encounter start-up problems, from getting clients, to developing the right contacts at insurance companies, to figuring out your fees.

This is one reason why for some people, it is wise to start this business as only a part-time venture initially. Without leaving the security of your paycheck, you can learn the ropes of the business and move cautiously to build up a clientele through word of mouth and networking. Remember that this business depends on being available during the day to see clients and especially to make phone calls, so avoid having your other job interfere with your ability to follow such a schedule.

Here are a few additional guidelines on common start-up problems.

NOT ENOUGH CLIENTS Determine why you may not have enough clients, or fewer than you expected. Are you spending enough time marketing (60 percent or more in the beginning of a new business)? When you tell people what you do, are they aware of your business? Are you generating leads but not closing them? Do you have competition from another business that is doing well?

Each one of these reasons calls for a different response. If you are spending only a few hours per week marketing, you probably need to get out and generate more leads. Get your publicity campaign in gear; print up more flyers and distribute them in new locations; give some talks to a few groups and get feedback on how you present. If after some publicity in your area, you find that people are still not aware of your business, you need to continue educating the public about your service. Step up your publicity campaign, and do more networking. If you are getting people to call you but they don't sign, examine your communication style and sales pitch to see if you are alienating them. Are your prices too steep for your area? If you have a competitor who is doing well, you probably need to change something in your pricing or service.

CASH FLOW   If you feel you cannot change your price, perhaps you can offer more services, such as in-home assistance on paying bills, organizing, and errands. Your own organized personality could prove useful to your clients. More services mean more money for you.

In addition, consider running a medical billing service because it taps into the same background and skills as being a CAP. Lori Donnelly of Donnelly Benefits Consulting offers both services to maximize her expertise and her cash flow.

FEW REFERRALS   People often don't know whether a business wants referrals, or they don't stop to think about it. It is perfectly acceptable to let people know that you appreciate any referrals they can make for you, without badgering them. Most services provide a "reward" for referrals, such as a discount on next year's fees or a free one-time consultation. You might even print on your flyer or business card something like "We appreciate your referring us to your friends" and mention what you will offer in return for the courtesy.

Building Your Business

Developing an ongoing CAP business is done client by client. Few businesses get off the ground without hard work, overtime hours, and tight times. But as every CAP confirmed, you need not worry about the future of this profession. Unfortunately, it appears that America will always have a need for claims professionals, even if we move to a national healthcare system. Our country's medical preferences seem to demand flexibility and choice in healthcare providers and insurance policies—both of which mean that we will continue to have a confused, even chaotic claims system in which mistakes are inevitable.

4

Medical Transcription Services

A medical transcription service may seem easy to describe. A transcriptionist types up dictated reports and documents for healthcare professionals of all kinds (including doctors, nurses, counselors, physical therapists, and psychologists). The transcribed reports are then stored either in the patient files of private physicians or in hospital medical records departments.

Although this simple definition captures the essence of the job, it only scratches the surface in portraying the importance and value that medical transcriptionists play in our healthcare system. Medical transcription is actually a vital occupation that is highly underrated and in great demand. The shortage of transcriptionists is one reason some American hospitals send their transcription work overseas (another reason is to take advantage of inexpensive labor). Nevertheless, the demand for new transcriptionists is predicted to remain high. In fact, the Bureau of Labor projected a 51 percent increase in the need for medical transcriptionists by the year 2000.

In this chapter, I'll cover the complex skills that are needed to become a medical transcriptionist, the day-to-day work issues faced by people in the profession, and the best methods by which you can enter the business. You will read about the emerging digital technology that is changing the profession. By the end of the chapter, you will have a clear idea of the advantages and disadvantages of this profession, and how you can enter this career if you decide it is for you.

Section I: Background

What a Medical Transcriptionist Does

Each day, healthcare providers in hospitals, clinics, and private offices dictate literally tens of thousands of reports about their patients that range from a few paragraphs to a dozen pages. Dictations must be done for every hospitalization admission or discharge (more than 30 million each year), for every physical exam or radiological study, for every surgical operation performed, and for dozens of other procedures. Dictations include why the patient was seen, what examinations and procedures the healthcare provider performed, and the provider's diagnosis and recommended treatment. These dictations are useless unless they are transcribed into documents that can be read by any physician who might see the patient at a later stage. Dictations may be permanently filed in a patient's private record at the physician's office, or they may be sent to an insurance company or be stored in the hospital's medical records department.

The medical transcriptionist is thus the link between the healthcare provider and the printed report. It is estimated that medical transcriptionists transcribe billions of lines of dictations each year. Table 4-1 lists the numbers and types of operations performed in the United States in a typical year, just one indication of the number of transcriptions that are made. (Note: the table reflects 1991 data, the latest available because of the time lag in collecting information and preparing it for publication.)

Transcriptions are actually medical-legal documents and are important for many reasons:

- They become part of the medical history for a patient who may later need continued treatment.
- They are an important source of information for any healthcare provider to whom the patient may be referred for additional treatment.

- They are increasingly required in managed care settings, where primary physicians control patient treatment and must obtain approvals for patients to see specialists. The specialists must also send their reports back to primary care physicians and managed care boards.
- They are frequently required for the payment of insurance claims, because Medicare and commercial insurance companies need to verify procedures and may sometimes dispute fees.
- Statistical information from medical reports is critical in medical research to track diseases and provide clues in understanding symptoms and illnesses.
- Medical reports are often required by lawyers and insurance companies whenever litigation occurs between two parties following an accident, a work injury, a crime, or a medical malpractice case.
- Reports are required in many states for Medicaid and other state-funded health insurance programs.

The role of medical transcriptionists throughout the country is thus pivotal in our healthcare system. Without high-quality transcription, reports can be inaccurate, leading to poor decisions by an attending physician or to an unfair settlement in an insurance dispute. Transcriptionists are the major link between healthcare providers and hospitals and insurance companies, effectively protecting everyone involved from mistakes, lost money, and even the loss of life.

In the past, transcriptionists have been perceived as being glorified typists, but today more and more transcriptionists are taking up the banner and fighting for increased respect and pay. As Linda C. Campbell, CMT, Director of Product Development for Health Professions Institute, told me, "Transcription is moving to the forefront; the need has always been there, but people's awareness of it is finally increasing." Like court reporters, transcriptionists perceive themselves as "language" specialists, not as typists, and today they are aggressively fighting to have the medical community recognize this distinction. For support, they point to a significant factor behind their work: transcriptionists must have a broad education and knowledge of medical terminology and procedures. Transcription work requires highly specialized education and preparation. In short, medical transcriptionists should be considered professionals.

Most people don't examine the training required to understand the typical physician's report. Stop for a moment and think what it takes to transcribe the words of a cardiologist who has performed an operation, or

TABLE 4-1

Procedures Undergone by Patients Discharged from Short-Stay Hospitals by Sex and Age (1991) (numbers in thousands)

Procedure	Sex			Age			
	Total	**Male**	**Female**	**Under 15**	**15—44**	**45—64**	**over 65**
All procedures	43,922	17,264	26,658	2,235	17,090	9,524	15,073
Operations on the nervous system	970	500	470	236	328	196	210
On the endocrine system	103	28	75	NA	41	22	25
On the eye	399	189	210	25	65	85	224
On the ear	129	75	54	66	36	15	13
On the respiratory system	956	561	396	60	173	290	433
On the cardiovascular system	4,123	2,383	1,740	148	477	176	2,022
On the hemic and lymphatic systems	392	212	180	20	77	110	185
On the digestive system	5,559	2,319	3,241	221	1,571	1,400	2,367
On the urinary system	1,558	884	674	47	376	386	750
On the male genital organs	584	584	NA	46	40	116	382
On the female genital organs	2,308	NA	2,308	8	1,624	445	231
Obstetrical procedures	6,867	NA	6,867	24	6,839	NA	NA
On the musculo-skeletal system	3,323	1,710	1,614	208	1,323	798	994
On the integumentary system	1,324	552	773	75	488	330	431

Note: Details may not add to total due to rounding.

Source: National Center for Health Statistics, Advance Data (reported in 1993).

the medical text of a doctor involved in a worker's compensation case in which the patient was paralyzed, or the autopsy report of a coroner. For instance, get someone right now to read the following passage aloud to you, while you close your eyes, and imagine yourself hearing the text dictated by a Pakistani doctor who is eating lunch as he talks rapidly:

Procedure in Detail: With the patient in the dorsal supine position, a thorough prep and drape of the face and neck was done. The vibrissae were shaved, the nose infiltrated with 0.75percent Marcaine with 1:100,000 adrenaline and the airways were packed with cotton moistened with 4 percent cocaine.

Initial incision in the patient's left nasal sill. The entire face was draped with a sterile plastic sheet with gauze over the eyes to protect the eyelashes. A sterile 4 × 4 was placed over the exposed parts to protect my gloves from touching the skin.

The initial incision was made in the patient's left nasal sill and carried anteriorly along the columella for 4—5 mm. A Joseph elevator was used to dissect tissue away from the nasal spine going laterally past the alar facial grooves bilaterally. A Cottle periosteal elevator was then used to make certain all soft tissues were dissected away from the site. A 3-mm roll of Marlex mesh saturated with Ancef was placed in the pocket, making certain that the marked center of the implant was over the maxillary spine....

Well, that should suffice for now (and that wasn't even the good part!). If you can imagine yourself listening to such dictations on tape, then you know what it would be like to be a medical transcriptionist. If, however, you feel turned off by this poetic passage, this may not be the profession for you.

Note though that there are many types of dictations, just as there are many kinds of physicians. Some dictation is clearly harder than others, and there is a major difference between hospital and office medical dictation. Some transcriptionists handle office work that is typically focused on physical exams, consultations, and referral letters, while others do transcription for hospitals that requires a much deeper knowledge of surgery, radiology, and various medical specialties.

In general, medical transcriptionists must have the skills and experience commensurate with the tasks. They must know at least several of the following subject areas, depending on their area of specialization: anatomy, physiology, biology, chemistry, pharmacology, psychology, neurology, cardiology, pediatrics, surgical procedures, and medical technology. They also must know the special formats used for transcribing medical reports so that headings stand out and readers can find information easily. They must know correct English grammar, punctuation, and patterns of capitalization and abbreviation. And finally, they must be able to type fast enough to make it worth their own time, if not their employer's (usually 60 to 80 words per minute or higher). We'll look at these requirements in more detail shortly.

Let's turn our attention now to the nitty-gritty truth behind medical transcription: what does a medical transcriptionist do while on the job, and how does he or she cope with the pressures of the work?

Transcriptionists' Work Styles

A transcriptionist might have three different work styles:

1. *Employee.* Many transcriptionists are employed by hospitals, clinics, or managed care facilities, where they work onsite transcribing dictations from the many practitioners in the facility. Transcriptionists are also employed by large transcription services that obtain contracts from hospitals and private physicians to do transcription for them; such transcriptionists work onsite at the service.

2. *Telecommuters.* In recent years, communications technology has allowed many hospitals and healthcare facilities to take advantage of using off-site transcriptionists rather than requiring them to come in and take up office space. Telecommuting transcriptionists are still employees, but they have the flexibility to work from their own homes.

3. *Independent.* This is perhaps the fastest growing segment of transcriptionists, those who are independent and may be home based or work out of an office. One reason for the growth of independent transcriptionists is the downsizing of many hospitals and even services. Staff transcriptionists have been laid off because of the savings achieved by outsourcing the work to independent contractors. The independent home-based transcriptionist is self-employed and has the flexibility to choose his or her own schedule and clients.

In general, telecommuting and independent transcriptionists may work in any of three ways:

1. They may pick up cassettes from hospitals and private medical offices and do the work at home.

2. Doctors may call them directly and dictate over the phone into specialized dictation/transcription machines located in their office or home.

3. They may call a recording station located at a hospital, service, or private office into which physicians have dictated; once they are connected to this central "server," they may transcribe while listening to the dictation over the phone line, or they may have specialized equipment that downloads the dictations into their home-based transcriber or computer.

We'll examine more details about the technologies for each of these arrangements later.

Note: this chapter is oriented toward describing the independent tran-scriptionist, although most of the information also pertains to telecom-muters.

The Types of Transcription

The type of work performed by transcriptionists depends greatly on whether they are doing hospital or doctor's office transcription. Each set-ting generates its own types of reports, and there are many distinctions among them.

Hospital transcription includes the following types of reports:

The Basic Four

History and Physical Report (H&P)

Consultation Report

Operative Report

Discharge Summary

Specializations

Medical Imaging Report

Pathology Report

Radiology Report

Electroencephalograms (EEG)

Electrocardiograms (EKG or ECG)

Autopsy Report

Labor and Delivery Notes (L&D)

Death Summary

Rehabilitation Notes

Emergency Room Notes (ER)

Psychological Report

Social Services Report

Transcriptionists must learn the format for each of these types of reports. The four basic reports generally adhere to a certain format with specific headings, subheadings, and styles for body text. The standardization of medical reports is actually fairly recent and is partially due to an agreement among several industry organizations, including the Joint Commission for Accreditation of Healthcare Organizations (JCAHO), to require physicians to include specific content in each type of report. Transcriptionists must therefore be familiar with these formats and be able to recognize them when heard on a dictation. Note that even with standardization, there are still variances in reporting formats from hospital to hospital, as each health information manager (formerly called medical records director) has his or her own preferences.

Medical office transcription formatting is different from hospital formatting. Medical offices more commonly follow one format for "chart notes" and another for consultations and referral letters. Chart notes usually appear in paragraph form, with the patient's name and date at the top. The most common chart note style is called SOAP:

- **S**—Subjective—the patient's complaint
- **O**—Objective—the physician's findings
- **A**—Assessment—the diagnosis
- **P**—Plan—the goals and direction of the treatment

Another common chart style is called HPIP.

- **H**—History
- **P**—Physical exam
- **I**—Impression
- **P**—Plan

Some physicians merge the two formats and dictate chart notes in the following form: Subject, History, Impression, Plan. Similarly, letters often follow a specific organization and content. Chart notes may be typed in standard block form or modified block form just as business letters. Whichever format is used, each physician usually has a preference that he or she wants a transcriptionist to follow.

Figures 4-1 and 4-2 illustrate two types of reports. Figure 4-1 shows an operative report; note the headings on the sides that have become standard in this type of report. Figure 4-2 shows a letter format from a specialist physician to a patient's primary care physician.

▬ ▬ ▬ ▬
Figure 4-1
Transcription of an
Operative Report.
(Courtesy of
Joan Walston,
Words Times 3
Medical Transcription,
Santa Monica, CA)

XXXXXXXXX AMBULATORY SURGERY CENTER
XXXXXXXXXXXXXXXXXXXXXXXXXXXXX SUITE XXXX
XXXXXXXXXXXXX, CA. 90034

PATIENT NAME: xxxxxxxx xxxxxxx   **MEDICAL RECORD: #xxxx**

DATE Of SURGERY: xx-xx-9x   **SURGEON: xxxxxxx xxxxx, M.D.**

ANESTHESIOLOGIST: xxxxxxxxxxx, M.D.

OPERATIVE REPORT

PREOPERATIVE DIAGNOSIS: Stenosing tenosynovitis, right thumb.

POSTOPERATIVE DIAGNOSIS: Same.

PROCEDURE: Release of flexor tendon sheath, right thumb.

PROCEDURE IN DETAIL: Under 2% Nescacaine, a local infiltration anethesia,
augmented by intravenous sedation, the right upper
extremity was prepped and draped in the usual fashion. The operation was done under
tourniquet control and using 3.5 power loupe magnification. A V-shaped incision was made
at the volar base of the right thumb. Dissection was carried down to the underlying flexor
tendon sheath. Bilateral digital nerves were carefully identified and preserved. The A1
pulley appeared stenotic and thickened. The patient had reproducible clicking on active
flexion. The A1 pulley was then incised longitudinally and this allowed free and
unencumbered excursion of the flexor tendon. The wound was irrigated and closed with
nylon sutures.

Dictated: xx/cms
Date Dictated: xx-xx-9x
Transcribed: xx-xx-9x

_____

xxxxxxxxxxxxxxx, M.D.

The Technology of Transcription

We discussed earlier that transcriptionists may work in any of three styles:
picking up tapes, having doctors call their home or office directly, or calling a central server from which they listen to the dictations or download
them to their own units at home. The way in which you work thus
depends extensively on the technology you have.

There are currently two technologies behind medical dictation and
transcription—analog cassette tapes and digital computer-based technology. As you might imagine, digital technology is quickly gaining ground
and will likely change the profession entirely over the next few years. Let's
examine each one.

Figure 4-2
Transcription of a
physician to
physician letter.
(Courtesy of Rochelle
Wexler, Medical
Transcription Service,
New York, NY)

xxxxxx, 199x

xxxxxx xxxxxxx M.D.
xxxxxxx Street
xxxxxxx, NY xxxxxxx

Re: xxxxxx   xxxxxxxx

Dear Dr. xxxxxxx:

Thank you for allowing me to once again see your patient, Ms. xxxxxx xxxxxx.

xxxxxx is a 55-year old woman with stage 0 CLL. I initially saw Ms. xxxx in 199x. Since that juncture, you have been following her. She has remained well with no evidence of infection, bleeding, pulmonary or skin manifestations nor adenopathy. On history, her review of systems is negative.

Physical examination reveals a blood pressure 140/88 mm Hg. There are no palpable nodes. Her chest is clear, her cardiac exam is normal. There is no palpable hepatosplenomegaly. Similarly, there is no skin infiltration nor neurological disease. On repeat CBC, her hemoglobin is 13.6 with a hemocrit of 40. Her white count is 73,000 of which 80% are lymphocytes which are mature in appearance. Her platelet count is 217,000. Her immunoelectrophoresis reveals a decreased IgM at 49, but otherwise is normal. Her LDH is not elevated, and her SMA-20 is normal except for a cholesterol of 291.

I believe that Ms. xxxxxxx is still "stage 0." Although the white count has increased over the three-year period, I do not at this point feel it indicates the need for therapy. I would ask that her hemotologic parameters be repeated when you see her. Hopefully, this would be in periods of roughly four months. I would be interested in discussing with you your hemotological findings.

Thank you once again for allowing me to participate in her care.

Sincerely,

xxxxxxxx xxxxxx, M.D., P.C.

THE OLD WORLD: ANALOG TAPES Cassette tapes are the basic technology that has dominated the medical transcription profession for decades. In general, cassette tapes are used as follows: doctors dictate into handheld cassette recorders or into desktop recording units that look like specialized telephones with microphones rather than a handset. Either of these dictation devices may use standard size or microcassettes. A transcriptionist then picks up the tapes—or perhaps a messenger service delivers them. The transcriptionist uses a machine called a transcriber that allows him or her to play the tape using a foot pedal that controls the speed of the play and the direction. The transcriptionist can advance the tape and type or rewind it if he or she needs to review a passage. When the transcriptionist is done, he or she must then return the hard copy of the dictation along with the original tapes to the physician.

In the 1970s and early 1980s, advances in communications equipment and tape technology led to further options. Both in hospital settings and medical offices, better phone systems and dictating units came on the market that allowed physicians to forgo a dictating unit in his or her office. Instead, the doctor could call an offsite transcriptionist from any phone. Using the phone keypad, he or she could control the tape for rewinding, reviewing, and re-recording the dictation as needed. These improvements in equipment greatly boosted offsite transcription services, but they also increased opportunities for telecommuting and home-based transcriptionists who likewise could now receive dictations called in directly to their offices without having to run around picking up cassettes.

Tape technology still largely dominates the medical transcription field, and new tape-based products continue to improve the equipment to this day. Companies such as Dictaphone and Lanier still produce tape-based dictation and transcribing equipment for use in hospital settings and offsite locations such as offsite transcription services and small- and home-based businesses. Today's best tape machines have multiple input ports and cassette trays that allow several physicians to call in and dictate simultaneously—while a transcriptionist can be playing another cassette and transcribing. The newest tape-based machines also include many sophisticated features, such as the ability to remove tapes without losing one's place and inserting another tape that contains priority work; voice-activated motion so that there is less wasted tape (the tape will stop moving when the physician is thinking rather than dictating); and LCD displays that show the amount of work contained on a cassette.

One reason that tape technology continues to lead is the sheer number of tape-based machines already in the field. Another reason is that many physicians still prefer to dictate into their own handheld dictation recorders or desktop units. The price range for sophisticated multiport tape systems is also within the budget of most small and home-based businesses that encourage physicians to call them directly.

However, tape technology has certain drawbacks. Despite the improvements, it is awkward and time-consuming to find a specific location on a tape. When the doctor or transcriber is searching for a specific text, the tape must be physically advanced or rewound. Second, tapes have a limited recording capacity (usually 60 or 90 minutes), so they must be watched and changed just before they run out of recording space. Finally, tapes can suffer from deterioration in voice quality, or become damaged, or worse, get lost.

THE NEW WORLD OF DIGITAL TECHNOLOGY Beginning in the early 1980s, the birth of digital technology began to revolutionize the transcription business. Digital technology allows dictation to be done directly onto a magnetic disk (just like the hard disk of your computer). As the physician dictates, special voice software samples the sound at rapid intervals and stores the data as series of 0s and 1s (bytes) just as your software stores your word-processed documents or spreadsheet data.

The advantages of digital technology are especially applicable to medical transcription, since there are no tapes to change and no unreasonable limits on length of time recordings can go on, and a passage of text can be found very quickly (called random access). This makes dictating easier, because the doctor can quickly go back and revise a dictation, or insert new text, or jump ahead to another passage.

Digital technology also makes the transcriptionist's job easier. First, the displays on digital transcribers are like telephone LCD displays that automatically capture the "demographic" data on a recording, such as patient's name, date, priority rating, and so on. This makes identifying the passage much easier for transcriptionists. Second, the transcriptionist can use the random access feature to move through a dictation, quickly advancing or going back to passages as necessary. Finally, the quality of digitized voice is generally better than the analog recording found on tapes. Digital technology also allows passages to be speeded up without distortion, so that fast typists can plow through a dictation faster than it was recorded.

Digital technology was very expensive when it first came out, so it was mostly purchased by large hospitals and services that had thousands of reports to transcribe each day. Physicians were able to call a central server and dictate their reports over the phone right from their offices or from workstations on the hospital floors, assured that their voices were accurately recorded digitally. When their dictations were finished, either an *onsite* transcriptionist would then log onto the server with a transcribing unit to do the work, or an *offsite* transcriptionist would call the central server and transcribe the dictations while listening over the phone lines. In general, the offsite transcriptionist also needed special equipment to control the playback—fast/slow, advance/rewind—so that the transcription could be properly done. This equipment was often a proprietary desktop unit specifically coordinated with the digital machine at the hospital or a special phone with a foot pedal.

New technology, however, never seems to solve all problems at once. Despite the significant improvements digital technology offered, some glitches and drawbacks remained. The principal one was the cost of communications to get the digital documents. Offsite transcriptionists who called in to retrieve dictations needed to spend hours on the phone listening to the dictations and transcribing them. Because it can take up to four times as long to transcribe a dictation than to record it, offsite transcriptionists who lived far away either could not be used or would incur huge phone bills!

One way to avoid the high cost of phone charges for dial-up transcription was to "re-record" the digital dictations all at once to the offsite service or home-based transcriptionist rather than having the work done while the transcriptionist remained on the phone. Ironically, much re-recording was being done from a sophisticated digital server in a hospital to old-fashioned tape-based transcribers still in use at independent transcription services and home-based businesses.

The glitches do not end there, however. One problem still existed: re-recording took a great deal of time. In fact, re-recording took the same amount of time it took to record the original dictation, practically defeating the purpose. If 10 doctors called a central server and dictated 10 hours of material that eventually had to be re-recorded to home-based transcriptionists, the re-recording would then take 10 more hours to accomplish. This was a time-consuming drain on hospitals, services, and independent transcriptionists.

As a result, the newest technology today in the digital arena is special compression software that reduces re-recording time to a fraction of the original recording time. Some products can download 10 hours of dictation in 30 minutes. This new phase of digital re-recording technology allows telecommuters and home-based transcriptionists to dial up the server in a hospital, clinic, or service at any time of day or night, download their assigned dictations, and transcribe them at a later time without tying up phone lines or incurring large communications costs. Downloads can even be programmed to occur automatically in the middle of the night, so that the transcriptionist will have a body of dictations all ready to start on in the morning.

One major company in this field, Dictaphone, describes how this technology has helped its customers. A mid-size independent transcription service in North Carolina that used Dictaphone products was serving dozens of hospitals in several southern states and even had some physicians calling from as far away as Hawaii and California. The service had a staff of 25 transcriptionists, but many of them were offsite and needed to obtain the dictations by calling in and transcribing while on the phone. The service was thus chalking up huge phone bills from the offsite workers. For instance, one of its best offsite transcriptionists was a woman based in Louisiana; when she called in to do two hours of dictation, she would log about eight hours of phone time.

With the new re-record technology, this service now has a Dictaphone server unit, called a Dictaphone Digital Express 7000®, which automatically dials the offsite transcriptionist in the middle of the night to download her work. At her end, she has a corresponding Dictaphone unit called the Dictaphone Straight Talk®, which features the company's proprietary ExpressNet™ re-record technology that transfers the voice data in a fraction of the real time. As Dictaphone points out, "When the home-based transcriptionist is ready to start work at 8 A.M., her desktop system is full of high-quality, re-recorded digital dictation that is ready to be transcribed, eliminating the need for lengthy long distance calls." See Figure 4-3 for an illustration depicting how Dictaphone's ExpressNet™ technology works for this type of arrangement. (Note: several other companies produce similar equipment. Dictaphone is used only for example here.)

As good as this sounds, a problem with such re-record technology is that it requires the transcriptionist working with a large facility such as a hospital or service to invest in the proprietary equipment needed to coordinate with the server at the host site. For example, in the case just described, the service ended up buying every one of its transcriptionists a Dictaphone Straight Talk® unit. This can become expensive for a small business that subcontracts out to independents but cannot afford to buy each of them a unit. On the other hand, a home-based transcriptionist who wants to work with hospitals or services can voluntarily invest in the equipment but needs to know which brand to buy, based on which brand is used by potential clients. Most of the companies selling dictation/transcription equipment lease the units to make them more affordable.

However, an interesting development has occurred recently to eliminate the proprietary equipment dilemma. Several PC-oriented companies have entered the market with specialized hardware and software that allows ordinary personal computers to become dictation/transcription units. For example, one company called Narratek produces software called *VoiceWare*™ that gives an ordinary PC (assuming it has a sound card) the capability to record digital dictation. If the PC is located in a physician's office or hospital, physicians can thus record the dictation right into it (or if the physician prefers, he or she can use a standard handheld tape recorder and then have the secretary replay the tape into the microphone on the PC). Once the dictations are stored on the sound card in the PC, they can be sent by modem to an offsite transcriptionist who has installed Narratek's corresponding *VoiceScribe*™ software, which decompresses the voice data. The transcriptionist then has a foot pedal attached

Figure 4-3
Brochure from
Dictaphone shows how
to go from dictation to
documentation in
minutes! "A physician in
Hawaii picks up a
phone, calls the Digital
Express® located at a
transcription service in
Durham, NC, then
dictates the report
The Digital Express,
equipped with
ExpressNet™
technology, transfers
voice file data at an
accelerated speed to
Straight Talk® in
Louisiana. The
transcriptionist plays
back the report,
transcribes it, then
transmits the completed
report back to the
service via modem or
fax. The service then
sends the finished
report either back to the
dictating physician or to
a referring physician.
The entire process, start
to finish, can be done
within 30 minutes with
ExpressNet. (Illustration
and text courtesy of
Dictaphone,
Stratford, CT.)

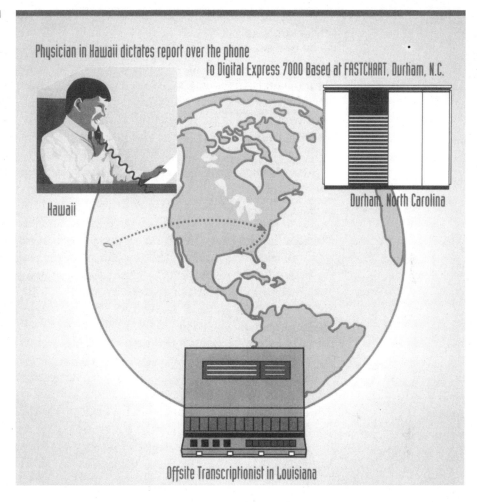

Physician in Hawaii dictates report over the phone to Digital Express 7000 Based at FASTCHART, Durham, N.C.

Hawaii

Durham, North Carolina

Offsite Transcriptionist in Louisiana

to the PC sound card to control the playback. Once the work is done, the transcriptionist can send the word-processed file back to the physician or hospital via modem, or, if preferred, he or she can fax, mail, or messenger the actual hard copies.

Narratek's software also works with DVI digital dictation systems (DVI is another of the leading companies in this arena). Just as with the re-recording scenario discussed earlier with the Dictaphone products, doctors call into a central DVI system and dictate their reports. However, rather than having the telecommuting or independent transcriptionist owning an expensive proprietary system, an ordinary PC can call up the DVI server and download the dictations to the PC's soundcard. The transcriptionist can then transcribe the reports using a foot pedal attached to the soundcard.

Narratek's systems are very cost-effective compared to traditional proprietary systems and may begin to attract an audience among small and home-based independent transcriptionists. However, some industry sources criticize PC-based software products such as Narratek's, claiming that these systems are not yet sophisticated enough and lack the security mechanisms that must be in place to protect patient confidentiality. You will need to judge this equipment for yourself.

One problem that transcription industry officials admit is that, at this time, there is still no standard data file format for compressing and storing voice data. Whatever file format is selected, it must take into account medical transcription's special requirements, such as the need to have digitized voice data capable of being played back at any speed without distortion, the need to have flexibility in the system so that physicians can insert and delete at will, and the need to have demographic data accompany the voice data. All of this means there will likely be many competing systems for quite a while, and that transcriptionists will need to choose from among them.

See Figures 4-4 and 4-5 for illustrations of some of the products offered by two of the leading companies in the transcription business, Lanier and Dictaphone.

Figure 4-4
Dictaphone transcription products. The ExpressWriter Plus™ uses microcassette technology. The Straight Talk® Plus unit uses digital technology and can link to Dictaphone dictation products used in hospitals and independent services, such as shown in Figure 4-3. (Photos courtesy of Dictaphone, Stratford, CT.)

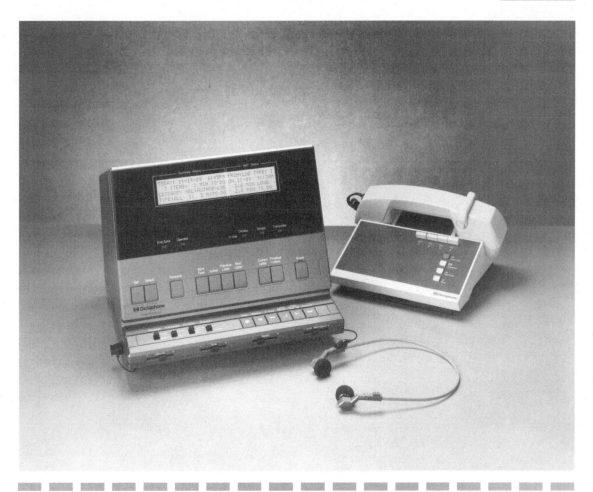

Figure 4-4 Transcription equipment from Dictaphone (Continued)

THE FUTURE WORLD: ONLINE TRANSCRIPTION As you can see, there are many exciting developments occurring in medical transcription. Digital technology is opening many new vistas for telecommuters and home-based independent transcriptionists. Furthermore, the future portends even more exciting developments, especially because of the Internet. Many industry insiders see the Internet as the eventual delivery vehicle for dictation and transcription.

Attaché IV

The Attaché IV combines the convenience of handheld dictation with standard cassette compatibility. Handy features, like one-button control and instructional queuing, help you stay productive anywhere your business takes you. Its superb sound quality ensures that your recorded voice is crisp and clear every time. And when you're ready to relax, use it to play back instructional tapes or listen to prerecorded music.

VoiceWriter 110/210

VoiceWriter 110 and 210 desktop dictation units offer crisp, clear sound and a host of features, like a pistol-grip microphone, one-button control, document queuing, telephone recording and half-speed recording. Additional features include an automatic recall, digital transcriptionist display and an optional foot control and headset. If your office uses standard cassettes for dictation, choose VoiceWriter 110. If you use microcassettes, choose VoiceWriter 210.

VoiceWriter 160/260

The VoiceWriter 160 and 260 offer all the features of the VoiceWriter 110 and 210, plus other capabilities. Digital Voice Operated Recording (VOR) automatically starts and stops the tape when you start and stop talking, automatically guarding against wasted tape and missed words. An expanded display panel features a voice level indicator for instant confirmation that you're recording. And the "store recall" feature lets you switch tapes for priority dictation without losing the display information for the original tape. VoiceWriter 160 uses standard cassettes, VoiceWriter 260 uses microcassettes.

VoiceWriter 650

The VoiceWriter 650 lets you multiply the productivity of your dictation and transcription operations. Featuring a rotating carrousel with four tapes, it lets you assign each tape to a different individual, or separate routine work from priority work. It allows call-in dictation using remote dictate stations or ordinary telephones, and can even function as an answering machine. The VoiceWriter 650 also functions as a transcribe station, with time-saving features like special instruction queuing, automatic recall and a work indicator light that lets you know when dictation is ready to be transcribed.

VoiceWriter Executive

The VoiceWriter Executive brings the power of digital technology to you by converting voice to digital information for storage on a computer hard drive. Digital dictation offers capabilities not available on analog systems, like automatic priority assignment, instantaneous random access and interactive verbal prompts. And because the voice signal is digital, it can be speeded up or slowed down without affecting the pitch, for easier transcription.

Lanier dictation products

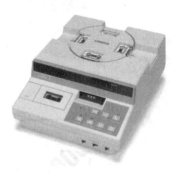

Figure 4-5   *Lanier transcription products. The VoiceWriter 650, for example, allows for simultaneous dictation and transcription with its four cassettes. The VoiceWriter Executive uses digital technology to improve the quality of the sound and to provide more flexibility for the transcriptionist. Photos courtesy of Lanier, Atlanta, GA.*

Imagine this scenario: the physician dictates into a recorder on her desk or at the station at the hospital. The recorder has a small credit-card size insert to store the dictation in digital form. When the doctor is finished, she removes the card and gives it to a clerk who inserts it into a PC. For each dictation, the PC automatically shows a screen containing the patient's name, age, and other identifying information. Meanwhile, the dictation is automatically digitized. The physician or secretary then presses one button and the PC connects to the Internet, locates the remote

Voice Recognition Software

Many transcription professionals have worried for years that voice recognition software would eliminate their jobs. Such software theoretically could take a dictated document and transform it into a printed one, using the ability of the computer to recognize sounds and identify them with an appropriate dictionary word that could be spelled out on the screen.

It now seems clear that voice recognition software is still a long way off from taking over medical transcription for many reasons. First, the software is simply not sophisticated enough to recognize the difference between many sound-alike words, such as ileum and ilium or perineal and peroneal. Second, the vocabulary of the medical profession changes rapidly with a steady stream of new drugs, procedures, and names for diseases. This means that the software would need constant updating. Finally, the most significant issue is that the current generation of voice recognition software requires physicians to speak in slow, monotone speech, at about 70 words per minute. The problem is, doctors tend to dictate at more like 200 words per minute, and they often do so while on the go, or eating lunch, or from a noisy room.

It may be that advances in chip speed and voice software algorithms will improve the software to the point that it can become a tool for transcriptionists. One potential use might be for a good voice recognition software product to create a first draft of a transcription, leaving holes or guesses at what the software thinks the word is. The transcriptionist could then work on the final draft by reviewing and editing the text with the correct words. If that were so, transcriptionists would probably welcome the technology because it would truly elevate them from the feeling of being rote typists to being medical language specialists.

site for the transcription company, and delivers the voice data and demographics within a few seconds. The transcriptionist—who may be located anywhere in the country—is notified of incoming mail and downloads it to his PC while working on another document. For the next few minutes, the PC decompresses the file in the background. When ready, the transcriptionist opens the file, and with an earphone connected to the PC, transcribes the report. The demographic data are automatically appended to the top of the file. Finally, the transcriptionist saves the file, logs onto the Internet, and e-mails the completed document back to the physician. All of this has taken about 30 minutes and has transpired with complete security and privacy for the information because of special keys used over the Internet to ensure data are delivered only to the appropriate destination.

If this future appeals to you, see the sidebar on page 222 for some interesting comments on technology from two industry leaders.

Comments from Two Industry Leaders

Scott Faulkner, Vice President, Healthcare, Western Region, Dictaphone

- In my view, the growth of the transcription industry cannot be underestimated. For example, new legislation requires that acute care facilities transcribe progress notes. This ties into the massive trend in healthcare for computerized medical records. There will likely be more and more work for people with less formal backgrounds and training (i.e., many medical reports of this nature, such as progress reports, are usually less technical). This means many excellent opportunities for people interested in medical transcription.
- One of the key developments in the medical transcription field is its expansion into the world of client/server architecture. A transcriptionist can dial into a central server (such as at a hospital) and download dictations and patient records from home. This erases the geographical boundaries that inhibit people from being able to work out of the home. Of course, we have had to overcome some limitations, such as the problems of telecommunications (the dilemma of local calls vs. long distance if the transcriptionist is calling in from far away). However, our view is that the next generation technology will utilize the Internet as the solution. The benefit of the Internet is that it makes a completely level geographic playing field. Anyone can download dictations from anywhere, do the work, and ship it back.
- Many people wonder about whether speech recognition technology will make a dent in medical transcription. In my view, it is unlikely, at least at present. Medical vocabulary is much too specialized, and there is a constant stream of new terms, such as for new drugs and pharmaceuticals. There will likely always be a need for human intervention.

Bernie Magoon, Marketing Manager, Voice Systems, Lanier

- The problem today is not having an appropriate technology to help the voice files go from point *a* to point *b*; the problem today is having enough transcriptionists to handle the workload.
- Technology is changing the profession today. It used to be that if physicians were calling your house to dictate, you were limited to your own geographic area for your customers. The market is now opening up and we will soon have a completely geographically free market. What we are trying to do today is take away the barriers so that you are not limited to your geographic location.
- What we will eventually have is real-time voice file movement and the ability to download quickly. It may very well be that transcriptionists of the future will work on ISDN lines.
- Ironically, technology today is helping home-based people get into the business at low cost; but it may eventually hinder them as the big players are able to lower their costs too. This remains to be determined.

The Transcriptionist's Lifestyle

Your lifestyle of a transcriptionist depends entirely on whether you are an employee, a telecommuter, or an independent.

An employed hospital transcriptionist usually has a hectic, pressure-filled, and demanding job. Transcribing many kinds of reports requires exceptional experience and knowledge, and many hospitals don't hire new entrants to the field; there is simply too much pressure to produce, and they cannot afford to have inexperienced people working on their reports. The advantage of a hospital boiler-room atmosphere is that it provides transcriptionists with a collegial atmosphere—friends to whom they can turn for help and support. Many transcriptionists report that they often get into a jam when they simply don't understand what the physician has said, but by checking with another transcriptionist who can offer a "fresh ear," they can finally figure it out.

On the other hand, the life of the telecommuter or independent transcriptionist is usually much more enjoyable—and less pressured. These transcriptionists have more time to spend with their families while having more flexible hours that allow them to work in the early morning, evening, or while a child is napping in the afternoon. Home-based transcriptionists also report that they are usually more productive because they can get to work without wasting time commuting. However, some independents say that they miss the company of colleagues and that maintaining self-discipline to work can be a challenge.

Many independent, self-employed transcriptionists cite that having their own business is what attracted them to the profession, and they would rather be independent than employed telecommuters. They like being able to choose their clients and schedules. Some of the home-based services work for only a few local physicians, while others do regular work for hospitals as well as handling physicians in private practice.

The sidebar on Terri Ford of Monarch Transcription and Joan Walston of Words Times 3 describes two successful transcription businesses. As you'll see, Terri is a good model of the home-based independent lifestyle, while Joan has a small agency working out of an office.

Knowledge and Skills Needed

Unlike medical billing services or even medical claims assistance, the preparation needed to become a transcriptionist is extensive and arduous. This is not to suggest that only the most gifted of individuals need apply,

Business Profiles: Terri Ford and Joan Walston

Terri Ford

Terri Ford owned a home-based daycare center in rural Maryland for nine years while her three children were growing up. When they entered school full time and she was left with only other people's kids, Terri decided it was time for a change. She already had a computer background, having been a bookkeeper for 10 years before her children appeared, and she now felt strongly that working with computers was the future.

A number of coincidences then followed. First, Terri read about medical transcription in an issue of *Money Magazine*, and learning that it was predicted to be a good business, she ordered the book *The Independent Medical Transcriptionist* by Donna Avila-Weil. From that book, she learned about the home-study program called the SUM Program for Medical Transcription Training. She contacted one of the vendors, Jennifer Martin, and purchased it. She was so ambitious to get her new career off the ground that she flew through the program in just five months. She loved the work and passed the exam with flying colors.

As coincidence would have it, Terri then saw an advertisement in her local newspaper from a service looking for home-based transcriptionists. The firm was looking to subcontract out some of its work. Although it did not pay her very much, Terri took the work to build her experience, especially since the owner would proof her work for mistakes. That was the start for Terri's company, Monarch Transcription.

Terri stayed with the service for four months, and then one day, she got a call from a family practice asking her to take over the transcription for their two doctors and part-time nurse practitioner. She accepted the job and began getting about two tapes per day, which amounted to nearly five hours of transcription plus another few hours for proofing and printing. (Terri notes that a typical family practice report is 10 to 20 lines long, and a report for a physical is about three pages.) Terri tries to provide 24-hour turnaround, and she picks up and delivers the tapes because the practice is only five miles away.

For her equipment, Terri uses a mini Pearlcorder and a standard transcriber made by Panasonic. She bought a Pentium IBM Aptiva P-100 with a 16 Mb hard drive, a 4-speed CD-ROM, and she uses *Microsoft Word*. She told me that she expected her family practice client to convert to digital soon, so she will be able to call in rather than driving each day to drop off her work and pick up new tapes.

Terri has found her new transcriptionist lifestyle perfect for her family. She achieved her exact goal: to work from home during the hours when her children were in school, without having to go out into the working world and be away from her children. The only downside is the loneliness of working solo (as many people who work from home experience). Terri would therefore love to have a partner so she could have some adult company during the day. To fill part of this need, she occasionally logs onto America Online's forum and chats with other transcriptionists (there's one on CompuServe too).

Joan Walston

Joan Walston is the antithesis of Terri Ford when it comes to the transcriptionist's lifestyle. When I first called Joan to interview her about her business, she told me she was so busy that I needed to schedule an appointment with her—two weeks later! Rather than working in a beautiful rural area for a small family practice,

(Continued)

Joan's business is located in a bustling medical area of Santa Monica, California. She leases an office amidst several hospitals and dozens of buildings containing thousands of private physician practices.

Joan Walston got into medical transcription 20 years ago, when the requirements for entry into the business were much less rigorous. She was an English major in college, and believing that she had excellent language skills, she decided to try medical transcription. Her first jobs were doing overflow work for hospitals. Today, Joan handles work for many physicians affiliated with one of the hospitals nearby, and she also works for several private practices. Over the years, Joan has developed expertise in nearly every area of medicine, so she can handle almost every type of medical dictation, from operative reports and patient visits to medical research papers and grant proposals. One doctor even has Joan keep his resume on file and regularly update it each time he adds a new paper or grant award to his credentials.

Joan's business has generally grown although it goes through ups and downs. Her company, Words Times 3 Medical Transcribers, generates enough work that Joan subcontracts some of it out, using anywhere from two or three independents at a time. She encourages phone-in dictations from her clients, so she has two four-line systems with multiport transcribers that allow both dictations and transcriptions to occur simultaneously. Because her office is in such a densely packed medical area, she also picks up tapes and delivers transcribed documents for some clients within the two to three block radius.

Joan believes strongly in providing a quality service. She says that "quality work is a distinguishing factor in my business." She notes that many doctors are very articulate but some of her clients depend on her to fix up their dictations into proper English. On that note, she advises that anyone interested in transcription needs to understand that there is only room for people who are really good if they want to have their own business. She feels that there is a greater possibility for lower standards in a big operation, so her goal is to continue growing but only large enough for her to maintain control on the quality her company produces.

but simply to help you understand that if you are planning a career in medical transcription, you should consider the training as a long-term endeavor and not become discouraged or disappointed with the path in front of you. You may need to devote 6 to 18 months to study, and then another few years in an apprenticeship position. In the long run though, a good education and training program will help you build a solid business or enable you to have your pick of employers.

The starting point for a career in medical transcription is not difficult for anyone with a high school diploma. In general, if you have a fairly good command of English, know how to spell and the rules of spelling, and can type from 50 to 80 words per minute on a computer, you are ready to begin a program for learning medical transcription. Following are the areas of knowledge you will need to develop:

- Medical terminology (word origins, spellings, meanings) and transcription styles

- Medical sciences—the basics, including anatomy, physiology, pathology, pharmacology, disease processes, as well as some areas of specialization such as radiology, neuroscience, cardiology, or psychology/psychiatry
- English grammar and punctuation as well as spelling
- Skills with PC computers and general word-processing software
- Business skills—marketing and sales

The section later in the chapter on "Resources and Training" explains in more detail the type of programs you can find to take such courses, but note for now that many community and junior colleges offer medical transcription training. You will also find several home-study programs such as the one mentioned in the profile of Terri Ford, the SUM program.

Medical Terminology and Transcription Styles

Medical dictations do not reflect the average daily speech of mortals. Although we can ask insurance companies and lawyers to write their documents in plain English rather than formal legalese, medical reports cannot be simplified to a level below the technical vocabulary used in medicine. There is no other way to express what happens in a surgical operation except to use the highly technical terms for body parts, chemicals and drugs, units of measurement, and medical equipment involved. Medicine is a field that, by its very nature, requires specialized terms for the thousands of body parts, diseases, processes, diagnoses, chemicals, and technical terms that physicians must describe and use.

How does a student learn all this terminology? One major aid to mastering medical terminology comes from the field of *etymology,* which focuses on the origins of words. Since most medical words are based on Greek or Latin roots, plus a prefix and/or suffix, a large part of your medical education focuses on learning a few hundred roots, prefixes, and suffixes. For example, the words neurology, neuritis, neuropathy, neurosurgery, and neurologist all use the root *neur-,* meaning *nerve.* You can learn to recognize many root words from related English words, but you may need to study extensively the hundreds of prefixes and suffixes used in medicine. For instance, consider the suffixes *-itis* (inflammation of), *-oma* (tumor), *-ology* (study of), and *-ectomy* (removal of).

Another medical language area you will need to study are homophones (words that sound the same) and antonyms (opposites), because these are critical to getting it right when you type a medical transcription. For example, you must be able to distinguish clearly between "The patient's hypertension" and "the patient's hypotension," since the first means high blood pressure and the second means low blood pressure. This can be difficult when listening to a doctor who speaks quickly or with an accent, unless you know and understand the context. Many medical words sound very similar, but you must be able to decipher them based on context.

You will also need to study how to punctuate, abbreviate, and capitalize medical terminology. For instance, you must know where to put periods when you type a series of blood tests, or where to put a comma when you list a group of statements. You must know how to type many proper nouns such as Bells palsy (capitalize the B and don't use an apostrophe on eponyms). An important standard is knowing to capitalize and underline any statements relating to allergies (THE PATIENT IS ALLERGIC TO IODINE) because it could save someone's life.

As indicated earlier in the chapter, you also need to learn the various styles and formats used in transcription. In short, you need to learn a multitude of conventions and terminology (and this book cannot do justice to teaching you even a few).

Furthermore, your learning does not stop once you complete your initial education. Each year, new medical equipment and surgical instruments are invented whose names you will need to learn. One of the major areas of change is pharmaceuticals. Each year, hundreds of new drugs are added to the list of prescriptions doctors may offer, and you need to learn to spell them. (Ironically, most doctors have no idea how to spell many of these new drugs, so you are often the keeper of such knowledge.)

Medical Science Training

A medical transcriptionist must have a solid understanding of the medical sciences: anatomy, physiology, pathology, pharmacology, and so on. This usually means taking an overview course in each area to become familiar with the terminology and procedures, though you do not need to go into the same depth as a pre-med student or nurse. Your goal is not to learn enough to identify and analyze a disease, but you must have at least an aural knowledge of this "foreign" language, that is, the ability to identify and understand the significance of the word when you hear it.

A transcriptionist cannot work in a vacuum, typing up reports as if the words were nonsense terms that simply need to be spelled correctly. The mark of high-quality medical transcription is that the documents make sense. While transcriptionists are not technically responsible for fixing errors dictated by a doctor, they should be able to recognize the meaning of a report and monitor it for sense and context. If a doctor starts a transcription discussing a procedure performed on the right side of the body and then accidentally uses terminology related to the left side, the transcriptionist needs to recognize that an inconsistency has occurred. He or she can then point out the problem to the physician or to the supervisor if the transcriptionist is working for a hospital or service.

English Language Skills

Transcriptionists still use English to connect the hard words. In other words, you still need to know how to write proper English, how to punctuate correctly, and how to maintain a consistent style. As Joan Walston and others I interviewed were all eager to say, physicians are not usually the best grammarians, often slipping into the passive voice or using misplaced modifiers (e.g., "The patient was examined by me on the table" instead of, "I examined the patient on the table"), or rambling when a single sentence would have done it. Although many transcriptionists, particularly those who work in hospital settings, are told to transcribe verbatim without making any changes whatsoever, many independent transcriptionists report that doctors expect them to improve the grammar in their documents. This means that although transcriptionists cannot change any medical terminology or phrasing, they need to use judgment in making a physician's report read intelligently, with well-articulated sentences and proper punctuation.

Computer Literacy

Today, all medical transcription is typed using computers and word-processing software. For telecommuting and independent transcriptionists, *WordPerfect 5.0* or *Word Perfect 5.1* for DOS (formerly owned by Novell and now owned by Corel) has long been considered the software of choice, but *Microsoft Word for Windows* has captured a growing share of the market as has the new version of *WordPerfect for Windows*. Many transcriptionists still use the DOS-based software, but as in all professions, Windows-based programs are becoming the new standard. (In the hospital environment, many other software packages are in use; these are actually interfaces built on top of *WordPerfect* or *Word* by independent companies that add such features as management reporting, digital dictation, autofaxing, e-mail, and electronic signature.)

Most transcriptionists now use a variety of productivity-enhancing add-on software products, the most important of which are specialized medical spelling checkers. These include programs such as *Stedman's 25/Plus* medical spell checker and dictionary containing more than 200,000 words.

Another new type of software product hitting the market recently is "word-expanding software," programs that allow you to type just one or two characters and then select from a list of frequently used words that start with those characters. Obviously, such software is intended to improve productivity, because some medical terms and pharmaceutical drugs are as many as 15 to 30 characters long. For example, consider the word esophagogastroduodenoscopy, a mere 26 characters; rather than type each of those characters, you simply need to type "eso" and then point to the word you want that appears at the bottom of the screen.

See Appendix C for a list of companies offering spell-checking software and word-expanding software. for medical transcription.

Business and Professional Skills

Many people believe that medical transcription is the right profession for them, so they obtain training and set off to get a contract with a physician, only to discover that they must sell themselves. They then become flustered and find they cannot attract clients.

In short, transcription is a business just as any other. You cannot become an independent transcriptionist without having the skills to get clients and operate your business with a profit. You must know how to market yourself, compete with other services out there, set your fees, and develop a reputation. If you want to be an independent or telecommuting transcriptionist, you also need self-management skills, since you largely work alone even if you report to a supervisor in a hospital or service setting.

As part of your business skills, you must also develop a highly professional demeanor and be able to tolerate the day-in, day-out nature of your work, while feeling proud of what you do. You must be extremely detail oriented, organized, and compulsive about doing a good job and handing in quality work. A medical transcriptionist needs to be as precise as a neurosurgeon, as sensitive as an interior designer, and as attentive as an orchestra conductor. While a small level of error can perhaps go unnoticed and may even be within a level of statistical tolerance, the transcriptionist's charter is truly to avoid mistakes and to be vigilant in monitoring the work. In short, you must be a person of high standards.

You must also enjoy the challenge of figuring out a puzzle, because you will find yourself truly stumped and unable to recognize the words used. Nevertheless, you must be patient, curious, and open to finding out exactly what was said on the dictation without becoming frustrated and willing to abandon your task easily.

You must also maintain a high degree of ethics because of the extremely privileged and confidential information you are working on. You must respect both the rights of the patient and the sanctity of the healthcare provider. In fact, the matter of confidentiality is so important in this profession that there are federal and state laws that protect patient privacy that you need to know about.

You must also keep some emotional distance from your work, as you are often transcribing tapes about people who are seriously ill or dying. While none of the transcriptionists I interviewed said they suffered from depression or sadness when transcribing reports, I am sure that there is an emotional challenge to spending your days transcribing reports about seriously ill or dying people.

Finally, while many people think that the best personality for this job is an "introverted" one, it actually helps to be at least a bit outgoing and interested in having an active lifestyle. Two of the primary detrimental aspects of the job are burnout and stress-related physical illnesses, such as carpal tunnel syndrome, radial entrapment in the arms, eye and ear strain, lower back problems, and a host of other ailments that stem from keyboarding and sitting. For that reason, the wise person recognizes that hobbies and physical exercise are important aspects of the work. You need to regularly seek out things to do outside of work and establish a regular schedule of outdoor activities for amusement and life enhancement.

Income and Earning Potential

Medical transcription offers an excellent opportunity to make a good living in a consistently high-demand field. (I am sure you have never heard of medical transcriptionists who were laid off in the past few years! Or if they were, they probably went out and started their own business without any problems.) Other than the stability of the job, the important question is, how much can a transcriptionist actually earn?

Unfortunately, the answer to the income question varies considerably. For transcriptionists employed in hospitals, the starting pay ranges between $8 to $15 an hour, with an average salary for an experienced transcriptionist at $30,000 a year or slightly better. For independent transcriptionists, the earning potential can be much greater, going as high as $70,000 if you are highly qualified, type quickly, and work slightly more than full time.

The reason for these variances is that, as with the other professions in this book, there are many ways that independent transcriptionists price their services, and there is also a wide variation in the fees they can get depending on their location in the country. In the past, transcriptionists have charged according to any of the following three standards:

1. Hourly fees ($15 to $24 per hour)
2. Per page ($5 to $6 per page)
3. Per line ($0.08 to $0.19 per line)

In recent years, the per line method of charging has come to be the dominant method used by independent transcriptionists in many areas. One confusion that exists is what constitutes a line. In some areas, a typed line of any length counts as one line, regardless of length. You may set your margins to 60 characters or 80 characters, but regardless of how many words are on a line, each line counts. If a report you transcribe has 32 short lines (e.g., lines that have only 2 or 3 words on them) mixed in with 200 full-length lines (e.g., 70 characters), they all count the same, and you would charge for 232 lines.

The line-count method is easy to do and reasonable. Of course, you need to define with your client in advance what you call a line. Some transcriptionists like to set their margin to 65 characters, but some physicians like 70 or 80. You can end up battling over what constitutes a line.

Today, some transcriptionists are moving toward using 65 characters as the standard unit of measure to count lines. Regardless of what your margins are or how many words are on a line, you agree to call 65 characters one line. A good reason for this is that word-processing software easily and quickly counts characters. When a document is completed, you simply run the character count macro and divide the result by 65. For example, if you completed a transcript and the software counted 8,565 characters,

TABLE 4-2

Range of Line Rates for Medical Transcription (cents per line)

Region of the U.S.	Low Range	High Range
Northwest	10—12	17—19
Western	8—11	12—17
Middle	8—9.5	16—17
Eastern	10	12—15
Southern	10—12	13—16

Source: The Independent Medical Transcriptionist, by Donna Avila-Weil, CMT, and Mary Glaccum, CMT.

you divide 8,565/65. The result is 132 lines. You then multiply 132 × the line rate you have established. If you were charging 12 cents per line, you would earn $15.84 for that document.

Line rates vary greatly by location. In general, transcriptionists in major cities are able to charge much more than those in small towns and rural areas. What part of the country you live in also makes a big difference. According to a survey taken by Donna Avila-Weil and Mary Glaccum, authors of *The Independent Medical Transcriptionist*, most respondents charged by the line with rates as shown in Table 4-2.

Whatever the line rate, most transcriptionists charge a slightly higher fee for emergency work (called STAT work, "STAT" means immediately). They may also charge fees for special delivery, copies, faxing, or reprints of reports that have been lost. In all, the area of fees is open to negotiation for the independent transcriptionist. You can negotiate your best rate with each client based on the following:

- Determine if you want to charge by the "gross line count" regardless of how long a line is or how many words it contains, or by the measured line count (such as a 65-character line).

- Ask for samples of work done for the physician by other transcriptionists so you can measure the margins used to determine the line rate you might be able to get.

- Find out what the going rate is in your city or town and which method most people are using.

- Determine if you can charge your standard line rate for everything you put in a document, including headers and footers.

What then is the bottom line for income potential for an independent medical transcriptionist? The answer to this question depends entirely on your productivity and hours worked. For simplicity, let's make some assumptions: an experienced medical transcriptionist using the latest computer technology including macro abbreviations and word-extending software can type 300 lines per hour. A novice might be able to type from 100 to 200 lines per hour. Table 4-3 shows your income potential at various line rates per hour assuming you work an 8-hour day 250 days of the year.

As you can see, the potential for a decent income is high even for the novice. The table indicates that a novice who transcribes 100 to 150 lines per hour can gross between $20,000 and $50,000—a reasonable gross income range for either a single person or a spouse who wants to contribute to the family income. Note, however, that this table shows gross income and excludes business costs: equipment, supplies, faxes, delivery charges, marketing costs, utilities, phone bills, and so on. Expenses in this business average 20 percent to 30 percent of fees.

As the table also shows, if you are ambitious and seek more income, you can work harder to achieve a higher line production rate, moving far beyond the $50,000 bracket, especially if you can bill at a rate greater than 10 cents per line.

TABLE 4-3

Gross Income Projections for Medical Transcriptionists

	@ 10¢ per Line	@ 12¢ per Line	@ 14¢ per Line	@ 16¢ per Line	@ 18¢ per Line
100 Lines per Hour = 800 Lines per Day	$80/day × 250 = 20,000	96 per day × 250 = 24,000	112 per day × 250 = 28,000	128 per day × 250 = 32,000	144 per day × 250 = 36,000
150 Lines per Hour = 1,200 Lines per Day	120/day × 250 = 30,000	144/day × 250 = 36,000	168/day × 250 = 42,000	192/day × 250 = 48,000	216/day × 250 = 54,000
200 Lines per Hour = 1,600 Lines per Day	160/day × 250 = 40,000	192 per day × 250 = 48,000	224/day × 250 = 56,000	256/day × 250 = 64,000	288/day × 250 = 72,000
300 Lines per Hour = 2,400 Lines per Day	240/day × 250 = 60,000	288/day × 250 = 72,000	336/day × 250 = 84,000	384/day × 250 = 96,000	432/day × 250 = 108,000

Deciding If This Business Is for You

By now, you have read about the rigorous preparation medical transcriptionists must have, the lifestyle they lead, and the potential rewards. The following checklist can help with your decision. Take a moment now to do this 15-question checklist before reading the remainder of the chapter.

- Do I enjoy medical terminology and descriptions of cases?
- Do I enjoy working behind the scenes, without contact with the public?
- Do I like words, details, and working on documents?
- Do I like working on my own?
- Will I enjoy listening to voices of physicians, some of whom I haven't met?
- Do I like figuring out puzzles and trying to identify missing pieces?
- Do I enjoy constantly learning new words and vocabulary?
- Do I have a good ear for sounds, language, and voices and a good eye for spelling, punctuation, and grammar?
- Am I willing to listen to something over and over again until I get it right?
- Do I have good concentration skills and an ability to block out distractions that interfere with my ability to work?
- Am I accurate, organized, and fastidious?
- Do I like writing, typing, and working with computers?
- Can I read or write about serious illnesses without becoming upset or sensitive?
- Am I trustworthy and able to not disclose medical information about people whose names I know?
- Do I mind working in a profession that is sometimes given short shrift?

If you have answered yes to the majority of these questions, or if you have some doubts but want to proceed, the next section provides brief guidelines on how to get started. This material will be organized differently from the preceding chapters, since it is unlikely you will start your business immediately. The next section includes the location of resources for training and education, information on equipping and furnishing your office for medical transcription, and a discussion of how to build your career once you've finished an educational program.

Section II: Getting Started

Resources and Training

In general, if you have a good educational background, such as a college degree and general language aptitude, you can learn medical transcription using one of the high-quality home-study programs. However, if you are not linguistically oriented or do not have a good general educational background, you may wish to consider attending a community college program in medical transcription. These can take from two to four semesters to complete. Let's start by looking at home-study courses, since my assumption is that for most readers of this book, full- or part-time school is not an option.

HOME-STUDY PROGRAMS Perhaps the most noted home-study course that has received excellent marks is the SUM (Systems Unit Method) Program for Medical Transcription Training, available from Health Professions Institute in Modesto, California. As the SUM program literature explains:

> The SUM Program for Medical Transcription Training was developed to educate medical transcription students to the level where they are productive from their first day of employment. The SUM program is used mostly in schools and hospitals, but has also been made available to transcription companies and to individuals by popular demand. The program uses carefully selected authentic physician dictation, sequenced by medical specialty on standard-size cassette tapes, along with academic textbook reading assignments and exercises. As a self-directed student, you will transcribe the dictation to the best of your ability, using all references at your disposal, then check your work against the corresponding transcript answer keys.

This SUM program is modular. The Beginning Medical Training (BMT) course is the first segment. This module consists of 12 hours of authentic dictation, including:

- 1.5 hours of narration on relevant topics by well-known authors and educators in the field
- 1.5 hours of narrative instruction for transcribing pharmacology, lab procedures, and the medical history and physical examination
- 9 hours of authentic dictation, including chart notes, letters, initial office evaluations, history and physicals, consultations, emergency department reports, and discharge summaries in 11 specialties (cardiology, dermatology, endocrinology, gastroenterology, neurology, ophthalmology, orthopedics, otorhinolaryngology, pulmonary medicine, urology, and obstetrics and gynecology)

Students can take the beginning program and seek employment in a physician's office, group practice, or small clinic. It normally takes 480 hours to complete the basic program, including all the recommended readings (12 weeks if you study for 40 hours per week; or 24 weeks at 20 hours per week).

Students can then follow the basic program with any or all of five specialty modules that prepare them for more advanced work in hospital settings, including cardiology, gastroenterology, orthopedics, pathology, and radiology. Each advanced course contains four hours of authentic physician dictation (except for radiology, which has three). Students should plan on spending 80 hours for each advanced course.

The SUM program has received excellent marks from many people in the industry for its comprehensive and authentic training, and also for its ease of use among self-motivated people. As Linda Campbell, director of Product Development for Health Professions Institute (HPI) told me,

> We sell our program to hospitals and colleges but also to individuals. Before our program, there was very little quality among college programs, in part because there were no standards for training in this industry. There was no federal agency or anyone to mandate standards. We brought out our program in 1987, and since then, we have proven that given the right program, a motivated individual can learn medical transcription on his or her own. Is self-study an ideal situation? No, the ideal situation would be to have a trained medical transcriptionist teaching students in a facility. But that is not realistic for many adults today who are changing careers for one reason or another, and for whom self-study is their only option. We have done the best we can in this program, and we now have hundreds of people who have passed the certification (CMT) exam given by the American Association for Medical Transcription (AAMT).

The Basic Medical Transcription course costs $840, plus a few hundred dollars for various textbooks that are required reading. The course includes the tapes, the answer keys, and a student manual, which contains the suggested curriculum. According to Linda Campbell, if you are uncertain, you can purchase the first tape separately to see if you like the program; the cost is $85.

The advanced courses are $280 each, except for Radiology, which costs $210. Each advanced course comes with a student guide, answer key, and a word and phrase reference book.

HPI also offers a 10-hour video program called *Building a Successful Medical Transcription Business.* This video is directed at students who have completed the basic SUM program and/or advanced courses and are interested in starting their own business. The videos cost $495 and also include a binder of reference materials such as sample contracts.

Finally, HPI offers its students an opportunity to join a network, the Medical Transcription Student Network. The benefits of joining include a quarterly newsletter and a 10 percent discount on many reference and word books that HPI sells by catalogue.

Contact HPI at P.O. Box 801, Modesto, CA 95353 or call 209-551-2112 for information. HPI also sells a wide assortment of reference and word books for medical transcriptionists, and it publishes a quarterly magazine, *Perspectives on the Medical Transcription Profession.* See Figure 4-6 for samples showing various items available from HPI.

Note that the SUM program as offered by HPI is not an interactive course; students do not submit their practice transcriptions by mail to an instructor at HPI. It is completely self-study. No degree is awarded when you complete the program, because the Institute is not an accredited school, but rather a for-profit research and development facility providing educational materials. As its brochure states, however, "independent study students who have properly completed The Sum Program should not encounter difficulty finding employment."

If you prefer to have an instructor work with you as you complete the SUM program, and/or a degree, consider the following two options:

- **Review of Systems (ROS).** This educational training program is offered by Jennifer Martin and contains the same SUM program basic modules (BMT) along with interactive instruction. Ms. Martin is a former instructor at Maple Woods Community College in Kansas City, Missouri, and has been a home-based medical transcriptionist for more than nine years. Essentially, when you purchase Review of

Figure 4-6
Brochures and
training materials
from Health
Professions Institute

Figure 4-6
Brochures and training materials from Health Professions Institute

Systems, you get the very same beginning 12-hour SUM program offered by HPI, plus all necessary textbooks, a variety of reference and word books, and the expertise of Ms. Martin to correct assignments that you mail in as you complete them. ROS is sold in five modules, each costing $300, for a total of $1,500, slightly more than the fee charged by HPI for the basic program. You can contact Ms. Martin at 800-951-5559 or 816-468-4403. She is also available on e-mail at MTMonthly@AOL.com or at www.mtmonthly.com.

- **California College for Health Sciences (CCHS).** If you prefer to have an instructor plus earn a college degree, the entire SUM program is also offered as a home-study course through CCHS, an accredited degree-granting private postsecondary institution. CCHS offers the SUM program as part of an Associate of Science degree, which may entitle you to tuition assistance or reimbursement from an employer. You can contact the school at 222 West 24th Street, National City, CA 91950; phone 800-221-7374. See Appendix C for more information on CCHS.

Another home-study program is offered by a private company called At-Home Professions. This company began as a developer of home-study courses for court transcriptionists. The company realized that a related medical transcription course could also help many people who wanted to learn from home.

At-Home Professions' medical transcription course was developed under the guidance of Dr. Caroline Yeager, a UCLA physician who helped establish the Teaching Department at the UCLA School of Medicine, Martin Luther King Hospital. Caroline explained to me that in addition to being a radiologist, she had a long background in "instructional design" (the field of designing learning units for people, be it in banking or medicine), and so her interest in this area spurred her to write the course with At-Home Professions. In outlining the course, she pointed out that it follows "objective-based training" principles, meaning that you don't get an A, B, C, or D grade, which is a subjective view of your skills, but instead you move through the course by demonstrating that you have mastered one topic at a time. Caroline admitted quite modestly that the course won a prestigious award from a professional society of instructional designers of which she is a member.

The At-Home Professions program consists of five modules, with each module containing many lessons of written explanations, activities, and tapes that you do one at a time. According to company director Cole Thompson, At-Home Professions estimates that a student who studies an average of 20 hours per week can complete all five modules in about six months, although a few people have done it faster. "It's a completely self-paced program," he told me, "in which the students do the lessons at a pace they feel comfortable in. There are specific milestones in each module, and activities and assignments that students do that are self-correcting, followed by an activity that they mail in to us for correction." Cole added that in this program, students have regular one-on-one conversations with their instructors using At-Home's 800 phone number, so that it is not just a mail-order program with no contact between faculty and students.

Both Caroline and Cole were eager to reinforce that this program has tried to be as realistic as possible in teaching medical transcription. The course includes several hours of practice tapes using a broad range of voices similar to those of doctors—voices from Korea, India, Pakistan, Mexico, and many other locales, as well as voices eating lunch while dictating. The five modules teach all necessary medical transcription skills: specialty reports, hospital terminology, and operative reports, as well as essentials of anatomy and physiology. Cole also indicated that students are exposed to all the common specialties of medicine, such as orthopedics, chiropractic, internal medicine, and radiology.

The cost of the At-Home Professions program is $450 for each module, thus a total of $2,250. (Note: price is subject to change.) You can reach At-Home Professions at 800-528-7907, or by writing to 2001 Lowe Street, Fort Collins, CO 80525. The sidebar on Rochelle Wexler presents a profile of a transcriptionist who received her training using At-Home Professions' materials.

ACADEMIC STUDY   Home-study programs are often the only way that adults can learn a new profession, but if you have time or need the extra study, you might consider a broader based academic program offered through a college or community college. Academic programs differ in quality, so be sure to investigate the types of courses offered and the qualifications of the instructors.

The American Association for Medical Transcription (AAMT) recommends a model curriculum that it would like to see colleges adopt throughout the country. This curriculum includes two semesters of medical terminology and three to four semesters of practical experience in transcription, including one semester in a practicum. As you can see, this type of curriculum will take several years to complete. However, the advantages of attending a credentialed program are that you may get a more comprehensive education and that you may achieve a higher level of credibility in finding a job, especially in a hospital environment.

Business Profile: Rochelle Wexler

Rochelle came to medical transcription after a career in musical theater and a brief stint in publishing. She decided that she wanted to find a profession she could call her own, something that allowed her to work from home and to start up with a minimal investment in equipment and training. She had read the first edition of this book; and although she had no medical background, she realized that medical transcription fulfilled her needs.

Rochelle saw an advertisement for At-Home Professions in a magazine and called to receive its information. She double-checked the company's credentials and opted to purchase its training. Rochelle completely dedicated herself to completing the At-Home course quickly; she finished it within six months by working between 30 and 50 hours per week.

Rochelle says that the support staff at At-Home Professions gave her good advice about marketing her newfound career. Within two weeks, Rochelle obtained two clients using fliers that she created on her PC and samples of her work. Living in Manhattan, she was able to canvass a small area and give out 150 fliers in two days, which generated about six calls from various specialists.

Rochelle now has a variety of physicians for clients, including a urologist, cardiologist, oncologist, hematologist, endocrinologist, physical therapist, podiatrist, and pediatric pulmonologist. Some clients give her work sporadically, but she has several she "can count on." Rochelle points out that much of her work consists of referral letters and reports between primary care physicians and specialists. Her biggest client is a diabetes specialist who must heavily document patient visits.

Rochelle charges a line rate; she started at 13 cents per line and has been able to move most of her clients up to 16 cents per line. Her business philosophy is to do the best she can and to provide high-quality service. To this end, she does pick up and deliver tapes and documents. For her work, she used a plain vanilla 486 PC with *WordPerfect*. She has two transcribers, one for standard cassettes and one for micros.

Rochelle was kind enough to send in the photo in Figure 4-7 showing her workspace.

EVALUATING THE BEST PROGRAM FOR YOU Whichever method you prefer, academic or at-home study, degree or not, you should find out as much as you can about how the program works, how long it takes, how much it costs, who the instructors are, and what kind of instruction you will actually receive. In particular, ask if the program covers hospital transcription, physician transcription, or both (since hospital transcription tends to be more rigorous, with more technical vocabulary and more surgical procedures), and if it covers all of the major types of special reports. Then ask how many hours of listening you will receive, and if the audio component of the program includes a variety of accents and voices that increase the level of difficulty.

Following those questions, your next issue is to find out how well the graduates of the program have fared. Ask for a referral list so that you can speak to graduates to learn firsthand what they thought of the program

Figure 4-7
Rochelle Wexler, medical transcriptionist

and how many of them got the jobs they were hoping to find. A good program will not hesitate to give you such a referral list as a good-faith demonstration that its graduates were qualified enough to have landed positions somewhere in the industry.

If you are considering a full-time A.A. or B.A. degree program, find out how many other general curriculum courses you will need to take; these will add time and expense to finishing your degree.

For comparison, many sources in the medical transcription industry prefer the SUM program to the At-Home Professions program. The SUM is generally considered to be more professionally oriented and more attentive to the rigorous demands of the profession. However, you should evaluate both of these programs and others you may find, as well as programs available at your local community college; find out which is the best option for you. Also, if you are investigating other home-study courses, be wary of any course that suggests that you can finish it in six weeks or three months, as any comprehensive program worth paying for will challenge you and take time to learn. It is simply a waste of your money if your program doesn't properly train you for the demands of real-life medical transcription.

ASSOCIATIONS The most noted association in the industry is the American Association for Medical Transcription (AAMT), with approximately 8500 members. Deeming themselves "medical language specialists," AAMT members lobby around the country, encouraging those in the medical community to better understand and reward more appropriately the high level of knowledge and professionalism that a duly-trained transcriptionist brings to the job. Through its own publication, the *Journal of the American Association for Medical Transcription* (JAAMT), the association informs its members about new technologies, new ways to get training and improve skills, and new ideas for making hospitals and physicians treat them more professionally.

AAMT is actively involved in nearly every aspect of the industry, from recommending a model curriculum to be used in college programs to working with many industry groups to establish new national standards for transcription formats. AAMT offers a certification exam that any transcriptionist can sit for, even if he or she is not a member. Upon successful completion of the exam, the individual receives the title CMT, or Certified Medical Transcriptionist. The exam actually consists of two parts: the first is a written portion and the second is a practical test. Each exam costs $150.

In recent years, AAMT has been mostly oriented toward full-time medical transcriptionists with professional or academic backgrounds. If you are a student working from a home-study program, you may find that the benefits of joining AAMT are not worth the membership expense. (AAMT has generally disapproved of home-study programs and does not produce one itself.) However, depending on your interests, you should obtain information about the organization and its potential benefits for you by writing to P.O. Box 576187, Modesto, CA 95357-6187 or by calling 800-982-2182 or 209-551-0883. Ask for the Director of Member Services.

Another organization that may be of growing importance to telecommuting transcriptionists is the Medical Transcription Industry Alliance (MTIA). Although this is a trade association for corporations such as large transcription services, it has formed an affiliate category for the transcriptionist employees. See Appendix C for more information about contacting MTIA.

NEWSLETTERS To fill a large gap in information available to the independent, former transcriptionist Jennifer Martin started a newsletter, *MTMonthly.* The newsletter contains a variety of articles, including updates on technology and medical terminology (especially new drugs that come onto the market regularly), as well as business tips and advice.

The annual fee for the *MTMonthly* is $48. To order, write *MTMonthly,* Suite 100, 1633 NE Rosewood Drive, Gladstone, MO 64118 or call 800-951-5559 or 816-468-4403.

ONLINE RESOURCES   The world of online resources is growing in the medical transcription business. You can now find networks of people discussing medical transcription on CompuServe (in the Working from Home forum) and on America Online. The Internet is teeming with Web sites of interest to the new transcriptionist, including information from many of the companies that manufacture hardware and software for the industry, such as Dictaphone, Lanier, DVI, Narratek, and others. There is also a newsgroup dedicated to transcriptionists and other health professionals. See Appendix C for a list of sites to explore.

BOOKS   There is one book that can especially enlighten the person interested in becoming an independent transcriptionist. Aptly titled *The Independent Medical Transcriptionist,* its authors Donna Avila-Weil and Mary Glaccum have a combined total of more than 50 years in the transcription business. The book includes extensive information on every topic touched on in this chapter, including education and training, setting up your business, legal issues, pricing, contracts, and more. You can order the book from its publisher Rayve Productions Inc., P.O. Box 726, Windsor, CA 95492; order phone is 800-852-4890.

Equipment and Furnishings

TRANSCRIPTION EQUIPMENT   As described earlier in the sections of this chapter that discussed technology, the equipment you need to enter the business depends extensively on three factors:

1. Which type of business you are in (employee vs. telecommuter vs. independent)
2. What type of technology your customers use (digital vs. tape-based)
3. How you organize your service (physicians calling you vs. you calling into a server)

All these factors determine if you end up picking up cassettes from your clients and transcribing them at home using an inexpensive transcriber as Terri Ford does; or if you end up purchasing a multiport transcriber that allows for simultaneous call-in and transcription, such as the one Joan Walston uses; or if you invest in propriety digital technology equipment, such as the Straight Talk® unit from Dictaphone that coordinates with a large server at a hospital or service; or if you purchase PC-based software to turn your standard sound card into a dictation device or downloader device that allows you to decompress files that are sent to your machine via modem.

In general though, you may not need to worry about these decisions if you are just starting out. Most training programs, such as the SUM program and At-Home Professions and even college courses, simply require that you own an inexpensive standard cassette transcriber (not the micro-cassette size). This transcriber unit is made by many companies, including Lanier, Dictaphone, Sony, VDI, Phillips, and Panasonic, and the cost is usually less than $250. Some machines have adapters that allow you to use either standard cassettes or microcassettes. The more sophisticated of these transcriber units have many fancy buttons, such as ones that control the speed of the dictation, the volume, and the tone and know how many dictations are on the tape, and how long they are. It is generally recommended that you buy your transcriber unit from an authorized dealer or sales representative of a company rather than an office supply store, which tends to sell lower quality brands.

As you come closer to being ready to open your business, you can then decide if you want to invest in a multiport system and have doctors call you, or if you want digital equipment that coordinates with a large national service or a local one, or if you want PC-based software that enhances your PC. It is likely that the price of digital technology will come down by the time you are reading this book, and more facilities will adopt it. If so, you may still need to choose among various setups, such as purchasing proprietary hardware from Dictaphone, Lanier, or another major company versus the use of generic re-recording technology.

COMPUTER   Most medical transcription today requires a 386 or 486 PC using DOS-based word-processing software such as *WordPerfect*. However, it would not make sense to get into business—unless you absolutely had to—using this type of equipment. Prices on Pentiums are dropping dramatically, and a Windows-based environment will generally improve your productivity.

The common recommendation made today is to purchase a Pentium with 16 Mb of RAM, a 500 Mb hard drive, and a CD-ROM to use for the increasing amount of reference materials such as dictionaries and word books that are now available in that format. It also helps to have a backup tape unit or other backup equipment. You cannot risk losing completed reports to accidents, vandalism, or breach of security (such as a computer virus that destroys your hard disk).

PRINTER   For your printer, a good dot matrix printer is acceptable, as long as it has "near-letter-quality" output. However, more and more people are moving to using laser printers, as their purchase cost and per page expense go down.

SHREDDER   Because of the high level of patient confidentiality that you must maintain as an independent transcriptionist, it is also recommended that you own a paper shredder to destroy drafts of documents and transcriptions. Small shredding machines are now quite inexpensive and well within the budget for a home business.

OFFICE FURNISHINGS   Because you will be spending so much time at a keyboard, be sure to find an ergonomic desk that allows your arms and wrists to rest on a pad to avoid muscle spasms, inflammation of the wrist, and nerve entrapment due to swelling of the wrist. Dr. Earl Brewer, M.D, a specialist in arthritis in Houston, Texas, and author of *The Arthritis Sourcebook* (Lowell House), cautions that overuse of the wrists and arms by people who heavily use computers is one of the primary causes of long-term injury to the muscles and joints of that area, and therefore a contributing factor in arthritic problems.

It has also long been known that poor ergonomics (the study of how fit and function interrelate) combined with repetitive motions can lead to cumulative trauma disorders (CTDs), which include tennis elbow and carpal tunnel syndrome, a debilitating disease of the wrists. As a result, it is usually recommended that you have a chair with arm rests that allow you to relax your forearms. It is also useful for the chair to have castors so that you can move around easily to change positions, and that its height be adjustable. Ideally, you should aim to not need to stretch your neck, arms, or wrists to reach your keyboard. You can also purchase a keyboard platform to raise or lower your keyboard to accomplish this. (I have had this problem and it led to a very debilitating three months of bursitis in both shoulders, due to poor positioning of my arms relative to my keyboard and mouse.)

You also want your monitor to be at about a 20-degree angle lower than your line of sight, and positioned between 13 and 18 inches away from your eyes to avoid eyestrain. You might consider an antiglare filter, which absorbs reflected light on your screen that can overload the eyes.

Call BackSaver Products at 800-251-2225 for more information on back support products, and BackCare Corporation in Chicago at 312-258-0888 for information on their products to help typists. Read computer magazines for regular reports on new furniture, lighting equipment, and ergonomic computer designs that can improve your office or study conditions. One new product, for example, is called the HandEZE AE Fingerless Glove. As its name suggests, it is a glove worn while typing, but it has been ergonomically designed to alleviate muscle fatigue and pain caused from carpal tunnel, tendonitis, arthritis, and numbness. It costs only $19.95 per pair. Call for a catalogue and brochure from Therapeutic Appliance Group at 800-457-5535.

REFERENCE BOOKS Today's medical transcriptionist has a great need for a number of reference books on his or her desk. There are literally scores of dictionaries, word books, style guides, and medical reference sources. Some are general, but many are reference materials that you need to specialize in one medical field or another, from new technological vocabulary to psychology to pharmacology. Because new names are continually invented for diseases, procedures, diagnoses, instruments, and drugs, these books are constantly updated and so you need to purchase new editions frequently.

You can order reference materials and word books from several organizations and publishers of medical books. See Appendix C for details.

Building Your Career

If you finish a training program in medical transcription, you will probably be eager to get your new business going. However, it is commonly said that there is a Catch 22 in this industry for new transcriptionists: you can't get a job until you have two to three years of experience but you can't get experience without a job.

Nevertheless, because of the demand for transcriptionists everywhere, predictions are that even the newest graduates will find work, just as Terri Ford and Rochelle Wexler did within a few weeks of completing their programs. You may wish to start by interviewing in a medical records department of a hospital where you can obtain continued support and training. Because hospital work is so varied, you will also expand your breadth of knowledge and experience.

Alternatively, you might discuss opportunities for employment with a local service, such as that run by Joan Walston, who seeks out distinctive individuals to train. There is now a growing number of extremely large national services that hire hundreds of transcriptionists, many of whom are offsite. It is likely that many such services will need people and be willing to hire new recruits who can demonstrate quality work and a commitment to learning. It is expected that the next century will open up even more professional training programs in this field to handle the growing demand for transcriptionists.

Many industries have similar future outlooks. As with insurance, banking, and publishing, you will need to put in a few years to pay your dues and learn the ropes before you can move out on your own. There is actually some value in this, because obtaining real-world experience and getting paid for it benefit you in many ways. If you must obtain a job rather than start your own company, this is the time to learn about dealing with doctors, with poor dictations, with voices you didn't encounter in school or in your home-study program, and with the myriad other details that no one taught you. This is the time to perfect your working style so that when you go off on your own, you are not surprised at your mistakes or the little idiosyncrasies that you thought you never had when you were under pressure.

Many people say that one to two years of experience in a hospital are sufficient as background to start your own business or to work for a small service that provides flexible hours and possible telecommuting opportunities. One key to assuring that you can control your own destiny is to pick an area in which to specialize. Learn the vocabulary of one field and develop your knowledge of its trends. With medicine itself becoming an industry of specialists, you would be wise to imitate the doctors in this way. As a matter of fact, it is probably better to specialize in a few areas, to be sure you do not become attached to a small clientele. If one doctor for whom you do most of your work moves or changes practice, you would be left without a source of income.

Related to this issue of having only one client, if you are a free-lance independent medical transcriptionist (or any other professional for that matter), you must be careful about working exclusively for one client since the IRS may then determine that you are not really an independent contractor but a statutory employee. If that happens, the financial penalties for you are severe. Charging on an hourly basis is one indication the IRS may use against you, so be sure to charge by the page or line, and to have many clients so you will be perceived as an independent contractor. Be sure to consult your accountant and attorney to review the IRS questions that are used to determine if a person is an independent contractor or an employee.

ESTIMATING START-UP EXPENSES Like medical claims assistance, one advantage of this business is that, in general, start-up costs are very low for the home-based person. Your investment in office equipment (including a computer, printer, transcriber, and phone) and supplies such as books and reference materials can be as low as $2,000. If you can afford it, you may want to spend $2,500 to $6,000 for better computer and transcription equipment.

Your expenses might amount to

Office equipment (computer, printer)	$1,500—$3,000
Transcriber (if purchased new)	$300—$1,000
Business cards, letterhead, envelopes	$100—$200
Fliers	$100—$500
Office furniture	$400—$800
Phone	$100—$200
Books	$200—$300
TOTAL	$2,700—$6,000

Note: sophisticated tape-based or digital transcription equipment can be leased for as little as $150 to $250 per month.

MARKETING YOUR SERVICE A home-based medical transcriptionist is as much a businessperson as the other two medical professionals in this book. You must therefore know how to market to prospective clients if you want to remain in business.

The first avenue open to a qualified transcriptionist is to obtain overflow work from permanently staffed locations. Nearly every transcriptionist reported that hospitals and services are continually overloaded or need to fill in for vacationing staff, forcing them to farm out work to independent contractors on a regular basis.

The second avenue to marketing your service is to pursue a field of specialization and create a niche for yourself. When you have such a specialization, you can write a letter of introduction to every doctor in your area who performs that specialty and announce your new business. You can easily tailor a direct marketing letter to a small number of doctors who might use your services. One transcriptionist I interviewed used her background in both medical and legal transcription to specialize in personal injury (PI) and worker's compensation cases, since doctors involved in these cases must extensively document the patient's injuries. She obtained a list of all doctors who do worker's comp from the state board in California and then sent a letter to each one. She got many responses, some of whom became clients when she followed up with a personal call and an interview.

Finally, the next most useful marketing strategy is word of mouth. Like accountants, lawyers, and consultants, doctors use recommendations and referrals for finding services they need. You should do the same. After working with a doctor for a few months, ask for a referral to one of his or her colleagues. It's easy to get referrals if you have been performing well and the physician knows what kind of person you are.

As with many professions, starting up your own business can be slow and painful, but a few months of lean times can pay off big in the end.

PRICING   As discussed earlier in the chapter, your goal is to maximize your fees. At the same time, you are likely faced with a classic situation of needing to compete with a few others who lower their prices to get the business. This dilemma points to the fact that the transcription market is fairly price sensitive. For example, Joan Walston of Words Times 3 says that she can charge $24 per hour, but she has not been able to go above that figure for many years because of resistance in the market.

You therefore need to have a sense of what your competition charges and what your clients are willing to accept if they like your work. If you are a fast typist in an area in which per line rates are low, you may be better off charging by the page. On the other hand, if your product is high quality, but your work takes longer than another transcriptionist, you might do better charging by the hour to more fairly compensate you for the extra effort you put into making sure that your documents are perfect.

Ultimately, you need to watch out for what one medical transcriptionist called the "bad mental connection." She explained,

> What I mean is that your presence in the doctor's office signifies trouble to the physician, as in "Oh, no, here goes more of my money." You don't want the doctor to think like that. You want the physician to associate your presence with help, not with a drain on money. That's why you also learn to invoice physicians whenever they pay their other employees, so that they don't think that every time you walk in the door while there's a roomful of patients waiting for them, that they have to pull out their checkbook and pay you.

CONTRACTS   Many independent transcriptionists have only an informal contract with their clients, but most seek to operate formally and so ask the physician to sign a contract for their services. Given the efforts you may have expended to sign a new client, it is certainly advisable that you try to work with a contract as often as possible. Contracts can spell out the turnaround times, schedules, fees and method of pricing, and all the variables you need to protect you from the whims of new office personnel who want to fire you and put in their friend. Remember that turnover is rampant in medical staffing, and it is easy for a new office manager to suddenly dislike your work and insist on hiring someone else. Consult a lawyer to create your contract, and make it for at least a three- or six-month period of time to start, so that both you and the physician can make sure the relationship is working.

Finally, while medical transcriptionists are not technically responsible for the correctness of the documents, it is often suggested that you carry errors and omissions (E&O) insurance to protect yourself. Or if you don't, Donna Avila-Weil and Mary Glaccum recommend that your contract clearly state that you do not carry E&O insurance and that you are not responsible for errors in your documents unless proofed by the dictating physician. One transcriptionist I interviewed places a footer at the bottom of every page that reads, "Dictated but not read unless signed." This more or less forces the physician to sign each document to verify the accuracy of the transcription.

Building Your Business

Medical transcription demands rigorous training and in-depth technical knowledge and is an extremely intense occupation, but the rewards can be worth the effort. The current shortage of transcriptionists is critical, and it bodes well for a properly trained individual to enter the profession and find steady work with a good salary. For this reason, it is a profession on the forefront of the home-based business movement, allowing thousands of people to establish their own work schedules and run their own businesses from the comfort of their home.

While some predict that new technologies such as voice recognition and computer-based patient records (CPR) may change the face of the profession over the next decade, it is actually far more likely that the evolution of such technology will not remove the need for human intervention in this highly demanding field. For this reason, you can truly count on a fertile environment for good transcriptionists who have the knowledge and skills required in this business. In short, this is a profession in which you can be proud to participate.

CHAPTER 5

Ten Steps to Starting Your Business

The goal of this chapter is leave you with a way to think about a broad range of start-up business advice. Rather than throw out random suggestions and tips, I have developed a brief mnemonic scheme—a device that helps you remember—to assist you in recalling the steps you now need to take. The mnemonic is DREAM BIG for $, which stands for the following sequence of steps:

- Step 1: **D**ouble-check your decision
- Step 2: **R**esearch your business
- Step 3: **E**stablish goals and a business plan
- Step 4: **A**rrange your office
- Step 5: **M**otivate yourself
- Step 6: **B**e professional
- Step 7: **I**nvigorate your marketing
- Step 8: **G**row your business
- Step 9: $$—Make Money!—$$
- Step 10: —Enjoy Yourself!—

Notice that this mnemonic device is upbeat and bright; it even includes that trite little happy face that was popular years ago that most of us now hate. Nevertheless, it has come to represent a certain "Don't worry!" philosophy of life that even the most serious entrepreneurs need to recapture once in a while. The goal of this mnemonic is to remind you at all times of the 10 necessary functions that you must accomplish and keep in mind while undertaking your own business. A good mnemonic sticks in your head for years and years and thus becomes a permanent way to remember a great deal of data that would otherwise confound the mind. Like the mnemonics "Every Good Boy Deserves Fudge" (for the lines of the music staff: EGBDF) and "My Very Excellent Mother Just Sells Nuts Until Passover" (for the planets: Mercury Venus, Earth, etc.), I hope this mnemonic will come to be memorable and significant to you too.

Let's examine now the elements of the mnemonic, exploring what you need to remember at each step of the way.

Step 1: Double-Check Your Decision

It's truly amazing how many people want to be in business for themselves. Though there are no official figures, recent estimates indicate that nearly 36 million people are self-employed and work from home in either full-time or part-time businesses. Small businesses especially are growing, with hundreds of thousands of new incorporations each year, and hundreds of thousands more starting sole proprietorships and partnerships. Another statistic of note is that the fastest growing segment of these new businesses are those started by women.

However, statistics also show that many businesses fail each year, as many as two out of three (and usually within the first year) for a variety of reasons, including excessive spending, poor management, cash flow problems, inadequate marketing, and bad service/product. The point is: are you sure you are ready and able to launch your venture? While pessimism is not useful, and in fact can destroy a positive attitude that contributes to success, I simply suggest that you take time in this initial phase of your thinking to reflect upon your decision and explore its pros and cons in as much depth as you can. Although your choice of a business may arise from your previous background and experience, or from a strongly held desire to work in one of the medical fields, you need to ask yourself several critical questions about your plans:

- Do you have the personality traits that are needed to market a new business?
- Are you willing to learn what you don't know?
- How hard can you work to make your business a success?
- How much are you willing to sacrifice?
- Do you have the character to survive the challenges of start-up?

It can be difficult to force yourself to answer such questions objectively. We are all a product of our own minds and often cannot see our own faults. Some people have a higher opinion of their capabilities than is justified, and may answer such questions with the conviction that they can overcome any challenge. This is usually a good attitude to have, but overstating your qualifications can lead to serious business myopia. You can't afford to miss your own internal problems. This is why, in my opinion, so many people fail in new businesses: they just aren't willing to seek training when they need it, or they fail to ask the right questions because they think they know all the answers.

On the other hand, I also believe that many people discount their talents and shortchange their capabilities. They don't give themselves enough credit for their native intelligence and skills. Many people can prosper in their own business if they recognize that they truly have the talents, skills, and learning ability to succeed. The problem is, people often tend to glamorize entrepreneuring and exaggerate the personal talents and skills needed to do it. They end up fearing that they don't have these skills or abilities, or that their intelligence is insufficient to learn them.

The truth is, few people fit into the category of genius (and that kind of intelligence doesn't necessarily guarantee success anyway). Entrepreneurs are everywhere. Thousands of businesses are started by "ordinary people" every day, except these people believe in themselves and have a deep understanding of their strengths and weaknesses. Their self-knowledge gives them direction and reflection; they know where and how to focus their energy, when to say "I need to learn something new," and when to change course.

The secret to success is best expressed in the adage from Socrates, "Know Thyself." Knowing yourself well allows you to make more meaningful assessments of your skills, abilities, and interests. Don't jump to conclusions about your capability to start a business. Really think through your interests, motivations, strengths, and weaknesses to see if you are minimizing or overstating them.

Table 5-1 contains a list of questions you should consider in double-checking your decision to start a health service business. Rather than having you answer the questions with a simple yes or no, there's a column for your "qualifying thoughts" in which you can reflect deeply about why you said yes or no, and what additional factors you may need to consider to support your conclusion. Consider this column to be the "gray area" in which you are honest in admitting that you don't really know something, or that you actually do believe you could learn something in a relatively short period of time if you put your mind to it.

You might decide, for example, that although you said no to the question that asks about your mastery of accounting and bookkeeping, your qualifying thought might be that you have always enjoyed math. As a result, rather than letting your ignorance of the topic count as a simple *no* that could deter you from your entrepreneurial pursuit, your gray area points out that you recognize your potential to learn about accounting. This will help you see your *potential* energy, rather than your static energy.

Depending on your answers to these questions, you may be ready to get going—or to cancel your plans. If the latter is the case, this book may have saved you a lot of time, headaches, and money. You needn't feel bad about your decision or feel that you have failed. Not starting a health services business does not reflect a deficit in your abilities; it simply indicates that you have wisely chosen otherwise. Perhaps you can explore other entrepreneurial ventures that better match your personal interests and goals. With the growth of home-based work today, you can probably find a wide range of opportunities that might satisfy your personal and professional objectives.

For example, Daniel Lehmann and Patricia Bartello, of DAPA Support Services, the medical billing company mentioned in Chapter 2, spent more than a year evaluating career options. Both had a long-time interest in running their own business, but after a year of exploring franchises and business opportunities, they felt most comfortable choosing a business that matched Pat's previous background in the health field and Dan's background in business. Similarly, Nancie Cummins was coming from an insurance sales background when she decided she wanted to run her own business. She looked at many options, including accounting and medical transcription, but she finally chose medical billing after evaluating her skills and personal interests. In both situations, the individuals involved took their time exploring options and weighing the pros and cons of each.

If you haven't firmly decided to start your own business, you may wish to check the resources in Appendix D. These sources can assist you in eval-

TABLE 5-1

Questions to Ask to Double-Check Your Decision

QUESTIONS	Y	N	QUALIFYING THOUGHTS
Personal Questions			
■ Have you had an interest in running your own business for a long time?			
■ Have you worked in a related business area or had any experience relevant to medical billing, claims assistance, or transcription?			
■ If you haven't worked in a related field before, are you sure that you want to abandon the work experience you already have to learn a new field?			
■ Do you enjoy technical details, formal systems such as health insurance, and complex terminology?			
■ Are you willing to learn new things and to work in a profession that requires continual learning?			
■ Is income potential more important to you than enjoying your work and the people with whom you work?			
■ Are you independent and a self-starter?			
■ Are you persistent, organized, disciplined, trustworthy, creative, and not easily discouraged?			
■ Are you confident about yourself and comfortable working with professionals such as doctors, nurses, and medical personnel?			
■ Is your family supportive of your interest and effort to start your own business?			
■ Are you willing to change your lifestyle so that you can work more hours and more intensely, at least at the beginning of your enterprise?			
■ Do you enjoy working alone without feedback or praise from others?			
■ Have you considered working with a partner?			
Business Questions			
■ Have you had any business training in management, marketing, or sales?			
■ Do you know how much money you will need to get started?			

(Continued)

TABLE 5-1

Questions to Ask to Double-Check Your Decision   (Continued)

QUESTIONS	Y	N	QUALIFYING THOUGHTS
Business Questions (Cont.)			
■ Have you determined your minimum income needs?			
■ Do you know how to do bookkeeping and accounting?			
■ Do you enjoy taking classes on business issues or reading about business in newspapers and magazines?			
■ Do you enjoy working with computers?			
■ Are you open to learning to use new software in desktop publishing, accounting, database management, and other areas?			
■ Do you enjoy negotiating?			
■ Are you willing to do cold calling and selling?			
■ Are you willing to seek business advice from others and accept suggestions and criticism?			

uating your career options and clarifying your true desires. (Even if you have decided to start a medical billing, claims assistance, or transcription business, many of these books will be valuable to you.)

Step 2: Research Your Business

Many people do not like the idea of doing research, preferring to follow their gut feeling, intuition, or perhaps the advice of others. They think research is not action, but rather busywork that does not influence how they act and cannot accomplish what they want to do.

However, given that many new businesses fail during their first year, and that bankruptcy and failure are destructive patterns of behavior, it would seem to be clearly in your best interest to research your new venture. Why risk your money and your goals for lack of a few days of information seeking and asking the right questions? Research not only helps you prevent failure, it also allows you to maximize your potential. If research can help you earn $45,000 in your first year rather than $30,000 because you uncovered a new clinic opening in your community and were the first one to get there, wouldn't that put your business interests in better shape?

The goals of your research should be to find out about the size of the market for your business in your community; to scope out and know your competition, if any; to determine as best you can the optimal way to target your market; to define your company in terms of how your business fits into the industry; to understand the patterns of pricing for your business in your geographic area; and to learn what kinds of mistakes people typically make in your business.

These issues are all vital to making sure you have the best advantage when you get underway. The data you find in researching such issues can influence what title you pick for your company name, how large a geographic area you decide to cover, whether to use direct mail, how many clients you might be able to get in your first year, how long it may take you to break even, and a host of other critical issues that determine whether you remain in business. As you know, most first-year businesses fail, so if you intend to stay in the business, research allows you to better plan your activities and goals, and to be better prepared than the next guy to outlast your competition.

Don't underestimate the power of research! Make some phone calls to doctors' offices and speak with the staff or to the doctor himself or herself. Call a hospital healthcare information department (formerly called medical records) and ask to speak to the supervisor for transcriptionists. Call a local clinic and ask if it has anyone it recommends to those patients who need help filling out claims. Open up the *Yellow Pages* in your city and those within 50 miles, and find out how many companies are listed under Medical Transcription, Billing Services, or Insurance Claims Assistance. Log onto the Internet and search Alta Vista or another search engine for medical transcription or medical billing and review the entries listed. Visit the Web sites of the many organizations and companies involved in the allied health fields, such as NACAP, NEBA, AAMT, HPI, Dictaphone, Lanier, and DVI to learn about trends in your industry.

Call competitors and tell them your plans. Paul and Sarah Edwards report that this method is actually quite useful. If you find that competitors are open about the business and willing to talk, it is a good sign that there is enough business to go around. (You might even get some overflow work simply by doing this.) If you find that people are close-mouthed, you may conclude that times are rough and so you may need to rethink your plans. I found, in researching this book, that all the people I called were open and willing to speak about their businesses. Not only did this indicate to me that they were doing well, but that all the businesses I am covering have ample opportunity for additional players.

Another overlooked avenue for information are your own physicians. Why not use them for information and feedback on your business plans? You will probably find that they are flattered to be asked and might accept an offer to take them to lunch.

Through this footwork and phone calling, you can learn, for example, that you would fare best if you planned to focus on one specialty, such as anesthesiology, because there may already be enough competition in other specialties.

Through your research, you may also find a person who is interested in becoming a partner with you. Some people recognize that they cannot handle all the work, or that they would benefit greatly by having a partner who has different skills, such as marketing experience or a nursing background. You may recall from Chapter 2 that Mary Vandegrift and Heidi Kollmorgen each started out on her own, but both realized shortly thereafter that they didn't enjoy the marketing aspect of medical billing. Each met another woman who had just the talent needed, and now both have successful partnerships. While this option isn't for everyone (many people simply insist on being on their own), collaborations and partnerships, often called strategic alliances, are becoming a more popular and useful paradigm for doing business. (In fact, I have just finished authoring a book with Paul and Sarah Edwards on this topic. Called *Teaming Up*, the book explains how to develop any of ten different types of collaborations and provides legal and financial advice for doing so.)

So, there are many benefits to research. Whether your research period lasts a few days or months, just do it! Although you can also do too much research, and procrastinate starting your venture out of fear, statistics generally indicate that most people don't do enough.

Step 3: Establish Goals and a Business Plan

There are many ways to establish goals, but writing a business plan is the best one. A business plan can range from a formalized document if you are applying for a business loan, to a more informal outline of your future plans and financial projections. Whichever method you choose, a well-conceived written business plan is a map to your destination. It plots the route showing how you will get from point A to point B and serves as a continual reminder of your course.

A business plan usually begins with what is called your company's "mission statement," a terse articulation that explains the heart of your business. This statement expresses what you want customers to think about you, so don't include such statements as "I will make $100,000 within two years." An example of a mission statement for a billing service might be: "To be a dedicated service-oriented company that guarantees the satisfaction of its clients through consistent attention to detail and timeliness on electronic claims and full practice management services."

Don't assume you can eliminate this step if you already have a background in the medical area, such as working for a physician. Despite your experience, writing a business plan will prevent you from falling into the trap of believing that you know how to run a business. Working for someone else is not the same as working for yourself.

An outline of the remainder of a typical business plan is shown in Table 5-2. Each subsection serves a purpose in defining and qualifying your goals, financial expectations, and principles. The more precisely you identify and verbalize your objectives and responses, the better you will fare. Business planning enables you to weed out faulty thinking; it forces you to examine your goals accurately and in detail. By writing down your ideas and thoughts, you can discover inconsistencies and gaps that you failed to notice before.

One important aspect of your business plan is your company name. Now is the time to select it. Your company name is a critical factor in many businesses. You can choose a name to reflect your location, your service, your motto, or your personal attention. Think, for example, of the businesses described in the profiles in this book and the names their owners chose:

- *Billing:* Business Medical Services (Dave Shipton); Medical Management Billing (Nancie Cummins); H/D Medical Receivables, Inc. (Heidi Kollmorgen); Linda's Billing Service (Linda Noel); DAPA Support Services (Daniel Lehmann and Patricia Bartello); AccuMed Solutions (Sheryl Telles and Kathy Allocco)

- *Claims Assistance:* Claims Security of America (Harvey Matoren); In Home Medical Claims (Tom and Nancy Koehler); Claim Relief Inc. (Barbara Melman); Medical Claims Management (Rikki Horne)

- *Transcription:* Words Times 3 (Joan Walston); Monarch Transcription (Terri Ford); Medical Transcription Service (Rochelle Wexler)

TABLE 5-2

Business Plan Outline

I. EXECUTIVE SUMMARY

    1. General description of the business plan

    2. Introduction to the company

    3. Mission statement

    4. Brief description of your business goals and financial requirements

II. COMPANY ANALYSIS

    1. Strengths and weaknesses analysis

    2. Company history

    3. Product, program, and service offerings

    4. Technology and resources

    5. Major competitors and competitive positioning

    6. Factors determining success

III. INDUSTRY ANALYSIS

    1. Definition and description of industry

    2. Growth rate and key factors

    3. Financial characteristics of the industry

IV. MARKET ANALYSIS

    1. Size of total market

    2. Market segmentation and share

    3. Market barriers

    4. Market demand

    5. Price structures and policies

    6. Marketing mix (advertising, public relations, direct selling, and sales promotions)

V. STRATEGIC ANALYSIS

    1. Goals and objectives

    2. Key performance and indicators of success

    3. Tactical plans and completion schedules

    4. Operating assumptions

TABLE 5-2

Business Plan Outline   (Continued)

VI. MANAGEMENT ANALYSIS

      1. Identification of key personnel

      2. Organizational structure

      3. Management and customer service philosophy

VII. FINANCIAL ANALYSIS

      1. Budget projections and pro formas

      2. Financial schedules and statements

As you can see, some of these owners chose names to suggest their medical expertise, while others emphasized a function of their service or their own name. Spend some time considering your business name. Create several options, and then sound them out with friends and professional acquaintances. Choose one that is memorable and portrays a suitable image in your market. Avoid names that sound like other companies in your area.

For assistance in developing a business plan, consider the following sources:

Business planning software. If you are going into medical billing, the association NEBA has a partially formatted business plan on disk that you can use as a template for your own company. The plan comes with a copy of the well-known software program *Tim Berry's Business Plan Tool Kit,* which you can use to modify the template according to your needs. If you go into claims assistance or medical transcription, you can buy Tim Berry's software, as well as another program, *BizPlanBuilder* by JIAN Tools, in any software or office supply store. (A portion of the NEBA business plan for medical billing is included on the CD-ROM accompanying this book. See Appendix A for information about contacting NEBA and Tim Berry's company, Palo Alto Software.)

Books: There are literally several dozen books that teach how to write a business plan. Look in your local bookstore in the small business section.

Government assistance: Many states publish through their Department of Commerce pamphlets and publications that can help you organize yourself and learn about business planning. There are also various bureaus often affiliated with business schools that can assist you in developing your plans. You might also contact the Small Business Administration at 800-827-5722, from which you can obtain information on a host of topics ranging from business planning and financing to women's and minority business issues. There is also the SBA Office of Women's Business Ownership, which you can reach at 202-205-6673. Every state also has one or more branches of the Small Business Development Centers (SBDC) that are specifically intended to help new entrepreneurs create their business plans and objectives. Call your closest SBA office to find out the location of your nearest SBDC.

The National Association of Women Business Owners, founded in 1978 and now with over 10,000 members and scores of chapters across the country, can also be of service to women seeking information and mentoring when opening a new business. It can be reached at 1100 Wayne Avenue Suite 830, Silver Spring, MD 20910, 301-608-2590 phone, 301-608-2596 fax.

Step 4: Arrange Your Office

Now is the time to organize your home-based business. If you are not a neat, organized person by nature, you can benefit by taking a few days to plan your home office, organize your files, purchase supplies, and set up your computer system.

If you are purchasing new equipment, whether it is a new phone system, a computer, or new software, give yourself time to become comfortable operating it. Many software programs have a "quick start" lesson that teaches the basics in a few hours, but to take full advantage of the software's most powerful features, you need to spend time practicing and using it just as you would for your business.

One caution in setting up your home office according to Herman Holtz, author of several consulting books: don't spend excessive amounts of money equipping your business. A rule of thumb is to buy only when the equipment improves your productivity and pays for itself in your next job. For example, if you need to send out direct mail letters and by purchasing a laser printer, you can save $500 in typesetting and design, this purchase is worthwhile. Similarly, spending an additional $75 on a high-speed 28,800 modem rather than a 14,400 modem can pay off in faster transmissions and less wasted time on the Internet. In general, upgrading to better business equipment that significantly improves your productivity is worthwhile, even if you have to purchase it on credit (interest on business debt may be tax deductible for you; check with your accountant).

If you buy office equipment such as computers, furniture, chairs, or lamps, you can write off up to $18,000 (this amount will increase each year between 1997 and 2003 to $25,000) against your gross business income in that year (assuming you made a profit); you cannot write off expenses to create a loss as long as your earnings are at least $10,000 in that year! In other words, you can only write off against earnings; you cannot use business expenditures to create a loss.

Speaking of taxes, here's an important tip about setting up your home office. Be sure to do it so you can legally take a home office deduction for using part of your living quarters as office space. Even if you use part of a bedroom, you can deduct it as an expense (pro-rated according to its percentage of space compared to the total living space in your home) as long as you use it strictly for business purposes. If you make any improvements to your home office, you can also deduct those direct expenses. Of course, you can also deduct against business income standard business expenses, such as office supplies, stationery, business cards, software, shipping/postage charges, professional publications and books, business insurance, and advertising. Be sure to check with your accountant for advice on your specific situation before taking any business or home office deductions. If you take such deductions, make sure you have kept records of all your purchases and office supplies to verify them.

To handle their business finances, many home-based business owners use one of the easy-to-learn accounting programs, such as *Quicken, Cash-Graf, DacEasy Accounting 95, Peachtree Accounting,* or *OneWrite Plus.* These programs have become very easy to use, even for people unfamiliar with accounting and bookkeeping principles. Because none of the businesses covered in this book carry inventory, your accounting will generally be straightforward, and you can most likely keep your books on a "cash" rather than "accrual" basis. If you need assistance in understanding accounting for a home business, go to a bookstore and choose from the many books available on basic accounting procedures.

Step 5: Motivate Yourself to Work and Win

The field of personal performance improvement is growing quickly in the 1990s, as many people have come to recognize that concepts such as creativity, positive thinking, and peak learning are not New Age babble but scientific areas that are researched every day by training and development specialists, instructional designers, and even military planners. In fact, many fascinating general audience books have been published in the past decade that extrapolate on this research.

Starting your own enterprise demands that you maximize your work flow and personal habits. You need to stay motivated and upbeat, learn how to tackle challenges and overcome defeats, and work to your best ability if you want to succeed—and stay healthy. Poor management, one of the leading reasons for business failure, does not only indicate that the entrepreneur did not understand accounting, cash flow, or marketing mix. Poor management can also indicate that the owner has a bad attitude, alienated customers, or became so discouraged that an opportunity to save the business passed right in front of his or her eyes. It is probably an understatement that 50 percent of small business failures happen because people did not have the right personal management skills to keep their business going through rough times.

To motivate yourself, read some of the books listed in Appendix D. These books have helped many people gain greater control of their time, their productivity, and their creativity in business.

Step 6: Be Professional

This step encompasses the many bureaucratic tasks you must take care of to establish your business legally in your community. It also includes the actions you can take to enhance your business image in the eyes of your clientele and the public.

Nearly all home businesses must obtain proper city or county licenses to operate as businesses. You need to make sure that your neighborhood is zoned for home-based businesses, even if you don't have clients coming to your home. If you are doing medical claims assistance, and you have people coming to your home office, be sure that you don't incur the wrath of your neighbors and that you have the proper licenses to run the business from home. You can never tell what might upset a neighbor. One CAP who lived in a condominium complex related to me how her neighbors complained to her association because she had one or two clients per day coming during normal business hours.

In most locales, you need to pay your city or county a few hundred dollars in business license fees. To find out what you owe, check with your city hall or county clerk's office.

If your company uses a name other than your own, you should file a fictitious-name statement, which requires advertising your business name in a local newspaper for a few days and filing paperwork with your city or county. This ensures that you are not accidentally usurping another name already in use.

If you sell any type of product (and some types of services), you may need to register with your state's sales tax board and pay quarterly or monthly sales tax to the state. Check with your accountant about your specific city and state laws.

As mentioned in Chapter 3, if you become a CAP, you may need to be licensed by your state as an insurance broker or public adjuster.

Because you are self-employed and do not have federal taxes and Social Security withheld from a pay check, you will need to file and pay federal and possibly state estimated quarterly taxes on your income. These are due each year on April 15, June 15, September 15, and January 15 for income that was earned in each preceding three-month quarter. One component of what you pay is the "self-employment tax" for your share of Social Security and Medicare taxes. When you work for a company, one-half of this is paid by the employer and the other half is deducted from your paycheck. When you work for yourself, you pay both halves, according to a schedule tied to your net income. Consult your accountant for details about these payments, as there are methods to reduce your liability for the Social Security portion of the tax. Note that you need to keep good records of your income to file these estimates.

Last, you may wish to consider increasing your home insurance to include your home-based business equipment and liabilities. Such extra insurance can usually be done as a rider to your policy for a small additional premium. Whether or not you should buy "errors and omissions insurance" for protection in the event of mistakes you make in your business is difficult to judge. Consult your accountant and lawyer for advice on this issue, as it depends on what assets you need to protect and what risks you take in your business.

Regarding your business image, you can easily enhance the impression you make on your clients by having well-designed and neatly printed stationery and business cards. Try not to settle for the $29.95 special at the local office supply store, as standard business typefaces and logos are not distinctive enough if you want to give the impression of a professional business. Use a desktop publishing software to devise your own logo, or hire a designer to create a specialized logo for your company.

Invest in a high-quality answering machine or voice mail system that allows you to have separate messages for different purposes. A good phone system would have at least two message options (A and B) so that you can record one message for when you are in the office but busy and another message for when you are out. The message you leave on your answering machine or voice mail is important. Don't record an informal or unprofessional message. Call your own machine and listen to your message once in a while to make sure it is working properly and sounds professional. You'd be surprised at how fast, or long, or boring your message may sound to a caller. Many machines allow people to press the star (*) key to bypass the message if they are a frequent caller, so be sure to tell people that.

You should maintain a professional appearance in any of the professions in this book. If you are a male in the medical billing or transcription business, wear a jacket but no tie to meetings with your clients—and don't carry a briefcase. Several people told me that this will prevent receptionists from pegging you as a pharmaceutical salesman and blocking your access to the doctor. You'll have to try this out for yourself.

For many of these issues, it is best to consult a lawyer and an accountant to review your specific situation. For additional assistance in some of the areas of this step, consider joining the newly formed home-based business organization, Small Office Home Office Association (SOHOA). Members of this organization get a variety of benefits, including group health, life, and business insurance; access to a legal service plan that provides with legal advice; the capability to do credit checks on your customers using Dun & Bradstreet services; and the ability to take credit cards (which is difficult to obtain for most home-based businesses). You can reach SOHOA at 1765 Business Center Drive, Reston, VA 22090; phone: 1-888-SOHOA11. Another home-business association is the American Association of Home-Based Businesses, P.O. Box 10023, Rockville, MD 20849, phone 202-310-3130 or 800-447-9710.

Step 7: Invigorate Your Marketing

Each of the chapters in this book has focused on some of the most important marketing concepts for that business. Every home-based business must squarely face the marketing issue, because without customers, you aren't in business. There is no escaping the fact that you should constantly do marketing *all* the time, even when you have a few clients.

This step uses the term "invigorate" quite intentionally. As a home-based business, you don't have the wherewithal to compete with large companies in direct mail volume or in advertising dollars. You need to be creative, originating marketing ideas that make your potential client base take notice of you—and then take action to hire you. Appendix D contains a list of many useful books on marketing, sales, and publicity. Here are some important concepts to keep in mind:

1. Be classic in the design of your marketing materials; don't overdo glitz. This approach provides the professional appearance cherished in the medical market.

2. Have people come to you instead of going to them. Focus your marketing efforts on publicity, networking, and special promotions that make people want your service. Save presentations for someone who has already expressed a strong interest in your service.

3. Obtain personal meetings with your clients, so that they can see who you are and what you can offer. Be pleasant and professional. It's hard to turn down a request for business from a person with whom they've spent some time and have begun to develop a relationship.

4. Referrals are your very best source of business. Use networking to obtain as many leads as you can.

5. Don't lose sight of your cold prospects; call them occasionally to see if their situation has changed.

6. Test your marketing materials. Prepare several different versions of direct mail cards or letters of introduction so that you can test out which one seems to draw the most clientele.

7. Present your information in a simple way that concentrates on what value the customer will get from your service.

8. Devote at least 10 percent to 20 percent of your time on continuous marketing efforts, regardless of how many clients you have. If for some unforeseen reason, a client leaves you and you must replace that business, you will have a much shorter way to go if you have a few warm prospects waiting in the wings.

Step 8: Grow Your Business

When people start their own business, they often don't think they will achieve their target, and so are surprised when they become successful. However, it is important to grow your business slowly while paying attention to the quality of your service. For example, if you find yourself with too many clients to handle alone, your service may suffer and your customers will be disappointed.

Remember to do continuous planning to keep in step with your situation. Revise your plans every few months. Don't let old projections of business growth get stale. If you are to grow your business, you need to keep track of all the details that influence your rate of growth, such as cash flow, hours worked, number of clients, new clients each month, and productivity levels. Accurate record keeping and review will inform you when you might need to put in extra hours to get new clients, or when you might need to hire a temporary assistant.

You also need to grow at a pace that is right for your personality and work habits. You may have dropped out of a corporate job because you were tired of 12-hour days and coming home stressed. If your new home-based business causes you to feel the same stress, you have not gained much. By looking into your heart and taking stock of your true goals, you can reformulate your business direction and reduce the problems that detract from being your own boss. For example, the medical transcriptionist Terri Ford, mentioned in Chapter 4, knew that she wanted to run a home-based business that still gave her time to spend with her children, so she structured her day around that goal and did not force herself to take on more clients than she could readily handle.

Spend one day a month charting your progress. Although you may have started your business because you enjoy the specific work in that field, you still need to be like the president and CEO who stands vigil at the control tower to be sure there are no accidents.

Step 9: $$—Make Money—$$

How do you know if you are making money? Most people look in their checkbook to see if the balance is greater today than yesterday. But this does not mean that you are making money; balances can be deceptive. If you have invoices to get out or collections to make, you are missing money and your checkbook balance does not tell you that. That is why it is better to use an accounting program.

Don't be fooled by your mental or temporary picture of your financial status. Again, use your computer and an accounting package to keep track of your money. Know when you need to get clients to pay, or when you might delay paying a bill yourself to improve your financial picture.

Consider any hesitations you have about making money and refute them. Some people say that they are in business because they like the work, but this is often foolhardy if they are not making enough money to support their business or their families. Why should you settle for $25,000 when you could be making $35,000 or more if you worked more efficiently or priced your service more aggressively? Don't underestimate your potential. If you think you can charge an extra $65 registration fee, do so. If you think you can get the physician to pay $500 for you to do the setup of patients in your medical billing software, by all means ask for it. If the physician disputes your fees, say, "I am just not able to work for free. It will take me two days to enter all your patients, and just as you get paid for your work, I have to get paid for mine." You can always back down and settle for a compromise figure. You need to speak from a position of strength although you needn't hesitate to compromise when necessary. But it isn't worth going into a situation with a compromised position!

Step 10: —Enjoy Yourself!—

If you are going into business for yourself, you probably had a dream that included greater control of your life and more self-respect. On this basis, I highly recommend that you periodically take stock of your business and make sure that you enjoy your work.

One important element are your clients. Do you enjoy working with them and are they worth the financial rewards you gain? Entrepreneurs often feel desperate to accept business even though some customers bring in more problems than profits. We all know that the medical field has its share of egotistical doctors who can be bad businesspeople. There are also front office staff people who, when faced with tremendous pressure to do more than one job, may take their anger out on you. If you are experiencing personality problems with a client, or what appears to you to be an unusual number of snafus, you need to do something about the situation. Either speak up or get out. You do not need to increase your anxiety or financial distress with customers who blockade your success and happiness. This is not to suggest that you abandon clients at the drop of a dime if they are troublesome, but that you look for patterns of behavior that indicate to you that the client is disreputable, egotistical, sexist, or simply not worth your time. Conversely, situations like these may give you an opportunity to test out your personal communication skills. Can you make the situation better by trying to find a way to clear the air?

In short, run your business according to your pleasure and taste. If you are to succeed, you might as well do it your way! I wish you the best of luck in your venture, whatever that might be.

Appendix A

Medical Billing Business Opportunity Vendors

The companies listed on page 274 are all business opportunity vendors. They sell billing and practice management software *plus* some type of training to prepare you to enter the medical billing field. Some people may benefit from purchasing a business opportunity, especially if they do not have a background in health insurance, medical practice management, or sales/marketing. The training and support that a business opportunity vendor provides can improve the chances of success.

There are many medical billing business opportunity vendors in the country. However, it is important to be sure that you buy from a reputable business opportunity dealer. There are reports about vendors who use high-pressure sales techniques to entice you to buy their package, but then do not provide adequate training to help you understand how to use the software or develop a high-quality marketing program to get clients. To protect yourself, please see the suggestions in Chapter 2 for finding a good medical billing business opportunity vendor and some caveats to help you identify unscrupulous vendors.

To simplify your search, the following list includes vendors that, in my view, are among the most reliable and knowledgeable in this business. These vendors offer medical and dental software along with either live training onsite at their offices with professional trainers, or offsite training via phone conference calls and reference materials. Please be aware that purchasing from one of the vendors on this list is not a guarantee that you will succeed in medical billing, nor does it ensure that you will never encounter any problems.

Note that all vendors change their packages and prices, so specific information on prices is not included here. You are encouraged to call each vendor and obtain a brochure showing what is currently included in its package in terms of software (DOS or Windows-based), the extent of study materials provided in its package, the type and location of its training, the cost of ongoing technical and marketing support, and the amount of marketing assistance provided. Which vendor you finally select will be based on your own criteria. Be sure to get a firm understanding with each vendor about how much marketing support you will receive, because marketing your business is the key to success.

ClaimTek
President: Kyle M. Farhat
222 SE 16th Avenue
Portland, OR 97214
800-224-7450 phone
503-239-8316 phone
800-503-9461 fax

Electronic Filing Associates (EFA)
President: Ed Epstein
6900 East Camelback Road
Suite 800
Scottsdale, AZ 85251
800-596-9962 phone
602-481-0464 phone
602-994-9826 fax

Medical Management Software
President: Merry Schiff
1730 South Amphlett Blvd., Suite 217
San Mateo, CA 94402
800-759-8419 phone
415-341-9759 fax

Santiago Data Systems
President: Tom Banks
Director of Sales: Mary Lee Hyatt
1801 Dove Street
Newport Beach, CA 92660-2403
800-652-3500 phone
714-852-6600 phone
714-852-6626 fax

Medical Billing Software Companies

The following companies sell medical and dental billing software only. They do not sell support or training on how to market to healthcare providers. They supply only technical support on using their software.

You may wish to buy directly from one of the following software companies if you believe you have the skills and background to make it on your own. As an alternative to buying from a medical billing business opportunity vendor, you could supplement a direct purchase of software with a home-study course listed in a later section. However, note that this method of studying still requires that you have a good background in health insurance, medical practice management, and marketing. Home study for medical billing without the support of a trained professional is not recommended for those who have a minimal background in the field.

The Computer Place—Medisoft
Contact: Jeff Ward, Marketing Director
Darlene Pickron, Marketing
916 E. Baseline Road
Mesa, AZ 85204
800-333-4747 phone
602-333-4747 phone
602-892-4804 fax
Web site: www.azmedisoft.com

Lytec Software
Lytec Systems
7050 Union Park Center, Suite 390
Midvale, UT 84047
800-735-1991 phone
801-562-0111 phone
801-562-0256 fax
Web site: www.lytec.com

Oxford Medical Systems
President: Gary Boehm
230 Northland Blvd., Suite 223
Cincinnati, OH 45246
800-825-2524 phone
513-772-5102 phone

Associations

The following two organizations are important to join for anyone interested in medical billing:

National Electronic Biller's Alliance (NEBA)
2226 A Westborough Blvd., Suite 504
S. San Francisco, CA 94080
415-577-1190 phone
415-577-1290 fax
Web site: www.nebazone.com

NEBA is a new organization for people in medical billing. The association offers an extensive array of marketing support materials, a home-study course, a newsletter, a template business plan, and certification. Through the association, you can meet many other people who are in the profession and share information and assistance.

New Organization of Claims Assistance Professionals
c/o Lori A. Donnelly
Donnelly Benefit Consultants
2475 Willow Park Road
Bethlehem, PA 18017
610-974-8271 fax
E-mail: dbclad@aol.com

Based on the old NACAP organization, this emerging association, under the leadership of Lori Donnelly, has many members who perform both medical billing and CAP functions. NACAP went out of business just as this new edition of this book was going to press. You can contact Ms. Donnelly for more information about medical billing and claims assistance.

Online Resources

You can find excellent information and an opportunity to chat with colleagues and other people interested in medical billing by going online. The two largest online services in this field are CompuServe and America Online.

- *CompuServe.* First, use the Go command and type "Work." When you enter the Working from Home forum, go to the Library menu and select "Medical Transcription and Billing." This library contains dozens of files with information, reports, and transcripts of conversations or e-mail that are useful to anyone interested in medical billing.

- *America Online.* Enter the key word "Business Strategies," then go to the "Home Business Message Board." Then enter "New" and "Medical Claims Processing."

If you are not a member of either CompuServe or America Online, you can easily subscribe. Both services offer free sign-up disks, which can be found in computer magazines on newsstands everywhere. Otherwise call CompuServe at 800-487-0453 or America Online at 800-827-3338.

Newsletters and Directories

AQC Resource Newsletter
175 N. Buena Vista Avenue, Suite B
San Jose, CA 95126
408-295-4102 phone

Noted medical billing industry watcher Gary Knox publishes this excellent newsletter bi-monthly. The newsletter contains reviews of software, business opportunity companies, notes on healthcare trends.

AQC Resources also publishes **The Directory of Medical Management Software.** This is an excellent compilation of the many companies involved in the medical billing field, including software publishers, business opportunity vendors, clearinghouses, and associations. The directory includes reviews of most of the leading software products and business opportunity vendors.

NOTE: *Readers of this book can purchase the AQC Directory of Medical Management Software at a 10% discount off the usual AQC price. The discounted price is $40.00 including first class shipping and handling. (California residents: add 8.25% state tax, totaling $43.00.) Please make your check out to Rick Benzel and send it to: Benzel/AQC Order, 11670 National Blvd., Suite 104, Los Angeles, CA 90064. Allow 10-14 days for processing and first class delivery.*

Code Facts Newsletter
Published by Medicode
5225 Wiley Post Way, Suite 500
Salt Lake City, UT 84116
800-678-TEXT (8398) phone

This twice-monthly publication includes articles on coding tips, questions and answers, office management strategies, and Medicare policy changes.

Magazines and Professional Journals

Before subscribing to the following magazines and journals, look at a copy at a library or call to ask for a sample copy to determine your level of interest.

Journal of Medical Practice Management
  800-638-6423 or 410-528-4100
  $134 per year

Medical Economics
  800-223-0581
  $94/year

Clearinghouses

There are literally dozens of clearinghouses you can work with. Your software may require you to go through one specific clearinghouse. However, you can likely work with any clearinghouse you want. Contact the following clearinghouse for a competitive rate:

Electronic Translations and Transmittals Corporation (ET&T)
Frank Haraksin, President and Founder
Victorville, CA
619-955-1788 phone
800-950-3868 for information

The following clearinghouse is developing the capability to handle insurance eligibility requests electronically:

EDI Pathways Corporation
Kathy Allocco, Sheryl Telles, and Noreen Sachs
7898 East Acoma Drive, Suite 101
Scottsdale, AZ 85260-3480
888-EDI-CORP phone
602-368-9200 phone

Supplier of Medical Coding and Reference Books

Medicode
5225 Wiley Post Way, Suite 500
Salt Lake City, UT 84116
800-678-TEXT (8398)
Web site: www.medicode.com

Medicode publishes and distributes medical information books, such as ICD-9 and CPT coding books, as well as many others. Ann Jacobsen, Account Specialist, will help you with your reference book needs. For readers of this book, she offers a 15 percent discount on Medicode publications, and 10 percent on other publications. To receive your discount, identify yourself as a reader of this book.

Recommended titles from Medicode:

Understanding Medical Insurance: A Step-by-Step Guide, 3d Edition by Jo Ann C. Rowell

Coders' Desk Reference, published by Medicode

Reimbursement Manual for the Medical Office: A Comprehensive Guide to Coding, Billing, and Fee Management, published by PMIC.

PMIC
4727 Wilshire Blvd., Suite 300
Los Angeles, CA 90010
800-MED-SHOP

PMIC publishes a variety of medical reference books, including books on coding, billing, and practice management. Call for a catalogue. See especially the books on practice management, which can help you understand the physician's point of view.

Home-Study Courses

National Electronic Biller's Alliance (NEBA)
2226 A Westborough Blvd., Suite 504
S. San Francisco, CA 94080
415-577-1190 phone
415-577-1290 fax
Web site: www.nebazone.com

NEBA offers a detailed home-study course in medical billing. The course contains in-depth information on what you need to know to get into medical billing and how to market your services.

At-Home Professions
2001 Lowe Street
Ft. Collins, CO 80525-9949
800-528-7907

At-Home Professions offers a multivolume home-study course in medical billing and also one in medical transcription.

Marketing Support Materials

National Electronic Biller's Alliance (NEBA)
2226 A Westborough Blvd., Suite 504
S. San Francisco, CA 94080
415-577-1190 phone
415-577-1290 fax
Web site: www.nebazone.com

NEBA offers a wide variety of marketing support materials, including an excellent tape program, templates you can use for your brochures and fliers, phone consultations, and software you can use during your presentations.

Communications Plus
Brenda Borneman
28 Coy Park Drive
Newark, IL 60541
815-695-5223 phone

This company supplies mailing lists of medical providers who do not file electronically—exactly what you need for your business. You can order from Brenda directly.

General Business Books

See Appendix D for a list of books on entrepreneuring and marketing your business.

In addition, if you are interested in software to help write your business plan or to assist with your marketing planning, contact the following company about their software products: *Tim Berry's Business Plan Pro* and *Tim Berry's Marketing Plus.* These are two of the best software products available for entrepreneurs.

Palo Alto Software
144 East 14th Avenue
Eugene, OR 97401
800-229-7526 phone
541-683-6162 phone
E-mail: info@palo-alto.com
Web site: www.palo-alto.com

Contact NEBA at the address and phone number on page 280 for a special version of *Tim Berry's Plan Pro* that contains a business plan template for a medical billing business. A sample of this template is included on the CD-Rom accompanying this book.

General Health Information

Health Care Financing Administration (HCFA)
U.S. Department of Health and Human Services
7500 Security Boulevard
Baltimore, MD 21244
Web site: www.hcfa.gov

HCFA is the federal government agency that operates Medicare and Medicaid. You must understand Medicare and Medicaid billing rules and regulations. You can download from HCFA's Web site the most current edition of the *Medicare Handbook,* which will give you a general overview of how Medicare works and what benefits it pays to enrollees. [Note: to view the document just as it is printed, you will need to first download the Adobe Acrobat Reader, which is available free at http://www.adobe.com/acrobat/readstep.html. Then when you go to the hcfa.gov Web site to download the *Medicare Handbook* as a "pdf" file, it will automatically appear on your screen exactly as printed in booklet form. Alternatively, you can visit the hcfa.gov Web site and download the handbook as a straight text (.txt) file, but it will not be formatted in columns and with photos as you would find in the printed document.]

However, this document is intended for the general public, so it is not specific enough to teach you about billing issues you may encounter as a professional medical billing service. To learn more about Medicare, check with the insurance carrier in your state or region that is responsible for handling Medicare claims. Enroll in the billing seminars it offers.

Health Insurance Association of America (HIAA)

1025 Connecticut Avenue NW
Washington, DC 20036-3998
800-828-0111 to order the *Source Book*

HIAA offers an excellent annual publication containing information and statistics about the healthcare industry, particularly relating to health insurance. If you enjoy facts and statistics or want to use such data in your presentations to potential clients, order a copy of the *Source Book of Health Insurance Data,* usually published in a new edition in March of each year.

Appendix B

Associations

New Organization of Claims Assistance Professionals
c/o Lori A. Donnelly
Donnelly Benefit Consultants
2475 Willow Park Road
Bethlehem, PA 18017
610-974-8271 fax
E-mail: dbclad@aol.com

As indicated in the text, the old NACAP organization went out of business just as this new edition of this book was going to press. A new organization is evolving, under the guidance of several active members of NACAP, spearheaded by Lori Donnelly. You can contact her about the status of the new organization and its membership. As the new organization develops, there will be many opportunities for leadership roles and networking.

Training Programs

Institute of Consulting Careers (ICC)
222 SE 16th Avenue
Portland, OR 97214-1488
800-829-9473 phone

ICC is a publisher of professional business training materials. ICC produces a home-study course coauthored by CAP Lori Donnelly and Rick Benzel. The course includes two manuals, two videos, and a diskette containing sample letters, forms, and agreements. The course sells for $495, but ICC will provide a 10 percent discount to readers of this book.

Claims Security of America
Harvey Matoren
3926 San Jose Park
P.O. Box 23863
Jacksonville, FL 32241-3863
904-733-2525 phone
800-400-4066 phone

Harvey Matoren offers workshops and seminars in CAP work. He also has a software program developed for use in his own business. Harvey is an extremely knowledgeable and experienced practitioner of CAP work.

Donnelly Benefit Consultants
Lori Donnelly
2457 Willow Park Road, Suite 219
Bethlehem, PA 18017
610-974-8447 phone
610-974-8271 fax

Lori Donnelly offers workshops and seminars to teach CAP work as well as medical billing. She will also come to your location for a fee to train you in either business.

Information on Medicare

Health Care Financing Administration (HCFA)
U.S. Department of Health and Human Services
7500 Security Boulevard
Baltimore, MD 21244
Web site: www.hcfa.gov

HCFA is the federal government agency that operates Medicare and Medicaid. You must understand Medicare if you work as a CAP. You can download from HCFA's Web site the current yearly edition of the *Medicare Handbook* to get a general overview of Medicare benefits. This publication is updated annually and contains a description of Part A and Part B benefits, deductibles, and copayments. The document is intended for the general public, but it is a good start if you have little knowledge of Medicare. [Note: to view the document just as it is printed, you will need to first download the Adobe Acrobat Reader, which is available free at http://www.adobe.com/acrobat/readstep.html. Then when you go to the hcfa.gov Web site to download the Medicare Handbook as a "pdf" file, it will automatically appear on your screen exactly as printed in booklet form. Alternatively, you can visit the hcfa.gov Web site and download the handbook just as a straight text (.txt) file, but it will not be formatted in columns and with photos as you would find in the printed document.]

General Books on Medicare and Health Insurance

Check your local bookstore for a variety of books that are continually published intended to help consumers understand Medicare and Medigap, such as *Medicare and Medigaps: A Guide to Retirement Health Insurance* by Susan and Leonard Hellman, and *Medicare Made Easy* by Charles Inlander and Charles MacKay. You can also benefit by reading *Understanding Medical Insurance* by Jo Ann C. Rowell, available from NACAP or Medicode (see Appendix A). These resources can add to your general knowledge, although you will need a more in-depth understanding developed through experience and networking with other CAPs.

Hospital Bill Auditing Business Opportunity

Healthcare Data Management, Inc.
President: Bill Conlan
60 Chestnut Avenue, Suite 103
Devon, PA 19333
800-859-5119 phone
610-341-8608 phone
610-989-0658 fax

HDM offers a business opportunity in "hospital and doctor bill auditing." This field is related to CAP work but focuses more specifically on auditing hospital bills. The business opportunity includes software, manuals about the hospital billing business, general business manuals, contact management software, sample marketing materials, and two days of training in the Philadelphia area (airfare not included).

Appendix C

RESOURCES FOR MEDICAL TRANSCRIPTION

Home-Study Programs

Many community colleges and vocational schools offer training for medical transcription. However, if you are not inclined to attend an academic program, consider the following home-study programs:

SUM (Systems Unit Method) Program for Medical Transcription Training
Health Professions Institute (HPI)
P.O. Box 801
Modesto, CA 95353
209-551-2112 phone
Website: www.hpisum.com

The SUM program is considered to be the top-ranked program for learning medical transcription. The basic program, called the Beginning Medical Training (BMT), consists of a specific syllabus of readings plus 12 tapes that utilize authentic dictations. It normally takes 480 hours to complete the basic program, including all the recommended readings. (That amounts to 12 weeks if you study for 40 hours per week; or 24 weeks at 20 hours per week.) The advanced program consists of five additional modules in various specialties: cardiology, gastroenterology, orthopedics, pathology, and radiology.

HPI also sells a wide assortment of reference and word books for medical transcriptionists, and it publishes a quarterly magazine, *Perspectives on the Medical Transcription Profession*.

Review of Systems (ROS)
Jennifer Martin
1633 NE Rosewood Drive
Gladstone, MO 64118
800-951-5559 phone
816-468-4403 phone
E-mail: MTMonthly@AOL.com
Web site: www.tyrell.net/~mtmonth

ROS uses the same materials from SUM program, but in an interactive format. Ms. Martin provides personal feedback on your assignments, grades your tests, and generally helps you with your progress in accomplishing the SUM program. ROS is useful for people who want to study independently but would like a watchful eye helping them along the way.

California College for Health Sciences
222 West 24th Street
National City, CA 91950
800-221-7374 phone
Web site: http://cchs.edu

CCHS offers an Associate of Science degree program specializing in medical transcription. CCHS is a recognized degree-granting institution for distance education. The program in medical transcription utilizes the SUM program materials.

Medical Management Software
President: Merry Schiff
1730 South Amphlett Blvd., Suite 217
San Mateo, CA 94402
800-759-8419 phone
415-341-9759 fax

Medical Management Software is a reseller of the SUM program. Contact Merry Schiff to learn about the discount offered for the beginning SUM program for readers of this book.

At-Home Professions
2001 Lowe Street
Fort Collins, CO 80525
800-528-7907 phone

At-Home Professions offers its own independent study course in medical transcription, consisting of five modules. Each module contains a study manual/workbook and tapes.

Newsletter

MT Monthly
Suite 100
1633 NE Rosewood Drive
Gladstone, MO 64118
800-951-5559 or 816-468-4403 phone
Published by Jennifer Martin
$48 per year or $90 for two years

The newsletter contains articles of interest to the home-based transcriptionist, including business issues, product reviews, updates on new terminology and technology, new drug information, and humor. You can download a copy from CompuServe, on the Working from Home forum, in the library section for medical transcription. You can also see a recent copy on the Internet at www.Tyrell.net/~mtmonth.

Business Training

For an in-depth examination of becoming an independent medical transcriptionist, see

The Independent Medical Transcriptionist
Donna Avila-Weil and Mary Glaccum
Rayve Productions, Inc.
Box 726
Windsor, CA 95492
800-852-4890 phone

This book contains a detailed presentation of the issues involved in becoming an independent transcriptionist. Recommended reading if you are serious about this profession.

Medical Terminology, Word, and Reference Books

Medical transcriptionists need an assortment of reference and words books to check spelling of terms and definitions. You can order a wide variety of reference and terminology books from Health Professions Institute and AAMT. See their listings for ordering information. You can also order reference materials from the American Medical Association; to obtain its catalog, call 800-621-8335 and ask for customer service.

In addition, there are many major publishers of medical reference and word books, including

- F.A. Davis Company, 1915 Arch St., Philadelphia, PA 19103, 800-523-4049

- J.B. Lippincott, East Washington Square, Philadelphia, PA 19105, 800-638-3030

- South-Western Publishing, 4770 Duke Drive, Suite 200, Mason, OH 45040, 800-242-7972
- Springhouse Publishing Company, 1111 Bethlehem Pike, Springhouse, PA 19477, 800-346-7844
- W.B. Saunders Company, 6277 Sea Harbor Drive, Orlando, FL 32887, 800-545-2522
- Williams & Wilkins, 428 East Preston Street, Baltimore, MD 21202, 800-638-0672

Spell Checking Software

The following companies produce specialized spell checking databases in the medical field that work either with a standard word processor such as *WordPerfect* or with a proprietary word processor:

- Spellex Development (medical spell check for DOS and Windows) 800-442-9673
- Sylvan Software (medical spell check for DOS and Windows) 800-235-9455
- W.B Saunders Company (medical spell check for DOS and Windows) 800-545-2522
- Williams & Wilkins (medical spell check for DOS, Windows, and Mac) 800-527-5597

Word-Expanding Software

Word-expanding software allows you to type just the first few characters of long medical words and have the entire word appear, saving keystrokes and time. The following companies provide such word-expanding software:

- Hawk Technologies, Inc.—Product: *ShortCut*—770-640-1151
- Narratek—Product: *Smartype*—617-566-1066
- Productive Performance—Product: *Medical Macro Expanders*—206-788-8300

- Productivity Software International—Product: *PRD + MedEasy*—212-818-1144
- Summit Software—Product: *FlashForward*—800-577-6665
- Textware Solutions—Product: *InstantText*—800-355-5251
- Twenty-First Century Research—Product: *Explode-It!*—800-563-5418

Associations

Health Professions Institute (HPI)
P.O. Box 801
Modesto, CA 95353
209-551-2112 phone
209-551-0404 fax

HPI is not actually an association, but if you are a student of medical transcription, you can join its network MTSN (Medical Transcription Student Network). Benefits include a free subscription to HPI's magazine *Perspectives* and to a special newsletter for students *MTSN Gazette.* You also receive a 10 percent discount on reference books purchased from HPI and Williams and Wilkins.

Medical Transcription Industry Alliance (MTIA)
Executive Director: Catherine Baxter
Houston, TX
713-313-6050 phone
713-313-6051 fax
e-mail: csbmtia@icsi.net
Web site: www.wwma.com/a2/mtia

Begun as an association for owners of large medical transcription services, MTIA has branched into representing transcription businesses of any size, including one- and two-person small-office and home-based independents. Today, MTIA is geared to meet the educational and networking needs of many transcription businesses and interested students who are planning a career in medical transcription. Among the goals of MTIA are to promote uniform performance standards, to educate transcriptionists about new technologies and industry changes, and to provide business information for committed entrepreneurs. MTIA has several membership categories, including an associate membership for those who are just getting under way in an independent business. The CD-ROM accompanying this book contains a document about the history of MTIA.

American Association for Medical Transcription
Pat Forbis—Associate Executive Director
P.O. Box 576187
Modesto, CA 95357-6187
800-982-2182 phone (Ask for Director of Member Services)
209-551-0883 phone
Web site: www.sna.com/aamt

AAMT is oriented toward promoting the continuing education and high-level ethical and professional standards for transcriptionists. In general, it is not oriented toward teaching you the entrepreneurial skills of starting and running a small or independent medical transcription business, although it now has a business issues subgroup. If you are a student in a full-time college program or a working transcriptionist, you may wish to join AAMT to obtain its benefits: an excellent quarterly journal, *JAAMT*, which contains many articles to help you continue your medical transcription education. AAMT has local subchapters in many areas as well. AAMT also offers a certification exam that may add credibility to your business. The exam is in two parts—written and practical; you must pass the first portion before you can take the second. You do not need to be a member of AAMT to take the certification exam.

Online Services

- *CompuServe.* To find the forum for medical transcriptionists, use the GO command and type WORK. This will take you to the Working from Home forum; then choose LIBRARY, and select "Medical Billing and Transcription." This library contains files of interest to medical transcriptionists, including transcripts of past conversations among transcriptionists and reviews of hardware and software.

- *America Online.* You will find the transcriptionists under EXCHANGE, Home/Health Careers, on the Careers Bulletin Board.

- *Prodigy.* You will find medical transcriptionists on the Careers Bulletin Board under the Medical Transcription Topic.

- *Genie.* Genie has its own software (Aladdin), which can be downloaded once you have registered and are online. You will find the MTs on the Medical Bulletin Board.

In addition, the Internet has become a burgeoning resource for transcriptionists. There is a medical transcription newsgroup called sci.med.transcription, where you can chat with many others and read previous conversations between transcriptionists who debate the fine points of which associations to join and which technology to use. There are also many home pages belonging to transcriptionists on the Net. For example, see the Web site, www.angelfire.com.

Appendix D

Resources for Double-Checking Your Decision

- *To Build the Life You Want, Create the Work You Love*, by Marsha Sinetar, St. Martin's Press
- *Finding Your Perfect Work*, by Paul and Sarah Edwards, Jeremy P. Tarcher/Putnam
- *Growing a Business*, by Paul Hawken, Fireside/Simon & Schuster
- *Honey, I Want to Start My Own Business: A Planning Guide for Couples*, by Azriella Jaffe, HarperBusiness
- *How to Find Your Mission in Life*, by Richard Bolles, Ten Speed Press
- *On Your Own: A Guide to Working Happily, Productively and Successfully at Home*, by Lionel Fischer, Prentice Hall

In addition to these books, contact the various associations listed in Appendices A to C, including NEBA, NACAP, AAMT, HPI, and MTIA, to obtain general information about the professions they represent. Speaking to people in these associations can often be useful in helping you decide if you want to enter the career they represent.

Resources for Motivation

- *Aha: Ten Ways to Free Your Creative Spirit and Find Your Great Ideas*, by Jordan Ayan, Random House
- *The Greatest Salesman in the World*, by Og Mandino, Warner
- *How to Succeed on Your Own: Overcoming the Emotional Roadblocks*, by Karin Abarbanel, Holt
- *How to Think Like an Entrepreneur*, by Michael B. Shane, Bret Publishing
- *The Secrets of Successful Self-Employment*, by Paul and Sarah Edwards, Jeremy P. Tarcher/Putnam

- *Seven Habits of Highly Effective People,* by Steven Covey, Fireside/Simon & Schuster
- *Seven Laws of Spiritual Success,* by Deepak Chopra, Amber Allen Publishing

Resources to Invigorate Your Marketing

- *Do It Yourself Marketing,* by David Ramacitti, Amacom
- *Grow Your Own Business with Desktop Marketing,* by Steven Morgenstern, Random House
- *How to Get Big Results from a Small Advertising Budget,* by Cynthia Smith, Carol Publishing
- *How to Get Clients,* by Jeff Slutsky, Warner
- *Secrets of Savvy Networking,* by Susan RoAne, Warner
- *Successful Presentations for Dummies,* by Malcolm Kushner
- *The Ultimate Sales Letter,* by Daniel Kennedy, Bob Adams Publishing
- *Street Smart Marketing,* by Jeff Slutsky, Wiley
- *The World's Best Known Marketing Secret,* by Ivan R. Misner, Bard & Stephen

SPECIALTY ITEMS

- *The Business Generator,* by Paul and Sarah Edwards, includes a copy of *Getting Business to Come to You* plus a special program created by the Edwardses to help you understand your preferred marketing methods and develop an effective marketing strategy. Call 800-561-8990 for orders.

Business Planning Books

- *Business Planning Guide,* by David Bangs Jr., Upstart
- *How to Write a Business Plan,* by Mike McKeever, Nolo Press
- *Preparing a Successful Business Plan,* by Rodger Touchie, Self-Counsel Press
- *Successful Business Plans: Secrets and Strategies,* by Rhonda M. Abrams, Oasis Press

SOFTWARE

- *BizPlanBuilder,* Jian Tools for Sales, Inc.
- *The Medical Billing Business Plan Template,* available from NEBA (see listing in Appendix A), includes a copy of Tim Berry's *Business Planning Software*

General Business Books

- *The E-Myth: Why Most Small Businesses Don't Work and What to Do About It,* by Michael Gerber
- *The Home Office and Small Business Answer Book,* by Janet Attard, Henry Holt
- *The Idiot's Guide to Starting Your Own Business,* by Edward Paulson with Marcia Layton, Alpha Books
- *Running a One Person Business,* by Claude Whitmeyer, Salli Rasberry, and Michael Philips, Ten Speed Press
- *Teaming Up,* by Paul and Sarah Edwards and Rick Benzel, Putnam/Jeremy P. Tarcher
- *Streetwise Guide to Small Business Startup,* Bob Adams, Bob Adams Publishing
- *Working from Home,* by Paul and Sarah Edwards, Jeremy P. Tarcher/Putnam

In addition to these books, visit the web site for Paul and Sarah Edwards at www.workingfromhome.com. Here you will find a wealth of information about home-based professions. The Edwards are also the hosts of a weekly radio show which you can hear in many cities on the Business Radio Network, or you can hear it live at the web site www.cfra.com (assuming you have installed audio plug-in software that allows you to download broadcasts and sounds off the Internet using Netscape or Microsoft Explorer). You can also order an interactive CD-ROM version of their noted book on marketing, *Getting Business to Come to You,* by calling 800-756-0339.

General Business Associations

National Association of Women Business Owners (NAWBO)
1100 Wayne Avenue, Suite 830
Silver Spring, MD 20910
301-608-2590 phone
301-608-2596 fax

NAWBO is the premier organization for women entrepreneurs. There are hundreds of local chapters that provide business information, support, and opportunities for networking.

Small Office Home Office Association (SOHOA)
1765 Business Center Drive
Reston, VA 22090
1-888-SOHOA11 phone
1-703-438-3049 fax

SOHOA provides networking and educational opportunities for self-employed individuals. Through the power of the association, you can purchase automobile, home, health, and life insurance at group rates. It also has a special program with a bank that allows you to accept credit cards for payment.

Appendix E

CONTENTS OF THE CD-ROM

The CD-ROM accompanying this book contains "demos" of seven medical billing software programs and a demonstration copy of the medical billing business plan template available from NEBA. In some cases, the demonstration versions are live working software, although they have been disabled or limited in some fashion, such as the number of patients they can store or actions they can perform. In other cases, the demonstration is a self-running presentation of the software.

Note: All of the software publishers included here may have put out newer versions of their software since this CD-ROM was compiled. Please call the vendors directly to obtain information about any new releases they have; their direct phone numbers are provided below.

The following information explains how to use the CD-ROM.

Installation Procedures

To install the software programs on your computer from the CD-ROM, follow these instructions:

For Windows 95 systems:

Save and close all programs and documents currently running. (One of the demos requires you to restart your computer after its installation, so you don't want to lose any data you may be in the middle of working on when this occurs. It is therefore important to save your data first and close all running applications before starting this installation procedure.)

Insert the CD-ROM into the drive. Select the [Start] button.

From the Start menu, select the "Run" option.

At the "Run" prompt, type the following: E:\SETUP.EXE (or use whatever drive letter is associated with your CD-ROM drive)

Follow the prompts on the screen to complete the installation. You will be prompted to select the programs you want to install, and you may "uncheck" any programs you don't want.

All the programs (except OneClaim Plus) will automatically be installed to your hard drive. These will be grouped together and listed as "Benzel Demos" on the Programs submenu of your "Start" menu.

The last program, OneClaim Plus, has its own installation program. After the first seven programs have been automatically installed, a separate installation wizard will automatically take over and install OneClaim Plus. It will then prompt you to restart Windows before continuing. **Note:** OneClaim Plus will not be listed as part of Benzel Demos; it has its own listing in your Programs submenu.

After the installation, look at the "Copyright and Contacts Readme" file before using any of the software. This file contains information about your warranty from McGraw-Hill, as well as listing all the addresses and phone numbers of the software companies included on this CD-ROM. You may wish to print out this file.

To run any program (except for OneClaim Plus), go to "Benzel Demos" and select it. Further details are provided below. To run OneClaim Plus, it is listed as a separate title on your Program menu. Some of the software programs also contain Readme files that explain the specifics of how to use them. Read these files for assistance in how to use each software product.

For Windows 3.1x systems

Save and close all running applications first to be sure you do not lose any data.

Insert the CD-ROM into the drive. From the "File" menu, select "Run."

At the Run prompt, type the following (use the drive letter associated with your CD-ROM drive): D:\SETUP.EXE.

Follow the prompts on the screen to complete the installation.

The presentation will be installed in a group folder named "Benzel Demos" which will appear on your desktop.

To run any software, click on its icon or on a Readme file associated with that software. Further details are provided below.

There is also a "Copyright and Contacts Readme" file which you should read first. This contains a listing of all the software companies and warranty information.

NOTE: *Santiago's OneClaim Plus operates only with Windows 95. When you are installing the other 7 programs, you will receive a prompt reminding you that this software will not install on your system if you are working under Windows 3.x. Be sure to "uncheck" this software from the install box if you are running Windows 3.x.*

Uninstall Procedures

For Windows 95 systems

For all Benzel Demo Applications:

Select the "Uninstall Readme" icon from the Benzel Demo Applications program group. This contains specific information about how to uninstall the programs, including OneClaim Plus.

For Windows 3.x systems

To uninstall the software, refer to the "Uninstall Readme" file under "Benzel Demos."

Detailed Guidance to Use Each Program

1. InfoHealth Demonstration Software: The Claims Manager
InfoHealth (a division of Synaps Corporation) has provided a demonstration of its medical billing software, The Claims Manager. The demonstration includes a working but limited version of the company's software with complete instructions for a walk-through.

To run the software:

Select "InfoHealth Presentation" from the program group Benzel Demos. A main menu screen will appear, containing 3 categories.

Opportunity—under this category, two buttons appear: The Industry and Synaps Corporation. Clicking on each button will reveal a document you can read.

The Solution—under this category, the Features and How to Order buttons also contain documents to read.

Software Showcase—under this category, there are 3 buttons:

Overview—this button provides a self-running tour. (Use the right arrow key to advance through the tour; hit the escape key if you want to exit it.)

Instructions—this button provides important information for using the demo.

Demonstration—this button launches you into a demo of the Info-Health software.

Important note: Before trying the demo, click on the "Instructions" button and print them out; you will need them to operate the software and get a feel for how to use it.

NOTE: *When trying the actual software, try printing out sample patient statements and monthly reports. If you want to do so, be sure to change the parameter for "Print Device" from "Output1.opt" by pressing the F1 key and selecting "Printer1."*

Additional note: Do not uninstall this demo from the main menu. Use the uninstall Wizard that comes with the Benzel Demos and uninstalls all the software programs at once (except for OneClaim Plus).

For more information, contact Synaps Corporation/InfoHealth at 800-455-2544.

2. Lytec Systems Demonstration Software: Lytec Medical for Windows Lytec has provided a working but limited copy of its medical billing software, Lytec Medical for Windows.

To run the software:

Open the instructions found in the file called Lytec Readme. Print out the file, as this contains a tutorial to help you walk through the software using sample data.

Select the software Lytec Medical from Benzel Demos. Follow the instructions for using the software in the Readme file. The demo includes hypothetical sample data that is automatically loaded, allowing you to practice with the software.

There is also a Lytec Help file in Benzel Demos that contains general Help screens about the software.

For more information, contact Lytec Systems at 800-735-1991.
Lytec is also sold by the following two business opportunity vendors:

Medical Management Software (800-759-8419)

Claim-Tek (800-224-7450).

3. Santiago SDS, Inc. Demonstration Software: OneClaim Plus
Santiago SDS, Inc. has provided a demonstration copy of its software, OneClaim Plus. This is a working but limited version of the software.

NOTE: *This software requires Windows 95, a Pentium processor, and 20MB of free space on your hard drive. Remember, this software does not appear under Benzel Demos on your Programs menu; it is listed separately. However, the Readme and Help files for this software are located in Benzel Demos.*

To run the software:

Open the "OneClaim Plus Readme" file located in Benzel Demos that provides complete instructions for using the demo. You may wish to print out this file before using the software.

Select "OneClaim Plus for Windows" located on your Programs menu of your Start Button. (Remember, this program is not located under Benzel Demos. It insisted on having its location on the Programs menu of your Start menu.)

There is also a Santiago Help file located under Benzel Demos. This file contains general help screens about the software.

For more information, contact Santiago SDS, Inc. at 800-652-3500.

4. ClaimTek Systems Demonstration Software: Data-Link
ClaimTek has provided a demonstration copy of its medical practice management software for Windows, Data-Link. This software is not a medical billing program; it is intended to be used in a physician's office, to which your independent medical billing service would be linked. The staff in a

physician's office uses Data-Link to record patient visits and perform practice management for the physician. The independent billing service links up with Data-Link over the modem to download the data that the office staff has keyboarded, with which it can perform the billing and electronic claims submission. The medical billing service then uploads updated account information back to the physician's office. Data-Link interfaces with Lytec Medical for Windows, which ClaimTek sells you with Data-Link.

To run the software:

NOTE: *There are no specific instructions with this demo program. Begin by clicking on the "Locate Patient" button and then type in "Smith." This will bring up a patient into the main field, and you can then click on any of the other buttons to peruse the screens.*

For more information, contact Claim-Tek at 800-224-7450.

5. Medisoft Demonstration Software á Medisoft Advanced Patient Accounting Medisoft has provided a demonstration copy of its software, Medisoft Advanced Patient Accounting (DOS-based). The software includes a self-running screen show demo that walks you through the software. Medisoft is developing a Windows-based version of this product.

To run the software:

Select "Medisoft Patient Accounting" from Benzel Demos. The program will load and begin. The main menu screen gives you the option of choosing a self-running demo or using an actual version of the software. It is recommended that you select the self-running demo first. Hit any key to walk through the self-running demo. Hit Escape to exit the demo and go to the actual software.

When you are working in the actual software, use your down arrow key on the main menu to select the option "Exit" when you want to quit. The escape key does not exit the software and return you to Windows.

For more information, contact Medisoft at 800-333-4747.

6. Oxford Medical Systems Demonstration Software: WinClaim IV for DOS Oxford Medical Systems has provided a demonstration version of its software WinClaim. (Note: the program is DOS-based.) The demo contains both a self-running presentation and a working but limited copy of the software that you can actually use to run a medical billing business. (The live software is limited to 500 patients, but it will keep records and print HCFA 1500 forms. However, it will not send electronic claims.)

To run the software:

Select "WinClaim Demonstration" from Benzel Demos to see a self-running demo of the software. Hitting any key will advance you through the demo.

Go to Benzel Demos and select "WinClaim Readme." This provides information on how to use the actual software. After you have printed out this Readme file, go to next step.

Select WinClaim Introduction" from Benzel Demos. The WinClaim software will start. Follow the directions in the Readme file.

For more information, contact Oxford Medical Systems at 513-772-5102.

7. Healthcare Data Management, Inc. Demonstration Software: Medical Bill Auditing This company has provided a self-running presentation of its medical bill auditing business opportunity. The demo does not include the software HDM sells for hospital bill auditing. Be sure to ask the company for a demo of its complete software before investing.

To run the demo:

Select "Healthcare Readme" from Benzel demos. Read the file for information on using the demo.

Select "Healthcare Presentation" from Benzel Demos to start the software.

Anytime you want to advance to the next slide, press the enter key.

When you see a blue box, click the left button of your mouse on this box and it will display additional information about the topic.

When you want to exit the program, press the escape key.

For more information, contact Healthcare Data Management, Inc. at 800-859-5119.

8. Business Plan Pro—Medical Billing Business Planning Software Demo The National Electronic Biller's Alliance has produced a business plan template for people starting a medical billing business. This template operates by using the well-known software program, Tim Berry's Business Plan Pro_, produced by Palo Alto Software. This demo version allows you to read the entire business plan and see the graphics that accompany it. However, you cannot print the business plan or edit it. (You need to purchase a copy to customize it for your business.)

To run the software:

Select "Business Plan Pro" from Benzel Demos.

When the main menu appears, click on the button for "Open a business plan." Choose the existing plan called "Ezclaim1.bps."

The medical billing business plan template will load and your screen will divide in half. The top half explains what section of the business plan you are in. This half of the screen provides directions on what to write if you were actually writing a business plan yourself. The bottom half of the screen shows you what is already written in the medical billing template. When you first open up the template, you are automatically placed into the first section of the business plan, Executive Summary.

You can read the existing business plan template, going from section to section to see what someone starting a medical billing business might have written. To see other parts of the business plan, click on the buttons on the bottom of the screen "Next Topic" or to go back to what you have already read, click on "Previous Topic." You can also see a list of the entire contents of the business plan by clicking on the "Select Topic" button. This will reveal a full listing of all business plan sections, and you can jump to any one of them.

As you read each section of the business plan, the top of the screen will occasionally reveal a "table" icon or a "graph" icon. This indicates that this section of the business plan has an accompanying table or graph. Click on the icon to view the table or graph.

You cannot print the business plan in this demo version, but you read the entire document in print preview mode. Go to "File" menu, select "Print," then "Print Preview." This allows you to read it more quickly. If you want, you can go back to each section of the business plan and read it in detail, as well as see the type of instructions the business planning software provides to people who are writing their own plans.

The "save" and "print" function of this software have been disabled out of consideration for the publisher and NEBA who sell them. Obviously, you must purchase a copy of the software and business plan template if you want to edit, rewrite, and customize it for your own business. To purchase a full working copy of the business planning software with the medical billing business plan template that you can customize for your business, contact NEBA at 415-577-1190. You can also contact Palo Alto Software at 144 E. 14th Ave., Eugene, OR 97401 (phone: 800-229-7526) to purchase just the business planning software. Note: only NEBA sells the combined software plus medical billing business plan template. Palo Alto Software sells only their business planning software.

For further information, contact NEBA for questions about the content of the business plan template, or for technical questions, contact Palo Alto Software at the phone numbers above.

NOTICE: *All software names are either Copyrighted, Trademarked, or Registered by their respective owners.*

Books Available from Rick Benzel
Ordering Information

Directory of Medical Management Software published by AQC Resource Books $36.00

Making Money in a Health Service Business on Your Home-Based PC $29.95

Working from Home, by Paul and Sarah Edwards $15.95

Finding Your Perfect Work, by Paul and Sarah Edwards $16.95

Teaming Up: The Small Business Guide to Collaborating with Others to Boost Your Earnings and $13.95
Expand Your Horizons, by Paul and Sarah Edwards and Rick Benzel

Aha! Ten Ways to Free Your Creative Spirit and Find Your Great Ideas, by Jordan Ayan, edited $15.00
by Rick Benzel

Note: California residents must add 8.25% sales tax to their total.

Add $4.00 for the first book ordered and $2.00 for **each** *book thereafter to cover shipping and handling fees.*

Send your check to
  Rick Benzel
  11670 National Boulevard, Suite 104
  Los Angeles, CA 90064

Indicate which title(s) you want, and clearly print your name, shipping address, and phone number. Allow 10-14 days for delivery. Remember to add shipping and handling fees as indicated.

Discounts are available for quantity purchases. Please write to the address indicated.

INDEX

About the Author

Rick Benzel is a freelance writer specializing in entrepreneurial opportunities and home-based business. He works closely with Paul and Sarah Edwards, and is the coauthor with them of *Teaming Up: The Small Business Guide to Collaborating with Others to Boost Your Earnings and Expand Your Horizons.*